# TimeOut
# Amsterdam

**Penguin Books**

PENGUIN BOOKS

Published by the Penguin Group
Penguin Books Ltd, 27 Wright's Lane, London W8 5TZ, England
Penguin Putnam Inc., 375 Hudson Street, New York, New York 10014, USA
Penguin Books Australia Ltd, Ringwood, Victoria, Australia
Penguin Books Canada Ltd, 10 Alcorn Avenue, Toronto, Ontario, Canada M4V 3B2
Penguin Books (NZ) Ltd, Private Bag 102902, NSMC, Auckland, New Zealand

Penguin Books Ltd, Registered offices: Harmondsworth, Middlesex, England

First published 1991
Second edition 1993
Third edition 1995
Fourth edition 1996
Fifth edition 1998
10 9 8 7 6 5 4 3 2 1

Colour reprographics by Precise Litho, 34–35 Great Sutton Street, London EC1
Printed and bound by William Clowes Ltd, Beccles, Suffolk NR34 9QE

## Edited & designed by

Time Out Guides Limited
Universal House
251 Tottenham Court Road
London W1P OAB
Tel +44 (0)171 813 3000
Fax +44 (0)171 813 6001
E-mail guides@timeout.co.uk
http://www.timeout.co.uk

## Editorial

**Managing Editor** Peter Fiennes
**Editor** Will Fulford-Jones
**Deputy Editor** Lesley McCave
**Consultant Editor** Steve Korver
**Researcher** Sue Cowell
**Proofreaders** Tamsin Shelton, Phil Harriss
**Indexer** Douglas Matthews

## Design

**Art Director** John Oakey
**Art Editor** Mandy Martin
**Designers** Benjamin de Lotz, Lucy Grant, Scott Moore
**Scanner Operator** Chris Quinn
**Advertisement Make-up** Paul Mansfield
**Picture Editor** Kerri Miles
**Picture Researcher** Emma Tremlett

## Advertising

**Group Advertisement Director** Lesley Gill
**Sales Director** Mark Phillips
**Advertising Assistant** Ingrid Sigerson
**Advertisement Sales (Amsterdam)** Boom Chicago

## Administration

**Publisher** Tony Elliott
**Managing Director** Mike Hardwick
**Financial Director** Kevin Ellis
**Marketing Director** Gillian Auld
**General Manager** Nichola Coulthard
**Production Manager** Mark Lamond

## Features in this guide were written and researched by:

**Introduction** Will Fulford-Jones. **Amsterdam by Season** Steve Korver. **History** Will Fulford-Jones, Mark Fuller, Steve Korver, Sophie Marshall, Kees Neefjes (*Hip to be Square* Willem de Blaauw; *The drugs do work* Steve Korver; *Squat thrusts* Jules Marshall). **Amsterdam Today** Willem de Blaauw. **Architecture** Rodney Bolt, Steve Korver. **Sightseeing** Steve Korver (*Pleins for the future* Willem de Blaauw). **Galleries** Jane Szita. **Museums** Vincent Hoberg, Aleida Strowger (*The appliance of science* Howard Shannon; *Subculture club* Will Fulford-Jones). **Accommodation** Dave Vickers. **Restaurants** Steve Korver. **Cafés & Bars** Pip Farquharson, Will Fulford-Jones, Vincent Hoberg, Steve Korver, Guy Thornton (*Rooms with a view* Willem de Blaauw; *Cheers & booze* Guy Thornton). **Coffeeshops** Pip Farquharson (*Courier X* Steve Korver). **Shopping** Kate Holder, Johanna Stoyva. **Services** Elaine Harvey. **Children & Parents** Rina Vergano. **Clubs** Merijn Hoorweg. **Dance** Lisa Sove. **Film** Manuel den Hollander. **Gay & Lesbian** Willem de Blaauw, Pip Farquharson. **Media** Jules Marshall (*Caught in the Net* Howard Shannon). **Music: Classical & Opera** Andrew May, Dirk van Spanjer. **Music: Rock, Roots & Jazz** Steve Korver. **Sport & Fitness** Guy Thornton. **Theatre** Vincent Hoberg. **Beyond Amsterdam** Vincent Hoberg, Steve Korver. **Excursions in Holland, The Randstad, The Provinces** Vincent Hoberg. **Directory** Sue Cowell, Will Fulford-Jones, Merijn Hoorweg, Lesley McCave.

## The Editor would like to thank the following:

Peter Carty, Matthew Collin, Jonathan Cox, Paul de Lara, Julie Emery, Danny Fryer, Tamsin Howe, Kevin Hudson, Marijn van der Jacht, Ruth Jarvis, Paul McManus, Rebekah McVitie, Andrew May, John Meyer, David Pepper, James Pretlove, Nigel Quested, Oep Schilling, NJ Stevenson, Johanna Stoyva, Sumo & Brokkoli, Caro Taverne, Chris Taylor, Amie Tridgell, Rina Vergano, and all the contributors, especially Sue Cowell, Steve Korver and Lesley McCave.

**Maps by** Mapworld, 71 Blandy Road, Henley-on-Thames, Oxon RG9 1QB; Amsterdam Transport map by Studio Olykan.
**Photography by Anthony Cassidy**, except for: page ii **Nick Feeney**; page 25 **AKG**; page 45 **Ed Marshall**. Pictures on pages 101, 154, 173, 220, 227, 230, 233, 238 and 240 were supplied by the featured establishments.

# Contents

# About the Guide

The fifth edition of the *Time Out Amsterdam Guide* represents the most radical rethinking of the Time Out format since our first Guide was published a decade ago. All listings information has been comprehensively updated, many sections have been rewritten, and all practical information has been moved to the Directory at the back of the book. In addition, the Sightseeing section has now been conveniently organised by area, while the maps have been revised and reordered and a comprehensive street index added. Now, every sight, museum, bar, restaurant, gallery, club – every place of interest, in fact – has been map-referenced, making the Guide infinitely easier to use.

Our team of resident writers and specialist researchers have trawled the streets of the city hunting down every last shop, concert hall and gallery that we think is worth visiting. All aspects of Amsterdam are covered in depth: from small, backstreet stores to major museums, and from local bars to landmark restaurants.

The *Time Out Amsterdam Guide* is part of an expanding series of city guides that now includes Barcelona, Berlin, Brussels, Budapest, Dublin, Edinburgh, Florence, Las Vegas, Lisbon, London, Los Angeles, Madrid, Moscow, Miami, New Orleans, New York, Paris, Prague, Rome, San Francisco and Sydney.

## CHECKED & CORRECT

All the listings information in this Guide was fully checked and correct at the time of going to press, but owners and managers can change arrangements at any time. It's always best to phone to confirm opening hours and the like before setting out.

The prices listed throughout should be regarded as guidelines, not gospel. Fluctuating exchange rates and inflation can cause prices to change unpredictably. However, if prices anywhere vary wildly from those we've quoted, ask if there's a reason. If not, go elsewhere – there's plenty of choice in most areas – and please let us know. We aim to give the best and most up-to-date advice, and always want to hear if you've been overcharged or badly treated.

## LANGUAGE

Most residents of Amsterdam speak English to a high standard, and communication is not usually a problem. However, there is a list of useful Dutch words and phrases on page 247 of this Guide.

## TELEPHONE NUMBERS

All numbers in Amsterdam can be dialled as listed in the Guide from within the city itself. However, if you are calling from elsewhere in Holland, add 020 – the area code for Amsterdam – at the front of the number. International dialling codes are given on pages 248-9.

## CREDIT CARDS

The following abbreviations have been used for credit cards in this guide: **AmEx** – American Express; **DC** – Diners' Club; **EC** – Eurocheque card; **JCB** – Japanese credit bank card; **MC** – Mastercard; **TC** – travellers' cheques in any currency ($TC, £TC denotes currency); **V** – Visa.

## RIGHT TO REPLY

Throughout this Guide, the information we give is impartial. No organisation, venue or business has been included because its owner or manager has advertised in our publications. Impartiality is one reason why *Time Out* guides are successful and well-respected. We hope you enjoy the *Time Out Amsterdam Guide*, but if you take exception to any of our reviews, please let us know. Readers' comments are always welcome, and are taken into account when preparing future editions. You'll find a reader's reply card at the back of this book.

There is an online version of this guide, plus weekly events listings for Amsterdam and other international cities, at http://www.timeout.co.uk.

# Introduction

Let's start with a word-association game. Ready? Good. So, what's the first word or phrase that comes to mind when you hear the word 'Amsterdam'? Canals, possibly? Or maybe it's drugs. Then again, it could be art, or history, or sex, or bicycles, or tulips, or…

Everyone thinks they know about Amsterdam. To some, it's the town of Rembrandt and Van Gogh, to others, the one city in the world where you can spliff up in the street without fear of arrest or social ostracism. To some, it's a wonderful picture-postcard world of windmills and water, to others, Sodom made flesh. Yup, Amsterdam is a strangely difficult city to get a handle on, which is why both visitors and residents look at the place in different ways.

Amsterdam's worldwide reputation is both its saving grace and its downfall. For one thing, its reputation draws a massive variety of people to the city, all attracted by different aspects of life in this most varied of towns. But conversely, its image leads some to write off the city before they've even experienced it, while others come, limit themselves to one cultural area that they've heard so much about – canals or coffeeshops, it matters not – and leave having barely tasted the flavour of the city.

It's the contradictions between past and present, between young and old, between convention and individuality, that keep the city alive. Samuel Johnson once wrote that when a man is tired of London, he is tired of life, and the same could be true of Amsterdam. After all, there are galleries and

museums aplenty for the culture vulture, stores for the shopaholic, tulips, clogs and windmills for the cliché-spotter, pot for the mellow-minded, canals for those in search of peace and quiet, the Red Light District for the curious and the desperate…

Despite its rich history – the Houtenhuis, the oldest remaining house in the city, was built in 1460, while the town itself has been here for almost 800 years – Amsterdam is undeniably a forward-thinking city, both politically and socially. The city's long-held liberal stances on prostitution and soft drugs are either brave and smart, or bloody-minded to the point of absurdity, depending on your frame of mind at any given moment. Less celebrated, though just as important in their own ways, are the ambitious new urban developments in the north of Amsterdam, the city's pioneering work in Internet and new media, and even the traffic system, wherein cars have been all but eliminated from the city centre. The latter, particularly, is an ideal that cities from London to New York have all considered at one time or other.

Like most countries in Europe, the Netherlands face a period of political uncertainty with the implementation in 1999 of the single European currency. It remains to be seen whether this closer European integration will result in a loss of the city's unique character, and whether the identities of individual countries will be subsumed in Euro-bureaucracy and over-zealous legislation. One would hope not. As things stand, Amsterdam remains one of Europe's liveliest, most surprising cities. Enjoy it while it lasts. *Will Fulford-Jones*

# Globaleyes

Global markets, global communications, global technologies...
the trend seems to be to globalize pretty well everything.
So how on earth do you keep on top of the daily developments?
Through the global eyes of the International Herald Tribune.

## THE WORLD'S DAILY NEWSPAPER

# Amsterdam In Context

# Amsterdam by Season

**Flowers, music, cannabis, pervs: Amsterdam has a festival for everything and everyone.**

When the original settlers of Amsterdam, the Batavians, arrived in the city, they brought with them a rich heritage of partying that involved song, dance and the slurping of brew from the skull of the slain enemy. As Amsterdam entered its Golden Age in the seventeenth century, parties tended to last for weeks. the *Zottenfeesten* ('Fool Fests'), in particular, were mass, drawn-out, drunken mind games that promoted insanity by role reversal: the kids hammed authority, while the adults went berserk and acted, as the saying had it, as if 'hit on the head by the windmill'.

The centuries-long ingraining of Calvinist morals may be the root of the Netherlands' healthy economy, but it did little for the survival of ancient off-the-wall traditions. Today, Amsterdammers' inner partying pagan beast only comes raging out on to the cobbled streets for **Koninginnedag** (Queen's Day) and **Oudejaarsavond** (New Year's Eve), the year's two consistently best bets for experiencing frolicsome mass psychosis. These only get topped when Ajax win an important championship match and thousands of supporters gather in and around Leidseplein and Rembrandtplein to tread that delicately fine line between celebratory partying and raucous rioting. But whether you want to get off your head on cannabis or on art, there is enough to interest everyone.

Where possible, exact dates are given; check the dates of others by phone. The **AUB** and **VVV** (*see chapter* **Directory**, *page 251*) have up-to-date information on all events in the city and the latter publishes a calendar in its *What's On In Amsterdam* magazine (f4). Also, check out *Time Out* magazine in London, which has a pick of Amsterdam's best events, and its website, at

*Keep abreast of the revelries on* **Queen's Day**. *See page 7.*

# Pedestrians

# Possibilities

TimeOut | London's Living Guide.

http://www.timeout.co.uk

*www.timeout.co.uk*. For a list of public holidays, *see chapter* **Directory**, *pages 251-2*, and see relevant chapters for details of other, smaller festivals. Unless stated, events listed below are free.

## Frequent events

### Arts & crafts markets

*Spui (tram 1, 2, 4, 5, 9, 14, 16, 20, 24, 25) &*
*Thorbeckeplein (tram 4, 9, 14, 20)*. **Date** Mar-Oct/Nov.
**Open** 10am-5pm Sun. **Map 5 D4; Map 6 E4**
Two open-air arts and crafts markets are held every Sunday from March until October or November (depending on the weather). These are pleasant places to browse if you're into pleasant browsing, but don't come here to buy a bovine in brine or a crucifix in urine: most of the jewellery, paintings, vases and bargain ornaments are rather more mediocre. Buskers touting CDs and tapes enhance the laid-back vibe.

### Rowing contests

*Amsterdamse Bos (information 646 2740). Bus 170,*
*171, 172.* **Date** Apr-July.
Come to this lovely green expanse to watch participants get wet. There are various rowing contests held here from April through to December; check local press or phone the VVV for details.

### Book markets

Four book markets spring up in summer: two along the Amstel (mid-May, mid-August) and two on Dam (mid-May, mid-July).

### Antiques market

*Nieuwmarkt. Tram 9, 14, 20/Metro Nieuwmarkt.* **Date** *mid-May-Sept* 10am-5pm Sun. **Map 2 D2**
Lovers of antiques and bric-a-brac should head for this small antiques market. There's a fair amount of naffness, but also a few gems, especially books, furniture and objets d'art.

## Spring

Spring is when the tulips and crocuses start cracking through the earth, and a winter's worth of doggy-do defrosts: those who know about this sort of thing estimate the amount at 20 million kilograms. However, it's also when the population of Amsterdam shrugs off the weight of existential drag that often defines the northern European mindset during winter. Motivated by a visible sun, the city dwellers take on the more shiny *joie de vivre* vibe that's usually associated with the Southern European terrace-café cultures. On the down side, bicycle paths start to clog up, not only with increased traffic, but also with lost, doe-eyed tourists stopping to check their maps. Cycling lanes are often red asphalt, so pedestrians be warned: avoid them or be prepared to become road pizza. Otherwise, relax and enjoy a city in a season when lounging in a park or on a terrace is seen as a well-deserved and respected thing to do after a long winter's cold rain and mental drain. For **Amsterdam Roots Festival, Blues Festival, Drum Rhythm Festival**, and **Amsterdam Pop Prijs/Wanted R&B Hip Hop Prijs Finals**, *see chapter* **Music: Rock, Roots & Jazz**, *page 211*).

### Stille Omgang (Silent Procession)

*(information 023 524 6229).* **Date** 21 Mar 1999; phone for 2000 date.
Every year on a Sunday in March, local Catholics commemorate the 1345 Miracle of Amsterdam with a silent night-time procession through the city. The apparently true story of the Miracle begins graphically: a dying man vomited up the bread given to him in communion as part of the last rites. The purged host was tossed on the fire, but was then found the next morning undamaged among the ashes, and the sick man is said to have subsequently recovered. The procession, with the very same piece of toast in tow (yum!), follows the road that pilgrims have used for centuries, called, for that reason, Heiligeweg (Holy Way). The sight of the procession moving through the bustling Red Light District at night is surreal. The route begins and ends at Spui, via Kalverstraat, Nieuwendijk, Warmoestraat and Nes. For information, write to Gezelschap van de Stille Omgang, Zandvoortseweg 59, 2111 GS Aerdenhout, or phone them on the above number after 7pm.

### World Press Photo

*Nieuwe Kerk, Dam (information 676 6096). Tram 1, 2,*
*5, 9, 13, 14, 16, 17, 20, 24, 25.* **Date** Apr-June.
**Admission** *f7; f5* under-12s. **Map 2 C3**
With exhibits chosen from tens of thousands of photos taken by thousands of different photographers, the world's largest photo competition takes place in the already sight-worthy confines of the Nieuwe Kerk (the ancient 'New Church'). Each year it kicks off in Amsterdam, before moving on to another 70 locations worldwide.

### National Museum Weekend

*Various venues in Amsterdam (information 670 1111).* **Date** mid-Apr. **Admission** varies.
During National Museum Weekend, many state-run museums offer reduced or free admission and mount special exhibitions and activities, such as treasure hunts. Although opening hours are often extended, most museums are busy. Phone the Vereniging Museum Jaarkaart on the above number for further information, or pick up the free *Museum Weekend* paper at the VVV, ANWB (auto association) and the museums themselves. *See chapter* **Museums**, *pp74-86*.

### Koninginnedag (Queen's Day)

*All over Amsterdam.* **Date** 30 Apr.
Party-lovers, bric-a-brac collectors and students of the stupendously surreal, listen up. If you only go to Amsterdam once in your life, make sure your visit coincides with 30 April. Queen's Day (Koninginnedag in the local lingo) is, in theory, a one-day celebration of Beatrix's birthday. In reality, though, the Queen is soon forgotten amid the revelry. More than a million folk come to the city, nearly tripling its population, and making every single street and canal dense with different sounds, suspicious smells and second-hand sales in the process. It's a day of excess, and the communal vision of a city becomes blurred. You might stagger along and discover a leather-boy disco party on one side street, boogie through and get to some local crooner singing of broken hearts and spilt beer on another, when suddenly a boat bellows by with a heavy metal band, whose amps get short-circuited at the next bridge as a gang of gabber-loving boys in orange (the royal colour) with shaven heads urinate on to it. If nothing else, you can at least come away with a few stories to tell your grandkids.

Even though Mayor Patijn played party pooper a couple of years ago by banning street selling on the Queen's Eve (29 April), he does have a point: you should really try to get some rest before the big day. If you've got kids in tow, head to Vondelpark, which is dedicated to children; gay celebrations are focused around the Homomonument and Reguliersdwaarsstraat (*see chapter* **Gay & Lesbian**, *p185*); and Dam becomes a fairground. The mind gets clogged with an overdose of senses and your pockets slowly empty as you

*The **Arts & crafts market** on Spui, held every Sunday from March to November:*

get tricked into buying just what you always (read: never) wanted: a fetching pair of orange clogs or silver platforms, a brain implant or some processed uranium… all for next to nothing. With performances, markets, crowds and, of course, alcohol, the scenic streets of Amsterdam have it all for one day only. Come and see what the fuss is all about.

### Herdenkingsdag & Bevrijdingsdag (Remembrance Day & Liberation Day)

**Remembrance Day** *National Monument, Dam. Tram 1, 2, 4, 5, 9, 13, 14, 16, 17, 20, 24, 25.* **Date** 4 May. **Map 2 D3**
**Liberation Day** *Vondelpark (tram 1, 2, 3, 5, 6, 12, 20) & Leidseplein (tram 1, 2, 5, 6, 7, 10, 20).* **Date** 5 May. **Map 5 C6; Map 5 D5**
On 4 May, those who died during World War II are remembered in a ceremony at the National Monument on Dam Square. The service starts at 7.30pm, the Queen lays a wreath at 8pm, and a two-minute silence follows before the Chief of the Armed Forces and other dignitaries lay wreaths. Although homosexuals who died during World War II are also now remembered in this ceremony, the Dutch gay organisation COC organises its own remembrance service at the Homomonument (*see chapter* **Gay & Lesbian***, p185*). Liberation is celebrated on the following day, with various activities throughout the city. Vondelpark, Museumplein, Leidseplein and Rokin are the best places to head for on 5 May: expect to find performances by local and national bands on hastily erected stages, speeches and information stands organised by political and ideological pressure groups, plus a free market where you can sell everything you bought in a drunken stupor on Queen's Day not one week earlier.

### Oosterparkfestival

*Oosterpark. Tram 3, 6, 9, 14.* **Date** first week of May. **Map 7 H3**
Located in the centre of the culturally eclectic east of Amsterdam, Oosterpark plays host to a one- or two-day free festival that emphasises community between nationalities. It has links with Remembrance Day (4 May), since many local Jews were deported during World War II, and is a great opportunity to experience different music, customs, food, games and sports.

### National Windmill Day

*(information 623 8703).* **Date** second Sat in May. **Admission** varies.
About 600 of the country's 1,035 windmills and 75 watermills turn their Ministry of Tourism-subsidised sails and open to the public. Among them are Amsterdam's six working mills (*see box* **Windmills on your mind***, p46*). Windmills open to the public carry a blue banner, but for full details, contact the Vereniging de Hollandse Molen on the above number.

### National Cycling Day

**Date** second Sat in May.
On National Cycling Day, the roads are even more full of cyclists than usual (if that's possible). About 230 routes are set up for the occasion, and if you want to be part of the action – or avoid it completely – contact the VVV for information nearer the time.

### KunstRAI (RAI Arts Fair)

*RAI Congresgebouw, Europaplein (549 1212). Tram 4, 25/NS rail to RAI station.* **Open** *office/enquiries*

*a great one-stop shop for gifts and presents. See page 7.*

9am-5pm Mon-Fri. **Dates** mid-May-early June.
**Admission** ƒ20.
This huge (and hugely mainstream) annual exhibition of contemporary art includes everything from ceramics and jewellery to paintings and sculpture. About a hundred Dutch and international galleries take part.

### EuroPerve
*Partycentrum 2000, Daniel Goedkoopstraat (information 620 5603/tickets 492 1232). Metro 53.* **Admission** *in advance* ƒ100; *on the door* ƒ150.
An annual event that herds thousands of Europe's most sexually adventurous folks together into the Partycentrum 2000 for one weekend at the end of May. Formal dress – leather, latex, PVC and adult-sized nappies – is required. You can also buy tickets from the above number, or via your favourite S&M or fetish outlet. If you go by Metro 53 (confusingly, it's a tram), get off at the Spaklerweg stop; Partycentrum is 300m down on the left.

### Open Ateliers
*Kunstroute de Westelijke Eilanden on Prinseneiland, Bickerseiland & Realeneiland.*
Neighbourhoods with large artist populations and artists' studio complexes hold open days (not necessarily every year) in the spring or autumn. Over a weekend or more, dozens of artists – both the starving and the successful – open their doors to the public. The Westelijke Eilanden – the largest and most popular – is situated on the wonderfully picturesque and peaceful islands around Prinseneiland, which are all connected by traditional 'skinny bridges'. Be sure, also, to check out the **Jordaan Open Ateliers**, held, not surprisingly, in the Jordaan; the next one is in May 2000. You can find out about the times and venues of all the Open Ateliers by picking up the *Kunstladder* (the official list) at VVV or AUB shops.

### Vondelpark Openluchttheatre (Open-air theatre)
*Vondelpark (information 523 7790/673 1499). Tram 1, 2, 3, 5, 7, 10, 12, 20.* **Date** Wed-Sun, end May-end Aug. **Admission** free. **Map 5 C6**
Throughout the summer months, the Vondelpark hosts a wide variety of theatre and music. The open-air theatre is in the middle of the park by the fountain. Cabaret, drama, concerts, kids' programmes and dance all feature. The atmosphere alone is worth experiencing, even if the performances turn out to be crap. *See chapters* **Music: Rock, Roots & Jazz**, *p208, and* **Theatre**, *p222.*

## Summer

With the consistent sunshine that summer brings, Amsterdammers move outdoors for their leisure time. Liberally undressed bodies pack like sardines on the nearby beaches at Bloemendaal and Zandfoort, festivals abound and Vondelpark gets gridlocked with skaters, joggers, sun-worshippers and bongo-players. Many locals vacate to vacationsville, while the city's tourist load reaches maximum density. Aside from the summer events listed below, there are plenty of others, such as **Dance Valley** (*see chapter* **Clubs**, *page 178*); **Over Het IJ Festival** and **International**

# Tales of the city **A Klaas act**

When the Church finally decided to tame the wild pagan partying that had always accompanied the end of the slaughter season, it began by ruling that the traditional celebration should be based around St Nicholas – or 'Sinterklaas' – the patron saint of children. The Dutch, whose bloodlust was legendary, were forced to lay down their arms and instead bake mounds of animal-shaped cookies of gingerbread and marzipan cakes. Adapting further, they soon began to exchange poems instead of spells, and a once-violent tradition was slowly reborn as a mellow and Christian family feast on 6 December, St Nick's birthday. Sinterklaas, as we all know, eventually emigrated to the States, mutated into Santa Claus, and shifted his birthday to 25 December in order to fill in for Jesus's failings of character when it came to the spirit of gross revenue.

While Christmas remained a purely religious holiday in the Old World, St Nick – with his white beard, bishop robes and ridged staff – has instead become every Dutch kid's favourite uncle, playing the good cop by controlling the distribution of sweets at the annual parade of the city. Meanwhile, his assisting bad cops, Zwarte Pieten, ('Black Peters') – Al Jolson-style elves – represent the threat to the naughty kids. Each year, people note how

staggeringly politically incorrect this all is. Klaas warriors, on the other hand, maintain that the elves are part of the tradition that has darkness representing evil: 'Black Peter' is actually the devil, and his colour and predilection for mischief-making are the only leftovers of an evil beaten out of him by St Nick. Others still reckon that the colour of Black Peter's skin is a result of his assigned job of delivering sweets to the awaiting shoes via that dirtiest of orifices, the old-fashioned chimney.

It doesn't end there, though: St Nicholas, quite aside from his festive responsibilities, is also the patron saint of sailors, merchants, prostitutes and thieves. So why does he attract such a motley crew? Well, legend has him as a forgiving sort: an evil butcher, for example, who killed and pickled two boys was 'punished' by St Nicholas with nothing more than a reprimand and an instruction to start living the good life. Nick, in fact, seems even softer on crime than Amsterdam itself, which usually copes with wimpier misdemeanours by condoning or legalising them. Now, is this really the kind of guy you want your children to hang out with? Well, as long as he brings joy to the hearts of kiddies, we can forgive some lapses in his character. 'Tis the season, after all…

*See opposite for details of the Sinterklaas parade.*

---

**Theatre School Festival** (for both, *see chapter* **Theatre**, *page 222*); and **North Sea Jazz Festival**, **Sonic Acts** and **A Camping Flight to Lowlands** (for all, *see chapter* **Music: Rock, Roots & Jazz**, *page 211*).

## Echo Grachtenloop (Canal Run)
*(information 585 9222).* **Date** second Sun of June.
**Admission** *participants f7-f9; spectators* free.
Around 5,000 people take part in either a 5½-, 9½- or 18km (three-, six- or 11-mile) run along the city's canals (Prinsengracht and Vijzelgracht). You can register on the spot half an hour before at the Stadsschouwburg (*see chapter* **Theatre**, *p221*), where the run starts and finishes. Most of the action kicks off at 11am. If you've left your sports gear at home, you can just observe the runners getting knackered from assorted vantage points around town. Leidseplein is a good place to watch, but it does get crowded; for a more relaxed experience, stand on the banks of Prinsengracht. Registration is from mid-May at VSB banks (Rozengracht 207; 638 8009). *See chapter* **Sport**, *page 215.*

## Holland Festival
*Stadsschouwburg, Leidseplein (information 530 7110).*
*Tram 1, 2, 5, 6, 7, 10, 20.* **Date** mid-June. **Admission**
*f18-f85.* **Map 5 C5**
A perennial fixture in the diaries of the Netherlands' posh

and civilised folk, the world-renowned Holland Festival features art, dance, opera, theatre and a whole lot more. The programme includes both mainstream and experimental works, and is held in the Stadsschouwburg and assorted venues around Amsterdam, with other events in The Hague. Advance programme information is available from Holland Festival, Kleine Gartmanplantsoen 21, 1017 RP Amsterdam (627 6566; open 9am-6pm Mon-Fri). There are also direct sales (from May) from the AUB Uitburo, VVV offices and individual theatres. The Holland Festival website – *www.hollandfestival.nl* – has full programme information.

## Parade
*Martin Luther Kingpark (information 033 465 4577).*
*Tram 25/Metro Amstel station.* **Date** first two weeks of Aug (3pm-1am Mon-Thur, Sun; 3pm-2am Fri-Sat).
**Admission** *f5; shows f2,50-f15.*
The Old World carnival spirit is alive and well at the Martin Luther Kingpark. The arty sideshows, depraved burlesque and demented theatre should not be missed.

## Uitmarkt
*Various locations, including Museumplein, Dam & sites along the Amstel.* **Date** last weekend of Aug.
The Uitmarkt previews the Netherlands' coming cultural season with a huge fair on and around Dam and the Nes, giving information on amateur and professional theatre, opera, dance and music of all sorts. There are also performances on outdoor stages and in the city's various theatres. Everything is free, so, not surprisingly, it gets very crowded. Theatres,

performing artists and companies preview and sell their programmes for the coming season. From Friday to Sunday, several outdoor stages are set up in squares around the centre of Amsterdam, with free music, dance, theatre and cabaret performances.

# Autumn

Amsterdam has been known to have the occasional Indian summer, but otherwise this season's sometime stormy disposition is a warning of the winter's despair that is sure to follow. It's a time when Amsterdammers renew their Prozac prescriptions and keep any razor blades out of sight. As a visitor, though, this might be just the right time to visit the city: with the tourist tide finally going out and touring bands arriving in their droves, the true essence and spirit of Amsterdam comes right to the surface.

### Jordaan Festival

*In the Jordaan.* **Date** Sept.
This annual neighbourhood festival features performances from local talents following in the footsteps of Johnny Jordaan and Tante Leen, artists who personified the spirit of the Jordaan by singing about lost love and spilt beer. Normally good fun.

### Bloemen Corso (Flower Parade)

*(information 029 732 5100).* **Route** *leaves from Aalsmeer at 9.30am; Olympic Stadium, Stadionplein, at 1pm (tram 16); Overtoom (tram 1, 6); Leidseplein (tram 1, 2, 5, 6, 7, 10, 20); Leidsestraat (tram 1, 2, 5); Spui (tram 1, 2, 5); Spuistraat (tram 1, 2, 5); Dam (tram 1, 2, 4, 5, 9, 13, 14, 16, 17, 20, 24, 25) around 4pm; Rembrandtplein (tram 4, 9, 14, 20); Vijzelstraat (tram 16, 24, 25); Weteringschans (tram 6, 7, 10).* **Date** first Sat of Sept.
Once a year for over 40 years, a spectacular parade of floats bearing all kinds of flowers – except tulips, amazingly, as they're out of season – has made its way from Aalsmeer (the home of Holland's flower industry; *see chapter* **Excursions in Holland,** *p226*) to Amsterdam. Crowds line the pavements for a glimpse of the beautiful and fragrant displays. At 4pm the parade reaches a packed Dam where there is a civic reception, after which it returns for an illuminated cavalcade through Aalsmeer (9-10pm).

### National Monument Day

*(626 3947).* **Date** second weekend of Sept.
Despite the name, this event is held over a full weekend. The National Monument Society arranges for hundreds of the Netherlands' listed buildings to open their doors to the public. In Amsterdam, this means you can see inside around 30 of the city's finest canal houses, as well as windmills and pumping stations. Phone for details, as the buildings that are open change annually.

### Kunstroute/Exchange WG Terrein

*WG Terrein, Marius van Bouwdijk Bastiaansestraat (information 618 7848).* **Tram** 1, 3, 6, 12. **Date** 18-20 Sept 1998. **Map 4 A6**
The Kunstroute/Exchange is held in the former womens' hospital turned artists' studios/living complex. One year it's a Kunstroute (meaning that an exhibition of local work is shown here), and the next year it's an exchange exhibition with another European city (they all exhibit here and then go off for a jolly old time over there... any excuse for a trip abroad). A combined route map and catalogue can be obtained from the VVV or AUB. Phone nearer the time for the 1999 dates.

### Cannabis Cup

*(information 624 1777).* **Date** Oct/Nov. **Admission** varies.
*High Times* magazine hosts this four-day ganja festival and hemp expo. Activities are city-wide, but the Melkweg (*see chapters* **Art Galleries,** *p72*, **Film**, *p184*, **Music: Rock, Roots & Jazz,** *p207*, and **Theatre,** *p222*) is normally at the centre of the bong vortex. Awards go to the wickedest weeds and the heaviest hashes, and American stoners fly in by the planeload. Phone for exact prices and dates nearer the time.

### Sinterklaas

**Date** mid-Nov. **Route** *Barbizon Palace Hotel, Prins Hendrikkade (tram 1, 2, 4, 5, 9, 13, 16, 17, 20, 24, 25); Damrak (tram 4, 9, 14, 16, 20, 24, 25); Dam (tram 1, 2, 4, 5, 9, 13, 14, 16, 17, 20, 24, 25); Raadhuisstraat (tram 13, 14, 17); Rozengracht (tram 13, 14, 17, 20); Marnixstraat (tram 7, 10); Leidseplein (tram 1, 2, 5, 6, 7, 10, 20).*
In mid-November, Sinterklaas (St Nicholas, the Dutch equivalent of Santa Claus) marks the beginning of the Christmas season when he steps ashore from a steamboat at Amsterdam's Centraal Station, before parading through the city on his traditional white horse. On the eve of 6 December, St Nick and his helpers slide down chimneys to leave goodies in the shoes that children have left by the fireplace. Or so the story goes. Families celebrate by exchanging small gifts and poems. *See box* **A Klaas act** *opposite.*

# Winter

The conversion of Leidseplein from patio into ice rink signals the advent of winter. With a little luck, the canals also turn solid enough for scenic skating later in the season. Otherwise, it's only two family-oriented festivals: St Nicholas's Day (6 December, with festivities the night before) – as important to the Dutch as Christmas – and New Year's Eve that break up the potential monotony of this most sleety of seasons.

### Oudejaarsavond (New Year's Eve)

*All over Amsterdam.* **Date** 31 Dec.
Along with Koninginnedag (*see above* **Spring**), New Year's Eve is Amsterdam's wildest and wackiest celebration. There's happy chaos throughout the city, but the best spots are Nieuwmarkt and Dam, both of which get seriously crowded. It's an evening to be avoided by those who suffer from combat flashbacks: the ample use of firecrackers is suggestive of the fall of Saigon (and almost as dangerous). The Dutch often begin their celebration with an evening of coffee, spirits and *oliebollen* ('oil-balls', which taste better than they sound: they're deep-fried blobs of dough, apple and raisins, made even yummier with a hefty sprinkle of icing sugar) with the family until midnight, which is why so many bars don't open until the witching hour.

### Chinese New Year

*Nieuwmarkt. Tram 9, 14, 20/Metro Nieuwmarkt.* **Date** end Jan. **Map 2 D2**
Centred around Nieuwmarkt in Amsterdam's Chinatown, dancing lions and dragons bring luck for the New Year. It's great for children but less great for the ears, as firecracker residue reaches knee-height before the day is out.

### Commemoration of the February Strike

*Jonas Daniel Meijerplein. Tram 9, 14, 20/Metro Waterlooplein.* **Date** 25 Feb. **Map 3 E3**
Every year a ceremony commemorating the dockworkers' protest strike of 1941 is held at the Dokwerker statue.

# Key Events

## Middle Ages

**1204** Gijsbrecht van Amstel builds a castle in the coastal settlement that is to become Amsterdam.
**1270** The River Amstel is dammed at Dam Square.
**1275** Count Floris V grants Aemstelle Dam a toll privilege charter, the first historical record of Amsterdam.
**1300** Amsterdam granted city rights by Bishop of Utrecht.
**1306** Work begins on the Oude Kerk.
**1313** The Bishop of Utrecht grants Aemstelledamme full municipal rights and leaves it to William III of Holland.
**1342** City walls (burgwallen) are built.
**1345** The 'Miracle of Amsterdam'. From this date Amsterdam attracts large number of pilgrims.

## 1400-1535

**1421** Saint Elizabeth's Day Flood; Amsterdam's first great fire.
**1452** Fire destroys most of Amsterdam's wooden houses. Building with slate and stone obligatory from this date.
**1489** Maximilian grants Amsterdam the right to add the imperial crown to its coat of arms.
**1534** Anabaptists seize the City Hall. They are captured and a period of anti Protestant repression begins.

## Under Spanish rule

**1562** Amsterdam has 5,728 houses, 30,000 inhabitants.
**1565** A winter crop failure causes famine among Calvinist workers; William the Silent organises a Protestant revolt against Spanish rule.
**1566** The Beeldenstorm (Iconoclastic Fury) is unleashed. Protestant worship authorised in public for the first time.
**1568** Eighty Year War with Spain begins.
**1572** William of Orange (1533-84) joins beggars revolt.
**1577** Prince of Orange annexes Amsterdam.
**1578** Catholic burgomasters and officials are replaced with Protestants in a coup known as 'The Alteration'.
**1579** The Union of Utrecht is signed, allowing freedom of religious belief but not freedom of worship.
**1585** Antwerp falls to Spain; mass exodus to the north.

## 1600-1700

**1602** Inauguration of Verenigde Oost Indische Compagnie (VOC).
**1606** Rembrandt van Rijn is born.
**1609** Amsterdam Exchange Bank established.
**1611** Zuiderkerk is completed.
**1613** Construction of the western stretches of Herengracht, Keizersgracht and Prinsengracht begins. Amsterdam's population is 105,000.
**1621** West Indische Compagnie (WIC) is inaugurated.
**1623** WIC colonises Manhattan Island. Peter Stuyvesant founds New Amsterdam two years later.
**1638** Athenaeum Illustre opens. Westerkerk is completed.
**1642** Rembrandt finishes 'The Night Watch'.
**1648** The Treaty of Münster, ending war with Spain. Jacob van Campen starts to build the City Hall on Dam. Daniel Stalpert finishes it in 1654.
**1654** England starts first war against United Provinces.
**1665** England is at war with the United Provinces again.

**1667** England and the Netherlands sign Peace of Breda.
**1663** The plague takes its toll: 23,000 people die.
**1672** England and the Netherlands are at war; Louis XIV of France invades the Netherlands.
**1674** West Indies Company is dismantled. Amsterdam has a population of 200,000.
**1675** The Portuguese Synagogue is completed.
**1685** French protestants take refuge in Amsterdam after the revocation of the Edict of Nantes.
**1689** William of Orange, Stadholder of the Netherlands, becomes King William III of England.
**1696** Undertakers riot against wedding and funeral tax.

## 1700-1815

**1780** Fourth war with England, Dutch fleet destroyed.
**1787** Frederick William II, king of Prussia, occupies Amsterdam in support of his brother-in-law.
**1795** French Revolutionary armies are welcomed into Amsterdam by the Patriots. The Batavian Republic is set up and administered from Amsterdam.
**1806** Napoleon's brother is made King of the Netherlands.
**1811** King Louis is removed from the Dutch throne.
**1813** Unification of the Netherlands. Amsterdam is no longer a self-governing city.
**1815** Amsterdam becomes capital of Holland.

## 1824-1940

**1824** North Holland Canal completed.
**1848** The city's ramparts are pulled down.
**1876** Noordzee Kanaal links Amsterdam with North Sea.
**1877** Gemeentelijk Universiteit (later UvA) set up, followed in 1880 by the Vrije Universiteit Amsterdam.
**1880s** Oil is discovered on the east coast of Sumatra; foundation of the Royal Dutch Company (Shell Oil).
**1883** Amsterdam holds the World Exhibition.
**1887** The Rijksmuseum is finished.
**1889** Centraal Station opens.
**1922** Women are granted the vote.
**1928** The Olympic Games are held in Amsterdam.
**1934** Amsterdam has a population of 800,000.

## WWII to present day

**1940** May 15, German troops invade Amsterdam.
**1941** February strike against the deportation of Jews.
**1944-1945** The Hunger Winter; over 2,000 people die.
**1945** May 8, Canadian soldiers free Amsterdam.
**1947** Anne Frank's diary is published.
**1966** Provo (Provocation) movement. Marriage ceremony of Princess Beatrix and Prince Claus ends in riots.
**1968** IJ tunnel opens.
**1973** Amsterdam's football team, Ajax, win the European Cup for the third successive year.
**1975** Cannabis is decriminalised.
**1978** First Metrolijn (underground) opens.
**1980** Riots on Queen Beatrix's Coronation Day (30 April) in Nieuwe Kerk. This day becomes National Squatters' Day.
**1986** Stopera is built amid much controversy.
**1992** Boeing 747 crashes into a block of flats in Bijlmermeer.

# History

*From the beer era to the Golden Age, the history of Amsterdam is almost as colourful as the city itself.*

*For a taste of early Amsterdam, visit the **Begijnhof** square, built in 1346. See page 14.*

## Early history

According to legend, Amsterdam was founded by two fishermen and a seasick dog, which ran ashore and threw up on the site of the city when their ship ran aground. The reality, sadly, is probably rather more mundane.

Although the Romans occupied other parts of Holland, they didn't reach the north. Waterlogged swampland was apparently not the stuff empires were built on, so the legions headed elsewhere in northern Europe. Archaeologists have found no evidence of settlement at Amsterdam before AD1000, although there are prehistoric remains further east in **Drenthe**. Amsterdam's site, in fact, was partially under water for years, and the River Amstel had no fixed course until enterprising farmers from around Utrecht began to build dykes during the eleventh century. Once the peasants had done the work, the nobility took over.

During the thirteenth century, the most important place in the newly reclaimed area was Oudekerk aan de Amstel. In 1204, the Lord of Amstel built a castle near this tiny hamlet on what is now the outskirts of Amsterdam. After the Amstel was dammed in about 1270, a village grew up on the site of what is now Dam Square, acquiring the name Aemstelledamme.

The Lord of Amstel at this time was Gijsbrecht, a pugnacious man continually in trouble with his liege lord, the Bishop of Utrecht, and with his nearest neighbour, Count Floris V of Holland. Tension increased in this power struggle when Floris bestowed toll rights – and some independence – on the young town in 1275. Events culminated in Floris's murder by Gijsbrecht at Muiden (where Floris's castle, Muiderslot can still be seen). Gijsbrecht's estates were confiscated by the Bishop of Utrecht and given to the Counts of Holland. Amsterdam has remained part of the province of North Holland ever since.

### ROLL OUT THE BARREL

The saying goes that Amsterdam's prosperity was launched in a beer barrel. This is based on the commercial boost the city enjoyed courtesy of a later

Count of Holland, Floris VI, who in 1323 made Amsterdam one of only two toll points in the province for the import of brews. This was no trivial matter at a time when most people drank beer; drinking the local water, in fact, was practically suicidal. Hamburg had the largest brewing capacity in northern Europe, and within 50 years a third of that city's production was flowing through Amsterdam. Thanks to its position between the Atlantic and Hanseatic ports, the city increased its trade in an assortment of essential goods.

### FIRE ALARMS

Although it was a major trading post, Amsterdam remained little more than a village until well into the fifteenth century. As late as 1425, the 'city' consisted only of a few blocks of houses with kitchen gardens and two churches, compactly arranged along the final 1,000-metre stretch of the River Amstel and bordered by what are now known as Geldersekade, Kloveniersburgwal and Singel. Virtually all these old buildings – like the **Houtenhuis**, still standing in the Begijnhof – were wooden, so fire was a constant threat; in the great fire of May 1452, three-quarters of the town was razed. Structures built after the fire had to be faced with stone and roofed with tiles or slates. These new architectural developments coincided with a certain amount of urban expansion in the city, as – most notably – foreign commerce led to developments in the shipbuilding industry.

### CAPTAIN KERK

In early medieval society, the Catholic Church permeated every aspect of life throughout Europe, and Amsterdam was no exception. Contemporary chronicles show that the city became an independent parish before 1334. Documents dating from this period also contain the first recorded references to the **Oude Kerk** (*see chapters* **Architecture**, *page 33*, and **Sightseeing**, *page 49*).

As the city expanded, more and more cloisters cropped up around the city: at one point, 18 were dotted around the tiny urban enclave, though the only remaining example is the **Begijnhof**, just off Spui (*see chapter* **Sightseeing**, *page 50*). The proliferation of the cloisters is thought, in part, to be down to the 'miracle' of 1345, when a dying man was given the last sacrament which he then vomited up into a fire; the host emerged unscathed from the fire, though, and the man remarkably recovered. The cloisters became the main source of social welfare, providing hospital treatment and orphanages, at least until the Protestant elite – which took over the city after the Reformation – obliterated every trace of popery. The Heiligeweg (Holy Way) was the road within the city which led to the chapel on Rokin, close to where the Miracle took place. Its length – roughly 70 yards – is an indication of just how small Amsterdam then was.

## War & Reformation

None of the wealth and glory of Amsterdam's Golden Age would have been possible without the turbulent events that preceded it. During the sixteenth century, Amsterdam's population increased five-fold, from about 10,000 (a low level even by medieval standards) to 50,000 by 1600. Its first major urban expansion accommodated the growth, but people flocked to the booming city only to find poverty, disease and squalor in the hastily built working-class quarters. Amsterdam's merchants, however, weren't complaining: during the 1500s, the city started to emerge as one of the world's major trading powers.

Amsterdam may have been almost autonomous as a chartered city, but on paper it was still subject to absentee rulers. Through the intricate and exclusive marriage bureau known as the European aristocracy, the Low Countries (the Netherlands and Belgium) had passed into the hands of the Catholic Austro-Spanish House of Habsburg. The Habsburgs were the mightiest monarchs in Europe and Amsterdam was a comparative backwater among their European possessions, but events in the sixteenth century soon gave the city a new prominence.

### REVOLT & REPRESSION

Amsterdam's burgeoning status as a trade centre led to the import of all kinds of radical religious ideas that were flourishing throughout northern Europe at the time, encouraged by Martin Luther's audacious condemnation of the all-powerful Catholic Church in 1517. The German princelings sided firmly with Luther, but the Habsburgs gathered all the resources of their enormous empire and set about putting the protesters back in the Catholic Church.

Although Luther's beliefs failed to catch on with Amsterdammers, many people were drawn to the austere creeds of the Anabaptists and, later, Calvin. Advocating a revolutionary Christian equality, the Anabaptists insisted on adult baptism. When they first arrived from Germany in about 1530, the Catholic city fathers tolerated the new movement. But when they seized the Town Hall in 1534 during an attempt to establish a 'New Jerusalem' on the River Amstel, the authorities clamped down. The leaders were arrested and executed, signalling a period of religious repression unparalleled in the city's history. Protesters of every persuasion had to keep a low profile: 'heretics' were burned at the stake on the Dam.

After the Anabaptists were culled, Calvinist preachers came to the city from Geneva, where the movement started, and via France (the Principality of Orange, in the south of France, had links with Holland and was one of the few pockets of Protestantism outside Switzerland and parts of

Germany). The arrival of the Calvinists, with their principles of sober, upright citizenship, caused a transformation in Amsterdam. In 1566, religious discontent erupted into what became known as the Iconoclastic Fury, the most severe of such outbreaks in European history. In the space of two months, a spontaneous uprising led to the sacking of many churches and monasteries. The Iconoclastic Fury had two major effects. One was that a church in Amsterdam, the Zuiderkerk, was allocated to the Calvinists, while the other was Philip II of Spain's decision to send an army to suppress the heresy.

## ALTERED STATES

The Eighty Years' War (1568-1648) between the Habsburgs and the Dutch is often seen as a struggle for religious freedom, but there was rather more to it than that: the Dutch were, after all, looking for political autonomy from an absentee king who represented little more than a continual drain on their coffers. By the last quarter of the sixteenth century, Philip II of Spain was fighting wars against England (to which he sent his Armada) and France, in the East against the Ottoman Turks, and in the New World, for control of his colonies. The last thing he needed was a revolt in the Low Countries.

During the revolt, Amsterdam toed the Catholic line, ostensibly supporting Philip II until it became clear that he was losing. Only in 1578 did the city patricians side with the rebels, who were led by the first William of Orange. The city and William then combined to expel the Catholics and dismantle their institutions in what came to be called the Alteration. A year later, too, the Protestant states of the Low Countries united in opposition to Philip when the first modern-day European Republic was born at the Union of Utrecht. The Republic of Seven United Provinces was made up of Friesland, Gelderland, Groningen, Overijssel, Utrecht, Zeeland and, most importantly, Holland. Although lauded as the start of the modern Netherlands, it wasn't the unitary state that William of Orange had wanted, but rather a loose federation with an impotent States General assembly.

Each province appointed a 'stadhouder' (or viceroy), who commanded the Republic's armed forces and had the right to appoint some of the cities' regents or governors. The stadhouder of each province sent delegates to the assembly, held at the **Binnenhof** in The Hague (*see chapter* **The Randstad**, *page 233*). The treaty enshrined freedom of conscience and religion, apart from for Catholics (at least until the Republic's end in 1795).

## CALVIN & NOBS

From its earliest beginnings, Amsterdam had been governed by four Burgomasters – mayors, basically – and a city council representing citizens'

interests. By 1500, though, city government had become an incestuous business: the city council's 36 members were appointed for life, and themselves 'elected' the mayors from among their own ranks. Selective inter-marriage meant that the city was, in effect, governed by a handful of families. When Amsterdam joined the rebels in 1578, the only change in civic administration was that the formerly Catholic elite was replaced by a Calvinist faction comprising equally wealthy families.

However, social welfare was transformed. Formerly the concern of the Catholic Church, welfare under the Calvinists was incorporated into city government. The Regents, as the Calvinist elite became known, took over the convents and monasteries, establishing charitable organisations such as orphanages and homes for the elderly. But the Regents' hard-work ethic and abstemious way of life would not tolerate any kind of excess: crime, drunkenness and immorality were all condemned and punishable by a spell in a house of correction. Law and order in the city was maintained by the civic guard or militia who, fortunately for artists like Rembrandt, had a penchant for having their portraits painted.

## TRADE & INDUSTRY

During the two centuries before the Eighty Years' War, Amsterdam had developed a powerful maritime force, expanding its fleet and broadening its trading horizons to include Russia, Scandinavia and the Baltic States. Even so, Amsterdam remained overshadowed by Antwerp until 1589, when that city fell to the Spanish.

The Habsburg Spanish, rather than engaging in pitched battles, adopted siege tactics, primarily in what is now Belgium. Amsterdam, therefore, was unaffected by the hostilities, and benefitted from the crippling blockades suffered by rival commercial ports. Thousands of refugees fled north, including Antwerp's most prosperous Protestant and Jewish merchants. These refugees brought with them the skills, the gold and, most famously, the diamond industry that would set Amsterdam on course to becoming the greatest trading city in the world and herald the beginning of what came to be known as the Golden Age.

## The Golden Age

European history seems to be littered with Golden Ages, but in Amsterdam's case the first six decades of the seventeenth century truly deserve the title. The small city on the Amstel came to dominate world trade and establish important colonies, resulting in a population explosion and a frenzy of urban expansion in Amsterdam: the elegant girdle of canals excavated around the city centre was one of the greatest engineering feats of that century. Extraordinarily, this all happened

*A portrait of the artist as a hairy man, on the window of his old house. See page 18.*

while the country was at war with Spain, the century's ailing superpower. Equally startling for the period, though, is the fact that this growth was presided over not by kings, but by businessmen.

The East India Company doesn't have much of a ring to it, but the name of the mighty Verenigde Oost Indische Compagnie (VOC), the world's first ever transnational company, definitely loses something in translation. The VOC was initially created by a States General charter in 1602 to finance the wildly expensive and hellishly dangerous voyages to the East. Drawn by the potential fortunes to be made out of trade in spices and silk, the shrewd Dutch saw sense in sending out merchant fleets, but they also knew that one disaster could leave an individual investor penniless. As a result, the main cities set up trading 'chambers', which evaluated the feasibility (and profitability) of ventures, then sent ships eastwards. The power of the VOC was far-reaching: it had the capacity to found colonies, establish its own army, declare war and sign treaties. The VOC's history is well charted in the **Nederlands Scheepvaart Museum** (*see chapter* Museums, *page 80*).

## DIRE STRAITS

The story of Isaac Lemaire, whose name was to become immortalised in atlases, is a good illustration of just how powerful the VOC became. Lemaire fled to Amsterdam from Antwerp in 1589 and became a founder member of the VOC, initially investing ƒ90,000 in the company (over ƒ90 million in today's money). Later, after being accused of embezzlement, he was forced to quit the company, and cast around for ways to set up on his own. However, the VOC had a monopoly on trade with the East via the Cape of Good Hope, and, at that time, there was no alternative route.

Lemaire was not so easily beaten, and heard Portuguese seamen claiming that the Cape route was not the only passage to the East: they believed the fabulous spice islands of Java, the Moluccas and Malaya could also be reached by sailing to the tip of South America, where a strait would lead into the Pacific. In 1615, Lemaire financed a voyage, led by one of his sons, that discovered the strait that still bears his name.

While the VOC concentrated on the spice trade, a new company received its charter from the Dutch Republic in 1621. The Dutch West India Company (*West-Indische Compagnie*, or WIC), though not as successful as its sister, dominated trade with Spanish and Portuguese territories in Africa and America, and in 1623 began to colonise Manhattan Island. The settlement was laid out on a grid system similar to Amsterdam's, and adopted the Dutch city's name. New Amsterdam flourished, and areas were named after other enterprising towns with a stake in the colony: the New York boroughs of Harlem and Brooklyn are named after Haarlem and Breukelen, while Staten Island took its moniker in honour of the States General, the 'national' council of the Republic.

However, the name didn't last. After the Duke of York's invasion in 1664, the peace treaty between England and the Netherlands determined that New Amsterdam would change its name to New York and come under British control. The Dutch got Surinam as a feeble consolation prize.

Though commerce with the Indies became extensive, it never surpassed Amsterdam's European business: the city had soon become the major European centre for distribution and trade. Grain from Russia, Poland and Prussia, salt and wine from France, cloth from Leiden and tiles from Delft all passed through the port. Whales were hunted by Amsterdam's fleets, generating a flourishing soap trade, and sugar and spices from

Dutch colonies were distributed to ports throughout Scandinavia and the north of Europe. All this activity was financed by the Bank of Amsterdam, which had been set up in the cellars of the City Hall by the municipal council as early as 1609. It was a unique initiative and led to Amsterdam being considered the money vault of Europe, its notes readily exchangeable throughout the trading world. Single European Currency, eat your heart out…

## WHERE THERE'S A WILL

The political structure of the young Dutch Republic was complex. When the Treaty of Utrecht was signed in 1579, no suitable monarch or head of state was found, so the existing system was adapted to fit new needs. The seven provinces were represented by a 'national' council, the States General. In addition, the provinces appointed a stadhouder, a viceroy figure.

The most popular and obvious choice for stadhouder after the treaty was William of Orange, the wealthy Dutchman who had led the rebellion against Philip II of Spain. William was then succeeded by his son, Maurits of Nassau, who was as militarily successful against the Spanish as his father had been, eventually securing the Twelve Years' Truce (1609-21). Although each province could, in theory, elect a different stadhouder, in practice they usually chose the same person. After William's popularity, it soon became something of a tradition to elect an Orange as stadhouder, and by 1641 the family had become sufficiently powerful for William II to marry a British princess, Mary Stuart. It was their son, William III, who, backed by Amsterdam money, set sail in 1688 to accept the throne of England in the so-called Glorious Revolution.

But the Oranges weren't popular with everyone. The provinces' representatives at the States General were known as regents, and Holland's – and therefore Amsterdam's – regent was in a powerful enough position to challenge the authority and decisions of the stadhouder. This power was eventually exercised in 1650, in a crisis precipitated by Holland's decision to disband its militia after the end of the Eighty Years' War with Spain. Stadhouder William II wanted the militia maintained – and, importantly, paid for – by Holland, and in response to the disbandment, he got a kinsman, William Frederick, to launch a surprise attack on Amsterdam.

After William II died three months later, the leaders of the States of Holland called a Great Assembly of the provinces. Even though there was no outward resistance to the Williams' earlier attack on the city, the provinces – with the exception of Friesland and Groningen, who remained loyal to William Frederick – decided that there should be no stadhouders, and Johan de Witt, Holland's powerful regent, swore no prince of

Orange would ever become stadhouder again. This became law in the Act of Seclusion of 1653.

## BUY THE POWER

During this era, Amsterdam's ruling assembly, the Heren XLVIII (a sheriff, four mayors, a 36-member council and seven jurists), kept a firm grip on all that went on both within and without the city walls. Although this system was self-perpetuating, these people were merchants rather than aristocrats, and anyone who made enough money could, in theory, become a member. The mayors and the council usually came from a handful of prominent families, the most powerful being the Witsen, Bicker, Six and Trip families; all are still commemorated with Amsterdam street names. The mayors' wives, nieces and daughters also got in on the act: in a blatantly nepotistic gesture, they were elected to form boards of governesses at the multitude of charitable institutions scattered throughout the city.

The less elevated folk – the craftsmen, artisans and shopkeepers – were equally active in maintaining their position. A system of guilds had developed in earlier centuries, linked to the Catholic Church, but under the new order, guilds were independent organisations run by their members. The original Amsterdammers – known as 'poorters' from the Dutch for 'gate', as they originally lived within the gated walls of the city – began to see their livelihoods threatened by an influx of newcomers who were prepared to work for lower wages.

Things came to a head when the shipwrights began to lose their trade to less expensive competitors in the nearby Zaan region and protested vigorously to the powers-that-be. The shipwrights' lobby was so strong that the city regents decreed that Amsterdam ships had to be repaired in Amsterdam yards. This kind of protectionism extended to almost all industrial sectors in the city and effectively meant most crafts became closed shops. Only poorters, or those who had married poorters' daughters, were allowed to join a guild, thereby protecting Amsterdammers' livelihoods and, essentially, barring outsiders from joining their trades.

## GROWING PAINS

Although Amsterdam's population had grown to 50,000 by 1600, this was nothing compared with the next 50 years, when it ballooned fourfold. Naturally, the city was obliged to expand to fit its new residents. The most elegant of the many canals circling the city centre was Herengracht (Lords' Canal): begun in 1613, this was where many of the Heren XLVIII had their homes. So there would be no misunderstanding about who was most important, Herengracht was followed further out by Keizersgracht (Emperors' Canal)

and Prinsengracht (Princes' Canal). (For all, *see box* **Passing Water**, *pages 54-5*.) Immigrants were housed rather more modestly in the Jordaan.

Despite the city's wealth, and the reputation of its people as masters of transport – they could, in theory, have food supplies shipped in – famine hit Amsterdam with dreary regularity in the seventeenth century. Guilds had benevolent funds set aside for their members in times of need, but social welfare was primarily in the hands of the ruling merchant class. Amsterdam's elite was noted for its philanthropy, but only poorters were eligible for assistance: even they had to fall into a specific category, described as 'deserving poor'. Those seen as undeserving were sent to a house of correction. The initial philosophy behind these places had been rather idealistic, and they were run on the premise that hard work would ultimately produce reformed, useful citizens. But soon, the institutions became little more than prisons.

Religious freedom was still not what it might have been, either. As a result of the Alteration of 1578, Roman Catholic worship was banned in the city during the seventeenth century, and Catholics were left to practise their faith in secret, if they dared practise at all. Some Catholics started attic churches, which are exactly what their name suggests they might be: of the several set up in the city during the 1600s, the **Amstelkring Museum** has preserved Amsterdam's only surviving example – Our Lord in the Attic – in its entirety (*see chapter* **Museums**, *page 79*).

## ART FOR ART'S SAKE

Amsterdam's seventeenth-century Golden Age encompassed both commercial life and the arts: Rembrandt and hundreds of other less notable artists made a good living during the period. Those artists united in the Guild of St Luke – even artists had a guild – are estimated to have produced an extraordinary 20 million paintings, with every family having at least three or four works of art in their home. Though Rembrandt famously died in poverty, he had a remarkably comfortable life, evidence of which can be seen at the rather grand house where he lived in Jodenbreestraat, now known, simply, as the **Rembrandthuis** (*see chapter* **Museums**, *page 76*).

However, unlike other European countries, the Netherlands wasn't liberally scattered with ancient universities: in fact, Amsterdam didn't have one at all. The first move towards establishing a centre of higher education came in 1632 when the Athenaeum Illustre was opened. It was attended by (male) members of the elite, who studied Latin, Greek, law and the natural sciences. But two of the era's most important scientific pioneers – physicist Christiaan Huygens and Anthonie van Leeuwenhoek, who pioneered microbiology – didn't go to a university at all, doing all their work in improvised laboratories at home. Amsterdam's guild of surgeons, as Rembrandt and other artists have recorded, held public demonstrations of anatomy, using the bodies of executed criminals for dissection practice.

## Decline & fall

Although Amsterdam remained one of the wealthiest cities in Europe until the early nineteenth century, its dominant trading position was lost to England and France after 1660. The United Provinces then spent a couple of centuries bickering about trade and politics with Britain and the other main powers. Wars were frequent: major sea conflicts included battles against the Swedes and no fewer than four Anglo-Dutch wars, from which the Dutch came off slightly worse. It wasn't that they didn't win any wars; more that the small country ran out of men and money.

Despite – or perhaps because of – its history with the Orange family, Amsterdam became the most vociferous opponent to the family's attempt to acquire kingdoms, though it strongly supported William III when this Orange crossed the sea to become King of England in 1688. The city fathers believed a Dutchman on their rival's throne could only be an advantage, and for a while they were proved correct. However, William was soon knocking on the Amsterdammers' doors for more money to fight even more wars, this time against France.

The admirals who led the wars against Britain are Dutch heroes, and the **Nieuwe Kerk** has monuments to admirals Van Kinsbergen (1735-1819), Bentinck (1745-1831) and, most celebrated of all, Michiel de Ruyter (1607-76). The most famous incident, though not prominent in British history books, was during the Second English War (1664-67), when de Ruyter sailed up the Thames to Chatham, stormed the dockyards and burnt the *Royal Charles*, the British flagship, as it lay at anchor. The *Royal Charles'* coat of arms was stolen, and is now displayed in the Rijksmuseum.

Despite diminished maritime prowess, Amsterdam retained the highest standard of living of all Europe until well into the eighteenth century. The Plantage district was a direct result of the city's prosperity, and tradesmen and artisans flourished: their role in society can still be gauged by the intricate shapes and carvings on gablestones.

### FRENCH BRED

The Dutch Republic began to lag behind the major European powers in the eighteenth century. The Agricultural and Industrial Revolutions didn't get off the ground in the Netherlands until later: Amsterdam was nudged out of the shipbuilding market by England, and its lucrative textile industry was lost to other provinces. However, the city managed to exploit its position as the financial

centre of the world until the final, devastating Anglo-Dutch War (1780-84). The British hammered the Dutch merchant and naval fleets, crippling the profitable trade with their Far-Eastern colonies.

The closest the Dutch came to the Republican movements of France and the United States was with the Patriots. During the 1780s, the Patriots managed to shake off the influence of the stadhouders in many smaller towns, but in 1787 they were foiled in Amsterdam by the intervention of the Prince of Orange and his brother-in-law, Frederick William II, King of Prussia. Hundreds of Patriots then fled to exile in France, where their welcome convinced them Napoleon's intentions towards the Dutch Republic were benign. In 1795 they returned, backed by a French army of 'advisers'. With massive support from Amsterdam, they celebrated the new Batavian Republic.

It sounded too good to be true, and it was. According to one contemporary, 'The French moved over the land like locusts.' Over $f$100 million (about $f$1 billion today) was extracted from the Dutch, and the French also sent a standing army, all 25,000 of whom had to be fed, equipped and billeted by their Dutch 'hosts'. Republican ideals seemed increasingly hollow when Napoleon installed one of his brothers, Louis, as King of the Netherlands in 1806, and the symbol of Amsterdam's mercantile ascendancy and civic pride, the City Hall of the Dam, was requisitioned as the royal palace. Even Louis was disturbed by the increasing impoverishment of a nation that had been Europe's most prosperous. However, after Louis had allowed Dutch smugglers to break Napoleon's blockade of Britain, he was forced to abdicate in 1810 and the Low Countries were absorbed into the French Empire.

Even so, government by the French wasn't an unmitigated disaster for the Dutch. The foundations of the modern Dutch state were laid in the Napoleonic period, a civil code was introduced and education improved. Conversely, though, trade with Britain ceased, and the growing price of Napoleon's wars prompted the Dutch to join the revolt against France. After Napoleon's defeat, Amsterdam became the capital of a constitutional monarchy, incorporating what is now Belgium; William VI of Orange was crowned King William I in 1815. But though the Oranges still reign in the northern provinces, the United Kingdom of the Netherlands, as it then existed, was to last only until 1830.

## Between the Occupations

When the French were finally defeated and left Dutch soil in 1813, Amsterdam emerged as the capital of the new kingdom of the Netherlands but very little else: extraordinarily, the city wasn't even the seat of government. With its coffers almost totally depleted and its colonies occupied by the British, Amsterdam would have to fight hard for recovery.

The fight was made tougher by two huge obstacles. For a start, Dutch colonial assets had been reduced to present-day Indonesia (then the Dutch East Indies), Surinam and the odd island in the Caribbean. Just as important, though, was the fact that the Dutch were slow to join the Industrial Revolution. The Netherlands had – indeed, still has – few natural resources to exploit and Dutch business preferred to keep its hands clean by relying on the power of sail. Add to all this the inconvenient fact that Amsterdam's opening to the sea, the Zuider Zee, was too shallow to accommodate the new, larger, steam-ships, and it's easy to see how the Dutch were forced to struggle.

In an attempt to link the city to the North Sea port of Den Helder, the circuitous Great North Holland Canal was dug in 1824. But because it had so many bridges and locks, it was slow and expensive, both to construct and to use. Rotterdam gradually took over the capital's position as the most progressive industrial centre.

## STATION TO STATION
Prosperity eventually returned to Amsterdam after the 1860s. The city readjusted its economy to meet modern demands, and its trading position was greatly improved by the building of two canals. The opening of the Suez Canal in 1869 sped up the passage to the Orient, producing a giant increase in commerce. But what the city needed most was easy access to the major shipping lanes of northern Europe. When it was opened in 1876, the North Sea Canal enabled Amsterdam to take advantage of German industrial trade and become the Netherlands' greatest shipbuilding port again, at least temporarily. Industrial machinery was introduced late to Amsterdam. However, by the late nineteenth century, the city had begun to modernise production of the luxury goods it would become famous for: chocolates, cigars, beer and cut diamonds.

Of course, not all of Amsterdam's trade was conducted on water. Although there had been a local railway track between Haarlem and Amsterdam since 1839, the city finally got a major rail link and a new landmark in 1889. **Centraal Station** was had been designed by influential architect PJH Cuypers in 1876, and was initially intended to be in the Pijp. When it was decided that the track should run along the Zuider Zee, shutting the city off from its seafront, much objection ensued. There was also controversy when the **Rijksmuseum** (*see chapter* **Museums**, *page 76*) was situated at what was then the fringe of the city, and about the selection of Cuypers as its architect. The result was, like Centraal Station, uniquely eclectic and led to the museum being ridiculed as a 'cathedral

of the arts' – a not entirely inappropriate label, given the contemporary boom in culture.

The city's powers decided to consolidate Amsterdam's position at the forefront of Europe, both commercially and culturally, with the building of a number of landmark structures. In 1877, the Carré Theatre opened, followed a year later by the **Concertgebouw**, then in 1894 by the **Stadsschouwburg**, in 1895 by the **Stedelijk Museum** and, in 1926, the Tropen Institute (now the **Tropenmuseum**). The city's international standing had soon improved to such a point that in 1928 it hosted the Olympic Games.

## AFFORDING THE POOR
Social welfare in Amsterdam, long dependent on charity and the goodwill of the elite, was also transformed in the nineteenth century. But until prosperity returned in the last third of the century, the living conditions of the working population continued to be appalling. Before 1850, Amsterdam's solution was to follow central government policy and round up the destitute, sending them off to do hard agricultural labour. Yet throughout this period, Amsterdam spent a relatively large amount of money on relief for the poor.

In the second half of the century, however, the idea grew that assistance only made the poor lazy, and relief was cut back. But towards the end of the 1800s, the newly formed trade unions set up some forms of poor relief for their members. Socialist ideas began to permeate, and the way was paved for the development of one of the best social security systems in the world.

## DIAMOND LIFE
The story of diamonds in Amsterdam is also the history of social change in the city. The first records of diamond-working in Amsterdam go back as far as 1586, and latterly, fabulous stones such as the Koh-i-Noor (Mountain of Light), one of the British crown jewels, were cut by an Amsterdammer. But as the industry was entirely dependent upon the discovery of rare stones, it was in a continual state of flux. In the early 1870s, diamond cutters could light cigars with $f$10 notes (the average weekly wage for the rest of the workforce was then $f$8). A decade later, though, the city prohibited diamond workers from begging naked in the streets. Thankfully for the impoverished diamond workers, however, the working classes had become more politicised in the intervening years, and the ideas behind the old guild system took on a new resonance. Funds were established to protect diamond workers during slumps, and this movement led to the formation of the first Dutch trade union.

In the early days of the union movement, socialists and the upper classes co-existed relatively harmoniously, but by the 1880s things were changing.

*Amsterdam's seventeenth-century expansion began with* **Herengracht**. *See page 18.*

The movement found an articulate leader in Ferdinand Domela Nieuwenhuis, who set up a political party, the Social Democratic Union. The SDU faded into obscurity after a split in 1894, but a splinter group, the Social Democratic Labour Party (SDAP), later won the first ever socialist city-council seat for the diamond workers' union chief, Henri Polak, in 1901. The SDAP went on to introduce the welfare state after World War II.

Educational reform was perhaps the greatest step forward made in the late nineteenth century. A network of free primary schools was set up to teach the working classes the rudiments of reading, writing and arithmetic.

## NEW DEVELOPMENTS

Amsterdam's population had stagnated at around a quarter of a million for two centuries after the Golden Age, but between 1850 and 1900 it more than doubled. The increased labour force was desperately needed to meet the demands of a revitalised economy, but the major problem was how to house the new workers. Today, the old inner city quarters are desirable addresses, but they used to be the homes of Amsterdam's poor. The picturesque Jordaan, where riots broke out with increasing regularity in the 1930s, was occupied primarily by the lowest-paid workers, canals were used as cesspits, and the mortality rate was high. Oddly, the Jordaan was the first area in the city to have Tarmac streets. The decision wasn't philanthropic, however: it came after Queen Wilhelmina had been pelted by Jordaan cobblestones.

Around the old centre, new neighbourhoods were constructed. The new housing developments – the Pijp, Dapper and Staatslieden quarters – weren't luxurious by any means, and most were cheaply built by speculators, but at least they had simple lavatory facilities (though no bathrooms). Wealthier city-dwellers, meanwhile, found elegance and space in homes built around Vondelpark and in the south of the city.

## WAR & DEPRESSION

The city didn't fare badly in the first two decades of the twentieth century, but Dutch neutrality during World War I brought problems. While the elite lined their pockets selling arms, the poor were confronted with continual food shortages. In 1917, with food riots erupting, especially in the Jordaan, the city had to open soup kitchens and introduce rationing. The army was called in to suppress another outbreak of civil unrest in the Jordaan in 1934. This time the cause was unemployment, endemic throughout the industrialised world after the Wall Street Crash of 1929: historians estimate that in 1936, 19 per cent of the workforce was unemployed.

Unfortunately, the humiliation of means testing for unemployment benefit meant that many families suffered in hungry silence. Many Dutch workers even moved to Germany where National Socialism was creating new jobs. At home, Amsterdam initiated extensive public works under the 1934 General Extension Plan, whereby the city's southern outskirts were developed for

# Hip to be square

All tourists in Amsterdam find themselves on Dam Square (or just Dam, as it's often called) at least once during a visit: it's simply unavoidable. Most visitors cross the square in a hurry, on their way from the tacky Kalverstraat to the even tackier Nieuwendijk, or en route to the Bijenkorf department store. Fighting their way through pigeons, street artists, ice-cream and hot dog vans and hundreds of fellow tourists, they're rarely aware of the square's prominent place in Amsterdam's history books.

It's hard to imagine that this is the same place that, over the centuries, has been the inspiration to so many artists. This inability to grasp the square's historical importance is understandable as, despite the crowds, today's square is surprisingly lacking in atmosphere. In fact, one of the few things that haven't changed over the years is the presence of people milling about, though the reasons for them being here might have.

Dam Square has one hell of a claim to fame. Located in the heart of the city, it marks the spot where, in about 1270, a dam over the Amstel (called Aemstelledamme) was built, which gave Amsterdam its name. There once was a harbour on the site where the prestigious Bijenkorf department store now stands. As a spot where goods were unloaded, it was the perfect location for the city's market.

Three eye-catching monuments are found on the square. The most striking of these is the **Koninklijk Paleis** (or Royal Palace). Architect Jacob van Campen originally designed the palace as a town hall in the seventeenth century, but when King Louis came to Amsterdam in 1808 he deemed the building grand enough to become his Royal Palace. From 1715 to 1815, Rembrandt's best-known painting, *The Night Watch*, was displayed inside. In hindsight the choice of location was disastrous, as the masterpiece had to be cut by about 29 inches (75cm) on each side in order to fit on a wall between two doors. Opposite the palace is the **Nieuwe Kerk**, originally built in the late fourteenth century but destroyed by fire several times. Though not exactly a spring chicken, it *is* new compared with the **Oude Kerk**.

Wherever you stand on the square you can't miss the **Nationaal Monument**, a 72-foot (22-metre) high pillar with statues and lions, erected in memory of the Dutch people who lost their lives during World War II. In contrast to the violence it commemorated, the monument became the epicentre of love and peace in the '60s: hippies from all over the world came to talk, kiss, smoke hash and sleep on its steps. Sadly, the spot has long since lost its innocence, and nowadays merely attracts aimless tourists and dubious characters trying to flog them drugs of equally dubious quality, and by 1997, the Nationaal Monument was falling apart and had to be stripped and renovated. Ironically, the ren-

---

public housing. The city was just emerging from the Depression by the time the Nazis invaded in May 1940.

## World War II

Amsterdam endured World War II without being flattened by bombs, but its buildings, infrastructure and inhabitants were reduced to a terrible state by Nazi occupation. The Holocaust also left an indelible scar on a city whose population in 1940 was ten per cent Jewish.

Early in the morning of 10 May, 1940, German bombers mounted a surprise attack on Dutch airfields and military barracks in order to destroy the Dutch Air Force. The government and people had hoped that the Netherlands could remain neutral, as they had in World War I, so the armed forces were unprepared for war. Even when it became apparent that this would not be so, the Dutch aimed to hold off the Germans until the British and French could come to their assistance. Their hope was in vain, though, and Queen Wilhelmina and the government fled to London to form a government in exile, leaving Supreme Commander Winkelman in charge of state authority.

Rotterdam, too, was destroyed by bombing, and when the Germans threatened other cities with the same treatment, Winkelman gave up the ghost on 14 May, 1940. The Dutch colonies of Indonesia and New Guinea were then invaded by the Japanese in January 1942. After their capitulation on 8 March, the Dutch colonials were imprisoned in Japanese concentration camps.

During the war, Hitler appointed Austrian Nazi Arthur Seyss-Inquart as Rijkskommissaris (State Commissioner) of the Netherlands, and asked him to tie the Dutch economy to the German one and to Nazify Dutch society. Although it won less than five per cent of the votes in the 1939 elections, the National Socialist Movement (NSB) was the largest and most important fascist political party in the ovation was carried out by a German company, the only firm with sufficient expertise to do it.

Behind the Nationaal Monument is the **Grand Hotel Krasnapolsky** (*see chapter* **Accommodation**, *page 91*), a massive, old hotel that stands in complete contrast to several seedy tourist traps around it: the sleazy Warmoesstraat on the left, the Damstraat, with its numerous junkies, on the right, and the Red Light District directly behind. Also cashing in on the square's status as a tourist hot-spot is the grandly named **Madame Tussauds Scenerama**, on the corner of Dam Square and Rokin.

Though its glory days are over, Dam Square can – and does – still have its moments, particularly when it is used for festivities. Massive fun fairs (in May), an annual open-air draughts (checkers) tournament, the **Remembrance Day** celebrations, the **Dam to Dam** marathon and the summer **Uitmarkt** all take place here (*see chapter* **By Season**, *pages 7, 8 & 10*). Then again, if you're here in December, you'll notice a Christmas tree that's seen better days. Don't bother asking yourself why the Amsterdam council can't afford anything better: it's actually an annual gift from the Norwegian town of Trondheim.

*See chapter* **Sightseeing**, *pages 41-43, for more on Dam Square's sights and sounds.*

Netherlands, and was the only Dutch party not prohibited during the occupation. Its doctrine greatly resembled German Nazism, but the NSB wanted to maintain Dutch autonomy under the direction of Germany.

During the first years of the war, the Nazis allowed most people to live relatively undisturbed. Rationing, however, made the Dutch vulnerable to the black market, while cinemas and theatres eventually closed because of curfews and censorship. When the Nazis' soft approach failed to have the desired effect on the locals, the Germans adopted more aggressive measures: Dutch men were soon forced to work in German industry, and economic exploitation assumed appalling forms. In April 1943, all Dutch soldiers, who'd been captured during the invasion and then released in the summer of 1940, were ordered to give themselves up as prisoners of war. In an atmosphere of deep shock and outrage, strikes broke out during April and May, but were violently suppressed.

To begin with, ordinary people, as well as the political and economic elite, had no real reason to make a choice between collaboration and resistance. But as Nazi policies became more virulent, opposition to them swelled, and a growing minority of people were confronted with the difficult choice of whether to obey German measures or to resist. There were several patterns of collaboration. Some people joined the NSB, while others intimidated Jews, got involved in economic collaboration or betrayed people in hiding or members of the Resistance. Amazingly, a small number even signed up for German military service. In Amsterdam, several social institutions gave information about Jews to the Germans, but the most shocking institutional collaboration was by the police, who dragged Jews out of their houses for deportation. The Dutch Railways also assisted the Nazis by transporting Jews to their deaths and received money for doing so. After the war, between 120,000 and 150,000 people were arrested for collaborating. Mitigating circumstances – as in the case of NSB members who helped the Resistance – made judgments very complicated, but, eventually, no fewer than 60,000 people were brought to justice.

## GOING UNDERGROUND

The Resistance was made up chiefly of Calvinists and Communists. Though the latter movement gained public support, the Calvinist elite ensured that there was no Communist takeover after liberation. Anti-Nazi activities took several forms, illegal newspapers – the only alternative to what was then a heavily censored press – keeping the population properly informed and urging them to resist the Nazi dictators.

Underground groups took many shapes, sizes and forms. Some spied for the Allies; others fought an armed struggle against the Germans through assassination and sabotage; and others still falsified identity cards and food vouchers. A national organisation took care of people who wanted to hide, and helped the railway strikers, Dutch soldiers and illegal workers being sought by the Germans, with other groups helping Jews into hiding. By 1945, more than 300,000 people had gone underground in the Netherlands.

## HUNGER WINTER

Worse was to follow towards the end of the war, when, in 1944, the Netherlands was plunged into the 'Hunger Winter'. Supplies of coal vanished after the liberation of the south and a railway strike, called by the Dutch government in exile to hasten German defeat, was disastrous for the supply of food. In retaliation for the strike, the Germans damaged Schiphol Airport and the harbours of Rotterdam and Amsterdam – foiling any attempts to bring in supplies – and appropriated everything they could. Walking became the only means of transport, domestic refuse was no longer collected, sewers overflowed, and the population, suffering from malnutrition and illnesses brought on by the cold, was vulnerable to disease.

To survive, people stole fuel: more than 20,000 trees were cut down and 4,600 buildings were demolished. Floors, staircases, joists and rafters were plundered, causing the collapse of many houses, particularly those left by deported Jews. Supplies were scarce and many people couldn't even afford to buy their rationing allowance, let alone the expensive produce on the black market. By the end of the winter, 20,000 people had died of starvation and disease, and much of the city was seriously damaged.

Hope, though, was just around the corner. The Allies finally liberated the south of the Netherlands on 5 September, 1944, Dolle Dinsdag (Mad Tuesday), and complete liberation came after the Hunger Winter on 5 May, 1945, when it became apparent that the Netherlands was the worst hit country in Western Europe. In spite of the chaos, destruction, hunger and the loss of so many lives, there were effusive celebrations. But tragedy struck in Amsterdam on 7 May, when German soldiers opened fire on a crowd who had gathered on Dam Square to welcome their Canadian liberators. Twenty two people were killed.

## THE HOLOCAUST

'I see how the world is slowly becoming a desert, I hear more and more clearly the approaching thunder that will kill us,' wrote **Anne Frank** in her diary on 15 July, 1944. Though her words obviously applied to the Jews, they were also relevant to the Gypsies, the homosexuals, the mentally handicapped, and the Nazis' political opponents, who were all severely persecuted during the war. Granted, anti-Semitism in Holland had not been as virulent as in Germany, France or Austria. But even so, most – though not all – of the Dutch population closed its eyes to the persecution, and there's still a feeling of national guilt as a result.

The Holocaust arrived in three stages. First came measures to enforce the isolation of the Jews: the ritual slaughter of animals was prohibited, Jewish government employees were dismissed, Jews were banned from public places such as restaurants, cinemas and libraries and, eventually, all Jews were forced to wear a yellow Star of David. (Some non-Jewish Dutch courageously wore the badge as a demonstration of solidarity.) Concentration was the second stage. From early 1942, all Dutch Jews were obliged to move to three areas in Amsterdam, isolated by signs, drawbridges and barbed wire. The final stage was deportation. Between July 1942 and September 1943, most of the 140,000 Dutch Jews were deported, via Kamp Westerbork. Public outrage at the first deportations provoked the most dramatic protests against the anti-Semitic terror, the impressive February Strike.

The Nazis had also wanted to eliminate Dutch Gypsies: more than 200,000 European Gypsies, about 200 of them Dutch, were exterminated in concentration camps. Homosexuals were also threatened with extermination, but their persecution was less systematic: public morality acts prohibited homosexual behaviour, and gay pressure groups ceased their activities. In addition, men arrested for other activities were punished more severely if they were found to be gay. In Dutch educational history books, the extermination of Gypsies and homosexuals is still often omitted, but Amsterdam has the world's first memorial to persecuted gays, the **Homomonument**, which incorporates pink triangles in its design, turning the Nazi badge of persecution into a symbol of pride.

## The post-war era

The Netherlands was deeply scarred by the German occupation, losing about ten per cent of all its housing, 30 per cent of its industry and 40 per cent of its total production capacity. The transport system, too, had been immobilised, and some of the country's dykes had been blown up, leaving large areas flooded. Though Amsterdam had escaped the bombing raids which devastated Rotterdam, it had borne the brunt of the deportations: only 5,000 Jews, out of a pre-war total Jewish population of 80,000, remained in the city.

Despite intense poverty and drastic shortages of food, fuel and building materials, the Dutch tackled the massive task of post-war recovery and restoration with the spirit of the Resistance. There was a strong sense of optimism and unity, which was sustained until the end of the '40s. In 1948, people threw street parties, firstly to celebrate the inauguration of Queen Juliana and, later, the four gold medals won by Amsterdam athlete Fanny Blankers-Koen at the London Olympics.

Some Dutch flirted briefly with communism directly after the war, but in 1948, a compromise was struck between the Catholic party, KVP, and the newly created Labour party, PvdA, and the two proceeded to govern in successive coalitions until 1958. Led by Prime Minister Willem Drees, the government resuscitated pre-war social programmes and laid the basis for the country's lavish welfare state. The Dutch reverted to the virtues of a conservative, provincial society: decency, hard work and thrift.

The country's first priority after the war was economic recovery. The Amsterdam city council concentrated on reviving the two motors of its economy: Schiphol Airport and the port of Amsterdam, the latter of which was soon boosted by the opening of the Amsterdam-Rhine Canal in

**Anne Frank**. *See page 24.*

1952. Joining Belgium and Luxembourg in the Benelux also brought the country trade benefits, and the Netherlands was the first to repay its Marshall Plan loans. The authorities then proceeded to dust off their pre-war development plans and embarked on rapid urban expansion. Garden cities such as Slotervaart, Geuzenveld and Osdorp were created in the west; the architecture was sober, the setting spacious. But as people moved out to the new suburbs, businesses moved into the centre, worsening congestion on the already cramped roads. Traffic casualties soared.

### COLONIAL CONNECTIONS
After the war, the Dutch colonies of Indonesia and New Guinea were liberated from the Japanese and were soon pushing for independence. With Indonesia accounting for 20 per cent of their pre-war economy, the Dutch launched military interventions on 20 July, 1947 and 18 December, 1948. However, the interventions could not prevent the transfer of sovereignty to Indonesia on 27 December, 1949, while the dispute with New Guinea dragged on until 1962 and did much to damage the Netherlands' international reputation. Colonial immigrants to the Netherlands, including the later arrival of Surinamese, and Turkish and Moroccan 'guest workers', now comprise 16 per cent of the population. Although poorer jobs and

housing have usually been their lot, racial tensions were relatively low until the mid-'90s, with the rise of neo-fascism in the shape of the CD party. But the CD's gains in previous elections were all but wiped out in 1998, as Dutch voters sent a message that they'd had enough of extremist politics.

Though the economy revived in the '50s, and the welfare state was back to its best, there was still civil unrest. Strikes flared at the port and council workers defied a ban on industrial action. In 1951, protesters clashed with police outside the Concertgebouw, angered by the appointment of a pro-Nazi as conductor. In 1956, demonstrators besieged the Felix Meritis Building, the base of the Dutch Communist Party from 1946 until the late '70s, hurling stones in outrage at the Soviet invasion of Hungary.

In the late '40s and '50s, Amsterdammers returned to pre-war pursuits: fashion and celebrity interviews filled the newspapers and cultural events mushroomed. In 1947, the city launched the prestigious **Holland Festival** (*see chapter* **Amsterdam by Season**, *page 10*), while the elite held their own annual event called the Boekenbal, where writers met royalty and other dignitaries. New avant-garde artistic movements emerged, notably the **CoBrA** art group, whose 1949 exhibition at the Stedelijk Museum caused an uproar, and the *vijftigers*, a group of experimental poets led by Lucebert. Many of these artists met in brown cafés around Leidseplein.

### FAREWELL TO WELFARE
The '60s were one of the most colourful decades in Amsterdam's history. There were genuine official attempts to improve society and make it more prosperous. The IJ Tunnel eased communications to North Amsterdam and the national economy took off. There were high hopes for vast rehousing developments like the **Bijlmermeer** (now Bijlmer), and influential new architecture from the likes of Aldo van Eyck and Herman Herzberger sprang up around the city.

Yet the generous hand of the welfare state was being bitten; 'welfare is not well-being' went one popular slogan. Discontent began on a variety of issues, among them the nuclear threat, rampant urban expansion and industrialisation, the consumer society and authority in general. Popular movements similar to those in other west European cities were formed, but with a zaniness all of their own. Because protest and dissent have always been a vital part of the Netherlands' democratic process, and because the Dutch have a habit of keeping things in proportion, many popular demonstrations took a playful form.

### PROVO PRANKS
The discontent gained focus in 1964, when pranks around 't Lieverdje statue, highlighting political or

# The drugs do work

A large part of the Netherlands' image abroad is defined by its seemingly lax attitude towards drugs: that, somehow, wobbly Dutch logic sees legalising crime as a viable way of dealing with crime. This image is but a shadow: in fact, soft drugs remain only semi-legal.

Back in the early 1970s, the famously pragmatic Dutch began to put drug laws into much-needed perspective. Swamped with heroin brought in by Chinese triads, and vocally reminded of the relatively benign and non-addictive effects of pot by ex-Provos and hippies then entering mainstream politics, the fight against wimpy drugs came to be regarded as a ludicrous waste of both time and money.

In 1976, a vaguely worded law defined a difference between hard and soft drugs – thereby effectively separating these markets from each other's influence – and allowed the use and sale of small amounts of soft drugs (less than 30 grams, or one ounce). The 'front door' of the then-embryonic 'coffeeshop' was now legal, but the 'back door', where produce arrived by the kilo, was still a gateway to an illegal distribution system. Still, it worked: time passed without the increase of drug use that doomsayers predicted, while the coffeeshop became an institution and a permanent part of the Amsterdam streetscape. Concerted efforts against hard drugs, meanwhile – mainly through education, methadone programmes, drop-in centres, needle exchanges and counselling – have resulted in one of the lowest junkie populations in the world.

Attempts at complete legalisation of soft drugs have always failed for a variety of reasons: misguided pressures from fellow EU members (mainly France, ironically home to Holland's pipeline for heroin), combativeness between government and coffeeshop owners who've come to enjoy testing the vague laws, and the lack of a local supply among them. This last reason is no longer a problem, though, at least not since the 'green wave' of the early '90s, when an American-designed reddish weed, Skunk, blew over and was found to grow very nicely indeed under artificial light. Technology has moved on so far that the Dutch can now produce their own hashes; foreign markets no longer have to be involved. A conservative stream in government has recently back-pedalled against home-growing, though, allowing only the growing of four plants at a time, and as a result, the black market has started to flourish again. People are allowed to be in possession of 500 grams of dope now, but this law was introduced more to cover up the absurdity of some coffeeshops selling 40 different varieties, meaning their display menus alone held more than the previously allowed 30 grams.

Many believe that now is the right time for the Netherlands to attempt to completely legalise the growing, distribution and use of soft drugs. After years of derision, neighbouring countries are now looking at the advantages of Dutch policy; the pro-legalisation campaign in the UK, for example, picked up pace in 1998 on the back of a campaign led by the *Independent On Sunday* newspaper.

After staying on the defensive for so many years, the Netherlands should now perhaps turn to a more offensive strategy wherein the government clearly explains what it has been attempting – since few actually know – and the positive results it has so far delivered.

---

social problems, became the springboard for a new radical subculture, the Provos. Founded by anarchist philosophy student Roel van Duyn and 'anti-smoke magician' Robert Japser Grootveld, the Provos numbered only about two dozen, but were enormously influential in the late '60s. Call them the flashiest of street scene-makers or call them proto-Yippies, but the Provos had a style that influenced the anti-Vietnam demos in America, and set the tone for Amsterdam's continuing love of liberal politics and absurdist theatre.

Grootveld had been considered an inspired freak of sorts ever since 1961 when he started his one-man campaign against consumerism. Hyping Amsterdam as the 'magical centre of the universe' and himself as some wacky voodoo high-priest of the 'K-temple', a hangout off the Leidseplein, he began to get noticed. However, it took responsible van Duyn to focus the chaos into an agenda. He shared with the artier types a sense of humour and a media savvy, but after years of experience with the 'Ban the Bomb' movement, he knew how to walk and talk some straight Fuck-the-State. He began distributing newsletters under the name of Provo (after 'provoke').

It was fun. Orchestrated mind-games had police, for example, busting houses for the possession of what turned out to be hay. The cops were baited, and started confiscating issues of Provo and being a little over-zealous with their truncheons. This only served to radicalise many bystanders, and the Provos soon gained wider support.

On 10 March, 1966, the Provos hit the big time, when protests about Princess Beatrix's wedding to ex-Nazi Claus von Amsberg turned nasty. The Provos let off a smoke bomb on the carriage route and a riot ensued. But the net result was not another jail sentence for Grootveld: instead, the chief of police, and then the mayor, were sacked. As opinion turned against the council's planning policies, the Provos won a seat on the city council in 1966. However, their manifesto – the so-called White Plans – tended towards the Utopian, and by May 1967, the Provos had outgrown themselves and disbanded.

## HIPPY HEAVEN

Meanwhile, foreign hippies flocked to the city, attracted by its tolerant attitude to soft drugs. Although the possession of up to 30g (1oz) of hash wasn't decriminalised until 1978, the authorities turned a blind eye to its use, preferring to prosecute dealers who also pushed hard drugs. The city subsequently suffered a heroin (and AIDS) epidemic, but has since developed a well-defined drugs policy (*see box* **The drugs do work**).

The focal points of hippy culture were the **Melkweg** and **Paradiso**, both of which emitted such a pungent aroma of marijuana that it could be smelt hundreds of metres away in Leidseplein. The city soon became a haven for dropouts and hippies from all over Europe until the end of the decade, when the Dam and Vondelpark turned into unruly campsites and public tolerance of the hippies waned. In the '70s, Amsterdam's popular culture shifted towards a tougher expression of disaffected urban youth. Yet Vondelpark, the Melkweg and the Dam remain a mecca for both ageing and new age hippies, even into the '90s.

## HOME SWEET HOME...

Perhaps the most significant catalyst for discontent in the '70s – which exploded into civil conflict by the '80s – was housing. Amsterdam's compact size and historic city centre had always been a nightmare for city planners. There was a dire housing shortage and many inner city homes were in need of drastic renovation. The population increased during the '60s, reaching its peak (nearly 870,000) by 1964. The numbers were swelled by immigrants from the Netherlands' last major colony, Surinam, many of whom were dumped in the forbidding Bijlmermeer housing project. It quickly degenerated into a ghetto, and when an aeroplane crashed there in October 1992, the number of fatalities was impossible to ascertain: many victims were illegal residents and not registered.

The Metro link to the Bijlmermeer is itself a landmark to some of the most violent protests in Amsterdam's history. Passionate opposition erupted against the proposed clearance in February 1975 of the Jewish quarter of the Nieuwmarkt, a particularly sensitive site. Civil unrest culminated in 'Blue Monday', 24 March, 1975, when heavy-handed police tactics once again sparked off violent clashes with residents and over 1,000 supporters. Police fired tear gas into the homes of those who had refused to move out and battered down doors with armoured cars. Despite further clashes just weeks later, the plans went ahead and the Metro was opened in 1980, though only one of the four lines planned for the city was completed.

City planners were shocked by the fervent opposition to their schemes for large, airy suburbs and the wholesale demolition of old neighbourhoods. It was simply not what people wanted: they cherished the narrow streets, the small squares and cosy corner cafés. The shortage of residential space in the city centre made it a target for property speculators, and the public felt that the council was selling out to big business, complaining that the city centre was becoming unaffordable for ordinary people. In 1978, the council decided to improve housing through small-scale development, renovating houses street by street. But with an estimated 90,000 people (13 per cent of the city's population) still on Amsterdam's housing list in 1980, public concern grew about the shortages.

## THE SQUAT MOVEMENT

Speculators who left property empty caused justifiable, acute resentment, which was soon mobilised into direct action: vacant buildings were occupied illegally by squatters. In March 1980, police turned against them for the first time and used tanks to evict them from a former office building in Vondelstraat. Riots ensued, but the squatters eventually came away victorious.

In 1982, as Amsterdam's squatting movement reached its peak with an estimated 10,000 members, clashes with police escalated: a state of emergency was called after one eviction battle. Soon, though, the city – led by new mayor Ed Van Thijn – had taken control over the movement, and one of the last of the city's important squats, Wyers, fell amid tear gas in February 1984 and was pulled down to make way for a Holiday Inn. The squatters were no longer a force to be reckoned with, though their ideas of small-scale regeneration have since been absorbed into official planning (*see box* **Squat thrusts**, *page 28*).

## BACK TO BASICS

Born and bred in Amsterdam, Ed Van Thijn embodied a new strand in Dutch politics. Although a socialist, he took tough action against 'unsavoury elements' – hard drug traders, petty criminals, squatters – and upgraded facilities to attract new businesses and tourists. A new national political era also emerged, with the election in

# Squat thrusts

During the '70s and '80s, Amsterdam was synonymous with squatting. But by the late '80s, the scene had become mired in outmoded lefty didactics and ineffectual confrontation, and, for the best part of the '90s, has been in decline. The tactics of playful yet direct environmental action, urban traffic disruption and unity with the free party scene used so effectively in the UK have been relatively slow to catch on in Amsterdam, where the grimmer, smash-the-state 'autonome' movement has traditionally held sway.

More concerned with intra-movement bitching than proposing radical new modes of social life, the Amsterdam squat movement began to find itself out of touch with once-generous middle class support in the '80s. Picked off one by one or stung in police raids, the once-vibrant squat scene has given way to tacky shopping arcades and expensive flats. Recent lost prime alternative real estate includes the last of the monumental, long-term artist squats: the Graan Silo (at its height, one of the coolest places in Europe) and Vrieshuis Amerika, whose days are probably numbered. In fact, the ADM building in the Western Docks is the main remaining squat building, and even that is under threat.

But there are still signs of life from the movement that did much to make Amsterdam the home of radical politics and liberal social experimentation. Ruigord, a village just outside the city that has been squatted by artists and hippies since the late '70s, has been marked as a toxic waste dump masquerading as a new dock. However, residents there are refusing to go quietly. In 1997, squatters established Groennord, an Earth First-style eco-protest camp complete with tunnels, treehouses, lock-ons and a fort. Repeatedly destroyed and rebuilt, it's become a symbol of the squatters' tenacious battle against authority. In addition, the proposed expansion of Schiphol airport is proving to be a popular rallying point, and protesters may yet adopt tactics reminiscent of the Manchester airport débâcle in the UK.

Other UK imports, such as the Reclaim the Streets guerrilla parties, have also been picking up support over the last couple of years. But ironically, alternative Amsterdam received its biggest boost following its massive defeat at 1997's EU summit hosted by the city, when a crowd of around 200 squatters and sympathisers were rounded up *en masse* on trumped-up civil disorder charges and held for several days. The summit, or the 'Euro Top', as it was dubbed here – conveniently spelt 'EU rot op' ('fuck off EU') on popular T-shirts – has made an indelible impression on Amsterdam's historically bolshie burghers, who were forced to endure a two-week police state.

If you want to make contact or just experience the atmosphere of the scene, a number of 'tame' squats can still be found, their occupants having long since cut a deal and gone legitimate: Vrankrijk (south of Dam on Spuistraat) and Korsakoff (Lijnbaansgracht 161) have fun bars behind their forbidding exteriors. With free entrance, cheap beer and late opening hours, and packed with energetic wannabe anarcho-syndicalists and students, they're well worth a look.

1982 of Rotterdam millionaire Ruud Lubbers as leader of the then centre-right coalition government of Christian Democrats and right-wing Liberals (VVD). He saw to it that the welfare system and government subsidies were trimmed to ease the country's large budget deficit, and aimed to revitalise the economy with more business-like policies. In February 1984, though, Van Thijn resigned to become Home Affairs Minister.

The price of Amsterdam's new affluence (among most groups, except the poorest) has been a swing towards commercialism. Van Thijn has found it hard to live down a clumsy remark he made about turning Amsterdam into a 'pleasure park'. Yet the evidence of his intentions can be seen in the casino, luxury apartments and shopping complex at the Leidseplein and the massive redevelopment of its docklands. Van Thijn also pushed through plans to build the **Stadhuis-Muziektheater** (City Hall-Opera House) complex, dubbed 'Stopera!' by its opponents (*see chapters* **Sightseeing**, *page 51, and* **Music: Classical**, *page 203*).

But the hordes of squatters were largely supplanted by well-groomed yuppies. Flashy cafés, galleries and nouvelle cuisine restaurants replaced the alternative scene and a mood of calm settled on the city. Still, a classic example of Dutch free expression was provoked by the city's mid-'80s campaign to host the 1992 Olympics. Amsterdam became the first city ever to send an (ultimately successful) official anti-Olympics delegation. It seems the city isn't yet ready to relinquish its rebel status.

# Amsterdam Today

**Drugs, crime, housing problems: it's the same old story in Amsterdam. But can the local council finally turn things around?**

You'd think that with the tourist dollar arriving in vast quantities on its shores every day, the Amsterdam powers-that-be would leave things just as they are. After all, foreign money is coming in, the tourist industry is thriving and business is booming.

Naturally, it's not that simple. Rather than play on its liberal image, Amsterdam is trying to get rid of the 'anything goes' badge that has been tightly pinned to the lapel of the Dutch capital for years. The sex, drugs and rock'n'roll label might be one way of attracting lots of tourists, but the authorities feel that a drastic change of image is needed if the city wants to survive the next century. Consequently, the Tourist Board is trying to draw in more moneyed tourists who'll spend freely in shops and restaurants, as opposed to the flocks of

backpackers whose holidays – and money – are spent wandering from coffeeshop to coffeeshop in a fug of pot smoke.

At the same time, Amsterdam council is trying to clean up the city, in a bid both to attract more companies, and to lure back professional couples, who invariably flee from Amsterdam as soon as their offspring arrives. Mayor Schelto Patijn has put a hold on the opening of new coffeeshops and ensured that existing ones need to comply with strict rules. Sex shops have been banned from displaying sexually explicit material in their windows, and the rules for festivities such as Queen's Day, which were once virtually non-existent, are seemingly tightened almost every year. Quite where this will leave the city in ten years' time is anyone's guess.

*With crime on the increase in the city, Amsterdam's police have their work cut out.*

## OFF-SHORE INVESTMENT

As with most major cities, there is a huge shortage of housing in Amsterdam. Unlike most major cities, though, Amsterdam has decided to do something about it. New suburbs are presently being developed in the city, with IJburg – two islands near the IJ – the most controversial of them (see box **Eye for an IJ**, page 37). After a long debate and a referendum, the ƒ500-million development has finally been given the go-ahead. Only 30 per cent of the 6,240 properties to be built on the islands will be council houses, though: the rest are to be luxury owner-occupied residences. The government is investing ƒ285 million in the fast IJrail tram – a public transport system that will link IJburg with Centraal Station – with another ƒ15 million set aside for the creation of a nature park and recreational area for the locals.

But there are also various projects to create new houses and upgrade areas closer to the city centre. Haarlemmermeerplein, for example, will eventually be home to an 1,800-seater cinema, 24 houses for the elderly, a supermarket, a grand café and an underground car park, while the Museumplein is also undergoing drastic restyling (see box **Pleins for the future**, page 62). To cope with the city's expansion – on both residential and commercial levels – the city's public transport system is to be expanded: the North-South Metro line, when completed in 2000, will link the World Trade Centre with Centraal Station, at a cost of ƒ816 million.

The Science Park in the Watergraafsmeer is also expanding. Dubbed 'the digital heart of the Netherlands', the Park is home to an astonishing 1,300 multimedia companies. A second building is currently being constructed to house the overflow, and the industry is growing at such a rate that plans for a third complex are currently being drawn up. Also on a technological front, the multinational Philips group decided to relocate its Dutch headquarters in 1997 from Eindhoven, in the south of the Netherlands, to Amsterdam. When it moved to the Rembrandt Tower near Amstel station and Watergraafsmeer, the spotlight was turned on the area: a second office building is currently being built and a third is on the way, while there are also plans for a huge car park and the renovation and extension of Amstel railway station.

So far, so good, then. But like every good story, this one has two very different sides. During the redevelopments, old buildings such as Vrieshuis Amerika, Graansilo, Villa Omval, and a couple of warehouses on the Entrepotdok have all been demolished, or are slated to be pulled down in the near future. Many of these formerly empty buildings had been turned into restaurants, concert venues and live/work artists' residences by squatters. The last point is particularly ironic: while Amsterdam council makes a great song and dance about mixing working and living in the centre of town – exactly what the squatters were doing – it quickly changes its mind when the real estate developers come calling with proposals to build yuppie flats.

The arguments are different with the Metro extension, but the new line to the World Trade Centre has still caused no end of debate among locals. Granted, major companies – like the ABN-Amro bank – are eager to relocate to the WTC, and the financial investments involved in this business district can only be good for the city on a purely economic level. On the whole, locals understand this, but even so, many are against the Metro extension: while some see it simply as unnecessary, others are rightly concerned that small shopkeepers will go broke due to the fact that during construction, large areas of the city will be unreachable. Frivolous types, though, point to the 'witte fietsenplan', a scheme that, in theory, aims to provide each Amsterdammer with a free white bike. After an unsuccessful trial period in the '60s, the scheme has made a tentative comeback, with experimental card-operated bike racks on Waterlooplein and near Artis Zoo where people can pick up bikes as and when they see fit. If it's a success, the white bike scheme will spread to other parts of the city. And if it does work, some say, then who needs a new Metro line?

## CRIME & VIOLENCE

Figures from 1997 show that there are just over 718,100 people living in Amsterdam, an increase of about 3,000 from 1994. Staggeringly, though, between 80,000 and 100,000 Amsterdammers are unemployed at any one time, while a recent study by the Erasmus University showed that there are 18,000 illegal immigrants living in Amsterdam (the actual figure might, in fact, be as much as double that, as the researchers had to base their study on the limited information supplied by the police).

Amsterdam has, perhaps, more than its fair share of crime. The council is putting almost ƒ10 million into a project to battle youth crime, while recent years have seen increases in both drug-related liquidations between organised crime gangs in broad daylight, and fights between partygoers on Leidseplein and Rembrandtplein in the wee small hours. Bar and club owners claim the latter problem is a direct result of legislation that forces all bars to keep the same hours, which results in crowds of alcohol- and drug-fuelled merrymakers spilling out on to the streets at the same time.

After a number of relatively minor incidents that hardly made world news, it took two events in 1997 to really bring the level of the problem home to ordinary Dutch citizens. A few weeks after student Joes Kloppenburg was kicked to death in a senseless attack on Voetboogsteeg, Meindert Tjoelker was murdered on his stag night after he made a comment to a group of men who were

**Centraal Station**, *soon to be renovated.*

throwing bikes in a Leeuwarden canal. He was buried on the day his marriage would have taken place. Both events stole the headlines in Holland, and resulted in a one-minute silence in bars, cafés and on national TV; even public transport in Amsterdam shut down for 60 seconds.

In memory of Joes, and as a protest against violence, a neon sign reading 'Help' was put up in the Voetboogsteeg – near the Café de Schutter – where he was brutally murdered. The response of the locals has been speedy. Although proposals that would have outlawed 'happy hours' in bars were quickly set aside after a storm of protest from bar owners, there is to be a special police post next to the RoXY club on Singel, dealing exclusively with nightlife safety. Others have suggested making the licensing laws less strict, with longer opening hours for establishments that serve non-alcoholic drinks and coffee. However, these were still a long way from becoming law at the time of writing.

### ENTERTAINMENT TONIGHT

Amsterdam's plans to transform the south-east into a glittery amusement area are finally materialising. For years, this suburban part of Amsterdam – also known as the Bijlmer – had a bad name, but recent development efforts have proved more successful. Run-down blocks have been demolished to make way for rows of semi-

detached houses housing professional couples; large shopping centres, such as Amsterdamse Poort, have been erected; and Ajax have now moved into the ArenA, a superb stadium in the area. Future developments include a cineplex and a huge amusement park, a venue for pop gigs, a hall for the Cirque du Soleil, a museum (devoted, ironically, to money), a casino and a luxury hotel. If all goes according to plan, the grand opening will be in 2003. Closer to the centre of town, 1998 saw construction start on an Oostelijke Handelskade building that will eventually be the Music Centre Amsterdam, comprising the jazz institutes Bimhuis and IJsbreker.

Centraal Station, too, is facing radical renovations in order to accommodate the North-South Metro line. The hall of the station, which is used by over 200,000 commuters and tourists every day, will be transformed into a bright and spacious area with a glass elevator, more shops and ticket windows and a late-opening supermarket. The many narrow and dark corners and corridors, which now attract many junkies, alcoholics, homeless people and prostitutes, will disappear.

At the start of 1998, after an increase in harassment of travellers and numerous fights between rival groups of junkies, police were granted a special jurisdiction to remove people from the station concourse. Organisations working for drug addicts and the homeless are furious about the new policy: they believe that the council should come up with a more constructive solution to what is definitely a major problem, instead of just shifting the street prostitutes, homeless and drug addicts to other parts of the town. However, the council realises that drug-related problems won't disappear just like that, and have set up three 'user room' projects to accommodate drug addicts. In theory, junkies will go to these designated buildings instead of lingering in the streets, causing trouble and shooting up in public. If the initiative works – basically, if junkie-related troubles on the streets of the city decrease – then another 12 user rooms will be set up. But it's a big if.

As the millennium approaches, Amsterdam is undergoing some of the biggest changes in recent memory. Since the '60s, the city has been known to foreigners primarily as the liberal capital of the world. But Mayor Patijn seems keen to tailor Amsterdam's image to fit in better with its growing reputation as a top business city. Will it work? It's hard to say: after all, Amsterdam is still the only place in Europe where you can walk into a shop, buy a joint and walk out again without a care in the world. But as corporate companies move to Amsterdam, the squat scene is largely eradicated, and young couples return to the city limits, one thing remains certain: for everyone else, despite the Tourist Board's attempts to project a contrary image, the party ain't over just yet…

# Architecture

**For a city built on slippy mud, Amsterdam has held up remarkably well over the last 700 years.**

'The colours are strong and sad, the forms symmetric, the façades kept new,' wrote Eugene Fromentin, the nineteenth-century art critic, of Amsterdam. 'We feel that it belongs to a people eager to take possession of the conquered mud.' The treacherously soft soil upon which the merchants' town of Amsterdam is built put strictures on most attempts at monumental display. Thanks to the make-up of the land – combined with the Protestant restraint that characterised the city's early developments – it's not palaces and castles that make up the architectural highpoints but, rather, warehouses, domestic architecture, the stock exchange and the city hall.

It doesn't take an expert to work out that Amsterdam's architectural epochs have closely followed the pulse of the city's prosperity. The dainty gables and decorative façades of wealthy seventeenth- and eighteenth-century merchants' houses still line the canals. A splurge of public spending in the affluent 1880s gave the city two of its most notable landmarks: Centraal Station and the Rijksmuseum. Conversely, social housing projects in the early twentieth century stimulated the innovative work of the Amsterdam School, while Amsterdam's late-1980s resurgence as a financial centre and transport hub led both to an economic upturn and to thickets of bravura modern architecture sprouting on the city outskirts.

Prime viewing-time for Amsterdam architecture is late on a summer's afternoon, as the sun gently picks out the varying colours and patterns of the brickwork. Then, as twilight falls, the canal houses – most of them more window than wall – light up like strings of lanterns, and you get a glimpse of the beautifully preserved, rather opulent interiors that lie behind the façades.

## MUD, GLORIOUS MUD

Amsterdam is built on reclaimed marshland, with a thick, soft layer of clay and peat beneath the topsoil. About 12 metres down is a hard band of sand, deposited 10,000 years ago during the Little Ice Age, and below that, after about five metres of fine sand, there is another firm layer, this one left by melting glacial ice after the Great Ice Age. A further 25 metres down, through shell-filled clay and past the bones of mammoths, is a third hard layer, deposited by glaciers over 180,000 years ago.

The first Amsterdammers built their homes on muddy mounds, making the foundations from tightly packed peat. Later, they dug trenches, filled them with fascines (thin, upright alder trunks) and built on those. But still the fruits of their labours sank slowly into the swamp. By the seventeenth century, builders were using longer underground posts and were rewarded with more stable structures, but it wasn't until around 1700 that piles were driven deep enough to hit the first hard sand layer.

The method of constructing foundations that subsequently developed has remained essentially the same ever since, though nowadays most piles reach the second sand level, while some even make the full 50-metre journey to the third hard layer. To begin, a double row of piles is sunk along the line of a proposed wall (since World War II, concrete has been used instead of wood). Then, a crossbeam is laid across each pair of posts, planks are fastened longitudinally onto the beams, and the wall is built on top. From time to time, piles break or rot. Amsterdam is full of buildings that teeter precariously over the street, tilt lopsidedly, or prop each other up in higgledy-piggledy rows.

## STICKS & STONES

Early constructions in Amsterdam were timber-framed, built mainly from oak with roofs of rushes or straw. Wooden houses were relatively light and so were less likely to sink into the mire, but after two devastating fires (in 1421 and 1452), the authorities began stipulating that outer walls be built of brick, though wooden front gables were still permitted. In a bid to blend in, the first brick gables were shaped in a direct imitation of their spout-shaped wooden predecessors.

Amsterdammers took to brick with relish. Granted, some grander seventeenth-century buildings were built of sandstone, while plastered façades made an appearance a hundred years later and reinforced concrete made its inevitable inroad this century. But Amsterdam is still essentially a city of brick: red brick from Leiden, yellow from Utrecht and grey from Gouda, all laid in curious formations and arranged in complicated patterns. Local architects' attachment to – and flair with – brick reached a zenith in the fantastical, billowing façades designed by the Amsterdam School early this century.

*The wooden* **In't Aepjen** *building.*

## TOUCH WOOD

Only two wooden buildings remain in central Amsterdam: one (built in 1460) in the quiet square of Begijnhof (No.34), and the other on Zeedijk. The latter, **In't Aepjen** (Zeedijk 1), was built around 1550 as a lodging house, getting its name from the monkeys that impecunious sailors used to leave behind in payment. Though the ground floor dates from the nineteenth century, the upper floors provide a clear example of how, in medieval times, each successive wooden storey protruded a little beyond the previous one, allowing rainwater to drip on to the street rather than run back into the body of the building. Early brick gables had to be built at an angle over the street for the same reason. This style of building also allowed objects to be winched to the top floors without crashing against the windows of the lower ones. Therefore, some of Amsterdam's apparent wonkiness is, in fact, intentional.

Amsterdam's oldest building is the **Oude Kerk** ('Old Church', Oude Kerksplein 23; *see chapter* **Sightseeing**, *p49*), which was begun in 1300, though only the base of the tower actually dates from then. Over the next 300 years, the church developed a barnacle crust of additional buildings, mostly in a Renaissance style (though some are unmistakably Gothic). Surprisingly, nearly all the buildings retain their original medieval roofs, mak-

ing the church unique in the Netherlands. The only full Gothic building in town – in the style of towering French and German churches – is the **Nieuwe Kerk** (at Dam and Nieuwezijds Voorburgwal; *see chapter* **Sightseeing**, *p42*), which is still called the 'New Church' even though building began at the end of the fourteenth century.

When gunpowder arrived in Europe in the fifteenth century, Amsterdammers realised that the wooden palisade that surrounded their settlement would offer scant defence against invaders, and so they set about building a new city wall. Watchtowers and gates left over from this wall make up a significant proportion of remaining pre-seventeenth-century architecture, though most have been considerably altered over the years. The **Schreierstoren** (Prins Hendrikkade 94-5; *see chapter* **Sightseeing**, *p66*) of 1480, however, has kept its original shape, with the addition of doors, windows and a pixie-hat roof. The base of the **Munttoren** (Muntplein; *see chapter* **Sightseeing**, *p50*) originally formed part of the **Reguliers-poort**, a city gate built in 1490. Another city gate from the previous decade, the **St Antoniespoort** (Nieuwmarkt 4), was converted into a public weighhouse ('Waag') in 1617, then further refashioned to become a Guild House.

## DUTCH RENAISSANCE

A favourite sixteenth-century amendment to these somewhat stolid defence towers was the addition of a sprightly steeple. Hendrick de Keyser (1565-1621) delighted in designing these spires, and it is largely his work that gives Amsterdam's present skyline a faintly oriental appearance. He added a lantern-shaped tower with an openwork orb to the Munttoren, and a spire that resembled the Oude Kerk steeple to the **Montelbaanstoren** (Oude Schans 2), a sea-defence tower that had been built outside the city wall. His **Zuiderkerk** (Zandstraat 17; *see chapter* **Sightseeing**, *p50-51*), built in 1603, sports a richly decorative spire said to have been much admired by Christopher Wren.

The appointment of de Keyser as city mason and sculptor in 1595 had given him free reign, and his buildings represent the pinnacle of the Dutch Renaissance style. Since the beginning of the seventeenth century, Dutch architects had been gleaning inspiration from translations of Italian pattern books, adding lavish ornament to the classical system of proportion they found there. Brick façades were decorated with stone strapwork (scrolls and curls derived from picture frames and leather work). Walls were built with alternating layers of red brick and white sandstone, a style that came to be called 'bacon coursing'. The old spout-shaped gables were replaced with cascading step-gables, often embellished with vases, escutcheons and masks (before house numbers were introduced in

Amsterdam in the eighteenth century, ornate gables and wall plaques were a means of identifying houses). The façade of the Vergulde Dolphijn (Singel 140-142), designed by de Keyser in 1600 for Captain Banningh Cocq (the commander of Rembrandt's Night Watch), is a lively combination of red brick and sandstone, while the Gecroonde Raep (Oudezijds Voorburgwal 57) has a neat step gable with riotous decoration featuring busts, escutcheons, shells, scrolls and volutes. However, de Keyser's magnificent 1617 construction, the Huis Bartolotti (Herengracht 170-172), is the finest example of the style.

This decorative step-gabled style was to last well into the seventeenth century. But, gradually, a stricter use of classical elements came into play; the façade of the Bartolotti house features rows of Ionic pilasters, and it wasn't long before others followed where de Keyser had led. The Italian pattern books that had inspired the Dutch Renaissance were full of the less-ornamented designs of Greek and Roman antiquity. This appealed to many young architects who succeeded de Keyser, and who were to develop a more restrained, classical style. Many, such as Jacob van Campen (1595-1657), went on study tours of Italy, and returned fired with enthusiasm for the symmetric designs, simple proportions and austerity of Roman architecture. The buildings that they constructed during the Golden Age are among the finest that Amsterdam has to offer.

## THE GOLDEN AGE

The 1600s were a boom time for builders as well as for business. Really, there was no way it could have been otherwise, as Amsterdam's population more than quadrupled during the first half of the century. Grand new canals were constructed, and wealthy merchants lined them with mansions and warehouses. Van Campen, along with fellow architects Philips Vingboons (1607-78) and his brother Justus (1620-98), were given the freedom to try out their ideas on a flood of new commissions.

Stately façades constructed entirely of sandstone began to appear, but brick remained the most popular building material. Philips Vingboons's Witte Huis (Herengracht 168) has a white sandstone façade with virtually no decoration: the regular rhythm of the windows is the governing principle of the design. The house Vingboons built in 1648 at Oude Turfmarkt 145, has a brick façade adorned with three tiers of classical pilasters (Tuscan, Ionic and Doric) and festoons that were also characteristic of the style. The crowning achievement of the period was Amsterdam's boast to the world of its mercantile supremacy and civic might: namely, the Stadhuis (City Hall) on the Dam, designed by Van Campen in 1648 and now known as the **Koninklijk Paleis** (*see chapter* **Sightseeing**, *p40-41*).

There was, however, one fundamental point of conflict between classical architecture and the requirements of northern European building. For obvious practical reasons, wet northern climes required steep roofs, yet low Roman pediments and flat cornices looked odd with a steep, pointed roof rising behind them. The architects eventually solved the problem by adapting the Renaissance gable, with its multiple steps, into a tall, central gable with just two steps. These simpler elevated neck-gables had a more suitable classical line. Later, neck-gables were built with just a tall central oblong and no steps. The right-angles formed at the base of neck-gables – and again at the step of elevated neck-gables – were often filled in with decorative sandstone carvings called claw-pieces.

Dolphins, sea monsters and other marvels of the world as explored by the Dutch East India Company ships became themes for claw-piece design. At Oudezijds Voorburgwal 187, exotic men with feather head-dresses recline on bales of tobacco. Later, the space occupied by the claw-piece was filled in with brick, rather than by sandstone carving, to form the aptly named bell-gable. These were often trimmed with sandstone decoration.

On exceptionally wide houses, it was possible to construct a roof parallel to the street rather than end-on, making a more attractive backdrop for a classical straight cornice. The giant Trippenhuis (Kloveniersburgwal 29), built by Justus Vingboons in 1662, has such a design, with a classical pediment, a frieze of cherubs and arabesques, and eight enormous Corinthian pilasters. It wasn't until the nineteenth century, when zinc cladding became more affordable, that flat and really low-pitched roofs became feasible.

## THE EIGHTEENTH CENTURY

Working towards the end of the seventeenth century, Adriaan Dortsman (1625-82) had been a strong proponent of the straight cornice. His exceptionally stark designs – such as for the Van Loon house at Keizersgracht 672-674 – ushered in a style that came to be known as Restrained Dutch Classicism. It was a timely entrance. Ornament was costly, and by the beginning of the eighteenth century, the economic boom was over.

The great merchant families were still prosperous, but little new building went on. Instead, the families gave their old mansions a facelift or revamped the interiors. A number of seventeenth-century houses got new sandstone façades (or plastered brick ones, which were cheaper), and French taste (said to have been introduced by Daniel Marot, a French architect living in Amsterdam) became hugely hip. As the century wore on, ornamentation regained popularity. Gables were festooned with scrolls and acanthus leaves (Louis XIV), embellished with asymmetri-

*Art or arse? The building of the **Stopera** on Waterlooplein led to riots in 1982. See page 36.*

cal rococo fripperies (Louis XV) or strung with disciplined lines of garlands (Louis XVI). The baroque grandeur of the house at Keizersgracht 444-446, for example, hardly seems Dutch at all. Straight cornices appeared even on narrow buildings, and became extraordinarily ornate: a distinct advantage, this, as it hid the steep roof that lay behind, with decorative balustrades adding to the deception. The lavish cornice at Oudezijds Voorburgwal 215-217 is a prime example.

### ONE FOOT IN THE PAST

Fortunes slumped even further after 1800, and during the first part of the century, more buildings were demolished than constructed. When things picked up after 1860, architects raided past eras for inspiration. Neo-classical, neo-Gothic and neo-Renaissance features were sometimes lumped together in the same building in a mix-and-match Eclectic style. The Krijtberg church (Singel 446) from 1881, for example, has a soaring neo-Gothic façade and a high, vaulted basilica, while the interior of AL van Gendt's Hollandse Manege

(Vondelstraat 140) from the same year combines the classicism of the Spanish Riding School in Vienna with a state-of-the-art iron-and-glass roof. On the other hand, the **Concertgebouw** (Van Baerlestraat 98; *see chapter* **Music: Classical & Opera**, *p201*), another Van Gendt construction from 1888, borrows heavily from the late Renaissance, with the **City Archive** (Amsteldijk 67) from 1892 little more than Hendrick de Keyser revisited. But the most adventurous building of the period is probably the Adventskerk (Keizersgracht 676), which somehow manages to cram in a classical rusticated base, Romanesque arches, Lombardian moulding and fake seventeenth-century lanterns.

The star architect of the period was PJH Cuypers (1827-1921), who landed the commissions for both the **Rijksmuseum** (Stadhouderskade 41; *see chapter* **Museums**, *p76*) of 1877-85 and **Centraal Station** (Stationsplein), built between 1882 and 1889. Both are in traditional red brick, adorned with a wealth of Renaissance-style decoration in sandstone and gold leaf. Cuypers made a conscious decision to move away from Eclecticism, and organise each building according to a single coherent principle. This idea became the basis for modern Dutch architecture.

## THIS IS THE MODERN WORLD

Brick and wood – good, honest, indigenous materials – appealed to HP Berlage (1856-1934), as did the possibilities offered by industrial developments in the use of steel and glass. A rationalist, he took Cuypers' ideas a step further in his belief that a building should openly express its basic structure, with just a modest amount of ornament in a strictly supportive role. His **Beurs** (Beursplein), built 1898-1903 – all clean lines and functional shapes, with the mildest patterning in the brickwork – was startling at the time, and earned him the reputation of being the father of modern Dutch architecture.

Apart from the odd shopfront and some well-designed café interiors, the art nouveau and art deco movements had little direct impact on Amsterdam, though there were a few eccentric flourishes at the time: de Jong's **Tuschinski Cinema** (Reguliersbreestraat 26; *see chapter* **Film**, *p183*) of 1918-21, for example, is a delightful piece of high-camp fantasy. Instead, Amsterdam architects developed a style of their own, an idiosyncratic mixture of art nouveau and Old Dutch using their favourite materials: wood and brick.

This movement, which became known as the Amsterdam School, reacted against Berlage's sobriety, producing whimsical buildings with waving, almost sculptural brickwork. Built over a reinforced concrete frame, the brick outer walls go through a series of pleats, bulges, folds and curls that earned the movement's work the nickname 'Schortjesarchitectuur' ('apron architecture'). Windows may be trapezoid or parabolic; doors are carved in strong, angular shapes; brickwork is decorative and often polychromatic; and brick and stone sculptures abound.

The driving force behind the Amsterdam School came from young architects Michel de Klerk (1884-1923) and Piet Kramer (1881-1961). Commissions for social housing projects from two Housing Associations – one for the Dageraad (constructed around PL Takstraat, 1921-23) and another for Eigen Haard (in the Spaarndammerbuurt, and built 1913-1920) – allowed them to treat entire blocks as single units, and the adventurous clients gave them complete freedom to express their ideas.

In the early 1920s, a new movement emerged that was the complete antithesis of the Amsterdam School. Developing on, rather than reacting against, Berlage's ideas, the Functionalists believed that new building materials such as concrete and steel should not be concealed, but that

the basic structure of a building should be there for all to see. Function was supreme; ornament was anathema. Their hard-edged concrete and glass boxes have much in common with the work of Frank Lloyd Wright in the USA, Le Corbusier in France and the Bauhaus in Germany. Not surprisingly, such radical views were not shared by everyone, and differences of opinion marked this as a turbulent period in Amsterdam's architectural history.

Early Functionalist work, such as 1937's Round Blue Teahouse (in Vondelpark) and the Cineac Cinema (Reguliersbreestraat 31) of 1934, has a clean-cut elegance, and the Functionalist garden suburb of Betondorp (literally, 'Concrete Town'), built 1921-26, is far more attractive than the name might suggest. But after World War II, Functionalist ideology became an excuse for dreary, derivative, prefabricated eyesores. The urgent need for housing, coupled with town-planning theories that favoured residential satellite suburbs, led to the appearance of soulless, high-rise horrors on the edge of town, much the same as in the rest of Europe.

A change of heart during the 1970s refocused attention on making the city centre a pleasant jumble of residences, shops and offices. At the same time, a quirkier, more imaginative trend began to show itself in building design. The ING Bank (Bijlmerplein 888), built in 1987 of brick, has hardly a right angle in sight. A use of bright colour, and a return to a human-sized scale, is splendidly evident in Aldo van Eyck's Moederhuis (Plantage Middenlaan 33) from 1981. New façades – daringly modern, yet built to scale – began to appear between the old houses along the canals. The 1980s also saw, amid an enormous amount of controversy, the construction of what became known as the **Stopera**, a combined city hall (**Stadhuis**) and opera house on Waterlooplein (*see chapters* **Sightseeing**, *p51, and* **Music: Classical & Opera**, *p203*). The eyecatching brick and marble coliseum of the **Muziektheater** is decidedly more successful than the dull oblongs that make up the city hall.

Housing projects of the 1980s and 1990s have provided Amsterdam with some of its most imaginative modern architecture. The conversion of a nineteenth-century army barracks, the Oranje Nassau Kazerne (Sarphatistraat/Mauritskade) into studios and flats, with the addition of a row of rather zanily designed apartment blocks, is one of the more successful examples. Building on the KNSM Eiland and other islands in the derelict eastern docklands has combined an intelligent conversion of existing structures with some highly inventive new architecture. It is hoped that the hard lessons of the 1950s and 1960s have been learned, and the architectural mistakes then will never be repeated.

## THE FUTURE

At the municipal information centre for planning and housing in the **Zuiderkerk** (Zuiderkerkhof 72), one can see various models of the many current and future developments set to transform Amsterdam in the next decades; most give some cause for optimism. Travesties of the past have politicised the populace, who now keep a sharp eye on development. The result is that referendums have become the latest trend. Though 130,000 votes against the construction of IJburg – a residential community to be built on a series of man-made islands in the IJmeer, just east of Amsterdam – was not enough to stop development around this ecologically sensitive area, it did inspire the promise that ƒ15 million would be invested in 'nature-development' (*see box* **Eye for an IJ**,

*below*). Similarly, the referendum result against the laying of the North-South metro line didn't halt the project still set to begin in 1998, but it did establish that the city needed to be more diligent in its thinking: the powers-that-be, after all, apparently skimmed over such details as financing, loss of revenue for proximate shopkeepers, and the potential for all this digging to cause the speedier sinking of above-lying historical buildings. The completion of these and other projects such as the **Museumplein** face-lift (*see box* **Pleins for the future**, *p62*), the construction around the Arena stadium – which, it is hoped, will pump some much needed economic life into the nearby architectural prison known as the Bijlmermeer – and the complete transformation of the harbourfront will prove if this general optimism is justified.

# Eye for an IJ

Think of a city on water and your thoughts probably turn to Venice. Indeed, it might surprise you to know that in terms of length of waterways, Amsterdam actually surpasses the famed Italian city, even though the Dutch capital is not strictly a city on the water in the way that Venice is. The shortage of housing and the lack of sites in Amsterdam's immediate environment on which to build has led to a radical solution: the construction of what will be the first true city *in* the water.

Amsterdam's history is linked to water. To the west, the Noordzee Canal from IJmuiden, completed in 1876, provides a link between the North Sea and the city's waterfront. On the other side of the city, the harbour area, once the centre of maritime activity, is now almost non-existent. Shipping and trade have been replaced by urban development; warehouses have been turned into accommodation; docks have been rebuilt with housing, offices and business premises. But still Amsterdam's housing shortage remains, and explains the need for IJburg (pronounced 'Eye-berg'), a new city being built on the water to the east of the harbour, in the mouth of the IJmeer (Lake IJ).

The Dutch, of course, are world leaders when it comes to land reclamation. Much of the Netherlands was formerly marshland, or even sea, but urban development was only part of the reason for reclamation: agriculture, coastal protection and safeguarding against flooding were equally, if not more, important. IJburg is unique among reclaimed land, though, in that it is being constructed purely for housing purposes. When it's completed in 2010, the six islands will be

home to some 45,000 people in 18,000 dwellings, complete with a complete infrastructure of commercial and industrial premises, shops, schools and other facilities.

However, the proposal is not without its enemies. Opponents, who claim that the IJmeer is an environmentally sensitive area of outstanding natural beauty and ecological importance, contest the assertion that disruption will be minimal. The campaign for the preservation of the IJmeer succeeded in forcing a referendum in April 1997, and, though the public voted against by a substantial majority, it was still not enough to stop the development going ahead, after the council tightened the conditions required for a referendum to succeed.

Dwellings in IJburg, which has been designed to echo the grandeur and openness of the IJmeer, will be floating or on platforms, with the high- and low-density housing incorporating mansions, maisonettes, urban villas, detached houses and single-person dwellings. Though some distance from Amsterdam, all islands will be connected to the city centre, and to each other, by a rapid tram system. The IJburg will also be cycle-friendly, with the use of cars discouraged; water transport for commuter and leisure traffic will carry passengers and bikes to the Amsterdam waterfront.

While there are still reservations about the project, there is also potential. And though IJburg promises much – homes for over 40,000 people, for a start – it remains to be seen what it will deliver. It's an ambitious development, certainly, but one thing is for sure: if anyone can pull off such a project, it's the Dutch.

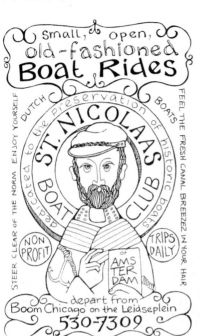

# Sightseeing

# Sightseeing

*Enjoy a city chock-full of sights for sore eyes.*

In a city the size of Amsterdam, it's entirely possible to walk around the centre of town and 'do' all the biggest and best sights in a couple of days. For whatever reason, though, few visitors to Amsterdam go beyond the borders defined by the *grachtengordel* (girdle of canals), except perhaps to stroll up to the area around Museumplein and Vondelpark, where several of the major museums are situated. The further you travel from the heart of town, the newer the areas become, and there's plenty out of the centre worth investigating if you take the time to escape from the main tourist drag.

Within the centre of town are the medieval buildings, the old port, the red lights that denote the world's (flourishing) oldest trade, the earliest and prettiest canals and the seventeenth-century merchants' houses. Slightly further out, though, are quarters built to house the various waves of incoming workers; some of these areas – the Jordaan, the Pijp and the Oost – are covered below, while others in the south and west, while not 'sightworthy' enough to cover in this section, are still worth a visit for specific architecture, shopping, eats or entertainment (*see relevant chapters*).

After World War II, new self-contained 'garden neighbourhoods' were built even further out of the centre, including those to the west at Osdorp and Slotermeer. More recent building projects have been completed nearer the centre: in the east, around the old port area, new homes have been built to replace the old housing, and many warehouses have being converted from squats into apartments. Across the River IJ behind Centraal Station, Amsterdam Noord has recently been made more accessible by the IJ tunnel. However, apart from the impressive Flora Park, there is little to see in the north, and the most interesting part of a trip there is probably the free ferry journey for pedestrians and cyclists, which leaves from just behind Centraal Station.

As with many major cities, the majority of Amsterdam's noteworthy sights are museums. To avoid duplication, these have been included in full in the **Museums** chapter (*pages 74-86*), where you can find full reviews and listings information; they have been cross-referenced wherever possible in this section. See other relevant chapters – including **Architecture**, **Shopping**, **Cafés & Bars** and **Restaurants** – for more details on the highlights of each area.

## The Old Centre

Boundaried, at least in theory, by the harbour behind Centraal Station, the Singel and the Kloveniersburgwal canals, the old city centre is bisected by Damrak, which turns into Rokin south of Dam Square. Within the Old Centre, the area to the east containing the Red Light District is the ancient **Old Side (Oude Zijde)**, while the area to the west, whose most notable landmark is Spui Square, is the not-really-that-new-anymore **New Side (Nieuwe Zijde)**.

## Around the Dam

Straight up from Centraal Station beyond the once-watery and now-paved and touristy strip called the Damrak lies the **Dam Square** (*see box* **Hip to be Square**, *page 22*), the heart of the city since the first dam was built here across the Amstel in 1270. Today, it's a convenient meeting point for many tourists, the majority of whom meet under its mildly phallic centrepiece, the **Nationaal Monument**. This 22-metre (70-foot) white obelisk is dedicated to the Dutch servicemen who died in World War II. Designed by JJP Oud, with sculptures by John Raedecker, it incorporates 12 urns: 11 are filled with earth collected from the then 11 Dutch provinces, with the twelfth containing soil from war cemeteries in Indonesia, a Dutch colony until 1949.

The monument, for years on the brink of collapse, has just been recently reinstalled after being completely refurbished (partly in Germany, of all ironic places). And though the Dam itself has lost some of its political spark since 1535, when the Anabaptists ran naked through the square to test the boundaries of religious freedom – and certainly since the '60s, when it was used as a chill-out zone for the hippies – there are nevertheless a number of important landmarks on and around it.

The west side is flanked by the **Koninklijk Paleis** (literally, 'Royal Palace'). Designed by Jacob van Campen in the seventeenth century along classical lines, and built on 13,659 wooden piles that were rammed deep into the sand, it was originally used as the city hall. The poet Constantijn Huygens hyped it as the 'the world's

*However you choose to travel, Amsterdam is an easy city to get around.*

Eighth Wonder', a monument to the cockiness Amsterdam felt at the dawn of its Golden Age. However, the exterior is only really impressive when viewed from the rear – where Atlas holds his load from a great height – and you'll have to go inside to understand what Huygens meant. The interior also helps the visitor realise that the confidence felt at the time was one laced with fear: God, the devil and their elements were always on hand to kick you in the teeth when you least expected it.

Inside the Palace, the epic Citizen's Hall, with its decoration in grand marble and bronze that images a miniature universe, is meant to make you feel about as significant as the nibbling rats seen carved in stone over the door above the Bankruptcy Chamber. Although much of the art reflects the typically jaded humour of a people who have seen it all, the overall impression is one of deadly seriousness: one screw-up and you could end up among the grotesque carvings of the Tribunal and sentenced to die in some uniquely torturous and public way. Gentler displays of creativity, though, can be seen in the chimney pieces, which were painted by artists such as Ferdinand Bol and Govert Flinck, both pupils of Rembrandt (who, ironically, had his own sketches rejected). The city hall was transformed into a royal palace in 1808 after Napoleon made his brother, Louis, King of the Netherlands (*see chapter* **History**, *page 19*), and a fine collection of furniture from this period can be seen on a guided tour of the building. The Palace became state property in 1936 and is still used occasionally by the royal family.

Beside the Royal Palace stands the **Nieuwe Kerk**. While the 'old' Oude Kerk in the Red Light District (*see below*) was built in the 1300s, the sprightly 'new' Nieuwe Kerk dates from 1408. It is not known how much damage was caused by the fires of 1421 and 1452, or how much rebuilding took place, but most of the pillars and walls were erected after that period (*see chapter* **Architecture**, *page 33*). Iconoclasm in 1566 left the church intact, though statues and altars were removed in the Reformation (*see chapter* **History**, *page 14*).

In 1645 the church was completely gutted by the Great Fire; the ornately carved oak pulpit and great organ (the latter designed by Jacob van Campen) are thought to have been constructed shortly after this. Also of interest here is the tomb of naval hero Admiral de Ruyter, who died in 1676. Behind his black marble tomb is a white marble relief depicting the sea battle in which he died. Poets and Amsterdam natives Pieter Cornelisz Hooft and Joost van den Vondel are also buried here. The Nieuwe Kerk is no longer used as a place of worship, but does host organ recitals, state occasions and consistently excellent exhibitions, such as

**World Press Photo** (*see chapter* **Amsterdam by Season**, *page 7*).

In painfully kitsch contrast is **Madame Tussauds Scenerama**, on the south side of Dam Square. The only branch of Tussauds outside the UK, the show is housed in the top two floors of the Peek & Cloppenburg department store. An express lift whisks visitors from ground level to be greeted by Claes Janszoon, Amsterdam Man, a five-metre (16-foot) figure decked out in all the clichés (windmills, tulips et al). Wander around the first floor and see cheese-textured representations from Holland's own Golden Age of commerce and empire, with merchants, peasants, artists and kings all depicted. Go to the second floor for another golden shower of hits: the Dutch royal family, local celebrities, international political leaders and renowned superstars. Oh, and make sure you bring a match to melt Madonna.

Backtrack towards Centraal Station past the shopping frenzy that takes place in the **Bijenkorf** ('Beehive') department store, and you'll come to the **Beurs van Berlage**. Designed in 1896 by Hendrik Petrus Berlage as the city's palatial stock exchange, the Beurs, while incorporating many different, more traditional, building styles, represents an important break with nineteenth-century architecture and prepared the way for the modern swoopy brickwork of the Amsterdam School (*see chapter* **Architecture**, *page 36*). No longer used as a stock exchange, the building now operates as a conference and exhibition centre with two concert halls, a café and a restaurant. If that sounds all a tad too cultural, a touch of good old-fashioned sex and violence can be had across Damrak at the **Sex Museum** and the **Torture Museum**.

Return to the Dam, and take the narrow theatre street known, succinctly, as Nes. Dating from the Middle Ages, this street was once home to the city's tobacco trade and the Jewish quasi-Buddhist Spinoza (1623-77), who saw body and mind as aspects of a single substance. You can stop, recharge and realign your own essence with a Smart Cocktail at the Nes Café (Nes 33). At the end of the Nes, either turn left to buy a bike off a junkie on the bridge, risking jail and deportation in the process; turn right and end up near the **Allard Pierson Museum**; or walk onward to the very euro-scenic **Oudemanhuis Book Market** (*see chapter* **Shopping**, *page 161*) on the University of Amsterdam campus.

### Beurs van Berlage

*Damrak 277 (626 5257/fax 620 4701). Tram 4, 9, 14, 16, 20, 24, 25.* **Open** *office & enquiries* 9am-5pm Mon-Fri; *museum* 10am-4pm Tue-Sun. **Admission** *museum f4.* **Map 2 D2**

### Dam Square

*Tram 1, 2, 4, 5, 9, 13, 14, 16, 17, 20, 24, 25.* **Map 2 D3**

### Koninklijk Paleis
*Dam (624 8698 ext 217). Tram 1, 2, 4, 5, 9, 13, 14, 16, 17, 20, 24, 25.* **Open** 12.30-5pm daily. **Admission** *f*7; *f*5 students; *f*2,50 under-13s; free under-4s. Group discounts (number of persons vary: phone for details). **Map 2 C3**
*Guided tours and group tours (by appointment only).*

### Madame Tussauds Scenerama
*Peek & Cloppenburg, Dam 20 (622 9239). Tram 4, 9, 14, 16, 20, 24, 25.* **Open** *Sept-June* 10am-5.30pm daily; *July, Aug* 9.30am-7.30pm daily. **Admission** *f*18,50; *f*15 5-14s; *f*60,75 family ticket A (two adults, two children), *f*68,25 family ticket B (two adults, three children). **Credit** AmEx, DC, EC, MC, V. **Map 2 D3**

### Nieuwe Kerk
*Dam (Nieuwe Kerk foundation 626 8168/recorded information 638 6990). Tram 1, 2, 4, 5, 9, 13, 14, 16, 17, 20, 24, 25.* **Open** hours vary depending on exhibitions and events: phone for details. **Admission** usually free, though some exhibitions may charge. **Map 2 C3**

## The Old Side & the Red Light District

The Red Light District, situated in an approximate triangle formed by Centraal Station, the Nieuwmarkt and the Dam, is the root of Amsterdam's international notoriety. The world's desperate and horny imagine breasts eagerly pancaked against red neon-framed windows, canals awash with bodily fluids. As if to give weight to this image, the postcards on sale in local shops present a sort of small, cutesy Vegas. If truth be told, though, the cheesy joke shop has here become the cheesy sex shop, with electric palm buzzers and comedy nose glasses being replaced by multiorificed inflatables and huge orbital dildos.

Most of the history of the Red Light District – of which there is plenty, this being the oldest part of Amsterdam – has been greasily veneered with that oldest of trades: marketing. Sex, while the hook upon which the area hangs its reputation, is actually secondary to window-shopping. People do buy (it's a *f*1 billion per year trade) but mostly they wander in groups, stopping here and there to gawp open-mouthed at the live exhibits. The choice is ample: an astounding 5,000 professionals ply their trade from here, of which 2,000 are available on any given day. Most of these window girls are self-employed, and even though prostitution is technically illegal, the women are taxed and have a union, De Rode Draad, that has represented them since 1984. They are, indeed, mostly women: despite attempts to launch male and transsexual prostitution, men have so far found it difficult to get their dicks into this particular door of opportunity.

As at more traditional markets like the Albert Cuyp, where cheese merchants line up alongside cheese merchants and fishmongers group with fishmongers, women of similar specialisations also tend to clump together. Sultry Latins gather on the Molensteeg and the beginning of Oudezijds Achterburgwal, African mamas on the Oudekerkplein, ambiguously sexed Thais on Stoofstraat, and the vaguely model-ish but definitely anorexic on Trompettersteeg, Amsterdam's smallest street. But there is much else to absorb in

*The tourists? They went that way...*

# Museums in the Old Centre

**Allard Pierson Museum**
*Oude Turfmarkt 127 (525 2556). See page 77.*

**Amsterdams Historisch Museum**
*Kalverstraat 92 (523 1822). See page 79.*

**Erotic Museum**
*Oudezijds Achterburgwal 54 (624 7303). See page 86.*

**Hash Marihuana Hemp Museum**
*Oudezijds Achterburgwal 148 (623 5961). See page 86.*

**Museum Amstelkring**
*Oudezijkds Achterburgwal 40 (624 6604). See page 79.*

**Sex Museum**
*Damrak 18 (627 7431). See page 86.*

**Tattoo Museum**
*Oudezijds Achterburgwal 130 (625 1565).*
*See page 84.*

**Torture Museum**
*Damrak 20-22 (639 2027).*
*See page 86.*

**Universiteitsmuseum de Agnietenkapel**
*Oudezijds Voorburgwal 231 (525 3341). See page 83.*

---

this most iconoclastic of neighbourhoods. Prostitutes, clerics, schoolkids, junkies, carpenters and cops all interact with a strange brand of social cosiness, and the tourists are mere voyeurs. It's all good fun and pretty harmless, just so long as you remember that window girls do not like having their pictures taken and that drug dealers react to eye contact like a dog to a bone.

## ZEEDIJK

Facing away from Centraal Station to the left are two churches, the **St Nicolaaskerk** (whose interior of funky darkness can be viewed from Easter to mid-October; open 1.30-4pm Mon, 11am-4pm Tue-Sat) and the dome and skull-adorned exterior of the **St Olafkerk** (locally known as the 'Cheese Church', having housed the cheese exchange for many years). Between the two, you can enter Zeedijk, a street with a rich and tattered history. Before this dyke was built around 1300, Amsterdam was a fishing village with barely enough bog to stand on. But by the fifteenth and sixteenth centuries, with the East India Company raking in the imperialist dollars, Zeedijk was where sailors came to catch up on their boozing, brawling and bonking (or 'doing the St Nicolaas' as it was fondly referred to in those days, as a tribute to their patron saint, a busy chap who also patrons children, thieves, prostitutes and the city of Amsterdam). Sailors who had lost all their money could trade in their pet monkey for a bed at Zeedijk 1, which still retains its old name – **In't Aepjen**, meaning 'In the Monkeys' – and is one of the oldest wooden houses in the city (*see chapters* **Architecture**, *page 33, and* **Cafés & Bars**, *page 125*).

Just off the street towards the harbour down Oudezijds Kolk, you can spot the **Schreierstoren**, the 'Weeping Tower'. Wives would cry there, perhaps with relief, when husbands set off on a voyage, and then cry again if the ship returned with the bad news that the husband was lost at sea. If

the latter ever happened, then – conveniently – it was but a short walk to Zeedijk, where the bereaved lady would often continue life as a 'merry widow'. Prostitution was often the female equivalent of joining the navy: the last economic option.

During the twentieth century, Zeedijk has been sparked by cultural diversity. In the 1930s, the first openly gay establishments appeared, and at the now-closed Café Maandje (Zeedijk 65), there is still a window shrine to legendary owner Bet van Beeren (1902-67), who will surely go down in history as the original Lesbian Biker Chick. In the 1950s, all the jazz greats, from Chet Baker to Gerry Mulligan, came to jam and hang out in the many after-hours clubs around here.

Unfortunately, this subculture marked Zeedijk as a place where heroin could be scored with comparative ease. By the '70s, the street was crowded with dealers, junkies and indifferent cops, with most of the restaurants and cafés renting their tables to dealers. The junkies' magic number back then was '27': ƒ25 for the drugs themselves, and ƒ2 for the drink the owners insisted the junkies purchase to maintain the façades of legality.

Amsterdam's reputation became littered with needles and bits of foil, never more so than when a wasted Chet Baker made his final moody decrescendo in 1988 on to a cement parking pole from a window of the **Prins Hendrik Hotel** at the entrance of the Zeedijk. In recent years, police claim to have cleaned the street up, and indeed, the scene is today much less intimidating and packed with new and new-ish business. The famed dance, ambient and easy tune label Outland Records has its store at no.22; **Demask** offers its posh line of leathers and latexes at no.64 (*see chapter* **Shopping**, *page 144*); and excellent cheap Chinese food can be found at the **New King** at Zeedijk 115-7 (*see chapter* **Restaurants**, *page 120*).

# Tales of the city
# Of bananas and Beelzebub

If one follows Camus's observation and follows the circles formed by Amsterdam's canals inward to what should be the very inner bowels of hell itself, one would find oneself – neatly enough – in the heart of the Red Light District. And here, once upon a time, dwelled the Church of Satan. Coincidence? Read on…

It all began in the '70s in a depraved pub called the Bananenbar. The naked barmaids had naughty bits that were highly trained and uniquely muscled: they could puff pompously on cigars, or be poetic on paper when appended with a pencil. If a customer leaned his head back on the bar with some cash balanced on his nose, it was taken as a cue for a rather exotic dance. With a foot on each side of his head, the assigned barmaid would groove and grind slowly downward to a position where the bill could be commandeered by a fairly singular and strange suction. This Hoover-effect could also be reversed, as shown with the schtick that gave this bar its name: the banana would be peeled, 'inhaled', and then gently discharged bit by bit to any peckish patron.

Legend has it that the Bananenbar only embraced Beelzebub when the owner realised he could circumvent the problems of impending taxation and a lapsed drinking licence by registering as a religion. A crafty move indeed, since religious tolerance has defined Amsterdam ever since the Anabaptists ran naked through the Dam over 450 years ago, starting the chain of events that led to the end of Catholic domination. And since the bar was located in the Neighbourhood of the Beast – or, at least, the district where his lusty appetites seemed most apparent – the choice of the devil as deity seemed logical. It soon all fell into place: the owner became a black bishop of sorts, the barmaids were promoted as nuns, the drinks were now served as elixirs, and the banana shenanigan became a ritual on a par with the taking of the host during mass. It was a scam that worked for years.

Publicity led to brisk business, but also attracted 'real' satanists who legitimised the whole affair by converting several houses down the street into a huge den of darkness, complete with a large S&M-tinged temple, a library and meditational coffins. Courses were offered, and marriages performed, where the happy couples exchanged vows of adultery. It was all fairly harmless. But in 1988, when the 'Church' started to claim a membership of 40,000 overseen by a council of nine anonymous persons, paranoia reached its peak. Who were these shrouded executives of Sodom? Was it the friendly local herringmonger, the Chief of Police or Prince Bernhard? No one was telling.

In any case, the tax police were soon called in to find the loopholes and bust the Church: it was to be an exorcism through audit. But the Fallen Angel's wings beat sweet mercy on the shady council, and the Bananenbar was tipped off. The houses and businesses were sold, the profits gathered, and the Church disbanded. Now under a new owner, the Bananenbar kept its name and returned to its traditional roots as a purveyor of specialised sleaze. But what, you may ask, became of the devil? Well, keep your eyes wide open in the Red Light District: you never know who you might see…

**Bananenbar**
*Oudezijds Achterburgwal 37 (622 4670). Tram 4, 9, 14, 16, 20, 24, 25.* **Map 2 D3**

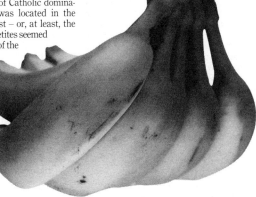

# Windmills on your mind

No self-respecting tourist should miss out on the windmills in Holland: after all, what are clichés for? And though the most impressive examples are outside Amsterdam in nearby **Zaanse Schans** (*see chapter* **Excursions in Holland**, *page 230*), there are actually six mills in the city. Though they're not open to the public, all the mills are capable of working, or at the very least turning their sails, and all do so on **National Windmill Day** (*see chapter* **Amsterdam by Season**, *page 8*).

With the exception of **D'Admiraal**, which was built in 1792 to grind chalk and is now empty, all are private homes or shops. The best example is **De Rieker**, on the banks of the Amstel, which can be reached by walking through Amstelpark. It was constructed in 1636 to drain the Rieker polder, and was a particular favourite of Rembrandt, who is commemorated nearby with a statue. No doubt he would still love it today: it's beautifully preserved, and is now a private home. There are two mills on the Haarlemmerweg: **1200 Roe** (circa 1632) – a 'roe' is an old-fashioned unit, used to calculate the distance of the windmill from the the the city centre – and the corn mill **De Bloem** (1768). **1100 Roe**, an old water mill in a western suburb, and **De Gooyer** (1725), a former corn mill and now home to **Bierbrouwerij 't IJ** (*see box* **Cheers & booze**, *p132*), complete the sextet.

## D'Admiraal
*Noordhollandschkanaaldijk, near Jan Thoméepad. Bus 26, 36, 37, 39.*

## De Bloem
*Haarlemmerweg, near Nieuwpoortkade. Bus 18.*

## De Gooyer
*Funenkade. Tram 6, 10/bus 22, 28.*

## 1100 Roe
*Herman Bonpad, Sportpark, Ookmeer. Bus 19, 23.*

## 1200 Roe
*Haarlemmerweg, near Willem Molengraaffstraat. Bus 85.*

## De Rieker
*Amsteldijk, near De Borcht. Bus 148.*

## NIEUWMARKT

At the bottom of Zeedijk, your eyes will immediately be drawn to the huge and menacing castle-like **De Waag**, or 'the Weigh House'. The Waag, previously called St Antoniespoort, stands in the centre of the Nieuwmarkt and dates from 1488, when it was built as a gatehouse for the city defences. If what motivates your walk through this area is a meditation on humankind's darkest sides, then try to imagine the body parts that used to garnish the Waag's south-east side, and let them act as a baleful warning: this is where the majority of Amsterdam's public executions took place. Here people were tortured, hanged, shot, or, when Napoleon's brother held influence, guillotined, and there were always plenty of corpses for the medical guild to dissect, or for Rembrandt to study and paint: *The Anatomy Lesson of Dr Nicolaes Tulp* stands as evidence. One can only hope that none of the leftovers were sold at the open-air market that has always existed here. Still more depressing is to imagine how, in the dark days of the Nazi occupation, this square was surrounded by barbed wire and used to hold those from the nearby Jewish quarter who were to be shipped off to concentration camps.

More recently, Nieuwmarkt was the site of many riots around 1980, when the city was busy demolishing housing in order to build the Metro. After recent renovation work, the Waag's Anatomical Theatre is now scrubbed clean and is open to the public by appointment, as is a trendy café and the **Society for Old and New Media** (*see chapter* **Media**, *page 199*), complete with free Internet room. The Waag's 500-year passage from torture to technology is now complete.

The streets leading north-east from Nieuwmarkt contain Amsterdam's small **Chinatown**, while the colourfully named side streets ('Monk', 'Blood' and 'Cow') on the southwest lead into the reddest part of the Red Light District. Heading south from the Nieuwmarkt along the Kloveniersburgwal canal, though, makes for a more interesting stroll. At Kloveniersburgwal 29 is the Trippenhuis, now home to the Dutch Academy of Sciences, and formerly, in the eighteenth century, home to the Rijksmuseum collection. During the Golden Age, the building was owned by the very powerful Trip family, whose fortune was made by arms dealing (as testified to by the cannon-shaped chimneys). Their riches meant they could easily afford the imposing gun-powder grey exterior, and they even indulged themselves in building the House of Mr Trip's Coachman at Kloveniersburgwal 26, erected in response to a one-liner the coachman

*The windmills at* **Zaanse Schans**, *just outside Amsterdam.*

allegedly made about being happy with a house as wide as the Trip's front door. He got his wish. The house is now home to a trendy clothing store complete with appropriately anorexic display figures in the window.

### De Waag
*Nieuwmarkt. Tram 9, 14/Metro Nieuwmarkt.*

### 'DE WALLEN'
The canals Oudezijds Voorburgwal and Oudezijds Achterburgwal, with their interconnecting streets, are where carnal sin screams loudest, and right in the middle of Sin City, you'll stumble across the **Oude Kerk**. Originally built in 1306 as a wooden chapel, and constantly renovated and extended between 1330 and 1571, the Oude Kerk is Amsterdam's oldest and most interesting church (*see chapter* **Architecture**, *page 33*). All its original furnishings were removed by iconoclasts during the Reformation, but the church has retained a wooden roof, which was painted in the fifteenth century with figurative images. Keep your eyes peeled, too, for the Gothic and Renaissance façade above the northern portal, and the stained-glass windows, parts of which date from the sixteenth and seventeenth centuries. Rembrandt's wife Saskia, who died in 1642, is buried under the small organ. The inscription over the bridal chamber, which translates as 'Marry in haste, Mourn at leisure', is in keeping with the church's location, though this is more by accident than design.

The Oudezijds Achterburgwal offers some of the more 'tasteful' choices for the eroto-clubber. The **Casa Rosso** nightclub (Oudezijds Achterburgwal 106-08; 627 8954) is certainly worth a look, if only for its peculiar marble cock-and-rotary-ball water fountain at its entrance. A short walk away is the **Bananenbar** (*see box* **Of bananas and Beelzebub**, *page 45*), where Olympic-calibre genitalia can be witnessed night after night working out (and, incidentally, spitting out an average of 15 kilos of fruit every evening in the process). But if your urges are more academic than participatory, then you can pay tribute to original S&M muse Betty Page at the **Erotic Museum**, which has some original photos of the lady on display among its five floors of quasi-erotic gadgetry.

Surprisingly, it's not all sex, sex, sex down here, though you'd be forgiven for thinking otherwise. Body manipulators can put their hobby into a cultural and historical perspective by visiting the **Tattoo Museum**, though if skin is really your thing you may want to take the trek to the outskirts of town to visit the anatomical **Museum Vrolik**, which has a few choice clippings of tattooed human rawhide alongside a remarkable collection of skulls and Siamese twin foetuses in brine (*see chapter* **Museums**, *page 85*).

The Oudezijds Voorburgwal was known as the 'Velvet Canal' in the sixteenth century due to the obscene wealth of its residents. Now, though, the velvet has been replaced by red velours, illuminated by scarlet lightbulbs and complemented by a steady stream of increasingly bored-looking girls sat twiddling their thumbs in the windows of the lovely canal houses. It's rather ironic, then, that this canal should be so densely populated with churches, chapels and orders. The **Museum Amstelkring**, formerly a clandestine attic church, can be found at Oudezijds Voorburgwal 40, while the former convent **Agnietenkapel** is at no.231; reps from the Salvation Army seem to lurk on every nearby corner. On the Spinhuissteeg, opposite the **Hash Marihuana Hemp Museum**, is the Spinhuis, another former convent that used to set 'wayward women' to work spinning wool as their penance. The male equivalent was a short walk away off Kalverstraat at Heiligeweg 9 – now an entrance to the new **Kalvertoren** shopping complex – where audiences once watched prisoners being branded and beaten with a bull's penis. In a further historical foreshadowing of this city's contemporary S&M scene, the entrance gate sports a statue resembling a scolding dominatrix.

### Oude Kerk
*Oudekerksplein 1 (625 8284). Tram 4, 9, 16, 20, 24, 25, 26.* **Open** *11am-5pm Mon-Sat; 1-5pm Sun.* **Admission** *f5; f3,50 students. Groups discounts (min 10 persons).* **Map 2 D2**
*Guided tours (by appointment).*

### WARMOESSTRAAT
It's hard to believe that Amsterdam's oldest street was once the most beautiful of lanes, providing a sharp contrast to its then-evil and rowdy twin, Zeedijk. The poet Vondel ran his hosiery business at Warmoesstraat 101; Mozart's dad would be trying to scalp tickets at the posh bars for his young son's concerts; and Marx would later come here to write in peace. But with the influx of sailors, the laws of supply and demand dictated a fall from grace. Adam and Eve in their salad days can still be seen etched in stone at Warmoesstraat 25, but for the rest, this street has fallen to accommodating the low-end traveller. Still, the recent appearance of a few galleries and shops – especially the **Condomerie Het Guiden Vlies** at no.141 (*see box* **The new curiosity shops**, *page 160*) – are bringing back some brighter colours to the strip.

## The New Side & around Spui

Rhyming with 'cow', the Spui is the square that caps the three main arteries that start down near the west end of Centraal Station: the middle-of-the-road walking and shopping street Kalverstraat (called Nieuwendijk before it crosses the Dam), Nieuwezijds Voorburgwal, and the Spuistraat. Coming up Nieuwezijds Voorburgwal –

translated literally as 'The New Side's Front of the Town Wall', to distinguish it from the Oudezijds Voorburgwal ('The Old Side's Front of the Town Wall') found in near mirror image in the Red Light District, though both fortress walls have long since been destroyed – the effects of tragically half-assed urban renewal are immediately noticeable. The **Crowne Plaza** (Nieuwezijds Voorburgwal 5; *see chapter* **Accommodation**, *page 91*) was formerly the site of the large Wyers squat, which was dramatically emptied by riot police in 1985 after a widely supported campaign by squatters against the mass conversion of residential buildings into commercial spaces that was taking place at the time. The multinational won, as did the **ABN-Amro Bank** slightly further up, with its in-your-face glass plaza at the corner with Nieuwezijdskolk. While an underground car park was being dug on this site, archaeological remains of a thirteenth-century castle believed to belong to the Lords of the Amstel were found. Once surrounded by marshland, the castle remains have now, unfortunately, been paved over for luxury office, shop and hotel space.

South of Dam, still on Nieuwezijds Voorburgwal, is one of the entrances to **Amsterdams Historisch Museum**. This elegant historical museum is a rambling cluster of buildings and courtyards, located on the site of St Lucy's Convent, which dates from 1414. The museum, in turn, connects to the **Begijnhof**. A quiet backwater also accessible via the north side of Spui square, the Begijnhof is a group of houses built around a secluded courtyard and garden. Established in the fourteenth century, it originally provided modest homes for the Beguines, a religious sisterhood of unmarried women from good families who, though not nuns, lived together in a close community and often took vows of chastity; the last sister died in 1971. Most of the neat little houses were modernised in the seventeenth and eighteenth centuries.

In the centre of the courtyard stands the **Engelsekerk** (English Reformed Church), built in around 1400 and given over to English-speaking Presbyterians living in the city in 1607. Now one of the principal places of worship for Amsterdam's English community (*see box* **Losing your religion?**, *page 263*), it's worth a look primarily to see the pulpit panels, which were designed by a young Mondrian. Also in the courtyard is a Catholic church, secretly converted from two houses in 1665 following the banning of the Roman Catholic faith after the Reformation. The wooden house at Begijnhof 34, meanwhile, is dated 1477 and is the oldest house standing in the city, while Begijnhof 35 is a café and information centre. This is the best-known of the city's numerous *hofjes* (almshouses); for details of others, *see below* **The Jordaan**.

The Spui square itself plays host to many markets – the most notable being the Book Market on Fridays – and was historically an area where the intelligentsia gathered for some serious browbeating and alcohol abuse, often after doing an honest day's graft at one of the many newspapers that were once located on the Spuistraat. The Lieverdje ('Little Darling') statue in front of the **Athenaeum Newscentrum** magazine store (*see chapter* **Shopping**, *page 141*) – a small, spindly and pigeon shit-smeared statue of a boy in goofy knee socks – was the site for Provo 'happenings' in the mid-'60s (*see chapter* **History**, *pages 25-7*).

You can leave the Spui by going up either the Kalverstraat or the Singel past Leidsestraat: both routes lead to the **Munttoren** (Mint Tower) at Muntplein. Just across from the floating flower market (*see chapter* **Shopping**, *page 150*), this medieval tower was the western corner of the Reguliersspoort, a gate in the city wall in the 1480s, and in 1620 a spire was added by Hendrik de Keyser, the foremost architect of the period. The tower takes its name from the time when it was used to mint coins after Amsterdam was cut off from its money supply during a war with England, Munster and France. There's now a shop on the ground floor selling fine Dutch porcelain, but the rest of the tower is closed to visitors. The Munttoren is prettiest at night when it's floodlit, though daytime visitors may be able to hear its carillon, which often plays for 15 minutes at noon.

From here, walk down Nieuwe Doelenstraat beginning at the **Hôtel de L'Europe** (familiar if you've seen Hitchcock's *Foreign Correspondent*; *see chapter* **Accommodation**, *page 90*). This street connects with the scenic Staalstraat: walk up here and you'll soon end up at Waterlooplein market.

### Begijnhof

*Tram 1, 2, 5, 20.* **Open** 9am-11pm daily. **Admission** free. **Map 5 D4**

### Munttoren (Mint Tower)

*Muntplein. Tram 4, 9, 14, 16, 20, 24, 25.* **Map 5 D4**

## Around Waterlooplein

Situated to the south-east of the Red Light District, the Waterlooplein and its immediate surroundings are a peculiar mix of old and new architectural styles. If you leave the Nieuwmarkt along St Antoniebreestraat, you'll pass several bars, coffeeshops and chic clothes shops: it's a good escape route out of the throbbing Red Light District. The modern yet relatively tasteful council housing that lines the street was designed by local architect Theo Bosch.

Pop through the ancient skull-adorned entrance between St Antoniebreestraat 130 and 132, and enter the former graveyard and now restful square around the **Zuiderkerk** (South Church). Designed by the ubiquitous Hendrik de Keyser, it was built between 1603 and 1614, the first Protestant church to appear after the Reformation. Now, it's the municipal information centre for the physical planning and housing of Amsterdam. Development plans are made to look promising with interactive scale models, but as you walk around the neighbourhood, it becomes obvious that shiny ideals can often create obtuse realities.

Crossing the bridge at the end of St Antoniebreestraat, you'll soon arrive at the historic **Rembrandthuis**. If you then take an immediate right down the steps, you'll find yourself in the **Waterlooplein Market** (*see chapter* **Shopping**, *page 162*). Although it's a bit touristy these days, the market can still be a bargain hunter's dream if you're patient and have a couple of hours to spare.

Just down from Waterlooplein is Mr Visserplein. Although both the **Portuguese Synagogue** and the **Joods Historisch Museum** (Jewish Historical Museum) are within spitting distance, Mr Visserplein is actually little more than a roundabout where five main roads conjoin. If you head west from here, you'll arrive almost immediately at the nineteenth-century **Mozes en Aäronkerk**. This former clandestine Catholic church, now covered in political murals, has been used as a social and cultural centre since 1970.

Also in this area, and dominating Waterlooplein, is the **Stadhuis-Muziektheater** (the City Hall-Music Theatre; *see chapter* **Music: Classical & Opera**, *page 203*). It wasn't always thus, though: the area where the Stadhuis-Muziektheater now stands was once a Jewish ghetto, and then – in the '70s – home to literally dozens of squatters, who made their homes in several gorgeous sixteenth- and seventeenth-century buildings. The new building was dogged by controversy from the start: it was first mooted in the 1920s, though it was not until 1954 that the city council selected Waterlooplein as the site, and it was 1979 before it was decided that the civic headquarters should be combined with an opera house. The decision was a controversial one, as was the design (by Wilhelm Holtzbauer and Cees Dam), and Amsterdammers showed their discontent by organising demonstrations and protesting during construction. Finally, in 1982, a riot caused a million guilders' worth of damage to construction equipment. These displays of displeasure are the

reasons why the ƒ300-million building, home to both the Netherlands Opera and Dutch National Ballet, is now universally known as the 'Stopera'.

It's rare that science and art meet on the level, but in the passage between City Hall and the Muziektheater there is a display of geological information, the Amsterdam Ordnance Project, which includes a device showing the NAP (normal Amsterdam water level) and a cross-section of the Netherlands showing its geological structure. Close by here is the **Blauwbrug** ('Blue Bridge'), linking Waterlooplein with Amstel, which used to be the main route into the city from the east. The current bridge was built in 1873, but a plaque depicting the original (taken from a demolished house) has been placed at the entrance of the Muziektheater car park.

### Portuguese Synagogue

*Mr Visserplein 3 (624 5351). Tram 4, 9, 14, 20.* **Open** *Apr-Oct* 10am-12.30pm, 1-4pm Sun-Fri; *Nov-Mar* 10am-12.30pm, 1-4pm Mon-Thur; 10am-12pm, 1-3pm Fri; 10am-noon Sun. **Admission** ƒ5; ƒ2,50 under-18s. **Map 3 E3**

## Around Rembrandtplein

Over the Blauwbrug away from Waterlooplein and on the other side of the Amstel is **Rembrandtplein**. Not much to look at now, this area used to be called Reguliersmarkt and once hosted Amsterdam's butter market. In 1876, the square was renamed in honour of Rembrandt; a statue of the Dutch master stands in the centre of the gardens, gazing in the direction of the Jewish quarter. Although there is no longer a market here, it's still the centre of probably more commercial activity than ever before, with neon signs and loud music blaring out of the cafés, bars and restaurants on all sides. Gloriously tacky, Rembrandtplein is full of sunbathers by day and funseekers by night: the square is home to a variety of places, from the faded fake elegance of traditional striptease parlours to seedy peep-show joints and nondescript cafés and restaurants. Nevertheless, there are a few exceptions to this exuberant display of trash, such as the zoological sample-filled grand café **De Kroon** (*see chapter* **Cafés & Bars**, *page 128*) and the extravagantly colourful art deco masterpiece, the **Tuschinski** cinema (*see chapter* **Film**, *page 183*). Just round the corner on the Amstel is a stretch of gay cafés (*see chapter* **Gay & Lesbian**, *pages 187-8*).

# Museums around Waterlooplein

**Holland Experience**
*Waterlooplein 17 (422 2233). See page 84.*

**Joods Historisch Museum**
*Jonas Daniel Meijerplein 2-4 (626 9945). See page 83.*

The city's oldest graffiti can still be made out on the façade of Amstel 216. Over 300 years ago, the former mayor Coenraad van Beuningen, drinking buddy of Louis XIV, scrawled – with his own blood – pentagrams, Hebrew letters and magical symbols that, according to his apparent madness, predicted the end of the world. Even modern chemical cleaning products have not been able to erase his ravings, and after 300 years, the word 'magog' is still visible as a warning. Coincidentally (or is it?), the nearby alleys between Reguliersbreestraat and Reguliersdwarsstraat were once referred to as the 'Devil's Triangle', back in the days when they were still home to the city's rat catchers and petty criminals.

From Rembrandtplein, walk along either the up-and-coming shopping street Utrechtsestraat, or explore the painfully scenic Reguliersgracht and the grotesquely pleasant oasis of **Amstelveld**. Kerkstraat, which runs along the edge of Amstelveld with the **Amstelkerk** – the white wooden church that used to act as a stable for Napoleon's horses – is also a fine street. Heading west towards Leidsestraat, you'll encounter a quirky array of funky houses, galleries and shops including 'shroom and smart drugs central **Conscious Dreams** (*see chapter* **Coffeeshops**, *page 138*). Heading east will get you to the **Magerebrug** ('Skinny Bridge'; *see box* **Passing water**, *page 55*) over the Amstel, a lovely spot for a stroll on a sunny summer's day.

### Rembrandtplein
*Tram 4, 9, 14, 20.* **Map 6 E4**

## Around Leidseplein

Leidseplein is, in a nutshell, the tourist centre of Amsterdam: the bastard child of Times Square in New York City and London's Leicester Square, it's permanently packed with merrymakers drinking at pavement cafés, listening to the buskers and soaking up the atmosphere. It lies on the southwest edge of the *grachtengordel*, and though it's called a square, it is in fact an L-shape, running from the end of Leidsestraat to the bridge over Singelgracht. In the current climate of city-centre traffic reduction schemes, this square is a reminder that such ideas are not new: during the Middle Ages, carts and wagons were banned from the centre of Amsterdam, and people heading for the city had to leave their vehicles in *pleinen*, or squares. At the end of the road from Leiden was a 'cart park', surrounded by warehouses and establishments catering for this captive clientele.

*The daily queues outside the hugely popular* **Anne Frankhuis***. See page 58.*

*The quickest way out of* **Leidseplein**...

The area around Leidseplein probably has more cinemas, theatres, nightclubs and restaurants than any other part of the city. The square is dominated by the **Stadsschouwburg** (the municipal theatre; *see chapter* **Theatre**, *page 222*), as well as numerous cafés that take over the pavements during the summer. This is also the time of year when fire-eaters, jugglers, acrobats, singers and small-time con-artists fill the square, but watch out for those pesky pickpockets. The development of Leidseplein in recent years has meant that there are now fast food restaurants on every corner, and many locals feel that the essential Dutch flavour of the district has been destroyed for a quick buck.

Leidseplein has always been a focal point of the town for one reason or another. Artists and writers used to congregate here in the 1920s and 1930s, when it was the scene of pre-war clashes between Communists and Fascists. During the war, it was a focus for protests, which were ruthlessly broken up by the occupying Nazis: there's a commemorative plaque on nearby Kerkstraat, where a number of people were killed. More recently, Leidseplein has become the venue for celebrations whenever Ajax, the local football team, win anything, which is quite often. The police take the mini-riots that usually ensue in their stride (and so they should: they've had enough practice at dealing with them by now).

The café society associated with Leidseplein began in earnest with the opening of the city's first bar incorporating a terrace, the Café du Théâtre. It was demolished in 1877, 20 years before completion of Kromhout's impressive **American Hotel** – now a prominent meeting place for the posh; *see chapters* **Accommodation**, *page 89*, and **Restaurants**, *page 107* – at the south-west end of the square. Opposite the American is a building, dating from 1882, that reflects Leidseplein's transformation into its current state as architectural billboard. The enormous illuminated Drum and Hitachi adverts add nothing to the building's former grandeur. Just off the square, in the Leidsebos, is the Adamant, a white pyramid-shaped sculpture given to Amsterdam by the city's

# Passing water

The Dutch call them *grachten*. There are 165 of them in Amsterdam. They stretch 75.5 kilometres (47 miles) around the city, and reach an average depth of three metres (10ft). They function to keep the sea and the surrounding bog at bay. About 10,000 bicycles, 100 million litres of sludge and grunge and 52 corpses (usually tramps, who trip while pissed and pissing) are dredged from their murky depths each year…

The major canals and their radial streets are where the real Amsterdam exists and where its past is most evident. What they lack in specific sights, they make up for as a focus for scenic coffee slurping, quirky shopping, aimless walks and meditative gable gandering.

The **Singel** was the original medieval moat of the city, while the other three major canals that follow its line outward were part of a Golden Age urban renewal scheme; by the time the building finished, Amsterdam had quadrupled in size. The **Herengracht** (named after the gentlemen who initially invested in it), the **Keizersgracht** (named for the Roman Emperor Maximillian I) and the **Prinsengracht** (named after William, Prince of Orange) are the canals where originally the rich lived, and though they're still residential in parts, many properties have been given over to offices, hotels and museums. The radially connecting canals and streets, originally built for workers and artisans, have a higher density of cosy cafés and smaller speciality shops, while the major shopping stretches of Rozengracht, Elandsgracht, Leidsestraat and Vijzelstraat are all former canals, filled in to deal with the advent of motor traffic. Smaller canals worth seeking out include Leliegracht, Bloemgracht, Spiegelgracht, Egelantiersgracht and Brouwersgracht.

## Singel

One of the few clues to the Singel's past as the protective moat surrounding the city's medieval wall is the bridge that crosses at Oude Leliestraat. It's called the Torensluis and did indeed once have a lookout tower; the space under the bridge was supposedly used as a lock-up for medieval drunks. But besides the **Bloemenmarkt** (*see chapter* **Shopping**, *page 150*) by day, and, perhaps, the **RoXY** (*see chapters* **Clubs**, *page 176*, and **Gay & Lesbian**, *page 190*) by night, there are few specific sights.

Still, while you're here, you may want to join the debate on whether Singel 7 or Singel 166 is the smallest house in Amsterdam. Always good for a laugh is the House with Noses at Singel 116, though arty types may be more interested in Singel 140-142, once the home of Banning Cocq, the principal figure of Rembrandt's *Night Watch*. Pussy lovers will adore the Poezenboot ('cat boat') at Singel 40, home to dozens of stray and abandoned felines. You may also want to stake out the town's poshest sex club, Yab Yum (Singel 295; 624 9503), to watch the country's elite enter for a service.

## Herengracht

As the first canal to be dug in the glory days, the Herengracht attracted the richest of merchants. This is where the houses are the most stately and overblown, especially in the stretch known as the 'Golden Bend', between Leidsestraat and Vijzelstraat. The **Museum Willet-Holthuysen** is a classic example of such a seventeenth-century mansion, densely furnished in eighteenth- and nineteenth-century styles. Excess also defines the Louis XVI style of Herengracht 475, while tales of pre-rock 'n' roll excess are often told about Herengracht 527, whose interior was completely trashed by Peter the Great.

Mischievous types (of which there are plenty in Amsterdam) may like to annoy the town's mayor: to do so, simply park your boat on his personal and pleasantly scenic dock in front of his official residence at Herengracht 502. If you're caught, quickly douse your spliff and try palming off the authorities with the excuse that you're just visiting **Het Kattenkabinet** (Herengracht 497), a nearby museum dedicated to cats.

Stone masons kept themselves busy at Herengracht 380, an exact copy of a Loire mansion, complete with coy reclining figures on the gable and frolicking cherubs and other mythical figures on its bay window. Try, also, to snatch a look into the windows of Van Brienenhuis at Herengracht 284: the excesses of bygone eras will soon become apparent.

## Keizersgracht

If you walk down Keizersgracht starting at its western end (by Brouwersgracht), you'll soon encounter the 'House with the Heads' at Keizersgracht 123, a classic of pure Dutch Renaissance. The official story has these finely chiselled heads representing classical gods, but the real scoop is supposed to be that these are actually the heads of burglars, chopped off by a vigilante and a lusty maidservant. She decapitated six and married the seventh, or so the story goes. Another classic is at Keizersgracht 174, an art nouveau masterpiece by Gerrit van Arkels and currently the headquarters of Greenpeace International.

The **Felix Meritis Building** (Keizersgracht 324) is hard to ignore, a neo-classical monolith with 'Happiness through achievement' chiselled over its door. And achieve it did: after housing a society of arts and sciences in the 1800s, it went on to house the Communist Party and is now a foundation for experimental art and theatre. This stretch was also the site in that time of the 'Slipper Parade' every Sunday, where the posh-footed rich strolled about to see and to be seen.

## Prinsengracht

Prinsengracht is the most charming of the canals. Pompous façades have been mellowed with shady trees, cosy cafés and some of the funkier houseboats in town. The streets of Prinsenstraat, Reestraat, Berenstraat and Runstraat, meanwhile, offer a diverse selection of smaller, artier speciality shops that perfectly complement a leisurely stroll down by the water.

If it's a Monday morning and you're doing the rounds at the weekly **Noorderkerk** market, stop for coffee at the nearby Papeneiland (Prinsengracht 2), a café that has remained unchanged through more than three centuries of service. A tunnel from the Papeneiland used to go under the canal to a Catholic church during the Protestant uprising. The scenic tower of the **Westerkerk** is also to be found here.

## Bridges

With so many canals, it's logical that Amsterdam should also have a fair number of bridges: there are, in fact, over 1,400 of them. Try to stop off at the point on Reguliersgracht, at the junction with Keizersgracht, where you can see seven parallel bridges. Floodlit by night, it's one of Amsterdam's most beautiful scenes.

One of Amsterdam's more unusual bridges is the **Magerebrug** ('Skinny Bridge'), built in the seventeenth century. The story goes that two sisters who lived either side of the Amstel were bored by having to walk all the way round to visit each other, so the bridge was built for them. Uniquely, it's made from wood, and has to be repaired every 20 years. The bridge links Kerkstraat and Nieuwekerkstraat and is opened by hand whenever a boat needs to pass. The only other bridge of note is the **Blauwbrug**, which links Amstelstraat with Waterlooplein and was inspired by the elaborate Pont Alexandre III in Paris.

# Museums on the Canals

**Anne Frankhuis**
*Prinsengracht 263 (556 7100). See page 79.*

**Bijbels Museum**
*Herengracht 366 (624 2436). See page 80.*

**Het Kattenkabinet**
*Herengracht 497 (626 5378). See page 84.*

**Museum Van Loon**
*Keizersgracht 672 (624 5255). See page 79.*

**Museum Willet-Holthuysen**
*Herengracht 605 (523 1870). See page 79.*

**Theatermuseum**
*Herengracht 168 (623 5104). See page 83.*

**Woonbootmuseum**
*Prinsengracht, by no.296 (427 0750). See page 84.*

# Museums around the Plantage

**Artis**
*Plantage Kerklaan 40 (623 1836). See page 84.*

**Hollandse Schouwburg**
*Plantage Middelaan 24 (626 9945). See page 80.*

**Hortus Botanicus**
*Plantage Middelaan 2A (625 8411). See page 78.*

**Verzetsmuseum Amsterdam**
*Plantage Kerklaan 61 (620 2535). See page 80.*

diamond industry in 1986 to commemorate 400 years of the trade. Designed by Joost van Santen at a cost of ƒ75,000, it uses light to create a rainbow hologram.

On leaving Leidseplein, you can take either Lijnbaansgracht to pass the **Melkweg** (*see chapters* **Art Galleries**, *page 72*; **Music: Rock, Roots & Jazz**, *page 207*, and **Theatre**, *page 222*); Leidsestraat, for a shopping expedition; or Weteringschans, which leads past the **Paradiso** (*see chapters* **Clubs**, *page 176*, and **Music: Rock, Roots & Jazz**, *page 208*) and eventually to the **Rijksmuseum** and the canal boat departure point. Before you get that far, though, you'll come to **Max Euweplein**, which backs on to the canal. Look out for the grand entrance to the square: pillars form a portal, upon which is inscribed a Latin motto, roughly translating as 'Man does not piss against the wind'. Formerly used for the internment of Resistance fighters during Nazi occupation, architects redesigned the square to resemble an Italian piazza, with a shallow waterfall and steps. To begin with, it was crammed with exclusive shops and cafés, but many ended up closing, leaving mostly tack and souvenir shops behind. It's still a pleasant alternative route to the Vondelpark, though, and you can even stop and play oversized chess in tribute to Max Euwe, the chess champion for whom the square is named.

## The Plantage & the Oost

The mostly residential area known as the Plantage lies south-east of Mr Visserplein and is reached via Muiderstraat, with the Portuguese Synagogue on the right. The wide, attractive Plantage Middenlaan winds past the **Hortus Botanicus**, passes close by the inspiring **Verzetsmuseum**, runs along the edge of the **Artis Zoo**, and heads onward towards the **Tropenmuseum**.

After a period during which the area was largely populated by rich citizens, Jews began to settle here some 200 years ago. Diamond cutting was, back then, one of only a few trades open to Jews, and after an era of poverty, the area was soon redeveloped on nineteenth-century diamond money. The splendid headquarters of the diamond cutters' trade union still stands on Henri Polaklaan, and other extant buildings such as the

Gassan, the **Saskiahuis** and the **Coster** stand as reminders that Amsterdam's most profitable trade was once based in this area (*see box* **A girl's best friend**, *page 154*).

The Plantage is still wealthy, even though its charm has faded somewhat over the years. Its graceful buildings and tree-lined streets provide a residential area much sought-after by those who want to live centrally but away from the tourist areas. The area has already undergone extensive redevelopment, and work is still continuing. As one would expect, results have been mixed: while Entrepotdok is a scenic and positive example of the renovations, the housing association flats and houses erected where the army barracks and dockside warehouses once stood (just past Muiderpoort city gate) are somewhat less attractive. Still, the area has maintained some of its heritage: the brightly coloured Van Eyck's Moedershuis on Plantage Middenlaan was a mother and child refuge during World War II, while on the other side of the road is the attractive Huize St Jacob, an old people's home rebuilt on the site of an earlier one using the original stone portal.

South of Mauritskade is **Amsterdam Oost** (East), where the happening **Arena** hostel complex (*see chapter* **Accommodation**, *page 95*) is located along the edge of another former graveyard that was long ago transformed into the green oasis known as **Oosterpark**. Just beyond the aforementioned Tropenmusem, also along the park's edge, is the **Dappermarkt** (*see chapter* **Shopping**, *page 161*), which defines one border of the Indische Buurt (Indonesian Neighbourhood), further east. The **Bierbrouwerij 't IJ**, a brewery in a windmill (*see boxes* **Windmills on your mind**, *page 46*, and **Cheers & Booze**, *page 132*), is a good place to sip on a culturally reflective beer.

## The Jordaan

The Jordaan area is roughly sock-shaped, with often-disputed borders at Brouwersgracht, Leidsegracht, Lijnbaansgracht and Prinsengracht.

*Enjoy some animal magic at the **Artis Zoo** in the Plantage.*

*Museums? Who needs 'em?*

Before the invention of noise pollution, it was said that if you could hear the bells of the **Westerkerk**, you were in the Jordaan. Nowadays, the church tower is merely a good place from which to view the Jordaan's streets and canals, provided you don't suffer from vertigo. At 85 metres (278 feet) high – one of the tallest structures in Amsterdam – it also makes a useful landmark.

The neo-classical church was built in 1631 by Hendrik de Keyser. Its tower is topped with a somewhat gaudy gold, blue and red crown marked 'XXX'. The story goes that in 1489, Maximillian, the Holy Roman Emperor, in need of medical help during a pilgrimage and grateful for the sanctuary, granted the city the right to include his crown on the city arms. The triple-X came to be used by the city's traders as a seal to denote quality and does not mark something as X-rated, as some people theorise when they witness, for the first time, the 'XXX'-marked and remarkably phallic parking poles – 'Amsterdammertjes' – that are found throughout the city.

It's worth climbing to the top of the tower (186 steps to the sixth floor) for the superb view of the city. While you recover from the exertion, ponder

the fate of one of Amsterdam's most famous sons, Rembrandt van Rijn. It's thought that the painter is buried somewhere in the graveyard here, though no one is entirely sure where. Rembrandt died a pauper, and is commemorated inside with a plaque. Although his burial on 8 October 1669 was recorded in the church register, the actual spot was not specified; there's a good chance he shares a grave with his son, Titus, who died the previous year and is buried here. Practical jokers are recommended to take their companions for a coffee at the historical **Chris Café** (Bloemstraat 42), which began as the local for the builders of the Westerkerk. The toilet's flusher has always been located – uniquely – by the bar, which makes it all too easy to shock a friend who's having an over-leisurely sit (sic).

A short saunter away from Westerkerk is **Anne Frankhuis**, one of the most visited attractions in town (*see chapters* **History***, page 24, and* **Museums***, page 79*). It's the seventeenth-century canalside house where the young Jewish girl Anne Frank spent over two years in hiding during World War II, from June 1942 to August 1944. It's definitely not a cosy recreation of a family home: the Nazis destroyed the furniture and the interior has been left bare, though you can still see the diary and the bookcase that concealed the entrance to the annexe where the family hid, sustained by friends. Regular exhibitions are held, but visit very early to avoid the crowds.

The Jordaan emerged when the city was extended in the early part of the seventeenth century and was originally designated for the working classes, as well as providing a haven for victims of religious persecution, such as Jews and Huguenots. In keeping with the modest economic circumstances of the residents, the houses tend to be small and densely packed, compared to the magnificent

# Tales of the city **Eel life drama**

Contrary to popular sporting myth, Amsterdammers have not just been obsessed with football, skating and cycling since the dawn of time. Quite the opposite: before the Lindengracht was filled in, this small canal was the city's premier venue for the sport of eel-pulling. The trick to this most peculiar of games was to yank an eel off a rope from which it was dangling over the canal, while passing in a fast-moving boat. Cricket it ain't. However, the sport – banned at the time – really hit the headlines in 1886, when a passing policeman elected to cut the rope from which the eel was hanging. This was perhaps

not the wisest idea: the residents of the Jordaan, then the city's main working-class neighbourhood, had long felt hard done-by, and the cop's interference was the final straw. The Eel Riot of 1886, as the incident came to be known, began by the corner of Lindengracht and Eerste Goudsebloemdwarsstraat, and escalated so quickly that the army had to be called in. After a few days, it was announced that 26 Jordaansers had died and 136 wounded. And the eel? Astonishingly, it survived the event, and its dry husk was auctioned in 1913 for the princely sum of *f*75.

# Keep on the grass

For such a small city, Amsterdam has a remarkable number of green spaces. Many are found in small residential neighbourhoods: Sarphatipark in the Pijp and Oosterpark in the east are the pride of their respective districts, particularly in spring and summer when the flowers are in full bloom. Still, few of the city's 28 parks – Amstelpark, Amsterdamse Bos, Beatrixpark, Flevopark and **Vondelpark** (pictured; *see also* **The Museum Quarter***, pages 62-63*) – are really worth a visit.

**Amstelpark** was created for a garden festival in 1972, and now offers recreation and respite to locals in the suburb of Buitenveldert, near the RAI business centre. A formal rose garden and rhododendron walk are among the seasonal floral spectacles, while there are also art shows at the Glass House (Glazenhuis), pony rides and a children's farm, plus tours on a miniature train. The Rosarium Restaurant serves expensive meals, though its outdoor café is somewhat less pricey.

**Amsterdamse Bos** predates Amstelpark: it was created in the 1930s, partly as a job-creation scheme to ease what was a chronic unemployment problem. The 800-hectare (2,000-acre) Bos ('wood') is a favourite retreat for Amsterdam families, especially at weekends. The man-made Bosbaan is used for boating and swimming, with canoe and pedalo rental available. Other attractions include a horticultural museum, play areas, jogging routes, a buffalo and bison reserve, a bike-hire centre (open from March to October), a watersports centre, riding stables and a picnic area. The non-subsidised goat farm sells various cheeses, milks and ice-cream: you can even feed the goats while you're there.

A little off the beaten tourist track, just by the RAI business centre, **Beatrixpark** is one of Amsterdam's loveliest parks. Extended and renovated in 1994, it's a wonderfully peaceful place, and handy if you want to avoid the crowds on a hot summer's day. The Victorian walled garden is worth a visit, as is the pond, complete with geese, black swans and herons. Amenities include a wading pool and well-equipped play area for kids, and there are concerts held here in July and August.

Supremely peaceful and much bigger than it looks on the map, **Flevopark** has both extensive wooded areas and wide open spaces. Its size means that there are always places to sit in peace and quiet; added bonuses are the two open-air swimming pools that, though highly popular in the summer, somehow always seem to have enough space on the surrounding grass for the late-coming sunbather.

### Amstelpark
*Bus 8, 48, 49, 60, 158, 173.* **Open** dawn-dusk daily.

### Amsterdamse Bos
*Bus 170, 171, 172.* **Open** 24 hours daily.

### Beatrixpark
*Tram 5.* **Open** dawn-dusk daily.

### Flevopark
*Tram 14.* **Open** *pool* 10am-5pm, 7-9pm (on days warmer than 25°C) daily. **Admission** ƒ4,25.

dwellings along the adjacent *grachtengordel*. The area is a higgledy-piggledy mixture of old buildings (many of them listed monuments), bland modern social housing and the occasional eyesore that has somehow sneaked past city planning. There are also odd, contemporary contributions in the area, such as the large, yellow tap 'sculpture' that protrudes from a house at Tuinstraat 157.

Despite its working-class associations, the properties are now highly desirable, and though the residents are mainly proud, community-spirited Jordaaners, the nouveaux riches are slowly moving in and yuppifying the 'hood. Brouwersgracht, arguably still the most charmed and charming canal in the area, is one obvious example, with its recently constructed trendy warehouse-conversion apartments.

There are several ideas as to the origin of the name 'Jordaan': some believe it to be a corruption of *joden*, Dutch for Jews, or of the French word for garden, *jardin*. The latter seems more plausible: the area was formerly a damp meadow, and many streets have been named after flowers or plants. Other streets are also named after animals whose pelts were used in tanning, one of the main industries in the Jordaan in the seventeenth century. Looiersgracht ('Tanner's Canal') is surrounded by streets such as Hazenstraat ('Hare Street'), Elandsgracht ('Elk Canal') and Wolvenstraat ('Wolf Street').

Part of the Jordaan's charm is what is hidden from the uninformed eye: the area has the highest concentration of *hofjes* (hidden garden courtyards) in the city. The better-known ones in the area are Claes Claesz Hofje (1e Egelantiersdwarsstraat 3), St Andrieshofje (Egelantiersgracht 107-114), Suyckerhofje (Lindengracht 149-163), Venetiae (Elandsstraat 106-136), and the oldest, Linden Hofje (Lindengracht 94-112). The Jordaan has no major sights as such, but is more of an area where you just stumble across things. It provides a welcome, relaxing break from the crowded tourist areas: it's constantly surprising to wander through its streets and hardly see a soul. In general, the area north of the shop-dense Rozengracht (formerly a wide canal, now filled in) is more interesting and picturesque, with the area to the south more residential and commercial.

A washed-up Rembrandt lived from 1659 until he died ten years later at Rozengracht 184, where all that remains of his former home is a plaque on the first floor bearing the inscription 'Hier Stond Rembrandts Woning 1410-1669' ('Here Stood Rembrandt's Home 1410-1669'). However, with its many galleries and resident artists, the Jordaan's association with art is still alive today. The area also contains some of the best vegetarian restaurants in the city, the most noteworthy of which are arguably **De Bolhoed** and **De Vliegende Schotel**. **De Koophandel** (Bloemgracht 49) is a late-night drinking bar that doesn't start filling up until close on the witching hour, while **'t Smalle** (Egelantiersgracht 12), set on a small, picturesque canal, was where Peter Hoppe (of Hoppe & Jenever, the world's first makers of gin) founded his distillery in 1780. For a more unique, local

*Escape to the wonderfully calm* **Hortus Botanicus**. *See page 56.*

# Museums around Museumplein

**Nederlands Filmmuseum**
*Vondelpark 3 (589 1400). See page 78.*

**Rijksmuseum**
*Stadhouderskade 42 (673 2121). See page 76.*

**Rijksmuseum South Wing**
*Hobbemastraat 19 (673 2121). See page 76.*

**Stedelijk Museum of Modern Art**
*Paulus Potterstraat 13
(573 2737).
See page 77.*

**Van Gogh Museum**
*Paulus Potterstraat 7 (570 5200).
See page 77.*

experience, try to sing along at the marvellously kitschy **Café Nol**. For all, *see chapters* **Restaurants**, *pages 105-121*, and **Cafés & Bars**, *pages 122-134*.

Between scenic coffees or debauched daytime beers, you might want to check out one of the many specialist shops in this area. Some of the best of the outdoor markets are found nearby: the **Noordermarkt** and the **Boerenmarkt** share the same site around the Noorderkerk – the city's first Calvinist church, built in 1623 – on different days. The remains of the former livestock market next to the Boerenmarkt can be a disturbing sight, with cages crammed with tropical birds, ducks and even kittens. Adjacent to the Noordermarkt is **Westermarkt**, while another general market fills the Lindengracht on Saturday mornings (for most of the above, *see chapter* **Shopping**, *pages 161-2*).

More quirky shopping opportunities are to be found on Haarlemmerdijk, which runs parallel to, and behind, Brouwersgracht. Though not officially part of the Jordaan, the street and its side streets do share a comparable ambience. Where it ends at Haarlemmerplein, you can see the imposing **Haarlemmerpoort**, built as a city gate for William II's visit in 1840. Behind it you can enter the eminently wanderable Westerpark, which connects up to the **Westergasfabriek** (*see chapters* **Theatre**, *page 222*), a large terrain that's evolved from gas factory to underground squat village to its present state as an official and surprisingly cutting-edge centre for culture, art, exhibitions and music.

The area south of Rozengracht has two excellently browse-worthy indoor antique markets, **Rommelmarkt** and **Looier**, both of which have cafés. There are also a number of interesting shops, including curio store **Het Winkeltje** (Prinsengracht 228), and the **English Bookshop** (Lauriergracht 71). For all, *see chapter* **Shopping**, *page 141, 160-2*).

Elandsgracht, meanwhile, is lined with a mix of shops that cater to every need. Elandsgracht 71-77 used to be home to the maze-like Sjakoo's Fort. Sjakoo is often referred to as the 'Robin Hood of

Amsterdam', glossing over the fact that he sometimes neglected to give to the poor after stealing from the rich. Still, he had style: robbing prescouted houses while dressed in white, accompanied by his black-clad henchmen. His head ended up spiked on a pole where the **Shell Building** now stands behind Centraal Station, but a local band (Sjakoo!) and an anarchist-oriented bookstore keep his name alive. Another tribute can be paid where Elandsgracht hits Prinsengracht: here you'll find statues of Tante Leni, Johnny Jordaan and Willi Alberti, who all personified the 'Spirit of the Jordaan' by crooning of lost love and spilt beer in many of the local cafés.

## Westerkerk

*Prinsengracht 281 (624 7766/tower 552 4169). Tram 13, 14, 17, 20.* **Open** *church opening times vary: phone for details; tower* June-Sept 10am-4pm Wed-Sat. **Admission** *tower f3.* **Map 2 C3** *Disabled access.*

## The Museum Quarter

Part of the Oud-Zuid (Old South) and one of the wealthiest areas in the city, the Museum Quarter's borders run along the Rijksmuseum and Vondelpark in the north, down Emmastraat to Reijnier Vinkeleskade and up along the Hobbemakade in the east. A century ago, the area was still officially outside the city limits and consisted of little more than vegetable patches. Towards the end of the century, though, the city expanded rapidly, and the primarily upper-class city fathers decided to build an upper-class neighbourhood between the working-class areas to the west and south. Most of the beautiful mansions, with their characteristic art deco gateways and stained-glass windows, were built around the turn of the century, and the exclusive shopping streets of PC Hooftstraat and Van Baerlestraat are today known throughout the country for their élite selection of designer shops and expensive restaurants.

The heart of the area is **Museumplein**, the city's largest square, which is bordered by the **Rijksmuseum**, the **Stedelijk Museum of Modern Art**, the **Van Gogh Museum** and the

# Pleins for the future

Museumplein, situated in the rich, residential Museum Quarter, has long been thought of as the jewel in the city's cultural crown. Given that it's bordered by three of the city's most-visited museums – the **Rijksmuseum**, the **Van Gogh Museum** and the **Stedelijk Museum** – plus the famed **Concertgebouw** (*see chapter* **Music: Classical & Opera***, page 201*), this is hardly surprising. However, visit the square before early 1999 and you'll wonder what all the fuss is about: Museumplein is currently a mess, as it undergoes massive renovations that aren't due to be completed until March '99.

Developed in 1872, Museumplein was originally the location of the World Exhibition of 1883. The city's largest square, it has hosted plenty of large outdoor events, most memorably a 40,000-strong anti-nuclear demo in the early '80s. But most of the time it's deserted, used only as a car park by coaches ferrying tourists to the museums, and by basketball players and skaters showing off their tricks among the exhaust fumes of the Museumstraat. This large road that divides the square in two has been dubbed 'the shortest motorway in the world', and has always ensured that no one in their right mind spends more time on the square than it takes to cross it.

Until now, that is. In 1996, the local borough put into motion plans for a major redevelopment of the square, at a cost of around ƒ175 million. Rotterdam town planner Stefan Gall and Danish landscape architect Sven-Ingvar Anderson, the latter best known for his work on La Grande Arche in Paris, have come up with some striking ideas for the square. Importantly, Museumstraat is to go, and both the Stedelijk and Van Gogh museums are to be extended, redesigns that would be radical enough by themselves. However, among other additions to the area are a large pond (which, when frozen over, will no doubt be used as a public skating rink), a sports area for boules and basketball, half-pipes for skaters, a shop near the Rijksmuseum, and a café with a terrace near the pond. Two underground car parks will also be constructed, one for 600 cars and one for 25 coaches, and an underground supermarket will complete the picture.

So far, so good. Well, sort of: local residents are up in arms about the proposals. In their opinion, the creation of the car parks, combined with the loss of the Museumstraat – until now, a useful short cut – will attract more cars to the already traffic-jammed streets of the neighbourhood. Locals are also outraged that 250 of the 330 or so trees on the square will have to be cut down to make way for the car parks, and that the building of the museum annexes, shop, café and pond mean there will be little room left to stage major outdoor events. Whether they're right to be worried is something only time will tell: no one's really sure whether Museumplein will be a museum piece or a monstrosity. But one thing *is* for sure: Messrs Gall and Anderson have their fingers firmly crossed…

**Concertgebouw** (*see chapter* **Music: Classical & Opera***, page 201*). The Museumplein is not really an authentic Amsterdam square, either in shape or character: its irregular oblong shape has been causing the city problems since its development in 1872. It originally served as a location for the World Exhibition of 1883, and was then rented out to the Amsterdam ice-skating club between 1900 and 1936. During the Depression, the field was put to use as a sports ground, and during World War II the Germans built four bunkers and a concrete shelter on it, which remained until 1952.

In 1953, Museumstraat was completed. However, radical renovations are under way to make the square more pivotal for the city (*see box* **Pleins for the future***, above*): the motorway is no longer, an underground car park is being constructed, and the Van Gogh and Stedelijk museums are being expanded. Nearby Roemer Visscherstraat is a quiet street leading into Vondelpark, and is easily passed by. For those interested in architecture, it's worth taking a look at the houses from nos.20 to 30. Each represents a different country built in the appropriate 'national' style: Russia comes complete with a miniature dome, Italy has been painted pastel pink, and Spain's candy stripes have made it one of the street's favourites. Fans of luxury, though, will probably head for one of the diamond factories in the area, for which *see box* **A girl's best friend***, page 154.*

## Vondelpark

The Vondelpark, Amsterdam's largest green space, is named after the city's most famous poet, Joost van den Vondel (1587-1679), whose spicily controversial play *Lucifer* caused a backlash from the religious powers of the time against those who engaged in 'notorious living'. The concerted campaign from the moral majority helped bring about the downfalls of both Rembrandt and Vondel, who ended his days as a pawnshop doorman, a sometimes chilly job that inspired him to write his own tear-jerking epitaph: 'Here lies Vondel, still and old/Who died because he was cold.'

Vondelpark is the most central of Amsterdam's major parks, though it's slowly sinking into the bog from which it came. Its construction was inspired after the development of Plantage, which had formerly provided the green background used by the rich for their leisurely walks. It was designed in the 'English style' by Zocher, with the emphasis on natural landscaping; the original four hectares (ten acres) were opened in 1865. There are several ponds and lakes in the park – no boating, though – plus a number of cafés (the most pleasant, and therefore busy, being the Nederlands Filmmuseum's **Café Vertigo**, which backs on to the park; *see chapter* Film, *page 184*), and assorted children's play areas. The park gets fantastically busy in Amsterdam on sunny days and on Sundays, when bongos abound, dope is toked, and impromptu football games take up any space that happens to be left over. The dicky-tickered can avoid a seizure by keeping one eye out for rollerbladers. Theatre productions, film screenings and pop concerts are also held here, including open-air theatre in summer (*see chapter* **Amsterdam by Season**, *page 9*).

### Vondelpark

*Tram 1, 2, 3, 5, 6, 7, 10, 12.* **Open** dawn-dusk daily. **Map 5 C6**

## The Pijp

Not to be confused with the suggestive slang in Dutch for the act of 'piping' – translatable as 'giving a blow job', to be frank – doing the Pijp can still be a fairly colourful experience: the district has definitely got a spunky verve about it. And though it's hardly a treasure trove of history, the Pijp's time is the present, with its global village vibe very much alive.

The area is the best known of the working-class quarters built in the late nineteenth century, when a population boom burst the city's seams. Harsh economics saw the building of long, narrow streets, which soon inspired the change in name from the official double yawn-inducing 'Area YY' to its more appropriate nickname, 'The Pipe'. Because rents were still too high for many tenants, they were forced, in turn, to let rooms out to students. And it was the students who gave the area its bohemian character, together with numerous Dutch writers who lived here, including Heijermans, De Haan and Bordewijk, who famously described World War I-era Amsterdam as a 'ramshackle bordello… a wooden shoe made of stone'. Many painters had studios here, too, and the area was packed with brothels and bohemian drinking dens. In the basement of Quellijnstraat

64, the Dutch cabaret style, distinguished by its witty songs with cutting social commentary for lyrics, was formulated by Eduard Jacobs and continues to live on through modern proponents like Freek de Jong.

At the turn of the century, the Pijp was a radical socialist area. Although the area has lost much of its radicalism since those halcyon days, the students remain, even though many families with children have fled to suburbia. The number of cheap one- or two-bedroom apartments, combined with the reasonably central location, makes the area very attractive to students, young single people and couples. The area also has the densest gay population in Amsterdam.

During the last 40 years, many immigrants have also found their way into the area and set up shop. The Pijp now houses a mix of nationalities, providing locals with plenty of Islamic butchers, Surinamese, Spanish, Indian and Turkish delicatessens, and grocery stores selling exotic food. Restaurants offer authentic Syrian, Moroccan, Surinamese, Thai, Pakistani, Chinese and Indian cuisine. Thanks to all these generally low-priced exotic eats, the Pijp is the best place in town for quality snacking treats, the ingredients for which are mostly bought fresh from the largest daily market in the Netherlands.

**Albert Cuypmarkt** is the hub around which the Pijp turns, attracting thousands of customers every day. It's the core of the Pijp streetlife and generally spills into the adjoining roads: the junctions of Sweelinckstraat, Ferdinand Bolstraat and 1e Van der Helststraat, north into the lively Gerard Douplein, and south towards Sarphatipark. The chaos will undoubtedly be enhanced over the next few years by the construction of the controversial North-South subway line that will run underneath the Ferdinand Bolstraat.

The grass-, pond-, and duck-dappled **Sarphatipark** was designed and built as a miniature Bois de Boulogne by the inspired and slightly mad genius Samuel Sarphati (1813-66). Aside from also building the **Amstel Intercontinental** hotel (*see chapter* **Accommodation**, *page 90*) and the Paleis voor Volksvlijt, Sarphati also showed philanthropic tendencies as a baker of inexpensive bread for the masses, and as initiator of the city's garbage collection. Fittingly, the park – and its centrepiece fountain, complete with a statue of Sammy himself – received a fresh scrubbing in 1994.

On the corner of Stadhouderskade and Ferdinand Bolstraat stands the old **Heineken Brewery**. Beer production here stopped at the beginning of 1988 amid some outcry: after all, Heineken is virtually the Dutch national drink, even though connoisseurs refer to it as 'paarden pis' due to its resemblance to 'equine urine'. Now the building acts purely as a propaganda centre for the company, which still runs its infamous brewery tours here. The tour climaxes with an all-you-can-drink taste-test, which, for about the same price as real horse piss (or so we reckon) – $f2$ – is a fine deal indeed.

Beyond the stall-filled stretch of Albert Cuypstraat, across Ferdinand Bolstraat, is a cluster of cheap Indonesian restaurants excellent for gelling a queasy post-Heineken tour belly. A few doors from here is the famed **Sang Photo Studio** (Albert Cuypstraat 57; 679 6906; open 9.30am-6pm Mon-Sat), where one can have a black and white portrait taken and then painted in by the gentleman proprietor, a sublimely kitsch gift idea for a not unreasonable $f37,50$. And after passing the coach-party attraction of **Van Moppes & Zoon Diamond Factory** (*see box* **A girl's best friend**, *page 154*), diamond turns to ruby around the corner along the Ruysdaelkade, the location of the Pijp's very own mini red light district. Watch horned-out motorists caught in their own traffic gridlock while you lounge around casually along an otherwise restful canal.

Over 250 artists live in and around the Pijp, and the current crop is slowly gaining more status in a district where most streets are named after their illustrious forebears: Jan Steen, Ferdinand Bol, Gerard Dou and Jacob van Campen are just a few who have been honoured in this way. Steen (1625-79), barkeeper and painter of rowdy bar scenes, even has a bar named after him (the Jan Steen Café at Ruysdaelkade 149), which still represents him well: the beer is cheap and the crowd is loud. And why view his work in the Rijksmuseum when you can see it in action? Back to the present, the **Kunstroute de Pijp** (*see chapter* **Amsterdam by Season**, *page 11*) is a yearly exhibition of local art work, displayed in the windows of shops, cafés and offices in the area.

Crossing the Albert Cuypmarkt from Gerard Douplein is 1e Van der Helststraat. This little square, with its cafés, coffeeshops, chip shops and authentic Italian ice-cream parlour, turns into one big terrace during the summer, and is hugely popular with the locals. Bargain second-hand Euro knick-knacks can be bought at the nearby Stichting Dodo (no.21), while the cheapest raw herring in town can be gotten for the gullet at Volendammer Vis Handel at no.60. Nearby, Café De Duvel serves international cuisine to a plethora of young locals and students in the evenings. On the corner of 1e Van der Helststraat and Govert Flinckstraat is one of the area's best bakeries, Bakkerij Runneboom. Apart from selling a huge variety of Dutch bread – including 'Rembrandt' bread – and pastries, it also stocks various typical Turkish, Moroccan and even Irish (buttermilk) breads. There is always a queue outside the little shop, no matter what time of day. Hidden halfway down 1e Jan Steenstraat is a

rather special bric-a-brac shop, **Nic Nic**, a paradise for '50s and '60s freaks (*see chapter* **Shopping**, *page 161*).

Running parallel to Albert Cuypstraat, the Ceintuurbaan offers little of note for the visitor, with the exception of the buildings at nos.251-5 near the crossing over the Amstel. Why? Well, there aren't many other houses in the city that incorporate giant ball-playing green gnomes with red hats in their wooden façades. The unique exterior of the 'Gnome House' was inspired by the owner's name: Van Ballegooien translates literally (and somewhat clumsily) as 'Of the ball-throwing'.

### Heineken Brewery

*Stadhouderskade 78 (523 9239/recorded information 523 9666). Tram 6, 7, 10, 16, 20, 24, 25.* **Tours** 9.30am, 11am Mon-Fri. **Admission** $f2$ (goes to charity). No bookings; over-18s only. **Credit** AmEx, DC, EC, MC, V. **Map 6 E5**
*Disabled access (limited).*

## The Waterfront

Amsterdam's historical wealth owes a lot to the city's waterfront: it was here that all the goods were unloaded, weighed and prepared for storage in the many warehouses still found in the area. During Amsterdam's trading heyday in the seventeenth century, most maritime activity was centred east of Centraal Station, along Prins Hendrikkade and on the artificial islands east of Kattenburgerstraat. At the time, the harbour and its arterial canals – many of which have been filled in since the rise of land traffic – formed a whole with the city itself. A drop in commerce led slowly to unbalancing this unity, and the construction of Centraal Station late in the nineteenth century served as the final psychological cleavage. This neo-Gothic monument to modernity (as it was seen then) blocked the city's view of the harbour and its own past.

This is not to say, though, that the harbour started slacking. While Rotterdam is by far the world's largest port, Amsterdam and the nearby North Sea Canal ports of Zaanstad, Beverwijk and IJmuiden together rank among the world's 15 largest ports, handling 45 million tonnes per year. Amsterdam is now the centre of Nissan's European distribution, and is still the world's largest cocoa port: in 1997, a storage warehouse for these most oily of nuts caught fire and stayed burning for a week, spewing dramatic dark smoke over the city. Since 1876, access to the sea has been via the North Sea Canal, running west from Amsterdam, and because the working docks are also to the west, there is little activity on the IJ

*Okay: try and tiptoe through this lot...*

behind Centraal Station beyond a handful of passenger ships and the free ferry that runs across to Amsterdam Noord.

The previously mentioned Schreierstoren, or 'Weeping Tower', is the first thing you'll notice on the right if you walk east from Centraal Station, and is the most interesting relic of what's left of Amsterdam's medieval city wall. Some historians claim that 'schreiers' was actually originally 'schreye', the Dutch word for 'sharp', and, indeed, the tower has a sharp edge where it once formed an acute corner on the city wall. Built in 1487, it was successfully restored in 1966.

In 1927, though, a bronze memorial plaque was added by the Greenwich Village Historical Society of New York: its text states that it was from this point, on 4 April 1609, that Henry Hudson departed in search of shorter trade routes to the Far East. He ended up colonising a small island in the mouth of a river in North America. The river was later named after him and the colony was called New Amsterdam, only to have its name changed by the English to New York. (Today, some of the boroughs still have a nederstamp on them: in particular, Harlem, after Haarlem, and Brooklyn, after Breukelen). In 1956, stones from the Schreierstoren were taken to Chicago and placed into the wall of the Chicago Tribune building, alongside similar chunks from famous buildings around the world, including the Parthenon in Athens, Paris's Notre Dame cathedral and the Great Wall of China.

The next eye-opener you'll come across is a green building that looks like the *Titanic* in midsink. It's the new **newMetropolis Museum** (*see box* **The appliance of science**, *page 75*), from whose accessible sloped roof you not only get an impressive view of the city and its harbour, but get to look at a replica of a very 'Shiver me timbers, Matey, ever been masted at sea before?' East India Company sailing ship. Indeed, the wharf of the VOC (the Dutch acronym for the company) was

once here and a small naval base remains, though the Admiralty has been converted into the **Nederlands Scheepvaart Museum**. The museum itself is an impressive Venetian-style building, designed by Daniel Stalpaert and completed in 1657. It houses a collection of naval emphemera second only to London's National Maritime Museum in Greenwich. Nearby is another nautical museum, **Werf 't Kromhout**.

The old harbour is now virtually disused and the whole **IJ-Oevers** (docklands) are undergoing massive redevelopment, a big issue within the city, concerning both locals and environmental groups (*see box* **Eye for an IJ**, *page 37*). It is said to be the country's only remaining upmarket area for new housing and office development, and plans for development – estimated to cost ƒ6 billion – are continually subject to alteration because of the lack of financial backing, pressure from local residents and new *stadsdeelraden* (local councils), and the ever-changing traffic control plans. Squats, cheap housing and artists' studios are being replaced with new low-cost housing, office buildings and business premises, together with a Metro extension and a dual carriageway.

While you're up this way, be sure to visit the Vrieshuis Amerika (Oostelijke Handelskade 25) while it's still possible. The former cold-storage warehouse for goods coming from America is now the most happening squat on the planet, with its many artists' studios, indoor skateboard park, Wild West roller-skating rink, bar-restaurant, and occasional exhibitions and parties. It's an inspired cultural centre that, sadly, is due to be demolished in the near future (*see chapter* **Amsterdam Today**, *page 30*). There remains some hope that this fate can still be avoided, and that the Vrieshuis can evolve in a similar manner as the Westergasfabriek did on the other side of town.

Look east and you'll espy **KNSM Island**, where the KNSM shipping company originally docked its boats and unloaded cargo. In recent years, it's been transformed from a squatters' paradise to a newly developed and largely residential area, featuring some striking modern architecture and some newish bars and venues, such as Kanis & Meiland and the AMP Studios. As for the squatters in this area, many of them have now made the transition to legal tenants and homeowners.

The **Westelijke Eilanden** (Western Islands), north-west of Centraal Station, are artificial islands, created in the seventeenth century for shipping-related activities. There are now trendy warehouse flats and a yacht basin on Realeneiland, Prinseneiland and Bickerseiland, where shipyards, tar distillers, fish-salters and smokers were once located. If friends recommended visiting the famed, sprawling Silo squat, don't bother: it's been emptied and is now being transformed into an apartment complex.

# Museums around the Waterfront

**Nederlands Scheepvaart Museum**
*Kattenburgerplein 1 (523 2222). See page 80.*

**newMetropolis**
*Oosterdok 2 (0900 919 1100). See page 75.*

**Werf 't Kromhout**
*Hoogte Kadijk 147 (627 6777). See page 80.*

# Art Galleries

*It's very pretty... It's very adventurous... But is it art? Who cares? You can probably find it in the galleries of Amsterdam.*

Given the concentration of galleries and art dealers in the city, not to mention the profusion of public monuments around town, you'd be forgiven for thinking that Amsterdammers are avid consumers of art. You'd be right: there are few apartments or offices in the city that don't have an original artwork on display. This is no new phenomenon. Even back in the Golden Age – Rembrandt's era – visitors to the city were remarking on the large numbers of paintings for sale, and how common they were in both homes and workplaces.

This long-running trend, as with so many other aspects of modern-day Amsterdam, can be traced back to the city's Calvinist roots. The secular, egalitarian climate of the seventeenth-century city gave rise to the early creation of a large middle class who formed the artists' main market. Consequently, the habit of buying art to hang on the wall as decoration (rather than as an investment or status symbol), and the treatment of art as a commodity (rather than as some mystical phenomenon above considerations of money) is firmly ingrained into the consciousness of the locals, and the art trade, in all its forms, continues to thrive. With such a down-to-earth attitude in the ascendant, the Dutch are remarkably supportive and savvy of *kunst* in all its forms, though their appreciation can often appear rather earnest to foreign observers.

## THE CONTEMPORARY SCENE

Twentieth-century Dutch art has been heavily influenced by modern international movements such as Cubism, but the locals have made one major contribution of their own to art as we know it today. The bold abstractionism of De Stijl (simply, 'The Style') has had an enormous impact on modern art in all its forms, and its influence should not be understated. Less well-known is the Bergen School, an expressionist movement whose main progenitor Charley Toorop (a woman) was instrumental in founding the modern realism movement of the '30s. Later still, the abstract expressionist CoBrA movement burst onto the scene after World War II. Since then, hundreds of Dutch artists have been helped hugely by the government's extraordinary social welfare programme, though this indulgent policy of – basically – paying artists to be artists eventually had to be pruned almost to pieces with the dawn of harder times.

## THE CURRENT SCORE

The Golden Age of subsidies is long gone, but the arts remain relatively well funded in Holland. Today's young artists have the additional influences of new media, new technology and new attitudes to consider, not to mention the host of artistic traditions from all over the world that have found a home in Amsterdam. The painterly tradition continues to thrive, but headlines in recent years have been grabbed by the likes of Inez van Lamsweerde, a photographer whose manipulated images make a disturbing comment on contemporary party sexuality; Dadara, who started out designing party flyers, and now sells T-shirts to clubbers and oil paintings to their parents; and Droog Design, a group of young designers whose pared-down but witty creations have won them enormous international acclaim. So varied is art in Amsterdam these days that generalisations are, more often than not, ill-advised. What history will make of Dutch art in the '90s, though, is anybody's guess.

## WHAT'S IN A NAME?

In addition to its galleries, the Netherlands boasts five of the world's greatest museums: the wonderful **Stedelijk Museum** in Amsterdam, the **Haags Gemeentemuseum** in The Hague; the **Rijksmuseum Kröller-Müller** in Otterlo; the **Groninger Museum** in Groningen, and the **Van Abbemuseum** in Eindhoven (*see respectively chapters* **Museums**, *page 77,* **The Randstad**, *page 233, and* **The Provinces**, *pages 240-242*). All have shows that spotlight new and established artists – from both home and abroad – and set a high standard that the smaller galleries would have to work miracles to match.

To complicate matters further, though, galleries are but a part of the city's art trade, sharing the market with innumerable *kunsthandels* (art dealers). As a rule, *kunsthandels* operate on a buy-from-the-artist, sell-to-the-public basis. They stock a selection of original works and/or prints that are not necessarily contemporary; they feature more established artists; and, generally speaking, they do not put on exhibitions. Galleries, though, don't usually buy the artists' work; rather, they sell it for them on a commission basis. You'll find younger artists in the changing programme of exhibitions in the city's galleries, which could be anything

*The number of young artists who exhibit at **Bloom** must be a record. See page 70.*

from large spaces staging group exhibitions, to small atelier-galleries, where individuals or collectives show their own work and that of friends.

New galleries open up in Amsterdam all the time. For an up-to-date list, buy the monthly *Alert* magazine (available at **Athenaeum Newscentrum**; *see chapter* **Shopping**, *page 141*): though it's in Dutch, galleries are sorted into areas and clearly marked on maps. Many of the galleries listed below close during July or August and have a relaxed attitude to opening hours, so it's best to phone before setting out. Unless otherwise specified, galleries listed do not accept credit cards, and admission is free.

For KunstRAI, the city's annual art fair, and the Open Ateliers, *see chapter* **Amsterdam By Season**, *page 9*; for artists' bookshop **Boekie Woekie**, *see chapter* **Shopping**, *page 141*.

## Galleries

### Animation Art

*Berenstraat 19 (627 7600/fax 422 8646). Tram 13, 14, 17, 20.* **Open** 11am-6pm Tue-Fri; 11am-5pm Sat; 1-5pm Sun. **Credit** AmEx, DC, EC, MC, V. **Map 5 C4**
As you'd expect, Animation Art is entirely devoted to animation, with displays of original Disney works and other animators' 'cels' (outlines or line drawings of cartoon char-

acters, which are then painted on to cellulose acetate). Hand-inked originals on display are often for sale.

### De Appel
*Nieuwe Spiegelstraat 10 (625 5651/fax 622 5215). Tram 16, 24, 25.* **Open** noon-5pm Tue-Sun. **Map 5 D4**
An Amsterdam institution, and the first gallery in Holland to recognise video art. Housed in the former ICA (Institute of Contemporary Arts) building, the gallery holds varied exhibitions of new art, mainly by young unknowns. *Disabled access.*

### ArCam
*Waterlooplein 213 (620 4878). Tram 9, 14, 20/Metro Waterlooplein.* **Open** 1-5pm Tue-Sat. **Map 6 E3**
ArCam is a keen promoter of contemporary Dutch architecture: there are exhibitions of architectural drawings and

models, plus lectures and discussion forums. The group is online at *www.arcam.nl.*

### Art Affairs
*Lijnbaansgracht 316 (620 6433). Tram 16, 24, 25.* **Open** 1-6pm Wed-Sat; 2-5pm first Sun of month. **Credit** AmEx, DC, EC, MC, V. **Map 5 D5**
Art Affairs' international programme includes paintings, printing, photography, sculpture and performance art, with artists such as Morellet and Smejkal often on show. *Disabled access.*

### Aschenbach
*Bilderdijkstraat 165C (685 3580). Tram 3, 7, 12, 13, 17, 20.* **Open** 1-6pm Wed-Sat. **Map 5 D5**
The first gallery in Amsterdam to show Russian artists, Aschenbach concentrates on international painting, sculpture

When is a table not a table? When it's part of an installation at **Galerie Fons Welter**.

and photography, and happily mixes famous – and, therefore, expensive – young artists with upstarts who have yet to really make it.
*Disabled access with assistance.*

### Bloom
*Bloemstraat 150 (638 8810/fax 638 8918). Tram 13, 14, 17, 20.* **Open** *1-6pm Tue-Sat; 2-5pm first Sun of month.* **Map 1 B3**
Founded in 1992, Bloom is one of Amsterdam's most exciting young galleries, regularly exhibiting ground-breaking artists and switching easily between traditional media and conceptual and installation works.
*Disabled access.*

### BMB
*Kerkstraat 127-129 (622 9963/fax 625 1189). Tram 1, 2, 5.* **Open** *12.30-5.30pm Wed-Sat; 1-5pm first Sun of month; also by appointment.* **Map 6 E4**
For several years now, BMB has specialised in young artists from Holland, Italy, France, Spain and other countries. Exhibitions always feature paintings, based in the figurative tradition.
*Disabled access.*

### Boomerang
*Boomstraat 12 (tel/fax 420 3516). Tram 3.* **Open** *noon-6pm Thur-Sun.* **Credit** EC. **Map 1 B2**
There are several galleries for Australian aboriginal art in Amsterdam now, but Boomerang was there first in 1992, and it shows. That's a compliment: the exhibitions are excellent,

covering a variety of styles in traditional crafts of aboriginal and non-aboriginal Australian art. A new space called Immaculate Conceptions has just opened at Marnixstraat 94 (427 3716; open by appointment only) featuring Australian art and a World Art Collection.
*Disabled access (both branches).*

### Clement
*Prinsengracht 845 (625 1656). Tram 16, 24, 25.* **Open** *11am-5.30pm Tue-Sat.* **Map 5 D5**
Clement (previously called Printshop) is the grandaddy of printmakers' studio-galleries: it's been an atelier since 1958, and a gallery since 1968. Artists do their own prints and the gallery also exhibits their drawings and paintings. Standards are mixed.

### Collection d'Art
*Keizersgracht 516 (622 1511). Tram 1, 2, 5, 20.* **Open** *1-5pm Wed-Sat.* **Map 5 C4**
An established gallery – it was founded in 1969 – with a stable of established artists. Armando, Benner and Constant are among the names, with Baselitz the only exception in an otherwise Dutch line-up.

### Donkersloot Galerie
*PC Hooftstraat 127 (572 2722). Tram 2, 3, 5, 12, 20.* **Open** *9am-6pm Mon-Sat, first Sun of month.* **Credit** AmEx, DC, EC, MC, V. **Map 5 C6**
One of the city's newer galleries, holding regular exhibitions featuring established artists. Past shows have included the gorgeous fruit and babies' bottoms montages of Belgian pho-

tocopy artist Lieve Prins and the monomaniac butterfly paintings of Hans Verhoff. There are special events every month: phone for details.
*Disabled access.*

## D'Eendt
*Spuistraat 270 (626 5777). Tram 1, 2, 5, 20.* **Open** noon-6pm Thur-Sat; 2-6pm Sun. **Map 2 C3**
Once a trendsetter of the cutting-edge variety, D'Eendt has had its ups and downs in recent years. The gallery features paintings and installations by young international artists. Shows are of variable quality; modern and naïve figuratives are the strongest work.

## Espace
*Keizersgracht 548 (624 0802). Tram 1, 2, 5, 20.* **Open** 1-5pm Wed-Sat; 2-5pm first Sun of month. **Map 5 C4**
Based in the city since 1960, Eva Bendien is one of the city's *grandes dames* of Amsterdam art. Her gallery shows the likes of Lucassen, Lucebert and Pierre Alechinsky, while Co Westerik's popular but odd Dutch realism is another frequent highlight.

## De Expeditie
*Leliegracht 47 (620 4758). Tram 13, 14, 17, 20.* **Open** 1-6pm Wed-Sat. **Map 2 C3**
The one-man shows at De Expeditie take months of preparation. International names such as Siguidur Gudmunsson and Barry Flanagan have exhibited here, as have many notable Dutch artists.

## The Frozen Fountain
*Prinsengracht 629 (622 9375). Tram 1, 2, 5, 20.* **Open** 1-6pm Mon; 10am-6pm Tue-Fri; 10am-5pm Sat. **Credit** EC (all cheques and foreign currency). **Map 4 C4**
Specialising in furniture and functional design items, The Frozen Fountain is really a shop – stocking Droog Design products, among others – but its exhibitions, mainly spotlighting young Dutch designers, is the reason why it's to be found here and not in the shopping chapter. The gallery was instrumental in giving a leg-up to a generation of then-promising and now-famous thirtysomething talent, such as Piet Hein Eek.
*Disabled access.*

## Galerie Akinci
*Lijnbaansgracht 317 (638 0480). Tram 16, 20, 24, 25.* **Open** 1-6pm Tue-Sat; 2-5pm first Sun of month. **Map 5 D5**
A reliably exciting gallery in a warren-like complex, opened in 1993 to help seven local gallery members fight the recession together. The shows are very mixed, combining the known with the unknown, the local with the far-flung.
*Disabled access.*

## Galerie Barbara Farber/Rob Jurka
*Singel 28 (627 6343/fax 627 8091). Tram 1, 2, 5, 13, 17, 20.* **Open** 1-6pm Wed-Sat; 2-5pm first Sun of month. **Map 2 C2**
A top gallery and an Amsterdam phenomenon, showing new, experimental paintings and photography. The owners have a good eye for young talent, and it's usually well worth a look.

## Galerie Binnen
*Keizersgracht 82 (625 9603). Tram 1, 2, 5, 13, 17, 20.* **Open** noon-6pm Tue-Sat; 2:5pm first Sun of month. **Credit** EC, MC. **Map 2 C2**
The city's foremost gallery for industrial and interior design and the applied arts ('binnen' means 'indoors'). The owners have a great roomy space used for showing new work by Dutch designers, including installations, spatial projects, glass, ceramics and jewellery.
*Disabled access.*

## Gallery Delaive
*Spiegelgracht 23 (625 9087). Tram 6, 7, 10.* **Open** 11am-5.30pm Tue-Sat; noon-5pm Sun, also by appointment. **Credit** AmEx, EC. **Map 5 D5**
Internationally acclaimed, Delaive is an upmarket, high-quality gallery, though the emphasis on names rather than talent sometimes backfires, resulting in the occasional less than impressive exhibition. Still, it's generally a safe bet: the majority of shows – often by artists with international reputations – are excellent.

## Galerie Fi Beiti
*Prinsengracht 157 (622 8465). Tram 13, 14, 17, 20.* **Open** 1-6 pm Thur-Sat, first Sun of month. **Map 2 C2**
A newcomer to the Amsterdam scene, Fi Beiti specialises in art from the Middle East and Central Asia; hardly surprising, really, since owner Nico Duyvesteijn taught art in Cairo for many years. Exhibitions feature both young and established artists who work in painting, sculpture and photography, with both the traditional, orthodox idioms of the region and more Westernised styles represented in their regular shows.

## Galerie Fons Welters
*Bloemstraat 140 (423 3046). Tram 13, 14, 17, 20.* **Open** 1-6pm Tue-Sat; 2-5pm first Sun of month. **Map 1 B3**
Another big name in the city, with a preference for work from innovative young sculptors. The owner, Fons Welters, is passionate about Dutch sculpture, and the gallery shows an excellent range of home-grown talent. Exhibitions here – which include installations and spatial projects – are of a high standard.

## Galerie Foundation for Indian Artists
*Fokke Simonszstraat 10 (623 1547). Tram 16, 24, 25.* **Open** 1-6pm Wed-Sat, first Sun of month. **Map 6 E5**
Devoted to the promotion of contemporary Indian art in the Netherlands, the exhibitions at the Galerie Foundation for Indian Artists are of reliably high quality and incredible diversity. Successful international artists such as Dilip Sur, Bhupen Khakhar and Jaya Ganguly are regular exhibitors, along with many artists who are as yet unknown in Amsterdam and, indeed, the West as a whole.
*Disabled access.*

## Galerie Paul Andriesse
*Prinsengracht 116 (623 6237). Tram 13, 14, 17, 20.* **Open** 11am-6pm Tue-Fri; 2-6pm Sat; 2-5pm first Sun of month. **Map 2 C2**
When Paul Andriesse takes you on, you know you've made it. It's a gallery that largely concentrates on experimental work by artists who already have something of a reputation. Names to look out for include Marlene Dumas and Pieter Laurens Mol.

## Galerie van Gelder
*Planciusstraat 9A, off Haarlemmerplein (627 7419). Tram 3.* **Open** 1-5.30pm Tue-Sat, first Sun of month. **Map 1 A1**
One to watch, this: Van Gelder regularly picks up new talent. International artists along the lines of Nam June Paik and Sylvie Fleury feature in the group shows, which are consistently excellent.
*Disabled access.*

## Galerie Van Wijngaarden
*Lijnbaansgracht 318 (626 4970). Tram 16, 20, 24, 25.* **Open** 1-6pm Tue-Sat. **Map 5 D5**
This is essentially a gallery exhibiting young Dutch talent from the Rietveld Akademie and other notable art schools. The work exhibited is mainly figurative, with an emphasis on new developments. Situated, like a number of other galleries, on Lijnbaansgracht.

## GO Gallery

*Prinsengracht 64 (422 9580). Tram 13, 14, 17, 20.*
**Open** noon-6pm Wed-Sat; 1-5pm Sun. **Credit** EC, MC.
**Map 1 B2**
GO Gallery is the new project of Oscar van den Voorn, one
of the trendiest of Amsterdam's art entrepreneurs of recent
years and a man blessed with an infectious enthusiasm for
making art accessible. GO Gallery is welcoming and unpre-
tentious, veering between populist theme shows (a St
Valentine's Day, for example) and genuine oddities: the
Human Chair, an exhibition of chairs made out of plastic
human body parts, might give you an idea of what to expect.
*Disabled access.*

## Heaven On Earth

*Prinsengracht 175 (427 5147). Tram 13, 14, 17, 20.*
**Open** 1-5pm Wed-Sat, first Sun of month. **Credit** EC.
**Map 2 C2**
A new gallery – it opened in January 1998 – with an inclu-
sive attitude. Though the owners claim to want to show all
kinds of art, in reality the exhibits tend to be from well-
established international artists such as Croatian painter
Velimir Trsnski.
*Disabled access.*

## Kokopelli

*Warmoesstraat 12 (421 7000). Tram 4, 9, 14, 16, 20,
24, 25.* **Open** 11am-10pm daily. **Credit** AmEx, DC, MC,
V. **Map 2 D2**
A young, trendy gallery, run by the former Conscious
Dreams team and mostly promoting new artists, some of
whom come from the Amsterdam club scene.
*Disabled access with assistance.*

## Lieve Hemel

*Nieuwe Spiegelstraat 3AB (623 0060/fax 627 2663).
Tram 6, 7, 10, 20.* **Open** 11am-6pm Tue-Sat. **Credit**
AmEx, DC, EC, MC, V. **Map 5 D4**
Lieve Hemel is well worth a look if you're interested in
new work by new Dutch realist painters, a group to which
owner Koen Nieuwendijk now confines himself. Others on
show might include Ben Snijders, Theo Voorzaat and Olaf
Cloefas van Overbeek.
*Disabled access.*

## Lumen Travo

*Lijnbaansgracht 314 (627 0883). Tram 6, 7, 10, 16, 24,
25.* **Open** 1-6pm Wed-Sat; 2-5pm first Sun of month.
**Map 5 D5**
Another member of the Lijnbaansgracht gallery complex,
Lumen Travo is a reliable bet for good, well thought-out con-
ceptual art, while it also shows a generally impressive selec-
tion of other international contemporary art.
*Disabled access.*

## Melkweg

*Lijnbaansgracht 234A (624 1777). Tram 1, 2, 5, 6, 7,
10, 20.* **Open** 2-8pm Wed-Sun. **Map 5 D5**
The Melkweg ('Milky Way') is something of a mixed bag of
a venue, though its gallery, devoted to contemporary photography, is always worth a visit. Artistic director Suzanne
Dechart is open to anyone with good ideas, which means the
shows are varied and usually excellent. *See chapters* **Music:
Rock, Roots & Jazz**, *p207, and* **Theatre**, *p222.*
*Disabled access.*

## Mokum

*Nieuwezijds Voorburgwal 334 (624 3958/625 8025).
Tram 1, 2, 5.* **Open** 11am-6pm Wed-Sat; 1-5pm first Sun
of month; also by appointment. **Map 2 D3**
Mokum specialises in Dutch realism, an extremely well-
developed school throughout Holland. Magic (or fantastic)
realists are also represented.
*Disabled access (ground level only).*

## Montevideo/TBA

*Keizersgracht 264 (623 7101/fax 624 4423). Tram 13,
14, 17, 20.* **Open** 1-6pm Tue-Sat. **Map 2 C3**
Montevideo is a media artists' organisation whose innovative gallery features electronic art as well as photography,
sculpture and installations. More information can be snaf-
fled from its website (*www.montevideo.nl*).
*Disabled access (ground floor only).*

## Nanky de Vreeze

*Lange Leidsedwarsstraat 198-200 (627 3808/fax 622
8405). Tram 1, 2, 5, 20.* **Open** noon-6pm Wed-Sat, first
Sun of month. **Map 5 D5**
One of the largest and most attractive commercial galleries
in Amsterdam, with a wide variety of shows that cover
sculpture, installations or two-dimensional art.
*Disabled access.*

## De Opsteker

*Noorderstraat 61 (638 6904). Tram 16, 24, 25.* **Open**
1.30-5.30pm Thur-Sun; also by appointment. **Map 6 E5**
Opened originally as a photo gallery for young, upcoming
artists in 1992, De Opsteker's tiny gallery is now home to
mixed exhibitions of photography, painting and small-scale
sculpture, with abstract and figurative work both represented. There is a second exhibition space in Durgerdam's
old village church (Dropskerk Durgedam, Durgedammerdijk
76; 638 6904): take bus 33 from Centraal Station to
Waterlandplein, then change to bus 30.
*Disabled access.*

## Ra

*Vijzelstraat 80 (626 5100). Tram 4, 9, 14, 16, 20, 24,
25.* **Open** noon-6pm Tue-Sat. **Credit** AmEx, DC, EC,
MC, V. **Map 5 D4**
There are several jewellery galleries (and good designers) in
Amsterdam, but Ra really sets the standard that others try
and follow. Sculptural creations in unexpected materials
such as Bakelite are on show, but though the pieces are definitely intriguing, they are more collectors' items than
wearable accessories.
*Disabled access (ground floor only).*

## Reflex Modern Art Gallery

*Weteringschans 79A (627 2832). Tram 6, 7, 10.* **Open**
11am-6pm Tue-Sat. **Credit** AmEx, DC, EC, MC, V.
**Map 5 D5**
Monthly exhibitions at Reflex feature top international
artists such as Arman, Ben and Kriki, and Amsterdam success stories including former club flyer artist Dadara. The
gallery stocks excellent graphics and lithos by Corneille and
Appel, and there's also a branch at number 83 on the same
street (open 11am-6pm Tue-Sun).
*Disabled access (both branches).*

## Scheltema

*Koningsplein 20 (523 1411/fax 622 7684). Tram 1, 2, 5.*
**Open** 1-6pm Mon; 9.30am-6pm Tue, Wed, Fri; 9.30am-
9pm Thur; 10am-6pm Sat; noon-5.30pm Sun. **Credit** (min
*f*50) AmEx, EC, MC, V. **Map 5 D4**
Although, strictly speaking, it's actually a bookshop,
Scheltema does have good exhibitions displayed along its
staircases, featuring photography that's more often than
not related to travel, landscapes and portraiture. Well worth
a visit.

## Stedelijk Museum Bureau Amsterdam

*Rozenstraat 59 (422 0471/fax 626 1730). Tram 13, 14,
17, 20.* **Open** 11am-5pm Tue-Sun. **Map 4 B4**
Opened in October 1993, the Stedelijk's most recent venture
promotes young Amsterdam-based artists. It holds solo and
group exhibitions, with lecture series accompanying the
shows and selections of artists' videos.
*Disabled access.*

### Steendrukkerij Amsterdam

*Lauriergracht 80 (624 1491/fax 624 6569). Tram 13,
14, 17, 20.* **Open** *1-5.30pm Wed-Sat; 2-5pm first Sun of
month; closed July, Aug.* **Map 5 C4**
This gallery shows woodcuts, experimental prints and lithos
(*Steendruk* means 'lithography'). It has a down-to-earth
approach, and tends to show technique-driven pieces rather
than so-called 'artistic' works.
*Disabled access with assistance.*

### Steltman

*Spuistraat 330 (622 8683). Tram 13, 14, 17.* **Open**
11am-6pm Tue-Sat. **Credit** AmEx, DC, EC, MC, V.
**Map 2 C3**
A light, airy space, where exhibitions often feature the whimsical baroque fantasies of Czech-born designer Borek Sipek
(glass, ceramics and furniture) and dreamy magic realism
from painters like Michael Parkes.

### Stichting Oude Kerk

*Oudekerksplein (625 8284/fax 620 0371). Tram 4, 9,
14, 16, 20, 24, 25.* **Open** 11am-5pm Mon-Sat; 1-5pm
Sun. **Map 2 D2**
Oude Kerk, Amsterdam's oldest church, situated in the heart
of the Red Light District, is one of the most beautiful – and
bizarre – exhibition spaces. Since the spaces are openly available for rent, the shows vary enormously in quality. *See chapter* **Sightseeing**, *page 49.*
*Disabled access.*

### Taller Amsterdam

*Keizersgracht 607 (624 6734/fax 627 1539). Tram 16,
24, 25.* **Open** 1-5pm Tue-Sat. **Credit** EC. **Map 6 E4**
An artists' collective, still producing inspirational work some
30 years after its creation; founders and linchpins Armando
Bergallo and Hector Vilche are still very much involved.
Situated in a beautifully converted former coach house, the
gallery space is large and accommodating. *See chapter*
**Music: Classical**, *page 204.*
*Disabled access.*

### Torch

*Lauriergracht 94 (626 0284/fax 623 8892). Tram 7, 10,
20.* **Open** 2-6pm Thur-Sat; also by appointment. **Credit**
AmEx, DC, EC, MC, V. **Map 5 C4**
One of Amsterdam's classier and more prestigious galleries,
courting impressive international names such as Cindy
Sherman. Group exhibitions are owner Adriaan van der
Have's speciality, with fabulous themed shows. Reliable and
highly recommended.
*Disabled access.*

### 2 / x 4 /

*Prinsengracht 356 (tel/fax 626 0757). Tram 13, 14, 17,
20.* **Open** 1-5pm Wed-Sat. **Map 5 C4**
This is the sole survivor of a number of galleries exclusively devoted to photography (the Canon Image Center, for
example, was transformed into a shoe shop in 1994). The fact
that this gallery has survived has a lot to do with the invariably high quality of its work: the solo shows, in particular,
can be excellent.

### Vromans Gebouw Atrium

*Strawinskylaan 3101 (642 7295). Tram 50, 51/Bus 48,
51, 63.* **Open** 9am-5pm Mon-Fri; noon-3pm Sat, first Sun
of month.
It's worth going (slightly) out of the centre for this one.
Housed in a fine example of modern office architecture,
Vromans is a big gallery in Holland, not just Amsterdam. In
the main space – at the base of a huge glass atrium tower –
you can expect to see painting, sculpture and sometimes
ceramics and jewellery from new and established artists,
with a number of international names featured.
*Disabled access.*

### W139

*Warmoesstraat 139 (622 9434). Tram 4, 9, 14, 16, 20,
24, 25.* **Open** 1-7pm Wed-Sun. **Map 2 D2**
Founded by art students more than 15 years ago, W139 still
aims to be the city's premier alternative art space. Huge by
Amsterdam standards, the gallery shows work by young
international artists like Bob and Roberta Smith and Jane
Bendix, with a particular emphasis placed on installations.
The exhibitions here are reliably good, and the location
agreeably central.
*Disabled access.*

### De Witte Voet

*Kerkstraat 135 (tel/fax 625 8412). Tram 1, 2, 5.* **Open**
noon-5pm Wed-Sat; 2-5pm first Sun of month. **Map 5 D4**
Ceramics have been a national strength ever since Delftware
was first produced. De Witte Voet continues the tradition by
exhibiting a number of talented Dutch ceramic designers on
a regular basis.
*Disabled access.*

### XY

*2e Laurierdwarsstraat 42 (625 0282). Tram 10.* **Open**
noon-5pm Tue-Fri; noon-4pm Sat. **Credit** AmEx, DC,
MC, V. **Map 4 B4**
One of the better Jordaan galleries, XY regularly produces
interesting shows. Among its claims-to-fame is the invention of the Supermart, the first supermarket devoted entirely to affordable art.

### De Zaaier

*Keizersgracht 22 (420 3154). Tram 1, 2, 5, 13, 17, 20.*
**Open** 10.30am-6.30pm daily. **Credit** EC. **Map 2 C2**
Group exhibitions, changing every three weeks, from a wide
variety of painters' cooperatives and associations. The work
on show is mostly Dutch, with some international guests: a
recent exhibition spotlighted a women's collective from
SoHo, New York.

## Artoteeks

If you're staying in town for a while, you can borrow works of art as you would books from a
library, from the city-run *artoteek* or the govern-
ment-funded *kunstuitleen* (libraries). There are also
a few artists and studios which now lend out their
work on the same principle, with an option to buy.
However, the **SBK** (Stichting Beeldende Kunst, or
Fine Arts Foundation) is probably the best place
to start: its library offers 22,000 works by some
2,000 artists (not all Dutch or contemporary), and
also has a separate sculpture department. You
select your work from what's on show at the time
you visit.

### SBK Kunstuitleen

*Nieuwe Herengracht 23 (623 9215/fax 622 4961). Tram
4, 9, 20/Metro Waterlooplein.* **Open** 1-8pm Tue, Thur; 1-
5pm Fri; 9am-5pm Sat; 1-5pm first Sun of month. **Hire
cost** *f8-f40 a month.* **Map 3 F3**
You need to show your passport and proof of address to bor-
row art from the SBK Kunstuitleen. Of your fee, 60-75%
is banked by the SBK and can be used if you buy a work
later on.
**Branches**: Zeilmakerstraat 15, Bickerseiland (427 5862);
KNSM-laan 307/309, KNSM Eiland (419 0064);
Wingardweg 28 a/b, Noord (632 1336); Keurenplein 28-30,
Osdorp (619 5782); Van Limburg Stirumstraat 15,
Westerpark (688 0520); Van Eeghenstraat 59,
Zuid (673 2640).

# Museums

**There's a whole lot more than just art in the city's museums.**

Sex, drugs, torture, tattoos and a whole heap of Van Goghs. Yup, Amsterdam's museums are far from conventional, but since the Netherlands is home to a daunting 830 museums, a little bit of diversity in this most liberal of cities is only to be expected. Whatever your interests, they're probably covered at one of the city's museums.

Holland has produced some of the best-known and most prolific artists the world has ever seen, and, naturally, can also boast some of the finest art museums anywhere in Europe. The Dutch public's relationship with art has always been a healthy one, a tradition that has its roots in the Golden Age. As a result, many of the finest works by the likes of Rembrandt, Vermeer and Frans Hals are part of the national heritage and are now housed in the **Rijksmuseum**, while the life and works of Van Gogh are documented in the **Van Gogh Museum**. Rembrandt is also celebrated in the **Rembrandthuis**, while modern art is stored and exhibited in the excellent **Stedelijk Museum**. A word of advice, however: leave yourself enough time to pay each museum the respect it deserves. The Rijksmuseum, in particular, is huge, and a quick hour-long jaunt around it won't do it justice.

Art lovers should also consider a couple of trips out of town: the **Frans Hals Museum** in Haarlem houses some fine work by Hals and his contemporaries, while the **Boymans-Van Beuningen** in Rotterdam has works by Van Eyck, Rembrandt, Bosch and others (see **Further afield** *below*, and **Trips out of town**, *pages 223-243*). Both are excellent museums.

But it's not all art, not by any stretch of the imagination. There are plenty of museums devoted to history, for example, including the excellent **Amsterdams Historisch Museum**, the hugely and justifiably popular **Anne Frankhuis**, the **Verzetsmuseum** (detailing the history of the Resistance) and the criminally undervalued **Museum Amstelkring**; for more background on these and other historical museums, *see chapter* **History**, *pages 12-28*. Nature types should head forthwith to the **Hortus Botanicus**, while the **Scheepvaart Museum** will appeal to anyone of a nautical bent. Nevertheless, it's lovers of trash who are best catered for, with museums devoted to sex, tattoos, torture and drugs all out to grab your tourist dollar. Don't be drawn in…

A few of Amsterdam's museums have recently undergone expansion, refurbishment or rehousing, while others have the builders in as you read this. The new restored south wing of the Rijksmuseum, for example, was reopened in 1996, and the new **newMetropolis** has been drawing kids from all over the country to sample its hi-tech mix of science education and interactive entertainment (*see box* **The appliance of science** *opposite*). Meanwhile, a generous ƒ37.5-million donation has enabled the Van Gogh Museum to build a new wing. Designed by Japanese architect Kisho Kurokawa, who created the Hiroshima City Museum of Contemporary Art, this extension will open in May 1999.

All in all, then, the city has more than enough museums to amuse even the most hardened traveller. What's more, in a town the size of Amsterdam, the majority of the museums are within a short walk of each other, which can make for a lovely few days strolling around town and popping in to whichever exhibitions take your fancy at the time.

## TICKETS & INFORMATION

While the majority of Amsterdam museums charge an admission fee, most are priced extremely reasonably: ƒ5 to ƒ10 is usual. However, if you're thinking of taking in more than a few – either in Amsterdam or elsewhere in the country – the **Annual Museum Card** ('Museumjaarkaart') is an absolute steal at ƒ45 or ƒ32,50 for under-18s and pensioners. The ticket offers free or reduced admission to almost 400 museums throughout the Netherlands, and though special exhibitions are normally not covered by the ticket, you may be entitled to a reduction. The card can be purchased at one of the participating museums (check the listings below for details of which ones) or at **VVV** tourist offices. Reductions on entry fees can also be obtained with a valid student identity card, available at the **AUB** (*see chapter* **Directory**, *page 252*).

The value-for-money deals don't end there, though: National Museum Weekend, held around the second week of April each year, sees 350 museums throughout the country open free of charge (*see chapter* **Amsterdam by Season**, *page 7*). There's a catch with this one, though: you'll have to vie with all the locals taking advantage of this popular freebie, and the museums can get exceptionally busy. Also to be avoided if at all possible are the major museums' temporary exhibitions on the weekends, and almost any museum on Wednesday afternoons:

# The appliance of science

As almost any parent will tell you, getting kids interested in learning ain't always easy. And when you bear in mind the ever-increasing distractions of the modern world – computer games, the movies, and, of course, TV – it's easy to sympathise with the little 'uns. Still, the folks behind Amsterdam's newMetropolis museum have hit upon a neat idea: get the kids interested in learning by using all the usual distractions in a positive way. Thus, the museum is full to bursting with computers, movies, TVs and a whole host of other interactive exhibits that both educate and entertain.

Don't confuse the newMetropolis with, say, London's Science Museum: this is definitely a place designed for kids, with more hands-on exhibits and less straight displays. Touted as a 'hands-on science and technology centre', the massive structure – in some ways, a replacement for the Technologie Museum, which closed in the mid-'90s – is virtually new, as is everything inside, bar one exhibit. Funded in part by the Dutch government and in part by Amsterdam city council, with about half the building costs raised through sponsorship, it finally opened on 4 June 1997, having cost a cool ƒ330 million (it now supports itself through entrance fees). With the museum situated on a man-made island in the main harbour, the architects have gone for a maritime theme in appearance, most striking when viewed some way back on the main road by the entrance to the neighbouring Scheepvaart Museum. From here, the impression created by the building – of a green ship rising out of the harbour – is quite spectacular.

Spread over five floors, the exhibits are grouped in age ranges from 6-9, 9-12 and over-12s, with some exhibits for those under six. Curiously, there's almost no history here: the exhibitions – split into five zones, covering, in essence, banking and communication, energy, light, cars and the brain – are all far more about the future than the past. When we visited, the centre was so full and each experiment so popular that the adults we spoke to said it quickly became second nature for them to give way to kids in the queue. And though the museum plans to target adults in the future, the only grown-ups there during our visit were teachers or parents accompanying herds of hyperactive kids.

Experiments are well spaced and with exceptionally clear multilingual instructions printed on brightly coloured boards (in Dutch, English, French and German). There are also plenty of multilingual 'human hosts' ready to answer questions, plus a liberal sprinkling of computer terminals. This being a techno museum, bog-standard paper tickets have been consigned to the dustbin of history. Instead, both entrances issue tickets that are then swiped through an electronic turnstile and which allow the user to exit and re-enter the building up to three times.

### newMetropolis

*Oosterdok 2 (information 0900 919 1100/e-mail info@newmet.nl). Bus 22/Apr-Oct shuttle boat from Centraal Station.* **Open** *museum* 10am-6pm Sun-Fri; 10am-9pm Sat; *shop* 1-6pm Tue-Fri; 11am-7pm Sat; 11am-6pm Sun. **Admission** *ƒ23,50; ƒ15,50 4-16s; free under-3s; ƒ13,50 over-4s after 5pm. Group discounts (min 20 persons).* **Credit** *AmEx, DC, MC, V. Disabled access. Guided tours (intro tour min 15 persons, highlight tour min 10 persons; ƒ7,50).*

most primary schools have Wednesday afternoons off, and it can get a little hellish.

Other things worth noting include the fact that many museums – though by no means all – are closed on Mondays and public holidays (always phone to check, if you're unsure). And if you're worried about the language barrier, don't: while museums don't always have captions and explanations in English, many sell reasonably priced English guidebooks, and several museums also offer guided tours in English for groups, though you'll need to phone ahead to book.

## Museumboot

*Office & main boarding point: Stationsplein 8 (625 6464/622 2181). Tram 1, 2, 4, 5, 9, 13, 14, 16, 17, 20, 24, 25. Departs June-mid-Sept every 30 mins, mid-Sept-May every 45 mins, 10am-5pm daily.* **Stops at** Prinsengracht (Anne Frankhuis, Theatermuseum); Singel (Museumplein, Rijksmuseum, Van Gogh Museum, Stedelijk Museum); Herengracht/Leidsegracht (Bijbels Museum, Amsterdams Historisch Museum, Allard Pierson Museum); Amstel/Zwanenburgwal (Rembrandthuis, Joods Historisch Museum, Hortus Botanicus, Tropenmuseum); Oosterdok/Kattenburgergracht (Scheepvaart Museum, Werf 't Kromhout); Centraal Station (Madame Tussauds, Museum Amstelkring). **Day tickets** ƒ22; ƒ18 with Museum Card, under-13s. Group discounts (min 20 persons). Tickets can also be bought from the office opposite the Rijksmuseum.

The Museumboot is remarkably good value, especially for those on a particularly tight budget. Tickets entitle holders to get on and off at any of seven stops serving 16 of the city's 40-odd museums located on or near one of the concentric canals, or by the River IJ near Centraal Station. Bearing in mind that the larger museums – such as the Rijksmuseum and the Stedelijk – demand at least half a day each, the Museumboot is better used to take in more of the smaller ones that aren't so easily accessible via public transport. Tickets for the Museumboot also give discounts of as much as 50 per cent on admission prices to assorted museums; phone for details.

# Art

## CoBrA Museum of Modern Art

*Sandbergplein 1, Amstelveen (547 5038). Tram 5, Metro 51.* **Open** 11am-5pm Tue-Sun. **Admission** ƒ7,50; ƒ5 with CJP card, over-65s; ƒ3,50 under-16s; free with Museum Card. Group discounts (min 15 persons).

To say that the CoBrA is one of Amsterdam's major museums would be pushing it: it has yet to cement its position on every art-loving tourist's itinerary. Still, this small museum is more than just a cute diversion among the city's more noted halls. The CoBrA group of artists – who took their name from the cities in which they worked (Copenhagen, Brussels and Amsterdam) – attempted to radically reinvent the language of paint in the '50s. Preaching an ethos of participation – they wanted to see everyone creating art, regardless of competence or education – artists like Karel Appel, Eugene Brands and Asger Jorn were long regarded as a troupe of eccentric troublemakers whose work was of little artistic worth. Time, naturally, has mellowed their impact, and they've now got their own museum. Sure, it might not be the most technically adept art you've ever seen, but that's the point. The CoBrA Museum provides a sympathetic environment from which to trace the development of the most relevant Dutch art movement of the twentieth century. *Café. Disabled access (with assistance) & toilets. Shop.*

## Rembrandthuis

*Jodenbreestraat 4-6 (520 0400). Tram 4, 9, 14, 20/Metro Nieuwmarkt.* **Open** 10am-5pm Mon-Sat; 1-5pm Sun, public holidays. **Admission** ƒ7,50; ƒ5 10-15s; free with Museum Card, under-12s. Group discounts (min 15 persons). **Map 3 E3**

Though he died a pauper, Rembrandt at least kept himself busy during his life: aside from all his famous works (some of which are on display in the Rijksmuseum), he also found time to knock up hundreds of etchings. About 250 of them are on display at this charming three-storey house (built 1606), where the artist lived for almost 20 years. Visitors to the Rembrandthuis can trace the artist's development through his etchings, though, disappointingly, the only paintings on show here are by Rembrandt's teacher, Pieter Lastman, and those painters who worked under Rembrandt in his studio. Still, be sure not to miss Rembrandt's amusing drawings in the basement, depicting the men's and women's toilets, the miniature self-portraits on the first floor, and the temporary exhibitions all the way up top. The museum also does guided tours and etching demonstrations by arrangement, and since the opening of the Holland Experience next door (*see below* **Miscellaneous**), it offers a combined ticket for both venues.
*Disabled access. Guided tours (by arrangement).*

## Rijksmuseum

*Stadhouderskade 42 (673 2121). Tram 2, 5, 6, 7, 10, 20.* **Open** 10am-5pm daily. **Admission** ƒ15; ƒ12 over-65s; ƒ7,50 6-18s; free with Museum Card. Group discounts (min 20 persons). **Map 5 D5**

Designed by PJH Cuypers – the architect responsible for Centraal Station – and opened in 1885, the Rijksmuseum is, statistically speaking, the most popular museum in Amsterdam. The collection was started when William V started acquiring pieces just for the hell of it, and has been growing ever since: it now includes paintings from the fifteenth century until around 1850, as well as decorative and oriental arts. If you only have a limited amount of time, head for the Dutch Masters section on the first floor. Here's where you'll find Rembrandt's *Night Watch*, and *The Kitchen Maid* and *The Young Woman Reading a Letter* by Johannes Vermeer, each capturing a moment in the lives of two women from totally different backgrounds. There are also excellent selections of work by the likes of Pieter de Hooch, Jan Steen, Jacob van Ruisdael and Paulus Potter, all offering an excellent insight into life during the Golden Age. Other attractions here include superb examples of Delftware, porcelain, pottery, silverware and oriental art, while the Gallery Room is devoted to seventeenth- and early eighteenth-century dolls' houses, furnished and decorated in the materials that would originally have been used in the life-sized equivalents. Since the coming of the ARIA Interactive computer system, it's much easier to find your way around the enormous place. Operational every day from 10am to 5pm, ARIA can give the visitor information on the entire collection or establishes connections between certain works of art. It is now possible to find every piece of Argentinian art in the museum, for example, in seconds. The use of ARIA is free, unless you want to make a printout of data. The Rijksmuseum is also the only place where you can get tickets for the Six Collectie, the Six family's small but perfectly formed collection of paintings by the likes of Rembrandt and Hals: ask at the information desk, and take your passport as ID
*Café. Disabled access with assistance. Educational department. Films and slide shows. Guided tours (by arrangement).*

## Rijksmuseum South Wing

*Hobbemastraat 19 (673 2121). Tram 2, 5, 6, 7, 10, 20.* **Open** 10am-5pm daily. **Admission** included in Rijksmuseum price (see above). **Map 5 D5**

Although part of the Rijksmuseum building, the South Wing has its own entrance. The admission fee covers the entire

The **Stedelijk Museum of Modern Art**.

museum and it is possible to access the main building internally, but it's a complicated procedure: a far better idea is to go out and come back in again through the other entrance. Reopened in 1996 after a three-year renovation programme, the South Wing now provides a home for eighteenth- and nineteenth-century paintings, Asiatic art objects – paintings, statues, statuettes and other artefacts including lacquer work, ceramics, jewellery, weaponry, bronze and jade – and the Textile and Costume collection.
*Disabled access & toilets. Garden. Shop.*

### Stedelijk Museum of Modern Art

*Paulus Potterstraat 13 (Dutch & English recorded information 573 2737). Tram 2, 3, 5, 12, 16, 20.* **Open** *Apr-Oct 10am-6pm daily; Nov-Mar 11am-5pm daily; 11am-5pm public holidays.* **Admission** *f9; f4,50 with CJP card, under-17s; free with Museum Card, under-7s.* **Credit** *(shop only) AmEx, EC, MC, V.* **Map 5 D6**
The best collection of modern art in Amsterdam, no question. Alongside the permanent displays, the regularly changing temporary exhibitions, drawn from the collection, tend to focus on particular trends or specific artists and the works. After occupying various locations around the city, the Stedelijk finally settled in its present neo-Renaissance abode, designed by AW Weissmann in 1895. In time, the building became too small for the ambitions of its directors and an ugly new wing was tacked on in 1954. Even so, the rooms themselves are agreeably spacious and sympathetically lit, with the highlights including paintings by Monet, Cézanne, Picasso, Matisse, Kirchner and Chagall. The museum also has a prized collection of paintings and drawings by the Russian artist Kasimir Malevich. The Dutch De Stijl group, of which Piet Mondrian is probably the most famous, is also well represented, along with other post-1945 artists including De Kooning, Newman (whose works have been mutilated twice in the last few years by a deranged hater of his art),

Ryman, Judd, Stella, Lichtenstein, Warhol, Nauman, Middleton, Long, Dibbets, Van Elk, Kiefer, Polke, Merz and Lounellis. The Nieuwe Vleugel Stedelijk Museum (New Wing) is used as a temporary exhibition space, often focusing on design and applied art, while the Appelbar and restaurant are decorated with the designs of CoBrA artist Karel Appel; the latter has a terrace overlooking the sculpture garden, and is a lovely place to sit on a sunny day.
*Café and restaurant. Disabled access & toilets. Guided tours (f200 incl entrance fee; max 15 persons; book at least two weeks ahead). Library (open Sept-Jun to library card-holders only; phone for details). Shop.*

### Van Gogh Museum

*Paulus Potterstraat 7 (570 5200). Tram 2, 3, 5, 12, 16, 20.* **Open** *10am-5pm daily.* **Admission** *f12,50; f5 under-18s; free with Museum Card. Group discounts (min 20 persons).* **Map 5 D6**
Apart from the bright colours of his palette, Van Gogh is also known for his productivity, and both are clearly reflected in the 200 paintings and 500 drawings that form part of the permanent exhibition at this staple of Amsterdam's museum scene. Aside from this massive collection, there are also examples of his Japanese prints, as well as works by the likes of Toulouse-Lautrec and Gauguin, which add perspective to Van Gogh's own efforts. Changing exhibitions, created from the museum's archives and private collections, also feature here. Because of a major refurbishment, the museum will be closed for a while (from 1 September 1998), but 140 pieces will be moved to the South Wing of the Rijksmuseum until the Van Gogh Museum reopens in May 1999. A new wing will house temporary exhibits, while the enlarged Rietveld building remains the base for the permanent collection.
*Disabled access & toilets. Library. Restaurant. Shop.*

## Archaeology

### Allard Pierson Museum

*Oude Turfmarkt 127 (525 2556). Tram 4, 9, 14, 16, 20, 24, 25.* **Open** *10am-5pm Tue-Fri; 1-5pm Sat, Sun, public holidays.* **Admission** *f9,50; f7 students; f3 12-15s; f2 with Museum Card; f1 4-11s.* **Map 2 D3**
Established in 1934, the Allard Pierson Museum claims to now hold the world's richest university collection of archaeological exhibits, gathered from Egypt, Greece, Rome and other ancient civilisations. Although the exhibits are undeniably interesting, the building has a disappointingly subdued atmosphere, and many statues, sculptures, clay tablets and ceramics are unimaginatively presented. There is a more creative, if limited, selection of scale maquettes (of the pyramids, Olympia and so on), as well as a full-scale model of a Greek chariot and sarcophagi, but, more often than not, the accompanying English text is minimal and not very enlightening. The temporary exhibitions on the first floor (usually costing around f5) draw large-ish crowds.
*Disabled access with assistance. Guided tours (f35; book at least three days ahead).*

## Botanical

### Bosmuseum

*Koenenkade 56, Amsterdamse Bos (643 1414). Bus 170.* **Open** *10am-5pm daily.* **Admission** *free.*
The Bosmuseum recounts the history and use of the Amsterdamse Bos, the extensive forest built in the 1930s to provide Amsterdammers with work and a place to spend their days off. Its mock woodland grotto, which turns from day to night at the flick of a switch, is wonderful for kids (*see chapter* **Children***, p169*).
*Disabled access. Guided tours of the forest (phone for details). Restaurant. Shop.*

*Join James Stewart and Kim Novak for a drink at the **Nederlands Filmmuseum**.*

## Hortus Botanicus
## (University of Amsterdam)

*Plantage Middenlaan 2A (625 8411). Tram 7, 9, 14,
20/Metro Waterlooplein.* **Open** *Apr-Sept* 9am-5pm Mon-
Fri; 11am-5pm Sat, Sun; *Oct-Mar* 9am-4pm daily.
**Admission** ƒ7,50; ƒ4,50 5-14s; free under-5s. **Map 7 G3**
You don't have to be the green-fingered type to enjoy these
beautiful gardens, a true oasis of calm just a stone's throw
from Waterlooplein. It was established in 1682, when ships
from the East India Company brought back tropical plants
and seeds that were originally intended to supply doctors
with medical herbs and shrubs. The highlight is the relatively new greenhouse, with three differing but extraordinarily hot climates, while the terrace is one of the nicest in
Amsterdam: only the distant sounds of the city remind you
where you are. One shop sells small plants, seeds and bulbs,
while another specialises in environmental books. *See box*
**Keep on the grass***, p59.*
*Café. Disabled access. Shop.*

## Hortus Botanicus (Vrije Universiteit)

*Van der Boechorststraat 8 (444 9390). Tram 5/bus
96, 169, 170, 171.* **Open** 8am-4.30pm Mon-Fri.
**Admission** free.
This small but perfectly formed garden is, rather curiously,
wedged between the high buildings of a university and a
hospital. Built in 1967, it doesn't have the charm of its coun-
terpart in the city centre (*see above*), but it's a pleasant
enough place for a stroll if you're in the neighbourhood. The
fern collection is one of the largest in the world, while the
Dutch garden shows the great variety of flora originally
found in this country.
*Disabled access.*

## Cinema

### Nederlands Filmmuseum (NFM)

*Vondelpark 3 (589 1400/library 589 1435). Tram 1, 2,
3, 5, 6, 12, 20.* **Open** *box office* 10am-9.30pm Mon-Fri; 1-
9.30pm Sat, Sun; *library (no loans)* 10am-5pm Tue-Fri;
11am-5pm Sat; *screenings* 7pm, 7.30pm, 9.30pm, 10pm
daily; kids' matinée 3pm Sun. **Tickets** *cinema* ƒ11; ƒ9

students; ƒ6 members. Group discounts (min 10 persons).
**Membership** ƒ30 per year. **Map 5 C6**
A great three-in-one visit for real film buffs, the NFM is a
cinema, a museum and an extensive library. Housed in a
grand former nineteenth-century tearoom on the edge of the
Vondelpark, the NFM, like some other Amsterdam cinemas,
is a museum in itself. Actual exhibitions are held only spo-
radically, but the two-screen cinema – furnished with original period artefacts acquired from an old cinema – has
several screenings every day. The museum vaults hold some
35,000 national and international films, which are screened
in imaginatively thematic blocks, while the library (round
the corner at Vondelstraat 69-71) houses the country's largest
collection of film books and mags, scripts, photos, archives,
videos and biographies. Plans are currently being formulated to move parts of the museum out of the city, but at the
time of writing no decision had been made. *See also chapter*
**Film***, p184.*
*Disabled access (preferably with prior arrangement).*

## Ethnography

### Tropenmuseum

*Linnaeusstraat 2 (568 8215). Tram 9, 10, 14.* **Open**
10am-5pm Mon-Fri; noon-5pm Sat, Sun, public holidays.
**Admission** ƒ10; ƒ5 6-18s, students; free with Museum
Card (special exhibitions extra ƒ2,50), under-5s.
**Map 7 H3**
Amsterdam's Tropical Museum takes an honest look at daily
life and problems in the tropical and sub-tropical regions of
the Third World. Ironically, the vast three-storey building
was originally designed and erected in the 1920s to glorify
the colonial activities of the Dutch. Now, though, it's host to
a stimulating, imaginatively presented and colourful collection of articles, including costumes, musical instruments,
puppets and domestic utensils. Visitors are encouraged to
experience the exhibitions by smelling samples of herbs and
spices, as well as stroll in and around walk-through lifesize
reproductions of bazaars (including an African compound
and an Indian village) accompanied by tapes of street sounds
and music. Excellent temporary exhibitions are creatively
mounted in the large hall on the ground floor, and the shop

has a good selection of souvenirs and books from or dealing with Third World countries. Attached to the main Tropenmuseum is the **Kindermuseum**, for children aged between six and 12 (see chapter **Children**, *p170*), and a small cinema where Third World pictures are shown (*see chapter* **Film**, *p184*). Hugely enjoyable for both adults and children.

*Café, restaurant and terrace. Disabled access & lifts. Guided tours (f50/hour weekdays, f75/hour weekends; max 25 persons).*

## Golden Age

### Museum Amstelkring: Ons' Lieve Heer op Solder (Our Lord in the Attic)

*Oudezijds Voorburgwal 40 (624 6604). Tram 4, 9, 14, 16, 20, 24, 25.* **Open** 10am-5pm Mon-Sat; 1-5pm Sun. **Admission** *f7,50; f6 under-19s; free with Museum Card, under-5s. Group discounts (min 10 persons).* **Map 2 D2.**

The Amstelkring is undeservedly neglected by most visitors. Sited in the heart of the Red Light District, the building houses the only remaining attic church in Amsterdam, rescued from demolition in the late 1800s by a group of historians called the Amstelkring (hence the museum's name). The church itself was built in 1663, and was used by Catholics during the seventeenth century when they were banned from worshipping after the Alteration. The lower floors of the house include furnished living rooms that could have served as the setting for one of the seventeenth-century Dutch masters, while upstairs, the chaplain's room has a small cupboard bed. The pilgrimage upwards leads visitors to the highlight of the museum: the beautifully preserved attic church, the altarpiece of which features a painting by eighteenth-century artist Jacob de Wit. The church is often used for services and a variety of other meetings. Don't miss it.

*Guided tours by prior arrangement.*

### Museum Willet-Holthuysen

*Herengracht 605 (523 1870). Tram 4, 9, 14, 20.* **Open** 10am-5pm Mon-Fri; 11am-5pm Sat, Sun. **Admission** *f5; f2,50 under-16s.* **Map 6 E4**

Originally built in 1689, the interior of this pleasant patrician's mansion is more reminiscent of a French château than a Dutch canal house: both the Louis XV and neo-Louis XVI styles are very much visible. The latter was mainly introduced by the Willet-Holthuysens, the family who acquired the house in 1860 and gave it its name. Their passion for over-embellishment is also apparent in their legacy of rare objets d'art, glassware, silver, fine china and paintings. English texts accompany the exhibits, and there's also an English-language video explaining the history of the house and the canal system. A view from the veranda into the recently renovated eighteenth-century garden almost takes you back in time, but the illusion is somewhat disturbed by the adjoining modern buildings. Still, well worth a look.

*Guided tours for groups by prior arrangement.*

### Museum Van Loon

*Keizersgracht 672 (624 5255). Tram 16, 24, 25.* **Open** 11am-5pm Fri-Mon; **Admission** *f7,50; free under-12s. Group discounts (min 10, max 40 persons).* **Map 6 E4**

Behind the classical façade of this canal house lies a classically furnished interior, showing how wonderful it was to be a wealthy resident of Amsterdam in the seventeenth century. Designed by Adriaan Dortsman – the same architect, incidentally, who designed the New Lutheran Church on Singel – this patrician's house was the home of Ferdinand Bol, one of Rembrandt's former pupils, and another artist commemorated with a street (Ferdinand Bolstraat, in the Pijp). Apart from the Louis XV décor, the museum has an unusually large collection of family portraits from the sev-

enteenth and eighteenth centuries, added after the purchase of the house in 1884 by Hendrik van Loon. The eighteenth-century garden, laid out in the French style, contains a coach house from the same period; it's now, charmingly, a private residence.

*Guided tours (by prior arrangement; min 10 persons).*

## Historical

### Amsterdams Historisch Museum

*Kalverstraat 92 (523 1822). Tram 1, 2, 4, 5, 9, 14, 16, 20, 24, 25.* **Open** *museum* 10am-5pm Mon-Fri; 11am-5pm Sat, Sun; *library* 1-5pm Mon-Fri. **Admission** *f11; f5,50 under-17s; free with Museum Card. Group discounts (min 15 persons).* **Map 2 D3**

The courtyard of the Amsterdam Historical Museum is a welcome oasis of peace in the Kalverstraat. However, the entrance is a bit hard to find: look out for a tiny alley and a lopsided arch bearing the three crosses of the city's coat of arms. The museum itself is in a former convent and orphanage dating from the sixteenth century, and details the development of the city from the thirteenth century to the present day with various objets d'art, archaeological finds and interactive displays. The best view of the Civic Guard Gallery – a covered street gallery with several massive group portraits commissioned by wealthy burghers in the sixteenth and seventeenth centuries – is from the second floor of the museum. Another attraction is the adjacent Begijnhof (*see chapter* **Sightseeing**, *p50*), though larger groups of tourists are banned from this lovely little courtyard. The Amsterdams Historisch Museum is also the starting point for **Mee In Mokum** tours (*see chapter* **Directory**, *p258*), which leave at 11am (Tue-Thur, Sun), last around two hours and cost only *f4*, a charge that includes a series of money-saving coupons entitling you, among other things, to a 50 per cent reduction on admission to the Amsterdams Historisch Museum. Booking is essential (phone 523 1743, 1-5pm Mon-Fri).

*Disabled access. Library. Restaurant.*

### Anne Frankhuis

*Prinsengracht 263 (556 7100). Tram 13, 14, 17, 20.* **Open** *Jan-Mar, Sep-Dec* 9am-5pm daily; *Apr-Aug* 9am-9pm daily; *1 Jan, 25 Dec* noon-5pm. **Admission** *f10; f5 10-17s; free under-10s. Group discounts (min 10 persons).* **Map 2 C3**

As anyone who's read her diary or seen the film will tell you, Anne Frank's house isn't the largest of properties. But that hasn't stopped it becoming one of the city's most visited sights, attracting about half a million people every year. Having already fled from persecution in Germany in 1933, Anne Frank, her sister Margot, her parents and four other Jews went into hiding on 5 July 1942. Living in an annexe behind Prinsengracht 263, they were sustained by friends who risked everything to help them; a bookcase marks the entrance to the sober, unfurnished rooms that sheltered the eight inhabitants for two long years. Eventually, on 4 August 1944, the occupants of the annexe were arrested and transported to concentration camps, where Anne died along with Margot and their mother. Her father, Otto, survived, and decided that Anne's moving and perceptive diary should be published. The rest, as they say, is history. Anne Frankhuis is home to an exhibition on the Jews and the persecution they suffered during the war, and other displays charting current developments in racism, Neo-Fascism and anti-Semitism, complete with explanatory texts in English. There's also a display of different editions of the diary. The museum is managed by the Anne Frank Foundation, which aims to combat prejudice, discrimination and oppression. A statue of Anne Frank by Mari Andriessen (dated 1977) stands nearby, at the corner of Westermarkt and Prinsengracht.

*Bookshop. Documentation department (Keizersgracht 192; 556 7100). Educational department. Guided tours by prior arrangement. Videos.*

*Sea the sights at the* **Werf 't Kromhout**.

## Hollandse Schouwburg

*Plantage Middenlaan 24 (626 9945). Tram 7, 9, 14, 20.*
**Open** 11am-4pm daily. **Admission** free. **Map 3 F3**
A small but very impressive exhibition about the tragic historical role of this former theatre. During World War II, the building functioned as a collection point for Jews who were to be sent to camps. Strangely, given its history, the façade of the Schouwburg has been left intact, even though most of the main structure was removed to make way for a memorial monument.

## Verzetsmuseum Amsterdam

*Plantage Kerklaan 61 (620 2535). Tram 7, 9, 14, 20.*
**Open** 10am-5pm Tue-Fri; noon-5pm Sat, Sun.
**Admission** ƒ8; ƒ4 under-15s; free with Museum Card, under-6s. **Map 3 F3**
The collection that makes up the Verzetsmuseum (the Museum of the Resistance) used to be housed in a former synagogue in the Rivierenbuurt, the part of town where Anne Frank lived between escaping the Nazi Germans in 1933 and hiding in the attic on Prinsengracht. Now it's situated near Waterlooplein, in the former Jewish quarter. The permanent collection holds artefacts, documents and interactive displays explaining matters such as sabotage, espionage and the February Strike (*see chapter* **History**, *p24*). You can hear radio broadcasts, look around a mock-up of a hiding place, and see a bicycle-powered machine used to print illegal papers. Much of today's Dutch press started underground: early editions of *Het Parool* ('The Password'), *Vrij Nederland* ('Free Netherlands') and *Trouw* ('Loyalty') are on display here (*see chapter* **Media**, *p196-7*). Exhibitions on the first floor highlight contemporary developments such as extreme right-wing Dutch political parties, though only basic information is supplied in English.
*Guided tours (by prior arrangement; 8-15 persons, ƒ5 per person). Reference library.*

## Maritime

### Nederlands Scheepvaart Museum

*Kattenburgerplein 1 (523 2222). Bus 22, 32.* **Open**
10am-5pm Tue-Sun; *14 June-13 Sept* also 10am-5pm
Mon. **Admission** ƒ14,50; ƒ8 6-18s; free with Museum
Card, under-6s; ƒ37 family ticket. Group discounts (min
20 persons). **Map 3 F2**
It takes some time to see the whole nautical collection based in this monumental building, which dates from 1656. However, once you've made your way all the way round, you'll be glad you took the time. Originally used as a warehouse for the upkeep of the city's fleet of ships, it stands in what was the sea arsenal of the United Provinces, in the heart of Amsterdam's nautical district. The history and techniques of navigation and overseas trade from its very simple beginnings are shown using wooden models, old paintings, drawings and ship parts, with informative, clear and interesting explanations. The best part of this polished exhibition, though, is the full-size replica of the seventeenth-century East India Company ship, harboured right behind the museum. Here you can see a burial at sea while mingling with overacting 'sailors' on the decks and in the holds. They'll happily tell anything you want to know about the ship. One of the largest museums of its kind in the world, and one of the best.
*Disabled access except for ship. Restaurant. Shop.*

### Werf 't Kromhout

*Hoogte Kadijk 147 (627 6777). Bus 22.* **Open** 10.30am-4pm Mon-Fri. **Admission** ƒ4; ƒ2,50 under-15s. Group discounts (min 20, max 40 persons).
A nostalgic museum, full of old, silent ship engines and tools. The shipyard is obviously very proud of the fact that it's one of the few remaining original yards still in use, but its eighteenth-century heritage is no longer very apparent, nor is the yard as active as it once was. The museum will be undergoing major renovations at some point during 1998 or 1999, though plans were sketchy and it's advisable to phone to check it's still open before you visit.
*Bar. Disabled access (ground floor only) & toilet. Guided tours (by arrangement).*

## Religion

### Bijbels Museum

*Herengracht 366 (624 2436). Tram 1, 2, 5.* **Open** 10am-5pm Mon-Sat; 1-5pm Sun. **Admission** ƒ5; ƒ3,50 6-18s; free with Museum Card. Group discounts (min 10 persons). **Map 5 C4**
Although the Biblical Museum is undeniably well put together, many tourists visit the site simply for the two adjoining patricians' houses that accommodate it. Built in 1660-62 by the renowned Dutch architect Philip Vingboons, the houses feature stunning early eighteenth-century ceiling paintings by Jacob de Wit, and are really rather beautiful. Anyway, back to the museum itself... The emphasis of the permanent exhibition is on life in biblical times, and is illustrated by archaeological finds from Egypt and the Middle East, a reconstruction of a Palestinian house, models of Solomon's temple and various audio-visual displays. As you'd expect, there is also a fine collection of Bibles. Some displays are in English, and there is an English guidebook for borrowing. Like so many museums in Amsterdam, the Bijbels Museum is currently undergoing major refurbishments; things should be back to normal by the end of 1999.

*Rembrandt's* Night Watch, *on show at the wonderful* **Rijksmuseum**. *See page 76.*

*Head straight for the* **Bijbels Museum**, *p80.*

### Joods Historisch Museum

*Jonas Daniel Meijerplein 2-4 (626 9945). Tram 9, 14, 20.* **Open** *Nov-Aug* 11am-5pm daily; *Sept, Oct* closed for Yom Kippur. **Admission** ƒ8; ƒ2 10-16s; ƒ4 with ISIC card; free with Museum Card, under-10s. Group discounts (min 10 persons). **Map 3 E3**

Housed in what was once a High German synagogue in the heart of the former Jewish quarter of Amsterdam – it's a short walk from both Waterlooplein market and the Muziektheater (*see chapter* **Music: Classical & Opera**, *p203*) – the Jewish Historical Museum is full of interesting articles from past and present. Exhibits illustrate many aspects of Judaism in the Netherlands, though the main permanent displays concentrate on personal history, religion and the influence of Dutch culture on Jewish culture. The museum organises walks around the neighbourhood and visits to the nearby Portuguese Synagogue. The shop and excellent kosher café can be found in the narrow Shulgass, which links the building with the synagogue.

*Café. Disabled access. Guided tours (by arrangement).*

## Theatre

### Theatermuseum

*Herengracht 168 (623 5104). Tram 13, 14, 17, 20.* **Open** 11am-5pm Tue-Fri; 1-5pm Sat; 1-5pm Sun (museum only). **Admission** ƒ7,50; ƒ4 students, 4-9s; free with Museum Card. **Map 2 C3**

Now open again after extensive renovations, the Theatermuseum (built in 1638 by Philip Vingboons) is an architectural gem. The outside is lovely enough, but inside, the eighteenth-century plasterwork, ceiling paintings by Jacob de Wit and the spiral staircases are simply magnificent, and would make this museum worth a visit even without all the theatrical ephemera relating the story of Dutch

theatre. Go in summer and stop in the lovely old garden behind the house for tea and cakes, a practically perfect way to while away a lazy afternoon.

*Café. Guided tours (ƒ75, by prior arrangement; max 20 persons). Library.*

## Transport

### Aviodome

*Schiphol Centre (604 1521). NS rail to Schiphol Airport.* **Open** *Apr-Sept* 10am-5pm daily; *Oct-Mar* 10am-5pm Tue-Fri; noon-5pm Sat, Sun. **Admission** ƒ12,50; ƒ10 4-12s; free under-4s. Group discounts (max 20 persons).

Aeroplane enthusiasts will loop the loop over the displays in this exhibition: over 30 historic aircraft are neatly parked or suspended at the Aviodome museum, a short trip from Schiphol Airport. The exhibition starts with the first motorised plane – the Wright Flyer from 1903 – and the Spider, designed by Dutch pioneer Anthony Fokker, and also takes in recent aeronautical developments and space travel. You don't always have to stay behind the lines: kids enjoy playing Biggles and clambering into a cockpit, though adults may prefer the more realistic flight-simulator demonstrations (available by prior arrangement only). There are also film screenings and collections of models, photos and aeroplane parts, and the Aviodome also organises markets and fairs as well as occasional theme weekends.

*Bar. Disabled access (ground floor only) & toilet. Guided tours (ƒ40; max 25 persons). Shop.*

### Electrische Museum Tramlijn Amsterdam

*Haarlemmermeerstation, Amstelveenseweg 264 (673 7538). Tram 6, 16.* **Open** *Apr-June, Sept* 10am-5.30pm Sun; *July, Aug* 10am-4pm Tue-Sat. **Trams** depart every 20 mins. **Admission** ƒ5; ƒ2,50 4-11s; free under-4s.

When open, the Electric Tram Museum is almost always on the move. Some of the antique trolleys, collected from cities throughout Europe, are still in use: kids in particular love going for a 30-minute ride in one of the museum's colourful conveyances through the nearby and surprisingly rural Amsterdamse Bos (*see box* **Keep on the grass**, *p59, and chapter* **Children**, *p169*). Fun.

*Café at Haarlemmermeer station.*

### Schipholscoop

*Arrivals Hall 1, Schiphol Airport (601 2000). NS rail to Schiphol Airport.* **Open** 10am-6pm Mon-Fri; 10am-5pm Sat, Sun.

The visitors' centre at Schiphol Airport, which opened in June 1994, is no more and no less than a semi-decent way to kill time while waiting for your plane. The Schipholscoop has interactive exhibitions that provide information about Schiphol's economic and environmental significance, as well as details on noise pollution and job opportunities, should you fancy working in what will be – after the renovations – an extremely efficient airport.

## University history

### Universiteitsmuseum de Agnietenkapel

*Oudezijds Voorburgwal 231 (525 3341). Tram 4, 9, 14, 16, 20, 24, 25.* **Open** 9am-5pm Mon-Fri; open weekends on National Museum Weekend (*see above* **Tickets & information**) and every National Day of Science (second weekend of Oct). **Admission** free; *special exhibitions* ƒ3,50. **Map 2 D3**

In a city rich with architectural gems, the Agnietenkapel, built in 1473 and part of the university since its foundation in 1632, is actually one of the few Gothic chapels to have escaped the wrecking ball. The chapel, with its austere, Calvinistic beauty, lovely stained-glass windows and old wooden beams and benches, is more stimulating than the collection, which focuses on the history of education, research and student life at the University of Amsterdam. Still, the Grote Gehoorzaal ('Large Auditorium'), where respected seventeenth-century academics Vossius and Barlaeus gave their first lectures, has a beautiful wooden ceiling, decorated with soberly painted, ornamental Renaissance motifs such as angels, masks, flowers and a portrait of Minerva, the Roman goddess of science and arts. An absolute beauty.

## Zoological

### Artis

*Plantage Kerklaan 40 (623 1836). Tram 7, 9, 14, 20.* **Open** 9am-6pm; buildings close at 5.30pm daily. **Admission** ƒ23,50; ƒ15,50 4-12s; free under-4s. Group discounts (min 20 persons). **Map 7 G3**

This zoo, planetarium, geological and zoological museum is a great day out for children young and old. Apart from the usual range of animals, there's a special section for nocturnal creatures and a fascinating aquarium. The 150-year-old zoo contains a small but interesting museum featuring thematic exhibitions and a collection of stuffed animals. The narration in the planetarium is in Dutch but a short English translation is available if you want to keep yourself informed. Handily, the feeding ground for humans is ideally situated between the pond with flamingoes, and a popular children's playground. *See chapters* **Sightseeing**, *p56*, and **Children**, *p169*.

*Café. Disabled access. Guided tours (by arrangement). Restaurant. Shop.*

## Miscellaneous

### Ajax Museum

*Arena Boulevard 3 (311 1469). Metro Bijlmer.* **Open** 10am-6pm daily (opening hours on match days vary). **Admission** ƒ12,50; ƒ10 under-12s. Group discounts (min 20 persons).

A great outing for footie fans of all ages, the Ajax Museum takes you on a tour through the long and rich history of this legendary club. The exhibitions trace the development of the team from their humble beginnings to the big business enterprise of today. Unique photographs and memorabilia taken from the club's and players' collections are on display, as are all the cups, in the trophy cabinet: Ajax won the league and cup double in 1998, and are presently the dominant force in Dutch football. Highlights from the splendid audio-visual collection include clips from the cup finals, the eternal war between Ajax and Feyenoord, and, of course, footage featuring one of the greatest players who ever lived, Johan Cruyff, who personally welcomes the visitor in a video shot in the dressing rooms. Don't miss the eight-minute compilation film on three screens at the end of the tour, where you can enjoy some of the all-time great goals scored in the last 25 years by alumni such as Rijkaard and Van Basten. *See chapter* **Sport**, *p213*.

*Bar/restaurant. Shop.*

### Max Euwe Centrum

*Max Euweplein 30A (625 7017). Tram 1, 2, 5, 6, 7, 10.* **Open** 10.30am-4pm Tue-Fri, first Sat of month. **Admission** free. **Map 5 D5**

Named after the only chess world champion the Netherlands has ever produced – as is the square in which it stands – the Max Euwe Centrum harbours an international chess library, various chess artefacts from Euwe's inheritance, vast archives, and chess computers that the public can use and abuse at their leisure. Housed in the city's old House of Detention, it should please chess aficionados from all over the world.

*Disabled access. Guided tours on request.*

### Holland Experience

*Waterlooplein 17 (422 2233). Tram 9, 14, 20.* **Open** *Apr-Sept* 9.30am-7pm daily; *Oct-Mar* 9.30 am-6pm daily. **Admission** ƒ17,50; ƒ15 under-16s. **Credit** AmEx, DC, EC, MC, V. **Map 3 E3**

This brand new addition to Amsterdam's wide variety of sights and museums is an assault on the senses, throwing in every Dutch cliché bar the finger in the dyke during a multi-dimensional film focusing on life in the Netherlands. Viewers follow the 'comic' mishaps of a bunch of tourists on screen, while sounds, images and smells bombard you from every direction. Young children and bored, busy businessmen may enjoy this, but the 'experience' is so brash and over the top that you only remember half of what you have seen when it's all over: kids in clogs, windmills and tulips, the best of the Rijksmuseum, a waxen statue of Queen Beatrix… The only real plus is the combined ticket admission to both the Holland Experience and the Rembrandthuis next door, but overall the entrance fee is better spent in the adjacent Waterlooplein market.

*Cafés. Disabled access with assistance. Gift shop.*

### Het Kattenkabinet

*Herengracht 497 (626 5378). Tram 4, 9, 14, 16, 20, 24, 25.* **Open** 10am-2pm Mon-Fri; 1-5pm Sat, Sun. **Admission** free. **Map 5 D4**

The Kattenkabinet boasts that it's the only museum in the world to have a permanent exhibition exclusively devoted to cats. The multicultural collection includes paintings, statuettes, posters and more, with some living felines thrown in for good measure. The exhibition is spread over two spacious rooms, and is worth a visit alone for the beautiful location: it's housed in a seventeenth-century patricians' mansion, complete with murals by Jacob de Wit.

### Tattoo Museum

*Oudezijds Achterburgwal 130 (625 1565). Tram 4, 9, 16, 20, 24, 25.* **Open** noon-5pm Tue-Sun. **Admission** ƒ5. Group discounts (min 15 persons). **Map 2 D3**

Henk Schiffmacher, the force behind the world's only official tattoo institute, is a renowned figure in the tattoo world. Not only has he run the famous tattoo parlour Hanky Panky (*see chapter* **Services**, *p166*), in the heart of the Red Light District, for some 16 years, but he is also responsible for organising the annual Tattoo Convention, as well as appearing on numerous TV programmes about the art form. Housed in a former liquor factory, the Tattoo Institute – open since May 1996 – is a non-profit-making venture that includes a surprisingly interesting museum, a public library, an archive and an information centre. The exhibition, detailing the history of tattoos, includes hundreds of ancient and ethnographical tools, thousands of drawings, photographs and prints and even some preserved pieces of tattooed skin. Nice. Internationally renowned tattoo artists also make guest appearances.

*Disabled access. Guided tours by prior arrangement.*

### Woonbootmuseum 'Hendrika Maria'

*Prinsengracht, near no.296 (427 0750). Tram 10, 13, 14, 17, 20.* **Open** 10am-5pm Tue-Sun. **Admission** ƒ3,75; ƒ2,50 children under 152cm (5ft). **Map 5 C4**

And you thought that living on a houseboat was cramped, smelly, cold and uncomfortable? Well, hop inside the Woonbootmuseum and be stunned by the space and comfort of this beautiful boat, a former commercial sailing ship built in 1914. Although the museum is rather small, it's an experience not to be missed and gives a good idea of this unique Amsterdam way of life. There are models, photos and a slideshow explaining the perils and maintenance of a houseboat, among other things. The former cargo hold has been transformed into a cosy living space, with all the conveniences one can find in a 'normal' home. An illustrated guide in English is available, along with tea, coffee and soft drinks.

## University & specialist collections

Amsterdam has a variety of small, specialised collections, dealing with subjects ranging from the life and times of famous Dutch authors to embryological specimens. 'Museum' is perhaps too grand a word for some of the smaller collections, which are only really interesting for connoisseurs. Many of the collections listed below can only be visited by arrangement and are free unless otherwise stated.

### Museum Vrolik

*Entrance on south side of AMC medical faculty, Meibergdreef 15 (566 9111). Bus 59, 60, 61, 120, 126/Metro Holendrecht.* **Open** 2-5pm Tue, Wed; also by appointment. **Admission** *f*1 group tour (min 12 persons).
The Museum Vrolik, an anatomical embryological laboratory, contains eighteenth- and nineteenth-century specimens of human embryos, human anatomy and congenital malformations collected by Professor Gerardus Vrolik and his son. Not recommended for those with weak stomachs.

### Bedrijfsmuseum ENW Amsterdam

*Spaklerweg 20 (597 3107). Bus 46, 169/Metro Spaklerweg.* **Open** by appointment; phone 8am-4pm Mon-Fri.
Industrial artefacts relating to gas and electricity production and distribution.

### Bilderdijkmuseum

*De Boelaan 1105 (645 4368). Bus 8, 23, 26, 48, 49, 64, 65, 67, 158, 173, 197.* **Open** by appointment, at the Oude Drukken room on first floor of the Vrije University. The life and times of Dutch writer and academic Willem Bilderdijk (1756-1831) is illustrated with displays of his manuscripts, etchings and personal belongings.

### Historisch Documentatiecentrum van de Vrije Universiteit

*De Boelaan 1105 (444 7777). Tram 51.* **Open** 9am-5pm Mon-Fri.
The history of the Dutch Protestant University and its founder Abraham Kuyper.
*Disabled access.*

### Instituut voor Sociale Geschiedenis

*Cruquiusweg 31 (668 5866). Tram 6, 10/bus 22.* **Open** 9am-5pm Mon-Fri, 9.30am-1pm Sat.
An international library, run by the Institute for Social History, specialising in the social history of the world. The library contains original writings by Marx and Engels.

### Multatuli Museum

*Korsjespoortsteeg 20 (638 1938/624 7427). Tram 1, 2, 5, 13, 17, 20.* **Open** 10am-5pm Tue; noon-5pm Sat, Sun; also by appointment. **Map 2 C2**
The life of the nineteenth-century writer Eduard Douwes-Dekker (who wrote under the pseudonym Multatuli) is illustrated by photos and other objects. There's also a library.

### Vakbonds Museum

*Henri Polaklaan 9 (624 1166). Tram 7, 9, 14, 20.* **Open** 11am-5pm Tue-Fri; 1-5pm Sun. **Map 3 F3**
A permanent exhibition showing aspects of the Labour Union in Dutch history. The building was designed by Berlage to house the offices of the Netherlands' first trade union. *Disabled access.*

### Werkspoormuseum

*Oostenburgergracht 77 (625 1035). Bus 22, 28.* **Open** by appointment; phone 9am-5pm Mon-Fri.
Paintings, prints, models and other objects illustrate the history of the Dutch railroad.

*Skin rules at the* **Tattoo Museum***.*

## Further afield

### Catherijneconvent

*Nieuwegracht 63, Utrecht (030 231 7296). Bus 2, 22 from Utrecht Centraal Station.* **Open** 10am-5pm Tue-Fri; 11am-5pm Sat, Sun, public holidays. **Admission** *f*7; *f*3,50 under-18s; free with Museum Card, under-6s. Group discounts (max 20 persons).
This fifteenth-century convent illustrates the history of Dutch Christian culture. The exhibition contains the biggest collection of medieval paintings, sculpture, gold and silver, textiles and manuscripts in the Netherlands. The *bogenkelder* (vaulted cellar), complete with many old Bibles with silver cast covers, and the beautiful stained-glass windows in the adjoining church should not be missed. An English guidebook is available.
*Café. Disabled access. Shop.*

### Frans Hals Museum/De Hallen, Haarlem

*Groot Heiligland 62, Haarlem (023 511 5775)/ Grotemarkt 16 (023 511 5840). Bus 1, 4, 5, 6, 71, 72 from Haarlem Centraal Station.* **Open** *both museums* 11am-5pm Mon-Sat; 1-5pm Sun, public holidays. **Admission** *Frans Hals Museum Apr-Sep f*8; *f*3,75 10-17s; free with Museum Card, under-10s; *Oct-Mar f*7; *f*3,25 10-17s; free with Museum Card, under-10s. *De Hallen Museum Apr-Sep f*4,50; *f*2,75 10-17s; free with Museum Card, under-10s; *Oct-Mar f*3,50; *f*1,75 10-17s; free with Museum Card, under-10s. Group discounts for both museums all year (min 20 persons).
Some of Hals's finest canvasses are on display here, while there are also paintings by many of his illustrious contemporaries. Reconstructed rooms illustrate the building's original use as the Oudemannenhuis (an almshouse for elderly men). Hals is famous for his group portraits of civic and almshouse regents; two of the eight displayed here depict

# Subculture club

Famed for its glorious history, ancient art and grandiose architecture, Amsterdam is a city that can rightly claim to be one of the most culturally exciting in Europe. Still, as some science guy once pointed out, for every force there is an equal and opposite force; for every Van Gogh Museum, there is a…

'Museum' is perhaps too strong a word for some of the tourist traps that clutter up the centre of Amsterdam. Our dictionary defines a museum as 'a place or building where objects of historic, artistic or scientific interest are exhibited, preserved or studied'. Hmmm. Only the most liberal language student would allow the **Erotic Museum** – in a nutshell, five floors of tawdry, asexual tackiness – into such a category. One can only assume the staggering array of sex toys on display are of scientific interest: they're hardly of historical worth, and the only art lies, perhaps, in working out exactly what some of them are for. Still, it does boast some original John Lennon erotic sketches, which are worth the meagre price of admission (ƒ5) by themselves.

The **Sex Museum**, sadly, can boast no such exhibits, and draws most of its trade from tourists passing on their way to and from Centraal Station. The highlight – at least if visitor popularity is anything to go by – is a couple of walls covered in tatty photographs of women engaged in unmentionable and probably illegal acts with assorted farmyard animals. We repeat: this is the *highlight*.

The **Torture Museum**, thankfully, is a little better. For a start, the displays are, at least, competently labelled, and some effort has gone into their presentation. Some of the stuff from the Spanish Inquisition, too, is actually interesting. But the whole thing reeks of cheapness, and besides, once you've seen one set of manacles, you've seen them all.

Amsterdam, of course, wouldn't be Amsterdam without a druggie museum, which is where the clumsily named **Hash Marihuana Hemp Museum** comes in. Like the Torture Museum, it has its moments, but then spoils it by getting all educational and worthy. The owners occasionally seem to lose sight of the whole point: namely, that you can smoke the stuff, not that you can knit it into a vile pair of sackcloth trousers. Incidentally, the Hash Marihuana Hemp Museum costs more to enter than Rembrandthuis. Make of this what you will.

## Erotic Museum
*Oudezijds Achterburgwal 54 (624 7303). Tram 4, 9, 14, 16, 20, 24, 25.* **Open** *11am-1am Sun-Fri; 11am-2pm Sat.* **Admission** *ƒ5. Group discounts (min 10 persons).* **Map 2 D2**

## Hash Mariihuana Hemp Museum
*Oudezijds Achterburgwal 148 (623 5961). Tram 4, 9, 14, 16, 20, 24, 25/Metro Nieuwmarkt.* **Open** *11am-10pm daily.* **Admission** *ƒ8.* **Map 2 D3**
*Disabled access with assistance.*

## Sex Museum
*Damrak 18 (622 8376). Tram 4, 9, 14, 16, 20, 24, 25.* **Open** *10am-11.30pm daily.* **Admission** *ƒ4,50.* **Map 2 D2**
*Disabled access.*

## Torture Museum
*Damrak 20-22 (639 2027). Tram 4, 9, 16, 20, 24, 25.* **Open** *10am-11pm daily.* **Admission** *ƒ7,50; ƒ5,50 students; ƒ4 under-13s.* **Map 2 D2**

---

the regents of the Oudemannenhuis itself. There is also a modern and contemporary art collection, including outstanding examples of work by artists from Haarlem and surrounding areas. Most explanations are in English. Well worth the trip.
*Bookshop/shop. Café. Disabled access. Guided tours (in English, 1.30pm Sun).*

## De Lakenhal, Leiden
*Oude Singel 28-32 (071 516 5360). NS rail to Leiden.* **Open** *museum 10am-5pm Tue-Fri; noon-5pm Sat, Sun, public holidays; library 10am-12.30pm Tue, Thur, Fri; 2-5pm Wed.* **Admission** *ƒ5; ƒ2,50 6-18s; free with Museum Card, under-6s.*
An awe-inspiring collection combining local history with decorative arts and paintings of just the right proportions. Don't overlook the extraordinary *Last Judgement* by Lucas van Leyden, the landscapes of Jan van Goyen and the wonderful genre scenes of Jan Steen.
*Disabled access. Guided tours (ƒ1,50, groups of 20) by arrangement three weeks in advance. Library.*

## Mauritshaus, The Hague
*Korte Vijverberg 8 (070 302 3456). NS rail to Den Haag (The Hague) Centraal Station.* **Admission** *ƒ12,50; ƒ6,50 under-18s; free with Museum Card.*
One of the country's finest Golden Age houses, holding magnificent masterpieces by Rubens, Van Dyck, the Flemish School, Rembrandt, Jan Steen, Holbein and Vermeer.
*Disabled access.*

## Museum Boymans-Van Beuningen, Rotterdam
*Museumpark 18-20 (010 441 9400). NS rail to Rotterdam Centraal Station, then tram 4.* **Open** *10am-5pm Tue-Sat; 11am-5pm Sun.* **Admission** *ƒ7,50; ƒ4 with Museum Card, under-16s; free under-4s.*
Some real gems by Van Eyck, Rembrandt, Bosch and other masters, along with French and surrealist art, modernist paintings and sculpture, and industrial design. It reopens on 1 January 1999 after refurbishments.
*Disabled access. Guided tours by prior arrangement.*

IN DE
WILDEMAN
BEER CAFE

18 BEERS ON TAP
200 BOTTLED BEERS

WINES
SOFT DRINKS
COFFEE & TEA

# Consumer Amsterdam

# Accommodation

*Whether you're after luxury or simplicity, Amsterdam will accommodate you.*

With an already overloaded multicultural population packed into a space that is, on average, only four storeys high and that takes just ten minutes to cycle across, Amsterdam has little room for its millions of visitors each year. Couple the small size of the city with the fact that an increasing number of rooms are reserved for business folk, and you soon see why you should try to book your rooms well in advance, especially during the peak season and around public holidays.

Unfortunately, high demand can equal high prices. This is not without its benefits. Most of the city's hotels are excellent, and you do get value for money here. Indeed, it's rare to see hoteliers in other cities injecting so much effort to provide that little something extra. The majority are also very helpful to tourists.

Coming to Amsterdam in a car isn't a great idea: if you do manage to find a parking space, you'll have to pay through the nose to avoid getting a big yellow wheel-cosy. However, some hotels offer reduced-fee parking, while others will gladly point the way to the nearest public car park. Of course, if you really splash out, you may just get a valet parking service to allay your automotive worries. Bikers should beware, though: thieves here could nick a Chieftain tank with a hairpin, so bring a cover and an impossibly complicated set of locks.

All the places listed in this section are classified into price groups on the basis of the cost of a double room with WC and shower en suite (where applicable) for one night in the high season. Unless otherwise stated, breakfast is included in the room price. Note that, as with other cities, the star rating applies to the hotel's facilities, rather than its overall appeal or charm. Disabled travellers should note that many hotels located in old houses do not have lifts; always check before booking.

For listings of other hotels, *see chapter* **Gay & Lesbian***, page 195.*

### RESERVATIONS

There are several ways of making reservations. Booking a travel and hotel package direct with your local travel agent is a reliable option and can work out cheaper. Many hotels offer special discounts in winter or if you book a package deal; it's worth doing a bit of research before you decide on one. If you book yourself, advance bookings need

to be made in peak periods as demand is high. Most hotels will require a deposit; if the establishment does not accept credit cards, this will have to be sent by post. Alternatively, you can make use of the free Dutch hoteliers' reservation service (*see below*), which handles bookings for the whole of the Netherlands. For those already in the country, the **VVV** tourist information offices at Centraal Station and Schiphol Airport (*see chapter* **Directory***, page 252*) also offer a national hotel booking service. In Amsterdam, this costs *f*5 per person (plus a deposit of *f*5 per person, later deducted from your hotel bill). Enquiries are only taken in person. The VVV also produces a comprehensive guide to hotels in the city, available from its offices, priced at *f*5.

### Nederlands Reserverings Centrum

*PO Box 404, 2260 AK Leidschendam (070 419 5500/fax 070 419 5519).* **Open** 8am-8pm Mon-Fri; 8am-2pm Sat. Many of the hotels recommended by the VVV can be booked through this bureau for a fee of *f*5. The VVV can provide a brochure of the hotels the centre deals with. If you decide to book through the VVV, it will send confirmation of your reservation by post, fax or e-mail (*info@hotelres.nl*).

## Hotels

### Deluxe (*f*500 and up)

All Deluxe hotels have a bar, café or brasserie, conference rooms, fitness facilities, laundry and dry cleaning, lifts, parking (valet or otherwise) and a restaurant. Room services for all include air-conditioning, 24-hour room service, a telephone, and a TV with in-house movies.

### American Hotel

*Leidsekade 97 (624 5322/fax 625 3236). Tram 1, 2, 5, 6, 7, 10, 20.* **Rates** *single f*395-*f*450; *double f*525-600; *extra bed f*75; under-12s free.* **Credit** AmEx, DC, JCB, MC, all TC, V. **Map 5 C5**
The American's classic art deco exterior, plush, modernised interior and spacious, luxurious rooms make it an attractive choice for those seeking deluxe lodgings. Not least among its visitors are numerous rock stars who seem to enjoy the hotel's proximity to the city's two main music venues – the Melkweg and Paradiso – along with the Stadsschouwburg theatre. Situated on the ground floor is the impressive Café Americain (*see chapter* **Restaurants***, p107*), the hotel's focal point, which overlooks the bustling Leidseplein. In complete contrast, the tranquil Vondelpark is just two minutes' walk away, and the museums a little further on. Breakfast is an extra *f*31,50.
**Hotel services** *Gift shop. Sauna. Terrace.* **Room services** *Babysitting. Minibar.*

*Live it up in the lap of luxury at the **American Hotel**. See page 89.*

## Amstel Intercontinental Amsterdam

*Professor Tulpplein 1 (622 6060/fax 622 5808). Tram 6, 7, 10, 20.* **Rates** *single f775-f875; double f825-f925; suite f1,100-f4,600; extra bed f100; babies free.* **Credit** AmEx, DC, JCB, MC, all TC, V. **Map 6 F4**
The alluring Grand Hall foyer gives just a hint of what lies beyond in this, the most luxurious, formal (and, thus, expensive) five-star hotel in the city. With a ratio of two staff to each of the 79 antique- and Delft-adorned rooms, you can expect to be pampered. The high expectations of guests seem to be met, too, given the extraordinary list of returning celebs and royals. The hotel's excellent cuisine can be enjoyed either in sumptuous indoor surroundings or on the riverside terraces, where the spectacular setting – just by the Amstel – can be truly appreciated. Breakfast is an additional f42,50.
**Hotel services** *Banqueting halls. Business centre. Cruise boat. Diamond shop. Disabled access with assistance. Limousine service. Secretarial services. Swimming pool. Terrace.* **Room services** *Fax. Minibar. Stereo CD player. VCR.*

## Amsterdam Hilton

*Apollolaan 138-40 (678 0780/fax 662 6688). Tram 5, 24.* **Rates** *single f415-f585; double f445-f615; suite f1,100-f2,000; under-12s free in same room as parents.* **Credit** AmEx, DC, JCB, MC, all TC, V.
Though it is famed for the John and Yoko 'bed-in' event of 1969, the huge five-star Amsterdam Hilton is actually pretty unexciting, both in terms of style and atmosphere. However, it does offer a wide spectrum of top-brass services: there are no less than 271 air-conditioned rooms – including executive rooms and suites – and great Mediterranean cuisine in the restaurant. The hotel's location is not ideal, but then again, there's no room for a yacht club and marina in the city centre.
**Hotel services** *Banquet facilities. Boat hire. Business facilities. Disabled access with assistance. Hairdresser. Shops. Terrace.* **Room services** *Minibar. Safe. Stereo. Voicemail & modem.*

## The Grand

*Oudezijds Voorburgwal 197 (555 3111/fax 555 3222). Tram 4, 9, 14, 16, 20, 24, 25.* **Rates** *single f660; double f760; suite f900-f2,500; extra bed f90; under-12s free.* **Credit** AmEx, DC, JCB, MC, all TC, V. **Map 2 D3**
Prince William of Orange was the first of many illustrious guests to stay at this centrally located, old town five-star when it opened as an inn in the late sixteenth century. Since then, the site has been the home of the great Dutch Admiralty and the dull city council. You get a glimpse of the history as soon as you enter the spacious courtyard, and the 182 rooms, suites and apartments are decorated accordingly. Monsieur Albert Roux, holy founder of the white sauce, presents excellent dishes in the restaurant and **Café Roux** (*see chapter* **Restaurants,** *p109*).
**Hotel services** *Babysitting. Banqueting room. Flower shop. Limousine service. Sauna & steam room. Swimming pool & Jacuzzi.* **Room services** *Fax. Non-smoking rooms. Safe. VCR. Voicemail & modem.*

## Hôtel de L'Europe

*Nieuwe Doelenstraat 2-8 (531 1777/fax 531 1778). Tram 4, 9, 14, 16, 20, 24, 25.* **Rates** *single f480-f530; double f580-f680; suite f820-f2,000; extra bed f65; under-12s free.* **Credit** AmEx, DC, JCB, MC, all TC, V. **Map 2 D3**
Looking out from one of the 100 individually decorated rooms, you might think this five-star hotel has a moat. It doesn't; it's just that its location on the Amstel river gives a great view of the city centre's main functional waterways. The hotel's charm is further enhanced by the Excelsior restaurant (jacket and tie required), serving haute cuisine and champagne on its river-level terrace facing the historic Munttoren. With its Victorian-period lounge and foyer, this truly is an elegant place, and caters for all, from business types to honeymooners (the bridal suite comes complete with Jacuzzi). Breakfast costs from f42,50.
**Hotel services** *Babysitting. Boat landing. Business facilities. Disabled access. Gift shop. Limousine service. Massage parlour. Safe. Sauna. Swimming pool. Terrace.* **Room services** *Minibar. Safe. Voicemail & modem.*

## Okura Hotel Amsterdam

*Ferdinand Bolstraat 333 (678 7111/fax 671 2344).*
*Tram 12, 25.* **Rates** *single ƒ385-ƒ505; double ƒ435-ƒ555;*
*suite ƒ655-ƒ2,475; extra bed ƒ105; under-12s free.* **Credit**
AmEx, DC, JCB, MC, all TC, V.

Perfectly situated and equipped for business, the luxury five-star Okura boasts 321 rooms, 49 suites and ten banqueting and conference rooms. Granted, the location isn't as central as it might be, but the fact that it's only a ten-minute walk from RAI Congress and the World Trade Centre is an obvious advantage to business travellers. Commerce aside, there are two bars and four restaurants to be enjoyed, one of which is on the 23rd floor and offers an incredible panoramic view of the entire city. There is also a fully equipped health centre with pool, Jacuzzi, sauna and Japanese torture facilities (aka multi-gym). Breakfast is an extra ƒ39,50.

**Hotel services** *Babysitting. Banquet facilities. Disabled access. Internet. Non-smoking rooms. Sauna & swimming pool. Secretarial services. Shops.* **Room services** *Fax. Minibar. Safe. Trouser press. Voicemail.*

# Expensive (ƒ300-ƒ500)

All hotels in this category have a bar or café, and dry cleaning and laundry. Room services for all includes room service, a telephone and a TV, normally with in-house movies.

## Ambassade Hotel

*Herengracht 341 (626 2333/fax 624 5321). Tram 1, 2, 5.* **Rates** *single ƒ260; double ƒ325; extra bed ƒ60; babies ƒ25.* **Credit** AmEx, DC, MC, all TC, V. **Map 5 C4**

The centrally located three-star Ambassade is a bit of a favourite with writers and publishers: after all, the atmosphere here is peaceful and groups are not encouraged. The hotel is made up of ten seventeenth-century canal houses, each with a very impressive canal view (particularly through the floor-to-ceiling windows in the swanky lounge). It's all done out in traditional Amsterdam style, complete with frighteningly narrow stairs. If you're suffering from writer's block, try and revive your creativity in the hotel's flotation and massage centre. Well, it's an excuse to pamper yourself, anyway. Breakfast is served beneath crystal chandeliers.

**Hotel services** *Lift.* **Room services** *Hairdryer. Safe.*

## Amsterdam Marriott Hotel

*Stadhouderskade 12 (607 5555/fax 607 5511). Tram 1, 2, 5, 6, 7, 10, 20.* **Rates** *single/double ƒ455; suite ƒ1,500* (discounts at weekends); *extra bed ƒ50; under-18s free.* **Credit** AmEx, DC, MC, all TC, V. **Map 5 C5**

The Marriott is a large five-star executive hotel with some delicate, subtle reminders of Uncle Sam: American football games are screened in Character's Bar & Grill, while there are also pool tables and an integrated Pizza Hut. The 392 rooms and suites are very comfortable, and all include a business working desk with modem outlet. The hotel is just off Leidseplein in between Vondelpark and the Casino, near the museums. Breakfast is an extra ƒ33,50.

**Hotel services** *Air-conditioning. Babysitting. Banquet rooms. Business centre. Conference rooms. Currency exchange. Disabled access. Fax. Hairdresser. Internet. Lift. Limousine service. Non-smoking rooms. Parking. Restaurant. Shop. Fitness facilities. Valet.* **Room services** *Hairdryer. Iron. Safe. Voicemail & ISDN/modem.*

## Crowne Plaza Amsterdam City Centre

*Nieuwezijds Voorburgwal 5 (620 0500/fax 620 1173). Tram 1, 2, 5, 13, 17, 20.* **Rates** *single ƒ385-ƒ510; double ƒ435-ƒ695; suite ƒ950-ƒ1,250 (ex 5% tourist tax); under-12s free (incl breakfast), 12-18s free (excl breakfast).* **Credit** AmEx, DC, JCB, MC, all TC, V. **Map 2 C2**

This cumbersomely named hotel, just a stone's throw from Dam Square, offers luxury and comfort in its 270 rooms.

Parents will no doubt be interested in the kids' suite, which comes complete with bunk beds: children under 19 stay for free, so they can stay in and play Nintendo while their parents go sightseeing. Or maybe it's the other way round. Restaurant Dorrius, situated in one of the two seventeenth-century houses incorporated in the hotel, serves delightful Dutch dishes in a welcoming, relaxed atmosphere. Breakfast is an additional ƒ34.

**Hotel services** *Babysitting. Bar. Brasserie. Business facilities. Conference rooms. Currency exchange. Disabled access (limited). Fitness centre. Gift shop. Internet. Lift. Limousine service. Non-smoking rooms. Parking. Restaurant. Safe. Sauna. Solarium. Swimming pool.* **Room services** *Air-conditioning. ISDN. Minibar.*

## Estherea

*Singel 303-309 (624 5146/fax 623 9001). Tram 1, 2, 5.* **Rates** *single ƒ215-ƒ300; double ƒ285-ƒ390; triple ƒ330-ƒ450; quad ƒ370-ƒ505; under-12s free; second child half price.* **Credit** AmEx, DC, JCB, MC, all TC, V. **Map 2 C3**

Estherea, a central four-star hotel, is a plot of eight canal houses accommodating 70 traditional rooms, all decked out in bright, happy colours with an array of antiques on show. The resident family prides itself on its home-from-home atmosphere: take advantage of the (free) option of breakfast in bed. Tea and coffee is also complimentary all day. If only all hotels were made this way.

**Hotel services** *Air conditioning. Babysitting. Bar. Fax. Internet. Lift. Lounge. Non-smoking rooms. Valet. Disabled access.* **Room services** *Minibar. Safe.*

## Grand Hotel Krasnapolsky

*Dam 9 (554 9111/fax 622 8607). Tram 1, 2, 4, 5, 9, 13, 14, 16, 17, 20, 24, 25.* **Rates** *single ƒ400-ƒ575; double ƒ455-ƒ575; suite ƒ850-ƒ1,400; extra bed ƒ80; under-2s free; under-12s half price in parents' room.* **Credit** AmEx, DC, JCB, MC, all TC, V. **Map 2 D3**

This huge five-star hotel, situated right in the bullseye of Amsterdam, was first established in 1866 as a modest coffee house (no, not a coffeeshop). Since then, it has expanded enormously, and now incorporates over 469 rooms and two very impressive national monuments (one of which is the cooling, glass-roofed Winter Garden restaurant, a very exotic lunch location). Business types are well catered for, with 21 convention rooms holding up to 1,500 suits. You can even throw away all those post-meeting formalities in the tent-adorned Bedouin-style restaurant, lay back on a cushion and be served delicious desert delicacies. Breakfast is an extra ƒ35.

**Hotel services** *Babysitting. Beauty parlour. Conference rooms with Internet. Disabled access. Excursions. Gym. Lift. Non-smoking rooms. Parking. Shopping arcade. Restaurants. Water taxi service.* **Room services** *Air-conditioning. Coffee/tea-maker. Minibar. Radio. Safe. Voicemail, fax & modem. Trouser press.*

## Hotel Dikker & Thijs Fenice

*Prinsengracht 444 (626 7721/fax 625 8986). Tram 1, 2, 5.* **Rates** *single ƒ280-ƒ365; double ƒ315-ƒ450; under-12s free.* **Credit** AmEx, DC, JCB, MC, V. **Map 5 C5**

A bit of a landmark in the centre of town, this cosy little hotel makes a point of keeping things on a personal level. It's not too difficult, mind: there are only 26 rooms here, all spacious and classically styled, and some boast a canal view. Given the myriad business-heavy hotels in the city, it's refreshing to learn that what was one the conference room here has been turned into a penthouse suite with a lovely panoramic view. There is good French/Italian food in the hotel's fine restaurant.

**Hotel services** *Bar. Conference room. Fax. Internet. Lift. Limousine service. Private jetty. Restaurant. Safe. Secretarial services. Sport/fitness facilities nearby.* **Room services** *Babysitting. ISDN. Minibar.*

## Hotel Pulitzer

*Prinsengracht 315-31 (523 5235/fax 627 6753). Tram 13, 14, 17, 20.* **Rates** *single* ƒ405-ƒ610; *double* ƒ470-ƒ675; *suite* ƒ1,495; *extra bed* ƒ90; under-12s free. **Credit** AmEx, DC, JCB, MC, all TC, V. **Map 2 C3**

Certainly the most traditional of the five-stars, the centrally located Pulitzer comprises 24 seventeenth-century canal houses accommodating 224 rooms and a labyrinth of connecting corridors linking rooms, restaurants and the new terrace, situated in the central courtyard gardens. The cultural essence of the Pulitzer goes beyond its architecture: the art gallery holds regular exhibitions, while hidden in its foundations is an award-winning wine cellar holding some of the best plonk around. Moored a step away from the front entrance is the hotel's swish 1909 canal boat, there for the benefit of guests. Breakfast is an extra ƒ22,50-ƒ33.

**Hotel services** *Air-conditioning. Airline reservations. Babysitting. Business services. Conference rooms. Currency exchange. Fax. Garden. Lift. Limousine service. Non-smoking rooms. Restaurant. Valet parking.* **Room services** *Minibar. Safe. Voicemail & modem.*

## Jan Luyken Hotel

*Jan Luykenstraat 58 (573 0730/fax 676 3841). Tram 2, 3, 5, 12, 20.* **Rates** *single* ƒ290; *double* ƒ330-ƒ435. **Credit** AmEx, DC, JCB, MC, all TC, V. **Map 5 D6**

In a quiet location near Vondelpark and the museums, this friendly yet formal four-star caters for business types and the more mature, refined customer. Design-wise, there are echoes of the late nineteenth century throughout: in fact, it feels like nothing has changed, though the kitschy '70s bar stools and the recently added solarium with steam baths and Jacuzzi do give the game away a little. The hotel has 62 well-furnished rooms, each with a business desk.

**Hotel services** *Babysitting. Business services. Conference facilities. Currency exchange. Disabled access with assistance. Fax. Lift. Limousine service. Non-smoking rooms.* **Room services** *Minibar.*

## Park Hotel

*Stadhouderskade 25 (671 1222/fax 664 9455). Tram 1, 2, 5.* **Rates** (incl all taxes and service charges) *single* ƒ325-ƒ410; *double* ƒ350-ƒ435; *triple* ƒ450-ƒ535; *suite* ƒ625-ƒ695; *extra bed* ƒ75; *under-6s* free (excl breakfast); *6-12s* free (excl breakfast). **Credit** AmEx, DC, JCB, MC, all TC, V. **Map 5 D5**

The manager at the Park is adamant that his hotel is in the best location. Why? 'Because it's the best, that's why!' He is biased, naturally, but not completely mistaken. This smart 187-roomed four-star is close to the Vondelpark, just minutes from the museums and Leidseplein. There is a canal, too, just across a busy road (thankfully, double glazing stops the intrusion of traffic noise). The price doesn't include the American buffet breakfast, but does entitle you to free entrance for the nearby Holland Casino and the Diamond Factory.

**Hotel services** *Air conditioning. Babysitting. Business centre. Conference room. Currency exchange. Fax. Hairdresser. Internet. Lift. Limousine service. Parking. Restaurant. Shops.* **Room services** *Coffee/tea-maker. Hairdryer. Safe. Trouser press. Voicemail.*

## Schiller Hotel

*Rembrandtplein 26-36 (623 1660/fax 624 0098). Tram 4, 9, 14, 20.* **Rates** *single* ƒ245-ƒ270; *double* ƒ315-ƒ340. **Credit** AmEx, DC, MC, V. **Map 6 E4**

A touch of class in the otherwise touristy tack of the centre's famous Rembrandtplein, the four-star Schiller is a known hangout for artists and poets. They seem to enjoy the hotel's recent return to its original Jeugenstil style: indeed, the hotel is well worth checking out, having been beautifully refurbished in a largely successful bid to restore style and comfort. The work of artist Frits Schiller, the benefactor, is displayed throughout. *See chapter* **Cafés & Bars***, page 129.*

**Hotel services** *Business facilities. Lift. Restaurant.*

## Victoria Hotel Amsterdam

*Damrak 1-5 (623 4255/fax 625 2997). Tram 4, 9, 14, 16, 20, 24, 25.* **Rates** *single* ƒ420-ƒ475; *double* ƒ455-ƒ510; *suite* ƒ600-ƒ900; *extra bed* ƒ60; *executive rooms* extra ƒ50; under-12s free (maximum two children). **Credit** AmEx, DC, JCB, MC, all TC, V. **Map 2 D2**

Conveniently located opposite Centraal Station, this deluxe four-star hotel is a businessman's palace. There are many comforts to enjoy after a hard day's work, including an indoor pool and a health club. If that's too much effort, enjoy great views of Dam as you take coffee and cakes on Vic's Terrace (there is no Bob's Terrace, by the way). Breakfast is an additional ƒ29,50.

**Hotel services** *Air-conditioning. Babysitting. Beauty salon. Business facilities. Conference rooms. Currency exchange. Disabled access. Fax. Fitness centre. Gift shop. Hairdresser. Internet. Lift. Limousine service. Swimming pool. Restaurant. Terrace.* **Room services** *Minibar.*

# Moderate (ƒ150-ƒ300)

All Moderate hotels have a telephone in the rooms, and the vast majority also have a TV.

## Acro

*Jan Luykenstraat 44 (662 0526/fax 675 0811). Tram 2, 5, 20.* **Rates** *single* ƒ105-ƒ150; *double* ƒ140-ƒ195; babies free. **Credit** AmEx, DC, JCB, MC, all TC, V. **Map 5 D6**

A good, modern hotel, stylishly and comfortably refurbished and very handy for the museums and Leidseplein. The bar (open all hours) is pleasant, while free breakfast is served downstairs in the comfortable self-service dining room.

**Hotel services** *Bar. Beauty salon. Hairdresser.* **Room services** *Hairdryer.*

## Agora

*Singel 462 (627 2200/fax 627 2202). Tram 1, 2, 5.* **Rates** *single* ƒ105-ƒ180; *double* ƒ115-ƒ210. **Credit** AmEx, DC, MC, JCB, all TC, V. **Map 5 D4**

This small, historic canal house in the centre of town has only 16 rooms, which keeps things pretty personal: the family room in the loft, for example, has olde worlde beams and angular ceilings. The Agora is also stuffed with plants, hardly surprising as it's just by the city's flower market.

**Room services** *Room service.*

## Amstel Botel

*Oosterdokskade 2-4 (626 4247/fax 639 1952). Tram 1, 2, 5, 9, 13, 17, 20, 24, 25.* **Rates** *single* ƒ115-ƒ135; *double* ƒ133-ƒ153; *triple* ƒ165-ƒ190; under-4s free. **Credit** AmEx, DC, JCB, MC, all TC, V. **Map 3 E1**

Docked near Centraal Station, the Botel appears to be the cross-channel ferry that never got away: some of the similarities are P&O (plain and obvious). However, this roll on/nod off hotel is a three-star, and offers quiet and relative comfort at good prices. Half the rooms have a pleasant view of the river IJ, while the other half look over the central post office. The Botel doesn't sway much at all, so you should be able to hold down your breakfast (an extra ƒ11).

**Hotel services** *Breakfast room. Fax. Hairdryer. Parking.* **Room services** *Safe.*

## Amsterdam Wiechmann

*Prinsengracht 328-32 (626 3321/fax 626 8962). Tram 1, 2, 5, 7, 17, 20.* **Rates** *single* ƒ135-ƒ150; *double* ƒ200-ƒ250; *triple* ƒ275; *quad* ƒ300. **Credit** AmEx. **Map 5 C4**

If there was a section in this Guide devoted to the handful of traditional, old-fashioned bed and breakfast hotels in the city, the Wiechmann would be at the top. It's located in the better part of the canal district, near Anne Frankhuis. The friendly owner prides himself on his antiques, wooden beams and panelling, and his 'good old days' hospitality. A lovely hotel.

**Hotel services** *Lounge.*

The beautiful **Canal House Hotel**.

## Best Western AMS Hotel Terdam

*Tesselschadestraat 23 (612 6876/fax 683 8313). Tram
1, 2, 3, 5, 6, 12, 20.* **Rates** *single* ƒ180*; double* ƒ260*;
extra bed* ƒ64*; under-2s free.* **Credit** AmEx, DC, JCB, MC,
all TC, V. **Map 5 C5**
A bit of a mouthful to relay to a taxi driver, but probably
just about worth the effort. This recently renovated corner-
house just off Leidseplein offers both homely and formal
rooms. All 93 of them have private facilities, and are
coloured in soft reds and yellows. There are big family
rooms (ƒ390 per night) and six lovely apartments for up to
two adults and a child (on a monthly basis, ƒ240 per night
including breakfast).
**Hotel services** *Bar. Currency exchange. Fax. Internet.
Lift. Lounge.*

## Bridge Hotel

*Amstel 107-11 (623 7068/fax 624 1565). Tram 4, 6, 7,
9, 10, 20.* **Rates** *single* ƒ100*-* ƒ140*; double* ƒ160*-* ƒ185*;
triple* ƒ240*-* ƒ250*; babies free.* **Credit** AmEx, DC, JCB,
MC, all TC, V. **Map 3 E3**
Only three minutes from Waterlooplein, this 28-room hotel
is located on the Amstel in a quiet and historic neighbourhood. The hotel is so named because it overlooks the famous
'skinny bridge'. With its abundance of staff, it offers plenty
of individual attention to clients, and the prices are pretty
good, too.
**Hotel services** *Dry cleaning. Parking coupons.*

## Canal House Hotel

*Keizersgracht 148 (622 5182/fax 624 1317). Tram 13,
14, 17, 20.* **Rates** *single* ƒ215*-* ƒ280*; double* ƒ235*-* ƒ280*;
no under-12s.* **Credit** AmEx, DC, JCB, MC, ƒTC, V.
**Map 2 C3**
Staying in a canal house is one thing; staying in *the* Canal
House is an experience to be treasured. From the amazingly
ornate ceilings and beautiful antiques to the patchwork
quilts and evenings around the bar listening to Sinatra, the
whole experience slides you all the way back to the Golden
Age (though Frank probably wasn't around at the time). A
friendly family-run three-star, and great value for money
to boot.
**Hotel services** *Bar. Garden. Lift.* **Room services**
*Hairdryer.*

## Concert Inn

*De Lairessestraat 11 (305 7272/fax 305 7271). Tram
16.* **Rates** *single* ƒ120*-* ƒ200*; double* ƒ165*-* ƒ215*;
apartments & studios for weekly or monthly rental* ƒ100
*per day; extra bed* ƒ65*; babies free.* **Credit** AmEx, DC,
JCB, MC, $TC, V. **Map 5 D6**
This friendly, neat and extremely clean hotel near to the
museums seems to cater for everyone. There are spacious
apartments and studios, and all rooms have en suite facilities. The garden is huge – by Amsterdam standards, at

least – and there is also a double garage, allowing drivers
and bikers a worry-free night's sleep. Breakfast is 'as much
as you can handle'. The enthusiastic manager generously
offers a discount (5% in summer, 10% in winter) if you
show him this Guide.
**Hotel services** *Disabled access with assistance. Fax.
Garden. Lift. Safe.* **Room services** *Hairdryer. Hot
drinks bar. Trouser press.*

## Eden Hotel

*Amstel 144 (530 7878/fax 623 3267). Tram 4, 9, 14,
20.* **Rates** *single* ƒ195*-* ƒ275*; double* ƒ275*-* ƒ300*;
triple* ƒ325*-* ƒ350*; quad* ƒ375*-* ƒ425*; bridal suite* ƒ300*;
under-13s free.* **Credit** AmEx, DC, MC, V, all TC.
**Map 3 E3**
One of the biggest three-stars in the centre, the Eden has a
smart outlook and has very friendly and efficient service.
Beyond the general 'garden of Eden' theme, the hotel has a
couple of hidden surprises. There are four art guest rooms
in the building, one of which is heaven for insomniacs: 49
glow-in-the-dark sheep have been painted on the ceiling to
help you nod off. But if you still can't sleep, then at least
you'll find plenty to do in the wee small hours in nearby
Rembrandtplein.
**Hotel services** *Bar/Brasserie. Business centre.
Conference room. Disabled access. Exchange. Hairdryer.
Laundry. Lift. Photo service.* **Room services**
*Babysitting. Video.*

## Hotel de Filosoof

*Anna van den Vondelstraat 6 (683 3013/fax 685 3750).
Tram 1, 6/bus 171, 172.* **Rates** *single* ƒ125-155*; double*
ƒ155*-* ƒ185*; triple* ƒ185-235*; quad* ƒ225-295*.* **Credit**
AmEx, MC, V. **Map 4 B6**
A hotel geared towards the thoughtful: each of the rooms has
a theme dedicated to one of history's great philosophers.
There is an interesting Plato room and a beautiful Japanese
room, while the Eros room is a virginal white bridal suite.
Ponder over your eggs in the small breakfast room, which
also doubles as a library.
**Hotel services** *Bar. Room service.*

## Hotel de Munck

*Achtergracht 3 (623 6283/fax 620 6647). Tram 4, 6, 7,
10, 20.* **Rates** *single* ƒ85*-* ƒ115*; double* ƒ125*-* ƒ165*; triple*
ƒ165*-* ƒ210*; quad* ƒ240*-* ƒ300*.* **Credit** AmEx, DC, MC, all
TC, V. **Map 6 F4**
A captain's canal house from the old East India Company
days restored back to its original style, with traditional furnishings and quaint narrow stairs. Original, that is, until you
notice the album covers spread on the walls in the '60s-style
restaurant, where you can eat your brekky to the sound of
Nat King Cole or Elvis. The '60s theme spreads to some of
the rooms, too, in the form of kitschy neon lamps and clocks.
In the summer, take advantage of the lovely breakfast garden. A very pleasant hotel.
**Hotel services** *Bar. Garden. Hairdryer.* **Room
services** *Radio.*

## Hotel Prinsen

*Vondelstraat 36-38 (616 2323/fax 616 6112). Tram 1,
2, 3, 5, 6, 12, 20.* **Rates** *single* ƒ130*-* ƒ175*; double* ƒ175-
ƒ225*; triple* ƒ225*-* ƒ295*; quad* ƒ275*-* ƒ350*; extra bed* ƒ55*.*
**Credit** AmEx, DC, JCB, MC, all TC, V. **Map 5 C6**
The Prinsen brags a friendly atmosphere in a nicely renovated building next to the Vondelpark. It's in an excellent
location for peace and quiet, while there's plenty of action
just minutes away at Leidseplein. All rooms have en suite
facilities and there is a lovely secluded garden in which to
get away from it all.
**Hotel services** *Bar. Garden. Lift.* **Room services**
*Coffee/tea-maker. Cot (*ƒ15*). Hairdryer.*

## Hotel Prinsenhof

*Prinsengracht 810 (623 1772/fax 638 3368). Tram 4.*
**Rates** *single ƒ85; double ƒ125-ƒ175; triple ƒ175-ƒ210;*
*quad ƒ210-ƒ290; babies free.* **Credit** AmEx, MC, ƒTC, V.
**Map 6 E4**

A charming canal house. The ten rooms are decorated in traditional old Amsterdam green – very snappy – while the friendly staff are flexible with check-out times and the like. Good value, this one, and scrupulously clean to boot.
**Hotel services** *Fax. Safe.*

## Hotel Washington

*Frans van Mierisstraat 10 (679 7453/fax 673 4435).*
*Tram 3, 5, 12, 16, 20, 24.* **Rates** *single ƒ90-ƒ120; double*
*ƒ120-ƒ225.* **Credit** AmEx, DC, MC, all TC, V. **Map 5 D6**
In a quiet street near the Museumplein, this small, clean and intimate hotel is popular with classical music lovers and visiting musicians playing at the nearby Concertgebouw.

## Owl Hotel

*Roemer Visscherstraat 1 (618 9484/fax 618 9441).*
*Tram 1, 3, 6, 12.* **Rates** *single ƒ115-ƒ155; double ƒ150-*
*ƒ205; triple ƒ195-ƒ250.* **Credit** AmEx, DC, JCB, MC, V.
**Map 5 C5**

A small and super-friendly family-run hotel. It's very handy for the Vondelpark, which is at the end of the garden, and the museums. All the rooms have en suite facilities. The hotel name comes from room number 282820.
**Hotel services** *Babysitting. Bar. Disabled access with*
*assistance. Fax. Garden. Internet. Laundry. Lift. Safe.*

## Parkzicht

*Roemer Visscherstraat 33 (618 1954/fax 618 0897).*
*Tram 1, 2, 3, 5, 6, 12, 20.* **Rates** *single ƒ65-ƒ90; double*
*ƒ120-ƒ160.* **Credit** AmEx, MC, all TC, V. **Map 5 C5**
This is a simple, quiet hotel close to the park and museums. The Parkzicht has an authentic Dutch feel to it, helped no end by the comfortable furnishings.

## Seven Bridges

*Reguliersgracht 31 (623 1329). Tram 16, 24, 25.* **Rates**
*single ƒ120-ƒ200; double ƒ140-ƒ300.* **Credit** AmEx, MC,
all TC, V. **Map 6 E4**

A stylish little hotel near the viewpoint of the famous seven bridges. Some of the furnishings in the 11 rooms are real treasures: how about combing your hair in a Napoleonic mirror, while your feet sink into a hand-woven Russian carpet? The lack of a dining area means breakfast in bed. What a shame.
**Hotel services** *Safe.* **Room services** *Radio.*

## Toren

*Keizersgracht 164 (622 6352/fax 626 9705). Tram 13,*
*14, 17, 20.* **Rates** *single ƒ85-ƒ270; double ƒ120-ƒ295;*
*triple ƒ230-ƒ250; quad ƒ250-ƒ270; suite ƒ400; under-12s*
half price. **Credit** AmEx, DC, MC, all TC, V. **Map 2 C3**
A former prime minister's canal house turned love-nest, this friendly hotel definitely has a romantic edge: there are bridal suites with double Jacuzzis and Laura Ashley-style rooms, all with en suite facilities. The hotel retains its dignity and tradition in the seventeenth-century bar and breakfast room.
**Hotel services** *Bar. Conference room. Dining room.*
*Fax.* **Room services** *Coffee/tea-maker. Hairdryer.*
*Minibar. Modem. Room service. Safe.*

# Budget (under ƒ150)

## De Admiraal

*Herengracht 563 (626 2150/fax 623 4625). Tram 4, 9,*
*14, 20.* **Rates** *single ƒ95-ƒ135; double ƒ120-ƒ175.* **Credit**
AmEx DC, MC, ƒTC, V. **Map 6 E4**

A friendly and homely hotel close to the Rembrandtplein. Room six has four beds and a stunning view of the lovely Reguliersgracht and Herengracht. The hearty Dutch

breakfasts are ƒ10. However, the hotel is normally closed from mid-November to mid-March, so if you want to book during these times, call well ahead.
**Hotel services** *Hairdryer. Telephone.* **Room services**
*Safe. TV.*

## Arena

*'s-Gravesandestraat 51 (694 7444/663 2649). Tram 3,*
*6, 9, 10, 14/Metro Weesperplein.* **Rates** *double ƒ90-ƒ115;*
*triple ƒ120-ƒ150; quad ƒ160-ƒ200; four/six/eight-bed*
*apartments ƒ32,50-ƒ37,50 per person; large dormitories*
*ƒ20-ƒ27,50 per person; under-12s free; linen rental for*
*dorms ƒ5.* **Key deposit** *ƒ10.* **Map 7 G3**
More of a youth and tourist culture centre with lodgings than a hotel, the Arena is a great budget option. It's housed in an old listed convent next to Oosterpark (the Reverend Mother would turn in her grave if she heard the live music programme going down in the old church), with a swanky restaurant and bar serving good food, and even an on-site car park. All the rooms and dorms are basic but neat and clean, and, while the Arena isn't exactly centrally located, the plethora of funky youngsters more than compensates in terms of atmosphere. *See chapter* **Music: Rock, Roots &**
**Jazz,** *p207* for details of the on-site club and bar.
**Hotel services** *Bar. Currency exchange. Disabled*
*access. Fax. Gift shop. Internet. Lift. Live music. Lobby*
*garden. Pool table. Restaurant. Safe. Tourist information.*

## Euphemia Hotel

*Fokke Simonzstraat 1-9 (tel/fax 622 9045). Tram 16, 24,*
*25.* **Reception open** 8am-11pm daily. **Rates** *single ƒ45-*
*ƒ120; double ƒ75-ƒ180; triple ƒ27,50-ƒ60 per person; quad*
*ƒ22,50-ƒ50 per person; breakfast ƒ7,50.* **Credit** AmEx,
DC, MC, V. **Map 6 E5**
On a quiet side street in a handy location, the gay-friendly Euphemia offers cheap and comfortable accommodation for young travellers. The hotel has a relaxed atmosphere – there's a cosy lounge where you can hang out in front of the TV and video – and the breakfast costs around ƒ6. Check its website at *www.channels.nl/amsterdam/euphemia.html* for more information.
**Hotel services** *Disabled access. Fax. Internet. Safe.*
**Room services** *TV in most rooms.*

## Hans Brinker Budget

*Kerkstraat 136-138 (622 0687/fax 638 2060). Tram 1,*
*2, 5, 16, 24, 25.* **Rates** *single ƒ78-ƒ90; double ƒ122-ƒ148;*
*dormitory ƒ43-ƒ50,50.* **Credit** AmEx, DC, MC, all TC, V.
**Map 6 E4**
This centrally located hotel's award-winning advert campaign offers free use of the fire escape in emergencies, which, while not exactly reassuring, may give you some indication that this is not a dull place. Hans Brinker Budget is definitely big – 530 beds – but everything in the hotel is well-maintained and clean, and staff are friendly. Enjoy happy hour in the bar, 5-6pm daily.
**Hotel services** *Café. Disabled access with assistance.*
*Disco. Kitchen. Lift.*

## De Harmonie

*Prinsengracht 816 (625 0174/fax 622 8021). Tram 4.*
**Rates** *single ƒ75-ƒ80; double ƒ110-ƒ140; triple ƒ150-*
*ƒ200; reduced rates for children.* **Credit** AmEx, DC, JCB,
MC, V. **Map 5 D5**
The friendly, up-front Irish owner of De Harmonie, Thereza Martin, describes her good-value hotel – a canal house, with ten clean and comfy rooms – as 'a bit of a laugh: it's like Fawlty Towers'. She enjoys accommodating groups who've come over for stag parties and the like, though anybody who enjoys having a good time is more than welcome and she can offer plenty of advice on where to enjoy the thrills of Amsterdam. Breakfast can be served in bed if you can't move in the morning.
**Hotel services** *Hairdryer. Ironing facilities. Safe.*

### Hotel Wilhelmina

*Koninginneweg 167-169 (662 5467/fax 679 2296).
Tram 2, 16.* **Rates** *single f55-f125; double f115-f155;
extra bed f35.* **Credit** AmEx, DC, MC, TC, V.
With unlimited tea and coffee throughout the day, this very
comfortable hotel is a great base for visiting museums and
spending hard currency in the nearby elegant shopping area.
The culturally savvy staff can advise you on places to go
during your stay in the city.
**Room services** *Radio. TV.*

### King Hotel

*Leisdekade 85-86 (624 9603/620 7277). Tram 1, 2, 5, 6,
7, 10, 17, 20.* **Rates** *single f65-f75; double f115-f130;
triple f165-f175; quad f185-f200; five-bed rooms f220-
f250.* **Credit** MC, V. **Map 5 C5**
A bit of a bargain, this one: a budget hotel in a canal house
with a touch of historical value. The King Hotel is the previous home of Mata Hari, executed in Paris during the war
for her espionage exploits. Nowadays, the hotel has a nice
ambience: it's basic but excellently located, and offers a
hearty buffet breakfast.
**Hotel services** *Safe. Telephone.*

### PC Hooft

*PC Hooftstraat 63 (662 7107/fax 675 8961). Tram 2, 3,
5, 12.* **Rates** *single f75-f85; double f110-f120.* **Credit**
MC, all TC, V. **Map 5 D5**
Plenty of international visitors stay at the cosy 16-room PC
Hooft, and the regulars just keep on coming back, which is
usually a good sign. It's probably something to do with the
hotel's proximity to Vondelpark, the museums and the super-
posh shops on this street, though the cheerful atmosphere
and top breakfasts might also have something to do with it.
Good value.
**Hotel services** *Breakfast room. Telephone.*

### Van Ostade

*Van Ostadestraat 123 (679 3452/fax 671 5213). Tram
3, 12, 24, 25.* **Rates** *single f80; double f90-f150.*
**Map 6 F6**
This two-wheel-friendly hotel in the Pijp offers bicycle hire,
shelter for motorbikes and two car spaces. The rooms are
clean and basic, and there is also a real cosy communal area.
The hotel is in a really nice area of town, near the Albert
Cuyp market.
**Hotel services** *Telephone.* **Room services** *TV.*

# Camping out

There are a number of camping grounds in and
around Amsterdam; we list four, all recommended by the VVV. Two are just a 15-minute
bus ride north from the centre, with the other
two further out and in more rural settings.
Remember that though the climate is changeable, you can always hire a cabin if it rains.
During the summer, the weather is reliably mild.
Vliegenbos and Zeeburg are classified as youth
campsites, while the other two are more family-
orientated campsites with separate areas for
youth camping.

### Gaasper Camping Amsterdam

*Loosdrechtdreef 7 (696 7326/fax 696 9369). Metro
Gaasperplas/bus 59, 60, 158.* **Reception open** *June-
Aug 9am-10pm daily; Sept-May 9am-8pm daily.* **Rates**
*per person per night f6,50; under-12s f3,50; car f6;
camper f11; caravan f9; motorbike f3; tent f7-f9;
electrics f4,50; hot showers f1,50; dog f3,75.*
This campsite is in the south-east of greater Amsterdam,
easily accessible by either Metro or bus. It's on the edge
of the Gaasperplas park, which has a lake with a watersports centre and facilities for canoeing, swimming (for
children, too), rowing and sailing, plus a surfing school.
Ground facilities include a shop, café, bar and restaurant,
a terrace, launderette and service station for fuel.

### Het Amsterdamse Bos

*Kleine Noorddijk 1, 1432 CC Aalsmeer (641 6868/fax
640 2378). Bus 171.* **Reception open** *Apr-15 Oct
9am-12.30pm daily.* **Rates** *per person per night f8,50;
under-4s free; 4-12s f4,25; car f4,25; caravan f6,50;
camper f10,75; motorbike f2,25; tent f5,50; electricity
for caravan/camper f3,50.*
The site is several miles from Amsterdam, a long and
dreary cycle ride. However, half-hourly bus services for
the 30-minute trip into town stop 300 metres from the
grounds, which are on the southern edge of the beautiful

Amsterdamse Bos, a large park with facilities for horse-
riding and watersports. Wooden cabins sleeping up to
four people can be hired for f60 per night. These are
equipped with stoves and mattresses, but you will have
to provide your own cooking utensils and sleeping bags.
Site facilities include phones, a shop, a bar and a restaurant, lockers, and bike hire in July and August. In high
season, the campsite has its own express bus service one-
way to Centraal Station (f5).

### Vliegenbos

*Meeuwenlaan 138 (636 8855/fax 632 2723). Bus 32,
36, 110, 111, 114/night bus 73.* **Reception open**
*Apr-June, Sept 9am-9pm daily; July-Aug 9am-10pm
daily.* **Rates** *under-3s free; 3-14s f8,80; over-14s
f13,75; car plus person f19,25; motorbike plus person
f16,50; car f11; camper plus two people f33-f38,50; log
cabin with up to four people f77; groups of max 12
people f225. Stays of less than three nights extra f1.
Launderette wash & dry f16,50. All prices incl
showers, tent pitch and tax.*
The grounds are close to the River IJ to the north of
Amsterdam, a five-minute bus journey from Centraal
Station. Facilities include a bar, a restaurant, a safe at
reception, and a small shop with exchange service. Cabins
sleeping up to four people cost f63 per night.

### Zeeburg

*Zuider Ijdijk 20 (694 4430/fax 694 6238). Tram
14/Bus 22/night bus 97.* **Reception open** *April-May
9am-1pm daily; June-Aug 8am-11pm daily.* **Rates** *per
person per night f6,50; under-5s free; 5-12s f2,50; tent
for 3-4 people f3,50; motorbike f3,50; car f6; camper
f10,50; electricity f4; hot showers f1,50.*
Facilities at these grounds, just north of the River IJ,
include a bar, a small restaurant, lockers, a shop and bike
hire. Log cabins sleeping two or four people cost f20 per
person including bedding. There is also a dorm with 24
beds for f15 per person (including launderette but
excluding bedding). Be sure to reserve for the cabins in
high season.

*Rock the boat on the **Amstel Botel**. See page 93.*

## Winston Hotel

*Warmoestraat 123-9 (623 1380/fax 639 2308). Tram 4, 9, 16, 20, 24, 25.* **Rates** *single ƒ73-ƒ116; double ƒ95-ƒ149; triple ƒ115-ƒ183; eight-person room ƒ44 per person; under-6s free; 6-12s half price.* **Credit** AmEx, DC, MC, all TC, V. **Map 2 D2**

It's impossible to get any more central than the Winston: it's right in there with the nightlife on the edge of the Red Light District. The hotel has its own entertainment, too, with a 24-hour bar for guests, and live music next door in the Winston Kingdom bar. It's obviously not the quietest of places, but it is friendly and spacious. There's also a forever-changing collection of exciting local art displayed throughout the hotel, and nine of the 66 rooms have their own sponsored arty themes. Breakfast costs an extra ƒ10.

**Hotel services** *Bar. Café. Conference/banquet room. Disabled facilities. Fax. Lift. Safe. Telephone. VCR.* **Room services** *TV (ƒ10 per night).*

## Hostels

The whole youth hostel scene in Amsterdam is a very laid-back, please-yourself affair: you just pay and enjoy. In fact, there are only two hostels (NJHF Hostels) listed below that require a valid IYHF membership. This can easily be obtained for an extra ƒ5 per night: you get a stamp on a IYHF card each night, and after six nights you can trade this in for a membership. Some hostels close for a couple of hours in the day and many impose a curfew.

### Bob's Youth Hostel

*Nieuwezijds Voorburgwal 92 (623 0063/fax 675 6446). Tram 1, 2, 5, 13, 17, 20.* **Rates** *dormitories ƒ24 per person; apartments for 2 or 4 persons ƒ150-ƒ250 (incl TV, kitchen, shower).* **Map 2 D3**

Many a backpacker seems willing to sacrifice a bit of privacy – almost all dorms, this one – for the low prices and heart of the city location of Bob's. Most of the dorms are mixed (though some are women only), and all have in-room showers. There's a friendly café/bar open from 8am to 3am, where you can bore everyone with your Eurorail stories. Curfew is at 3am, and sheets are included in the price.

**Hotel services** *Bar. Lockers (ƒ25 deposit).*

### Flying Pig Hostels

**Flying Pig Downtown** *Nieuwendijk 100 (420 6822/fax 428 0811). Tram 1, 2, 3, 5, 13, 17, 20.* **Flying Pig Palace** *Vossiusstraat 46-47 (400 4187/fax 470 5159). Tram 2, 5, 20.* **Reception open** 24 hrs daily (both branches). **Reservations** for more than four persons via head office (421 0583/fax 421 0802). **Rates (Downtown)** *double ƒ110; quad ƒ36,50-ƒ39,50 per person; six-person room ƒ32-ƒ35,50 per person; eight-person room ƒ30-ƒ34 per person; dormitory ƒ24,50-ƒ25 per person; no children.* **(Palace)** *double ƒ110; quad ƒ33-ƒ36,50 per person; six-person room ƒ31,50-ƒ35 per person; eight-person room ƒ30-ƒ33,50 per person; dormitory ƒ24,50-ƒ25 per person.* **Credit** MC, V. **Map 2 D2 (Downtown)/ Map 5 C6 (Palace)**

The Flying Pig (on the Net at *www.flyingpig.nl*) has two hostels in Amsterdam, one on the edge of the Vondelpark and one conveniently situated right by Centraal Station. Both are clean and laid back establishments, and are run by an enthusiastic crew who themselves are seasoned travellers and therefore understand the needs of the thousands of backpackers who pass through their doors each year. Both hostels offer a fully equipped kitchen and good tourist information facilities, and almost all rooms have showers and WCs. There is no curfew, but both hostels have lively on-site bars open to guests only if you don't want to go out. A good deal all round.

**Hotel services** *Bar. E-mail. Kitchens. Lockers. Safe. TV with filmnet. Tourist information.*

### International Budget Hotel

*Leidsegracht 76 (624 2784/fax 626 1839). Tram 1, 2, 5.* **Reception open** 9am-11pm daily. **Rates** *double ƒ75-ƒ150; quad ƒ25-ƒ40 per person.* **Credit** AmEx, DC, MC, V. **Map 5 C4**

There's nothing really flashy about this hostel – save the traditional beamed ceilings – but it comes into its own as the only inexpensive youth hostel to offer a canal view, and a nice one at that. The general set-up promotes a relaxed and familiar atmosphere: smoking is permitted in communal areas, so you don't have to be in the seedy centre of town to enjoy some of Amsterdam's finest. There's no curfew, either, which makes a night on the town that much easier.

**Hotel services** *Drinks machine. Fax. Safe. TV lounge with in-house movies.* **Room services** *Lockers.*

## Meeting Point

*Warmoesstraat 14 (tel/fax 627 7499). Tram 4, 9, 16, 20, 24, 25/Metro Centraal Station.* **Reception open** 24 hrs daily. **Rates** *four-six bed dorms ƒ35-ƒ40 per person; eight-18 bed dorms ƒ25-ƒ35 per person (incl linen).* **Map 2 D2**

An excellent location for young budget travellers seeking a good weekend blast in the city. The Meeting Point offers all you need to experience the fun and freedom of downtown Amsterdam: the spliff-friendly bar is open round the clock, and there is even a smart drugs shop next door. The hostel is basic but cheap, with breakfast an extra ƒ5.

**Hotel services** *Bar. Safe deposit boxes. Showers. TV.*

## NJHC Hostels

**Stadsdoelen** *Kloveniersburgwal 97 (624 6832/fax 639 1035). Tram 4, 9, 14, 16, 20, 24, 25.* **Vondelpark** *Zandpad 5 (589 8996/fax 589 8955). Tram 1, 2, 5, 6, 7, 10, 20.* **Receptions open** 24hrs daily. **Rates (Stadsdoelen)** *dormitories ƒ24-ƒ40,50.* **(Vondelpark)** *single ƒ67-ƒ77; double ƒ80-ƒ100; triple or quad ƒ148-ƒ168; five-/six-bed rooms ƒ195-ƒ219; dormitories ƒ32,50-ƒ36,50.* Non-members extra ƒ5 per night for both hostels; prices incl breakfast & tourist tax. **Credit** MC, all TC, V. **Map 2 D3 (Stadsdoelen)/Map 5 C6 (Vondelpark)**

The Stadsdoelen branch of the NJHC sits in the steamy cauldron of the very central Red Light District, which can be fun, but if you prefer tree-climbing to window-shopping, go for the more relaxed location at the Vondelpark. Both are spotless, friendly, and open 24 hours, but the latter is in a spacious renovated lovely listed building. There's a new block and a group room annexe, together with amenities including a brasserie, restaurants and gardens, creating a complete mecca for the budget traveller. The Vondelpark hostel gets full marks, too, for accommodating up to 18 disabled people.

**Hotel services (Stadsdoelen)** *Bar. Bus booking. Laundry. Internet. Luggage lockers. Safe. Self-catering facilities. TV.* **Hotel services (Vondelpark)** *Bar/Brasserie. Disabled access. Fax. Internet. Lift. Lockers. Safe. TV.*

## Young Budget Hotel Kabul

*Warmoesstraat 38-42 (623 7158/fax 620 0869). Tram 4, 9, 14, 16, 20, 24, 25.* **Reception open** 24 hrs daily. **Rates** *single ƒ70-ƒ95; double ƒ95-ƒ135; triple ƒ125-ƒ150; four-16 bed dorms ƒ27-ƒ40 per person.* **Credit** AmEx, DC, MC, V. **Map 2 D2**

Five minutes' walk from Centraal Station and located next to the Red Light District, this hostel is a no-frills basic budget option. It's a bit dark and dingy, but is nonetheless functional and right in the thick of Amsterdam's nightlife. The hotel has a bar for those who can't be bothered going out, and there's no curfew.

**Hotel services** *Bar. Breakfast room. Lockers. Pool table. Telephone.*

## Private accommodation/B&B

The B&B ideal is growing in the Netherlands, but is still not as popular – nor as widespread – as in Britain. Arguably the best way to track down a B&B is through either **Holiday Link** or **Simon's Euro Service**, both of which also deal with private accommodation and long-term stays. It's a good idea to check details and availability well in advance of your stay: private accommodation can get very busy, especially during peak season and holidays.

## Holiday Link

*Postbus 70-155, 9704 AD Groningen (050 313 4545/fax 050 313 3177).* **Open** 9.30am-4pm Mon-Fri.

An organisation dealing with B&B and budget accommodation. Its annual guide, *B&B and Budget Accommodation in Holland*, is available in bookshops, VVV tourist offices, by post or from its website (*www.holidaylink.com*) for ƒ10, and has 600 pages on all types of accommodation, from B&Bs to worldwide holiday home swaps.

*Comfort and history at* **Seven Bridges**. *See page 96.*

## Marcel van Woerkom

*Leidsestraat 87 (tel/fax 622 9834). Tram 1, 2, 5.* **Rates**
*ƒ100-ƒ125 per person.* **Map 5 D4**
Designer and graphic artist Marcel van Woerkom started
letting his rooms out to help pay the bills. Now, 28 years on,
they're all paid, but Marcel carries on the business in his now
lovingly restored and self-designed home. Marcel offers four
en suite rooms in his museum-piece of a home for two, three
or four people sharing. He says he is a people person and
likes to create a home-from-home atmosphere for his guests,
including sound tourist tips and information. We think he
does enough to warrant not providing breakfast.

## Simon's Euro Service

*Singel 417 (tel/fax 618 9435). Tram 1, 2, 5.* **Open** 10am-
6pm Mon-Fri. **Map 5 D4**
Simon says he has between 50 and 100 B&Bs in Amsterdam,
and 2,500 in total throughout the Netherlands; prices start
at around ƒ80 per person. It doesn't stop there, though: the
organisation can arrange your entire short break, including
board, trips, tours and railcards. The staff will even get you
a car and sort out a route through Holland, linking you up
with B&Bs on the way. They can also arrange apartments
and hotels for you. Book well in advance for all services.

## Flat-hunting

Looking for a flat in Amsterdam can be the biggest
challenge you will encounter in this four-storey
sardine can of a city. To its credit, this is a beautiful place to live in, but unfortunately everybody
else thinks so too and wants, like you, to live
smack bang in the centre of town. Basically, to get
a flat, you need friends, money and loads of luck.

In Amsterdam, there are two main price sectors:
below ƒ700 per month, and above ƒ700 per month.
Anything above ƒ700 is considered free sector
housing and can be found through housing agencies or by checking daily newspapers (in particular, the Wednesday, Thursday and Saturday
editions of *De Telegraaf* and *De Volkskrant*), and
every Thursday in the ads paper *Via Via*. Both
these methods can be pricey: people tend to ask for
a lot of money when advertising; with agencies,
you'll need to pay a hefty commission and high
rent but you'll usually get a place. Flatshares are
not really the done thing here.

Under ƒ700, there are two main choices. If you
have lived in Amsterdam for over two years (registered at an official address) or you study here and
have a resident's permit, then you can register with
one of the three main non-commercial housing cooperatives, **Woonwerk** (524 4566), **Archipel**
(511 8911) and **Spectrum** (489 0085). For a charge
of ƒ35, these agencies will supply you with a bul-
letin giving information on available accommodation. If you see something you like you can apply
for it, but you won't be the only one and – more
likely than not – the others applying will have been
on the list much longer than you. This can, of
course, take a very long time. The other alternative, apart from a cardboard box in Leidseplein, is
to register with one of the many non-profit housing agencies that hold regular lotteries. This may

sound bizarre, but you do have a good chance of
eventually obtaining a room in a house with this
system (for more details, contact **ASW
Kamerbureau** on 523 0130). When all's said and
done, though, by far the best way to find a place
here is by word of mouth.

## Apartment rentals

### Amsterdam Apartments

*Kromme Waal 32 (626 5930/fax 622 9544). Tram 4, 9,
16, 20, 24, 25.* **Open** 9am-5pm Mon-Sat. **Map 3 E2**
Amsterdam Apartments has details of furnished, self-contained flats in central areas of town. Rates start from ƒ700
a week for a one-person studio or one-bed flat. The minimum
let is for one week and the maximum two months.

### Apartment Services AS

*Maasstraat 96 (672 3013/1840/fax 676 4679). Tram 4,
12, 25.* **Open** 9.30am-5pm Mon-Fri.
This reliable, friendly agency deals with a wide variety of
mainly furnished accommodation, from simple short let flats
whose owners are away, to apartments and whole houses.
Rentals start at around ƒ1,000 per month and a minimum
let of three months is usual. There is a registration fee of ƒ50,
but the bureau will refund this after taking one month's rent
as commission.

### Intercity Room Service

*Van Ostadestraat 348 (675 0064). Tram 3, 4.* **Open**
10am-5pm Mon-Fri. **Map 6 F6**
The place to try if you are in Amsterdam and require something – anything – very quickly. This agency specialises in
flatshares, but occasionally offers entire apartments too; flatshares in the centre of town cost from ƒ400 per month, with
self-contained flats from ƒ1,000. The minimum stay is one
day, and the agency charges two weeks' rent as commission.

### Riverside Apartments

*Amstel 138 (627 9797/fax 627 9858). Tram 4, 9, 14,
20.* **Open** 9am-5pm Mon-Sat; by appointment other
times. **Credit** AmEx, DC, MC, V. **Map 3 E3**
These privately owned, luxurious flats in central Amsterdam
cost ƒ6,000 per month for two people, or, for a minimum of
six months, ƒ2,500 per month. Occasionally there are flats
available for three to four people, costing from ƒ7,500 per
month. Services include telephone, fax, laundry, linen and a
cleaner. Apartments are available for a minimum of one week.

## Registration

To register in the city, first you have to go to the
**Dienst Vreemdelingenpolitie** (Aliens' Police
Service), and register at the immigration desk. If
you would like to register for a house from the city
council, then you need a housing permit which
means you have to meet certain criteria (for example, you need to show that you are living, working
or studying in the city). If you meet these criteria
you can then register with the **Stedelijke
Woning Dienst** (City Housing Service). Bank on
a very long wait.

### Dienst Vreemdelingenpolitie

*Johan Huizingalaan 757 (559 6214). Tram 2/Bus 19, 63.*
**Open** 8am-5pm Mon-Fri.

### Stedelijke Woning Dienst

*Frederik Hendrikstraat 47 (581 0800). Tram 3, 10.* **Open**
9am-noon Mon; 9am-noon, 5-7pm, Thur. **Map 1 A3**

# Restaurants

*Pass up on a pie, say 'bye' to a burger, and enjoy the quality and variety of Amsterdam's excellent eateries.*

The term 'Dutch cuisine' usually raises a laugh or two. With a reputation built on the use of the bare essentials – meat, veg and cheese products – and the shunning of 'taboo' herbs and spices, Dutch food has always served but one purpose: to fill bellies. Such a stereotype is born from Calvinism, the scapegoat for all things Dutch. Combine this with the (wrong) assumption that a flat, grey land must surely offer flat, grey food and you soon see why the country is not exactly famed for its cuisine.

Yet you only have to pop into the Rijksmuseum for the real story. As far back as the Golden Age, bulimia had its grip on the country: take, for example, the works of Jan Steen and Adriaen van Ostade, whose paintings often depict the traditional 'fat kitchen' in their full richness and colour. As always, there's a flipside to the coin, namely an equal number of paintings showing a 'thin kitchen', where the calm and holy occupants and their victuals would give Kate Moss a run for her money. Yep, the Dutch, just like the rest of us, know there's nothing better than a huge blowout to put paid to a bit of abstention.

Time and colonialism have massaged the Dutch palate. As the Occupied under Napoleonic rule, they were, thankfully, seduced by the more refined southern cuisine, an influence which is still strongly felt in the city's more highly regarded restaurants. And as the Occupiers, the Dutch took on the spicy cuisine of Indonesia. Add to the mix the influx of workers after World War II, which gave birth to a multitude of Chinese, Philippine, Middle Eastern and Mediterranean eating places, and, more recently, travellers returning from India and Thailand, and the result is that this small corner of the world has finally provided the city with true culinary diversity. Today, the gourmand galloping through Amsterdam would hardly know the trouble the country has gone to in order to reach its high culinary standards.

In addition to the many restaurants listed below, there are many cafés serving decent – even inspired – food at reasonable prices; for these, *see* chapter **Cafés & Bars**, *page 122-134*. For other restaurants and cafés, *see chapter* **Gay & Lesbian**, *page 189*.

*Dine in civilised comfort at* **Café Roux**. *See page 109.*

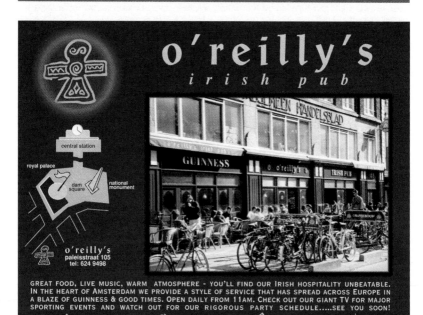

## LEISURELY DINING

Dining in Amsterdam is a laid-back affair, though the uninitiated should note that the Dutch tend to eat early – between 6.30pm and 9pm – with most kitchens shut by 10pm. However, once the meal is ordered, customers are usually welcome to linger over coffee and dessert until after midnight. Bills include 17.5 per cent tax and a 15 per cent service charge, though it's customary to leave some small change as well, if the service merits it. If you have any special requirements, such as high chairs or disabled access, it's best to phone the restaurant before setting out. For more places to take the kids, *see chapter* **Children**, *page 171.*

Credit cards are only accepted where specified. The average price listed below is based on the cost of a main course or equivalent, except where the restaurant specialises in set menu deals: these are marked as such. The prices listed should only be used as a guideline. If you want to find a restaurant in a particular area, *see box* **Area index**, *page 121.*

## City Landmarks

### 1e Klas

*Centraal Station, Line 2B (623 0131). Tram 1, 2, 4, 5, 9, 13, 16, 17, 20, 24, 25.* **Open** 5-11pm daily. **Average** ƒ45. **Credit** AmEx, DC, EC, MC, V. **Map 2 D1**
The former Grand Café brasserie for first-class commuters is now open to all who can afford its French cuisine… or perhaps just a coffee. Its high ceiling and original art nouveau interior can take you back to the turn of the century when Centraal Station was first built. Very Euro.
*Disabled access.*

### Café Americain

*Leidseplein 28 (624 5322). Tram 1, 2, 5, 6, 7, 10, 20.* **Open** 7am-1am daily (non-guest breakfast from 10am); *kitchen* 11am-11.30pm. **Average** ƒ45; *breakfast buffet* ƒ31,50. **Credit** AmEx, DC, EC, MC, V. **Map 5 C5**
The glorious art deco interior of the Café Americain is a listed monument decorated with murals and marbled lampshades: Mata Hari is said to have held her wedding reception here. Now, theatrical personalities, the theatre crowd and tourists meet under the high, vaulted roof or on the terrace.
*Disabled access.*

### Bodega Keyzer

*Van Baerlestraat 96 (671 1441). Tram 3, 5, 12, 16.*
Open noon-midnight daily. **Average** ƒ45. **Credit** AmEx, DC, EC, MC, V. **Map 5 D6**
Located near the Concertgebouw, this restaurant caters to concertgoers who can afford its extravagant prices. Don't try to order from a concert violinist, who often has the same style sense as the waiters. Fine fish, especially the sole meunière.
*Disabled access.*

### Brasserie Schiller

*Rembrandtplein 26-36 (554 0700).Tram 4, 9, 14, 16, 20, 24, 25.* **Open** 11am-11pm Mon-Thur, Sun; 11am-midnight Fri, Sat. **Average** ƒ35. **Credit** AmEx, DC, EC, MC, V. **Map 6 E4**
Part of the Schiller Hotel (*see chapter* **Accommodation**, *p93*): with its classic Jeugenstil interior and vaulted ceiling intact, it's a choice spot to chow down on such very French dishes as Petite Marmite Henri IV and Filet Véronique. If you really want to go for it, try the Russian Egg.
*Disabled access.*

### Christophe

*Leliegracht 46 (625 0807). Tram 13, 14, 17, 20.* **Open** 6.30-10.30pm Tue-Sat. **Average** ƒ60. **Credit** AmEx, DC, EC, MC, V. **Map 2 C3**
Hyper-posh and mega-expensive, Christophe's serves inspired French cuisine to movers and shakers with ample expense accounts. Strap a booster to your tastebuds and blast off to those Michelin stars.
*Disabled access (ground floor only).*

### La Rive

*Amstel Hotel, Prof Tulpplein 1 (622 6060). Tram 6, 7, 10, 20/Metro Weesperplein.* **Open** *breakfast* 7-10.30am Mon-Fri; 7am-noon Sat, Sun; *lunch* noon-2pm Mon-Fri; *dinner* 6.30-10.30pm Mon-Sat. **Average** *breakfast* ƒ42,50; *lunch* ƒ100; *dinner* ƒ150. **Credit** AmEx, DC, EC, MC, V. **Map 6 F4**
This elegant waterside restaurant in the Amstel Hotel is the home of Robert Kranenborg, one of the most famous chefs in the Netherlands. The lunch menu is an ideal introduction to his refined, regional French cuisine.
*Disabled access.*

### Maison Descartes

*Vijzelgracht 2A (622 1913). Tram 6, 7, 10, 16, 20, 24, 25.* **Open** noon-2.30pm, 6-11pm Mon-Fri. **Average** ƒ27,50. **Credit** EC. **Map 6 E5**
The setting of this small French restaurant, the walls of which are covered with original seventeenth-century Delft tiles, is pure Dutch. Don't bother coming on a weekend: it's closed for 'security reasons', as it's based in the same building as the French Consulate. You need to book days – no, make that months – in advance.

### Restaurant Pier 10

*De Ruijterkade, Steiger 10 (624 8276). Tram 1, 2, 5, 9, 13, 14, 16, 17, 20, 24, 25.* **Open** 6.30-10.30pm daily. **Average** ƒ32. **Credit** AmEx, EC, MC, V. **Map 2 D1**
One of Amsterdam's most surprising restaurants, set in a former shipping office. An unusual combination of functional décor, candlelight, shipside vistas, innovative food from chef Steve Muzerie and a casual atmosphere attracts a regular following. Reserve a table in the glass room.
*Disabled access.*

### 't Swarte Schaep

*Korte Leidsedwarsstraat 24 (622 3021). Tram 1, 2, 5, 6, 7, 10, 20.* **Open** noon-11pm daily. **Average** *lunch* ƒ48; *dinner* ƒ77,50. **Credit** AmEx, DC, EC, JCB, MC, V. **Map 5 C5**
Based in this 300-year-old building since 1937, this restaurant is noted for its wines (especially reds), authentic antiques and blend of classic, nouvelle and post-modern cuisine. A favourite hangout of the Dutch Royal Family.

### D'Vijff Vlieghen

*Spuistraat 294-302; entrance Vliegendesteeg 1 (624 8369). Tram 1, 2, 5, 13, 17, 20.* **Open** 5.30-10pm daily. **Set menu** ƒ60. **Credit** AmEx, DC, EC, MC, V. **Map 2 C3**
'The Five Flies' is an institution that sprawls over five houses and tries hard to pump up a Golden Age vibe – it has a Rembrandt's Room featuring some of his sketchings – but does better as a kitsch hot-spot. It serves poshed-up Dutch food, though the boar is no doubt imported.

## African

### Cul-de-Sac

*Oudezijds Achterburgwal 99 (625 4548) Tram 4, 9, 16, 20, 24, 25.* **Open** 3pm-1am Sun-Thur; 3pm-3am Fri, Sat. **Average** ƒ23. **Credit** AmEx, DC, EC, MC, V. **Map 2 D2**
Named after the Roman Polanski film, Cul-de-Sac offers 'an oasis in a world of madness': the madness is the surround-

*Veggie dishes galore at* **De Bolhoed**. *See page 116.*

ing Red Light District, and the oasis is the courtyard, the charm of which is enhanced by the tinklings of the music student neighbours. From Monday to Wednesday, the safariesque restaurant opens its kitchen to a talented Ivory Coast cook.
*Disabled access (ground floor only).*

## Chinese

### Hoi Tin
*Zeedijk 122-124 (625 6451). Tram 4, 9, 16, 20, 24, 25/Metro Nieuwmarkt.* **Open** 11.30am-11.30pm daily.
**Average** ƒ25. **Map 2 D2**
Busy but with patient and helpful service, Hoi Tin is worth a visit. Its menu is written in five languages, and lists over 200 dishes, including vegetarian options. They also don't mind if you feel a bit creative and fancy making your own variations on existing dishes.

### Nam Kee
*Geldersekade 117 (624 3470). Tram 4, 9, 16, 20, 24, 25/Metro Nieuwmarkt.* **Open** noon-11.30am daily.
**Average** ƒ15. **Map 2 D2**
A small restaurant, with greasy tiles covering the floor and walls and service slow enough to put many people off. But Nam Kee's customers come back again and again because the food is cheap and the fish dishes supreme. There's a take-away service.
*Disabled access with assistance.*

### Oriental City
*Oudezijds Voorburgwal 177-179 (626 8352). Tram 4, 9, 14, 16, 20, 24, 25.* **Open** noon-10.30pm daily. **Average**
ƒ35. **Credit** AmEx, DC, MC, V. **Map 2 D3**
The views overlook Damstraat, the Royal Palace and the canals. And that's not the best bit: some of Amsterdam's most authentic dim sum can be had here. Understandably, it's popular with Chinese locals as well as tourists.

## Dutch

### De Blauwe Hollander
*Leidsekruisstraat 28 (623 3014). Tram 6, 7, 10, 20.*
**Open** 5-10pm daily. **Average** ƒ22. **Map 5 D5**
The four big tables – there's no separate seating – are always busy, but small parties seldom have to wait long to be seated in De Blauwe Hollander. One of only a few decent restaurants in a very touristy area, serving rich and tasty food.

### Claes Claesz
*Egelantiersstraat 24-26 (625 5306). Tram 7, 10, 17, 20.*
**Open** 6-11pm Tue-Sun. **Average** ƒ30. **Credit** DC, EC, MC, V. **Map 1 B3**
The guy who this restaurant is named for was a blanket dealer: he built this as an orphanage in 1600, complete with courtyard (*hofje*). Chaos and social cosiness abound as the seasonal menu of modernised Dutch cuisine is served to the sounds of live music.
*Disabled access with assistance.*

### Haesje Claes
*Spuistraat 275 (624 9998). Tram 5, 12.* **Open** noon-10pm daily. **Average** ƒ28. **Credit** AmEx, DC, MC, V. **Map 2 C3**
The hearty Dutch fare at Haesje Claes is reasonably priced. Even so, the menu is just that bit too tempting: the extravagant décor may inspire you to order the (lovely) caviar.
*Disabled access.*

### Oud Holland
*Nieuwezijds Voorburgwal 105 (624 6848). Tram 1, 2, 5.*
**Open** noon-9.30pm Mon-Sat. **Average** ƒ25. **Credit** AmEx, DC, EC, JCB, MC, V. **Map 2 C3**
This building dates from 1649, but in the 1920s, the café was a regular meeting place for journalists. How times change: as a nod to passing tourists, Oud Holland now offers traditional Dutch dishes like pea soup, smoked eel and herring.

### Pancake Bakery

*Prinsengracht 191 (625 1333). Tram 13, 17, 20.* **Open** noon-9.30pm. **Average** *f*15. **Credit** AmEx, MC, V.
**Map 2 C2**
This quaint restaurant in the basement of one of Prinsengracht's lovely old houses claims to serve 'the best pancakes in town'. Maybe, maybe not, but you can't quibble with its range: there are over 70 different varieties. They're all large, so you can eat your fill of typically Dutch fare with a variety of toppings for less than *f*15.
*Disabled access with assistance.*

## Ethiopian

### Genet

*Amstelveenseweg 152 (673 4344). Tram 1, 6.* **Open** 5-11pm daily. **Average** *f*20.
Located by Vondelpark, this is a great spot to unwind after a long day of leisure in the greenery. The proprieter is quick to make you feel at home, and the food calls for restraint: you'll want to keep eating regardless of how full you feel.
*Disabled access with assistance.*

### Lalibela

*1e Helmerstraat 249 (683 8332). Tram 1, 3, 6, 12.* **Open** *kitchen* 5-11pm daily. **Average** *f*20.
**Map 5 C5**
This restaurant claims to be the most authentic Ethiopian restaurant in Amsterdam. It's certainly popular: reservations are recommended, especially at the weekend when the place fills up quickly.
*Disabled access with assistance.*

## Fish

### Albatros

*Westerstraat 264 (627 9932). Tram 10.* **Open** 6-11pm Mon, Tue, Thur-Sun. **Average** *f*30. **Credit** AmEx, DC, EC, JCB, MC, V. **Map 1 B2**
Great fishy cuisine in a fishy setting. All dishes are cooked to perfection, and the fine wine can be bought by the centimetre. Tiramisu to die for.
*Disabled access.*

### Julia

*Amstelveenseweg 160 (679 5394). Tram 6/bus 146, 147, 170, 171, 172, 173.* **Open** 5-10pm daily. **Average** *f*32,50. **Credit** AmEx, EC, MC, V.
For a real neighbourhood Dutch dinner, head out of the centre of town to Julia's. The special menu of ten different kinds of fish for *f*32,50 is tremendous value, as is the salmon trout at *f*27,50 for the whole fish.
*Disabled access with assistance.*

### Lucius

*Spuistraat 247 (624 1831). Tram 1, 2, 5.* **Open** 5pm-midnight Mon-Sat. **Average** *f*40. **Credit** AmEx, DC, EC, MC, V. **Map 2 C3**
Lucius is a fish-eater's paradise, serving a dinner of fresh ocean fish (as opposed to the normal North Sea variety), poached, grilled or fried, and shellfish when in season. Lobster should be ordered in advance.
*Disabled access.*

### Le Pêcheur

*Reguliersdwarsstraat 32 (624 3121). Tram 1, 2, 5.* **Open** *lunch* noon-3pm Mon-Fri; *dinner* 6-11pm Mon-Sat. **Four-course menu** *f*65,50. **Credit** AmEx, DC, EC, JCB, MC, V. **Map 5 D4**
Choose from the à la carte or the menu of the day, both of which are provided in Dutch, French and English. The service is friendly but formal, and the clientele are mature and

worry more about the quality of the food than the price. Excellent mussels and oysters.
*Disabled access.*

### Sluizer

*Utrechtsestraat 43-45 (626 3557). Tram 4.* **Open** 5-11pm Sun-Thur; 5pm-midnight Fri, Sat. **Average** *f*30. **Credit** AmEx, DC, EC, V. **Map 6 E4**
With interior design inspired by Charles Rennie Mackintosh and a luxury terrace on the top floor, this restaurant is chic yet unpretentious. It offers an extensive menu of grilled, baked or poached fish. Children's dishes are available.
*Disabled access with assistance.*

## French

### Beddington's

*Roelof Hartstraat 6-8 (676 5201). Tram 3, 5, 12, 20, 24.* **Open** 6-10.30pm Mon, Sat; noon-2pm, 6-10.30pm, Tue-Fri. **Average** *f*45. **Credit** AmEx, DC, EC, MC, V.
French cuisine is complemented by original touches gleaned from long trips through the Far East. The menu includes some beautifully presented fish dishes.

### Begijntje

*Begijnesteeg 6-8 (624 0528). Tram 1, 2, 5.* **Open** 6-10pm daily. **Three-course menu** *f*40. **Credit** AmEx, DC, EC, MC, V. **Map 5 D4**
The 'Little Nun' is the former coach-house of the old nunnery in Begijnhof (*see chapter* **Sightseeing**, *page 50*), and has a lovely terrace on which you can eat the set meal offered that day. Chef John Arents relies on French cuisine that edges towards what can tentatively be termed nouveau Dutch.
*Disabled access.*

### Belhamel

*Brouwersgracht 60 (622 1095). Tram 1, 2, 5, 13, 17, 20.* **Open** 6-10pm daily. **Average** *f*35. **Credit** AmEx, DC, EC, MC, V. **Map 2 C2**
A fresh approach to French cuisine and brilliant value for money characterise this beautiful art nouveau place. As a special treat, reserve a table overlooking the canal.

### Bordewijk

*Noordermarkt 8 (624 3899). Tram 3.* **Open** 6.30-10.30pm Tue-Sun. **Set menus** *f*62,50, *f*74,50, *f*84,50. **Credit** AmEx, EC, MC, V. **Map 1 B2**
This is a perfectly balanced restaurant, offering the very best of original food and palate-tingling wines in a designer interior. Service and atmosphere are relaxed. Recommended.
*Disabled access.*

### Café Roux

*The Grand, Oudezijds Voorburgwal 197 (555 3111). Tram 4, 9, 14, 16, 20, 24, 25.* **Open** 5.30-11am, noon-3pm, 6-11pm, daily. **Average** *f*40. **Credit** AmEx, DC, EC, JCB, MC, V. **Map 2 D3**
The same food is served in Café Roux as in the Grand Hotel itself, and is supervised by head chef Albert Roux. Despite the cook's superstar status, food here is good value, as is the afternoon tea. *See chapter* **Accommodation**, *p90.*

### Crignon Culinair

*Gravenstraat 28 (624 6428). Tram 1, 2, 4, 5, 9, 14, 16, 20, 24, 25.* **Open** 6-9.30pm Tue-Sat. **Average** *f*30. **Credit** EC. **Map 2 C3**
Cheese shop by day, restaurant by night. It's not as bizarre as it sounds: this small establishment's speciality is fondues. It's run by Adriaan Jaspers, an award-winning chef whose cuisine is very cheese-centred. Meat and fish dishes are also on the menu, but with a student price of *f*23,50 for a cheese fondue, the choice should be an easy one.
*Disabled access with assistance.*

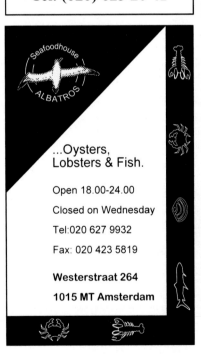

## Le Garage

*Ruysdaelstraat 54-56 (679 7176). Tram 3, 5, 6, 12, 16, 20.* **Open** noon-2pm, 6-11pm, Mon-Fri; 6-11pm Sat, Sun. **Average** ƒ55. **Credit** AmEx, DC, MC, V. **Map 6 E6**
Dress up to eat in this trendy brasserie, which is great for people-watching. The authentic French regional food – and 'worldly' versions thereof – is pretty damn fine. *Disabled access.*

## Kikker

*Egelantiersstraat 128-30 (627 9198). Tram 10, 13, 14, 17, 20.* **Open** 5.30-10pm Mon-Thur, Sun; 5.30-11pm Fri, Sat. **Three-course menu** ƒ34,50. **Credit** AmEx, DC, EC, MC, V. **Map 1 B3**
A two-storey restaurant tucked away in the Jordaan. The waiters are friendly, the art deco interior tasteful and the atmosphere intimate at this brasserie serving French/Portuguese grub. Weekends offer entertainment in the form of music, cabaret or comics. *Disabled access.*

## Nostradamus

*Berenstraat 8 (624 4292). Tram 1, 2, 5.* **Open** 6-11pm Mon, Wed-Sun. **Average** ƒ30. **Credit** AmEx, DC, EC, MC, V. **Map 5 C4**
A cannily themed restaurant that will surely be booked solid for the coming millennial celebrations. The candlelit Middle Ages of Nostradamus are further evoked with astrologically aligned pillars and frescos. Chef Jan Kesting reinvents French cuisine with edges of the Orient; veggie options and free Tarot readings round out the schtick.

## D'Theeboom

*Singel 210 (623 8420). Tram 1, 2, 5, 13, 14, 17, 20.* **Open** 6-10.30pm daily. **Average** *à la carte* ƒ60. **Credit** AmEx, DC, EC, MC, V. **Map 2 C3**
The three-course ƒ47,50 menu at d'Theeboom is one of the best quality/price ratios in town. The generous portions of classical French cooking and the strange absence of crowds make this one of Amsterdam's best kept secrets. *Disabled access with assistance.*

# Indian

## Balraj

*Binnen Oranjestraat 1 (625 1428). Tram 3.* **Open** 5-10pm daily. **Average** ƒ18. **Credit** EC. **Map 1 B2**
A small, cosy eating house just off Haarlemmerdijk. Food is reasonably priced and particularly well done, with vegetarians generously catered for. Highly recommended. *Disabled access with assistance.*

## Balti House

*Albert Cuypstraat 41 (470 8917). Tram 6, 7, 10, 16, 20, 24, 25.* **Open** 4-11pm daily. **Average** ƒ25. **Credit** AmEx, DC, EC, MC, V. **Map 6 E6**
The portions at Amsterdam's only balti eaterie are large, though the balti and tandoori dishes are slightly mellowed for the Dutch palate: if you want the full spicy works, let them know and they'll happily oblige. *Disabled access.*

## Himalaya

*Haarlemmerstraat 11 (622 3776). Tram 1, 2, 5, 13, 17, 20.* **Open** 5-11.30pm daily. **Average** ƒ40. **Credit** AmEx, DC, EC, MC, V. **Map 2 C2**
Terrific Indian cuisine at reasonable to attractive prices. The staff can make any dish more or less spicy than usual, and the service is invariably welcoming and friendly. Less pretentious than most, despite the wonderful art and designs on the walls. *Disabled access.*

## The India Cottage

*Ceintuurbaan 111 (662 8873). Tram 3, 12, 16, 20, 24, 25.* **Open** 5-11pm daily. **Average** ƒ26. **Credit** AmEx, DC, EC, MC, V. **Map 6 E6**
Just out of the centre of town, the India Cottage is a real find, particularly if you're a fan of balti dishes. The restaurant is warm and traditionally decorated, while service is friendly without being over-attentive. There's a ten per cent discount for takeaway: why not take it to the nearby Sarphati Park? *Disabled access*

## Koh-I-Noor

*Westermarkt 29 (623 3133). Tram 13, 14, 17, 20.* **Open** 5-11pm daily. **Average** ƒ25. **Credit** AmEx, DC, EC, MC, V. **Map 2 C3**
Named after the famed diamond, Koh-I-Noor is a prime curry house with a cosy interior and friendly service. The food is rather decent, too. *Disabled access*

## Shiva

*Reguliersdwarsstraat 72 (624 8713). Tram 4, 9, 14, 16, 20, 24, 25.* **Open** 5-11pm daily. **Average** ƒ30. **Credit** AmEx, DC, EC, MC, V. **Map 5 D4**
Air-conditioning keeps the heat down in Shiva's relaxed and elegant interior. The menu holds a carefully selected choice of dishes, from classic curries to speciality plates. *Disabled access*

## Swaagat

*Lange Leidsedwarsstraat 76 (638 4702). Tram 1, 2, 5.* **Open** 5-11pm daily; *summer also* 12.30-3pm daily. **Average** ƒ35. **Credit** AmEx, DC, MC, EC, V. **Map 5 D5**
A nice Indian restaurant with good vegetarian options and a delivery service. Go for one of the fish dishes. *Disabled access.*

# Indonesian

## Bojo

*Lange Leidsedwarsstraat 51 (622 7434). Tram 1, 2, 5.* **Open** 4pm-2am Mon-Fri; noon-4am Sat, Sun. **Average** ƒ20. **Map 5 C5**
One of the few restaurants open into the small hours. A whole range of large-portioned, tasty Indonesian dishes are available, including all the classics, such as *gado gado* and *cummi cummi* (squid). The vegetarian special (including a bit of everything) is both delicious and enormous. *Disabled access.*

## Kantjil & de Tijger

*Spuistraat 291-293 (620 0994). Tram 1, 2, 5.* **Open** 4.30-11pm daily. **Average** ƒ40. **Credit** AmEx, DC, EC, MC, V. **Map 2 C3**
Well-cooked, authentic food at pleasing prices. The service can be rather too relaxed at times and the interior is bare and bright, but the food makes it all worthwhile. *Disabled access.*

## Mas Agung

*Kinkerstraat 304 (689 3994). Tram 7, 17.* **Open** 10am-7.30pm Mon-Fri; 9am-5.30pm Sat, Sun. **Average** ƒ10. **Map 4 B5**
Deliciously exotic delicacies in a small but impeccable take-away where the friendly owners give their customers a warm reception. The fine Indonesian Bintang beer is available.

## De Orient

*Van Baerlestraat 21 (673 4958). Tram 2, 3, 5, 12, 20.* **Open** 5-10pm daily. **Average** ƒ30. **Credit** AmEx, DC, EC, MC, V. **Map 5 C6**
A beautiful, cosy restaurant with a dauntingly large menu: there are four pages of dishes for vegetarians to choose from,

for example. The food is varied, with subtle and understated use of spices.
*Disabled access.*

## Puri Mas
*Lange Leidsedwarsstraat 37-41 (627 7627). Tram 1, 2, 5.* **Open** 5pm-12.30am daily. **Average** *f*35. **Credit** AmEx, DC, MC, V. **Map 5 D5**
Impeccable service and excellent food characterise this classy restaurant. A variety of dishes are served, from light meals to full meals plus vegetarian meals and *rijsttafels*.

## Sama Sebo
*PC Hooftstraat 27 (662 8146). Tram 2, 3, 5, 12, 20.* **Open** noon-3pm, 6-10pm, Mon-Sat. **Average** *f*50. **Credit** AmEx, DC, EC, MC, V. **Map 5 C6**
A comfortable and spacious restaurant. If you're not familiar with Indonesian dishes, staff are more than willing to help out and will also adapt any set menu for non-meat eaters. There is no minimum charge and the atmosphere is refreshingly relaxed, so if you just fancy a snack, this is a good choice.
*Disabled access.*

## Tempo Doeloe
*Utrechtsestraat 75 (625 6718). Tram 4, 6, 7, 10.* **Open** 6-11.30pm daily. **Average** *f*35. **Credit** AmEx, DC, EC, MC, V. **Map 6 E4**
This upmarket restaurant is adorned with fresh linen tablecloths and flowers. A spiciness rating is given for each dish on the menu: be warned, as the 'hot' dishes are just that. One of Amsterdam's best.

# International

## Amsterdam
*Watertorenplein 6 (682 2666/2667). Tram 10.* **Open** 11am-1am Mon-Thur, Sun; 11am-2am Fri, Sat; *kitchen* 11.30am-11.30pm daily. **Average** *f*27. **Credit** AmEx, DC, EC, MC, V.
Until a few years ago, this remarkably spacious monument to industry used to pump water from the coast's dunes, and had been doing so for around a century. Now, you can eat honest Dutch and French dishes here, under a ceiling you have to squint at to see and beneath floodlighting culled from the old Ajax and Olympic stadium. A unique experience.

## Bep
*Nieuwezijds Voorburgwal 260 (626 5649). Tram 1, 2, 5, 13, 17, 20.* **Open** *summer* 11am-1am Mon-Thur, Sun; 11am-3am Fri, Sat; *winter* 5pm-1am Mon-Thur; 11am-3am Fri, Sat; 11am-1am Sun. **Average** *f*12,50. **Credit** EC. **Map 2 D3**
A slick and smooth-lined lounge that provides an intriguingly quirky menu at good prices. Depending on the night and your mood, the crowds come across as either advertising folk winding themselves up or artists winding themselves down.
*Disabled access with assistance.*

## Café Cox
*Marnixstraat 429 (620 7222). Tram 1, 2, 5, 6, 7, 10, 20.* **Open** 10am-1am Mon-Thur, Sun; 10am-2am Fri, Sat. *lunch* 12.30-2.30pm daily; *dinner* 5.30-10.30pm Mon-Wed, Sun; 5.30-11.30pm Thur-Sat. **Average** *f*30. **Credit** AmEx, DC, EC, MC, V. **Map 5 C5**
Imaginative French and modern Dutch cooking in a lively environment. Prices are reasonable.

## Melkweg Café-Restaurant De Komeet
*Marnixstraat 409 (420 7469). Tram 1, 2, 5, 6, 7, 10, 20.* **Open** 2-9pm Wed-Sun; *dinner* 5.30-9pm. **Average** *f*20. **Credit** EC. **Map 5 C5**
This international kitchen renews its menu choice of a fish, meat and vegetarian dish every day. Rock groupies should

note that 'The Comet' is your chance to watch your hero chew: whichever artist is booked to play at the Melkweg that night will probably chow down in here.
*Disabled access (entrance on Lijnbaansgracht).*

## Duvel
*1e Van der Helststraat 59-61 (675 7517). Tram 16, 24, 25.* **Open** noon-1pm Mon-Thur, noon-3am Fri; 11am-2am Sat; noon-1am Sun. **Average** *f*30,50. **Credit** AmEx, DC, EC, MC, V. **Map 6 E6**
A fine neighbourhood – and neighbourly – café, cooking up dishes with a French twist. Ingredients come fresh from the nearby Albert Cuyp market.

## Hemelse Modder
*Oude Waal 9 (624 3203). Tram, 1, 2, 4, 5, 9, 13, 16, 17, 20, 24, 25.* **Open** Tue-Sun 6-10pm. **Average** *f*30. **Credit** AmEx, DC, EC, MC, V. **Map 3 E2**
Oriental, French, Italian and Dutch cuisine merge together in the dishes – many of then vegetarian – served here. A full three-course menu is available at *f*45,50.

## Kort
*Amstelveld 12 (626 1199). Tram 16, 24, 25.* **Open** noon-1am daily; *kitchen* noon-10pm daily. **Average** *f*35. **Credit** AmEx, DC, EC, MC, V. **Map 6 E4**
With one of the most painfully scenic terraces in Amsterdam, this wooden church – once the stable for Napoleon's horses – is a lovely place to indulge. The set menu is *f*49,50.

## Kuipers
*Boomstraat 41A (622 2402). Tram 3, 10.* **Open** 6pm-1am Tue-Sun. **Average** *f*32. **Credit** AmEx, DC, EC, MC, V. **Map 1 B2**
In an ancient Jordaan house, this freshly scrubbed and modern restaurant effortlessly achieves a feeling of social cosiness, particularly when the patio is open. The menu happily jumps from national to international dishes: from Thai curry to sushi, for example. Perfect for a date.

## Lof
*Haarlemmerstraat 62 (620 2997) Tram 1, 2, 4, 5, 9, 13, 16, 17, 20, 24, 25.* **Open** 6.30pm-1am Tue-Sun; *kitchen* 6.30-11pm Tue-Sun. **Three-course menu** *f*52,50. **Credit** EC. **Map 2 C2**
During daylight hours, you'd be forgiven if you mistook Lof for some sort of soup kitchen. At night, it's a different story: the lighting works miracles, as does the chef, who magically improvises dishes that drawn equally from Mediterranean tradition and Far East cuisine. The fish is sublime.
*Disabled access with assistance.*

## Lulu
*Runstraat 8 (624 5090). Tram 1, 2, 5, 7, 10.* **Open** 6-11pm daily. **Average** *f*32. **Credit** AmEx, DC, EC, MC, V. **Map 5 C4**
This small French-Indonesian restaurant offers a *f*49 menu that is so good you wonder how they do it. Stop wondering, and enjoy the food: it's fine stuff, with the fish dishes especially well-prepared.

## Ondeugd
*Ferdinand Bolstraat 15 (672 0651) Tram 3, 6, 7, 10, 12, 16, 20, 24, 25.* **Open** 6pm-1am Mon-Thur; 6pm-3am Fri, Sat; *kitchen* 6-11pm daily. **Average** *f*30. **Credit** AmEx DC, EC, MC, V. **Map 6 E6**
A very popular and flashily kitsch restaurant in the Pijp, perfect for a casual evening out. The menu is primarily French, with outside influences.
*Disabled access.*

## Prego
*Herenstraat 25 (638 0148). Tram 1, 2, 5, 13, 17, 20.* **Open** *lunch* noon-2.30pm Tue-Sat; *dinner* 6-10.30pm

daily. **Average** ƒ38. **Credit** AmEx, EC, MC, V.
**Map 2 C2**
A small, comfortable restaurant frequented largely by locals, where the imaginative chefs change the Mediterranean-based menu on a daily basis.
*Disabled access.*

### De Smoeshaan
*Leidsekade 90 (627 6966). Tram 1, 2, 5, 6, 7, 10, 20.* **Open** *restaurant* 5.30-9pm Tue-Sat; *café* 11am-1am Mon-Thur, Sun; 11am-2am Fri, Sat. **Average** *restaurant* ƒ29. **Credit** AmEx, EC, MC, V. **Map 5 C5**
There's an old Dutch café-bar downstairs, which is usually busy, and a slightly more formal restaurant upstairs, with a more varied menu (and yep, you guessed it, higher prices). Both serve tasty Franco-Dutch food with lots of fresh vegetables and salads, and both attract a young, lively crowd.

### The Supper Club
*Jonge Roelensteeg 21 (638 0513). Tram 1, 2, 5, 13, 17.* **Open** 8pm-1am daily. **Three-course menus** ƒ55, ƒ85. **Credit** AmEx, DC, EC, MC, V. **Map 2 D3**
A very unique, very arty and very casual dining experience. The changing décor highlights the special set menu for the evening: a saloon one day, a psychedelic boudoir the next.
*Disabled access (by arrangement).*

### Trez
*Saenredamstraat 39-41 (676 2495). Tram 6, 7, 10, 16, 24, 25.* **Open** 6-11pm daily. **Average** ƒ31. **Map 6 E6**
A beautiful place in the Pijp with pretty tables and chairs, distinctive decorative themes, stylish glassware and an exposed kitchen in the middle of the restaurant. It offers an excellent light French menu and is good value for money.
*Disabled access.*

### Brasserie Van Baerle
*Van Baerlestraat 158 (679 1532). Tram 3, 5, 12, 16, 20.* **Open** noon-11pm Mon-Fri, 10am-11pm Sun. **Average** ƒ35. **Credit** AmEx, DC, EC, MC, V. **Map 5 D6**
The media crowd has been hanging out at this turn-of-the-century townhouse brasserie since it opened around ten years ago. The food is strictly modern, with Oriental salads and homemade soups. On warm days, the garden is a delight.
*Disabled access with assistance.*

### Van Beeren
*Koningsstraat 54 (622 2329). Tram 4, 9, 14, 16, 20, 24, 25/Metro Nieuwmarkt.* **Open** 4.30pm-1am daily; *kitchen* 5.30-10.30pm daily. **Average** ƒ20. **Credit** EC. **Map 3 E2**
An atmospheric and welcoming *eetcafé*: dish of the day is ƒ15, with succulent sole or steaks costing ƒ20-plus. There's a spacious and stunning back garden.
*Disabled access with assistance.*

## Italian

### Casa di David
*Singel 426 (624 5093). Tram 1, 2, 5.* **Open** 5-11.30pm daily. **Average** ƒ28. **Credit** AmEx, DC, EC, MC, V. **Map 5 D4**
Casa di David's beamed design and panoramic views make it a perfect spot for romantic meals. The pasta is made on the premises and is first-rate; the marvellous crusty pizzas are cooked in a wood-fired oven.
*Disabled access (ground floor only).*

### Hostaria
*2e Egelantiersdwarsstraat 9 (626 0028). Tram 10, 13, 14, 17, 20.* **Open** 6.30-10.30pm Tue-Sun. **Average** ƒ29,50. **Map 1 B3**
Owners Marjolein and Massimo Pasquinoli serve up a wonderful selection of classic Italian dishes, including salmon

carpaccio and a spectacular *insalata di polipo* (squid salad). Excellent, unpretentious food at good prices.
*Disabled access with assistance.*

### Toscanini
*Lindengracht 75 (623 2813). Tram 3, 10.* **Open** 6-11pm daily. **Average** ƒ25. **Credit** AmEx, DC, EC, MC, V. **Map 1 B2**
The authentic and excellet Italian food at this bustling restaurant is prepared in an open kitchen. Don't go expecting pizza, and book early (from 3pm) if you want to be sure of a table.
*Disabled access*

### Trattoria Toto
*1e Constantijn Huygenstraat 112 (683 0028). Tram 1, 3, 6, 12.* **Open** 6-11pm daily. **Average** ƒ25. **Credit** AmEx, DC, EC, MC, V. **Map 5 C6**
Named after Italian comic Antonio DeCurti, this light and open treasure trove of pure and simple Italian dishes makes everything from the very freshest of ingredients. The real thing.

### Yam-Yam
*Frederik Hendrikstraat 90 (681 5097). Tram 3.* **Open** 6-10.30pm Tue-Sun. **Average** ƒ22. **Map 1 A3**
Yam-Yam calls itself 'the first trattoria for world cuisine', with a menu made up not only of tasty Italian dishes, but also Thai and even sushi platters.
*Disabled access.*

## Japanese

### An
*Weteringschans 199 (627 0607). Tram 6, 7, 10, 20.* **Open** 6-10pm Wed-Sun. **Average** ƒ30. **Credit** EC. **Map 6 E5**
If you're going to eat at An, bring your own booze, as there is no alcohol licence in the restaurant. However, that's the only drawback at this fine eaterie. Its basic interior disguises the fact that An serves some of the best and most authentic Japanese cuisine in Amsterdam.
*Disabled access with assistance.*

### Morita-Ya
*Zeedijk 18 (638 0756) Tram 1, 2, 5, 13, 17, 20.* **Open** 6-9.30pm Mon, Tue, Thur-Sun. **Average** ƒ18. **Credit** AmEx, EC, MC, V. **Map 2 D2**
A cheap and cheerful place near Centraal Station. Opening hours are a bit erratic, but if you do manage to get there when it's open, you'll enjoy some fantastic sushi and sashimi.
*Disabled access.*

### Teppan Yaki Hosokawa
*Max Euweplein 22 (638 8086). Tram 1, 2, 5, 6, 7, 10, 20.* **Open** 5-10.30 pm daily. **Set menus** ƒ85-ƒ120. **Credit** AmEx, DC, EC, JCB, MC, V. **Map 5 D5**
Tables with built-in grills allow you to witness kung fu-esque cookery in action. Fear of the cook's seemingly erratic knife chopping/juggling is soon replaced with admiration for his culinary abilities. Just don't dare complain about the price…
*Disabled access.*

### Tokio Sushi
*Haarlemmerdijk 28 (638 5677). Tram 3.* **Open** 11am-9pm daily. **Average** ƒ25. **Credit** AmEx, DC, EC, MC, V. **Map 1 B1**
Got an urge for a protein surge? Check out this place for its prices: ƒ2,50 per mouthful of fresh sushi is not to be sniffed at. The choice is limited – there's no blowfish, for example – but it does have vegetarian dishes.
*Disabled access.*

### Yakitori
*Leidsekruisstraat 4 (620 4989). Tram 1, 2, 5, 6, 7, 10.*
**Open** 5pm-1am Mon-Thur, Sun; 5pm-12.15am Fri, Sat.
**Average** *f*35. **Credit** AmEx, DC, EC, MC, V. **Map 5 D5**
Just as blissful as sushi, yakitori are bite-sized skewered
meat and vegetables grilled over wood coal (starting at *f*3
each). Rice, noodles and miso soup round out the menu. Make
sure you reserve on Fridays and Saturdays, as Yakitori does
get very busy.
*Disabled access.*

## Korean
### Mokkalie
*Utrechtsestraat 42 (625 9251). Tram 4.* **Open** noon-
2pm, 6-11pm, daily. **Average** *set menu* *f*35-*f*60. **Credit**
AmEx, DC, JCB, MC, V. **Map 6 E4**
There are beer pumps affixed to four of the tables where you
can have a go at pulling your own beers. If you get around
to eating, the set menu at Amsterdam's finest Korean restaurant is good value.

## Mexican
### La Margarita
*Lange Brugsteeg 6 (624 0529). Tram 1, 2, 4, 5, 9, 13,
14, 16, 17, 20, 24, 25/Metro Centraal Station.* **Open**
5pm-1am Tue-Sun. **Average** *f*30. **Credit** AmEx, DC,
EC, MC, V. **Map 2 D3**
If you're going to La Margarita, work up a large appetite: the
portions here are absolutely massive. The extensive menu
caters for all palates, with decent seafood, vegetarian and
meat choices.
*Disabled access.*

### Rose's Cantina
*Reguliersdwarsstraat 38-40 (625 9797). Tram 1, 2, 5,
16, 20, 24, 25.* **Open** 5.30pm-1am Mon-Thur; 5.30pm-
2am Fri, Sat; 5pm-1am Sun. **Average** *f*25. **Credit**
AmEx, DC, EC, MC, V. **Map 5 D4**
Definitely not the place for a quiet night out, and more Tex-
Mex than purely Mexican, but the ingredients at Rose's
Cantina are good enough and the portions more than gener-
ous. As you'd expect, combining a burrito with a pitcher or
three of margaritas makes for a merry meal. Well worth a
visit if you're in an upbeat mood.
*Disabled access.*

## Middle Eastern
### Eufraat
*1e Van der Helststraat 72 (672 0579) Tram 3, 12,
24, 25.* **Open** 11am-11pm daily. **Average** *f*20.
**Map 6 E6**
This family-run Assyrian restaurant is named after one of
the rivers that is said to have flowed through the Garden of
Eden. The ancient recipes are brought to life with real care
and loving attention: Eufraat even makes its own pittas and
yoghurts from scratch, and very nice they are, too. Aside
from the succulent lamb, vegetarians are well catered for
here. Try the supreme Arabic coffee.

### Koerdistan
*Ferdinand Bolstraat 23 (676 1995) Tram 16, 24, 25.*
**Open** 5-11pm daily. **Average** *f*18. **Map 6 E6**
A tad dingy, but most friendly and definitely tasty, this small
restaurant rarely disappoints with its top-notch Middle
Eastern cookery. If you can bear to lay off the snacks all day,
then you'll be in good shape for their daily three-course
menu, priced at *f*20.

# Cheese Trek: The final fondue

Although it was a Swiss who first fused wine
and cheese to form the fondue, it was the Dutch,
renowned cheese junkies and lovers of social
interaction, who adopted this most democratic
of dishes – one pot, many forks – and turned it
into a national pastime. What began as broken
bread dipped into a primordial stew of cheesy
strands has evolved into a broad culinary dis-
pline with infinite variants. But this most frolicsome of party foods is not for all palates: a kilo
of cheese in the belly can be burdensome, while
restaurateurs refuse to take responsibility for
any resultant cholesterol seizure. Connoisseurs
of cheese recommend aiding digestion with
kirsch, wine or black tea.

**Café Bern** is suitably atmospheric place for
a proper cheese fest. The Swiss-inspired menu
is affordable and the bar fully stocked with a
variety of grease-cutting agents. La Fondue
stays delicious right until the last strand, mingling nicely with the meat fondue, the Entrecote
Café Bern, where the flesh is gently sautéed in
a pesto-like sauce. Lovely.

The artier café-gallery **Leg Af** also has a
relaxed and informal atmosphere. There are
plenty of intriguing fondues to choose from: the
Fondue Japonaise, with its bonito and sake
bouillion, and the Cheddar and Cider Fondue
are especially eye-catching. On weekends, a
Japanese food chef prepares sushi and sashimi.
But for a posher fondue, try the dearer **Groene
Lantaarn**. The bread comes pre-chunked, the
desserts are suitably decadent, and they even
do a Dim Sum fondue.

### Café Bern
*Nieuwmarkt 9 (622 0034). Tram 4, 9, 14, 16, 20, 24,
25/Metro Nieuwmarkt.* **Open** 4pm-1am daily; *kitchen*
6-11pm daily. **Average** *f*20. **Credit** EC.
**Map 2 D2**

### Leg Af
*Oude Leliestraat 9 (624 6700). Tram 1, 2, 5, 13, 14,
17, 20.* **Open** 6-10pm daily. **Average** *f*25. **Credit**
EC. **Map 2 C3**

### Groene Lantaarn
*Bloemgracht 47 (620 2088). Tram 10, 13, 17, 20.*
**Open** 6-9pm daily. **Average** *f*40. **Map 1 B3**

## Portuguese

### Girassol
*Weesperzijde 135 (692 3471). Tram 6, 7, 10, 20.* **Open** 6-10pm daily. **Average** ƒ28. **Credit** AmEx, DC, EC, MC, V. **Map 7 G5**
One of the best Portuguese restaurants in town, with a lively atmosphere and more than competent cooking. Specialities include seafood and swordfish.
*Disabled access.*

### Iberia
*Kadijksplein 16 (623 6313) Bus 22.* **Open** 5-11.30pm daily. **Average** ƒ35. **Credit** AmEx, DC, EC, MC, V. **Map 3 F3**
Across from the Scheepvaart and newMetropolis museums, Iberia offers both Spanish and Portugese dishes in an appropriately Mediterranean ambience. Indulge in sherry fresh from the keg during your meal.
*Disabled access.*

## Spanish

### Centra
*Lange Niezel 29 (622 3050). Tram 4, 9, 14, 16, 20, 24, 25.* **Open** 1-11pm daily. **Average** ƒ30. **Credit** EC. **Map 2 D2**
Known for good, wholesome, homely cooking. The cafétéria tables and fluorescent lighting don't make for an atmospheric meal, but the tapas, lamb and fish dishes are all great.
*Disabled access with assistance.*

### Duende
*Lindengracht 62 (420 6692). Tram 3.* **Open** 4pm-1am Mon-Thur; 2pm-2am Fri, 2pm-3am Sat; 2pm-1am Sun. **Average** *tapas* ƒ6. **Credit** EC. **Map 1 B2**
This little bit of Andalusia in the Jordaan serves a good and varied selection of tapas. Order at the bar and be prepared to share your table with an amorous couple or a flamenco dancer who might just offer you some free lessons.

### Tapas Bar
*Spuistraat 299 (623 1141). Tram 1, 2, 5.* **Open** 4pm-midnight Mon, Wed-Fri; noon-1am Sat, Sun. **Average** ƒ17; *tapas* ƒ4,50. **Credit** EC. **Map 2 C3**
An imaginatively named and splendidly atmospheric tapas bar, complete with all the saints staring down at you from the walls. But don't feel guilty as you tuck into tapas, which includes fresh seafood dishes.
*Disabled access.*

## Thai/South-East Asian

### Cambodja City
*Albert Cuypstraat 58-60 (671 4930) Tram 16, 24, 25.* **Open** 11am-10pm Tue-Sat, 2-10pm Sun. **Average** ƒ20. **Map 6 E6**
Despite the name, the dishes served here are culled from Thailand, Vietnam, Cambodia and Laos. Aside from the 3-D moving waterfall painting, the surrounds are simple. The helpful service and the food itself rarely disappoint.

### Pathum
*Willemsstraat 16 (624 4936). Tram 3/bus 18, 22.* **Open** 5-10pm daily. **Average** ƒ23. **Credit** AmEx, DC, EC, MC, V. **Map 1 B2**
A cheap and lively little place in the Jordaan, offering lovely Thai food at low prices. Ask the waiters for advice on how hot the dishes are if you don't want your head blown off. Which you probably don't.
*Disabled access.*

### Thaise Snackbar Bird
*Zeedijk 77 (420 6289). Tram 1, 2, 4, 5, 9, 13, 14, 16, 17, 20, 24, 25.* **Open** 2-10pm daily. **Average** ƒ18. **Map 2 D2**
Probably the most authentic and certainly the cheapest Thai place in town. Naturally, then, it's also the most crowded, but it's worth the wait, whether you settle on a tom yam soup, a snack or a meal.

## Turkish

### Lokanta Ceren
*Albert Cuypstraat 40 (673 3524). Tram 4, 16, 20, 24, 25.* **Open** 6pm-midnight daily. **Average** ƒ18. **Credit** EC. **Map 6 E5**
A small, friendly restaurant in the heart of a busy market street in the Pijp. The numerous starters (meze) are displayed on a huge tray, but quickly disappear when accompanied by fresh, warm Turkish bread and a glass of raki. Round off your feast with some fresh fruit.
*Disabled access.*

## Vegetarian

### De Bolhoed
*Prinsengracht 60 (626 1803). Tram 13, 14, 17, 20.* **Open** noon-10pm daily. **Average** ƒ20. **Credit** EC. **Map 1 B2**
You can choose your hearty vegan dishes à la carte or from the daily changing set-price menu at this great little place. The restaurant is licensed and there's a sumptuous selection of pastries: the banana cream pie is a *tour de force*, best tackled by two. The interior is a pleasantly eccentric mix of folk, New Age and modern design.
*Disabled access.*

### Burger's Patio
*2e Tuindwarsstraat 12 (623 6854). Tram 3, 10.* **Open** 6-11pm. **Average** ƒ25. **Credit** AmEx, DC, EC, MC, V. **Map 1 B3**
Both veg and flesh-eaters are equally well served by the Italian-ish cooking at this very popular restaurant (try the homemade pasta). Confusingly, there are no burgers on the menu, veggie or otherwise.
*Disabled access.*

### Esoterica
*Overtoom 409 (689 7226). Tram 1, 6.* **Open** noon-9pm Wed-Sun. **Average** ƒ15.
Wash down reasonably priced bio-vegetarian food – including some delicious tapas – with fresh vegetable and fruit juices at this nice eaterie. The takeaway option is popular – particularly with Vondelpark just around the corner – though many choose to stay and browse the selection of esoteric books.
*Disabled access.*

### Oibibio
*Prins Hendrikkade 20-21 (553 9328). Tram 1, 2, 4, 5, 9, 14, 16, 17, 20, 24, 25.* **Open** 5.30-10pm daily. **Average** ƒ27. **Credit** AmEx, DC, EC, MC, V. **Map 2 D2**
The menu changes every six weeks in this slick Mediterraneanesque monument to the New Age. The food is fresh and thoughtful, but that doesn't stop the staff from occasionally ordering takeaway from McDonalds for themselves. Most peculiar.

*The King is dead, long live the* **New King.** *See page 120.*

# Tales of the city **Grease is the word**

Vending machines: every country has 'em. Cigarettes, chocolate, soft drinks... all can be had from wall-mounted machines across the globe in exchange for a few meagre coins. Fans of these modern conveniences, though, should prepare to tick off another machine on their 'I Spy' list. In Amsterdam, it's possible to walk up to a hole in the wall, slip a few coins into a slot, and get a hot meal out, if 'meal' is really an appropriate word for the prefab globs of grease found at **Febo**.

For the uninitiated, a visit to Febo (pronounced 'Fay-bo') can give an almost eerie edge to a Saturday night. Witness a near-religious moment: the quietening of a loud, beer-fuelled crowd as they line up to slot some change into a glowing wall and, in exchange, receive a sacrament of grease in the form of hamburger, fries, kroket (a deep-fried meat and potato product), bamibal (a deep-fried spicy noodle product), nasibal (a deep-fried spicy rice product) or kaas soufflé (a deep-fried cheese product). One bite, and the drool emanating from the consumer quickly merges with the oily lipstick smackeroonie delivered by the food in question.

While some people may find this an odd sight, it is, when you think about it, the next logical step in the evolution of the fast-food industry. Let's face it: what better example is there of modern eating habits, whereby humanoid employees subsume their identities to the greater cause of speedy service and corporate growth? Welcome to the future, where automatisation stands as the one fully realised dream of the twentieth century.

Some people, though, are yet to be convinced, questioning the quality of food that sits indefinitely in a limp and lamp-hot state. These whingers, needless to say, have it all wrong: the whole point of the fast-food ritual is that the dread word 'quality' should never come into play for a second. In any case, after a visit to Febo, 'quality' will be just about the furthest word from your mind...

**Febo**
*Branches around town.* **Average** *f*6.

### Vliegende Schotel
*Nieuwe Leliestraat 162 (625 2041). Tram 13, 14, 17, 20.* **Open** *summer* 1-10.15pm daily; *winter* 5-10.15pm daily. **Average** *f*12. **Map 1 B3**
Popular with locals – expect a mixed, arty crowd – Vliegende Schotel is a particularly good place to go if you want to get away from it all, read the papers or swing the resident cat. A range of delicious veggie nosh is served in huge portions. *Disabled access.*

### Vrolijke Abrikoos
*Weteringschans 76 (624 4672) Tram 6, 7, 10.* **Open** 5.30-9.30pm daily. **Average** *f*32. **Credit** EC, MC, V. **Map 5 D5**
Experimental cuisine made from organic/biodynamic ingredients. Enjoy a balcony view over the garden. *Disabled access with assistance.*

## Cheap eats

### Al's Plaice
*Nieuwdijk 10 (427 4192). Tram 1, 2, 4, 5, 9, 14, 16, 17, 20, 24, 25.* **Open** 5-10pm Mon; noon-10pm Wed-Sun. **Average** *f*6. **Map 2 D2**
Brits will spot the pun from 50 paces: yep, Al's Plaice – terrible, huh? – is an old-fashioned English fish'n'chip tent. Besides bargain fish, there's a selection of pies and pasties, plus mushy peas for the true Brit. You can even buy Heinz and HP sauces by the bottle.

### Albine
*Albert Cuypstraat 69 (675 5135). Tram 16, 24, 25.* **Open** daily 10.30am-10pm. **Average** *f*10,50. **Map 6 E6**
One in a row of three cheap Surinami restaurants, Albine gets top marks for light-speed service and solid vegetarian or meat meals of *roti*, rice or noodles. A perfect place to gel your belly back together after the Heineken tour or to restfully dine after strolling around the Albert Cuyp market. *Disabled access.*

### Bagels & Beans
*Ferdinand Bolstraat 70 (672 1610). Tram 16, 24, 25.* **Open** 8.30am-6pm Mon-Fri; 9.30am-6pm Sat; 10am-5pm Sun. **Average** *f*5. **Map 6 E6**
Bagels have been slow to catch on in Amsterdam, but that may change soon, at least if this patioed success is anything to go by. Perfect for an econo-breakfast, lunch or snack. Sundried tomatoes are particularly well employed. *Disabled access.*

### 't Balkje
*Kerkstraat 46-48 (622 0566). Tram 1, 2, 5.* **Open** 9am-9pm daily. **Average** *f*14. **Map 5 D4**
Generous sandwiches, cheeseburgers, calamares, quiches and Dutch treats such as *uitsmuiters* at low prices at this spot just off Leidsestraat. *Disabled access.*

### Broodje Lekker
*Kinkerstraat 312 (616 1417). Tram 7, 17.* **Open** 8am-5pm Mon, Tue, Sat, Sun; 8am-7pm Thur. **Average** *f*4.
It's a bit out of the way, and the Dutch *broodje* – sandwiches – are pretty standard, but this is the only *broodje* emporium dedicated to the legacy of Frank Sinatra. Surrounded by his portraits, you can stuff your throat while listening to Ol' Blue Eyes.

### Einde van de Wereld
*Javakade, KNSM-laan Island (no phone). Bus 28.* **Open** 6pm-late Wed, Fri. **Average** *f*11.
This squatty boat-restaurant overlooking the IJ is not quite, as its name suggests, at the end of the world, but it is a bit of a trek. Still, the huge servings of vegetarian and meat dishes

at bargain prices – the drinks are cheap, too – make the trip well worth the effort. Go early before the food runs out.

### Falafel Dans
*Ferdinand Bolstraat 126 (676 3411). Tram 3, 12, 24, 25.* **Open** noon-1am Mon-Thur, Sun; noon-3am Fri, Sat. **Average** *f*5. **Map 6 E6**
A healthier restaurant surely does not exist: Falafel Dans even has an all-you-can-stuff salad bar. True absurdity kicks in every day between 3pm and 5pm, when the happy hour allows you to cram down all the falafel you can. It must be a buyer's market for chick peas…

### Falafel Maoz
*Reguliersbreestraat 45 (624 9290). Tram 4, 9, 14, 16, 20, 24, 25.* **Open** 6pm-2am daily. **Average** *f*5. **Map 6 E4**
Pretty similar to Falafel Dans, only without the happy hour.

### Fridge
*Vrieshuis Amerika, Oostelijke Handelskade 25 (no phone). Bus 39.* **Open** from 7.30pm Wed-Fri; closing time varies. **Average** *f*12,50.
The Fridge offers three-course vegetarian dinners, with décor changing themes every week. Dine within the apocalyptic splendour of Amsterdam's last great squat, the future of which, sadly, is uncertain.

### Gary's Muffins
*Prinsengracht 454 (420 1452). Tram 1, 2, 5.* **Open** 8.30am-6pm Mon-Sat; 9am-6pm Sun. **Average** *f*5. **Map 5 C5**
One of the best snack stops in town, serving bagels, brownies and muffins. Its popularity is such that it can become cramped, though if the weather is favourable you can sit outside by the canal and share your food with the sparrows. The Marnixstraat branch is the largest, while the branch on Reguliersdwarsstraat is Gary's Late Night, and is open until 3am nightly, and until 4am on Fridays and Saturdays. **Branches**: Jodenbreestraat 15 (421 5930); Marnixstraat 121 (638 0186); Reguliersdwarsstraat 53 (420 2406).

### Goodies
*Huidenstraat 9 (625 6122) Tram 1, 2, 5.* **Open** 10am-10.30pm Mon-Sat, 11am-10.30pm Sun. **Average** *f*16. **Map 5 C4**
The best designer sandwiches in town: lots of choice and lots of taste for not a lot of cash. Locals love it.

### Keuken van 1870
*Spuistraat 4 (624 8965). Tram 1, 2, 5, 20.* **Open** 12.30am-8pm Mon-Fri; 4-9pm Sat, Sun. **Average** *f*14. **Credit** AmEx, DC, EC, MC, V. **Map 2 C2**
Eating at this former soup kitchen puts you in touch with the Dutch populace: you'll often have to share a table with locals, while the menu contains nothing but authentic Dutch standards such as endive with rashers of bacon or rib of steak. *Disabled access.*

### Moeder's Pot
*Vinkenstraat 119 (623 7643). Tram 3, 10.* **Open** 5-10pm daily. **Average** *f*10. **Map 2 B1**
'Mother's Pot' serves up – you guessed it – simple and honest Dutch farmer's fare in woody and kitsch surrounds. Unfortunately, decades in the business has made the proprietor a bit grumpy. *Disabled access with assistance.*

### New King
*Zeedijk 115-117 (625 2180). Metro Nieuwmarkt.* **Open** 11am-midnight daily. **Average** *f*12. **Map 2 D2**
Over 500 Chinese dishes, of which more than half are under *f*15. There's a wide choice of rice, noodles, meat, chicken, fish and vegetarian dishes, and portions are so big that one plate serves three hungry people.

**Riaz**
*Bilderdijkstraat 193 (683 6453). Tram 3, 7, 12, 17.* **Open** 1-9pm Mon-Fri; 2-9pm Sun. **Average** ƒ14. **Map 4 B5**
Riaz, Amsterdam's finest Surinami restaurant, is where Ruud Gullit scores his *rotis* when he's in town. If the skies are sunny, take away a takeaway to nearby Vondelpark.

**Rimini**
*Lange Leidsedwarsstraat 75 (622 7014). Tram 1, 2, 5.* **Open** 11am-11pm daily. **Average** ƒ15. **Map 5 D5**
Rimini is one of those places that defies simple economic rules by producing large and flavoursome pizzas and pas-

tas at silly prices (everything always seems to be half-price). Don't miss.
*Disabled access.*

**Vlaamse Friteshuis**
*Voetboogstraat 31 (no phone). Tram 1, 2, 5.* **Open** 11am-6pm Mon-Sat; noon-5.30pm Sun. **Average** ƒ3. **Map 5 D4**
Just off the Spui is the best crisp and chunky Belgium chip shop in Amsterdam. There are a zillion toppings to choose from here, but to maximise calories and food groups, choose *oorlog*, which includes mayonnaisen peanut sauce and onions.

# Area index

# Cafés & Bars

*Drink to days gone by or to future trends in Amsterdam's imbiberies.*

Dutch courage? You're going to need it if you want to sample the full range of cafés and bars in Amsterdam. We're being neither cruel nor inaccurate when we say that the Dutch are a nation of drinkers, which is only good news for the visitor in search of an oasis that involves neither Liam nor Noel Gallagher. With – at the last count – 1,278 places in the city serving alcohol, there is, as the saying goes, something for everyone.

### FIRST CALL AT THE BAR, PLEASE

Normal café licences run from early morning until 1am during the week and until 2am or 3am on Fridays and Saturdays, but each area has a few bars that don't open until the evening and close a couple hours later than the standard places. Around the street markets, some bars and cafés open as early as five or six in the morning. Not that locals calling in at this unearthly hour will necessarily be looking for something alcoholic; many don't drink during the day at all. In neighbourhoods such as the Pijp and the Jordaan, and even in the centre of town, locals pop into the cafés not for a beer, but for a broodje (sandwich) or some other type of snack.

To sample Dutch culture at its most relaxed and charming, head to one of the plethora of old-style **brown cafés** scattered around the city. Named for their nicotine-stained walls and ceilings, they're the perfect place to lose an afternoon or evening in alcohol and conversation. For an equally traditional experience, head out of the centre to a local café for a game of biljarts, cards or cribbage, or make your way to a **proeflokaal**, where beer takes a back seat and liqueurs are drunk with alarming alacrity and enthusiasm. You'll pay a little bit more at the **grand cafés**, but it's often worth the extra few guilders for a glimpse at the often stunning interiors.

Still, with the twentieth century drawing to a close, it's not all tradition: **designer bars**, **alternative watering holes** and so-hip-it-hurts nightspots abound in town, all offering different atmospheres and opening at different times. And then there's the **Irish bars**, many of which are about as Irish as Jack Charlton but are massively popular nonetheless. Even if you don't drink, you'll be well looked after, with plenty of lovely **tearooms** and patisseries serving cakes, chocolates and confectionery to drooling locals, who wash it all down with a coffee or tea.

## HIGH SPIRITS & BRUTAL BREWS

Although there's a good choice of cafés in Amsterdam, there's an even bigger choice of beers. Heineken may be one of the world's largest breweries, but the days when you had a choice of Heineken, Heineken or Heineken in Dutch bars are long gone. In addition to the myriad local concoctions, many bars now stock a variety of imported foreign beers, with Belgian brews also popular. And then there's trappist beers, the mouth-puckering gueze beers, ales, strong pils, witbiers (wheat beers)… the choice is huge. Brits used to pint glasses may find the 250ml glasses small, but take care: generally speaking, this is strong stuff, and before you know it your head will be spinning with both alcohol abuse and regret for having given up your sobriety so quickly.

Don't forget the one genuine Dutch spirit: jenever. *The* Dutch drink for over 300 years, it's distilled from molasses and flavoured with juniper berries. Aside from the standard jenever, you can now get a variety of flavoured versions, and while it can be imbibed as part of a cocktail, the best way to drink it is neat, poured into a small glass filled to the brim: this way, you have to bend over it for fear of the dreaded spillage. All cafés worth their salt have jenever, but connoisseurs should head to a proeflokaal for the full experience.

## The Old Centre

### Around the Dam

#### Belgique

*Gravenstraat 2 (625 1974). Tram 1, 2, 5, 13, 14, 17, 20, 24, 25.* **Open** noon-1am Mon-Thur, Sun; noon-3am Fri, Sat. **Map 2 C3**
Unsurprisingly, a Belgian beer bar, and a decent one at that. *See box* **Cheers & booze**, *p132*.

#### De Drie Fleschjes

*Gravenstraat 18 (624 8443). Tram 1, 2, 4, 5, 9, 13, 16, 20, 24, 25.* **Open** noon-8.30pm Mon-Sat; 3-7pm Sun. **Map 2 C3**
A terrific proeflokaal just by Dam, serving a wide range of jenevers and liqueurs to local residents and workers. The padlocked barrels are rented by individuals and businesses.

#### Henri Prouvin

*Gravenstraat 20 (623 9333). Tram 1, 2, 5, 13, 14, 17, 20.* **Open** 4-11pm Tue-Fri; 4-9pm Sat. **Map 2 C3**
A charming drinks stop, albeit one for the more sophisticated palate. Henri Prouvin offers a spectacular variety of wines and champagnes by the bottle or the glass, at prices that range from reasonable to extortionate.

*Lose track of the afternoon at* **'t Loosje**, *right on Nieuwmarkt.*

## De Kuil

*Oudebrugsteeg 27 (623 4848). Tram 1, 2, 4, 5, 9, 13, 16, 17, 20, 24, 25.* **Open** noon-1am Sun-Thur; 10am-3am Fri, Sat. **Map 2 D2**
This perfect mix between brown café and coffeeshop is well hidden in a tiny side alley off the Damrak, and is even very likeable if you're not into the green stuff. A Boeing 747 ventilation system keeps things breezy, and there's '70s alternative music in abundance, though Frank Zappa fans have a head start. One of Amsterdam's best kept secrets.

## Noord Zuid Hollands Koffiehuis

*Stationsplein 10 (623 3777). Tram 1, 2, 4, 5, 9, 13, 16, 17, 24, 25.* **Open** *café* 9am-9pm Mon-Sat; 10am-9pm Sun; *kitchen* 10am-8.30pm daily. **Credit** AmEx, DC, EC, MC, V. **Map 2 D1**
Most people shoot straight past this lovely tearoom on their way out of Centraal Station. A shame, really: it's pleasantly relaxed, has a fine waterside terrace and serves reasonably priced light lunches.

## O'Reillys

*Paleisstraat 103-105 (624 9498). Tram 1, 2, 5.* **Open** noon-1am Mon-Thur, Sun; noon-2.45am Fri, Sat.
**Map 2 C3**
A massive and and massively popular Oirish bar. The location makes it a great meeting place, but the place has little else to recommend it.

## Oibibio

*Prins Hendrikkade 20-21 (553 9355). Tram 1, 2, 4, 5, 9, 13, 17, 20, 24, 25/Metro Centraal Station.* **Open** *bar* 9am-midnight Mon-Thur, Sun; 9am-1am Fri, Sat; *restaurant* 5-10pm daily. **Credit** AmEx, DC, EC, JCB, MC, V. **Map 2 D2**
Just opposite Centraal Station, this aesthetic and airy new Age bar has a wonderfully relaxed atmosphere and serves good, healthy snacks and meals. Also in the building is a Japanese-style tea garden and a sauna. *See chapters* **Shopping**, *p163*, and **Sport & Fitness**, *p216.*

## The Old Side & the Red Light District

### De Brakke Grond

*Nes 43 (626 0044). Tram 4, 9, 16, 20, 24, 25.* **Open** 12am-8am Mon, Sun; 10am-1am Tue-Thur; 10am-2am Fri, Sat. **Map 2 D3**
Part of the Flemish Cultural Centre, De Brakke Grond has a large range of Belgian beers, slugged back by connoisseurs and laymen alike. There's an excellent à la carte restaurant upstairs. *See box* **Cheers & booze**, *p132.*

### De Buurvrouw

*St Pieterpoortsteeg 29 (625 9654). Tram 4, 9, 14, 16, 20, 24, 25.* **Open** 8pm-2am Mon-Thur, Sun; 8pm-3am Fri, Sat. **Map 2 D3**
De Buurvrouw has quietened down considerably in recent years, but still remains lively, alternative and popular. A sawdust strewn floor, quirky art – including a figure of De Buurvrouw, 'the woman neighbour' who warmly watches over proceedings below – and a pool table all help give the place its atmosphere. Owned by the folks behind **De Koe** (*see* **Around Leidseplein**) and **Café Koenis & Meiland** (*see* **The Waterfront**).

### Café 't Loosje

*Nieuwmarkt 32-24 (627 2635). Tram 4, 9, 14, 16, 20, 24, 25/Metro Nieuwmarkt.* **Open** 9.30am-1am Mon-Thur, Sun; 9.30am-3am Fri, Sat. **Map 2 D2**
An outdoor terrace and old wooden interior make this subdued brown cafe a great place for late breakfasts, late nights and lazy, sunny afternoons. The tiles on the wall are nothing if not charming.

### Cul-de-Sac

*Oudezijds Achterburgwal 99 (625 4548). Tram 4, 9, 14, 16, 20, 24, 25/Metro Nieuwmarkt.* **Open** 3pm-1am Mon-Thur, Sun; 3pm-3am Fri, Sat. **Map 2 D3**
Hidden at the end of a little alley right in the heart of the Red

Light District, this bar-restaurant is a lovely escape. Buffets, barbecues and bulls are all on the often African-inspired menu, and there's a regular programme of sport on the bar's TV. *See chapter* **Restaurants**, *page 107.*

## Droesem

*Nes 41 (620 3316). Tram 4, 9, 14, 16, 20, 24, 25.* **Open** 5pm-1am Mon-Thur, Sun; 5pm-2am Fri, Sat. **Map 2 D3**
This small and cosy 'wine café' – a rare concept in beer-oriented Amsterdam – is barely a minute's walk from the Dam. House wine is served in carafes filled from barrels, and the fine selections of cheeses, breads, fish and meats are presented on wooden chopping boards.

## Durty Nelly's

*Warmoesstraat 115-117 (638 0125). Tram 4, 9, 14, 16, 20, 24, 25.* **Open** *bar* 8am-1am Mon-Thur, Sun; 9am-3am Fri, Sat; *kitchen* noon-10pm daily. **Map 2 D2**
Massive Irish bar in the heart of the Red Light District. The atmosphere is pretty relaxed, but it gets jam-packed at weekends. Popular with Brits.

## Engelbewaarder

*Kloveniersburgwal 59 (625 3772). Tram 4, 9, 14, 16, 20, 24, 25/Metro Nieuwmarkt.* **Open** noon-1am Mon-Thur; noon-3am Fri, Sat; 2pm-1am Sun. **Map 2 D3**
Live jazz brightens up Sunday afternoons in this pleasant literary café, frequented by quasi-academics and beer lovers enjoying the good range of brews. *See box* **Cheers & booze**, *p132.*

## Frascati

*Nes 59 (624 1324). Tram 4, 9, 14, 16, 20, 24, 25.* **Open** *bar* 4pm-1am Mon-Thur, Sun; 4pm-2am Fri, Sat; *kitchen* 5.30-10pm daily. **Map 2 D3**
A warm maroon colour complements the simple but sophisticated decor of the this traditional yet perversely modern bar. As with the nearby Flemish cultural centre **De Brakke Grond** (*see above*), the Frascati is popular with students and theatrical types from the several fringe venues in the street, providing the perfect pre- or post-theatre ambience.

## 't Gasthuis

*Grimburgwal 7 (624 8230). Tram 4, 9, 14, 16, 20, 24, 25.* **Open** noon-1am daily. **Map 2 D3**
Close to the university, 't Gasthuis's client base is largely made up of students, though others will feel at home. Excellent for lunches, and nice enough for an evening out, too.

## Gollem

*Raamsteeg 4 (626 6645). Tram 1, 2, 5.* **Open** 4pm-1am Mon-Thur, Sun; 4pm-2am Fri, Sat. **Map 2 D3**
A massive range of beers can be found at this brown café, which gets very busy in the evenings. *See box* **Cheers & booze**, *p132.*

## De Hoogte

*Nieuwe Hoogstraat 2A (626 0604). Tram 4, 9, 14, 16, 20, 24, 25/Metro Nieuwmarkt.* **Open** 10am-1am Mon-Thur; 10am-3am Fri, Sat; noon-1am Sun. **Map 3 E3**
A small but characterful drinking joint close to the Red Light District, catering to an alternative, hippyish crowd. Drinks are inexpensive compared to most bars, and De Hoogte is especially popular in the afternoons as a haven from the bustle of the tourist trap that is Nieuwe Hoogstraat.

## Maximiliaan

*Kloveniersburgwal 6-8 (624 2778). Tram 4, 9, 14, 16, 20, 24, 25.* **Open** noon-1am Tue-Thur, Sun; noon-2am Fri, Sat. **Map 2 D3**
A terrific brew-pub, established in 1992 and offering a great variety of beers. Food is also served at this popular establishment, which offers tours (by arrangement) of the premises. *See* **Cheers & booze**, *p132.*

## In't Aepjen

*Zeedijk 1 (626 8401). Tram 4, 9, 14, 16, 20, 24, 25.* **Open** 3pm-1am daily. **Map 2 D2**
Located in the oldest remaining wooden house in Amsterdam, this is a small and immensely characterful bar. The name – 'In the Monkeys' – comes from the days when the Zeedijk was frequented by sailors: those who couldn't pay their bills would bring back a monkey from the Dutch East Indies. It's quiet during the week but lively on Saturday night, when an accordionist plays sea shanties and old Amsterdam songs. *See chapter* **Architecture**, *p33.*

## In de Olofspoort

*Nieuwebrugsteeg 13 (624 3918). Tram 4, 9, 14, 16, 20, 24, 25.* **Open** 5pm-1am Mon-Thur, Sun; 5pm-2am Fri, Sat. **Map 2 D2**
Jenevers and liqueurs from Oud Amsterdam can be found at In de Olofspoort, a renaissance-type building dating from the seventeenth century. Worth a look if you fancy developing a taste for the hard stuff.

## Palmers

*Zeedijk 4-8 (427 0551). Tram 1, 2, 4, 5, 9, 13, 14, 17, 20, 24, 25.* **Open** *bar* 5pm-midnight daily; *kitchen* 5-11pm daily. **Map 2 D2**
This bar-restaurant in the old sailors' district has something of a trendy café feel to it, despite its history: the small, low-ceilinged room overlooking the bar was where ships' captains would recruit their crew at the end of an evening, from those who were too drunk to pay their bills. Food here is delicious and well presented, and the kitchen is open late.

## The Tara

*Rokin 89 (421 2654). Tram 4, 9, 14, 16, 20, 24, 25.* **Open** 11am-1am Mon-Thur, Sun; 11am-3am Fri, Sat. **Map 2 D3**
Running from the Rokin through to the Nes, this large yet cosy Irish bar has two bars, a pool table and a log fire. A television – mainly screening football – takes up one end of the bar, and there is also occasional live music here. As well as being one of the finest Irish bars in the city, it's also currently the only one where you're welcome to spliff up.

## De Waag

*Nieuwmarkt (422 7772). Tram 4, 9, 14, 16, 20, 24, 25/ Metro Nieuwmarkt.* **Open** 10am-1am daily. **Map 2 D2**
This 'castle', bang in the middle of Nieuwmarkt, can seem imposing, but walk through the doors of this former weigh-house, originally one of the gates to the old city dating from 1448, and you'll be transported back in time. There's no music here, and candles – a huge circular candelabra hangs from the ceiling – are the only lighting. The sole reminders of twentieth-century culture are the (free) Internet facilities. There's also a restaurant here. *See chapter* **Media**, *page 199.*

## VOC Café

*Schreierstoren, Prins Hendrikkade 94 (428 8291). Tram 4, 9, 14, 16, 20, 24, 25.* **Open** 10am-12pm Mon-Thur, Sun; 10am-3am Fri, Sat. **Map 2 D2**
Housed inside Amsterdam's oldest defence tower, the Schreierstoren, the VOC Café is a cosy bar with two terraces overlooking the quiet Gelderskade canal. There's regular live music (often courtesy of an accordionist), and they keep a good range of jenevers and liqueurs: try their own De Zeedijker Schoot An jenever, brewed to an old VOC recipe.

# The New Side & around Spui

## De Beiaard

*Spui 30 (622 5110). Tram 1, 2, 5.* **Open** 11am-1am Mon-Thur, Sun; 11am-2am Fri, Sat. **Map 2 D3**
A lovely, centrally located bar, with a huge range of beers and a decent food menu. This café, incidentally, is nothing

to do with De Beiaard on Herengracht. *See box* **Cheers & booze**, *p132*.

## Blarney Stone
*Nieuwendijk 29 (623 3830). Tram 1, 2, 5, 13, 17, 20.* **Open** 10am-1am Mon-Thur, Sun; 10am-3am Fri, Sat. **Map 2 C2**
Not the biggest Irish or Oirish bar in town, nor the most lavishly furnished, but its location means that it is often crowded and usually pretty lively.

## Café Dante
*Spuistraat 320 (638 8839). Tram 1, 5.* **Open** 11am-1am Mon-Thur, Sun; 11am-3am Fri, Sat. **Map 2 D3**
A bar, but a gallery, too: monthly exhibitions enliven the drinking area and the balcony above. Upstairs is Gallery Herman Brood, with paintings from the Dutch rock'n'roll icon, ex-junkie and overall bad-boy-turned-artist.

## Café Esprit
*Spui 10A (622 1967). Tram 1, 2, 4, 5, 9, 14, 16, 20, 24, 25.* **Open** *café* 10am-6pm Mon-Wed, Fri-Sat; 10am-10pm Thur; *kitchen* 10am-4pm Mon-Wed, Fri-Sat; 10am-9.15pm Thur. **Credit** AmEx, EC, MC, V. **Map 2 D3**
Owned by the neighbouring fashion store of the same name, this ultra-modern tearoom serves a full menu of Californian food as well as the more standard (but still classy) rolls and salads. It's at its best in the summer, when the terrace catches the sun and provides a welcome break from bargain-hunting on nearby Kalverstraat.

## Café Het Schuim
*Spuistraat 189 (638 9357). Tram 1, 2, 5.* **Open** 11am-1am Mon-Thur; 11am-2am Fri, Sat; 1pm-1am Sun. **Map 2 C3**
Het Schuim is a student haunt by day, but in the evenings arty thirtysomethings take over. Art is hung on the long, high walls, with exhibitions changing every six weeks. The perfect Sunday afternoon hangover cure.

## Café Luxembourg
*Spuistraat 22-24 (620 6264). Tram 1, 2, 5, 13, 17, 20.* **Open** *bar* 9am-1am Mon-Thur, Sun; 9am-2am Fri, Sat; *kitchen* 10am-11pm daily. **Credit** DC, EC, MC, V. **Map 2 C2**
Still going strong as the place to be seen for the trend-conscious and moneyed Amsterdammer, the Luxembourg is elegant, high-ceilinged and serves an excellent range of top quality snacks until midnight. If you're not up for hanging with the yuppies, the afternoon is your best bet to enjoy a quiet cappuccino. Dead posh.

## Hoppe
*Spui 18-20 (420 4420). Tram 1, 2, 4, 5, 9, 14, 16, 20, 24, 25.* **Open** 8am-1am Mon-Thur, Sun; 8am-2am Fri, Sat. **Map 2 C2**
An Amsterdam institution, this brown café allegedly dates from 1670. Always popular, it becomes impossibly crowded from 5pm to 6pm, when it's filled with stripey shirts having a quick one for the road on their way home from the office.

## De Jonge Roel
*Jonge Roelensteeg 4 (421 7521). Tram 1, 2, 5, 13, 14, 17, 20.* **Open** 4pm-1am Tues-Thur; 4pm-2am Fri, 2pm-2am Sat; 2pm-8pm Sun. **Map 2 D3**
A rather gothic bar, and one for the beer-lover: De Jonge Roel serves a great range of brews, many from Holland. *See box* **Cheers & booze**, *p132*.

## Ovidius
*Spuistraat 139 (620 8977). Tram 1, 2, 5, 13, 14, 17.* **Open** *bar* 10am-9pm Mon-Wed, Fri-Sun; 10am-11pm Thur; *kitchen* 11am-8pm Mon-Wed, Fri-Sun; 11am-10pm Thur. **Map 2 D3**
This tearoom is, perversely, the best place to get a coffee in Amsterdam. There's also a good array of sandwiches which, though not cheap, have to be tasted to be believed.

## Scheltema
*Nieuwezijds Voorburgwal 242 (623 2323). Tram 1, 2, 5, 13, 17, 20.* **Open** *bar* 8am-11pm Mon-Thur; 8am-2am Fri; 9am-9pm Sat; 11am-7pm Sun; *kitchen* opening times vary. **Map 2 D3**
Once thronged with journalists from the national dailies based down the road, this bar has become quieter now they've all moved out to the concrete wilderness. It retains an attractive, high-brow atmosphere.

## Seymour Likely
*Nieuwezijds Voorburgwal 250 (627 1427). Tram 1, 2, 5, 13, 17, 20.* **Open** *bar* 8pm-3am Mon-Thur, Sun; 8pm-4am Fri, Sat; *kitchen* 8pm-midnight Wed-Sun. **Credit** EC. **Map 2 D3**
Seymour Likely is the hangout of a young, self-consciously trendy crowd: listen to the conversation stop as you walk through the door, as Amsterdam's idea of the beautiful people all pause to give you the sartorial once-over. The drinks are nothing special, service is fashionably aloof and you'll never find a seat because it's always packed. Apart from that, it's all right.

## De Stil
*Spuistraat 326 (620 1349). Tram 1, 2, 5.* **Open** 10am-1am Mon-Thur, Sun; 10am-2am Fri, Sat. **Map 2 C3**
Sick of beer? Well, this is perhaps the place to head. De Stil stocks over 150 whiskies, including many single malts. Charmingly, there's a row of private bottles along the wall.

## De Wildeman
*Nieuwezijds Kolk 3 (638 2348). Tram 4, 9, 14, 16, 20, 24, 25.* **Open** noon-1am Mon-Thur; noon-2am Fri, Sat; 2-9pm. **Map 2 D2**
Around 200 bottled brews from various countries are always available here, and if you're missing your favourite pint, this is where it's most likely to be found: of the 18 draughts, many are international beers. The place is usually packed with a noisy and friendly mix of locals and visitors. The quieter side bar is strictly non-smoking.

*Art and alcohol mix easily at* **Café Dante** *in the centre of Amsterdam.*

# On the Canals

## Aas van Bokalen

*Keizersgracht 335 (623 0917). Tram 1, 2, 5.* **Open** *bar* 5pm-1am Mon-Thur, Sun; 5pm-2am Fri, Sat; *kitchen* 5.30-10.30pm daily. **Map 5 C4**
A friendly, unpretentious brown café with good value food and varied, though often young, clientele.

## De Admiraal

*Herengracht 319 (625 4334). Tram 1, 2, 5.* **Open** *bar* 4.30pm-midnight Mon-Fri; 5pm-midnight Sat; *kitchen* 5-10pm Mon-Sat. **Map 5 C4**
A popular, late-opening proeflokaal offering a wide range of liqueurs in a laid-back atmosphere: there are sofas for you to collapse on after you've drunk too much, though if you're planning on drinking a fair bit, try one of the decent meals before you get stuck in.

## De Beiaard

*Herengracht 90 (625 0422). Tram 1, 2, 5, 13, 14, 17, 20.* **Open** 4pm-1am Mon-Thur, Sun; 4pm-2am Fri, Sat. **Map 2 B2**
A large choice of beers can be drunk – slowly, mind – at this high-ceilinged, old-fashioned bar. Situated next door to Lieve, a fine Belgian restaurant.

## De Doffer

*Runstraat 12 (622 6686). Tram 1, 2, 5.* **Open** *bar* 11am-2am Mon-Thur; 11am-3am Fri, Sat; noon-2am Sun; *kitchen* noon-2.30pm, 6-10pm, daily. **Map 5 C4**
Two interconnecting cafés next to each other. One opens early and has the classic scruffy, friendly brown café ambience, while the other takes over at 8pm and stays open until the wee small hours.

## Felix Meritis

*Keizersgracht 324 (623 1311). Tram 13, 14, 17, 20.* **Open** 8.30am-7pm Mon-Fri; times vary Sat, Sun. **Map 5 C4**
An almost austere joint. The clientele at this open, high-ceilinged room – part of the theatre, for which *see chapter* **Theatre**, *page 221* – varies according to performance. There is also a restaurant, where you can eat prior to the show.

## Greenwoods

*Singel 103 (623 7071). Tram 1, 2, 5.* **Open** 9.30am-7pm Mon-Fri; 11am-7pm Sat, Sun. **Map 2 C3**
The service means this is hardly a fast food place, but everything here is freshly prepared, so we can forgive them: the cakes, scones and muffins baked daily on the premises. Try the cheesecake.

## Café Kalvertoren

*Singel 457 (427 3901). Tram 1, 2, 4, 5, 9, 14, 16, 20, 24, 25.* **Open** 10am-7pm Mon; 9am-7pm Tue, Wed, Fri; 9am-9pm Thur; 10pm-6pm Sat; noon-6pm Sun.
So-so café at the top of the Kalvertoren shopping centre, meriting a mention here purely for its spectacular vistas. *See box* **Rooms with a view**, *p129.*

## Land van Walem

*Keizersgracht 449 (625 3544). Tram 1, 2, 5.* **Open** *bar* 9am-1am Mon-Thur, Sun; 9am-2am Fri, Sat; *kitchen* 9.30am-10.30pm daily. **Map 5 D4**
One of the first designer bars, this long, narrow and bright filling station is currently being revamped. The food comes in good portions, with excellent vegetarian options.

## Lanskroon

*Singel 385 (623 7743). Tram 1, 2, 5.* **Open** 8am-5.30pm Tue-Fri; 8am-5pm Sat; 10-5pm Sun. **Map 5 D4**
Many regard this as the best *banketbakkerij* (patisserie) in town. The mouth-watering sacher tort, cakes, savouries, ice creams and chocolates can be wolfed down in the cramped tearoom, or bought as takeaway.

## Metz

*Keizersgracht 455 (520 7020). Tram 1, 2, 5.* **Open** 11am-5.30pm Mon; 9.30am-5.30pm Tue, Wed, Fri, Sat; 9.30am-9.30pm Thur; 12-5.30pm Sun. **Credit** AmEx, DC, EC, MC, V. **Map 5 D4**
The famous department store's café, with a fine lunch-style menu. *See box* **Rooms with a view**, *p129.*

## Morlang

*Keizersgracht 451 (625 2681). Tram 1, 2, 5.* **Open** *bar* 10am-1am Mon-Thur, Sun; 10am-2am Fri, Sat; *kitchen* 10am-11pm daily. **Credit** AmEx, MC, V. **Map 5 D4**
Morlang lacks the bright designer looks of Land van Walem next door, but is a pretty stylish hangout. The food here is good, and the selection of foreign spirits awesome.

## Pompadour

*Huidenstraat 12 (623 9554). Tram 1, 2, 5.* **Open** 9.30am-6pm Tue-Fri; 8.30am-5.30pm Sat. **Credit** EC. **Map 5 C4**
The cakes and crytal fruits are to die for, but it is the chocolates that Pompadour is most famous for. You can take your purchases away, but stop to enjoy a bite in the remarkable gilt-and-mirrors interior of the raised tearoom section.

## De Prins

*Prinsengracht 124 (624 9382). Tram 13, 14, 17, 20.* **Open** *bar* 10am-1am Mon-Thur, Sun; 10am-2am Fri, Sat; *kitchen* 6-10pm daily. **Map 2 C3**
Friendly and frequented by students, brown café De Prins is a great meeting place. The food is as good as the canal-side setting.

## Twee Prinsen

*Prinsenstraat 27 (624 9722). Tram 3, 10.* **Open** 10am-1am Mon-Thur, Sun; 10am-3am Fri, Sat. **Map 2 C2**
Tweedledum to the Tweedledee of the Vergulde Gaper opposite. There's a good range of beers here, and the clientele nicely mixed. The outdoor terrace is heated on chillier evenings.

## Van Puffelen

*Prinsengracht 377 (624 6270). Tram 1, 2, 5, 7, 10.* **Open** *bar* 3pm-1am Mon-Thur; 3pm-2am Fri; noon-2am Sat; noon-1am Sun; *kitchen* 6-11pm Mon-Sat; 5.30-10pm Sun. **Credit** AmEx, DC, EC, MC, V. **Map 2 C3**
The biggest brown café in Amsterdam and a haunt of the beautiful people, particularly on summer evenings when you can sit on the barge moored outside. There's live jazz on Sundays.

## Vergulde Gaper

*Prinsenstraat 30 (624 8975). Tram 3, 10.* **Open** 10am-1am Mon-Thur, Sun; 10am-2am Fri, Sat. **Map 2 C2**
A slightly more upmarket and larger version of the Twee Prinsen, Vergulde Gaper has an excellent selection of drinks, plus some sofas in which to snuggle up on a cold winter's evening.

# Around Waterlooplein

## Café de Sluyswacht

*Jodenbreestraat 1 (625 7611). Tram 9, 14, 20/Metro Waterlooplein.* **Open** 11.30am-1am Mon-Thur, Sun; 11.30am-3am Fri, Sat. **Map 3 E3**
Situated just across from the Rembrandthuis, this former lock-keeper's house was built in 1695, and has retained much of its charm from that era, as well as its foundations: the building leans heavily. The spacious terrace overlooks the waters of the Oude Schans, and is one of the most peaceful settings in Amsterdam.

*Escape to* **Kapitein Zeppos**.

### Dantzig

*Zwanenburgwal 15 (620 9039). Tram 9, 14, 20/Metro Waterlooplein.* **Open** *bar* 9am-1am Mon-Thur, Sun; 9am-2am Fri, Sat; *kitchen* 5.30-10pm daily. **Map 3 E3**
A spacious café/restaurant by the Stopera. For more, *see box* **Rooms with a view**, *p129.*

### De Druif

*Rapenburgerplein 83 (624 4530). Tram 1/Metro Waterlooplein.* **Open** 11am-1am Mon-Thur, Sun; 11am-2am Fri, Sat. **Map 3 E2**
A little-known brown bar of immense charm, right on the water's edge behind the harbour. If you make it out there you'll be the only non-local, but they're a very friendly bunch.

### De Jaren

*Nieuwe Doelenstraat 20 (625 5771). Tram 4, 9, 14, 16, 20, 24, 25.* **Open** *bar* 10am-1am Sun-Thur; 10am-2am Fri, Sat; *kitchen* 5.30-10.30pm daily. **Map 2 D3**
A beautifully restored old building with high ceilings, exposed brickwork and a tiled mosaic floor, De Jaren is the most elegant and unpretentious of Amsterdam's new grand cafés. *See box* **Rooms with a view**, *p129.*

### Kapitein Zeppos

*Gebed Zonder End 5 (624 2057). Tram 4, 9, 14, 16, 20, 24, 25.* **Open** *bar* 11am-1am Mon-Thur, Sun; noon-1pm Sun; *kitchen* 5.30-11pm daily. **Map 2 D3**
Used for storing horse-carriages in the seventeenth and eighteenth centuries, and then a cigar factory at the turn of the century, Kapitein Zeppos – named after a Belgian TV star from the '60s – has retained an olde worlde feel, despite the fact that it only opened in the mid-'90s. There is a charming restaurant in the conservatory area. Live jazz sounds out every Sunday from 7pm (except in summer), and Gypsy or Brazilian music can be heard during the week.

### Tisfris

*St Antoniesbreestraat 142 (622 0472). Tram 9, 14, 20/Metro Nieuwmarkt.* **Open** *bar* 9.30am-11pm daily; *kitchen* 9.30am-9.30pm daily. **Map 3 E3**
A bright, modern, trendy but undaunting split-level café decorated with paintings by Fabrice, a street artist whose works pop up with monotonous regularity all over town. The food is wholesome and delicious, the staff friendly and the clientele largely young and arty.

## Around Rembrandtplein

### Cooldown

*Rembrandtplein 45 (638 9242). Tram 4, 9, 14, 20.* **Open** 8pm-2am Mon-Thur, Sun; 8pm-4am Fri, Sat. **Map 6 E4**
Of all the bar/dancing meat markets in the city, this one is truly the pits. Avoid at all costs, unless you're extremely desperate for company. Loud seems to be the key word here, though the (usually drunk) people don't seem to care.

### Hooghoudt

*Reguliersgracht 11 (420 4041). Tram 4, 9, 14, 20.* **Open** 4pm-midnight Tues-Thur, 4pm-1am Fri; noon-1am Sat; noon-midnight Sun. **Map 6 E4**
A friendly proeflokaal, Hooghoudt specialises in the distillates of the Hooghoudt distillery. The bar at the front serves all sorts of vicious jenevers, while the restaurant at the back enables punters to line their stomachs before they get carried away.

### De Kroon

*Rembrandtplein 17-1 (625 2011). Tram 4, 9, 14, 20.* **Open** 10am-1am Mon-Thur, Sun; 10am-2am Fri, Sat. **Map 6 E4**
Several local TV companies and radio stations are housed in the same building as De Kroon, hence the proliferation of media types here. Huge, high-ceilinged, spacious and airy.

### Mulligans

*Amstel 100 (622 1330). Tram 4, 9, 14, 16, 20, 24, 25.* **Open** 4pm-1am Mon-Thur, Sun; 4pm-2am Fri; 2pm-2am Sat; 2pm-1am Sun. **Map 3 E3**
Yet another theme bar, but this one is more Irish than Oirish. The beer and the craic are both good, and there's a good programme of Irish music than runs almost daily. The pick of the pack.

### L'Opera

*Rembrandtplein 27-29 (627 5232). Tram 4, 9, 14, 20.* **Open** *bar* 10am-1am Mon-Thur, Sun; 10am-2am Fri, Sat; *kitchen* 11am-10pm daily. **Credit** AmEx, DC, EC, JCB, MC, V. **Map 6 E4**
The interior of this grand café is imposing and vaguely Parisian, with lots of mirrors and gilt. Unfortunately, the overall sense of style is not matched by the service, which is slow. The beer, incidentally, is expensive.

### Schiller

*Rembrandtplein 26 (624 9846). Tram 4, 9, 14, 20.* **Open** *bar* 4pm-1am Mon-Thur, Sun; 4pm-2am Fri, Sat; *kitchen* 5.30-10pm daily. **Credit** EC. **Map 6 E4**
This beautiful bar is a reminder of how things were on Rembrandtplein before neon was invented. A great art deco Amsterdam bar, it's part of the hotel of the same name (*see also* **Accommodation**, *p93*). If a lively atmosphere is what you're after, head elsewhere, but otherwise this is well worth a look.

### 't Madeliefje

*Reguliersdwarsstraat 76 (622 2510). Tram 4, 9, 14, 16, 20, 24, 25.* **Open** 9pm-3am Tue-Thur, Sun; 9pm-4am Fri, Sat. **Map 5 D4**
A real rarity: a smallish, trendy bar, crowded on weekends, that manages to maintain a very relaxed atmosphere. The

# Rooms with a view

Because of its compact size, the best way to explore Amsterdam is on foot. But when you're thirsty and the blisters on your feet are gradually creeping through your shoes and on to the pavement below, you can still explore the city from the comfort of a chair. All you need to do is find a café with a decent view, and your feet can rest easy for a while.

Named after Dutch ballet choreographer Rudi van Dantzig and situated right next to the Muziektheater, **Dantzig** (*see page 128*) is still as popular as when it opened in the late '80s. The library-style interior is spacious yet intimate, due to the skills of Dutch designers Pim Vlug and Peter Hertogh. However, the floor-to-ceiling windows force your eyes towards the beautiful Amstel just outside. In summer, the large terrace is a popular spot, with big parasols to make sure you won't lose your cool. The perfect place to relax after shopping at the adjoining Waterlooplein market.

Metz & Co, one of the last prestigious stores in the Leidsestraat, houses an equally prestigious café on the sixth. Paying ƒ6,50 for a pastry at **Metz** (*see page 127*) doesn't justify slow service and the staff's propensity to get orders wrong. But hey: the waiters probably think you're too busy admiring the views over Amsterdam to notice, and they might be right. From here, take in the various beauties of canal houses, gables, churches and other landmarks, which can be seen from four angles.

The Kalvertoren shopping centre (entered via Heiligeweg, Kalverstraat and Singel) houses more than thirty shops and a great café, up in a tower above the shops. Reached either by stairs or a glass elevator, the **Café Kalvertoren** (*see page 127*) has a nondescript interior, but that's easily forgotten: the floor-to-ceiling windows give you a dazzling, panoramic view of Amsterdam. See how many sights you can recognise. If it's too busy – it often is – take the stairs out. They're likely to be deserted, and the staircase, also made of glass, allows a voyeuristic glimpse out on the apartments and roof gardens surrounding the shopping centre.

A favourite with locals – and utter heaven compared to many of Rembrandtplein's tourist traps – the **De Jaren** café and restaurant (*see page 128*) has a terrace on the ground floor and a balcony on the first. Located on the corner of the Kloveniersburgwal canal and the Amstel, it offers magnificent views of both. While munching on one of the splendid sandwiches, gaze out and make up your mind whether to join the tourists opposite on a canal boat tour.

Although the **newMetropolis** museum (*see page 134*, and box **The appliance of science**, *page 75*) was built in 1997, it blends surprisingly well with the surrounding ancient harbour. It's quite a trek up there, mind: 120 steps to be precise, if you take the outside route. However, it's well worth the effort: here is where you'll find what are arguably the best panoramic views of old Amsterdam. Don't go inside the café unless you want to hear loud chart music. Instead, grab an ice-cream or a beer, sit outside and enjoy the awesomeness of it all.

music ranges from '70s R&B to classic soul, which may give you some idea. The salsa night on Wednesday is hugely popular. Try one of the shooters.

### De Korte Golf
*Reguliersdwarsstraat 41 (626 5435). Tram 4, 9, 14, 16, 20, 24, 25.* **Open** *8pm-2am Mon-Thur, Sun; 8pm-4am Fri, Sat.* **Map 5 D4**
For some bizarre reason, this two-storey brown café has become one of the most popular student hangouts in recent years. It's almost always packed, the drinks are overpriced, the music's too loud and the pool table is strictly grade Z. Still, regulars love it, so they must be doing something right.

## Around Leidseplein

### De Balie
*Kleine Gartmanplantsoen 10 (553 5130/restaurant 553 5131). Tram 1, 2, 5, 6, 7, 10, 20.* **Open** *July, Aug noon-2am daily; Sept-June 11am-2am daily.* **Map 5 D5**
Part of the cultural/political centre of the same name, De Balie is an open, marbled affair full of the arty and politically active watching the riff-raff of Leidseplein from large windows. The food upstairs is decent if unspectacular. *See chapter* **Theatre**, *p221.*

### Café Cox
*Marnixstraat 427 (620 7222). Tram 1, 2, 5, 6, 7, 10, 20.* **Open** *10am-1am Mon-Thur, Sun; 10am-2am Fri, Sat.* **Map 5 C5**
A pleasant, split-level bar and restaurant serving reasonably priced food. Thanks to its location – in the same building as the Stadsschouwburg – it attracts quite a theatrical crowd, particularly at night. *See chapters* **Restaurants**, *p112*, and **Theatre**, *p222.*

### Café de Koe
*Marnixstraat 381 (625 4482). Tram 7, 10, 17.* **Open** *4pm-1am Mon-Thur; 3pm-3am Fri, Sat; 3pm-1am Sun.* **Credit** EC. **Map 5 C4**
A friendly upstairs alternative bar decorated in a theme to suit its name (cows), along with a Scalextric track over the pool table. Staff are available for pinball competitions if it's not too busy, and the café/restaurant downstairs serves great food at reasonable prices. A terrific place.

*Beer at **Mulligans** puts a smile on everyone's face. Well, almost everyone. See page 128.*

## Het Molenpad

*Prinsengracht 653 (625 9680). Tram 1, 2, 5, 7, 10, 20.*
**Open** *bar* noon-1am Mon-Thur, Sun; noon-2am Fri, Sat; *kitchen* noon-3.30pm, 6-10.30pm, Mon-Fri; noon-4.30pm, 6-10.30pm, Sat, Sun. **Map 5 C4**
A long, dark and narrow brown bar with a large reading table at the back, good tapes, changing art exhibitions, exceptionally fine food, and a terrace to watch the scholarly enter the nearby public library. Very pleasant indeed, and there aren't many places near Leidseplein you can readily say that about.

## Reynders

*Leidseplein 6 (623 4419). Tram 1, 2, 5, 6, 7, 10, 20.*
**Open** 9am-1am Mon-Thur, Sun; 9am-2am Fri; 9am-3am Sat. **Map 5 C5**
Along with its neighbour Eylders, this brown café is probably the only bar worth considering on Leidseplein. Both are survivors of a bygone era, with white-aproned waiters and high-ceilinged interiors. Ignore the rest of the tacky joints, and head here for some much-deserved alcoholic relief.

## De Tap

*Prinsengracht 478 (622 9915). Tram 1, 2, 5, 6, 7, 10, 20.* **Open** 4pm-1am Mon-Thur, Sun; 4pm-3am Fri, Sat. **Map 5 D5**
A long, narrow, wood-panelled brown bar with character, not far from the generally frantic and characterless Leidseplein. De Tap has a pleasant ambience and a good range of snacks on offer. It's popular for office parties as its ancient, vomit-proof terracotta tiled floors make for an easy clean-up.

## De Zotte

*Raamstraat 29 (626 8694). Tram 1, 2, 5, 6, 7, 10, 20.* **Open** 4am-1am Mon-Thur, Sun; 4am-3am Fri, Sat. **Map 3 C4**
A really rather nice café just across from Leidseplein, whose speciality is Belgian beers. *See box* **Cheers & booze**, *p132.*

## The Plantage & the Oost

### Bierbrouwerij t'IJ

*Funenkade 7 (622 8325). Tram 6, 10.* **Open** 3-8pm Wed-Sun.
An excellent local brewery and bar based, oddly, in a windmill. Tours of the brewery can be arranged. *See box* **Cheers & booze**, *p132.*

## The Jordaan

### Café Nol

*Westerstraat 109 (624 5380). Tram 10.* **Open** 9pm-3am Mon-Thur, Sun; 9pm-4am Fri, Sat. **Map 1 B2**
Kitsch does not come any more hardcore: this over-the-top Jordaan bar/cultural institution, with its crowds of lustily singing locals, is supposed to sum up the true 'spirit' of the neighbourhood. Be warned: this brand of social cosiness comes with much jolly spittle flying through the air.

### Café Soundgarden

*Marnixstraat 164-166 (620 2853). Tram 10, 13, 14, 17, 20.* **Open** 1pm-1am Mon-Thur; 1pm-3am Fri; 3pm-3am Sat; 3pm-1am Sun. **Map 1 B3**
Popular with a grungey, alternative crowd and with music to match, Café Soundgarden has one of the best terraces in town, located most introspectively along a quiet stretch of canal. Pool, darts, pinball and table football help while away those rainy afternoons.

### Café Tabac

*Brouwersgracht 101 (622 6520). Tram 1, 2, 5, 13, 17, 20.* **Open** 11.30am-1am Mon-Thur, Sun; 11.30am-2am Fri, Sat. **Map 1 B2**
Despite a change of name – Tabac was formerly called 't Smackzeyl, after its 'shipsail' gablestone – this is still as brown a café as you could hope to find, perfectly situated on the corner of two canals. A standard menu is supplemented by a selection of club sandwiches.

# Cheers & booze

Drink a whiskey drink, drink a vodka drink, drink a lager drink, drink a cider drink... But what about a proper drink and, specifically, a proper beer? Sure, cafés are now offering a wider choice of liquid refreshments than ever before, but the choice is almost too much at times. Besides, not all cafés know how to actually serve the stuff. So, follow us as we head where few drinkers dare to go: in search of the perfect beer...

As a starter you can probably do no better than **In de Wildeman** (*see page 126*), arguably the best beer café in town. The friendly staff will take their time to help you make your choice – from over 200 bottled brews and 18 beers on tap – and the beer will be served with care and attention in the proper glass at the correct temperature. More variety can be found at **Gollem** (*see page 125*), actually the first café in Amsterdam to really offer a choice of brews. There are around 100 in stock at any one time, and this brown café is still worth visiting. Between these two is **Belgique** (*see page 122*), a small café just behind the Nieuwe Kerk with a good range of Belgian beers and – curiously – trappist cheese.

Just down on Spui is **De Jonge Roel** (*see page 126*). Another choice range of bottled and draught brews can be had here. From back when it was known as the Netherlands Beer Café, De Jonge Roel has been the perfect juxtaposition to **De Zotte**, the Belgium beer café just off Leidseplein (*see page 131*). Also on Spui is **De Beiaard** (*see page 125*), part of the Beiaard group that also has establishments in Enschede, Haarlem and Hoorn. The spacious enclosed terrace overlooking Spui makes for a lovely setting in which to sample their changing range of over 70 beers and, if you're hungry, enjoy a meal from the more than adequate menu. Belgian beer nuts are also well catered for at **De Brakke Grond** (*see page 123*), part of the Flemish Cultural Centre downstairs, while another excellent choice of brews can be had at the small but perfectly formed brown café **'t Smalle** in the Jordaan (*see page 134*).

Do not think you are confined to central Amsterdam for choice: beer-lovers could do a lot worse than **Welling** (*see page 134*), just behind the Concertgebouw. Run by the person who made the **Engelbewaarder** (*see page 125*) the good beer café it still is, there's a good range here, and you may find musicians dropping in after they've finished performing. Not far away

from here is **'t Ezeltje** (*see page 134*), where you can enjoy a selection of brown café beers and order from the bar menu.

While all the aforementioned establishments bring in their beer from outside sources – often from some of the 50 breweries in the Netherlands – there are a number of bars and cafés in town that even brew their own. One of the first was **Bierbrouwerij 't IJ**, started by former musician and songwriter Kaspar Petersen in 1984 and situated within an old windmill (*see page 131*, and *box* **Windmills on your mind**, *page 46*). The variety of beer here is compelling, with the range of seasonal brews particularly interesting. All bar one is bottle-conditioned, but the beers are frequently available on draught. Opening hours are limited and the place is understandably popular, but go in summer and you'll be able to sup your brew by the canal. Most civilised.

**Maximiliaan** (*see page 125*) is a multi-level homebrew pub – though beers are supplied elsewhere as well – started by brothers Albert and Casper Hoffman in 1992. They make a song about their products, too: the first thing you see as you walk in is a magnificent working copper at the end of the bar, used for producing top fermented beers, including the Kölsch-style Bethanien, and the dark, toffee-nosed Klooster, as well as several seasonal beers. Beers produced in conjunction with SNAB, an alternative brewers organization, are often in stock, and if you're hungry, rest assured: Maximiliaan is also a restaurant, with a (vegetarian-friendly) menu.

If you set up your visit carefully, you can coincide with one of the country's fine beer festivals. The autumnal Bok beers have their own festival on the last weekend in October held at the Beurs van Berlage; late April sees the Meibock festival, held at the Maximiliaan; and out of town, there's a winter beer festival in Delft in mid-January. And if you want to take some home with you, head to one of several beer-specialist off-licences in the city, of which the largest is **De Bierkoning** (*see chapter* **Shopping**, *page 155*). And if you're still thirsty after all that, well, we give up.

## PINT

*Postbus 3757, 1001 AN Amsterdam (0252 522909/010 411 2879).* **Open** *phone enquiries* 7.30-9.30pm Tue.
Contact PINT for details on beer festivals in Holland, and other beer-related activities. They're on the Internet at *www.pint.nl.*

*Moooove on over to the udder side of Amsterdam at the **Café de Koe**. See page 129.*

## Café West Pacific

*Haarlemmerweg 8-10 (597 4458). Tram 10/bus 18, 22.*
**Open** *bar* 11.30am-1am Tue-Thur, Sun; 11.30am-2am Fri,
Sat; members only after 10pm Thur-Sat (admission *f*15);
*restaurant* 6-10.30pm daily. **Map 1 A2**
This large alterna-bar has a huge fire, a dancefloor and a
decent menu. A mixture of music plays, but after 11pm
there's a cover charge and an emphasis on jazz-funky dance
music. There's also occasional live music on Sundays. The
café is part of the **Westergasfabriek**, a former gas factory (*see chapter* **Theatre**, *p222*).

## Koophandel

*Bloemgracht 49 (623 9843). Tram 10, 13, 14, 17, 20.*
**Open** 10pm-3am Mon-Thur, Sun; 10pm-4am Fri, Sat.
**Map 1 B3**
A late-night brown bar for the very dedicated. Situated in a
former warehouse beside the Jordaan's prettiest canal, it's
virtually empty before midnight, when things start to get
steadily livelier. Closing time is flexible but usually isn't
before dawn. Popping in after eating a fine fondue at its
neighbour, the **Groene Lantaarn** (*see box* **Cheese Trek**,
*p115*), makes for a culturally scenic evening.

## Du Lac

*Haarlemmerstraat 118 (624 4265). Bus 18, 22.* **Open**
4pm-1am Mon-Wed, Sun; 4pm-2am Thur-Sat. **Map 2 C2**
A beautiful grand café fitted out in an outrageously quirky
art deco style, including stuffed alligators and mutant trees.
It packs in trendies by the hundred, each of whom has a
favourite spot: the cosy snugs, raised gallery and glass-walled
conservatory are all popular. There's live jazz on Sundays.

## 't Monumentje

*Westerstraat 120 (624 3541). Tram 13, 14, 17, 20.*
**Open** 8.30am-1am Mon-Thur; 9am-3am Fri, Sat; 11am-
1am Sun. **Map 1 B2**
A nice, cosy brown café in the Jordaan, small but perfectly
formed and with a decent range of beers. A useful refreshment stop if you're visiting the Westerstraat market.

## Nieuwe Lelie

*Nieuwe Leliestraat 83 (622 5493). Tram 10, 13, 14, 17,
20.* **Open** 2pm-1am Mon-Thur; 2pm-2am Fri, Sat; 4-9pm
Sun. **Map 1 B3**
A charming split-level Jordaan brown bar, one of only a few
in the area where you can be pretty sure of getting a table
until quite late in the evening. It's very quiet and relaxed,
and if conversation's a bit stilted, then you can take advantage of the often unoccupied chessboards.

## Orangerie

*Binnen Oranjestraat 15 (623 4611). Tram 3/bus 18, 22.*
**Open** 4pm-1am Mon-Thur; 4pm-3am Fri; noon-3am Sat;
1pm-1am Sun. **Map 1 B2**
A delightful, relaxed and brown bar indeed (even though its
kitschified exterior may suggest otherwise), a stone's throw
from Brouwersgracht. It's good for a quiet evening out, holding private conversations while Pat Boone spins away on the
classic old skool jukebox.

## De Reiger

*Nieuwe Leliestraat 34 (624 7426). Tram 10, 13, 14, 17,
20.* **Open** *bar* 11am-1am Mon-Thur; 11am-2am Fri,
Sat; *kitchen* 6-10.30pm daily. **Map 1 B3**
The style-conscious alternative to the Nieuwe Lelie (*see
above*) down the street, this light and airy brown bar is
one of the most popular watering holes in the Jordaan. Get
there early, particularly if you want to eat from its much-
hyped menu.

## SAS

*Marnixstraat 79 (420 4075). Tram 7, 10, 17, 20.* **Open**
2pm-1am Mon-Thur, Sun; 2pm-3am Fri, Sat. **Map 1 B3**
Comfortable sofas and chairs sit among the wonderfully clut-
tered and intensely arty interior of this quasi-alternative café.
The décor changes whenever the owner feels like a change.
Good, homely meals at very low prices (and in very large
portions) are served downstairs and on the canalside terrace.
Candlelit, casual and charmingly romantic, this is a great little Amsterdam bar.

### 't Smalle

*Egelantiersgracht 12 (623 9617). Tram 13, 14, 17, 20.*
Open 10am-1am daily. **Map 1 B3**
't Smalle is a delightful café in the Jordaan: friendly, pleasingly situated by a canal, and lovely in summer. *See box*
**Cheers & booze**, *p132.*

### Thijssen

*Brouwersgracht 107 (623 8994). Tram 3.* **Open** 9.30am-1am Mon-Thur, Sun; 9.30am-2am Fri; 7am-2am Sat.
**Map 1 B2**
Owned by three local barflys, Thijssen's high windows and brown and nicotine-yellow highlighted interior blend in perfectly with the more ancient neighbouring cafés.

### De Tuin

*2e Tuindwarsstraat 13 (624 4559). Tram 3, 10, 13, 14, 17, 20.* **Open** 10am-1am Mon-Thur; 10am-2am Fri, Sat; 11am-1am Sun. **Map 1 B3**
A classic Jordaan brown café frequented by slightly alternative locals, De Tuin ('The Garden') is stone-floored, dark and always lively. Excellent apple tarts are served in the afternoons, and there's always someone in there looking for a game of chess or backgammon.

### Twee Zwaantjes

*Prinsengracht 114 (625 2729). Tram 13, 14, 17, 20.*
**Open** 8pm-1am Mon, Tue, Thur; 8pm-3am Fri, Sat; 3pm-1am Sun. **Map 1 B3**
A less rowdy version (but only just) of the Café Nol, this tiny bar is usually crammed to bursting point with oom-pah-pah accordion players and yodelling Jordaansers.

## The Museum Quarter

### Café Ebeling

*Overtoom 52 (689 1218). Tram 1, 3, 6, 12.* **Open** 11am-1am Mon-Thur; 11am-3am Fri, Sat; noon-1am Sun.
**Map 5 C5**
In the premises of an old bank, Ebeling is a well laid out, split-level bar which aims itself at the young and trendy without being snobby or needing to have the music so loud you can't think. One other plus point: Ebeling is one of the few non-Irish bars in town that serves Guinness.

### Welling

*Jan Willem Brouwerstraat 32 (662 0155). Tram 2, 3, 5, 12, 16, 20.* **Open** 3pm-1am Mon-Thur, Sun; 3pm-2am Fri, Sat. **Map 5 D6**
Just by the Concertgebouw, Welling offers plenty of choice in the beer department, and a welcoming, relaxed atmosphere. *See box* **Cheers & booze**, *p132.*

## The Pijp

### Carel's Café

*Frans Halsstraat 76 (679 4836). Tram 16, 24, 25.*
**Open** 10am-1am Mon-Thur; 10am-2am Fri, Sat; 11am-1am Sun. **Map 6 E6**
Although Carel's is basically a large neigbourhood café, people make the special trip from all over town for its excellent lunches and dinners. The Saenredamstraat branch is a night café just over the road.
**Branches:** Saenredamstraat 32 (676 0888); Voetboogstraat 6 (622 2028).

### 't Ezeltje

*Cornelis Troeststraat 56-58 (662 1703). Tram 12, 25.*
**Open** 4pm-1am Mon-Thur, Sun; 4pm-3am Fri, Sat.
An affable and popular brown café in the Pijp, loved by locals and visiting beer-lovers alike. *See box* **Cheers & booze**, *p132.*

### Gambrinus

*Ferdinand Bolstraat 180 (671 7389). Tram 16, 24, 25.*
**Open** 11am-1am Mon-Thur, Sun; 11am-2am Fri, Sat.
**Map 6 E6**
Live music on a Sunday is the perk here, at this otherwise pleasant local brown café in the Pijp. The reasonably priced menu offers a nice range of snacks, and the beer is served with due care and attention.

### O'Donnells

*Marie Heinekenplein (676 7786). Tram 16, 24, 25.*
**Open** *bar* 11.30am-1am Mon-Thur, Sun; 11.30am-3am Fri, Sat; *kitchen* 11.30am-3pm, 5.30-10pm, Mon-Fri; 11.30am-10pm Sat, Sun. **Map 6 E6**
A pretty standard Irish formula bar, complete with all the usual Gaelic schtick. It's a huge place, and hugely popular, too: there's regular live music out front, though Brits may be more interested in the Sky-equipped television out back, screening most of the big football and rugby games. Cheekily, O'Donnells is a Grolsch café… directly opposite the (disused) Heineken brewery.

### Wildschut

*Roelof Hartplein 1-3 (676 8220). Tram 3, 5, 12, 24, 25.*
**Open** *bar* 9am-1am Mon-Thur, Sun; 9am-3am Fri, Sat; *kitchen* noon-9pm daily.
This cavenous café/restaurant – complete with an impressive art deco interior – is still one of the places to be seen in Amsterdam. In summer, take a seat on the large terrace overlooking the Roelof Hartplein, a square surrounded by Amsterdam School architecture. Rooms can be hired out for private functions.

## The Waterfront

### Kanis & Meiland

*Levantkade 127 (418 2439). Bus 28, 32, 59.* **Open** *bar* 10-1am Mon-Thur, Sun; 10-3am Fri, Sat; *kitchen* 6-10pm.
Situated on KNSM island (hence the name), Kanis & Meiland is in the middle of Amsterdam's redeveloping docklands. The bright and spacious café – with a pool table and a waterfront terrace – is perfect for summer, while the international cuisine from the tiny kitchen includes Thai chicken, pasta and a large range of tasty salads.

### newMetropolis

*Oosterdok 2 (0900 919 1100) Bus 22/Apr-Oct shuttle boat from Centraal Station.* **Open** *museum* 10am-6pm Sun-Fri; 10am-9pm Sat. **Map**
The café at this new science museum is unremarkable save for its fantastic views over the city. Pleasingly, you don't have to pay the museum's admission charge to have a drink or snack in the café. *See boxes* **The appliance of science**, *p75,* and **Rooms with a view**, *p129.*

*Enjoy the craic at* **O'Donnells.**

# Coffeeshops

*Where to get more hash for your cash.*

Let's face it. Many of those visiting the historic city of Rembrandt and Van Gogh do so with but one thing on their mind: getting stoned. Amsterdam remains the one city in the world where people can stroll into what is ostensibly a café and purchase, over the counter and in full view of everyone, substances that would lead to arrest and possible criminal charges elsewhere in the world.

However, even here, da 'erb is not strictly legal, merely tolerated by the authorities (*see box* **Courier X**, *page 137*). Coffeeshops can sell soft drugs, but only in amounts of five grams or less; they can stock up to 500 grams (just over a pound) at a time for supply. If individuals are found with up to 30 grams for their own personal use, then it 'will still have no priority as far as investigation is concerned': basically, the police don't mind.

The attitude of the locals is, as with most things, a mixture of apathy and amused tolerance: coffeeshops here are used by locals and tourists alike. The exceptions – the gaudier, touristy establishments in the centre of town, like the **Bulldog** – are to be avoided. Instead, check out one of the infinitely better and cheaper places listed below.

## HASH ON DEMAND

What all coffeeshops have in common is the manner in which hashish and marijuana is sold (anything stronger is definitely frowned upon). Almost all coffeeshops have a menu card either on the bar or just behind it. Most hash and weed is sold in bags of *f*10 (around a gram's worth, depending on quality) or larger *f*25 bags. Prices are much of a muchness, but quality can vary hugely.

Good coffeeshops have a bewildering array of comestibles. The hash side of things is fairly clear, as varieties are generally named after the country of origin. Weed is a bit more complicated. It divides roughly into two categories: bush weeds grown naturally, such as Thai; and Nederwiet or Skunk, an indigenous Dutch product grown under UV lights for maximum toxi-hydro carbons (THC, the active ingredient). As with Guinness in Ireland, the skunk here is worlds away from anything available elsewhere, and caution is advisable if you are at all interested in remembering anything. The same caution should be exercised when it comes to most of the space cake on offer: return to planet Earth can be a protracted affair. Don't mix alcohol and smoking if you're not used to it, and if you do overdo it, eat or drink something sweet.

*A very different type of Tupperware party.*

The only don't that really needs to be stressed is that you should never, ever buy anything from street dealers. Junkies proliferate in certain areas of town, and if a street deal is not a precursor to a mugging, then you can count yourself lucky. Common sense is all that's needed: there are coffeeshops everywhere. It's also important to bear in mind that there are places where smoking is frowned upon. Not everyone in Amsterdam is going to smile and wave a peace sign if you have a joint in your hand. If in doubt, don't be afraid to ask: the worst you will get is a 'no'. But in the meantime, happy smoking…

## Coffeeshops

For **The Otherside**, Amsterdam's only gay coffeeshop, and for details of lesbian bar **Saarein**'s home-growing contest, *see chapter* **Gay & Lesbian**, *pages 189-90*.

### Barney's Breakfast Bar
*Haarlemmerstraat 102 (625 9761). Tram 13, 14, 17, 20.* **Open** 8am-8pm daily. **Map 2 C2**
If a huge, greasy breakfast washed down with HP sauce and a joint is your preferred hangover cure, then Barney's is undoubtedly your kind of place. The friendly staff serve breakfast – and cannabis – all day long, in an environment brimming with both Britpop (music) and Britpoop (the UK tabloids).

Take a toke on the **T-Boat**, Amsterdam's only floating coffeeshop.

## Free City

*Marnixstraat 233 (625 0031). Tram 3, 10.* **Open** noon-12.30am Mon-Thur, Sun; noon-2am Fri, Sat. **Map 4 B4**
Free City is more of a bar than a coffeeshop (most coffeeshops don't have a licence to sell alcohol), though it does have a reasonable selection of weed and hash. The pavement terrace looks out on to the ugliest street in town.

## Global Chillage

*Kerkstraat 51 (639 1154). Tram 1, 2, 5.* **Open** 11am-midnight daily. **Map 5 D4**
Amsterdam's own little piece of Goa, tucked away in a side street near Leidseplein. It's popular with a horizontal crowd (seating is low but comfortable), and the DJs at the weekend, playing ambient and mellow sounds, make it cooler still.

## Grasshopper

*Oudebrugsteeg 16 (626 1529). Tram 4, 9, 16, 24, 20, 25/Metro Centraal Station.* **Open** 8am-1am Mon-Thur; 7am-1am Fri-Sun. **Map 2 D2**
Situated close to Centraal Station, the Grasshopper is often the first stop for visitors. It's not bad as a starting point: the décor is a lot less tacky than many of the surrounding coffeeshops, and the selection of dope is pretty good.
**Branch**: Nieuwezijds Voorburgwal 59 (624 6753).

## Greenhouse

*Oudezijds Voorburgwal 191 (627 1739). Tram 4, 9, 14, 16, 20, 24, 25.* **Open** 9am-1am Mon-Thur, Sun; 9am-3am Fri, Sat. **Map 2 D3**
The Greenhouse comes with quite a reputation: it was voted the best coffeeshop in Amsterdam during the prestigious High Times Festival of 1997 (*see below* **Events**), and won the Cannabis Cup five years in succession from 1993 to 1997. Connoisseurs will delight in the hash/grass and seeds menu (from its own Greenhouse Seed Co); the knowledgeable staff will talk you through the different effects and highs of each purchase. Smaller amounts are available, as is alcohol.
**Branches**: Tolstraat 91 (673 7430); Waterlooplein 345 (622 5499).

## The Grey Area

*Oude Leliestraat 2 (420 4301). Tram 1, 2, 5, 13, 14, 17, 20.* **Open** noon-10pm Tue-Sun. **Map 2 C3**
Originally a hemp seed restaurant, this place is small but friendly, with the emphasis definitely on the quality of weed:
the menu is particularly good here. The Grey Area also do free refills of coffee.

## Homegrown Fantasy

*Nieuwezijds Voorburgwal 87A (627 5683). Tram 1, 2, 5, 13, 17, 20.* **Open** 9am-midnight Mon-Thur, Sun; 9am-1am Fri, Sat. **Map 2 D2**
Although Homegrown Fantasy is rather an average coffeeshop, it holds one of the widest selections of weed in Weedsville. This menu, and its central location, make it a popular smoker's venue.

## Kadinsky

*Rosemarijnsteeg 9 (624 7023). Tram 1, 2, 5.* **Open** 10am-1am daily. **Map 2 D3**
Pastels, plants and comfy sofas decorate this split-level coffeeshop, a perpetually popular and hip Amsterdam hangout. The menu lists a wide and impressive selection of hash and grass, including descriptions, tastes and effects (from 'well high' to 'very stoned'). The prices are above average, but it will do smaller deals, including *f*5 amounts.

## Paradox

*1e Bloemdwarsstraat 2 (623 5639). Tram 10, 13, 14, 17, 20.* **Open** 10am-8pm daily. **Map 1 B3**
A bright, characterful joint in the Jordaan that serves healthy, organic food and drinks on top of all the usual dope. A welcome change from the usual dingy pit-in-Marrakech atmosphere that pervades many coffeeshops.

## Pi Kunst en Koffie

*2e Laurierdwarsstraat 64 (622 5960). Tram 7, 10, 13, 14, 17, 20.* **Open** 10am-8pm Mon-Sat. **Map 4 B4**
A high-ceilinged coffeeshop looking out on to a quiet canal. The two rooms – one with loud orange and blue walls, the other a dubious mock-Egyptian theme presumably created while under the influence – are linked by a huge, wooden, semicircular bar. There are Internet facilities in the basement, and the choc chip cookies are practically legendary.

## De Rokerij

*Lange Leidsedwarsstraat 41 (622 9442). Tram 1, 2, 5, 6, 7, 10, 20.* **Open** 10am-1am Mon-Thur, Sun; 10am-3am Fri, Sat. **Map 5 D5**
A marvellous discovery on an otherwise hideously touristy street by Leidseplein, De Rokerij is a veritable Aladdin's

cave: lit by wall-mounted candles and beautiful metal lanterns, it's decorated with colourful Indian art and a variety of seating ranging from mats on the floors to decorative 'thrones'. The music is upbeat, and it also serves alcohol.
**Branches:** Amstel 8 (620 0424); Singel 8 (422 6643).

### Samementereng

*Tweede Laurierdwarsstraat 44 (624 1907). Tram 10, 13, 14, 17, 20.* **Open** noon-8pm Mon-Sat. **Map 4 B4**
If you're after an unusual experience on a par with one of Mr Benn's visits to the fancy dress shop, then pop into what is ostensibly a bric-a-brac shop crammed to the nines. At the back of the store is an African hut-style coffeeshop-cum-conservatory, complete with reggae, rastas and table football.

### Siberia

*Brouwersgracht 11 (623 5909). Tram 1, 2, 4, 5, 13, 17, 20/Metro Centraal Station.* **Open** 11am-11pm Mon-Thur, Sun; 11am-midnight Fri, Sat. **Map 2 C2**
Escape from the busy Haarlemmerstraat and take advantage of the peaceful pavement terrace overlooking this particularly beautiful canal. Inside, it's spacious and light: the low, wide tables are ideal for whiling away a rainy afternoon playing board games, while table football and pinball keep the more energetic regulars amused. There are regular exhibitions by local artists, and coffee and tea costs just ƒ1 a cup.

### T-Boat

*Oudeschans, by no.143 (423 3799). Tram 9, 14, 20.* **Open** 10am-midnight daily. **Map 3 E2**
The ultimate 'Amsterdam' experience: a coffeeshop on a boat. Score downstairs in the huge hull, where you can also catch a quirky film or chill to the music. Up on the deck, the views over the water towards the charming, leaning canal house – actually a bar, the Café de Sluyswacht, for which *see chapter* **Cafés & Bars**, *p128* – are lovely.

### La Tertulia

*Prinsengracht 312 (no phone). Tram 7, 10, 13, 14, 17, 20.* **Open** 11am-7pm Tue-Sat. **Map 4 C4**
A rather impressive depiction of a stoned-looking Van Gogh is painted on the outer walls of this charming, spacious split-level corner coffeeshop where, incidentally, Michelle from *EastEnders* took her first toke some years ago. In summer, the terrace overlooking the city's poshest canal is a delightful place to take.

### Tweede Kamer

*Heisteeg 6 (627 5709). Tram 1, 2, 5.* **Open** 10am-1am Mon-Thur, Sun; 10am-2am Fri, Sat. **Map 2 D3**
Situated off the Spui, Tweede Kamer is a bit of an insider's place, and is frequented more by locals as a result of its deserved reputation for having a wide range of imported grass. Rather smoky, poky and 'old Dutch style', you might do well to purchase your grass here but head elsewhere to actually smoke the stuff.

### Yo-Yo

*Tweede Jan van den Heijdenstraat 79 (664 7173). Tram 3, 4.* **Open** noon-8pm daily. **Map 6 F5**
A popular neighbourhood coffeeshop in the Pijp area, spacious and simply but pleasingly designed. The atmosphere is intrinsically mellow and chilling all day, but on Saturdays, you can also have a personal horoscope reading while you smoke.

# Tales of the city **Courier X**

You strut through the front door of the coffeeshop, smugly engage in a simple transaction, and then smoke the sweet smoke. You exit the front door: wiggly, wasted, and, most importantly – for you have done no wrong – free of paranoia. What a wonderful town.

Well, sort of. The glitch is that the wobbly law that allowed you this simple pleasure neglected to allow for how the wacky weed got there in the first place. Or rather, the lack of a law: as detailed above, possession is, while not legal, tolerated by the authorities. Known coffeeshops can sell up to five grams at a time. But where do they get the stuff from?

From the world of Courier X, who brought that weed in through the 'back door': the door that leads back into a legal void where growers, 'importers', and wholesale 'offices' must run their slickly operated weed-supply businesses on the sly. This tragically underpaid Johnny – or Jenny – Appleweed is the missing link, shuttling the goods from the darkness of the black market to the light of your ganga-addled skull. Be thankful to Courier X, for he is being squeezed for your sins: squeezed between the worlds of the legal and illegal, squeezed between the laws of supply and demand, and squeezed for time as he hastens between forgotten appointments (this is an industry fraught with short-term memory loss, for obvious reasons).

Wandering around Amsterdam, you may have noticed many speedy cyclists with large bags of what looks like laundry slung over their shoulders. No, the Dutch are not especially obsessed with cleaning their clothes. Yes, you may have had a fleeting encounter with Courier X during one of his rounds. With about two kilos to a bag, and maybe a couple of hundred guilders earned per kilo, he's carrying a nice day's profit over his shoulder. Assuming he sells it, of course: Amsterdam has a surplus of soft drugs, and the goods carried by the courier must be just right to be bought up.

The coffeeshop owners deal on the legitimate half of this economy, and can fearlessly redirect their profits into other legal ventures; some invest in nightclubs and hotels. The suppliers and importers experience the profitability of being illegal. But Courier X remains in a limbo land where such twentieth-century clichés as 'Kafkaesque' or 'Catch 22' are very real: he is, put simply, stuck right in the middle.

## Events

For details of the **Cannabis Cup**, *see chapter* **Amsterdam by Season**, *page 11*.

### Global Days Against the Drug War

*Stichting Legalize, Postbus 225, 2300 AE Leiden (070 380 8433).*
Events are organised concurrently in around 30 cities worldwide in an attempt to raise awareness of drugs issues. Spread over three days in June, it includes a remembrance ceremony in Dam Square for victims of drug warfare, a political forum, and a 'Legalize' street party, where party and political animals march together on a high-profile route through the centre of town.

### Highlife Hemp Exhibition

*Highlife, Discover Publishers BV, Huygensweg 7, 5482 TH Schijndel (073 549 8112/fax 073 547 9732).*
A new annual initiative, organised by *Highlife* magazine and held at the Jan Massinkhal in Nijmegen (*see chapter* **The Provinces**, *p241*), celebrating the cannabis plant, with an emphasis on the industrial uses of hemp. The exhibition holds informative displays detailing the many uses for the plant, and there are around 100 stalls selling smart drugs, weed tea and coffee, tins of magic mushroom soup (not quite your average Campbell's), plus bongs and other soft drugs paraphenalia.

### Nederwiet Festival

*Details as Highlife Hmp Exhibition above.*
The Dutch answer to the High Times Festival, organised by its own bi-monthly *Highlife* magazine. A one-day event held in February at the unavoidable Melkweg (*see chapter* **Music: Rock, Roots & Jazz**, *p207*), its highlight is the Highlife Cup awards. Tickets cost around *f*22,50.

## Smart drugs shops

It's somewhat ironic that while so-called 'smart drugs' were originally introduced for purposes of 'memory enhancement', they're now mostly just another alternative (and legal) way of getting off your face. The smart shops listed below stock a selection of relatively harmless products such as energy drinks, aphrodisiacs, guarana and echinacea chewing gum, and that centuries-old organic alternative to LSD, magic mushrooms. The latter should be taken with caution: instead of discovering the secrets of the universe, the only trip you could end up taking is one to the toilet. Always ask for advice, and if it isn't forthcoming, go elsewhere.

Also on sale are 'after party' drugs, which aim to counteract the harmful effects of illegal drugs, and restore your vitamin, mineral and amino-acid levels. Many of the products on sale, such as 'smart oxygen' and 'herbal love joints', should perhaps be taken with a pinch of salt. It remains up to the individual to discover whether these drugs are indeed smart or just plain silly.

### Chills & Thrills

*Nieuwendijk 17 (638 0015). Tram 13, 14, 17, 20.* **Open** noon-9pm Mon, Sun; 11am-9pm Tue, Wed, Thur; 11am-10pm Fri, Sat. **Map 2 C2**
A dedicated and super-friendly team of staff – plus a resident black dog – run this store near Centraal Station, which is crammed with a positively overwhelming selection of

products: an innovative range of pipes and bongs sits alongside postcards, T-shirts, mushrooms and hemp products, including a snowboard and seeds. Staff will happily explain how you can hallucinate from cacti buds, or show you the portable mini-vaporiser that vaporises pure THC, giving you a clean, smokeless hit. The branch at Force Blue serves mushroom tea.
**Branch**: basement of Force Blue, Nieuwendijk 41-43 (638 0015).

### Conscious Dreams

*Kerkstraat 117 (626 6907/fax 638 8865). Tram 1, 2, 5.* **Open** 11am-7pm Mon, Tue, Wed; 11am-8pm Thur, Fri, Sat; 2-6pm Sun. **Map 4 D4**
Conscious Dreams was the original proponent of the smart drugs wave in Amsterdam, and the owners are keen to point out that they're interested in the idealism behind smart drugs rather than the commercialism. Staff here are extremely knowledgeable – the owner worked as a drugs advisor for five years – and you're guaranteed to find what you're after.

### Kokopelli

*Warmoesstraat 12 (421 7000). Tram 4, 9, 14, 16, 20, 24, 25.* **Open** 11am-10pm daily. **Map 2 D2**
Kokopelli is the second store opened by Conscious Dreams (*see above*) and is within tripping distance of Centraal Station. What looks from the front to be a small shop turns out to be huge, with a canal view at the back that you can contemplate while you sample smart drinks, take in some literature, or watch a psychedelic video in the chill-out space. There's also a selection of arts and crafts from around the world, Internet terminals and occasional exhibitions.

### The Magic Mushroom Gallery

*Spuistraat 249 (427 5765). Tram 1, 2, 5.* **Open** 11am-10pm Mon-Thur, Sun; 10am-10pm Fri, Sat. **Map 2 C3**
A large store with the usual smart drugs products. All the gear – including 'magic mushroom joints' – is simply displayed in glass cases with information in English. There's a small chill-out area, where you can consume a smart drink, read the literature or check out the party and club flyers.
**Branch**: Singel 524 (422 7845).

## Smoking accessories

### The Head Shop

*Kloveniersburgwal 39 (624 9061/fax 620 8250). Tram 4, 9, 14, 16, 20, 24, 25/Metro Nieuwmarkt.* **Open** 11am-6pm Mon-Sat. **Map 2 D3**
Little has changed at the Head Shop since the '60s, and the store is well worth a visit for nostalgic reasons, if nothing else. There are wide selections of pipes, bongs, jewellery, incense, clothing, postcards and books, and mushrooms and spores (for growing your own) can also be purchased here.

## Information

### BCD (Cannabis Retailers Association)

*(627 7050).*
The coffeeshops' union. Not all coffeeshops belong to it, but members can be identified by a green and white rectangular sticker usually placed near, or on, their door.

### Drugs Information Line

*(0900 1995).* **Open** 9am-5pm Mon-Fri; Dutch recorded message at other times.
A national advice and information number. Phone operators – who speak English – deal with a wide variety of enquiries, from specific questions concerning drug laws to the effects and risks of drugs. They can put you in contact with other appropriate organisations.

# Shopping

**Amsterdam may not be world-renowned for its shops, but whether it's a miniature windmill or a Gucci suit you're after, you can find it here.**

So you've told your mum, your gran and your pet iguana that you're off to Amsterdam for a period of culture, refinement and museum-going. Now get rid of that self-righteous look and come clean: you're here to shop, so be proud of it. With over 10,334 shops in Amsterdam and only 40-odd museums, it's about time you got your priorities right. Arm yourself with our tips on shopping (*see* **How to shop 'til you drop**, *page 153*) and you'll be laughing.

## WHERE TO SPLASH YOUR CASH

Amsterdam's shopping scene isn't just about chain stores. The streets are lined with speciality shops, many of which hold quirky ranges of goods. However, that's not the whole story. What follows is a 'cheat sheet' detailing the general characteristics of the main shopping districts.

*The beautiful **Magna Plaza** shopping centre.*

**Damstraat**: This street is heavily laden with souvenir shops, elitist clothes shops and 'head shops' (selling drugs paraphernalia but not drugs), but has more than its fair share of drop-outs and pickpockets. Think summer of love meets grunge.

**The Jordaan**: Chock-a-block with all the things that make Amsterdam great: canals, bridges, bakeries, boutiques bursting with everything from glass and funky hats to bags and jewellery, plus a load of outdoor markets.

**Kalverstraat/Nieuwendijk**: These two streets, divided by Dam Square, are the most popular shopping areas in Amsterdam, and are made up mainly of high street shops with one or two boutiques thrown in for good measure. The streets are pedestrian-access only, so you can finally let down your guard against the dreaded bikes. The area is now open seven days a week, though be warned: it gets ridiculously busy on Sunday.

**Magna Plaza**: Located just behind Dam Square, this architectural treat was, believe it or not, formerly a post office. Its conversion into a five-floor mall has been embraced by tourists, though the locals are yet to be converted.

**The Pijp**: A bustling little neighbourhood famous for the Albert Cuyp market as well as for its abundance of wonderful ethnic food shops.

**Leidsestraat**: Connecting Koningsplein and the Leidseplein, Leidsestraat is peppered with lots of fine shoe shops and clothing boutiques. Unfortunately, you'll have to dodge the cyclists and trams that compete for space with pedestrians and delivery lorries on this very lively street.

**PC Hooftstraat**: If money's no object, make this your destination. PC Hooftstraat (the PC stands for Pieter Cornelisz) caters to dedicated followers of fashion who don't bat an eyelid at spending $f500$ on a shirt and who can give a shop assistant with an attitude a good run for their money. Top designer labels – for men, women or children – are the street's bread and butter.

**Spiegelkwartier**: Across from the Rijksmuseum and centred on the Spiegelgracht, this area is famous for antique shops offering authentic treasures at accordingly high prices.

Unless otherwise stated, credit cards are not accepted by the shops listed below. *See chapter* **Services**, *pages 164-166*, for details of other places of commercial interest.

**Athenaeum Nieuwscentrum**, *a great one-stop news shop.*

## Art & art supplies

For commercial galleries, *see chapter* **Art Galleries**, *pages 67-73*, and check out the shops at the main museums if it's prints and postcards you're after.

### Art Unlimited

*Keizersgracht 510 (624 8419). Tram 1, 2, 5, 20.* **Open** 10am-6pm Mon-Sat; noon-5pm Sun. **Credit** AmEx, DC, EC, MC, V. **Map 5 C4**

Art Unlimited claims to have the largest collection of postcards in Western Europe: a gob-smacking 40,000, sorted by artist and subject. The shop also has the most comprehensive collection of international photographs and posters in Holland. The range is staggering; it's easy to spend hours browsing in here (helped by the classical music in the background). Calendars and T-shirts complete the picture.

### J Vlieger

*Amstel 52 (623 5834). Tram 4, 9, 14, 16, 20, 24, 25.* **Open** noon-6pm Mon; 9am-6pm Tue-Fri; 10am-5pm Sat. **Credit** AmEx, DC, EC, MC, V. **Map 3 E3**

This shop is separated into two parts. The ground floor specialises in papers and cards of every description, weight and colour – including tissue, Fabriano and corrugated card – and a good variety of glues and tapes. Upstairs is a limited selection of paints, pens and inks, as well as small easels and hobby materials such as fabric paint and calligraphy sets.

### Peter van Ginkel

*Bilderdijkstraat 99 (618 9827/fax 683 7854). Tram 3, 7, 12, 17.* **Open** 10am-5.30pm Mon-Fri; 10am-4pm Sat. **Credit** EC, MC. **Map 4 B5**

The biggest art supplier in Amsterdam sells something for every creative persuasion. The rows of shelves are stacked with an inspiring range of paints and pigments, rolls of canvas, stretcher parts and many types of paper, including Fabriano and the shop's own cheaper brand.

### Van Beek

*Stadhouderskade 63-65 (662 1670/fax 671 1651). Tram 6, 7, 10, 16, 24, 25.* **Open** 1-6pm Mon; 9am-6pm Tue-Fri; 10am-5pm Sat. **Credit** AmEx, EC, MC, V. **Map 5 D5**

A large, well-stocked shop with everything from oil paints to ready-cut wood and pre-made stretchers. There's always something on special offer if you look around, and the shop runs a discount scheme for regular customers. There's a frame-making branch on the same street (Stadhouderskade 62; 662 6445), while the branch at Weteringschans 201 (623 9647) specialises in graphic art equipment.

## Auctions & antiques

**Sotheby's** (550 2200) and **Christie's** (575 5255) each has a branch in Amsterdam. *See also* **Looier**, *below* **Markets**.

### Veilinghuis De Nieuwe Zon

*Elandsgracht 68 (623 0343/fax 624 3447). Tram 7, 10, 17, 20.* **Open** 9.30am-6pm Mon-Fri; 10am-5pm Sat; occasionally open Sun. **Auctions** various times and dates; call for details. **Map 5 D4**

Art, antique and household goods are auctioned off once a month, except in the summer, when sales are less frequent. The organisers claim that their household auctions are unique: antiques are mixed with house clearance items, with items such as furniture and utensils sold off in boxed lots. Goods to be sold are on show the weekend before auction.

## Bookshops

Two weeks in the Dutch calendar are devoted to books: the third week in March, which celebrates Dutch literature with assorted events and special offers, and the second week in October, when bookshops focus their displays on children's books. Be warned: English-language books are expensive in Amsterdam. For book markets, *see chapter* **Amsterdam by Season**, *page 7. See also chapters* **Gay & Lesbian**, *page 195*, **Media**, *page 199*, and **Theatre**, *page 222*.

## General

### American Book Center
*Kalverstraat 185 (625 5537/fax 624 8042). Tram 1, 2, 4, 5, 9, 14, 16, 20, 24, 25.* **Open** 10am-8pm Mon-Wed, Fri; 10am-10pm Thur; 10am-8pm Sat; 11am-6pm Sun. **Credit** AmEx, DC, EC, MC, V. **Map 3 D3**
Since 1972, this shop has specialised in English-language books and magazines from the UK and US, and the four floors are packed with titles on every conceivable subject. Students and teachers receive a 10% discount, though others can buy a 10% discount card for ƒ20. The Center is on the Net at *www.abc.nl.*

### Athenaeum Nieuwscentrum
*Spui 14-16 (bookshop 622 6248/fax 638 4901/news centre 624 2972). Tram 1, 2, 5.* **Open** *bookshop* 11am-6pm Mon; 9.30am-6pm Tue, Wed, Fri, Sat; 9.30am-9pm Thur; noon-5.50pm Sun; *news centre* 8am-9pm Mon-Sat; 10am-6pm Sun. **Credit** AmEx, EC, MC, V. **Map 5 D4**
A favourite hangout of highbrow browsers, Athenaeum stocks newspapers from all over the world, as well as a wide choice of magazines, periodicals and good-quality books in many languages.

### Book Exchange
*Kloveniersburgwal 58 (626 6266/fax 675 4093). Tram 4, 9, 14, 20/Metro Nieuwmarkt.* **Open** 10am-6pm Mon-Fri; 10am-5pm Sat; 11.30am-4pm Sun. **Map 2 D3**
An Aladdin's cave of second-hand English and American books (mainly paperbacks). The owner is a shrewd buyer who'll do trade deals, and offers a 10% discount to anyone carrying a copy of this Guide.

### The English Bookshop
*Lauriergracht 71 (626 4230/fax 626 3213). Tram 7, 10, 17, 20.* **Open** 1-6pm Tue-Fri; 11am-5pm Sat. **Map 4 B4**
English books, including fiction, non-fiction, children's books and cookbooks, are temptingly displayed here. The proprietor knows his stuff and can offer good reading suggestions.

### De Kinderboekwinkel
*Nieuwezijds Voorburgwal 344 (622 7741). Tram 1, 2, 5, 13, 17, 20.* **Open** 10am-6pm Tue-Fri; 10am-5pm Sat. **Map 2 D3**
As the name suggests, it's (exclusively) children's books here. The large selection of books in English and other languages is attractively displayed and arranged by suggested age. **Branch**: Rozengracht 34 (622 4761).

### Martyrium
*Van Baerlestraat 170-172 (673 2092/fax 676 3676). Tram 3, 5, 12, 20, 24.* **Open** 9am-6pm Mon-Fri; 9am-5pm Sat; noon-5pm Sun. **Map 5 D6**
A high percentage of the stock here is English-language hardbacks and paperbacks, including literature, art and photography, history and philosophy. As 40% of the books are remainders, there are real bargains to be found.

### Scheltema
*Koningsplein 20 (523 1411/fax 622 7684). Tram 1, 2, 5.* **Open** 1-6pm Mon; 9.30am-6pm Tue, Wed, Fri; 9.30am-9pm Thur; 10am-6pm Sat; noon-5.30pm Sun. **Credit** (minimum ƒ100) AmEx, EC, MC, V. **Map 5 D4**
Six wonderful floors of books, with the specialist areas medicine, law, economics and science.

### De Slegte
*Kalverstraat 48-52 (622 5933/fax 624 1620). Tram 4, 9, 14, 16, 20, 24, 25.* **Open** 11am-6pm Mon; 9.30am-6pm Tue, Wed, Fri, Sat; 9.30am-9pm Thur; noon-5pm Sun. **Credit** AmEx, EC, MC, V. **Map 2 D3**
One of the city's largest bookshops, De Slegte carries a vast number of volumes – including children's books and textbooks – in English, Dutch and other languages. Stock is a mix of antiquarian, remaindered and new, and prices are low.
*Disabled access.*

### Waterstone's
*Kalverstraat 152 (638 3821/fax 638 4379). Tram 1, 2, 4, 5, 9, 14, 16, 20, 24, 25.* **Open** 11am-6pm Mon; 9am-7pm Tue, Wed; 9am-7pm Fri; 9am-9pm Thur; 10am-7pm Sat; 11am-5pm Sun. **Credit** AmEx, EC, MC, V. **Map 2 D3**
Formerly WH Smith, Waterstone's carries thousands of book titles, as well as magazines and videos, all in English. The children's section is especially delightful.
*Disabled access (ground floor only).*

## Specialist

### Architectura & Natura
*Leliegracht 22 (623 6186/fax 638 2303). Tram 13, 14, 17, 20.* **Open** noon-6.30pm Mon; 9am-6.30pm Tue-Fri; 9am-6pm Sat. **Map 2 C3**
The name says it all: architecture and nature. The stock includes photographic books on architectural history, field guides and animal studies, and many of the books are in English. Leliegracht 22 is also home to Antiquariaat Opbouw, which specialises in antiquarian books on architecture and related subjects.

### Au Bout du Monde
*Singel 313 (625 1397). Tram 1, 2, 5.* **Open** noon-6pm Mon; 10am-6pm Tue, Wed, Fri; 10am-9pm Thur; 10am-5pm Sat. **Map 2 C3**
Specialising in Eastern philosophy and religion, Au Bout du Monde stocks a daunting selection of titles, all clearly marked, on subjects ranging from psychology to sexuality. It also sells incense, cards and a handful of specialist magazines, as well as over 100 different packs of tarot cards.

### Boekie Woekie
*Berenstraat 16 (639 0507). Tram 1, 2, 5, 13, 14, 17, 20.* **Open** noon-6pm Tue-Fri; noon-5pm Sat; 2-5pm first Sun of month. **Map 5 C4**
Boekie Woekie exhibits and sells graphics and books by artists. That's graphics in the Dutch sense of the word: it includes all forms of printmaking.

### Intertaal
*Van Baerlestraat 76 (671 5353/fax 675 2686). Tram 3, 5, 12, 16, 20.* **Open** 9am-6pm Mon-Wed, Fri; 9am-9pm Thur; 10am-5pm Sat. **Credit** AmEx, EC, MC, V. **Map 5 D6**
This shop deals exclusively in language books, records and teaching aids. Whether grappling with basic Dutch or advancing your English, you'll be well catered for here.
*Disabled access.*

### Jacob van Wijngaarden (Geographische Boekhandel)
*Overtoom 97 (612 1901/fax 689 2666). Tram 1, 6.* **Open** 1-6pm Mon; 10am-6pm Tue, Wed, Fri; 10am-9pm Thur; 10am-5pm Sat. **Credit** AmEx, DC, EC, MC, V. **Map 4 B6**
Every part of our planet comes up for inspection in the geography books, nautical charts, maps and travel guides sold at Wijngaarden, and a great deal of the stock is in English. You can also find cycling maps of the Netherlands and Europe.

## De Kookboekhandel

*Runstraat 26 (622 4768/fax 638 1088). Tram 1, 2, 5, 7, 10, 17, 20.* **Open** 1-6pm Mon; 11am-6pm Tue, Wed, Fri; 11am-5pm Thur; 11am-5pm Sat. **Map 5 C4**
This shop sells cookery books on every conceivable subject. There are good 'fresh' and 'green' sections, plus vegan, vegetarian and biological sections. The stock is largely English language.

## Lambiek

*Kerkstraat 78 (626 7543/fax 620 6372). Tram 1, 2, 5.* **Open** 11am-6pm Mon-Fri; 11am-5pm Sat. **Credit** AmEx, DC, EC, MC, V. **Map 5 D4**
Established in 1968, Lambiek claims to be the world's oldest comic shop, and has thousands of comic books – including collectors' items – from around the world. There's a cartoonists' gallery here too, with new exhibitions of comic art for sale every two months.

## Pied-à-Terre

*Singel 393 (627 4455/fax 620 8996). Tram 1, 2, 5, 20.* **Open** *Sept-Mar* 11am-6pm Mon-Fri; 10am-5pm Sat; *Apr-Aug* 11am-9pm Thur. **Map 5 D4**
A wonderful little shop with helpful staff, supplying travel books, international guides and maps (including Ordnance Survey) for active holidays. Adventurous walkers, in particular, should head here before a trip out of town.

## Department stores

### De Bijenkorf

*Dam 1 (621 8080/fax 620 9949). Tram 1, 2, 4, 5, 9, 13, 14, 16, 17, 20, 24, 25.* **Open** 11am-6pm Mon; 9.30am-6pm Tue, Wed, Fri, Sat; 9.30am-9pm Thur; noon-6pm Sun. **Credit** AmEx, DC, EC, MC, V. **Map 2 D2**
De Bijenkorf is to Amsterdam what Harrods is to London and Bloomingdale's is to New York. There are good ranges of clothing – both designer and own-label – kidswear, jewellery, cosmetics, shoes, accessories and a wonderful household goods department. The new Chill Out department on the fifth floor features street and clubwear as well as '50s-style kitchenware and American products like Campbell's soup and marshmallow cream, while restaurant La Ruche is a good place for lunch. The Sinterklaas and Christmas displays are traditionally extravagant and hugely popular.
*Disabled access.*

### Hema

*Kalvertoren, Kalverstraat 208 (422 8988/fax 422 8942). Tram 1, 2, 4, 5, 9, 20.* **Open** 11am-7pm Mon; 9.30am-7pm Tue, Wed, Fri; 9.30am-9pm Thur; 9.30am-6pm Sat; noon-6pm Sun. **Map 2 D3**
A slightly upmarket version of the American five-and-dime store. Prices are low here, but quality is amazingly high: good buys are casual clothes, kids' clothing, swimwear, underwear, household items, stationery and other accessories. Hema also sells pastries, bread, delicatessen foods and reliable wines. The main four branches are listed here, but there are six others around town: call 311 4411 for details.
**Branches**: Ferdinand Bolstraat 93 (676 3222); Kinkerstraat 313 (683 4511); De Kolk Shopping Centre, Nieuwendijk 156 (623 4176).
*Disabled access.*

### Maison de Bonneterie

*Rokin 140-2 (626 2162/fax 620 6139). Tram 1, 2, 4, 5, 9, 14, 20, 24, 25.* **Open** 1-5.30pm Mon; 10am-5.30pm Tue, Wed, Fri, Sat; 10am-9pm Thur; noon-5.30pm Sun. **Credit** AmEx, DC, EC, MC, V. **Map 2 D3**
At this venerable institution – 'By Appointment to Her Majesty Queen Beatrix', apparently – you'll find men's and women's clothing of the highest quality. By and large, things here are pretty conservative: the Ralph Lauren boutique

within the store is about as wild as it gets. It also has a fine household goods department.
*Disabled access.*

## Metz & Co

*Keizersgracht 455 (520 7020). Tram 1, 2, 5, 20.* **Open** 11am-6pm Mon; 9.30am-6pm Tue, Wed, Fri, Sat; 9.30am-9pm Thur; noon-5pm Sun. **Credit** AmEx, DC, EC, MC, V. **Map 5 D4**
Reminiscent of London's Heals, Metz & Co is a good place to shop for special gifts: designer furniture, glass and Liberty-style fabrics and scarves are all sold. The top-floor restaurant is popular for business lunches and has a terrific view of the city. At holiday time, Metz & Co's Christmas shop puts even the most Scrooge-like customer back into the spirit of the season. *See box* **Rooms with a view,** *p129.*
**Branch**: Schiphol Airport (649 9123).
*Disabled access.*

## Vroom & Dreesmann

*Kalverstraat 201-203 (622 0171/fax 620 8109). Tram 4, 9, 14, 16, 20, 24, 25.* **Open** 11am-7pm Mon; 9.30am-7pm Tue, Wed, Fri; 9.30am-9pm Thur; 9.30am-6pm Sat; noon-6pm Sun. **Credit** MC, V. **Map 2 D3**
V&D equals good quality at reasonable prices. Since its recent remodelling, this branch has taken on a new, snazzy look to go with its new, snazzy merchandise. You'll find an impressive array of toiletries, cosmetics, small leather goods and watches, clothing and underwear for the whole family, kitchen items, suitcases, CDs and videotapes. The ground-floor bakery, Le Marché, sells excellent bread, ready-made quiches and sandwiches, with the La Place restaurant offering just about every other thing you might want to put in your mouth. Prices are a step up from Hema (*see above*).
**Branch**: Bilderdijkstraat 37-51 (618 0104).
*Disabled access.*

## Fashion

See *chapter* **Directory,** *page 267,* for a size conversion chart.

## Children

### Boon & Co

*Gravenstraat 11 (620 8438). Tram 1, 2, 4, 5, 9, 14, 16, 20, 24, 25.* **Open** 11am-6pm Wed-Fri; 11am-5pm Sat. **Credit** AmEx, DC, EC, JCB, MC, V. **Map 2 C3**
Own-label environmentally friendly baby clothes and basics for ages 0-2 in their Boontje ('little bean') range. Aaah.

### Geboortewinkel Amsterdam

*Bosboom Toussaintstraat 22-24 (683 1806). Tram 3, 7, 10, 12.* **Open** 1-5.30pm Mon; 10am-5.30pm Tue-Fri; 10am-5pm Sat. **Credit** EC. **Map 5 C5**
Beautiful maternity and baby clothes (including premature sizes) in cotton, wool and linen, baby articles, cotton nappy systems and ethnic woven baby slings, and birth information and videos about childbirth.

### 't Klompenhuisje

*Nieuwe Hoogstraat 9a (622 8100). Tram 4, 9, 14/Metro Nieuwmarkt.* **Open** 10am-6pm Mon-Sat. **Credit** AmEx, DC, EC, MC, V. **Map 3 E3**
A delightful selection of well-made and reasonably priced shoes, traditional clogs and handmade leather and woollen slippers from baby sizes up to size 35.
*Disabled access with assistance.*

### Prénatal

*Kalverstraat 40-42 (626 6392). Tram 1, 2, 4, 5, 9, 14, 16, 20, 24, 25.* **Open** 11am-6pm Mon; 9.30am-6pm Tue,

*Suits you, sir: the spectacularly posh **Emporio Armani**. See page 144.*

Wed, Fri; 9.30am-5pm Sat; 9.30am-9pm Thur; noon-5pm Sun. **Credit** AmEx, MC, V. **Map 2 D3**
Four floors of goods for expectant mothers and small children (newborns to five-year-olds). There are stacks of clothing, toys and furniture, plus cotton nappies for babies. Call for details of their three branches, out of the centre of town.

### 't Schooltje
*Overtoom 87 (683 0444). Tram 1, 2, 5, 6.* **Open** 1-6pm Mon; 9am-6pm Tue, Wed, Fri; 9am-9pm Thur; 9.30am-5pm Sat. **Credit** AmEx, DC, EC, MC, V. **Map 4 B6**
The well-heeled, well-dressed child is fitted out here. The clothing and shoes for babies and children aged up to 16 are attractive but expensive.
*Disabled access.*

### Warmer Kinderschoenen
*Bilderdijkstraat 134 (616 9627). Tram 3, 7, 12, 13, 14, 17, 20.* **Open** 1-6pm Mon; 10am-6pm Tue, Wed, Fri; 10am-9pm Thur; 9.30am-5.30pm Sat. **Credit** AmEx, EC, MC, V. **Map 4 B5**
Very pretty, soft leather shoes for children, in Mediterranean designer styles, and at reasonable to expensive prices.
*Disabled access.*

## Clubwear

### Clubwear House
*Herengracht 265 (622 8766). Tram 1, 2, 5, 13, 17, 20.* **Open** 11am-7pm Tue, Wed, Fri; 11am-9pm Thur; 11am-5pm Sat. **Credit** AmEx, DC, EC, JCB, MC, V. **Map 3 C3**
A wide selection of groovy clothes from around the world plus its own clothes label, Wearhouse 2000, and an in-house designer. If it's club information, flyers or pre-sale tickets you want, the staff of enthusiastic clubbers are helpful and know what they're talking about. A good selection of local and international DJ tapes is available and occasionally DJs play in the shop on Saturdays. Check out its website at *www.xs4all.nl/~cwh. See chapter* **Clubs,** *p178.*

### Housewives & Haircuts on Fire
*Spuistraat 130 (422 1067/fax 421 7371). Tram 1, 2, 5.* **Open** noon-6pm Mon, Sun; 11am-7pm Tue, Wed, Fri, Sat; 11am-10pm Thur. **Credit** EC, MC, V. **Map 3 C3**
Clubwear, new and second-hand clothes and accessories, an in-house hair salon offering colours, extensions and dreads, henna tattoos and gaudy make-up, nail polishes and body paints. Throw in Rush Hour Records with new and second-hand vinyl, and a slew of in-house DJs, and you've got the perfect one-stop club shop. Housewives & Haircuts on Frie are on the Net at *www.xs4all.nl/~housew.*

### Razzmatazz
*Wolvenstraat 19 (420 0483/fax 427 6247). Tram 13, 14, 17, 20.* **Open** noon-6pm Mon-Sat. **Credit** AmEx, DC, EC, JCB, MC, V. **Map 5 C4**
If you ignore the naff name, and the rather stern scolding at the implication that the shop sells club clothes (where else would you wear an orange cut-out Dexter Wong halter neck?), you'll find a good selection of men's and women's funky designer clothes at prices just below heart-stopping.
*Disabled access.*

### ZX Fashion
*Kerkstraat 113 (620 8567). Tram 1, 2, 5.* **Open** noon-6pm Mon-Wed, Fri, Sat; noon-9pm (winter 7.30pm) Thur. **Credit** AmEx, DC, EC, JCB, MC, V. **Map 5 D4**
ZX stocks comfortably styled, street/clubwear and accessories made in the Netherlands, as well as imports from the UK and US and a stash of party tickets and flyers. The Hair Police, based in the back of the shop, specialises in alternative hairstyles such as dread perms and extensions.
*Disabled access (ground floor only).*

## Designer

### Cora Kemperman
*Leidsestraat 72 (625 1284/fax 427 8439). Tram 1, 2, 5.* **Open** noon-6pm Mon, Sun; 10am-6pm Tue,

9am-5pm Sat; 1-5pm first Sun of month. **Credit** AmEx, DC, EC, JCB, MC, V. **Map 5 C6**
If it's casual designer clothing you're looking for, Reflections has a multitude of choices for men and women from Dolce e Gabbana, Gucci, Issey Miyake, Yohji Yamamoto and others.

## Erotic & fetish

### Absolute Danny
*Stromarkt 13 (421 0915). Tram 1, 2, 4, 5, 9, 13, 16, 17, 20, 24, 25.* **Open** 11am-7pm Mon-Fri; 11am-6pm Sat; 1-6pm Sun. **Credit** AmEx, DC, EC, JCB, MC, V. **Map 2 C2**
Surround yourself in the erotic at this saucy shop that sells everything from rubber clothes to erotic toothbrushes.

### Demask
*Zeedijk 64 (620 5603). Tram 4, 9, 16, 20, 24, 25.* **Open** 10am-7pm Mon-Wed, Fri, Sat; 10am-9pm Thur; noon-5pm Sun. **Credit** AmEx, EC, MC, V. **Map 2 D2**
Demask mainly stocks leather and rubber fetish clothing for both sexes, but it also sells some PVC. High heels, bondage wear and S&M accessories are available. Pre-sale tickets can be bought here for the Demask parties, and it's on the Net at *www.demask.com.*
*Disabled access.*

### Mail & Female
*Berenstraat 9 (623 3916/fax 624 8835). Tram 13, 14, 17, 20.* **Open** noon-7pm Mon-Fri; 11am-6pm Sat. **Credit** AmEx, DC, EC, MC, V. **Map 5 C4**
A relaxed environment and friendly staff make this shop a haven for women (only) looking for erotic toys, videos, books and the like. If you'd rather not pass through customs with your new bounty, don't fret: it also does mail order.

## Eyeglasses & contact lenses

*See anything you like here?*

Wed, Fri, Sat; 10am-9pm Thur. **Credit** EC, MC, V. **Map 5 D4**
Here, the discerning but budget-minded customer will find designer clothes at high street prices. If you're after a fur bolero jacket and hip huggers, or maybe a simple long black evening dress, then this is the place for you.
*Disabled access.*

### DKNY
*PC Hooftstraat 60 (671 0554). Tram 3, 12.* **Open** 1-6pm Mon; 10am-6pm Tue, Wed, Fri; 10am-9pm Thur; 9am-5.30pm Sat; noon-6pm first Sun of month. **Credit** AmEx, DC, EC, JCB, MC, V. **Map 5 C6**
Donna Karan classics for men, women and children.
**Branch**: Kalvertoren Singel 457 (422 7384).

### Emporio Armani
*PC Hooftstraat 39-41 (471 1121/fax 471 3323). Tram 3, 12.* **Open** 1-6pm Mon; 10am-6pm Tue, Wed, Fri; 10am-9pm Thur; 10am-5pm Sat; noon-5pm first Sun of month. **Credit** AmEx, EC, JCB, MC, V. **Map 5 C6**
This shop carries Armani, and lots of it.

### Khymo
*Leidsestraat 9 (622 2137). Tram 1, 2, 5.* **Open** noon-6pm Mon; 10am-6pm Tue, Wed, Fri, Sat; 10am-9pm Thur; 1-5pm Sun. **Credit** AmEx, DC, EC, MC, V. **Map 5 D4**
Trendy fashion for twenty- to fortysomethings, both male and female. Famous labels on offer include John Richmond, Jean-Paul Gaultier and Marithé & François Girbaud.
*Disabled access.*

### Reflections Men & Women
*PC Hooftstraat 66-8 (664 0040). Tram 3, 12.* **Open** 12.30-6pm Mon; 9am-6pm Tue, Wed, Fri; 9am-9pm Thur;

### Brilmuseum/Brillenwinkel
*Gasthuismolensteeg 7 (421 2414). Tram 1, 2, 5.* **Open** noon-5.30pm Wed-Sat. **Credit** EC. **Map 2 C3**
Although this is theoretically an opticians' museum, don't be put off. These folks specialise in glasses through the ages, and most of the exhibits are for sale.
*Disabled access.*

### Donald E Jongejans
*Noorderkerkstraat 18 (624 6888). Tram 3, 10.* **Open** 11am-6pm Mon-Sat. **Map 1 B2**
A great little shop in the Jordaan specialising in frames for glasses and sunglasses dating from the mid-1800s to the present day. The Mr Jongejans, is very particular about the fact that he sells not second-hand frames, but rather vintage frames that have never been worn. Well worth a visit.
*Disabled access with assistance.*

### Hans Anders Optitien
*Van Woustraat 160 (676 8995). Tram 4, 20.* **Open** 9am-6pm Tue, Wed, Fri; 9am-5.30pm, 7-9pm, Thur; 9am-5pm Sat. **Credit** AmEx, MC, V. **Map 6 F6**
The cheapest contact lenses in town. For ƒ75 you'll get a pair of off-the-peg contacts that'll last about six months (and a free corneal blister into the bargain, if you're not careful…).
**Branches:** Jan Evertsenstraat 84 (683 4791); Ferdinand Bolstraat 118 (664 1879).
*Disabled access.*

### De Kinderbrillenwinkel
*Nieuwezijds Voorburgwal 129-31 (626 4091/fax 622 1777). Tram 1, 2, 4, 5, 13, 14, 16, 17, 20, 24, 25.* **Open** 11am-6pm Tue-Fri; 11am-5pm Sat. **Credit** AmEx, DC, EC, MC, V. **Map 2 C3**
A vast collection of antique and new children's eyewear.
*Disabled access.*

### Schmidt Optiek
*Rokin 72 (623 1981). Tram 4, 9, 16, 20, 24, 25.* **Open**
1-5.30pm Mon; 9.30am-5.30pm Tue, Wed, Fri; 9.30am-
5.30pm, 6.30-9pm, Thur; 9.30am-5pm Sat. **Credit** AmEx,
DC, EC, MC, all TC, V, foreign currency. **Map 2 D3**
An expensive, high-class optician's, with over 2,000 frames
in stock at any one time. Brands and labels include everything from Gaultier to Ray-Ban. If you want it, then Schmidt
probably has it.
*Disabled access with assistance.*

## Handbags
### Cellarrich Connexion
*Haarlemerdijk 98 (626 5526). Tram 1, 2, 4, 5, 13, 14,
16, 17, 20, 24, 25.* **Open** 1-6pm Mon; 10am-6pm Tue-Fri;
10am-5pm Sat. **Credit** AmEx, DC, EC, MC, V. **Map 1 B2**
Sophisticated handbags in materials from leather to plastic.
Many of the bags on offer are designed and produced locally by four sassy Dutch designers. Cellarich Connexion also
sells jewellery.
*Disabled access.*

## Hats
### De Hoed van Tijn
*Nieuwe Hoogstraat 15 (623 2759). Tram 4, 9, 14, 16,
24, 25.* **Open** noon-6pm Mon; 11am-6pm Tue-Fri; 11am-
5pm Sat. **Credit** AmEx, DC, EC, MC, V. **Map 3 E3**
More of a curiosity than a shop, this old-style establishment
stocks a vast collection of headgear, including sombreros,
Homburgs, bonnets and caps. The range includes period hats
dating from 1900, as well as a range of second-hand, new
and hand-crafted items.
*Disabled access with assistance.*

*Jewellery emporium* **BLGK**. *See page 146.*

### Hoeden M/V
*Herengracht 422 (626 3038). Tram 1, 2, 5.* **Open**
1-6pm Mon; 10am-6pm Tue, Wed, Fri; 10am-9pm Thur;
10am-5pm Sat. **Credit** AmEx, DC, EC, MC, V.
**Map 5 C4**
Dreaming of Ascot in Amsterdam? Look no further. The top
quality hats here come from international designers such as
Philip Treacy, Sandra Phillips, Patricia Underwood, Mirjam
Nuver, Katja Langeveld and, for men, Borsalino.

### De Petsalon
*Hazenstraat 3 (tel/fax 624 7385). Tram 1, 2, 5, 13, 14,
17, 20.* **Open** noon-6pm Wed-Sat; by appointment Mon,
Tue. **Credit** EC, MC, V. **Map 5 C4**
Show some sass with a kooky handmade hat from local
designer Ans Wesseling, available at this small shop close
to Prinsengracht.
*Disabled access.*

## High street
### America Today
*Ground floor, Magna Plaza, Nieuwezijds Voorburgwal
182 (638 8447). Tram 1, 2, 5, 13, 14, 17, 20.* **Open**
11am-6pm Mon; 9.30am-6pm Tue, Wed, Fri; 9.30am-9pm
Thur; 10am-6pm Sat; noon-6pm Sun. **Credit** AmEx, DC,
EC, V. **Map 2 C2**
What started out as a tiny venture is now making millions:
America Today is able to sell new American classics
(Converse, Levi's, Timberland) at lower prices than
anywhere else because it imports stuff straight from the
States under a special tax agreement. It also has its own
clothing label.
**Branch:** Sarphatistraat 48 (638 9847).
*Disabled access.*

### Exota
*Hartenstraat 10 (620 9102). Tram 1, 2, 5, 13, 14, 17,
20.* **Open** 11am-6pm Mon; 10am-6pm Tue-Fri; 10am-
5.30pm Sat; 1-5pm Sun. **Credit** AmEx, DC, EC, MC, V.
**Map 2 C3**
A funky little shop with an original selection of simple yet
stylish clothes and accessories that crosses the borders
between high street and street fashion.
**Branch:** Nieuwe Leliestraat 32 (420 6884).
*Disabled access.*

### Hennes & Mauritz
*Kalverstraat 125-9 (624 0624). Tram 1, 2, 4, 5, 9, 14,
16, 20, 24, 25.* **Open** 1-6pm Mon; 10am-6pm Tue, Wed,
Fri; 10am-9pm Thur; 9.30am-5pm Sat; noon-5pm Sun.
**Credit** AmEx, DC, EC, MC, V. **Map 2 D3**
A fashion chain store, with clothes for men, women,
teenagers and wee kids. Prices: reasonable to jaw-droppingly low. Quality: reasonable to jaw-droppingly low. There are
loads of items that will appeal to trend-conscious guys and
gals of all ages, plus updates of timeless standards. Only the
branches at Kalverstraat 200 and Nieuwendijk 141 have Big
is Beautiful departments.
**Branches:** Kalverstraat 114-18 (624 0441); Kalverstraat
200 (530 1030); Nieuwendijk 141 (639 2021).
*Disabled access.*

### Miss Selfridge
*Kalverstraat 117 (638 0002). Tram 1, 2, 4, 5, 9, 14, 16,
20, 24, 25.* **Open** noon-6pm Mon; 10am-6pm Tue, Wed,
Fri, Sat; 10am-9pm Thur; 1-6pm Sun. **Credit** AmEx, DC,
EC, MC, V. **Map 2 D3**
One to make the Brits feel at home, this. The same glittery,
up-to-the-minute fashion for women (in teensy tiny sizes) that
you'd expect from this chain store, though the prices are
slightly higher than in the UK.
*Disabled access.*

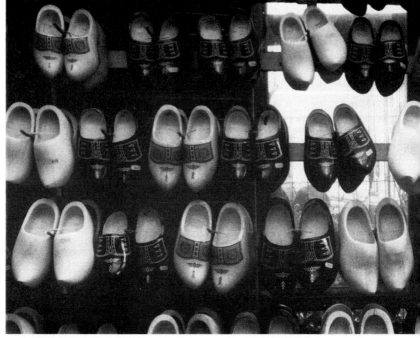

*Nike and Adidas ain't got nothing on these...*

## Jewellery

### BLGK

*Hartenstraat 28 (624 8154). Tram 13, 14, 17, 20.* **Open** 11am-6pm Tue, Wed, Fri; 11am-9pm Thur; 11am-5pm Sat; 1-5pm Sun. **Credit** AmEx, DC, EC, MC, V. **Map 2 C3**
Byzantinesque gold and silver jewellery: magnificent one-offs, as well as series pieces at reasonable prices.

### De Blue Gold Fish

*Rozengracht 17 (623 3134). Tram 13, 14, 17, 20.* **Open** 11am-6pm Mon-Sat. **Credit** AmEx, DC, EC, MC, V. **Map 1 B3**
Despite the fact that the staff here can be slightly harsh at times, they do have a great selection of funky jewellery and housewares for those lucky enough to have it all.

### Grimm Sieraden

*Grimburgwal 9 (622 0501). Tram 16, 20, 24, 25.* **Open** 12.30-6pm Mon; 9am-6pm Tue, Wed, Fri; 9am-9pm Thur; 9am-5pm Sat; noon-6pm Sun. **Credit** AmEx, DC, EC, JCB, MC, V. **Map 2 D3**
Owner Elize Lutz has a talent for bringing the freshest jewellery designers into her gallery shop, keeping the pieces at the cutting edge while remaining classic and wearable. *Disabled access.*

### Jorge Cohen Edelsmith

*Singel 414 (623 8646). Tram 1, 2, 5, 10.* **Open** 10am-6pm Mon-Fri; 11am-6pm Sat. **Credit** AmEx, DC, EC, JCB, MC, V. **Map 5 D4**
Argentinian-born Jorge Cohen uses a combination of sal-
vaged art deco jewellery, antique and new stones (onyx, citrine, carnelian and granite) and silver to produce art deco-inspired jewellery you'd be proud to pass off as the real thing. *Disabled access with assistance.*

## Large sizes

### Big Shoe

*Leliegracht 12 (622 6645). Tram 13, 14, 17, 20.* **Open** 10am-9pm Thur; 10am-6pm Fri, Sat; 1-5pm Sun. **Credit** AmEx, DC, EC, MC, V. **Map 2 C3**
Need a pair of red stilettos one foot long? Big Shoe stocks fashionable footwear for men and women in large sizes only. Every women's shoe on display is available in sizes 42-46.

### G&G Special Sizes

*Prinsengracht 514 (622 6339). Tram 1, 2, 5.* **Open** 9am-5.30pm Tue, Wed, Fri; 7-9pm Thur; 9am-5pm Sat. **Credit** AmEx, DC, EC, MC, V. **Map 5 D5**
A full range of men's clothing from size 58 to 75 is stocked by G&G. Staff also tailor garments to fit, though this service – as you'd expect – costs a bit extra. *Disabled access.*

### Mateloos

*Bilderdijkstraat 62 (683 2384). Tram 3, 12, 13, 14, 17, 20.* **Open** 1-6pm Mon; 10am-6pm Tue, Wed, Fri; 10am-9pm Thur; 10am-5pm Sat. **Credit** AmEx, DC, EC, MC, V. **Map 4 B5**
Two fabulous shops brimming with an enormous variety of large-sized clothing for women from sizes 44 to 60. Mateloos I offers a sumptuous collection of evening wear, lingerie and

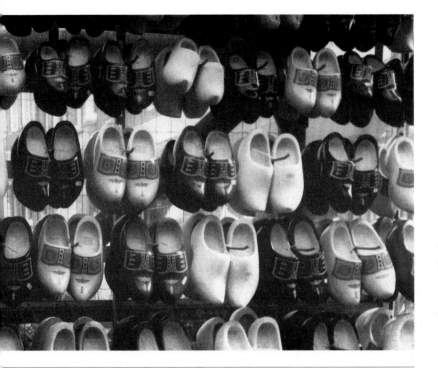

business clothes, while Mateloos II (Kinkerstraat 77; 689 4720) has a dizzying array of leisure- and sportswear, fake fur coats, hip hop pants, polyester shirts and denims. Owners Betty and Josine offer high-quality garments (including their own label, King Size Babes) at moderate to expensive prices. *Disabled access.*

## Lingerie

### Hunkemöller

*Kalverstraat 162 (623 6032). Tram 1, 2, 4, 5, 9, 14, 16, 20, 24, 25.* **Open** 11am-6pm Mon; 9.30am-6pm Tue, Wed, Fri; 9.30am-9pm Thur; 9.30am-5.30pm Sat; noon-5.30pm Sun. **Credit** AmEx, DC, EC, MC, V. **Map 2 D3**
Hunkemöller is a women's lingerie chain store with six branches in and around Amsterdam (call 035 646 5413 for details of other branches). It deals in attractive but simply designed and good quality underwear at reasonable prices.
**Branches:** Bilderdijkstraat 67 (618 2503); Ferdinand Bolstraat 61 (662 2020).
*Disabled access.*

### Robin's Bodywear

*Nieuwe Hoogstraat 20 (620 1552). Tram 4, 9, 14, 16, 24, 25.* **Open** 1-6pm Mon-Wed; 11am-6pm Thur-Sat. **Credit** AmEx, EC, MC, V. **Map 3 E3**
Sizeable for a women's lingerie shop, Robin's Bodywear has an extensive selection of reasonable and more expensive items of underwear, swimwear and hosiery by Naf-Naf, Calvin Klein, Aubade, Lou and others.
*Disabled access.*

### Tothem Underwear

*Nieuwezijds Voorburgwal 149 (623 0641). Tram 1, 2, 4, 5, 9, 13, 14, 16, 17, 20, 24, 25.* **Open** 1-5.30pm Mon; 9.30am-5.30pm Tue, Wed, Fri; 9.30am-9pm Thur; 9.30am-5pm Sat. **Credit** AmEx, DC, EC, MC, V. **Map 2 D3**
This men's underwear shop mainly sells designer items by Hom, Calvin Klein and Body Art.

## Local designers

### Fever

*Prinsengracht 192 (623 4500). Tram 13, 14, 17, 20.* **Open** noon-6pm Wed-Fri; 11am-5pm Sat; other days and times by appointment. **Credit** AmEx, EC, MC, V. **Map 2 C3**
Whether you drop in for the elegant modern clothes in lush colours and fabrics by Dutch designer Wilma Penning or the fantastic hand-painted floor by local artist Kate Wilkinson, this store is a real treat.
*Disabled access.*

### Studio Chazo

*Willem de Zwijgerlaan 280 (488 0082). Bus 21.* **Open** by appointment only. **Credit** EC.
Designer Karliyn Vriens creates one-of-a-kind wedding gowns that complement rather than overshadow each bride's individuality and spirit. Definitely one for the romantics: if you fancy a shotgun wedding while you're in Amsterdam, you'd do well to head here first.
*Disabled access.*

# Shoes

The best selections of shoes can be had at shops on **Leidsestraat** or **Kalverstraat**, while the best bargains in second-hand shoes are to be had at **Waterlooplein** and the **Noordermarkt** on Mondays; for both, *see below* **Markets**.

### Free Lance Shoes

*Rokin 86 (420 3205). Tram 4, 9, 14, 16, 20, 24, 25.* **Open** 1-6pm Mon; 10am-6pm Tue, Wed, Fri; 10am-9pm Thur; noon-5pm Sat, Sun. **Credit** AmEx, DC, EC, MC, V. **Map 2 D3**

The imaginative façade and interior décor immediately set this apart from other similar retailers. All the footwear is created by two French designers in classic and modern styles.

### Kenneth Cole

*Leidsestraat 20 (627 6012). Tram 1, 2, 5.* **Open** noon-6pm Mon; 10am-6pm Tue, Wed, Fri, Sat; 10am-9pm Thur; 11am-5pm Sun. **Credit** AmEx, EC, MC, V. **Map 5 D4**

Kenneth Cole stocks its own brand of conservatively styled shoes, plus a good range of boots, including Timberlands and Doc Martens. Stock changes often, and bargains are to be found during the frequent sales.
*Disabled access.*

### Palette

*Nieuwezijds Voorburgwal 125 (639 3207). Tram 1, 2, 5, 13, 17, 20.* **Open** 1-6pm Mon, Wed; 11am-6pm Tue, Thur, Fri; 11am-5pm Sat. **Credit** EC. **Map 2 D3**

Grab that bridesmaid's dress and head on down to Palette for shoes dyed to match in over 500 colours. White and ivory are stocked here, but expect to wait ten days for coloured shoes.
*Disabled access.*

### Pisa

*Muntplein 4 (624 5712). Tram 4, 9, 14, 20.* **Open** 1-6pm Mon; 10am-6pm Tue, Wed, Fri; 10am-9pm Thur; 10am-6pm Sat; 1-5pm Sun. **Credit** AmEx, DC, EC, MC, V. **Map 5 D4**

Men's and women's Italian designer shoes.

### Sacha

*Kalverstraat 161 (627 2160). Tram 1, 2, 4, 5, 9, 14, 16, 20, 24, 25.* **Open** 1-6pm Mon; 10am-6pm Tue, Wed, Fri; 10am-9pm Thur; 10am-5pm Sat; 1-5pm Sun. **Credit** AmEx, DC, EC, MC, V. **Map 2 D3**

The Dutch branch of the English shoe shop stocks a good selection of affordable shoes and boots for men and women, often in outrageous styles (from Spice Girly to goth queen) and colours.
**Branch**: Leidsestraat 29-33 (422 6060).
*Disabled access.*

### Shoe Baloo

*Koningsplein 7 (626 7993). Tram 1, 2, 5.* **Open** noon-6pm Mon; 10am-6pm Tue, Wed, Fri, Sat; 10am-9pm Thur; 10am-6pm Sat; noon-5pm Sun. **Credit** AmEx, DC, EC, MC, V. **Map 5 D4**

Shoes for men and women that make your mouth water: Gucci, Prada, Sergio Rossi, Costume National and more. The friendly staff make parting with your hard-earned dosh that much easier.
**Branch**: PC Hooftstraat 80 (671 2210).
*Disabled access.*

# Street

### Punch

*St Antoniesbreestraat 73 (626 6673). Tram 4, 9, 14/Metro Nieuwmarkt.* **Open** 10.30am-6.30pm Mon-Wed, Fri, Sat; 11am-9pm Thur. **Credit** AmEx, DC, EC, MC, V. **Map 3 E3**

Almost everything made by Dr Marten – boots, shoes, T-shirts and sweatshirts – is stocked here alongside Harrington jackets, Lonsdale wear, and sporty goods from Fred Perry and Ben Sherman. There is also a selection of Directions alternative hair colourants in vibrant shades.
*Disabled access with assistance.*

### RMF Streetwear

*Oudezijds Voorburgwal 189 (626 2954). Tram 4, 9, 14, 16, 20, 24, 25.* **Open** 11am-6pm Mon-Wed, Fri; 11am-9pm Thur; 11am-5pm Sat. **Credit** AmEx, EC, MC, V. **Map 2 D3**

RMF stocks a selection of American brands – OG Wear, Menace, No Joke, Top Dawg, South Pole and Capheads – that, until recently, have been difficult to find in Holland. It's not exactly a place for bargains, but the clothing is of good quality and you can be pretty confident that when you go out, you won't meet four other people wearing the same shirt.

### Rodolpho's

*Top floor, Magna Plaza, Nieuwezijds Voorburgwal 182 (623 1214). Tram 1, 2, 5, 13, 17, 20.* **Open** 11am-7pm Mon; 10am-7pm Tue, Wed, Fri, Sat; 10am-9pm Thur; noon-7pm Sun. **Credit** AmEx, DC, EC, MC, V. **Map 2 C3**

An in-line skate and skateboard outlet selling all the accessories needed to look the part: this is the best place to buy the coolest items currently fashionable on the streets. There's a large selection of T-shirts as well as the latest in trainers.
*Disabled access.*
**Branches**: De Bijenkorf, Dam 1 (621 8080 extension 894); Sarphatistraat 59 (622 5488).

### Stillet

*Damstraat 14 (625 2854). Tram 1, 2, 4, 5, 9, 13, 14, 16, 17, 20, 24, 25.* **Open** noon-6pm daily. **Credit** EC, MC, V. **Map 2 D3**

Stillet sells a huge collection of T-shirts with imaginative logos and designs, including ecological and political themes as well as cartoon images and club styles. The above opening times are approximate and depend on the owner's mood.
*Disabled access.*

### Vibes

*St Antoniesbreestraat 136 (420 3669/fax 421 1722). Tram 4, 9, 14, 20/Metro Nieuwmarkt.* **Open** 1-6pm Mon, Sun; 11am-6pm Tue, Wed, Fri, Sat; 11am-9pm Thur. **Credit** AmEx, EC, JCB, MC, V. **Map 3 E3**

Now in new premises, Vibes have lots of new stock (including an extensive collection of graffiti and breakdance videos), stacks of skaters and snowboarders' magazines and books, and all the hip labels (Stüssy, Carhartt, Inc and Haze) that you would expect in such a skater's paradise.
*Disabled access.*

# Vintage & second-hand

### Bebop Shop

*Nieuwendijk 164 (638 1306). Tram 1, 2, 4, 5, 9, 13, 14, 16, 17, 20, 24, 25.* **Open** 11am-6pm Mon; 10am-6pm Tue, Wed, Fri; 10am-9pm Thur; 9.30am-6pm Sat; noon-6pm Sun. **Credit** (min ƒ50) AmEx, DC, EC, MC, V. **Map 2 D2**

Two floors of vintage clothes, with one or two new retro pieces thrown in for good measure. Give things a good going over before you buy them, as some items can be stained or torn, and prices are not cheap.

### Lady Day

*Hartenstraat 9 (623 5820). Tram 1, 2, 5, 20.* **Open** 11am-6pm Mon-Wed, Fri, Sat; 11am-9pm Thur; noon-5pm Sun. **Credit** AmEx, EC, MC, V. **Map 2 C3**

Highly fashionable designs here, including beautifully tailored second-hand and period suits and sportswear classics

*Fabrics galore at the wonderful* **Capsicum**.

(including swimming costumes from the '40s and '50s). Period wedge shoes, pumps and accessories complete the collection.

### Laura Dols

*Wolvenstraat 7 (624 9066). Tram 1, 2, 5.* **Open** 11am-6pm Mon-Wed, Fri, Sat; 11am-9pm Thur. **Map 5 C4**
This small shop is packed with period clothing, mainly from the 1940s and 1950s. The emphasis is on women's clothing – well-crafted dresses are available in sumptuous materials – though there is also a limited selection of menswear.

### Wini

*Haarlemmerstraat 29 (427 9393). Tram 1, 2, 4, 5, 9, 13, 14, 16, 17, 20, 24, 25.* **Open** 1-6pm Mon; 10am-6pm Tue, Wed, Fri, Sat; 11am-9pm Thur; *summer* also 1-6pm Sun. **Credit** EC. **Map 2 C2**
A newcomer to Amsterdam's hugely competitive second-hand market, Wini sizzles with retro clothes that reflect today's tastes. Original pimp jackets, hipsters, Adidas and lots of polyester have made it the flavour of the month. *Disabled access with assistance.*

### Zipper

*Huidenstraat 7 (623 7302). Tram 1, 2, 5.* **Open** 11am-6pm Mon-Wed, Fri, Sat; 11am-9pm Thur; 1-5pm Sun. **Credit** AmEx, EC, MC, V. **Map 5 C4**
An excellent selection of jeans of various sorts, as well as 1970s hipsters and flares, and some clubwear. **Branch**: Nieuwe Hoogstraat 8 (627 0353).

## Fabrics & trimmings

### Capsicum

*Oude Hoogstraat 1 (623 1016). Tram 4, 9, 14, 16, 20, 24, 25.* **Open** 12.30-6pm Mon; 9am-6pm Tue, Wed, Fri; 9am-9pm Thur; 9am-5pm Sat; noon-6pm Sun. **Credit** AmEx, DC, EC, MC, V. **Map 2 D3**
The fabrics at Capsicum are made from splendidly textured natural fibres, such as cotton woven in India, and Thai silk

in glowing shades. The knowledgeable staff weaves the provenance and history of each fabric into the sale, making every purchase an event. One of the gems of Amsterdam's shopping scene.
*Disabled access.*

### Coppenhagen 1001 Kralen

*Rozengracht 54 (624 3681). Tram 10, 13, 17, 20.* **Open** 1-5.30pm Mon; 10am-6pm Tue-Fri; 10am-5pm Sat. **Map 1 B3**
Create your own designer jewellery or decorate a garment from thousands of different beads: the staff provide all the bits you need for self-assembly. Both standard and unconventional work is sold here in an awesome array of colours, sizes and shapes.
*Disabled access.*

### Het Kantenhuis

*Kalverstraat 124 (624 8618). Tram 4, 9, 14, 16, 20, 24, 25.* **Open** 11.45am-6pm Mon; 9.15am-6pm Tue, Wed, Fri, Sat; 9.15am-9pm Thur; noon-5pm Sun. **Credit** AmEx, DC, EC, JCB, MC, V. **Map 2 D3**
In business for nearly a century, the 'Lace House' sells reasonably priced tablecloths, place-mats, doilies and napkins that are embroidered, appliquéd or printed with Delft blue designs. There are also lace curtain materials, and kits with which to cross-stitch pictures of cutesy Amsterdam canal houses. An excellent place to pick up presents for the folks at home.
*Disabled access.*

### Knopen Winkel

*Wolvenstraat 14 (624 0479). Tram 1, 2, 5.* **Open** 1-6pm Mon; 11am-6pm Tue-Fri; 11am-5pm Sat. **Map 5 C4**
This button specialist is reputedly the only shop of its kind in Holland. The vast selection of buttons – one-third old and two-thirds new – comes from all over the world, including Spain, Istanbul and Italy. Buttons have been fashioned from raffia, coral, horn, bone and wood as well as plastic.
*Disabled access.*

*Sweets for your sweet at* **Puccini Bomboni**.

### Stoffen & Fourituren Winkel A Boeken

*Nieuwe Hoogstraat 31 (626 7205). Tram 4, 9, 16, 20, 24, 25.* **Open** noon-6pm Mon; 10am-6pm Tue, Wed, Fri, Sat; 10am-8pm Thur; 10am-5pm Sat. **Credit** EC. **Map 3 E3**
One of the most varied fabric stores in Amsterdam. The Boeken family has been hawking theatrical fabrics since 1920, but still manages to keep up to date. Just try to find another shop with as much variety: latex rubber, Lycra, fake fur (it even sells furry bolts of the Stars and Stripes) and sequins galore.
*Disabled access.*

## Flowers

It's tempting to bring home bulbs from Amsterdam, where bouquets and blooms are a part of everyday life. Unfortunately, import regulations often either prohibit the entry of bulbs entirely or require them to have a phytosanitary (health) certificate. An unlimited amount of bulbs can be taken into the UK and the Irish Republic without a certificate, and you can also carry an unlimited amount into the USA and Canada with the appropriate phytosanitary certificate(s). However, Australia and New Zealand allow no import of bulbs whatsoever, while Japan allows the import of no more than 100 certified bulbs. Some bulb packaging is marked with national flags, indicating the countries into which they can safely be taken. By and large, Dutch wholesale dealers know the regulations and can ship bulbs

to your home. This can be arranged at the **Keukenhof Flower Show** (held from the end of March to the end of May; call 025 246 5555 for details) or by mail order from **Frans Roozen Nurseries** (023 584 7245), where the minimum order varies depending on where you live (*see* chapter **Excursions in Holland**, *page 227-8*).

You are allowed to take an unlimited quantity of cut flowers back to the UK and Eire, as long as none is gladioli or chrysanthemums. In the US, regulations on cut flowers vary from state to state. You can buy flowers and bulbs at **Bloemenzaak Fleurtiek** (653 1702) at Schiphol Airport, where staff claim to know all the various regulations. However, you must buy a minimum of ten bulbs, and prices are higher than in the city.

### Bloemenmarkt (Flower market)

*Singel, between Muntplein and Koningsplein. Tram 1, 2, 4, 5, 9, 14, 16, 20, 24, 25.* **Open** 9am-6pm Mon-Sat. **Map 5 D4**
The world's only floating flower market is a fascinating collage of colour: it stretches along the southern side of Singel, with 15 florists and garden shops permanently ensconced on barges. Though the market attracts loads of tourists, the plants and flowers generally last well and are good value.

### Plantenmarkt (Plant market)

*Amstelveld, on Prinsengracht between Utrechtsestraat and Vijzelstraat. Tram 4, 6, 7, 10.* **Open** 9.30am-6pm Mon. **Map 6 E4**
The only other market in Amsterdam entirely devoted to botanical life. Although the emphasis is on plants, vases and pots, some flowers can be bought here, too. In spring, most plants on sale are intended for the balcony or living room, while later in the year, there are more garden plants and bedding plants for flower boxes.

## Florist

### Jemi

*Warmoesstraat 83A (625 6034/fax 638 6047). Tram 4, 9, 16, 20, 24, 25.* **Open** 9am-6pm Tue-Sat. **Map 2 D2**
The first stone-built house in Amsterdam is now home to this beautifully colourful florist's, which makes stunning bouquets, offers courses in arranging, hosts floral brunches, and stocks loads of pots and plants. Staff are very friendly.

## Food & drink

As far as snacking goes, there aren't many cities to rival Amsterdam in terms of variety, exoticism and sensible prices. The ubiquitous broodje, or sandwich, is available on nearly every street corner. In the past 20 years, the quality of bakers has improved, and most snack shops offer freshly baked French and Italian rolls for sandwiches.

How the Dutch maintain their smooth, peaches-and-cream complexions is a mystery: aside from the gorgeous chocolates, their favourite snack is chips drenched with great dollops of mayonnaise. The best stall is **Vlaamse Frites** at both Voetboogstraat 33 (off Spui) and Lange Leidsedwarsstraat 5. Fresh raw herring served with raw onions is almost as popular; purists down the fish in just one gulp head first, dangling the thing by the tail. Nice. *See also box* **The new curiosity shops**, *page 160.*

## Bakeries

For bread, rolls and packaged biscuits, go to a *warme bakker*, for pastries and wickedly delicious cream cakes, you need a *banketbakker*.

### JG Beune

*Haarlemmerdijk 156-158 (624 8356). Tram 3/bus 18, 22.* **Open** 8.30am-6pm Mon-Fri; 8.30am-5pm Sat. **Map 1 B2**
In business for over 100 years, this bakery has a full range of cakes and chocolates, plus speciality items such as chocolate tulips and wooden shoes. It also has the technology to take a photo and transfer the image onto a cake. The results will have you both smiling and licking your lips.
*Disabled access.*

### Mediterranee

*Haarlemmerdijk 184 (620 3550). Tram 3/bus 18, 22.* **Open** 8am-9pm Mon-Fri, Sun; 8am-8pm Sat. **Map 1 B2**
French, Moroccan and Dutch baking traditions are all practised under one roof here, and the results are delicious. Famous for the best croissants in town.
*Disabled access.*

### Oldenburg

*Beethovenstraat 17 (662 5520). Tram 5.* **Open** 9am-6pm Mon-Fri; 9am-5pm Sat.
This is one of two Oldenburg *banketbakkerijen* in Amsterdam, specialising in fancy dessert cakes, bavarois and chocolate mousse tarts. You can also buy home-made chocolates and marvellous marzipan confections in winter and chocolate eggs at Easter.
**Branch**: Maasstraat 84 (662 2840).

### Paul Anne

*Runstraat 25 (623 5322). Tram 1, 2, 5, 7, 10, 20.* **Open** 8.45am-6pm Mon-Fri; 9am-5pm Sat. **Map 5 C4**
Everything here is freshly baked daily from organically grown grains: try the cakes and popular sour-dough bread. There are also health food products such as soy milk, organic jam and apples, and sweets made without sugar.

### Puccini Bomboni

*Staalstraat 17 (626 5474). Tram 9, 14, 20/Metro Waterlooplein.* **Open** 9am-6pm Tue-Fri; 9am-5.30pm Sat. **Map 3 E3**
This highly regarded bakery specialises in sweets and gorgeous desserts made on the premises without artificial ingredients. It's close to the Muziektheater and the Waterlooplein flea market, which makes it a great place to relax after shopping or for a pre-performance pick-me-up.
**Branch**: Singel 184 (427 8341).
*Disabled access.*

### Runneboom

*1e Van der Helststraat 49 (673 5941). Tram 16, 24, 25.* **Open** 7am-5.30pm Mon-Fri; 7am-5pm Sat. **Map 6 E5**
This tiny bakery in the Pijp is a favourite with locals, and after just one bite, you'll know why. An enormous selection of French, Russian, Greek and Turkish loaves is on offer, with rye bread the house speciality. Delicious cakes and pastries are also sold.

## Cheese

It's considered derogatory to call the Dutch 'cheese heads', but you are what you eat, and the Dutch average 14 kilos per person per year.

Luckily, there is plenty to choose from. In general, the younger (*jong*) the cheese, the creamier and milder it will be, while riper cheeses (*belegen*) will be drier and sharper-tasting; driest and sharpest of all is old (*oud*) cheese. The most popular cheeses, meanwhile, are Goudse (from Gouda), Leidse, flavoured with cumin seeds, and Edammer (better known as Edam), with its red crust. However, there are plenty of other interesting cheeses available, such as Friese Nagelkaas, a ripe cheese whose sharp flavour is enhanced by cumin seeds and cloves; Kernhem, a good dessert cheese; and Leerdammer and Maaslander, which are both mild with holes. S*ee chapter* **Excursions in Holland**, *pages 226-7.*

### De Kaaskamer

*Runstraat 7 (623 3483). Tram 1, 2, 5.* **Open** 10am-6pm Tue-Fri; 9am-6pm Sat. **Credit** EC. **Map 5 C4**
Over 200 domestic and imported cheeses to choose from, plus pâtés, olives, fresh pasta and wines. While you're there, be sure to give Vinz the cat a cuddle.
*Disabled access.*

### Kef, French Cheesemakers

*Marnixstraat 192 (626 2210). Tram 3, 10.* **Open** 10am-6pm Tue-Thur; 9am-6pm Fri; 9am-4pm Sat. **Map 1 B3**
French cheesemaker Abraham Kef set up shop over 40 years ago and his shop still imports the finest selection of French cheeses – around 70 – in Amsterdam. The range of goat's cheeses is particularly good.

### Wegewijs

*Rozengracht 32 (624 4093). Tram 13, 14, 17, 20.* **Open** 8.30am-6pm Mon-Fri; 8.30am-5pm Sat. **Map 1 B3**
This authentic Dutch cheese emporium has been run here by the Wegewijs family for over a century. On offer are 50 foreign cheeses and over 100 domestic varieties, including *gras kaas*, a grassy-tasting cheese available only in summer. You can sample the Dutch cheeses before buying.

## Chocolate

You might not find true love in Amsterdam, but you can get at least halfway there with a piece or seven of fabulous Dutch chocolate. Once you've tasted these beauties, you'll forget the Swiss and the Belgian varieties in a heartbeat. Look out for Droste and Verkade, sold everywhere.

### Hendrikse Le Confiseur

*Overtoom 448-450 (618 0260). Tram 1, 6.* **Open** 8.45am-5.30pm Mon-Fri; 8.30am-4.30pm Sat. **Map 4 B6**
Hendrikse specialises in excellent handmade chocolates: try gianduja, a fudge-like chocolate log made with ground hazelnuts and almonds. Marzipan and chocolate figures are also a forte (and can be designed to order), as are the delicious fruit preserves.

### Huize van Wely

*Beethovenstraat 72 (662 2009). Tram 5.* **Open** 9am-6pm Mon-Fri; 8.30am-5pm Sat.
The most upmarket chocolatier in Amsterdam, Huize van Wely has been making sweet treats by hand at its factory in Noordwijk, on the west coast of Holland, since 1922. Its confections are so sublime that it's the only Dutch company that has been invited to become a member of the prestigious Relais Desserts and Académie Culinaire de France.
*Disabled access.*

## Patisserie Pompadour

*Huidenstraat 12 (623 9554). Tram 1, 2, 5, 7.* **Open**
9.30am-6pm Tue-Fri; 8.30am-5.30pm Sat. **Credit** EC.
**Map 5 C4**
This small bonbonnerie and tea room – with an eighteenth-
century interior imported from Antwerp – is likely to bring
out the little old lady in anyone, even men. The handmade
chocolates and pastries are inspired by traditional Belgian,
French and German recipes, and offer the best price/quality
ratio in town.

## Delicatessens

### Eichholtz

*Leidsestraat 48 (622 0305). Tram 1, 2, 5.* **Open** 10am-
6.30pm Mon; 9am-6.30pm Tue, Wed, Fri; 9am-9pm Thur;
9am-6pm Sat; 1-6pm Sun. **Credit** AmEx, MC, V.
**Map 5 D4**
This is the place where Yanks will find their chocolate chips
and Brits their Christmas puddings. There are lots of imported foods here – including some from the UK and US – plus
Dutch souvenirs (chocolate tiles and the like).
*Disabled access with assistance.*

### Hellas

*Hobbemastraat 26B (662 7238). Tram 6, 7, 10.* **Open**
9am-6pm Mon-Fri; 9am-5pm Sat. **Map 5 D5**
Greek delicacies and wines, freshly made snacks and salads,
cheeses, filo pastries and vine leaves fill the shelves here.
*Disabled access.*

### Loekie

*Prinsengracht 705A (624 4230). Tram 1, 2, 5.* **Open**
9am-5pm Mon-Sat. **Map 5 D4**
Premium sandwiches at premium prices. Whether it's Parma
ham, Parmesan or pesto, Loekie will serve it in distinctive
combinations on French bread, fresh ciabatta or rye. There's
also a selection of wines, sauces and flavoured cooking oils.
*Catering service. Disabled access with assistance.*

### De Pepperwortel

*Overtoom 140 (685 1053). Tram 1, 6.* **Open** noon-8pm
Mon-Fri; 4-8pm Sat, Sun. **Credit** EC. **Map 4 B6**
Pop out of the Vondelpark and into De Pepperwortel for lus-
cious sandwiches and salads, a tasty selection of wines and
complete picnic hampers from late spring until early autumn.

## Ethnic

### Casa Molero

*Gerard Doustraat 66 (676 1707). Tram 16, 24, 25.*
**Open** 9am-6pm Tue-Sat. **Map 6 E6**
Aside from stocking plenty of cheeses, spices, sausages and
hams from Spain, Casa Molero is also the exclusive Dutch
distributor for several Spanish and Portuguese wines, hence
its vast Iberian wine collection.
*Disabled access.*

### Oriental Commodities

*Nieuwmarkt 27 (638 6181). Tram 4, 9, 14, 16, 20, 24,
25/Metro Nieuwmarkt.* **Open** 9am-6pm Mon-Sat.
**Map 2 D2**
The largest Chinese food emporium in Amsterdam covers
the full spectrum of Asian foods and ingredients, from
shrimp- and scallop-flavoured egg noodles to fried tofu balls,
spicy crisp snacks and fresh vegetables. It also has a fine
range of Chinese cooking appliances and utensils.

### Sancho Panza Tapas

*Berenstraat 41 (620 1103). Tram 1, 2, 5.* **Open** 3-8.30pm
Tue-Fri, Sun; 3-8pm Sat. **Credit** EC. **Map 5 C4**
Blink and you'll miss this tiny tapas joint in the heart of the
Jordaan. Try the fabulous albóndigas (meat balls) and

pickled vegetables. If you simply can't wait to wrap your lips
around their mouth-watering treats, then walk to the picturesque bench by the canal close by and indulge.
*Disabled access with assistance.*

### Sareleng Atin

*1e Sweelinckstraat 20 (673 4309). Tram 3, 4, 16, 20,
24, 25.* **Open** 10am-6pm Mon-Sat. **Map 6 F5**
A fantastic selection of Filipino food, from shrimp fry to
coconut vinegar to dried salted fish. Sweets include cassava
cookies and halo-halo (mixed fresh fruits in crushed ice, milk
and ice-cream) on hot summer days.

### A Taste of Ireland

*Herengracht 228 (638 1642). Tram 13, 14, 17, 20.*
**Open** 1-6pm Mon; 10am-6pm Tue-Fri; 11am-5pm Sat.
**Credit** EC. **Map 2 C3**
This shop stocks many of the goodies you may be missing
from home: fresh sausages, bacon and puddings are flown
in fresh from Ireland every week, and there is also an extensive selection of British and Irish beers and ciders on sale.

### De Thai Shop

*Koningsstraat 42 (620 9900). Tram 4, 9, 14, 16, 20, 24,
25/Metro Nieuwmarkt.* **Open** 10am-6.30pm Mon-Fri;
10am-6pm Sat. **Credit** EC. **Map 3 E2**
A small shop stocking a selection of Thai ingredients, including freshly made curry, imported salted fish and fresh ingredients such as lemongrass and other herbs.
*Disabled access.*

### Toko Ramee

*Ferdinand Bolstraat 74 (662 2025). Tram 16, 20, 24,
25.* **Open** 9am-6pm Tue-Fri; 9am-5pm Sat. **Map 6 E6**
All the spices and ingredients used in Indonesian cooking
are sold here, along with Chinese and Thai ingredients and
some takeaway dishes.
*Disabled access.*

## Fish

### Viscenter Volendam

*Kinkerstraat 181 (618 7062). Tram 7, 17.* **Open** 8am-
6pm Mon-Sat. **Credit** EC. **Map 4 B5**
The family that runs this popular shop commutes from
Volendam, a major fishing village on the east coast of
Holland. Choose from a large selection of fresh water and sea
fish, shellfish, cured fish (try the smoked eels, or *gerookte
paling*), takeaway snacks and seafood salads.
*Disabled access.*

## Health food

*See also* **Noordermarkt**, *below* **Markets**.

### Biologische Boerenmarkt

*Noordermarkt, corner of Noorderstraat and
Brouwersgracht. Tram 3, 10/bus 18, 22.* **Open** 10am-
4pm Sat. **Map 2 B2**
A weekly market, and a terrific place to find organic fruit,
veg, cheese, breads and dairy products.

### Deshima Freshop

*Weteringschans 65 (423 0391). Tram 6, 7, 10, 16, 24,
25.* **Open** 10am-6pm Mon-Fri; 10am-5pm Sat. **Credit** EC.
**Map 5 D5**
This basement macrobiotic shop sells foods that contain no
dairy products, meat or sugar, and also offers macrobiotic
cookery courses in Friesland as part of the Kushi Institute
(phone 625 7513 for details). Above the shop is a curiously
subdued restaurant serving macrobiotic lunches from noon
until 2pm on weekdays.
*Disabled access.*

# How to shop 'til you drop

Your first challenge when shopping in Amsterdam is to bring yourself level with the locals. A grasp of the Dutch language is, dare we say it, totally unnecessary, as English is spoken by nearly everyone here. What you need instead are sharp wits and loads of determination. The Dutch are not a nation of mollycoddlers, and shopping here can be a rather invigorating exercise that challenges you mentally, physically and spiritually. The following is a list of pointers to help bring you up to par with even the most sophisticated of local shoppers.

● The conversation the sales person is having a) on the phone or b) with a colleague takes precedence over helping you. Know this and use it to your advantage. Enjoy those moments of solitude by meditating on your purchases and keeping your energies focused on other shopping issues, such as…

● Finding clothing, shoes and so on in your size. Whatever you do, do not expect the staff to convert clothing sizes for you. They've got better things to do like, well, chatting to their mates on the phone. It's up to you to look at the conversion chart on page 267 of this Guide.

● Stop regularly for frites met (chips with mayonnaise), or koffie verkeerd (café au lait) and apple gebak met slagroom (apple pie with cream). Shopping is a leisurely and social activity in Holland, so enjoy all the lovely cafés dotting the canals and keep your blood sugar level on a steady keel.

● Remember that front and honesty are respected in Holland: give as good as you get. Here, shopping is not for the timid. For those people lacking self-assertiveness skills, think of this as retail therapy. Shape up or ship out.

● Occasionally, you might think you're standing in a queue. Oh no you're not. Queues in Holland are mythical and fleeting things. Go back to your assertiveness training, take a deep breath, and plunge ahead. This is particularly vital at Amsterdam's outdoor markets, where any genteel rules that do exist are left at the wayside and shopping becomes high art.

● Without being too bossy (you may, after all, be travelling with someone whose first priority is not shopping), try to arrange your shopping around the erratic schedules of the city's shopkeepers. Sunday afternoons, in particular, are only for the hardiest of shoppers. At one time a ghostly calm pervaded the streets of Amsterdam on the Lord's Day, as no shops were allowed to open. However, times have changed, and shoppers can now indulge every Sunday along the Kalverstraat.

● Don't try to haggle: the Dutch are canny when it comes to making a buck and though it may work in a second-hand market, under no circumstances should you attempt it elsewhere.

● Finally, remember you can extricate yourself from even the stickiest shopping situations with a saucy wink and a smile. You might end up in hospital, but, hey: at least you *tried*…

## Gimsel
*Huidenstraat 19 (624 8087). Tram 1, 2, 5.* **Open** 12.30-6.30pm Mon; 9.30am-6.30pm Tue-Fri; 9am-5pm Sat. **Credit** EC. **Map 5 C4**
A popular and centrally located health food shop with organic fruit and veg and excellent freshly baked bread, cakes and savouries. The place to head if you've overdone it at Febo (*see box* **Grease is the word**, *page 119*) and want to get your body back on an even keel. *Disabled access.*

## De Natuurwinkel
*Weteringschans 133-7 (638 4083). Tram 6, 7, 10.* **Open** 7am-8pm Mon-Wed, Fri, Sat; 7am-9pm Thur; 11-6pm Sun. **Credit** AmEx, EC, MC, V. **Map 6 E5**
De Natuurwinkel is easily the largest health food supermarket in Amsterdam, with branches scattered all around town. You'll find everything here healthy and natural here, from organic meat, fruit and veg (all delivered fresh to the stores daily) to surprisingly tasty sugar-free chocolates and organic wines and beers.
**Branches**: 1e Constantijn Huygensstraat 49-55 (685 1536); 1e Van Swindenstraat 30-32 (693 5909); Haarlemmerdijk 174 (626 6310). *Disabled access.*

## Night shops
It's 11pm, and you're in dire need of ice-cream/toilet roll/condoms/beer (delete as applicable). This is where Amsterdam's night shops come in handy. Although prices are often pretty steep, you're paying for the convenience, and let's face it: shops that stay open until 2am are worth their weight in gold.

## Avondmarkt
*De Wittenkade 94-6 (686 4919). Tram 10.* **Open** 4pm-midnight Mon-Sat; 2pm-midnight Sun. **Credit** EC. **Map 1 A2**
The Avondmarkt is the biggest and best night shop in town: it's basically a supermarket, albeit a late-opening one. Recommended, and well worth the tram ride.

## Big Bananas
*Leidsestraat 73 (627 7040). Tram 1, 2, 5.* **Open** 11am-1am Mon-Fri; 11am-2am Sat. **Map 5 D4**
A reasonable selection of wines, some dubious-looking canned cocktails and a variety of sandwiches are available here. Expensive, even for a night shop. *Disabled access.*

# A girl's best friend

Amsterdam's association with diamonds dates back to the sixteenth century, when refugee Jews brought the trade to the city. The largest diamond ever found, the Cullinan, and the world-famous Koh-I-Noor, part of the British Crown Jewels, were cut by Amsterdam workers. Another claim to fame is that the smallest 'brilliant cut' diamond (a brilliant cut has 57 facets) was also cut here: it's a tiny sliver of sparkle – just 0.0012-carat – and can be seen in **Van Moppes & Zoon**.

There are still numerous diamond-polishing factories and shops in Amsterdam. The four bigger firms listed below are members of the Diamond Foundation and welcome visitors (you are under no obligation to buy). All offer similar tours, lasting from around 20 minutes to an hour, with the guides giving a brief history of the diamond industry and Amsterdam's strategic importance in it. You'll probably be shown a worker polishing or setting a diamond, but the real thrill (only offered to those in large groups) is when the guide nonchalantly pours diamonds from a black velvet bag onto a table for your inspection. If this happens, try not to nick any. It's not a good idea.

If you're set on buying a stone, you'll find that prices in Amsterdam are competitive, but not particularly cheaper than elsewhere. Still, **Gassan Diamond House**, built in 1879 as a diamond factory, offers one of the more enjoyable tours. There's not much to choose between the others – the **Amsterdam Diamond Centre**, **Coster Diamonds** and **Stoeltie Diamonds** all run free tours throughout the day on request, with a *gratis* drink at the end – but be prepared for an unenthusiastic commentary and a very brisk walk around to the sales room if you're not part of a group. Tours can be given in any European language.

### Amsterdam Diamond Centre
*Rokin 1-5 (624 5787). Tram 4, 9, 14, 16, 20, 24, 25.* **Open** 9.30am-6pm Mon-Wed, Fri-Sun; 9.30am-8.30pm Thur. **Credit** AmEx, DC, EC, JCB, MC, V. **Map 2 D2**
*Disabled access.*

### Coster Diamonds
*Paulus Potterstraat 2-6 (676 2222). Tram 2, 3, 5, 12, 20.* **Open** 9am-5pm daily. **Credit** AmEx, DC, EC, JCB, MC, V. **Map 5 D6**

### Gassan Diamond BV
*Nieuwe Uilenburgerstraat 173-175 (622 5333). Tram 9, 14, 20/Metro Nieuwmarkt.* **Open** 9am-5pm daily. **Map 3 E2**
*Disabled access.*

### Stoeltie Diamonds
*Wagenstraat 13-17 (623 7601). Tram 4, 9, 14, 20.* **Open** 8.30am-5pm daily. **Credit** AmEx, DC, EC, JCB, MC, V. **Map 3 E3**
*Disabled access.*

### Van Moppes & Zoon Diamond Factory
*Albert Cuypstraat 2-6 (676 1242). Tram 16, 24, 25.* **Open** 8.30am-5pm daily. **Credit** AmEx, DC, EC, JCB, MC, V. **Map 6 E6**
*Disabled access.*

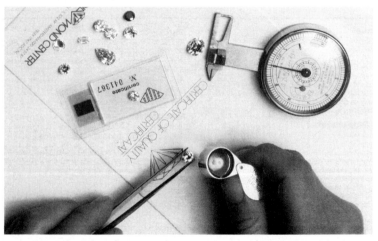

### Avondmarkt
*De Wittenkade 94-6 (686 4919). Tram 10.* **Open** 4pm-midnight Mon-Sat; 2pm-midnight Sun. **Credit** EC.
**Map 1 A2**
The Avondmarkt is the biggest and best night shop in town: it's basically a supermarket, albeit a late-opening one. Recommended, and well worth the tram ride.

### Big Bananas
*Leidsestraat 73 (627 7040). Tram 1, 2, 5.* **Open** 11am-1am Mon-Fri; 11am-2am Sat. **Map 5 D4**
A reasonable selection of wines, some dubious-looking canned cocktails and a variety of sandwiches are available here. Expensive, even for a night shop.
*Disabled access.*

### Dolf's Avondverkoop
*Willemsstraat 79 (625 9503). Tram 3.* **Open** 4pm-1am Mon-Sat; 11am-1am Sun. **Credit** EC. **Map 2 B2**
One of the best night shops in the Jordaan. It stocks all the urgent products you might suddenly need late at night, including toilet paper, toothpaste and bread. As pricey as most night shops.
*Disabled access.*

### Heuft's First Class Night Shop
*Rijnstraat 62 (642 4048). Tram 4, 25.* **Open** 5pm-1am Mon-Sat; 3pm-1am Sun. **Credit** AmEx, MC, V.
If you can't make it all the way out to Heuft's – it's way out just beyond the Pijp – you can phone for a delivery of anything from champagne and oysters to full meals: Heuft's has it all, if you're willing to pay over the odds. Definitely the classiest night shop in Amsterdam.

### La Noche
*Linnaeusstraat 24 (665 0440). Tram 3, 6, 9, 10, 14.* **Open** 6pm-midnight Mon-Fri; 5pm-midnight Sat; 2pm-midnight Sun. **Credit** EC. **Map 7 H3**
Basics such as beer, wine, coffee, milk and biscuits can be had here, along with a fine selection of takeaway meals and some decent sweets, which the staff will wrap in a cute little box for you.
*Disabled access with assistance.*

### Sterk
*Waterlooplein 241 (626 5097). Tram 9, 14, 20/Metro Waterlooplein.* **Open** 8am-2am daily. **Credit** AmEx, EC, MC, V. **Map 3 E3**
Sterk is more of a deli than a night shop: quiches, pastries, salads and more are made on the premises, and there's even a range of fresh fruit and veg on the shelves. It's also a good bet for a decent bottle of plonk and some nice confectionery. Be prepared to ask for whatever you want here, as there's no self-service. The branch on De Clercqstraat is known as 'Champagne Corner', which may give you some idea as to what's on offer.
*Disabled access.*
**Branches**: Vijzelstraat 125 (427 0711), open 5pm-1am Mon-Fri, 11am-midnight Sat, Sun; Champagne Corner, De Clercqstraat 1-9 (618 1727), open 1pm-1am Mon-Fri, 11am-1pm Sat, Sun.

## Off-licences (Slijterijen)

### De Bierkoning
*Paleisstraat 125 (625 2336). Tram 1, 2, 5, 13, 14, 16, 17, 20, 24, 25.* **Open** 1-6.30pm Mon; 11am-6.30pm Tue, Wed, Fri; 11am-9pm Thur; 11am-6pm Sat. **Map 2 C3**
'The Beer King', named for its location behind the Royal Palace, stocks approximately 850 different brands of beer from around the world, and a range of nice beer glasses.

Say it with flowers! See page 150.

### Chabrol, Adviseurs in Wijnen en Gedistilleerd
*Haarlemmerstraat 7 (622 2781). Tram 1, 2, 5.* **Open** 9am-8pm Mon-Wed, Fri; 9am-9pm Thur; 9am-7pm Sat; noon-5.30pm Sun. **Credit** AmEx, EC, MC, V. **Map 2 C2**
Offering wine, beer and spirits from all over the world as well as expert advice, this clumsily named shop is great value for money. Added bonuses include free delivery within Amsterdam and glasses available for rent.
*Disabled access.*

### De Cuyp
*Albert Cuypstraat 146 (662 6676/fax 673 6112). Tram 4, 16, 24, 25.* **Open** 9am-6pm Tue-Sat. **Map 6 F5**
De Cuyp stocks a large assortment of international wines and spirits, including drinks from Brazil, Surinam, and the owner's favourite, Pisco, from Chile. It also specialises in extremes: there are over 3,000 miniatures in stock, plus some huge bottles, such as a 21-litre bottle of champagne. There's free delivery within Amsterdam, and rental glasses on offer.
*Disabled access.*

### Wijnkoperij Woorts
*Utrechtsestraat 51 (623 7426). Tram 4.* **Open** 1-6pm Mon; 9am-6pm Tue-Sat. **Credit** EC. **Map 6 E4**
A wine-lover's paradise, offering over 600 varieties with an emphasis on Italian booze. Tasting sessions are held on request for groups of up to 12 (reservations necessary), and there's free delivery on weekdays within Amsterdam.
*Disabled access with assistance.*

## Supermarkets

That the Netherlands is one of the world's most densely populated countries is perhaps most

*Shoppers on busy Leidsestraat.*

apparent on Saturday afternoons at the supermarket. Thankfully, because Amsterdam is a city that stays up late, Saturday mornings are a different story and are a good time to get out and get the goods. Otherwise, prepare to brave the horrendously crowded aisles and long queues at the cash registers.

A few tips: unless a per piece (*per stuk*) price is given, fruit and vegetables must be weighed by the customer. Put your produce on the scale, press the picture of the item, and press the 'BON' button to get the receipt. You must pack your groceries yourself, and if you want a plastic bag (usually 35c), you have to ask for it.

### Albert Heijn
*Nieuwezijds Voorburgwal 226 (421 8344). Tram 1, 2, 4, 5, 9, 13, 14, 16, 17, 20, 24, 25.* **Open** 8am-10pm Mon-Sat; 11am-7pm Sun. **Credit** EC. **Map 2 D3**
This massive new branch of Albert Heijn, aptly named the 'Food Plaza', is located behind Dam Square. There are over 40 branches of Heijn within Amsterdam (some of which are listed below), but the extended hours at this branch are an exception to those of most others.
**Branches**: Van Baerlestraat 118 (662 0416); Haarlemmerdijk 1 (625 6931); Kinkerstraat 89 (618 0088); Koningsplein 6 (624 5721); Nieuwmarkt 18 (623 2461); Overtoom 454 (618 3065); Vijzelstraat 117 (625 9405); Waterlooplein 131 (624 1249); Westerstraat 79-87 (623 6852).
*Disabled access.*

### Dirk van den Broek
*Marie Heinekenplein 25 (611 0812). Tram 16, 24, 25.* **Open** 8am-8pm Mon-Wed, Fri; 8am-9pm Thur; 8am-6pm Sat. **Map 6 E5**
A perfectly decent, unflashy grocery store. There's less choice and less luxury than at Albert Heijn, but it's far cheaper in just about every area.
**Branches**: Bilderdijkstraat 124 (612 2658); Lijnbaansgracht 31 (625 3949); 2e Nassaustraat 23 (686 0132); Wittenburgerstraat 18 (620 0070).
*Disabled access.*

### Hema
*See above* **Department Stores** *for listings.*
Hardly the place for weekly basics – it doesn't sell milk, for one thing – but Hema has everything you need for a picnic, along with a terrific range of cheap and eminently munchable snacks.
*Disabled access.*

### Marks & Spencer
*Kalverstraat 66-72 (531 2468). Tram 4, 9, 14, 16, 20, 24, 25.* **Open** 11am-6pm Mon; 10am-6pm Tue, Wed, Fri; 10am-9pm Thur; 9.30am-6pm Sat; noon-6pm Sun. **Credit** EC, MC, V. **Map 2 D3**
Full of the food, clothing and underwear Brits already know and love, albeit at higher prices than in the UK. Many expats can be found here stocking up their cupboards.
*Currency exchange. Disabled access.*

## Tea & coffee

### Brandmeester's Koffie
*Van Baerlestraat 13 (675 7888). Tram 3, 12, 20, 24.* **Open** noon-6pm Mon; 9am-6pm Tue, Wed, Fri; 9am-9pm Thur; 9am-5.30pm Sat; noon-6pm first Sun of month. **Credit** AmEx, DC, EC, MC, V. **Map 5 D6**
Coffee beans from around the globe, roasted on the premises. The smell, as you'd imagine, is fantastic.
*Disabled access.*

### Geels & Co
*Warmoesstraat 67 (624 0683). Tram 4, 9, 14, 16, 20, 24, 25.* **Open** *shop* 9am-5.45pm Mon-Sat; *museum* 2-5pm Tue, Fri, Sat. **Map 2 D2**
Although it's not as old as some of its rivals, Geels is cheaper for some varieties of coffee beans and loose teas. It has a large stock of brewing contraptions and serving utensils, while upstairs is a small museum of old brewing equipment.
**Branch**: 't Zonnetje, Haarlemmerdijk 45 (623 0058).

### Levelt
*Prinsengracht 180 (624 0823). Tram 13, 14, 17, 20.* **Open** noon-6pm Mon; 9am-6pm Tue-Fri; 9am-5pm Sat. **Map 1 B3**

*Flying high at Joe's Vliegerwinkel.*

### Kramer/Pontifex
*Reestraat 18-20 (626 5274). Tram 13, 14, 17, 20.* **Open**
10am-6pm Mon-Fri; 10am-5pm Sat. **Map 2 C3**
Mr Kramer is a doctor for old-fashioned dolls and teddies
who has held his surgery on these premises for 25 years; he
can fix anything from a broken Barbie to a battered teddy.
Pontifex, on the same premises, sells a multitude of candles.
*Disabled access.*

### Scale Train House
*Bilderdijkstraat 94 (612 2670/fax 612 2817). Tram 3, 7,
12, 13, 14, 17, 20.* **Open** 1-5.30pm Mon; 9.30am-5.30pm
Tue-Fri; 9.30am-5pm Sat. **Credit** AmEx, DC, EC, MC, V.
**Map 4 B5**
With a DIY kit from here, you can build a replica of St Peter's
Basilica or the Arc de Triomphe. The ready-made parade
includes electric trains (with steam or diesel engines, and all
rolling stock) plus tracks, stations, houses and scenery.
There is also a huge variety of modern and vintage vehicles.
*Disabled access.*

### Schaak en Go het Paard
*Haarlemmerdijk 147 (624 1171). Tram 3/bus 18, 22.*
**Open** 10.30am-6.30pm Tue-Fri; 10.30am-5.30pm Sat.
**Credit** EC, MC, V. **Map 1 B1**
A fine selection of beautiful and exotic chess sets, ranging
from African to ultra-modern, as well as sets for the Japanese
game Go.
*Disabled access.*

### De Zeiling
*Ruysdaelstraat 21-3 (679 3817). Tram 2, 3, 5, 12, 16,
20.* **Open** noon-6pm Mon; 9am-6pm Tue-Fri; 9am-5pm
Sat. **Credit** AmEx, DC, EC, MC, V. **Map 6 E6**
This gem of a shop is stocked with Rudolf Steiner-inspired
artefacts, including handmade wooden toys, rattles, puzzles,
music boxes and night lights, baby clothes in natural materials, dyes, doll-making materials, cards and candles.

## Health & beauty

*See also chapter* **Services**, *page 164*, and *box* **The
new curiosity shops**, *page 160*.

### The Body Shop
*Kalverstraat 157-9 (623 9789). Tram 4, 9, 14, 16, 20,
24, 25.* **Open** 11am-6pm Mon; 9.30am-6pm Tue, Wed,
Fri; 9.30am-9pm Thur; 10am-5.30pm Sat; 1-5pm Sun.
**Credit** AmEx, DC, EC, MC, V. **Map 2 D3**
The usual wonderful array of shampoos, lotions and soaps
for pampering your body, along with gift-wrapping and refill
services. Prices are higher than in Britain.
**Branches:** Kinkerstraat 251 (683 7157); Nieuwendijk
196E (626 6135).
*Disabled access.*

### Kruiderij 'De Munt'
*Vijzelstraat 1 (624 4533). Tram 4, 9, 14, 16, 20, 24, 25.*
**Open** 9.30am-6pm Mon, Tue, Fri, Sat; 9.30am-9pm Thur;
2-6pm Sun. **Credit** AmEx, DC, EC, MC, V. **Map 5 D4**
This tiny, picturesque store is chock-a-block with all it takes
to turn your bathroom into a spa, including a wide range of
essential oils and treatment products from Neal's Yard,
Kiehl's and Weleda. If you have a taste for herbs you can't
find in coffee shops, come here for Celestial Seasonings teas,
Solgar Vitamins and bee pollen in capsule form.

### Lillian
*Leidsestraat 74-6 (627 1900). Tram 1, 2, 5.* **Open** 9am-
10pm Mon-Sat; 11am-10pm Sun. **Credit** AmEx, EC, JCB,
V. **Map 5 D4**
All the big name cosmetic lines and vitamin brands can be
picked up at this fine store on the busy Leidsestraat. Lillian

also sell homeopathic products and a large selection of body,
hair care and beauty aids.
*Disabled access.*

## Interior & housewares

### Frozen Fountain
*Prinsengracht 629 (622 9375). Tram 1, 2, 5.* **Open** 1-
6pm Mon; 10am-6pm Tue-Fri; 10am-5pm Sat. **Credit** EC
(all cheques and foreign currency). **Map 5 D4**
Frozen Fountain defies description: its thing is cutting-edge
designer furnishings that embrace the millennium, yet are
deeply seated in tradition. Don't miss.
*Disabled access.*

### Galerie KIS
*Paleisstraat 107 (620 9760). Tram 1, 2, 4, 5, 9, 11, 13,
16, 17, 20, 24, 25.* **Open** noon-6pm Wed-Sun. **Credit**
EC. **Map 2 C3**
Over 200 square metres (massive by Amsterdam standards)
of sensational furniture, lighting and housewares from independent designers, artists and architects. KIS keeps the numbers in each series small, so you can be sure you'll be the only
one on the block with one of these original pieces.
*Disabled access (ground floor only).*

### Kitsch Kitchen
*1e Bloemdwarsstraat 21 (622 8261). Tram 13, 17, 20.*
**Open** 11am-6pm Mon-Fri; 10am-6pm Sat. **Map 2 B3**
Kitsch Kitchen sends even the most hardy kitsch queens
weak at the knees. A staggering variety of culinary and
household objects (including wacky '60s wallpapers) have
been imported from Mexico, Guatemala, India, China and
parts of Africa, and there's also tons of plastic stuff.
*Disabled access.*

### Marañón Hangmatten
*Singel 488-90, at the flower market (420 7121). Tram 1,
2, 5, 20.* **Open** 10am-6pm Mon; 9am-6pm Tue-Sat; 11am-
5pm Sun. **Credit** AmEx, DC, EC, MC, V. **Map 5 D4**
Europe's biggest collection of hammocks for indoors and out
is available in a variety of colours and designs. The most
expensive and colourful are the hand-woven ones from South
America and Mexico (from ƒ60).
*Disabled access with assistance.*

### Pas-destoel
*Westerstraat 260 (420 7542). Tram 3, 10/bus 18.* **Open**
9.30am-5pm Fri, Sat; also by appointment. **Credit** EC.
**Map 1 B2**
Pas-destoel sells a massive range of kiddie stuff, including
toys, textiles, and delightful children's pressies. After browsing through the ladybird armchairs, toy boxes shaped like
trains and hand-painted wooden windmills, you'll long for a
second childhood.
*Disabled access with assistance.*

### Toele
*Overtoom 430-2 & 438 (618 1179). Tram 1, 6.* **Open**
10am-6pm Tue-Fri; 10am-4.30pm Sat. **Credit** EC.
**Map 4 B6**
A totally unpretentious shop that has been supplying
Holland with Persian rugs, sisal and coco matting and other
floor coverings from around the world since 1952. The
opening hours tend to vary, so it's best to phone ahead.
*Disabled access.*

### What's Cooking
*Reestraat 16 (427 0630). Tram 13, 14, 17, 20.* **Open**
noon-7pm Tue-Fri; 11am-6pm Sat. **Credit** EC, MC, V.
**Map 2 C3**
Every object in this zingy culinary gift shop seems chosen
for its retina-searing colours: vivid pink salad bowls, kiwi

# The new curiosity shops

Looking for records? Go to a record shop. Want to buy some toys for your kids? Check out the section on page 159. It's all pretty straightforward, really. Until, that is, you get the urge to buy some exotic Christmas decorations. In April. Or until you suddenly become overcome by a thirst for Chilean mineral water. Don't laugh: it could happen to you. And this is what to do when it does.

Amsterdam's wonderfully quirky speciality stores are the jewels in the crown of what is already an excellent shopping scene. Take **Christmas World**, for example, which sells nothing but cheery Yuletide decorations from around the world, including stockings and Delft blue ornaments. Or **De Witte Tandenwinkel** – literally, 'The White Teeth Shop' – which has hundreds of quirky toothbrushes, toothpicks and the like for the dentally minded. Anyone turned off by the grubby stores in the Red Light District should head for **Condomerie Het Gulden Vlies**, the first store of its kind in the world, which sells a trouser-boggling variety of condoms.

On a less febrile level, **Klamboe Imports** sells mosquito nets (because of its canals, Amsterdam has a real problem with mosquitoes in summer); **Olivaria** has bottle upon bottle of olive oil, including plenty of organic varieties; and **PGC Hajenius**, founded in 1826, is a terrific tobacconist's, stocking traditional Dutch clay pipes (14-inch or 20-inch stem) and its own famed brand of cigars.

Once you've been round all those, you'll need a drink: shopping is thirsty work, after all. Well, for once, pass by the brown café, and don't just pop down to the oh-so-convenient hotel bar: instead, head straight for **Waterwinkel**. Owner Jan Willem Bakker stocks over 100 different varieties of mineral water from all around the world...

### Christmas World

*Nieuwezijds Voorburgwal 137-9 (622 7047). Tram 1, 2, 5, 13, 17, 20.* **Open** 10am-6pm Mon-Fri; 10am-5pm Sat. **Credit** AmEx, MC, V. **Map 2 C3** *Disabled access.*

### Condomerie Het Gulden Vlies

*Warmoesstraat 141 (627 4174/fax 638 9265). Tram 4, 9, 14, 16, 20, 24, 25.* **Open** 11am-6pm Mon-Sat. **Credit** EC. **Map 2 D2** *Disabled access.*

### Klamboe Imports

*Prinsengracht 232 (622 9492). Tram 13, 14, 17, 20.* **Open** *mid-Apr-mid-Sept* 11am-5pm Tue-Sat; *mid-Sept-mid-Apr* noon-5pm Fri, Sat. **Credit** AmEx, DC, EC, MC, V. **Map 2 C3** *Disabled access.*

### Olivaria

*Hazenstraat 2A (638 3552). Tram 7, 10, 20.* **Open** 2-6pm Mon; 11am-6pm Tue-Sat. **Credit** EC. **Map 5 C4**

### PGC Hajenius

*Rokin 92-6 (625 9985). Tram 4, 9, 14, 16, 20, 24, 25.* **Open** noon-6pm Mon; 9.30am-6pm Tue, Wed, Fri, Sat; 9.30am-9pm Thur; noon-5pm Sun. **Credit** AmEx, DC, EC, MC, V. **Map 2 D3** *Disabled access with assistance.*

### Waterwinkel

*Roelof Hartstraat 10 (675 5932). Tram 3, 12, 20, 24.* **Open** 9am-6pm Mon-Fri; 9am-5pm Sat. **Credit** AmEx, DC, EC, MC, V.

### De Witte Tandenwinkel

*Runstraat 5 (623 3443). Tram 1, 2, 5.* **Open** 1-6pm Mon; 10am-6pm Tue-Fri; 10am-5pm Sat. **Credit** AmEx, DC, EC, MC, V. **Map 5 C4** *Disabled access.*

---

green sauces, and acid orange peppermills are just the tip of the proverbial iceberg; all are capable of putting pep into the most humdrum of kitchens. Cooking will never be the same again.

### Xenos

*Kalverstraat 228 (422 9163). Tram 1, 2, 4, 5, 9, 14, 16, 20, 24, 25.* **Open** 9.30am-6pm Mon-Wed, Fri, Sat; 9.30am-9pm Thur; noon-6pm Sun. **Map 2 D3**
If you're setting up house on a tight budget or for a short period of time, this is the place to find much of what you'll need at very low prices.
**Branch:** Nieuwendijk 200-206 (622 2576). *Disabled access.*

## Glass & crystal

### Glasgalerie Kuhler

*Prinsengracht 134 (638 0230). Tram 13, 14, 16, 20.* **Open** noon-6pm Tue-Sat; 1-4pm first Sun of month. **Credit** AmEx, DC, MC, V. **Map 1 B3**
A large collection of contemporary European glass and crystal is available at Glasgalerie Kuhler. Most pieces are unique, dated and signed by well-known artists, some of whome are Dutch. Glass-blowing is well represented, along with pate verre and cold laminated sculptures. Prices range from ƒ85 to a cool ƒ10,000.
*Disabled access with assistance.*

## Van Tetterode

*Singel 163 (620 6382). Tram 1, 2, 5, 13, 17, 20.* **Open** 10.30am-6pm Tue-Sun. **Credit** AmEx, DC, EC, MC, V. **Map 2 C3**

Since 1919, Van Tetterode's atelier has been turning out unique glass objets d'art, as well as monumental commissions and public pieces. One-day glass workshops are available by appointment.

# Vintage

## Fifties-Sixties

*Huidenstraat 13 (623 2653). Tram 1, 2, 5.* **Open** 1-6pm Tue-Fri; 1-5.30pm Sat. **Map 5 C4**

Every available inch of space in this shop is packed with authentic period pieces – toasters, blenders, lamps and even vacuum cleaners – all in good working condition (220 volts). Non-electrical goods include floor-standing chrome ashtrays.

## Nic Nic

*Gasthuismolensteeg 5 (622 8523). Tram 1, 2, 5, 13, 17, 20.* **Open** noon-6pm Mon-Fri; 10am-5pm Sat. **Credit** AmEx, DC, EC, MC, V. **Map 2 C3**

There is certainly no shortage of shops of this ilk in Amsterdam, but this one definitely has the best selection of '50s and '60s furniture, lamps, ashtrays and kitchenware, most in mint condition. Opening times can vary.
**Branch:** 1e Jan Steenstraat 131 (675 6805).
*Disabled access.*

## Quadra Original Posters

*Herengracht 383-9 (626 9472). Tram 1, 2, 4, 5, 14, 16, 20, 24, 25.* **Open** 10am-4.30pm Tue-Sat. **Credit** DC, EC, MC, V. **Map 5 D4**

Celebrate the millennium with an original *fin de siècle* advertising poster, or decorate your room with a circus poster from the 1930s. Whatever your tastes – from beer ads to B-movies – you're sure to find it here.
*Disabled access.*

## Markets

The biggest and best market of all is held on **Queen's Day** (*see chapter* **Amsterdam by Season**, *pages 7-8*). Amsterdam's neighbourhood markets, particularly **Albert Cuypmarkt** and the **Dappermarkt**, are the best places to find cheap food and clothes, while aficionados of second-hand goods should head to Monday's **Noordermarkt**. *See also* **Flowers** *above*.

## Albert Cuypmarkt

*Albert Cuypstraat. Tram 4, 16, 24, 25.* **Open** 9am-5pm Mon-Sat. **Map 6 E5**

Amsterdam's biggest general market, selling everything from pillows to prawns at excellent prices. It's also worth visiting for the material stalls, a firm favourite with painters who can pick up untreated canvas from around ƒ3,95 a metre. Clothes tend to be run-of-the-mill cheapies, but the odd bargain can be found.

## Boerenmarkt

*Westerstraat/Noorderkerkstraat. Tram 3, 10.* **Open** 10am-3pm Sat. **Map 2 B2**

Every Saturday, the Noordermarkt is transformed into the organic farmers' market. Products include organic fruit and vegetables (with opportunities for food- and wine-tasting) as well as essential oils, herbs, candles and the like. Groups of singers or medieval musicians sometimes make a visit here feel more like a day trip than a mere shopping excursion.

## Dappermarkt

*Dapperstraat. Tram 3, 6, 10, 14.* **Open** 9am-5pm Mon-Sat. **Map 7 H3**

A true locals' market, far less touristy than its famous counterparts: for a start, the prices here do not seem to rise in accordance with the number of visitors. It sells the usual market fodder, with plenty of cheap clothes and underwear.

## Looier

*Elandsgracht 109. Tram 7, 10, 17, 20.* **Open** 11am-5pm Mon-Wed; 11am-9pm Thur; 9am-5pm Sat. **Map 5 C4**

The Looier is more upmarket than the nearby Rommelmarkt: it's mainly antiques here, with plenty of collectors' items on offer. Hidden behind a façade of shop fronts, the entrance appears at first to be that of a rather smart antique shop. However, once inside, it's easy to get lost in the quiet, warehouse-like premises and find yourself standing alone by a stall crammed with antiquated clocks eerily ticking away.

## Noordermarkt

*Noorderstraat. Tram 3, 10/bus 18, 22.* **Open** 7.30am-1pm Mon. **Map 2 B2**

A bargain-hunter's paradise. Tagged on to the end of the utilitarian Westermarkt (*see below*), the Noordermarkt is compact and frequented by the serious market shopper. The piles upon piles of new and (mainly) second-hand clothes, shoes, jewellery and hats need to be sorted through with a grim determination in order to sift the dross from the delights. Prices can be laughably low, but like all the best second-hand markets, if you don't arrive early, the best stuff will already have been snapped up.

## Oudemanhuis Book Market

*Oudemanhuispoort. Tram 4, 9, 14, 16, 20, 24, 25.* **Open** 11am-4pm Mon-Fri. **Map 2 D3**

People have been buying and selling books, prints and sheet music at this charming arcade since the nineteenth century. When the alley was built in 1601, it was the entrance to a home for the elderly, hence the name.

## Postzegelmarkt

*Nieuwezijds Voorburgwal, by no.276. Tram 1, 2, 5, 13, 17, 20.* **Open** 11am-4pm Wed, Sun. **Map 2 D3**

A specialist market for collectors of stamps, coins, old postcards and commemorative medals.

## Rommelmarkt

*Looiersgracht 38. Tram 7, 10, 17, 20.* **Open** 11am-5pm daily. **Map 5 C4**

A flea market where, nestled among the household junk, you are likely to come across dubious bargains like a boxed set of Demis Roussos discs.

## Waterlooplein

*Waterlooplein. Tram 9, 14, 20/Metro Waterlooplein.* **Open** 9am-5pm Mon-Sat. **Map 3 E3**

Amsterdam's top tourist market, but no less entertaining for that. Basically a huge flea market, it's great for clothes (though they can be a bit pricey), with the usual selections of jeans, leathers and batik T-shirts and some excellent second-hand stuff. Bargains can be had, but they're often hidden among defunct toasters and shoes that are down at heel (literally). Musos will enjoy rifling through the boxes of battered vinyl.

## Westermarkt

*Westerstraat. Tram 3, 10.* **Open** 9am-1pm Mon. **Map 2 B2**

A general market, selling all sorts of things. The amount of people packing the pavement is proof as to the entirely reasonable prices and the range of goods, which includes new watches, pretty (and not so pretty) fabrics and cheap factory reject clothes.

*Just about anything can be found in **Waterlooplein Market***. *See page 161.*

## Music

### Blue Note from Ear & Eye
*Gravenstraat 12 (428 1029). Tram 1, 2, 4, 5, 9, 13, 16, 20, 24, 25.* **Open** 11am-7pm Mon-Sat; noon-5pm Sun. **Credit** AmEx, DC, EC, MC, V. **Map 2 C3**
Jazz is the speciality here at this clunkily-named CD-only store: the full spectrum, from '30s stompers to mainstream, avant garde and Afro jazz, can be seen on the packed shelves. *Disabled access.*

### Boudisque
*Haringpakkerssteeg 10-18 (623 2603/fax 620 6079). Tram 1, 2, 4, 5, 9, 13, 14, 16, 17, 20, 24, 25.* **Open** 1-6pm Mon, Sun; 10am-6pm Tue, Wed, Fri, Sat; 10am-9pm Thur. **Credit** AmEx, DC, EC, MC, V. **Map 2 D2**
A wide selection of pop, rock, heavy metal, ambient house, jungle and world music CDs, plus T-shirts and CD-Roms. *Disabled access.*

### Charles Klaasiek en Folklore
*Weteringschans 193 (626 5538). Tram 6, 7, 10, 16, 24, 25.* **Open** 1-6.30pm Mon; 10am-6.30pm Tue, Wed, Fri; 10am-9pm Thur; 10am-5.30pm Sat. **Credit** AmEx, DC, EC, MC, V. **Map 6 E5**
A specialist shop dealing in classical and folk. It's a good place to find stuff on some of the smaller German and French labels, and, bucking trends, it also still sells some vinyl. *Disabled access.*

### Concerto
*Utrechtsestraat 52-60 (626 6577/624 5467/623 5228). Tram 4.* **Open** 10am-6pm Mon-Wed, Fri; 10am-9pm Thur; 10am-6pm Sat; noon-6pm Sun. **Credit** AmEx, DC, EC, MC, V. **Map 6 E4**
New and second-hand records and CDs of all types: this is where to look for historic Bach recordings, obscure Beatles

items, or that favourite Diana Ross album that got lost in the move. There's also a large section of second-hand 45s and new releases for slightly less than the usual prices. Nick Hornby types will love it. *Disabled access.*

### Get Records
*Utrechtsestraat 105 (622 3441). Tram 4.* **Open** noon-6pm Mon; 10am-6pm Tue, Wed, Fri, Sat; 10am-9pm Thur; noon-6pm Sun. **Credit** AmEx, DC, EC, MC, V. **Map 6 E4**
The space liberated with the clearout of much of the vinyl at Get Records has been filled with a considerable selection of alternative and independent-label CDs. The back of the shop is deceptive: a little corner to the left is partially dedicated to cheapies and is well worth investigating. *Disabled access.*

### Midtown
*Nieuwendijk 104 (638 4252). Tram 1, 2, 5, 20.* **Open** 10am-6pm Mon-Sat; 10am-9pm Thur. **Credit** AmEx, DC, EC, MC, V. **Map 2 C2**
A more than adequate array of dance music can be had here: hardcore, gabber, trance, club, mellow house and garage are among the styles on the shelves. Midtown is also a good source of information and tickets for hardcore parties. *Disabled access.*

### Sound of the Fifties
*Prinsengracht 669 (623 9745). Tram 6, 7, 10, 20.* **Open** noon-6pm Mon-Sat. **Credit** AmEx, DC, EC, MC, V. **Map 5 C4**
Collectable vinyl from the '50s, from Liberace to Yma Sumac. Records and sleeves are in good condition, and prices are accordingly high.

### Virgin Megastore
*Magna Plaza, Nieuwezijds Voorburgwal 182 (622 8929). Tram 1, 2, 5, 13, 17, 20.* **Open** 11am-7pm Mon; 10am-

7pm Tue, Wed, Fri, Sat; 10am-9pm Thur; noon-7pm Sun.
**Credit** AmEx, EC, MC, V. **Map 2 C3**
Looking firmly to the future, Virgin doesn't stock vinyl, but it does have some of the largest selections of CDs, videos, computer games and T-shirts in the city.
*Disabled access.*

## New Age & eco

*See also* **Health Food** *above.*

### Greenlands, Hemp Eco Store
*Utrechtsestraat 26 (625 1100). Tram 4.* **Open** 11am-6pm Tue-Sat. **Credit** AmEx, DC, EC, MC, V. **Map 6 E4**
Greenlands' stock includes clothes, food, a small selection of stationery and lots of other bits and bobs made from hemp.
*Disabled access.*

### Hemp Works
*Niewendijk 13 (421 1762). Tram 1, 2, 5, 13, 17, 20.* **Open** noon-7pm daily. **Credit** AmEx, DC, EC, JCB, MC, V. **Map 2 C2**
If it's hemp you're looking for, you'll find it here. If it's quality, style, originality or a bargain you want, look elsewhere.

### Himalaya
*Warmoesstraat 56 (626 0899). Tram 1, 2, 4, 5, 9, 16, 17, 20, 24, 25/Metro Centraal Station.* **Open** 1-6pm Mon; 10am-6pm Tue, Wed, Fri, Sat; 10am-8.30pm Thur; 1-5pm Sun. **Credit** AmEx, EC, MC, V. **Map 2 D2**
Shop/gallery/teahouse Himalaya is a haven of calm amid seedy, bustling surroundings. The shop stocks an extensive range of books and magazines, crystals, tarot cards and jewellery, plus New Age CDs and tapes. The light and airy teahouse/gallery is a cosy place to relax, and there are daily readings in the shop in, for example, Mahabote (Burmese astrology), tarot and Sacred Path Cards: phone for details.
*Disabled access.*

### Jacob Hooy & Co
*Kloveniersburgwal 10-12 (624 3041). Tram 4, 9, 14, 16, 20, 24, 25/Metro Nieuwmarkt.* **Open** 10am-6pm Mon; 8.30am-6pm Tue-Fri; 8.30am-5pm Sat. **Credit** EC.
**Map 2 C3**
Established in 1743, this old-fashioned chemist sells around 600 kitchen and medicinal herbs, spices, natural cosmetics, health foods and homeopathic remedies.
*Disabled access with assistance.*

### Oibibio
*Prins Hendrikkade 20-21 (553 9355). Tram 1, 2, 4, 5, 9, 13, 17, 24, 25/Metro Centraal Station.* **Open** *café* 9am-midnight Mon-Thur, Sun; 9am-1am Fri, Sat; *restaurant* 5-10pm daily; *shop* noon-6.30pm Mon; 10am-6.30pm Tue, Wed, Fri; 10am-9pm Thur; 10am-6pm Sun; *sauna* 10am-midnight daily; *tea garden* noon-7pm daily. **Credit** AmEx, DC, EC, JCB, MC, V. **Map 2 D2**
This impressive centre is home to many resident therapists and there is a diverse range of workshops and lectures (mainly in Dutch, with a handful in English). A huge designer bar on the ground floor is overlooked by a gourmet vegetarian restaurant, and there's also a Japanese-style tea garden serving oriental delicacies. The Passage, a shop selling eco-friendly clothing, vitamins and minerals, runs between Nieuwendijk and Prins Hendrikkade, and the basement bookshop stocks a selection of books, CDs and videos. *See chapters* **Cafés and Bars**, *p123,* and **Sport & Fitness**, *p216.*
*Disabled access.*

### De Roos-Centrum voor Creatieve en Spirituele Groei
*Vondelstraat 35 (689 0081/bookshop 689 0436/tea house 689 5477). Tram 1, 2, 3, 5, 6, 12.* **Open** *centre*

8am-11pm Mon-Sat; 9am-6pm Sun; *shop* 10am-6.30pm Mon-Fri; 11.30am-5.30pm Sat; noon-4pm Sun; *tea house* 9am-10.30pm Mon-Sat; 9am-5pm Sun. **Map 5 C5**
A New Age centre with regular workshops and daily open sessions in yoga, Zen meditation and healing. There's a great range of books and leaflets on esoteric subjects, as well as magazines, candles, crystals, herbs, tarot cards and incense. The delightful tea shop – with a leafy garden at the back – will calm you down even more.

### Vitals Vitamine-Advieswinkel
*Nieuwe Nieuwstraat 47 (625 7298). Tram 1, 2, 5, 13, 17, 20.* **Open** 11am-6pm Mon; 9.30am-6pm Tue-Fri; 11am-5pm Sat. **Credit** AmEx, DC, EC, MC, V. **Map 2 C2**
The emphasis at this friendly shop is on educating yourself about food supplements and vitamins.
*Disabled access.*

## Souvenirs

### C-Cedille
*Lijnbaansgracht 275, near Spiegelgracht (624 7178). Tram 6, 7, 10.* **Open** *Jan, Feb* 11am-6pm Tue, Thur-Sat; noon-5.30pm Sun; *Mar-Dec* 1-6pm Mon; 11am-6pm Tue-Sun. **Credit** AmEx, DC, JCB, MC, V. **Map 5 D5**
In one half of this lovely shop, you'll find designer jewellery, mostly made by hand in the Netherlands. The other half has wooden toys, mobiles, glove puppets, music boxes and hand-made dolls in traditional Dutch costumes, plus some etchings and aquarelles of typical Amsterdam scenes.
*Disabled access.*

### Hans Brinker Village
*Nieuwe Hoogstraat 11 (427 3862). Tram 4, 9, 16, 20, 24, 25.* **Open** 11am-6pm daily. **Credit** AmEx, DC, EC, MC, V. **Map 3 E3**
How Dutch can one shop be? Well, if there were a competition, Hans Brinker Village would win hands-down: it stocks mountains of hand-crafted clogs, wooden children's toys and windmills. The perfect one-stop souvenir shop; you'll even find that cow print coffee cup you've always wanted.

### Holland Gallery De Munt
*Muntplein 12 (623 2271/fax 638 4215). Tram 4, 9, 14, 16, 20, 24, 25.* **Open** 9am-6pm Mon-Sat. **Credit** AmEx, DC, MC, V. **Map 5 D4**
Stockists of antique Delftware and royal and Makkumer pottery, plus other hand-painted objects such as traditional tiles and beautifully decorated wooden trays and boxes. Other highlights include miniature ceramic canal houses and dolls in traditional Dutch costumes. De Munt is located in the **Munttoren** (*see chapter* **Sightseeing**, *p50*).
*Disabled access.*

### Tesselschade: Arbeid Adelt
*Leidseplein 33 (623 6665). Tram 1, 2, 5, 6, 7, 10, 20.* **Open** 10am-6pm Tue-Fri; 10am-5pm Sat. **Credit** EC.
**Map 5 D5**
Toys and dolls, decorations and more utilitarian items – including tea cosies, embroidered tea towels and decorated clothes hangers – are crafted and sold on a non-profit basis by an association of Dutch women, Arbeid Adelt ('work ennobles'), founded in 1871.
*Disabled access.*

### Wooden Shoe Factory/De Klompenboer
*Nieuwezijds Voorburgwal 20 (623 0632). Tram 1, 2, 5.* **Open** *Apr-15 Sept* 10am-9pm daily; *16 Sept-Mar* 10am-6pm daily. **Credit** AmEx, DC, EC, MC, V. **Map 2 D3**
Wooden clogs (*klompen*) may not be the height of fashion, but they do make a tasteful souvenir of the Netherlands. Buy them large enough to wear over heavy socks. Brush up on your clog history at the exhibition in the back of the shop.

# Services

**Patience isn't just a virtue in Amsterdam's service sector: it's an absolute necessity.**

The variety of services in Amsterdam is great. The prices are, by and large, pretty decent. So, that'll be the good news, then. And the bad? Well, most people in the Amsterdam service industry don't seem to know the meaning of the phrase 'service with a smile', and you'll be expected to tip at least ten per cent for the privilege. Everyone's favourite shopping rule – 'the Customer is King' – is also anathema to most in the city's service sector. However, when all's said and done in this city where anything goes, a little patience goes a long way. Keep your head and you'll get what you want. Eventually.

Generally speaking, the more expensive the shop, the greater the number of services and attitude it has to offer. Every department store (*see* chapter **Shopping**, *page 142*), for example, has a customer service division (*klantenservice*) which will advise on packaging and shipping arrangements. Business-related services are listed in the **Directory** (*pages 259-62*), as are emergency services, car hire companies and bicycle hire firms. For florists and glasses and contact lenses, *see* chapter **Shopping**, *pages 150* and *144-5* respectively. And unless otherwise stated, the services listed below can not be paid for with credit cards.

## Beauty services

*See also chapter* **Shopping**, *page 159*.

### AYK Suncentre
*Rokin 58 (421 3046). Tram 4, 9, 16, 20, 24, 25.* **Open** 8am-10.30pm Mon-Sat; 10am-10.30pm Sun. **Map 2 D3**
Frazzle yourself to pieces in this clean and hygienic sun centre. There are six Power Titan beds for any interested melanomaholics, as well as regular beds for those with more patience. Prices start at ƒ15 for 15 mins.

### Beauty Planning
*Grand Hotel Krasnapolsky, Dam 9 (620 2610). Tram 4, 9, 16, 20, 24, 25.* **Open** 10am-10pm Mon-Thur; 10am-6pm Fri-Sun. **Map 2 D3**
Smack-bang in the middle of the city, this small salon, whose main product is Clarins, is here to pamper. Treatments include facials, manicures, waxings and massage, all at extremely reasonable prices. Ask for Elaine.

### Body Soul
*Runstraat 4 (623 4382). Tram 13, 14, 17, 20.* **Open** noon-9pm Tue-Sat; also by appointment. **Map 5 C4**
Body Soul has an extremely relaxed atmosphere, which makes the cleansing and rejuvenating process that much easier. A hot oil massage – lasting up to 80 mins – will set

you back a mere ƒ95, while those in a rush should try the relaxng 20-minute head and neck massage (ƒ42,50); Ayurveda is also practised here. Bliss.

## Camera, TV & radio hire

### Ruad BV
*Jan Tooropstraat 47 (669 8336). Bus 18.* **Open** 9.30am-6pm Tue-Fri; 9.30am-5pm Sat. **Credit** EC, V.
You'll need a spare ƒ500-ƒ1,000 and a passport as deposit should you wish to hire yourself a camcorder, TV or video from this bunch, and you'll also need to book in advance.

## Clothing care

### Clean Brothers
*Westerstraat 26 (627 9888). Tram 3, 10.* **Open** 8am-8pm daily. **Map 1 B2**
If your undies are turning into some cosmic life force at the bottom of your rucksack, then this launderette is the place to head. You can wash your own gear here or have it dry-cleaned, and they'll iron your stuff for a mere ƒ3 per item. **Branch**: Jacob van Lennepkade 179 (618 3637).

### Cleaning Shop Express
*Huidenstraat 24A (623 1219). Tram 1, 2, 5.* **Open** 9am-6pm Mon-Fri; 9am-5pm Sat. **Map 5 C4**
Dry-cleaning, laundering, leather and carpet cleaning, repairs, alterations and invisible mending are all on offer here. Staff can also hand-launder and press shirts and sheets.

### Het Strijkpaleis
*Molukkenstraat 200-s3 (665 6606). Tram 6, 10, 14.* **Open** 9.30am-4.30pm Mon-Fri.
Among the services on offer in this basement store are ironing, dry-cleaning (45c for a hanky; ƒ3,10 for a shirt) and shoe repair, while there's also a mobile car-wash and a shopping service. All are competitively priced, and they'll even collect and return your stuff within 24 hours from anywhere in town, so you needn't trek all the way out east. Unbeatable.

### Luk's Schoenservice
*Prinsengracht 500 (623 1937). Tram 1, 2, 5.* **Open** 8.30am-5.30pm Tue-Fri; 9am-5pm Sat. **Map 5 D5**
Luk provides a quick, professional, top-quality shoe cleaning and repair service, and he's quick to boot. You can totally trust him with your favourite ruby slippers.

## Costume hire

### Party House
*Rozengracht 93A-B (624 7851). Tram 13, 14, 17, 20.* **Open** 10am-6pm Mon-Wed, Fri; 10am-9pm Thur; 10am-5pm Sat. **Map 1 B3**
If you're not out to win any prizes, then the costumes on offer here will suffice. While you're at it, pick up a variety of bits and bobs, jokes and masks to irritate your mates, or pop into **Party Balloon**, its other shop a few doors down (Rozengracht 65; 420 1272), for a quick helium hit.

# Food delivery

## Bel Menu

*(669 3834/fax 669 3495).* **Open** 11am-8pm daily.
All you need for an evening in front of the telly. Bel Menu offer over 500 different dishes – including Indian, French, Italian and Chinese fodder – and you can order cigarettes and alcohol from them as well. Orders can take up to 45 minutes to arrive, but variety makes it worth the wait.

## Bojo Rijsttafel Express

*(694 2864).* **Open** 4-9pm daily.
Mammoth proportions of rice, crackers, satay, egg, meat, chicken and veg all come as part of the rice table. Prices start at ƒ29,50 for the works, though delivery costs ƒ2,50 if you only fancy a quick snack and the total is less than ƒ25.

## Het Internet Menu

*(488 8056/website www.eten.com).* **Open** hours vary.
Standard fare on offer – pasta, rice, noodles, etc – but the novelty value makes them worth a try.

## New York Pizza

*(445 0000).* **Open** 4-11pm daily.
Pizza, pizza and even more pizza. A huge cheese and tomato costs ƒ19 including delivery, plus ƒ3 per topping. Yummy.

# Formal dress hire

## Joh Huijer

*Weteringschans 153 (623 5439). Tram 6, 7, 10.* **Open** 9am-6pm Mon-Wed, Fri; 9am-6pm, 7-9pm Thur; 9am-4pm Sat. **Credit** AmEx, DC, MC, V. **Map 6 E5**
Men's formal dress hire, with nearly all clothing taken from the German Master Hans range, in British sizes 36 to 50. A complete outfit, including cuff-links and bow-tie, can be hired for around ƒ150.

## Maison Van Den Hoogen

*Sarphatipark 88-90 (679 8828). Tram 3, 20.* **Open** 9am-6pm Mon-Wed, Fri; 9am-8.30pm Thur; 9am-4pm Sat. **Map 6 F6**
A formal dress-hire outlet. There's a choice of shimmering frocks and smocks in sizes 8 to 16 for the chicks, and plenty of penguin suits for the blokes. Fabulous, dahlings.

# Hairdressers

*See also chapter* **Shopping**, *p143.*

## Headline

*Herengracht 148 (624 5355). Tram 13, 14, 17, 20.* **Open** 9am-6pm Tue; 9am-9pm Wed, Thur; 9am-6pm Fri; 9am-4pm Sat. **Map 2 C3**
Spacious, modern and relaxed hairdressers. Wash, cut and blow-dry begins at ƒ80, with colouring from ƒ50.

## Lemonhead

*Nieuwe Leliestraat 29 (427 1940/06 5134 5239). Tram 13, 14, 17, 20.* **Open** 11am-8pm Mon-Sat, or by appointment. **Credit** EC. **Map 1 B3**
This cool and funky hairdresser's near Anne Frankhuis is so laid back that you can even order a beer, wine or absinthe from the café across the street to sup on while you're shorn. Expect to pay around ƒ55 (excluding tip) for a wash, cut and blow-dry.

## Nederlandse Kappers Academie

*Weteringschans 167 (626 3430). Tram 6, 7, 10.* **Open** 9am-4.30pm Mon-Fri. **Map 6 E5**
If you look like something the cat dragged in but don't have the cash to splash on a trendy new cut, this training

institute, where advanced students do the cuts, will re-invent you for a mere ƒ19,95 (and send you home still looking like something the cat dragged in… maybe).

## Toni & Guy

*Magna Plaza (second floor), Nieuwezijds Voorburgwal 182 (620 0662). Tram 1, 2, 5, 13, 17, 20.* **Open** 11am-7pm Mon; 10am-6pm Tue, Wed; 10am-9pm Thur; 10am-7pm Fri, Sat; noon-7pm Sun. **Credit** AmEx, DC, EC, MC, V. **Map 2 C3**
Perenially rrendy experts in colour, cut and curl, who promise you a haircut to suit your face and personality (if you're a moody old bat, bring a paper bag, then). Prices range from ƒ65 to ƒ85 (plus tip, of course) for a wash, cut and blow-dry.

# Internet Service Provides (ISPs)/ Online Service Providers (OSPs)

## CompuServe

*(sales 0800 022 4968/free support 0900 227 3738/ e-mail 70006.101@compuserve.com).* **Open** 8am-midnight daily. **Credit** AmEx, MC, V.
The good thing about CompuServe is that there are no start-up costs, and in the first month you'll get a whopping 750 free hours, which means you can surf the net free for the entire month (assuming you have no life, that is). After this initial period you'll receive an automatic subscription at a cost of ƒ18 for the first five hours online, with each subsequent hour costing ƒ6, or opt to pay ƒ42.50 a month for 20 hours, with each hour thereafter costing ƒ4. Phone for details of other services.

## Euronet

*(reception 625 6161/help desk 535 5300).* **Open** *reception* 9am-5.30pm Mon-Fri; *help desk* 9am-9pm Mon-Fri; 10am-4pm Sat. **Credit** V.
A start-up set costs ƒ64,95, including the first month online and various other services, including e-mail and a Web browser. After that, it's ƒ45 a month for unlimited hours, or ƒ450 for 12 months.

## UUNET

*(024 365 3653/e-mail info@inter.uunet.nl).* **Open** 9am-9pm Mon-Fri; 10am-3pm Sat.
Internet access and an e-mail address costs ƒ23,50 for a start-up set, and ƒ17,50 a month (plus ƒ3,50 per online hour) thereafter: good value if you don't plan on spending hour upon hour surfing. However, there's a minimum subscription time of one month, and one month's notice is required for cancellation, so it's hardly convenient if you're just passing through.

## Xs4all

*(information 398 7654/help desk 398 7666).* **Open** noon-8pm Mon-Fri; information 10am-6pm Mon-Fri.
An Internet access company: getting connected costs ƒ30, after which it's ƒ30 a month for unlimited hours. Unfortunately, Xs4all (*see chapter* **Media**, *p199*) has become just a wee bit too popular, and getting online can be as difficult as getting a Big Mac in Moscow.

# Packing & removals

## De Gruijter

*Industrieweg 11-13, 2382 NR Zoeterwoude (071 589 9313). NS rail to Zoeterwoude.* **Open** 8am-5pm Mon-Fri.
De Gruijter will package and send your purchases or household belongings anywhere in the world by sea or air: handy to get all those rash bulk purchases home after your stay. It also offers storage facilities.

## Photocopying

### Lowie Kopie Copycentre
*Rozengracht 63 (420 0247). Tram 13, 14, 17, 20.* **Open**
9am-6pm Mon-Fri; 10am-5pm Sat; 11am-5pm Sun.
**Map 1 B3**
Full colour copies, business cards, invitations and even T-
shirts can be copied or printed here, and you can also use its
computers – equipped with DTP programs – for ƒ2,50 for
10 minutes. Regular black-and-white copies cost 6c
per sheet.

### Printerette
*Spuistraat 128 (624 8520). Tram 1, 2, 5, 13, 14, 17, 20.*
**Open** 9am-6pm Mon-Fri.
One of the cheapest copy shops in town: it's just 6c per sheet
for do-it-yourself copying.

## Photo processing

### Hema Foto Service
*Kalverstraat 208 (626 8720). Tram 1, 2, 4, 5, 9, 14, 16,
20, 24, 25.* **Open** 11am-7pm Mon; 9.30am-7pm Tue,
Wed, Fri; 9.30am-9pm Thur; 9.30am-6pm Sat; noon-6pm
Sun. **Map 2 D3**
With a one-hour service at ƒ4,75 for development and 79c
for each print – you only pay for successful shots – you'll
not find a cheaper service in town. It also sells frames,
albums and spool.

### Super Photo
*Max Euweplein 60 (420 2870). Tram 1, 2, 5, 6, 7, 10,
20.* **Open** 9am-6pm Mon-Fri; 9am-5pm Sat; 11am-5pm
Sun. **Credit** AmEx, DC, EC, MC, V. **Map 5 D5**
Open 365 days a year, these Kodak-owned shops offer top
quality dependable processing at great prices. They have 17
branches in Amsterdam; phone 0346 266044 for details of
addresses and phone numbers.

## Tattoos & body piercing

### Body Manipulations
*Oude Hoogstraat 31 (420 8085). Tram 4, 9, 14, 16, 20,
24, 25/Metro Nieuwmarkt.* **Open** noon-6pm Mon-Wed,
Fri, Sat; noon-9pm Thur; 1-5pm Sun. **Map 2 D3**
Rates begin at ƒ15 for an earlobe, ƒ20 for face piercing and
ƒ50 for any other hole, with jewellery starting at ƒ40. No
appointment necessary.

### Bodycult
*Warmoesstraat 101 (421 3939). Tram 4, 9, 16, 20, 24,
25.* **Open** noon-7pm Mon-Sat. **Map 2 D2**
Bodycult is a relatively new arrival on the tattooing/pierc-
ing scene in Amsterdam; like a lot of weird and wonderful
places, it's based on the Warmoesstraat in the Red Light
District. Bodycult will pierce and tattoo any orifice and/or
body part you desire. Tattoos cost from ƒ100, and booking
is advisable on weekends.

### Hanky Panky
*Oudezijds Voorburgwal 141 (627 4848). Tram 4, 9, 16,
20, 24, 25.* **Open** *summer* 11am-9pm daily; *winter* 11am-
6pm daily. **Map 2 D2**
If piercing, painting and puncturing your privates is your
thing, then follow in the footsteps of the Red Hot Chili
Peppers, Cypress Hill, Pearl Jam and, er, Robbie Williams,
and head to this dungeon parlour for the best prick in town.
Proprietor Henk Schiffmacher has run this shop in the Red
Light District for some 16 years, and also has a nice little
sideline with his **Tattoo Museum**, situated on the same
street (*see chapter* **Museums**, *p84*).

## Travel agents

For details of rail, coach and bike travel in Holland,
*see chapter* **Beyond Amsterdam**, *pages 224-5.*
For travel to the Netherlands from other European
countries and for airlines, *see chapter* **Directory**,
*pages 252-4.*

## General

### Budget Air
*Rokin 34 (626 5227). Tram 4, 9, 14, 16, 20, 24, 25.*
**Open** 9.30am-6pm Mon-Fri; 10am-5pm Sat. **Credit**
AmEx, MC, V. **Map 2 D3**
Low-cost fares to worldwide destinations, with discounts for
students, young people and senior citizens.

### Eurolines
*Rokin 10 (information 560 8787). Tram 4, 9, 14, 16,
20, 24, 25.* **Open** *information line* 9am-8pm Mon-Fri;
10am-4pm Sat; *offices* 8am-10pm Mon-Sat; 7.30am-
7.30pm Sun. **Credit** MC, V. **Map 2 D3**
Bus tickets for Europe and Morocco; discounts for those
under 26. Reservations are not taken over the phone.
**Branch**: Amstel station *(information 560 8787).*

### NBBS
*Dam 17 (620 5071). Tram 1, 2, 4, 5, 9, 13, 14, 16, 17,
20, 24, 25*0pen 6am-6pm Mon-Wed, Fri; 8am-9pm Thur;
9am-5pm Sat. **Map 2 D2**
Low-cost flights to worldwide destinations, with reductions
for students and young people, and a Eurotrain discount for
under-26s. The Leidsestraat branch keeps the same hours.
**Branch**: Leidsestraat 53 (638 1736).

### Travel Express
*Rokin 38 (626 2952). Tram 4, 9, 14, 16, 20, 24, 25.*
**Open** 9.30am-6.15pm Mon-Fri. **Map 2 D3**
Travel Express arrange bus travel to European destinations.
There are also 'bike' buses – buses with space allocated for
bicycles – to some locations in the summer, package trips to
London by air, city trips by train and cross-country world
travel. Travel Express has plans to move its office, though
its phone number will stay the same.

## Quick getaways

### KLM Call & Go
*(023 567 4567).* **Open** 1-11pm daily.
A last-minute phone-booking service, with information on
cheap European and international flights. The minimum
stay is two nights, the maximum four weeks.

### Last Minute
*Rokin 40 (0900 202 3008). Tram 4, 9, 14, 16, 20, 24,
25.* **Open** 9am-7pm Mon-Fri; 10am-5pm Sat; noon-6pm
Sun. **Map 2 D3**
Not only cheap flights here, but also package deals for those
who want to take off within a matter of days.
**Branch**: Schiphol Airport, Departure Lounge 3
(501 6196).

## Watch & jewellery repairs

### Elke Watch Company
*Kalverstraat 206 (624 7100/623 6386). Tram 1, 2, 4, 5,
9, 14, 16, 20, 24, 25.* **Open** 10am-5pm Mon-Fri. **Credit**
AmEx, DC, EC, MC, V. **Map 5 D4**
Besides selling portable timepieces, Elke carries out quick
repairs to watches and some jewellery.

# Arts & Entertainment

# Children & Parents

*Where to take the young and the young at heart.*

As with most other things in this most laid-back of countries, the Dutch have a relaxed approach to parenting. Naturally, then, Amsterdam kids are more spontaneous, more indulged and more boisterous than their counterparts elsewhere in Europe. And why not? The city is small and compact, making a visit with kids far easier than, say, a trip to London. This is especially true during the summer, when many free or cheap activities are organised for school-age children in the city's plethora of parks and playgrounds.

You needn't wait for summer, however: Amsterdam is bursting with cultural events for children all year round, from concerts to theatrical ents. The **AUB** ticket office on Leidseplein (621 ; *see also* **Directory**, *page 252*) is a good s e of information, as is the *Uitkrant* (look u leugd'). Its listings are mostly in Dutch, but a p call to the relevant organisation will normally r up anything you're not sure of.

For dren's bookshops, clothing and shoe stores, y shops, *see chapter* **Shopping**, *pages 141-143, 7 and 159.*

# Sch l holidays

Primary sch ildren have every Wednesday afte ree. The other main school holidays for sterdam region are listed below. For gen ools information, call the **Onderwijs foon** (School Telephone) on 0800 1608.

## 1998
17-25 Oct; 19 Dec-3 Jan.

## 1999
20-28 Feb; 30 Apr-9 May; 17 Jul-5 Sept; 23-31 Oct; 25 Dec-9 Jan.

## 2000
21 Feb-1 Mar; 29-13 Apr; 29 Apr-7 May; 15 Jul-3 Sept; 12-29 Oct; 23 Dec-7 Jan 2001.

## Transport

Amsterdam's size and layout mean that most interesting places for youngsters are reachable on foot, though manoeuvring a pushchair over the older cobbled sections can be frustrating. The other fastest and most convenient ways to get around are by tram, bus or metro, though some of the older vehicles can be difficult to board with a pushchair: remember that the bottom step on a tram must be pressed down to hold the doors open.

Children, understandably, tend to love Amsterdam's myriad waterways. Water taxis might be a little expensive, but what they lack in value for money they more than make up for in fun quotient. Not quite as pleasant but better value for money – it's free – is a trip on the River IJ ferry to Amsterdam North; boats leave from behind Centraal Station about every ten minutes. If you have older children, then you might like to rent a canal bike, but remember to navigate on the right-hand side of the waterway. For more information on public transport, water taxis and renting a boat, *see chapter* **Directory**, *pages 255-9.*

### Electrische Museum Tramlijn Amsterdam
*Haarlemmermeerstation, Amstelveenseweg 264 (673 7538). Tram 6, 16. See chapter* **Museums**, *p83, for full listings information.*
Less of a museum than a pleasure ride, particularly for the youngsters. The antique electric tram carriages here come from cities all over Europe and the 60-minute round trip in one of the colourful old trolleys along the edge of the Amsterdamse Bos (*see below, and box* **Keep on the grass**, *p59*) is particularly enjoyable.
*Café at Haarlemmermeerstation.*

## Outdoor entertainment

When winter arrives, many parents take their kids skating at the **Jaap Edenhal** rink (*see chapter* **Sport**, *page 216*), though the more daring head out on to the canals: when the weather is cold enough, many of the city's canals freeze over.

Skaters of a different kind, however, should prepare to be disappointed. The Museumplein renovations have meant that the skateboarding ramp that once stood by the Rijksmuseum is no longer.

*Kids always have a tree-mendous time in* **Vondelpark**.

However, when the developments are completed in mid-1999 – *see box* **Pleins for the future**, *page 62* – there will be new and improved facilities for inliners and skateboarders.

## Parks

One of the greenest cities in Europe, Amsterdam has 28 parks, and almost every one has a play-ground, usually with a sandpit and, sometimes, a paddling pool. Watch out, though, for unleashed pooches and their droppings.

Quite aside from boasting the best children's park in Amsterdam, **Vondelpark** (information 673 1499; *see chapter* **Sightseeing**, *pages 62-3*) is famous for its summer programme of free after-noon entertainment, which includes children's the-atre, concerts, mime artists and acrobatic displays. **Amstelpark**'s attractions include a miniature train, a maze, a small children's farm and pony rides. **Flevopark** (*see box* **Keep on the grass**, *page 59*) is the wildest and least used of the city's parks, and as such is a nice peaceful spot for a pic-nic or a kickabout. The adjacent Flevoparkbad has two fantastic outdoor swimming pools and a tod-dlers' paddling pool in a spacious grassy recre-ation area (*see chapter* **Sport**, *page 218*).

Amsterdam's largest green areas are on the edge of town. The **Amsterdamse Bos** is easily the pick of them, with boating lakes, an open-air theatre and large playgrounds. Plane spotters can watch low-flying aircraft coming in to land at near-by Schiphol, while nature lovers will be entranced by the wild deer. The Amsterdamse Bos is also where you'll find the magical **Bos Museum** (*see chapter* **Museums**, *page 77*), which has maps of the park, including walking routes, and **Geitenhouderij Ridammerhoeve** (645 5034; open 10am-5pm Mon, Wed-Sun), a goat farm with 120 milk goats and loads of cute goatlets. It sells biodynamic goat's milk, cheeses and ice-cream, and has a small recreation area and sandpit. Finally, **Gaasperpark** has some superb sport and playground facilities, including a paddling pool and lake for swimming (*see chapter* **Sport**, *page 218*). For more on Amsterdam's parks, including travel information, *see box* **Keep on the grass**, *page 59*.

## Urban farms

Smaller farms are in the *Amsterdam Yellow Pages* under 'Kinderboerderijen'; admission is often free.

### Artis Zoo Children's Farm

The Children's Farm at the Artis Zoo (*see chapter* **Museums**, *p84*) has a variety of animals, including pigs, calves, chickens, sheep and goats. The latter are small and frisky and will nibble bags and pushchairs, so it's best to park these outside the gate, removing your valuables first. Artis also has a great (dog-free) play area.

### De Dierenpijp

*Lizzy Ansinghstraat 82 (664 8303). Tram 3, 12, 24, 25.* **Open** 1-5pm Mon, Wed-Sun.
All the usual farm beasts live here in the Pijp, but it's nowhere near as busy as Artis Zoo, and is consequently

rather more pleasant. The resident sow produces regular litters of pink piglets, and you can buy fresh farm eggs. Look out for the special children's activity days, held on some Wednesdays and, occasionally, on Saturdays and Sundays.

### De Uylenburg
*Staalmeesterslaan 420 (618 5235). Tram 7, 13, 17/bus 18.* **Open** 10am-5pm daily.
A children's farm in Rembrandtpark, which has a simple play-and-do area for children, with pony rides and grooming.

## Indoor entertainment

### Children's films

There are a few special children's film shows at the **Kriterion**, **Rialto** and the **Filmmuseum** (for all, *see chapter Film, pages 183-184*), though most films for under-tens are dubbed into Dutch (indicated by the words 'Nederlands Gesproken' in the film listings). However, many other family-oriented films are in English with Dutch subtitles. In the autumn holidays, many theatres and cinemas take part in **Cinekid** (624 7110), a children's film festival with quality films from across the globe, many in English.

### Museums

Amsterdam boasts over 40 museums, many of which are practically taken over by kids, parents and teachers on Wednesday afternoons. The popularity of many of the city's museums has led to many of them organising special children's days at the weekends, with special events and activities that youngsters seem to love: check with the **AUB** (*see above*) for dates and times.

Obviously, not all of Amsterdam's museums are suitable for children. However, plenty do make for a terrific afternoon out. The best two are the **newMetropolis**, which replaces the now-closed Technologie Museum, and the **Tropenmuseum/ Kindermuseum**. At the maritime **Nederlands Scheepvaart Museum**, children can handle exhibits on the ships docked outside, including a reproduction of an eighteenth-century trading vessel, while the **Aviodome** at Schiphol Airport boasts an exciting flight simulator. The **Allard Pierson** archaeological museum has a small but worthwhile mummy collection and regular educational exhibitions, while the **Woonbootmuseum** offers a glimpse at what it's like to live on a houseboat. For details of all these museums, *see chapter* **Museums**, *pages 74-86*; for **Madame Tussauds Scenerama**, *see chapter* **Sightseeing**, *page 42*.

### newMetropolis
*Oosterdok 2 (general information 0900 919 1100 (premium rate)/e-mail info@newmet.nl). Bus 22/Apr-Oct shuttle boat from Centraal Station. See box* **The appliance of science**, *p75, for full details.* **Map 3 E2**
Kids of all ages are provided for here: older children will enjoy the museum's permanent and semi-permanent hands-on exhibits, while younger kids get their own special area where they play at being grown-up by dressing up as a geol-

*The* **Nederlands Scheepvaart Museum**.

ogist, doctor or scientist and watch themselves on TV afterwards (but hopefully they won't be glued to the box for as long as usual). There are also experiments with light and sound to keep 'em amused.

### Tropenmuseum/Kindermuseum
*Linnaeusstraat 2 (568 8215). Tram 9, 10, 14, 20/bus 22. See chapter* **Museums**, *p78, for full listings information.* **Map 7 H3**
'Step into another world' is the motto of the Tropenmuseum, and a children-friendly world it is too: exhibitions here educate youngsters and adults alike on the lifestyles and customs of different cultures, and do so in a way that tries to involve all the senses. The **Kindermuseum** (Children's Museum) here is good, but the specialised programmes that children have to follow are all in Dutch. For any visitors who want to take along their hosts' Dutch children, though, there's currently an interactive exhibition on the indigenous peoples of the Highlands of Bolivia, scheduled to run until 2000 (phone 568 8233 for information).

### Swimming pools & saunas

Good pools for kids are **De Mirandabad** (a subtropical pool with a wave machine, whirlpool, toddler pool and slide), the **Zuiderbad** and **Marnixbad** indoor pools, and the **Flevoparkbad** outdoor pool. For local pools, look in the phone directory under 'Zwembad' and check by phone for special children's hours. Most saunas tolerate quiet children, especially at off-peak hours. For saunas and pools, *see chapter* **Sport**, *pages 216 & 218*.

### Sportfondsbad Oost

*Fronemanstraat 3 (665 0811). Tram 3, 9.* **Open** *family swimming* 11.30am-12.45pm Sat; 11am-1pm Sun (11am-noon for families with children under 4); *family sauna* 9.30am-12.30pm Sun. **Admission** *sauna* ƒ15; ƒ12,50 under-12s (incl swimming in heated instruction pool).

## Restaurants

Aside from the specific kids' restaurants listed below, most cheaper restaurants and pizzerias welcome children. Youngsters are normally allowed in licensed bars and cafés, as long as they don't run amok. *See also chapters* **Restaurants** *and* **Cafés & Bars**, *pages 105-134.*

### Enfant Terrible

*De Genestetstraat 1 (612 2032). Tram 1, 3, 6, 12.* **Open** 9.30am-5.30pm Mon-Fri.
This small café attached to the Birth Centre is designed for parents and under-5s, though older kids are welcome. You can either eat here with your child, or eat in peace while a play-leader keeps your tot amused (ƒ2,50 per hour, half-price for second child). They'll even look after your kid(s) for you if you want to pop into town for a quick break (ƒ10 per hour, ƒ25 for three hours).

### KinderKookKafé (Children's café)

*Oudezijds Achterburgwal 193 (625 3257). Tram 1, 2, 4, 5, 9, 14, 17, 20, 24, 25/Metro Nieuwmarkt.* **Open** times vary; phone for details. **Map 2 D3**
This small restaurant is entirely run by children: they cook, serve, present the bill and wash up, all with a little help from the friendly grown-up staff, of course. The simple set menu includes main course and dessert: ingredients are fresh, the food is healthy, and prices are very low (ƒ5 1-4s; ƒ10 5-12s; ƒ15 over-13s, ƒ2,50 drinks). Children can even cook for their own guests: on Saturdays, kids aged between six and 12 can prepare dinner from 3.30pm onwards, and on Sundays over-5s can prepare and serve an English-style high tea. Booking is essential: phone for details.

### Pizzeria Capri

*Lindengracht 63 (624 4940). Tram 3, 10/bus 18, 22.* **Open** 5-10.30pm daily; *kitchen open* from 6pm. **Map 1 B2**
Children are welcome at this friendly pizzeria-cum-gelateria that boasts a small pavement terrace. Both staff and customers remain remarkably unfazed by kids dropping pasta on the floor, and there's plenty of real Italian ice-cream on hand for blackmail purposes. High chairs are available.

## Theatre & circus

The **Children's Theatre Phoneline** (622 2999) has recorded information in Dutch on kids' theatre, and you can also check under 'Jeugd' in the *Uitkrant*. If you're in Amsterdam for a while, you may want to get the theatre discount card: costing just ƒ12,50, it gives you a season's worth of discounts at six children's theatres. For information, call **Stichting Jeugdtheater Amsterdam** on 625 3284.

In addition to children's theatre companies, many theatres and music venues hold special children's concerts and the like throughout the year: check with the AUB (621 1211) for details.

### Circustheater Elleboog

*Passeerdersgracht 32 (626 9370). Tram 1, 2, 5, 7, 10.* **Open** *phone bookings* 10am-5pm; *activities/sessions* times

vary. **Admission** *non-members* day ƒ25; *club membership* ƒ140 for six months; ƒ45 for 3-morning pass (adult plus child; set mornings). **Shows** check *Uitkrant* for times; admission ƒ15 adults, ƒ10 under-17s. **Credit** EC. **Map 5 C4**
Kids aged from four to 17 can try out circus and clowning skills, learning tricks, make-up skills, juggling and tightrope walking. Activity days end in a performance for parents and friends. Non-member sessions are always busy, much as Dutch kids, but the staff speak English. They'll also do children's birthday parties (phone for details).
*Central hearing aid system (in Dutch) for deaf children. Disabled access & toilets.*

### De Krakeling

*Nieuwe Passeerdersstraat 1 (625 3284/reservations 624 5123). Tram 7, 10.* **Shows** 2pm Wed, Sun; 8pm Thur-Sat. **Admission** ƒ16 unaccompanied adult; ƒ11 adult with child; ƒ9 children; *some performances* ƒ3 extra. **Map 5 C5**
De Krakeling has separate productions for over-12s and under-12s: phone to check what's going on at any given time. For non-Dutch speakers, there are puppet and mime shows and sometimes musicals. Shows are listed in a programme available from the theatre and in *Uitkrant*.
*Disabled access.*

## Out of town

All the attractions below can be reached by rail with an **NS Rail Idee** ticket that includes the admission prices (*see chapter* **Beyond Amsterdam**, *page 224-5*). For details of other out-of-town attractions, *see chapter* **Trips out of town**, *pages 224-243.*

### Archeon

*Archeonlaan 1, Alphen aan den Rijn (0172 447744). 50km (31 miles) from Amsterdam; A4 to Leiden, then N11 to Alphen aan den Rijn.* **Open** *Apr-June* 10am-5pm Tue-Sun; *July, Aug* 10am-5pm daily; *Sept, Oct* 10am-5pm Wed-Sun. **Admission** ƒ20 adults; ƒ17,50 over-65s; ƒ15 4-11s; free under-4s. **Credit** EC, V.
The Archeon offers a trip through history, from when dinosaurs walked the earth – post-*Jurassic Park*, these exhibits are particularly popular – via the Bronze Age to Roman times. There are loads of interactive and hands-on displays, and an open-air plunge pool. Great fun.
*Disabled access & toilets; wheelchairs for hire. Gift shop.*

### Efteling

*Europalaan 1, Kaatsheuvel, Noord Brabant (0416 288111). 110km (68 miles) from Amsterdam; A27 to Kaatsheuvel exit, then N261.* **Open** *Apr-June, Oct* 10am-6pm daily; *July-Sept* 10am-9pm. **Admission** ƒ35; free under-4s. **Credit** AmEx, DC, EC, MC, V.
An enormous fairytale forest peopled with dwarves and witches, characters from Grimms' stories and the *Arabian Nights*, enchanted and haunted castles, and even talking rubbish bins. The massive (and massively popular) amusement park is packed with state-of-the-art thrills, as well as more traditional fairground rides for tinies. Busy in summer.
*Café/restaurant. Disabled access & toilets. Guidebook & map in English. Pram hire. Shops.*

### Linnaeushof

*Rijksstraatweg 4, Bennebroek (023 584 7624). 20km (13 miles) from Amsterdam; A5 to Haarlem, then south on N208.* **Open** *Apr-Sept* 10am-6pm daily. **Admission** ƒ11; free under-1s.
A huge leisure park near Haarlem, host to an astonishing 300 attractions: there's a Wild West train, cable cars,

mini-golf, trampolines, a water play area and go-karts. Children under five are happy in the new play area, and the price is most certainly right.
*Café/restaurant. Disabled access & toilets. Shops.*

### Madurodam
*George Maduroplein 1, The Hague (Den Haag); 070 355 3900). 57km (35 miles) from Amsterdam; take A4 to The Hague.* **Open** *Apr-June* 9am-8pm daily; *July, Aug* 9am-10pm daily; *Sept-Mar* 9am-5pm daily. **Admission** *f*19,50 adult; *f*14 4-11s; free under-3s. **Credit** AmEx, DC, EC, MC, V.
Madurodam claims to be the 'largest miniature village in the world', and who are we to argue? Kids adore the scale models of some of Holland's most famous sights – anything from Rotterdam's Erasmus Bridge to Schiphol Airport – all of which are built to scale on a 1:25 ratio. The best time to go is on a summer's evening, when the models are lit from inside by over 50,000 tiny lamps.
*Café/restaurant. Disabled access & toilets; wheelchairs for hire. Shop.*

### Museum van Speelklok tot Pierement
*Buurkerkhof 10, Utrecht (030 231 2789). 38km (24 miles) from Amsterdam; take A2 to Utrecht.* **Open** 10am-5pm Tue-Sat; noon-5pm Sun. **Admission** *f*9 adult; *f*5 4-12s; under-4s free.
A 20-minute walk from the Railway Museum, this has a unique antique collection of mechanical music boxes, circus, fairground and street organs and wondrous tin toys. A great double day out for junior machine freaks.
*Café. Disabled access & toilets; wheelchairs for use. Shop.*

### Nederlands Spoorwegmuseum
*Maliebaanstation 16, Utrecht (030 230 6206). 38km (24 miles) from Amsterdam; take A2 to Utrecht.* **Open** 10am-5pm Tue-Sat; 1-5pm Sun. **Admission** *f*13,50 adult; *f*11 over-65s; *f*9 4-12s; free under-4s.
The National Railway Museum is housed in an historic station, where over 60 old and new locomotives can be admired from inside and outside. There are also rides on a miniature Intercity and TGV line for under-12s.

## Parenting

## Babyminders
For babysitting services in the suburbs, look in the *Amsterdam Yellow Pages* under 'Oppascentrales'.

### Oppascentrale Kriterion
*(624 5848).* **Bookings** 5-7pm daily. **Rates** *7pm-midnight* *f*7/hour; *midnight-3am* *f*8/hour; *3am-7pm* *f*10/hour; *administration charge* *f*5; *f*5 supplement for Fri & Sat evenings; *minimum charge* *f*20.
This reliable babysitting service has been running for 45 years and uses male and female students over 18 years of age, all of whom are individually vetted. It's best to book in advance.

## Childbirth
Amsterdam is arguably the best place in the world to have a baby: over 40 per cent of births still take place at home, and the city's midwife and health visitor system is second to none. Options include an active birth, water birth and Leboyer, as well as 'domino' system hospital deliveries. Prenatal services, delivery and aftercare are all covered by *ziekenfonds* (national health) or private health insurance policies.

### Astrid Limburg Midwife Practice
*Sarphatipark 97 (671 0650). Tram 6, 7, 10.* **Map 6 E6**
A radical and friendly midwife practice, centrally situated. The midwives will also do water births at home.

### The Birth Centre
*De Genetetstraat 3 (685 3898). Tram 3, 7, 10, 12.* **Map 5 C5**
A midwife practice, a baby clinic, an information centre and a shop. It also runs courses.

## Children's rights

### Kinderrechtswinkel
*Staalstraat 19 (626 0067). Tram 4, 9, 14, 16, 20, 24, 25.* **Open** *walk-in consultations* 3-6 pm Mon; 2-5pm Wed, Sat. **Map 3 E3**
This children's rights office supplies under-18s with information about legal matters and the responsibilities of teachers, parents and employers. Kids may phone or visit, and while staff will answer questions from adults, they prefer dealing directly with the children involved.

### Kindertelefoon (Childline)
*(06 0432/0900 0432).* **Open** 2-8pm daily.
Young people from eight to 18 are welcome to phone this free line to get information on bullying, sexual abuse, running away from home and so on. Staff do not give information on children's entertainment.

## Crèches & playgroups
Crèches take children aged from three months to four years. There are long waiting lists for both council crèches (*kinderdagverblijven*) and playgroups (*speelzalen*), and though private crèches have shorter waiting lists, they're more expensive. For a list of childcare facilities in your area and a registration form (register early in pregnancy), contact your local Welfare Department office.

### Kinderbijslag (Family Allowance)
Parents from EC countries who live and/or work in the Netherlands are entitled to claim family allowance from the Dutch state for their children. For information and an application form call the **SVB** on 560 0911.

## Schools
Primary schooling is optional for children from four years, and compulsory from five years. Most schools are open from 8.45am to 3.15pm, and primary schools have Wednesday afternoons free. For more information about schools in your area, contact your local council office (*stadsdeelkantoor*). For information on English-speaking or international schools, contact the **British Council** on 676 4343.

## Toy libraries
There are several toy libraries in Amsterdam, where you can borrow toys large and small for your children. There is a registration fee, and a small borrowing charge. For details of your nearest toy library, in the *Amsterdam Yellow Pages* under 'Speel-o-theek'.

# Clubs

**Aided and abetted by late licences and a liberal drugs policy, Amsterdam's clubs will get you in the mood for dancing.**

While other European cities pride themselves on their constantly changing dance music scene, Amsterdam's clubs are still dominated by house, house, and, er, house. Other stuff is played in clubs here and there – drum'n'bass, hip hop, funk, soul and acid jazz all make appearances, while speed garage is slowly starting to catch on – but it'll often be at a night that also features house music. Even gabber (ludicrously fast hardcore house, pronounced with a throaty 'h') has at long last reached a cul-de-sac: only a few gabber parties are held in the city these days, and hardcore fans will have to venture to out-of-town places, like **De Hemkade** in Zaandam.

Although Amsterdam has a laid-back attitude to most things, the clubbing scene is the exception to the rule. Since Mayor Schelto Patijn came into office, all clubs have to close bang on 5am, otherwise they're liable for a penalty. And hard drugs are not tolerated: a while back, **Mazzo** was closed down for six months following a raid. (Soft drugs, naturally, are okay.) On top of this, the number of licences granted for major events at special venues

seems to be dwindling: **Westergasfabriek**, a huge hall which used to be a gasworks, is currently restricted to only one licence every two months. As a result, Amsterdam's nightlife tends to be concentrated on its clubs. Some of them, such as **RoXY**, **iT** and Mazzo, organise all their own nights, while others rent their club to party organisations (like the **Melkweg** and **Escape**), who have weekly or monthly club nights with their own door policies and membership systems.

Amsterdam's nightlife doesn't really get going until Thursday which, along with Saturday, is the most popular night; people looking for a decent night out on, say, Monday or Tuesday should not get their hopes up. And a night in Amsterdam doesn't come cheap: on top of the admission price, you have to pay to use the toilets (*f*1) in most clubs and parties, and you're also expected to tip the doorman (about *f*2,50). The latter isn't compulsory, mind, but doormen have long memories, and if you don't flash the cash, then don't expect to get in next time you turn up. Fortunately, drinks aren't usually overpriced (about *f*4), and even if the beers

*Get in with the in-crowd in Amsterdam and check out some* **RoXY** *music. See page 176.*

# Chemistry @ Escape

every saturday: world's #1 uplifting club event

Escape Rembrandtplein 11 Amsterdam |  |

are small, they're stronger than in most countries, so you need fewer to get you going.

Generally speaking, clubs are open from 10pm until 4am, or 5am on Fridays and Saturdays; *see below* **After hours** for ideas on what to do if you're still up for some dancefloor action after then. Dressing up is a good idea if you're going to **RoXY, Sinners in Heaven**, Chemistry (at **Escape**) or **iT**, but for most other clubs there is no strict dress code, though trainers are often frowned upon.

## Club venues

### Club Arena
*'s Gravesandestraat 51 (694 7444). Tram 3, 6, 7, 10.* **Open** 11pm-4am Thur; 11pm-5am Fri, Sat. **Admission** *f10-f15.* **Map 7 G3**
Regular parties and bands provide the entertainment at the club attached to the **Arena** hostel. All kinds of music is played: on Saturdays, for example, it's stuff from the '60s to the '80s. The venue is also used by private party organisers: look out for the flyers in all the usual places. The building used to be a convent and the parties are in what used to be the chapel, but that doesn't mean you have to feel guilty. *See chapters* **Accommodation,** *p96,* and **Music: Rock, Roots & Jazz,** *p207.*

### Dansen bij Jansen
*Handboogstraat 11 (620 1779). Tram 1, 2, 5.* **Open** 11pm-4am Mon-Thur, Sun; 11pm-5am Fri, Sat. **Admission** *f2,50-f5.* **Map 5 D4**
The music selection here is very safe, so why is the dancefloor always packed? There's only one possible explanation, and it's got nothing to do with free drink or drugs (dream on…). The reason it's so busy is because Dansen bij Jansen is a student club; you'll probably need a student card to get in. The good thing, of couse, is that admission is cheap and you can wear what you want.

### Escape
*Rembrandtplein 11 (622 1111). Tram 4, 9, 14, 20.* **Open** 8pm-1am Tue; 10pm-4am Wed, Thur, Sun; 11pm-5am Fri, Sat. **Admission** *f15-f35.* **Map 6 E4**
With a capacity of 2,000, Escape is the biggest venue in town. It is rented to different party organisers for their weekly club nights, resulting in a good mix of stuff. Though the club is big, the queues can be long and the door policy selective. Most popular is the trendy **Chemistry** on Saturdays where techno and its assorted offshoots are played by resident DJs Dimitri & Marcello and frequent international guests (recent visitors have included Kenny Larkin, Green Velvet, Basement Jaxx). **Hour Power**, held every Sunday (except for the last Sunday of the month) is also worth a look. On a more kitsch note, there's a roller disco on Tuesdays.

### Exit
*Reguliersdwarsstraat 42 (625 8788). Tram 1, 2, 4, 5, 9, 14, 16, 20, 24, 25.* **Open** 11pm-4am Mon-Thur, Sun; 11pm-5am Fri, Sat. **Admission** free-*f10.* **Map 6 E4**
This gay club – which admits men and women – attracts a trendy crowd. Spectacular lighting and a good mix of current and upbeat dance music make this small club well worth checking out. Very cruisey at weekends. *See chapter* **Gay & Lesbian,** *p188.*

### Havana
*Reguliersdwarsstraat 17/19 (620 6788). Tram 1, 2, 5, 16, 20, 24, 25.* **Open** 4pm-1am Mon-Thur; 4pm-2am Fri,

2pm-2.30am Sat; 2pm-1am Sun. **Admission** free, *upstairs f5.* **Map 5 D4**
An early-closing gay/mixed bar, with a small dancefloor upstairs. It's right on the main drag of the trendy gay area and tends to get completely packed at the weekend before the other clubs open. Once a year, the venue holds a Hollywood party: gays and drag queens gather here before being whisked off in limos to iT *(see below). See also chapter* **Gay & Lesbian,** *p185 & p188.*

### Industry
*Paardenstraat 17 (no phone). Tram 9, 14, 20.* **Open** 11pm-4am Thur, Sun; 11pm-5am Fri, Sat. **Admission** *f10-f17,50.* **Map 3 E3**
This club with a capacity of about 800 lies just around the corner from the Rembrandtplein. The music policy currently centres around R&B, but there are often live acts and theme parties, such as Turkish nights. Upstairs there's a bar area; the dancefloor is downstairs. Baseball caps are not allowed, but there are no further dress restrictions and staff are friendly to foreigners.

### iT
*Amstelstraat 24 (625 0111). Tram 4, 9, 14.* **Open** 11pm-4am Thur, Sun; 11pm-5am Fri, Sat. **Admission** *f12,50-f17,50.* **Map 3 E3**
Originally a gay club and one of the most extravagant nightclubs in Holland, iT now has a much more open door policy since the death of Manfred Langer, its flamboyant owner. It has also managed to hold onto some of its glamourous, exhibitionist atmosphere: there are loads of drag queens inside, and every hour, iT's own dancers give a show on stage. Saturday is for gay men only, though the other nights are mixed. And while the names of the club nights alter from time to time, the music is always the same: happy Ibiza house, played mainly by DJ Jean. *See also chapter* **Gay & Lesbian,** *p188.*

### Korsakoff
*Lijnbaansgracht 161 (625 7854). Tram 10, 13, 14, 17.* **Open** 10pm-3am Mon-Thur, Sun; 10pm-4am Fri, Sat. **Admission** usually free. **Map 5 C4**
An alternative grunge club where most of the audience is dressed in black. Sounds include hip hop, metal and heavy alternative rock. The venue is small but friendly, and is ideal for an all-night drinking session. Live bands are featured on Wednesday nights.

### Mazzo
*Rozengracht 114 (626 7500). Tram 13, 14, 17, 20.* **Open** 10pm-4am Wed, 11pm-4am Thur, Sun; 11pm-5am Fri, Sat. **Admission** *f10-f20.* **Map 4 B4**
Founded by the Rietveld Academy, Mazzo has always been a very relaxed club and is very friendly to foreigners. The music is trance and techno, played by resident DJs and international guests (along the lines of Laurent Garnier and Keith Fielder) and there is also a drum'n'bass night on Fridays. The club is quite small – the capacity is a mere 600 – so it sometimes fills up quickly, meaning you have to wait outside until other revellers leave. The good news, though, is that there are no dress restrictions.

### Melkweg
*Lijnbaansgracht 234A (624 8492). Tram 1, 2, 5, 6, 7, 10.* **Open** varies. **Admission** *HQ & Timemachine f27,50* in advance; *f32,50* on the door; *Concept f30; Sabotage Jungle Soldiers f15.* **Membership** (compulsory) *f4,40/month.* **Map 5 C5**
A big multi-media venue (capacity 2,000) near Leidseplein, which also stages more than its fair share of gigs: the bands are always followed by DJs. The 'Milky Way' also hosts several theme parties and monthly club nights. The four most popular gigs are **HQ** (last Friday of the month), featuring techno and hard house; **Timemachine** (once every

two months on a Saturday), hosted by happy-trance DJ Per; **Concept** (Fridays, monthly), playing drum'n'bass in one room and techno in another; and **Sabotage Jungle Soldiers** (monthly on Fridays), where you can jam to, um, jungle. The audience is very mixed, the atmosphere is good, and there are no dress restrictions at this staple of Amsterdam's cultural scene. *See chapters* **Art Galleries**, *p72*, **Film**, *p175*, **Music: Rock, Roots & Jazz**, *p207*, and **Theatre**, *p222*.

### Ministry
*Regulierdwarsstraat 12 (623 3981). Tram 16, 24, 25.* **Open** 4am-4am Wed, Thur, Sun; 11pm-5am Fri, Sat. **Admission** free-*f*15. **Map 5 D4**
A small club in a classy environment serving up different types of music every night. As with many clubs, Saturdays is the most popular night of the week: it's usually a speed garage gig, often featuring guest DJs from the UK. Sunday is mixed gay night.

### Odeon
*Singel 460 (624 9711). Tram 1, 2, 5.* **Open** 10pm-4am Mon-Thur, Sun; 10pm-5am Fri, Sat. **Admission** *f*2,50-*f*10; *students* *f*2,50-*f*5. **Map 5 D4**
Open seven nights a week, this large, down-to-earth club attracts a friendly mix of students, shop assistants and office clerks. There are three floors, each playing different music: jazz dance in the basement (when it's open), commercial house on the ground floor and classic stuff on the large first floor.

### Paradiso
*Weteringschans 6-8 (623 7348). Tram 1, 2, 5, 6, 7, 10, 20.* **Open** varies. **Admission** varies. **Membership** (compulsory) *f*4,50/month. **Map 5 D5**
In the '60s, hippies gathered at this old church venue, and in doing so cemented Amsterdam's reputation as the home of alternative culture. Nowadays, the hippies are few and far between, and the Paradiso is instead normally filled with sweaty clubbers. **VIP Club** on Fridays, which has a definite techno edge, is especially popular, and there are also some drum'n'bass nights. *See chapter* **Music: Rock, Roots & Jazz**, *p208*.

### RoXY
*Singel 465 (620 0354). Tram 1, 2, 4, 5, 9, 14, 16, 20, 24, 25.* **Open** 11pm-4am Wed, Thur, Sun; 11pm-5am Fri, Sat. **Admission** *f*12,50-*f*20. **Map 5 D4**
Situated in an old cinema, RoXY began its house-only nights ten years ago. Today, the house gigs are still going strong, but other musics – including drum'n'bass and speed garage – now get a look in with their own evenings. Wednesday is **Hard**, a long-running gay night, while Thursday sees the extremely popular **HTSM**, hosted by DJ Dimitri. RoXY is definitely the home of the in-crowd, and it's like Mission Impossible to get in if you haven't got a membership card: don't even think about coming unless you're absolutely determined to get in. If you *do* manage to get inside, however – preferably without scaling the walls – you'll have a great time. *See also chapter* **Gay & Lesbian**, *p190*.

SOUL OF ALL PEOPLE

### Sinners in Heaven

*Wagenstraat 3-7 (620 1375). Tram 4, 9, 14, 20.* **Open**
11pm-4am Thur, Sun; 11pm-5am Fri, Sat. **Admission**
*f*10-*f*20. **Map 3 E3**
Sinners is a trendy new club across from iT (*see above*),
attracting a chic and wealthy audience. It's great if you're
into (Dutch) celeb-spotting, especially as Martijn Krabbé, a
Dutch TV star, is a resident DJ here. The club isn't very
big, but the beautiful interior – all mirrors and designer
benches – and the three floors of different music more than
compensate. On Thursday night they play hip hop, quite a
rarity in Amsterdam. On other nights, the music leans more
towards commercial house and disco classics.

### Soul Kitchen

*Amstelstraat 32 (620 2333). Tram 4, 9, 14, 20.* **Open**
11pm-4am Thur; 11pm-5am Fri, Sat. **Admission** *f*10-
*f*12,50. **Map 3 E3**
This spacious club for lovers of soul music plays a truly varied selection of funky music, including '60s soul and
'70s disco.

### Trance Buddha

*Oudezijds Voorburgwal 216 (422 8233). Tram 4, 9, 14,
16, 20, 24, 25/Metro Nieuwmarkt.* **Open** 11pm-4am
Mon-Thur, Sun; 11pm-5am Fri, Sat. **Admission** free-*f*20.
**Map 2 D3**
This Goa trance club is one of the few in Amsterdam that
opens seven days a week. The dancefloor on the first floor
is surrounded by images of Buddha, while downstairs there

are more decks for visiting and regular DJs. The music
attracts a chilled-out bunch of spiritual types – you can spill
their pint without being killed – and, in keeping with the
image, there is a very relaxed door policy. Maaan.

## Out of town

Many hardcore clubbers regularly make the trip
out of Amsterdam. Though they're not too far out
of town, the best way to get there is by car, so try
and blag a lift. Flyers and word of mouth are the
best sources of up-to-date information.

### De Waakzaamheid

*Hoogstraat 4, Koog aan de Zaan (075 628 5829). NS
rail to Koogzanddijk.* **Open** 11pm-8am Sat.
**Admission** *f*25.
De Waakzaamheid is a cosy and always packed club right
in the middle of a housing estate in Koog aan de Zaan.
Pulling power comes in the form of great DJ line-ups, with
top international ones (such as Mike Dunn and Tony
Humphries) often putting in an appearance. The club is generally only open on Saturdays, but there are also monthly
club nights. The **11 till 11** parties (held on the third
Saturday of the month) are a particular fave, especially as
the door fee includes admission to an after-hours party.
There's also a separate bar area with different music, and in
summer you can sit outside on the terrace.

### De Hemkade

*Hemkade 48, Zaandam (no phone). NS rail to Zaandam.*
**Open** varies. **Admission** varies.
Formerly the Fun Factory, this place just north of
Amsterdam is basically a huge hall with different rooms for
different musics. Although there's no regular club night here,
expect at least one gig a week here: check the flyers to see
what's happening on any particular week.

## After hours

Although the clubs in town have to close by 5am
at the latest, there are plenty of late night/early
morning events to keep insomniacs busy. Most
clubs have permission to hold a few after-hours
parties every year, and there's normally at least
one late, late party going on. Look out for flyers
that are handed out in clubs, or keep your ears to
the proverbial grapevine. **Delta/Dino's**
(Coenhaveweg 26; no phone) and **After Hour
Power Surpreme** (Overtoom 65, Westzaan; 400
3391) – every first Sunday of the month – are two
of the best regular gigs: kicking off around 5am,
the final stragglers are booted out during the
afternoon. Expect to pay at least ƒ25 to get in.

## Club night organisers

Look out for events organised by the following
companies. Tickets can be bought in the stores listed below under **Tickets & information**.

### Club Risk

As well as Club Risk's monthly parties on the fourth
Saturday of the month at **De Waakzaamheid** (*see above*),
this bunch also host other big events from time to time.
Resident DJs are Eric de Man and the seemingly ubiquitous
Dimitri, and loads of international guests complete the bill.

### Dance Valley

*Spaarnwoude Recreation Area (tickets 0900 300
1250/travel information 038 423 5222). NS rail to
Sloterdijk, then free pendle buses to Spaarnewoude.*
**Tickets** ƒ80 in advance; ƒ100 on the door.
Started in 1995, Dance Valley has expanded to become the
biggest dance festival in Holland. Once a year, on a Saturday
in August, up to 30,000 people gather at Spaarnwoude
Recreation Area outside Amsterdam to chill out and listen
to everything from techno and hard house to speed and
garage. During the day, over 100 DJs and bands perform on
one main stage and in eight huge tents. Dance Valley also
holds monthly club nights – such as the aforementioned
**HQ** – at the **Melkweg** (*see above*), including **HQ**. Check out
its excellent website at *www.dancevalley.nl*, which has information on travel, camping and booking tickets.

### Healers

Three times a year, Healers' two **Love Boats** board near
Centraal Station for a unique clubbing experience off
Amsterdam's waterways. On certain holidays, such as
Queen's Day, Christmas and New Year, the boats are joined
together, with DJs on the decks spinning all sorts of
stuff for an enthusiastic crowd.

### MTC

The most hyped and extravagant parties in the Netherlands.
Most take place in Rotterdam, but are well worth the hour's
drive. The only drawback is that the events sell out about a

month in advance, and even if you can get hold of a ticket,
there's no guarantee you'll be let in due to MTC's erratic
door policy. Still, if you manage to get in, you'll have a
blinding night.

### Monumental

Monumental host the hugely popular Awakenings parties
at the **Westergasfabriek** (*see chapter* **Theatre**, *p222*) five
times a year. Gabbers and clubbers come together, while a
line-up of international DJs play techno until the early hours.

### No-One

No-One organise around four big techno and trance parties
every year, which are normally held at the **Meervaart**
(Osdorpplein 9, 610 7393). Not as hip as MTC or Silly
Symphonies, but pretty decent fun nonetheless.

### Silly Symphonies

Very hip parties, held all over Holland. Look out for the beach
partiesheld annually at Scheveningen, near The Hague (for
details on how to get to the town, *see chapter* **The
Randstad**, *pp234-5*). The music is techno and trance, spun
by DJ Remy and guests.

## Tickets & information

Listed below are the best places to pick up flyers
and tickets for clubs and parties in Amsterdam.
**Conscious Dreams** (*see chapter* **Coffeeshops**,
*page 138*) also has flyers for some events.

### Clubwear-House

*Herengracht 265 (622 8766). Tram 1, 2, 5, 13, 17, 20.*
**Open** 11.30am-6.30pm Mon-Wed, Fri; 11.30am-8.30pm
Thur; 11.30am-6pm Sat. **Map 2 C3**
A large clubwear shop with flyers and tickets for almost all
mellow and underground events. Check out its website at
*www.xs4all.nl/~cwh*. *See also chapter* **Shopping**, *page 143*.

### Dance Tracks

*Nieuwe Nieuwstraat 69 (639 0853). Tram 1, 2, 5.* **Open**
1-7pm Mon; 11am-7pm Tue, Wed, Fri; 11am-9pm Thur;
10am-6pm Sat; 1-6pm Sun. **Map 2 D2**
A record shop, with flyers and some tickets for events on the
more hardcore house scene.

### Groove Connection

*Sint Nicolaasstraat 41 (624 7234). Tram 1, 2, 5.* **Open**
2-6pm Mon, Sun; 11am-6pm Tue, Wed, Fri, Sat; 11am-
9pm Thur. **Map 2 C2**
A record shop which holds some tickets and flyers for underground events.

### Midtown Records

*Nieuwendijk 104 (638 4252). Tram 1, 2, 5, 13, 17, 20,
24, 25.* **Open** 10am-6pm Mon-Wed, Fri, Sat; 10am-9pm
Thur. **Map 2 D2**
This record shop has tickets and flyers for the hardcore and
gabber scenes. *See chapter* **Shopping**, *p162.*

### Outland Records

*Zeedijk 22 (638 7576). Tram 1, 2, 5, 13, 17, 20, 24, 25.*
**Open** 10.15am-6pm Mon-Wed, Fri, Sat; 10.15am-9pm
Thur. **Credit** AmEx, DC, EC, MC, V. **Map 2 D2**
A very popular record shop, with tickets for mellow house
events. Flyers are available only with record purchases.

### ZX Fashion

*Kerkstraat 113 (620 8567). Tram 1, 2, 5.* **Open** noon-
6pm Mon-Wed, Fri, Sat; noon-9pm (winter until 7.30pm)
Thur. **Credit** AmEx, DC, JCB, MC, V. **Map 5 D4**
Some flyers and occasional tickets at this clubwear store. *See
also chapter* **Shopping**, *page 143*.

# Dance

*Amsterdam's dance scene is one of the most adventurous in Europe.*

The Netherlands' traditional role as a link between countries across the ocean and those at its European back door is clearly reflected in the country's dance scene. In Amsterdam, Dutch choreographers and dancers are the minority. Foreign work regularly seen in Amsterdam includes that of William Forsythe, Anne Teresa de Keersmaeker, Pina Bausch, Lloyd Newson, Saburo Teshigawara and Trisha Brown. The dominant forces in Dutch dance are, strikingly, not Dutch: many touring companies pass through town, and guest choreographers or lead dancers are frequently invited to join forces with other companies for a limited engagement. Similarly, choreographies are often imported from repertoires abroad, and the core of the larger companies and schools are made up of foreign dancers.

A contributing factor is the state of flux in the financial structure upon which local dancers and choreographers depend. From top to bottom – government subsidy and policy organs to individual practitioners – a new form is being furiously sought with which to greet the millennium. The tendency seems to be towards bundling resources: space, administrations, pools of dancers and so on. The question remains as to whether this will serve the majority of those involved. Who will be left by the wayside? Young, inexperienced dancers just finishing their studies, most probably.

Having said that, even the established generation has not fared too well since the implementation of the new Art Plan at the start of the 1990s. As with other arts – and other countries – subsidies have been hard to come by, and many small companies and dancers struggle to survive in an increasingly competitive field. However, it's not all bad news, and there's plenty worth checking out here. Established dancers and companies worth catching – apart from the top two companies, **Nederlands Dans Theater** and **Het Nationale Ballet** – include Beppie Blankert, Shusaku Takeuchi, Jacqueline Knoops, Bianca van Dillen, Lisa Marcus and **Truus Bronkhorst**. Emerging names to watch are Suzy Blok and Chris Steel, Maria Voortman, Paul Selwyn Norton, Marcello Evelin, **Harijono Roebana and Andrea Leine**, Feri de Geus, and Anouk van Dijk.

Tickets for performances can be reserved and purchased at the specific venues, or from the **AUB Uitburo** or the **VVV** offices (*see chapter* **Directory**, *page 252*), both of which will charge

a booking fee. *Uitkrant* has information on dance events in the city.

## FESTIVALS AND EVENTS

In July each year, the **Stadsschouwburg** (*see chapter* **Theatre**, *page 222*) hosts **Julidans**, a month-long showcase of international dance. The **International Concours for Choreographers** in Groningen, meanwhile, is a competition, where prizes are awarded for ensemble choreographies. Details about festivals, competitions, performances, courses and workshops are available from the **Theater Instituut Nederland** (Herengracht 168; 623 5104; open 11am-5pm Mon-Sat).

## Venues

Dance is performed at a variety of venues in Amsterdam, many of which are listed below. For details of other venues – such as the **Bellevue**, the **Stadsschouwburg** and the **Melkweg** – *see chapter* **Theatre**, *pages 221-3*. Unless stated, credit cards are not accepted.

### Danswerkplaats Amsterdam

*Arie Biemondstraat 107B (689 1789). Tram 1, 17.* **Box office** 10am-5pm Mon-Fri. **Tickets** prices vary.
The dance studio at Danswerkplaats stages performances once a month, either here or at venues elsewhere in the city or country.

### Muziektheater

*Amstel 3 (625 5455). Tram 4, 9, 14, 16, 20, 24, 25/Metro Waterlooplein.* **Box office** 10am-6pm or until start of performance daily. **Tickets** *f*35-*f*120; concessions with CJP card. **Credit** AmEx, DC, MC, V. **Backstage tours** 3pm Wed, Sat; *f*8,50. **Map 3 E3**
The Muziektheater is Amsterdam at its most ambitious: the plush crescent-shaped building opened in 1986, holds 1,596 people and is home to both the Nationale Ballet (*see below* **Companies**) and the Nederlands Opera. The big stage is also used by visiting companies such as the Royal Ballet and the Martha Graham Company. The panoramic glass walls of the lobbies give an impressive view of the Amstel. *See chapter* **Music: Classical & Opera**, *p203*. *Disabled access & toilets.*

### Nes Theatres

**De Brakke Grond** *Nes 45;* **Frascati** *Nes 63 (both theatres 626 6866). Tram 4, 9, 14, 16, 20, 24, 25.* **Box office** 1pm until start of performance Mon-Sat. **Tickets** *f*15-*f*21; *f*12-*f*18 students; *f*9 children. **Map 2 D3**
Two theatres on Nes that stage a variety of dance pieces. The emphasis is on modern dance and improvisation: the Frascati holds the Night of Improvisation each year at the end of March, while the third Monday of every month sees an open improv session. *See chapter* **Theatre**, *pp221-2*. *Disabled access.*

The spectacular **Muziektheater**, home of the Nationale Ballet. See page 179.

### Tropeninstituut
*Linnaeusstraat 2 (568 8500). Tram 9, 10, 14, 20.* **Box office** *phone information & reservations* 10am-4pm Mon-Fri; *in person* noon-4pm Mon-Fri; also from one hour before performance. **Tickets** *ƒ*15-*ƒ*20; concessions with CJP card. **Map 7 H3**
The Tropeninstituut is home to two theatres – the Kleine Zaal and the Grote Zaal – that host a variety of performances: there are regular non-western dance events, as well as musical, theatrical and children's events. *See chapters* **Children & Parents**, *p170*, and **Music: Rock, Roots & Jazz**, *p208*. *Disabled access.*

### Het Veemtheater
*Van Diemenstraat 410 (626 0112). Tram 3/Bus 35.* **Box office** 10am-4pm Mon-Fri. **Tickets** *ƒ*15; *ƒ*12,50 with CJP card, over-65s.
A former warehouse next to the port, specialising in mime and movement theatre.
*Café.*

## Out of Town

### AT&T Danstheater
*Schedeldoekshaven 60, 2511 EN Den Haag (070 360 4930). NS rail to Den Haag Centraal Station.* **Box office** 10am-6pm or until start of performance Mon-Sat. **Tickets** *ƒ*30-*ƒ*45; concessions with CJP card. **Credit** AmEx, DC, EC, MC, V.
The home of the Nederlands Dans Theater (*see below* **Companies**) since 1987. It's considered a better venue than Amsterdam's Muziektheater, as it was designed exclusively for dance.
*Disabled access.*

### Rotterdamse Schouwburg
*Schouwburgplein 25, 3012 CL Rotterdam (010 411 8110). NS rail to Rotterdam Centraal Station.* **Box office** 11am until start of performance Mon-Sat; noon-

5pm Sun; *telephone bookings* 11am-7pm Mon-Sat; noon-5pm Sun. **Tickets** *ƒ*18-*ƒ*90; concessions with CJP card, over-65s. **Credit** AmEx, DC, EC, MC, V.
This large theatre opened in 1988, and due to its square shape, it has been nicknamed the 'Kist van Quist' ('Quist's box') after its architect. It plays host to the bigger national companies as well as dance troupes from abroad.
*Bar. Café. Disabled access & toilets. Shop.*

### Toneelschuur
*Smedestraat 23, 2011 RE Haarlem (023 531 2439). NS rail to Haarlem.* **Open** box office 3-9.30pm Mon-Sat; 2-3pm Sun. **Tickets** *ƒ*18; concessions with CJP card.
Many dance and theatre lovers from Amsterdam head to Haarlem for performances at the Toneelschuur. There are two halls here, and the venue is nationally renowned for its programmes of theatre and modern dance.
*Bar. Café. Disabled access.*

## Companies

### Nationale Ballet
*Information from Muziektheater (see above* **Venues**).
The largest company in the Netherlands, with over 20 Balanchine ballets in its repertoire (the largest collection outside New York). Since moving to the Muziektheater in 1986, its repertoire has included more classical ballet in a bid to fill the venue on a regular basis. Toer van Schayk and Rudi van Dantzig have been instrumental in developing this company's distinctive style within contemporary ballet.

### Nederlands Dans Theater
*Information from AT&T Danstheater (see above* **Venues: Out of Town**).
The design of the Nederlands Dans Theater's base suits the repertoire of the company, with the black stage walls directing all the attention towards the quality of the movement. The work of Hans van Manen and Jiri Kylin forms the core of the programming, with live music incorporated into every

performance. Apart from the main company, look out for NDT2, made up of novices and up-and-coming dancers, and NDT3, made up of veterans.

## Dance Company Leine & Roebana
*Theaterbureau, Korte Leidsedwarsstraat 12, 1017 RC Amsterdam (627 7555).*
Harijono Roebana and Andrea Leine's company perform their exciting, inventive modern dance works at various venues across Amsterdam. Worth investigating.

## Dansgroep Krisztina de Châtel
An outstanding modern dance company, created in 1976 by Hungarian-born Krisztina de Châtel. Her choreographies are an impressive example of minimalist modern dance. Amsterdam performances are usually held in the **Bellevue**.

## Het Internationaal Dansheater
*Kloveniersburgwal 87-89 (623 5359/623 9112). Tram 9, 14, 20/Metro Nieuwmarkt.* **Open** box office from one hour before performance. **Tickets** ƒ12,50-ƒ15; concessions with CJP card, over-65s. **Map 3 E3**
This Amsterdam-based company performs original dance from all over the world. The corps of 24 dancers works with guest choreographers from assorted countries.

## Stichting Dansers Studio
## Beppie Blankert
*Entrepotdok 4 (638 9398).*
Unique in the world of modern dance, Beppie Blankert offers a platform for a shifting group of freelance dancers and choreographers.

## Truus Bronkhorst
*Postbus 93044, 1090 BA Amsterdam (625 5572).*
A former solo dancer, whose group now explores a variety of themes and ideas. Bronkhorst's work is modern, adventuruous and well worth investigating. Her company has recently performed at **De Brakke Grond**, though they do tour the country regularly.

# Out of Town

The Amsterdam performances of the following companies are usually in the **Stadsschouwburg**.

## Raz
This new, large modern dance company, based in the southern city of Tilburg, has been making waves under the artistic leadership of Hans Tuerlings.

## Rotterdamse Dansgroep
*Information from Rotterdamse Schouwburg (see above* **Venues: Out of Town**).
The Rotterdamse Dansgroep is one of the most vigorous exponents of New York modern dance in the Netherlands. Imported dance routines are mixed with work by young Dutch choreographers.

## Scapino Ballet
*Information from Rotterdamse Schouwburg (see above* **Venues: Out of Town**).
The oldest dance company in the country. Until recently, the company's work was more oriented towards youth dance and 'family' programmes,but the company's image is now more in line with current, modern trends.

# Movement Theatre

## Griftheater
Griftheater is a giant on the international mime scene. The company produces both location movement theatre and

productions for existing theatre spaces. The work is an excellent combination of plastic arts and modern mime.

## Lisa Marcus
In recent years, the work of this transplanted New Yorker has become increasingly controversial due to the extreme images and eroticism found in her works.

## Shusaku and Dormu Dance Theatre
A veteran choreographer in Holland, Japanese Shusaku Takeuchi has been producing fascinating work for over 20 years. Specialising in huge location spectacles, often on or near bodies of water, Shusaku's work usually incorporates live music. Huge constructions, fire and impressive lighting typify his outdoor work. On a less grandiose scale, Shusaku's indoor work is highly influenced by his background in plastic arts.

# Events

*See chapter* **Amsterdam by Season**, *page 10-11*, for details of the **Holland Festival** and **Uitmarkt**, two multicultural festivals that both include a number of noteworthy dance performances each year.

## Spring Dance
*Information and bookings Keistraat 2, HV 3512 Utrecht (030 332 0332).*
Spring Dance – held annually in Utrecht in late April and early May – attempts to give an overview of recent developments in modern dance, film and music from around the world.

## Holland Dance Festival
*(information & reservations 070 361 6142/fax 070 365 0509).*
Held every two years in October and November – the next is to be held in 1999 – this festival takes place in one of three different venues, including The Hague's Dansheater. Many of the world's larger companies are attracted to the event and the quality of work is consistently high. Nederlands Dans Theater usually represents Holland.

## Cadans
*(information 070 363 7540).*
The Hague's exciting international festival of contemporary dance takes place in November on even-numbered years. Each piece is made specifically for the occasion.

# Courses & Workshops

## Trainingsfonds Moderne Theaterdans
*Danswerkplaats Amsterdam, Arie Biemondstraat 107B (689 1789). Tram 1, 6, 7, 17.* **Classes** 10.30am-noon Mon-Fri. **Cost** ƒ8,50-ƒ12,50/class.
Daily modern dance classes offered include barre lessons, advanced and intermediate technique.

## Singel Dans en Theater
*1e Nassaustraat 7 (681 0067). Tram 10.* **Classes** 10am-noon, 6pm-11pm, Mon-Sat. **Cost** ƒ5-ƒ12/class. **Map 1 A2**
Classes in both the morning and evening offered by a collective of eight members.

## Dansstudio Cascade
*Koestraat 5 (623 0597/689 0565). Tram 4, 9, 14, 16, 20, 24, 25/Metro Nieuwmarkt.* **Classes** 6-10pm Mon-Fri. **Cost** ƒ11-ƒ20/class. **Map 2 D3**
Modern dance technique, capoeira, stretching and contact improvisation is taught here. Most teachers here work within the 'new dance' technique.

# Film

**Dutch movies are becoming more popular in Amsterdam, but it's still 'Hooray for Hollywood' in many of the city's cinemas.**

Amsterdam is, as has hopefully been made clear over the previous 181 pages, different to most other cities in a number of important ways. However, when it comes to the cinema, one global truth remains unassaulted: the natives prefer to watch standard Hollywood fodder than flicks created by their fellow countrymen. But the recent international success enjoyed by films like *Antonia* and *Karakter* – both winners of the Best Foreign Language Film prize at the Oscars, in 1996 and 1998 respectively – have managed to fuel interest in national cinematic products, and what's on offer is often worth the effort. Just for starters, look out for anything that bears the name of Jos Stelling (*The Flying Dutchman*), George Sluizer (*The Vanishing*), Alex van Warmerdam (*Abel, The Dress*), Dick Maas (*Flodder, Amsterdamned*), Marleen Gorris (*Antonia*) or Mike van Diem (*Karakter*), all notable Dutch directors.

Still, some Dutch film folk have found a wider public – and a larger bank account – over in the US. Paul Verhoeven, director of *Robocop* and *Basic Instinct*, is probably the most famous, but don't forget Robby Muller (Wim Wenders' preferred cameraman), screenwriter Menno Meyes, and, of course, Jan de Bont, a former cameraman on films like *The Jewel Of The Nile*, and *Ruthless People* who's recently seen his flashy directorial efforts – *Speed* and *Twister* in particular – clean up all over the globe.

## THE CINEMAS

Although few in number, Amsterdam's cinemas offer as balanced and substantial a cinematic diet as any other European city, from Hollywood blockbuster junk food to the indigenous flavours of home-grown produce. As in many major cities, the cinemas can be divided into two main categories: First run cinemas, which show exactly what you'd imagine, and Revival and art houses (or 'filmhuizen'). Amsterdammers have a healthy appetite for foreign and art-house fare, and not only do the venues offer a cosmopolitan mix of art films, documentaries and retrospectives (as well as an informed selection of the more intelligent Hollywood flicks), but each also has a unique personality and charm. With the exception of the Uitkijk, all have marvellous cafés, while **The Movies**, especially notable for its lavish art deco interior, also has an enchanting restaurant. Of the

mainstream cinemas, the **Tuschinski**, with its sumptuous original deco architecture and fittings, is a marvel in itself.

## TICKETS & INFORMATION

Cinema programmes in the multiplexes change every Thursday. Weekly listings of the main venues are prominently displayed in virtually every café, bar and cinema, while other reliable sources of information include *Uitkrant*, the Wednesday edition of *Het Parool* and the *Amsterdams Stadsblad*. Look out for excellent monthly Dutch film mag *De Filmkrant*, which also has comprehensive movie information. Although these listings are in Dutch, they're easily understood by the non-native. Commercial-haters should be warned: the publicised starting time in multiplexes allows 15 minutes' grace while pre-film commercials are shown. Art houses, though, go straight into the movie without the often unwelcome appetiser of half-a-dozen soft drinks ads. It's advisable to reserve your tickets in advance if you think the movie of your choice is likely to be popular – on opening weekends, for example – cinemas usually charge a nominal fee of 50c; credit cards are not accepted.

As John Travolta pointed out in *Pulp Fiction*, you can drink a beer (from a glass, no less) in many of Amsterdam's cinemas, though this is where the decadence ends: smoking is invariably forbidden. All films are shown in the original language (normally English) with Dutch subtitles; films in Dutch are indicated by the words 'Nederlands Gesproken' after the title. Some movie houses offer student discounts with the appropriate ID. Purists should also note that for some inexplicable reason, many Dutch cinemas stick an interval in the middle of every film; call ahead if you really can't face it.

## First run & mainstream

### Bellevue Cinerama/Calypso
*Marnixstraat 400-402 (623 4876). Tram 1, 2, 5, 6, 7, 10, 20.* **Tickets** *day screenings* ƒ12,50 Mon-Fri; ƒ15 Sat, Sun; *evening screenings* ƒ15 daily. **Screens** 2 each. **Map 5 C5**
Two separate and glitzy complexes next door to each other, with a shared box office.

### City
*Kleine Gartmanplantsoen 15-19 (623 4579). Tram 1, 2, 5, 6, 7, 10, 20.* **Tickets** *day screenings* ƒ12,50 Mon-Fri;

*If the movie's bad, you can always check out the wall displays at the **Cinecenter**.*

ƒ15 Sat, Sun; *evening screenings* ƒ15 daily. **Late shows** around midnight Fri, Sat. **Screens** 7. **Map 5 D5**
The large frontage and huge electronic advertisement hoarding of the City dominate the Kleine Gartmanplantsoen, a small road off the Leidseplein. Inside, a bank of TV sets in the foyer runs a constant diet of trailers. Because of its central location, City is hugely popular with wandering tourists and loud youngsters.

### Tuschinski
*Reguliersbreestraat 26-28 (626 2633). Tram 4, 9, 14, 16, 20, 24, 25.* **Tickets** *day screenings* ƒ10-ƒ12,50 Mon-Fri; ƒ12,50-ƒ15 Sat, Sun; *evening screenings* ƒ12,50-ƒ15 daily; prices depend on screen. **Guided tours** Mon, Sun mornings by appointment; ƒ10. **Screens** 6. **Map 6 E4**
This cinema was built in 1921 by Polish tailor-turned-architect Abraham Tuschinski, originally as a variety theatre. It's now Amsterdam's most prestigious movie house, which inevitably means box-office queues spilling out into the street at evenings and weekends. Home to regular premières and occasional royal screenings, it offers a lively and occasionally inspired choice of films. The building's stunning art deco design (*see chapter* **Architecture**, *p36*) attracts many visitors, which explains the need for guided tours. If you've come with a group, splash out on the eight-person box, complete with glasses of champagne all round. There are plans to expand the Tuschinski to 13 screens by 1999.

## Revival & art houses

### Cinecenter
*Lijnbaansgracht 236 (623 6615). Tram 1, 2, 5, 6, 7, 10, 20.* **Tickets** ƒ13,50-ƒ16. **Screens** 4. **Map 5 C4**
The Cinecenter is a novel and welcoming venue, with beautiful *commedia dell'arte* prints adorning the walls and stairways. Each screen has its own name and décor – check out the tiny 52-seater Jean Vigo room – and the programme is pleasingly international.
*Café. Disabled access with assistance.*

### Desmet
*Plantage Middenlaan 4A (627 3434). Tram 7, 9, 14, 20/Metro Waterlooplein.* **Tickets** ƒ12,50; ƒ5 evenings Mon; ƒ7 3.30pm screenings Fri. **Screens** 2. **Map 3 F3**
Recently bought up by mainstream distributor Hungry Eye, this is another lovely art deco house, and another fine cinema: the selections are intriguing, the monthly mini-festivals ('Desmet Favourites') smart, and the café terrific. There are various events – lectures and interviews, for example – on the first Sunday of the month, while the monthly gay previews are well attended (*see chapter* **Gay & Lesbian**, *p186*).
*Café/bar. Disabled access with assistance.*

### Kriterion
*Roetersstraat 170 (623 1708). Tram 6, 7, 10/Metro Weesperplein.* **Tickets** ƒ12,50 Mon-Thur, Sun; ƒ13,50 Fri, Sat; *previews* ƒ8,50; *children's matinées* ƒ9. **Late shows** 12.15am Fri, Sat. **Screens** 2. **Map 7 G3**
Run by volunteer students, this local knows how to pick 'em: the ever-intriguing programme includes children's matinées (Wednesdays, Saturdays and Sundays) and preview screenings (Thursdays). Student flicks are shown here, while late shows cover cult US or erotic French films. The International Short Film Festival is held here every December.
*Café/bar. Disabled access (Screen 1 only).*

### The Movies
*Haarlemmerdijk 161 (624 5790). Tram 3.* **Tickets** ƒ13,50-ƒ15. **Late shows** 12.15am Fri, Sat. **Credit** EC, MC, V. **Screens** 4. **Map 1 B1**
Don't be fooled by the insipid name: The Movies is a great place to visit if you like, um, the movies. Built in 1928, it's a fine building: the 1930s-style café is worth a visit even if you're not catching a flick. If you do see a film, it will probably be international in origin and interesting in content. The seats aren't the most comfortable in town, but cinephile Brits won't mind: The Movies has been showing Stanley Kubrick's banned-in-the-UK *A Clockwork Orange* for over five years (every Friday and Saturday night at 12.15am).
*Café & restaurant. Disabled access with assistance.*

## Rialto

*Ceintuurbaan 338 (662 3488). Tram 3, 12, 24, 25.*
**Tickets** *f7,50-f15; five-visit card f50; ten-visit card f90.*
**Screens** 2. **Map 6 F6**
A stylish alternative cinema out in the Pijp, offering a mixed
diet of new and old international flicks and the occasional
European première. Thematic blocks change monthly and
there is always at least one classic oldie on show. The Rialto's
membership packages include ticket discounts and perma-
nent seat reservations.
*Café/bar. Disabled access (Screen 2).*

## De Uitkijk

*Prinsengracht 452 (623 7460). Tram 1, 2, 5, 6, 7, 10,
20.* **Tickets** *f12,50 Mon-Thur; f13,50 Fri-Sun.* **Screens**
1. **Map 5 D5**
Amsterdam's oldest cinema – the set-up dates from 1913 –
the staunchly independent De Uitkijk is an utterly charming
158-seat converted canal house; films that prove popular tend
to stay put for quite some time. Movie snobs, pay attention:
De Uitkijk doesn't serve food, so you're unlikely to be disturbed by annoying gits in the back row flicking popcorn at
your head.
*Disabled access with assistance.*

## Multi-media centres

### Melkweg

*Lijnbaansgracht 234A (624 1777). Tram 1, 2, 5, 6, 7,
10, 20.* **Tickets** *f7,50-f10; membership f4,50.* **Screens**
1. **Late shows** midnight Fri, Sat. **Map 5 C5**
The multi-purpose, multi-function Melkweg (*see also chapters* **Art Galleries**, *p72*, **Music: Rock, Roots & Jazz**,
*p207, and* **Theatre**, *p222*) runs a consistently imaginative
film programme in its cosy first-floor cinema, taking in anything from mainstream trash to cult and art-house movies.
*Café/bar.*

### Tropeninstituut Kleine Zaal/
### Grote Zaal

*Linnaeusstraat 2/Mauritskade 63 (both 568 8500).
Tram 9, 10, 14, 20.* **Tickets** *f10.* **Shows** 8.30pm Mon
(reservations 10am-4pm). **Screens** 2. **Map 7 H3**
Right next to the Tropenmuseum (*see chapter* **Museums**,
*p78, and* **Children & Parents**, *p170*), this venue stages
regular ethnic music and theatre performances, and, occasionally, interesting documentaries and feature films from
developing countries.
*Disabled access (Screen 2).*

## Film museum

### Nederlands Filmmuseum (NFM)

*Vondelpark 3 (589 1400/library 589 1435). Tram 1, 2,
3, 5, 6, 12, 20.* **Open** *library* 10am-5pm Tue-Fri; 11am-
5pm Sat; *screenings* 7pm, 7.30pm, 9.30pm, 10pm, daily;
*children's matinées* 3pm Sun. **Tickets** *f11; f9 students,
groups (min 10 persons); f6 members f6.* **Membership**
*f30* per year. **Screens** 2. **Map 5 C6**
This government-subsidised movie museum was established in the 1940s and has over 35,000 films in its vaults,
culled from every period cinematic style and corner of the
world. Dutch films and children's matinées take care of the
Sunday programme, while the occasional screenings of
silent movies are accompanied by live piano music. On
balmy Saturday evenings during the summer, there are outdoor screenings on the first-floor terrace. Students of cinema
can often be found poring over the Filmmuseum's unique
archives, parts of which have been transferred onto video.
**Café Vertigo**, in the basement, has one of Amsterdam's
most charming terraces. *See chapter* **Museums**, *p78*.

## Film festivals

### Exploding Cinema

*(information answerphone 419 6273).*
Exploding Cinema occasionally organises alternative events
around town where self-produced VHS, 8mm and 16mm
films are screened. The evenings often include live performances, installations, exhibitions, VJs and DJs, and a forum
where the directors field questions from the viewers. Keep
an eye out for flyers about the events.

### International Documentary
### Filmfestival Amsterdam

*(information 626 1939).* **Dates** 25 Nov-3 Dec 1998.
**Tickets** *one film f12,50; week f180.* **Credit** EC.
As the name suggests, documentaries are the staple of this
fascinating annual festival. A *f25,000* prize in the name of
the late Dutch documentary maker Joris Ivens is awarded to
the best film. Each afternoon, the public gets the opportunity to put questions to a few of the directors in the central festival location at **De Balie** (*see chapter* **Theatre**, *p221*).
Phone for the 1999 dates.

### International Film Festival Rotterdam

*PO Box 21696, 3001 AR Rotterdam (010 411 8080/
information 010 233 1401/reservations 010 233 1400).
NS rail to Rotterdam Centraal Station.* **Dates** 27 Jan-7
Feb 1999; 26 Jan-6 Feb 2000. **Tickets** phone for prices.
**Credit** EC.
The Rotterdam Film Festival is easily the biggest film festival in the Netherlands. It is international in scope, boasting
around 90 films in the main programme and up to 100 others thoughtfully compiled in retrospectives. The series of lectures and seminars by guest directors, actors, producers and
other industry figures is normally a highlight, while aspir-
ing movie-makers should check out the afternoon workshops
on film technique. The festival is non-competitive with an
emphasis on what can loosely be termed 'art' movies, and is
held in a number of different locations, all within walking
distance of each other (for more details on the city of
Rotterdam, *see chapter* **The Randstad**, *p236-7*). Enjoy this
festival, as it exposes Cannes as the mere schmoozefest that
it undoubtedly is.

### Nederlandse Film Festival

*Festival office: Oudegracht 158, Utrecht (030 2322 684).
NS rail to Utrecht.* **Dates** 23 Sept-2 Oct 1998. **Open**
office 10am-6pm Mon-Fri. **Tickets** *one film f10; three
films f25; f22,50 students; day card f40; f35 students;
entire festival f125; f95 students.*
An all-Dutch affair, aimed at the Dutch public and film industry and held in late September (phone for the 1999 dates).
The festival spotlights around 100 features in a variety of
venues, and there are also selections of shorts, documentaries
and TV programmes. Each new Dutch production is shown
here, along with a selection of flicks by students from Dutch
Film and Art Academies. The festival presents its own
awards to the year's best films and holds an annual retro-
spective of a Dutch film personality. Lectures and seminars
are also given.

### Weekend of Terror

*(information 623 1510).* **Dates** early Apr. **Tickets** *f45*
per night. **Map 6 E4**
For the last 14 years, the Tuschinski cinema (*see above*) has
held The Weekend of Terror, which, in a nutshell, is two
marathon nights of horror, suspense and sci-fi flicks. The
atmosphere is traditionally friendly and relaxed, and there
seems to be some sort of dark bonding between viewers:
every time a seriously bloody scene is displayed on the
screen, the crowd applauds. It's all quite, quite bizarre; don't
say you weren't warned. Tickets can be bought from the
AUB or the Tuschinski.

# Gay & Lesbian

**You too can have pride in the name of love in Europe's gay capital.**

Greased-up, black-capped leather boys clink down the Warmoesstraat (dubbed 'La Rue de Vaseline'); trendy boys pose down the Reguliersdwarsstraat; queens camp it up around the Amstel; and lesbians wander around searching for sapphic nightlife, invariably ending up at the only women-only bar in Amsterdam, the **Saarein**. Yup: for gay men, the opportunities are endless in this gay mecca, where just about anything is tolerated and, indeed, legal. For lesbians, though, the scene is limited: there's barely a handful of lesbian-owned but mixed bars, and no lesbian-only clubs, just one-nighters at various venues in town. Even so, Amsterdam's legendary tolerance makes it one of the most popular cities in Europe for the lesbian or gay traveller.

*Pay your respects at the* **Homomonument**.

## Landmarks

### Homomonument
*Westermarkt. Tram 13, 14, 17.* **Map 2 C3**
The Homomonument is the world's first memorial to persecuted gays and lesbians. Designed by Karin Daan, its three triangles of pink granite together form one large triangle that juts out into the Keizersgracht. Those victimised in World War II are commemorated here every year on 4 May, but flowers are laid daily in memory of more private grief, and also on World AIDS Day (1 December). During early 1998, the surrounding area was cleaned up for the summer's Gay Games.

### Pink Point
*Westermarkt. Tram 13, 14, 17.* **Map 2 C3**
At the start of 1998, plans were drawn up to place a 'gay booth' by the Homomonument for the duration of the Gay Games. The idea was to provide an information point for gay visitors to the city. Depending on its initial success – and funding – it hopes to have a permanent location at the site. If so, the booth should be open five days a week, noon-6pm.

## The queer year

For more information on gay events, phone the **Gay & Lesbian Switchboard** (*see below* **Help & information**).

### Spring
Gay celebrations on Queen's Day, held annually on 30 April (*see chapter* **Amsterdam by Season**, *page 7*), are based around the Homomonument: there are drag acts, bands and stalls, and the day closes with a huge open-air disco. Most gay and lesbian bars and clubs also organise their own celebrations, so head for your favourite bar or gay area.
**Remembrance Day** takes place on 4 May. Though gay and lesbian victims from World War II are remembered at this important event on Dam, the **NVIH/COC** have their own quiet tribute (with the laying of flowers) at the Homomonument. The next day, there is a more celebratory open-air party for **Liberation Day**.

**AIDS Memorial Day** takes place at the Beurs van Berlage on the last Saturday of May. Names of deceased loved ones are read out and candles lit. Everyone then walks to Dam, where symbolic white balloons are released.

### Summer
**Roze Zaterdag** (Pink Saturday; the Dutch equivalent of 'Gay Pride') is held on the last Saturday in June, but takes place in a different town in the Netherlands each year. Utrecht's **Midsummer Canal Party**, meanwhile, is held on or around 21 June. This three-day extravaganza includes performances on the canals with stages set up on them.
**Amsterdam Diners** is a two-day HIV/AIDS fund-raising event that takes place at the beginning of June and is held in a tent on the **Westergasfabriek** near Centraal Station. It includes the AmsterdaDiner, a huge charity evening with 1,600 guests.
**Walk for Life** takes place every year, usually on the first Sunday of July. This fund-raising walk includes a free open-air performance by Dutch stars that takes place in the Oosterpark. More details on Walk for Life and Amsterdam Diners can be found on the Net at *www.aidsfonds.nl.*
The **Hollywood Party** – held in August at iT – usually brings traffic on Reguliersdwarsstraat to a complete standstill: glitzy transvestite 'stars' leave their cocktails behind at the Havana and make their way to the iT in limousines.
**Amsterdam Pride** – held on the first weekend in August – is probably the most fun event of the year. This three-day extravaganza includes street parties, performances, and a gay parade on boats around the canals.

### Autumn
**Amsterdam Leather Pride** takes place annually at the end of October and usually encompasses ten days worth of parties and events, with activites organised by a huge variety of gay businesses in the city. **Wild Side** (*see below* **Help & information**) organises a range of events for women at this time. For more information, contact Amsterdam Leather Pride, Postbus 2782, 1000 CT Amsterdam.

### Winter
Various activities are organised by the Nationale Commissie AIDS-Bestrijding on and around **World AIDS Day** on 1 December. Events to look out for include Theater Action, a series of fund-raising performances by stars of the stage.

Get to **Getto** if you like good food, strong cocktails and bingo. See page 189.

## Cinema & media

For a real insider's view into gay life here, *Amsterdam Scene* (Gay Men's Press, London) is highly recommended. This handy pocket-sized book also includes an informative lesbian section.

### Broadcast media

The radio and TV stations below – mostly broadcast on Amsterdam cable – are mainly run by volunteers, which means quality can be a little dodgy at times. However, they can be a good source of information and entertainment. Try to check out the Urania's nationwide gay and lesbian Teletext page, on page 447 of NOS Teletext (on Nederland 1, 2 and 3 channels), or *De Gay Krant*'s Teletext service: it has pages 137, 138 and 139 on SBS6.

#### MVS Radio
*Cable 103.8 or 106.8 FM ether (620 0247).*
The major local gay and lesbian radio station, with news, events, interviews, and a gay chart on Saturdays. There are English-language programmes every Sunday evening.

#### MVS TV
*Cable 62.25 (620 0247).* **Times** 8-9pm Mon.
This mainly Dutch station offers coverage of the latest developments on the scene, plus *Mizz Mopsie's Talkshow*, gay/lesbian game show *Gay voor Twaalf*, and a monthly special on HIV/AIDS called *HIV Plus Puntjes*.

#### Pink TV
*Cable 62.25 (tel/fax 421 2152).* **Times** 9-10pm Mon.
Art films, interviews, lifestyle documentaries, gender studies and performances. At least half the content is in English.

### Cinema

Independent cinemas **Desmet**, **Rialto** and **Cavia** regularly screen gay and lesbian movies, as does the highbrow cultural centre **De Balie** (for all, *see chapter* **Film**, *pages 182-4*). Smaller gay porn

cinemas can be found in the centre of Amsterdam: for more information, check the ads in local gay publications. In addition, the **Gay & Lesbian Switchboard** (*see below* **Help & information**) has a list of cinemas and theatres with special gay and lesbian programmes.

### Publications

*Gay News Amsterdam*, in both Dutch and English, comes out monthly, and can be picked up for free in many gay establishments (it costs *f* 3,95 in some newsagents); you can also find it on the web at *www.gayamsterdam.com*. Catering for both tourists and locals, it's almost always an interesting read. Its main rival is *Gay & Night*, which hit the shelves during 1997. Published by a splinter group from *Gay News Amsterdam*, both look remarkably similar, though the latter makes for a more colourful read: it's published monthly, is free in bars, and is on the Net at *www.gay-night.nl*.

In addition, bi-weekly English-language *Queer Fish* – distributed free throughout Amsterdam, with a website at *www.xs4all.nl/~pipf* – has regularly updated listings of bars and clubs, as well as short articles and a good section on all the latest scene events. The **SAD-Schorerstichting** (*see below* **HIV/AIDS**) also produces a free gay tourist map and a safer-sex booklet (with a gay male bias) in English every year. Good Dutch-language publications include *De Gay Krant*, *sQueeze* and *Culture & Camp*.

## Clubs & bars

The gay scene in Amsterdam is mainly concentrated around four areas in the city, each with their own unique identity. Clubs and bars are listed here by area, with specialist establishments –

# Some things to bear in mind...

Amsterdam's reputation as an exceedingly liberal city didn't come about by accident: the town's tolerant policies on drugs and prostitution are well documented. Just as importantly, though, Amsterdam is also more tolerant of gays and lesbians than most major world cities. The good news: the Netherlands originally decriminalised homosexuality in 1811, with the age of consent for gay men lowered to 16 in 1971.

### Cruising

Cruising is generally tolerated in Amsterdam: public expressions of affection and even discreet sex in open spaces are all allowed, within reasonable limits and in places where offence is unlikely to be taken. Particularly popular are **Vondelpark** (by the rose garden: watch out for them thorns!) and the wooded **Nieuwe Meer**, in the south-west of the city. However, the last few years has seen the emergence of an increasingly less tolerant attitude towards cruising areas: the Nieuwe Meer area has just been redesigned to make it more open, largely due to public concern about the possibility of stumbling across amorous couples and used condoms.

### Darkrooms

Darkrooms, found in assorted bars and clubs in the city, must comply with strict regulations which force proprietors to make both safer sex information and condoms readily available.

### Marriage

Gay and lesbian marriage was introduced from 1 January 1998. However, it's little more than a legal contract in the form of a registered partnership dealing with practical

matters such as finance and property rights. Custody rights of same-sex couples and their children differ greatly from heterosexuals, and adoption, too, is still not possible for married gay or lesbian couples, though it is possible for unmarried heterosexual couples, and – since April 1998 – for individuals. If you are unable to get married officially but would like some sort of ceremony, the **Remonstrantse Broederschap** (Nieuwegracht 27A, 3512 LC Utrecht; 030 231 6970) is allowed to bless gay relationships even if you're not Dutch or don't belong to its church, provided you contact it six to 12 months in advance.

### Prostitution

The well-advertised, super-liberal prostitution laws in Amsterdam also apply to gays: there are several male brothels scattered throughout the city, and 'rent boy bars', mainly to be found on Paardenstraat, are legal. However, Paardenstraat is full of exploited, mainly Eastern European boys and can be rather dangerous, in terms of both personal safety and unsafe sex. Caution is strongly advised.

### Safer sex

Since the advent of HIV and AIDS, the Dutch have developed a highly responsible attitude towards the practice and promotion of safer sex, and condoms are available from most gay bars. *See below* **HIV/AIDS** for details of HIV- and AIDS-related organisations.

### SM

The practice of SM is legal here. Men should head for the Warmoesstraat area, where there are many leather bars with darkrooms and cellars, while women interested in SM should contact **Wild Side**, based at the **COC** (*see below* **Help & information**).

---

Bar-restaurants, **Cafés** and **Lesbian bars** – and the pick of the city's **One-off club nights** and **Sex parties** listed below that. For details on **Exit**, **iT** and **Havana**, *see chapter* **Clubs**, *pages 175.*

## Leidseplein: Kerkstraat

This quiet, innocuous street that crosses the Leidsestraat near the busy Leidseplein has no specific identity, unlike the other gay areas across town: it's home to a wide variety of gay establishments, and frequented by more locals than other areas tend to be. As well as the bars listed below, 'Church Street' is also where you can find the Greenwich Village Hotel (Kerkstraat 25; 626 9746), **The Bronx** (*see below* **Leather-rubber/sex shops**), **Thermos Night** (*see below* **Saunas**) and Sarah's Grannies (*see below* **Cafés**). In addition, a couple of mixed, low-key bars, open during the day and frequented mainly by more mature, gay men, are **Camp Café** at Kerkstraat 45 (622 1506), and **Meia Meia** at Kerkstraat 63 (623 4129).

### Cosmo Bar

*Kerkstraat 42 (624 8074). Tram 1, 2, 5.* **Open** midnight-3am Mon-Thur; midnight-4am Fri, Sat. **Map 5 D4**
A tarty, late-night bar for those who don't want to go on to a club but don't want to go home, either.

### De Spijker

*Kerkstraat 4 (620 5919). Tram 1, 2, 5.* **Open** 1pm-1am Mon-Thur, Sun; 1pm-3am Fri, Sat. **Map 5 C4**
A friendly, American-style bar where, though there is no dress code, you won't look out of place in your jeans, leathers or army outfit. Delightfully seedy and dimly lit, it can be cruisey. Porn videos and cartoons are shown side-by-side, and there is an upstairs darkroom; more balls are knocked around on the pool table. The daily happy hour (5-7pm daily) is popular. Incidentally, this is one predominantly male place that is welcoming to women.

## Around Rembrandtplein

This area, centred around the ghastly, neon-lit, touristy Rembrandtplein, has traditionally long been associated with the camp scene, and, as a result, most of the gay bars – all within earshot of each other – belt out either Dutch oom-pah music or Dutch pop songs and feature occasional drag acts. Paardenstraat is around here, as are women's bar Vive Le Vie (see below **Lesbian bars**), popular café Le Monde (see below **Cafés**) and the infamous iT club (see chapter **Clubs**, page 175).

Aside from the bars listed below, there are other bars located along the Amstel that provide a breather from the frenetic square behind. **Gaiety** (Amstel 14; 624 4271) was originally an underground gay bar in the '50s; **Mix** (Amstel 50; 420 3388) is a fairly nondescript place; **Café Milord** (Amstel 102; 622 8355) hosts female impersonator Sally Bowles every Friday from 10pm; and men-only hotel bar **Monopole** (Amstel 60; 624 6451), is the only place in town where gays still sport their '70s 'accessory of accessories', the clone moustache.

On the other side of Rembrandtplein is **Reguliersdwarsstraat**, a quite tremendously gay street: there are more pansies here than in the flower market just behind on Singel. A posey, young crowd of gays hang out here, and the bars and clubs reflect the trend: Café April, Exit, Downtown and Havana are owned by the same guy. It's also where the town's only gay coffeeshop, **The Otherside** (see below **Coffeeshop**), and **Reality** (Reguliersdwarsstraat 129; 624 7532), a tropical, multiracial gay bar, can be found.

### Amstel Taveerne

*Amstel 54 (623 4254). Tram 4, 9, 14, 16, 20, 24, 25.* **Open** 4pm-1am Mon-Thur, Sun; 4pm-2.45am Fri, Sat. **Map 3 E3**
If you want the real Dutch experience, this spacious brown café on the corner of Halvemaansteeg and Amstel is heavily traditional, from the ceiling full of beer tankards right down to the small copy of Rembrandt's *The Night Watch* and, of course, the music. A TV monitor proudly displays which song is currently being played: a mixture of both old and new Dutch sing-along songs get heavy rotation, with the odd Eurovision tune thrown in for bad measure.

### Café April

*Reguliersdwarsstraat 37 (625 9572). Tram 1, 2, 4, 5, 9, 14, 16, 20, 24, 25.* **Open** 2pm-1am Mon-Thur, Sun; 2pm-2am Fri; 2pm-3am Sat. **Map 4 D4**
A relaxed bar, with the added bonuses of friendly staff, and cakes made at the Downtown coffeeshop along the street. Relatively quiet by day, things liven up during happy hour (6-7pm Mon-Sat, 6-8pm Sun). One quirky feature of the café is its back bar, which revolves when the premises gets busy.

### Exit

*Reguliersdwarsstraat 42 (625 8788). Tram 1, 2, 4, 5, 9, 14, 16, 20, 24, 25.* **Open** *bar* 11pm-4am Mon-Thur, Sun; 11pm-5am Fri, Sat; *club* 11pm-4am Thur, Sun; 11pm-5am Fri, Sat. **Admission** free Mon-Wed; ƒ5 Thur, Sun; ƒ10 Fri, Sat. **Map 6 E4**
A smart disco for trendy, young gays (women are allowed in, but only in small doses). Reached via a comfortable bar area, the disco room was once a hayloft; plenty of hay-making activity still goes on. State-of-the-art equipment pumps out music for the benefit of an enthusiastic crowd.

### iT

*Amstelstraat 24 (625 0111). Tram 4, 9, 14, 20.* **Open** 11pm-4am Thur, Sun; 11pm-5am Fri, Sat. **Admission** ƒ12,50 (free for gays) Thur; ƒ17,50 (members ƒ12,50) Fri, Sun; ƒ12,50 (gay men only) Sat. **Map 3 E3**
Once one of Europe's most famous gay clubs, this convert-

ed cinema has definitely lost some of the glamorous, international appeal that helped make its name in the early '90s. Even so, old visitors to the club won't find much changed, except the inflated prices at weekends. On Saturdays, it's gay men only, though the odd fag hag may slip in.

### Havana

*Reguliersdwarsstraat 17/19 (620 6788). Tram 1, 2, 5, 16, 20, 24, 25.* **Open** *bar* 4pm-1am Mon-Thur; 4pm-2am Fri; 2pm-2am Sat; 3pm-1am Sun; *disco* 10pm-2am Fri; 10pm-2.30am Sat. **Map 5 D4**
One of the most popular gay bars along this stretch, Havana is a people-watcher's paradise where Gaultier clashes with Dolce e Gabbana. However, it gets very busy from around 10pm, and even earlier at weekends: DJs play souly sounds upstairs, and you can expect to pay ƒ5 to get in.

### Le Montmartre

*Halvemaansteeg 17 (620 7622). Tram 4, 9, 14, 16, 20, 24, 25.* **Open** 5pm-1am Mon-Thur; 5pm-3am Fri; 4pm-3am Sat; 4pm-1am Sun. **Map 3 E3**
This deliciously cheesy bar advertises itself with the slogan 'voted most popular bar in 1997', though the ad doesn't say who by. The lively crowd clearly love the pop and Dutch music played here, singing along and showing off on the tiny raised dancefloor at the back. Décor includes disco balls and flashing disco lights from a bygone era, with glitzy ornamental touches. Happy hours runs from 6pm to 8pm daily.

## Red Light District: Warmoesstraat

The Warmoesstraat is a rather seedy street running along the edge of the Red Light District. Although there is a high police profile and a police station on the street itself, it's advisable to take care when walking down here at night. Perverts and junkies dominate the area: avoid engaging in conversation with them.

Apart from the fabulously kitsch **Getto** (see below **Bar-restaurants**), and the trad Dutch bar **Casa Maria** (Warmoesstraat 60; 627 6848), this strip is dominated by most of the city's leather bars. The Web (see below) and **Cuckoo's Nest** (Nieuwezijds Kolk 6; 627 1752), a daytime opening bar (1pm-1am daily) that boasts Europe's largest playroom in its cellar, are located just a couple of streets away, as is the Queen's Head.

### Argos

*Warmoesstraat 95 (622 6595). Tram 4, 9, 16, 20, 24, 25.* **Open** 10pm-3am Mon-Thur, Sun; 10pm-4am Fri, Sat. **Map 2 D2**
The oldest and most famous leather bar in Amsterdam, Argos is also the cruisiest. There is a basement darkroom with cabins, one of which has a sling, and every last Sunday of the month they organise the SOS (Sex on Sunday) party: doors are open between 3pm and 4pm, it costs ƒ10 to get in, and the dress code is 'nude/shirtless'. Men only.

### Cockring

*Warmoesstraat 96 (623 9604). Tram 4, 9, 16, 20, 24, 25.* **Open** 11pm-4am Mon-Thur; 11pm-5am Fri, Sat. **Map 2 D2**
This free-admission nightclub is one of the few gay venues for which you need to queue at weekends, particularly after 1am. It attracts all types of gays aged under about 40, despite its location in the leather district, with an underground and hard house music policy. The Cockring's a cruisey place, with a darkroom reached through the industrial/hi-tech toilets. There are also regular live sex shows here. Men only.

### Queen's Head
*Zeedijk 20 (420 2475). Tram 4, 9, 16, 20, 24, 25/Metro
Centraal Station.* **Open** 3pm-1am Mon-Thur, Sun; 3pm-
3am Fri, Sat. **Map 2 D2**
A row of action men and a Dusty doll line the window of this
traditional '50s Dutch kitsch bar, opened by a gay couple –
Johan and Dusty – from the De Trut squatters group (*see
below* **One-off club nights**) in spring 1998. Decked out in
traditional '50s Dutch kitsch – from the light fittings and
wallpaper right down to the carpet on the tables – it has a
beautiful view out the back of all the old Dutch canal houses: you could almost forget which century you're in. Every
Tuesday, Dusty drags up and dons her magical wig to host
her very popular bingo nights from 10pm until last call.

### The Web
*Sint Jacobsstraat 6 (623 6758). Tram 1, 2, 3, 5.* **Open**
2pm-1am Mon-Thur, Sun; 2pm-2am Fri; 2pm-3am Sat.
**Map 2 D2**
Close to Centraal Station, this is one of the most popular
leather bars. Attractions include a small roof garden, a darkroom upstairs and porn videos in the downstairs bar. The
Web has a reputation for throwing wild parties – particularly at Hallowe'en – and for having the cleanest toilets of
any leather bar in town. Men only.

## Bar-restaurants

### Getto
*Warmoesstraat 51 (421 5151). Tram 4, 9, 16, 20, 24,
25.* **Open** 7pm-1am Tue (women only); 4pm-1am Wed-
Sat; 1-midnight Sun; kitchen 7-11pm Tue; 6-11pm Wed-
Sat; 1-11pm Sun. **Credit** AmEx, EC, MC, V. **Map 2 D2**
Undoubtedly the most exciting initiative to open on the gay
scene in recent years, and a place where gays and lesbians
really do mix. Getto is a trendy, kitsch establishment with a
candlelit restaurant at the back (delicious meals, including
vegetarian options, cost around *f*18.50 and are available
until 11pm) and a cool bar at the front. Happy hour is 5-7pm
and 8-9pm on Tuesday, and there's a popular bingo session
every Thursday.

### Hemelse Modder
*Oude Waal 9 (624 3203). Tram 1, 2, 4, 5, 9, 13, 16, 17,
20, 24, 25/Metro Nieuwmarkt.* **Open** 6pm-midnight Tue-
Sun; kitchen 6-10pm Tue-Sun. **Map 3 E2**
This gay-owned, mixed restaurant comes highly recommended for its romantic, candlelit meals, nice interior and
friendly staff. In fact, the only complaint we've heard is that
the tablecloths aren't long enough for you to have that discreet shag under the table. Food is Mediterranean, with vegetarian options always available.

### Huyschkaemer
*Utrechtsestraat 137 (627 0575). Tram 4, 6, 7, 10.* **Open**
*bar* 11am-1am Mon-Thur; 11am-3am Fri; 1pm-3am Sat;
1pm-1am Sun; kitchen 11am-3.30pm, 5-11pm Mon-Fri; 1-
3.30pm, 5-11pm Sat, Sun. **Map 6 E6**
Huyschkaemer's split-level designer interior – replete with
huge windows and wrought-iron features – attracts a mixed,
mainly young and artistic gay and lesbian crowd. Delicious
food costs around *f*20-25 for a main dish: staff are happy to
turn a slightly cheaper starter of your choice into a main dish
for around *f*16.

### La Strada
*Nieuwezijds Voorburgwal 93-95 (625 0276). Tram 1, 2,
5, 13, 17, 20.* **Open** 4pm-1am daily; kitchen 5-10.30pm
daily. **Map 2 D2**
This spacious and centrally located culinary café attracts a
rather artistic and cultural crowd, and is particularly popular with lesbians. Food here is delicious, and a three-course
meal costs around *f*25,50, with vegetarian dishes served.

## Cafés

### Backstage
*Utrechtsedwarsstraat 67 (622 3638). Tram 4, 6, 7, 10.*
**Open** 10am-6pm Mon-Sat. **Map 6 E4**
Sunglasses would be a definite bonus in this multicoloured
café/knitwear boutique that serves almost as a museum to
the half-Mohawk 'Christmas Twins'. Although Greg died in
1997, his identical twin Gary continues to run the place in
his own unique way, selling his knitwear, chatting to the customers and giving spontaneous horoscope readings.

### Downtown
*Reguliersdwarsstraat 31 (622 9958). Tram 1, 2, 4, 5, 9,
14, 16, 20, 24, 25.* **Open** 10am-8pm daily. **Map 5 D4**
Good-value snacks, salads and cakes are served by friendly
staff in this bright, modern café. To a background of mellow
music, you can peruse the exhibitions and selection of magazines and newspapers, while the outdoor terrace is, during
summer, one of the most popular gay haunts on the street.

### Le Monde
*Rembrandtplein 6 (626 9922). Tram 4, 9, 14, 20.* **Open**
8am-midnight daily; kitchen 8-11pm daily. **Map 6 E4**
A popular, early-opening café overlooking Rembrandtplein,
and a great place to have breakfast, lunch, dinner or a snack.

### Sarah's Grannies
*Kerkstraat 176 (624 0145). Tram 16, 24, 25.* **Open**
9.30am-5pm Tue-Fri; 10.30am-5pm Sat. **Map 5 D4**
This once lesbian-owned traditional café-gallery is still frequented by a largely lesbian clientele, though it now enter-
tains a more mixed crowd than it once did. A quiet delight.

## Coffeeshop

### The Otherside
*Reguliersdwarsstraat 6 (421 1014). Tram 1, 2, 5.* **Open**
11am-1am daily. **Map 5 D4**
A bright, modern coffeeshop in the heart of Amsterdam's
own piece of Soho. There is a good, varied hash/weed menu
– single joints are available from *f*6 to *f*11, depending on
strength – with space cake priced at *f*7,50 a slice and
cannabis tea at *f*10 a cup. Staff here are friendly and informative: don't hesitate to ask them if you have any doubts
about whether you should have your cake and eat it too.

## Lesbian nightlife

There is currently no lesbian club in Amsterdam.
However, a thriving – though small – scene does
still exist in the bars and clubs. Apart from the
refreshing **Getto Girls** every Tuesday at Getto
(*see above* **Bar-restaurants**), and **Hard** at the
RoXY (*see below* **One-off club nights**), there is
little for women during the week. Weekend-wise,
both **Flirt Party**, held on the first Sunday of the
month at Café Toon (Korte Leidsedwarsstraat 26),
and **Samura Sunday Party's** (sic), held on the
first Sunday of every other month at Margarita's
(Reguliersdwarsstraat 108), are both worth a look.
The latter, unusually, is followed by a happy
hour – 11pm-12.30am – at the nearby **Café
Reality** (*see* **Around Rembrandtplein** *above*).

### Saarein
*Elandstraat 119 (623 4901). Tram 7, 10.* **Open** 3pm-
1am Tue-Thur, Sun; 3pm-2am Fri, Sat. **Map 5 C4**
Amsterdam's legendary women-only bar opened as a political café in the late '70s, and still retains some 'character'

*Stroke the resident pussy at* **Saarein**, *the city's only lesbian bar. See page 189.*

from that decade. A split-level traditional brown bar with a sleepy resident cat, it's a great place to come for more of a low-key drink or two. Notable events include the Saarein's birthday party on the third Sunday in August, and the annual weed-growers contest on the last Friday in November.

### Vandenberg
*Lindengracht 95 (622 2716). Tram 3, 10.* **Open** 5pm-1am Mon-Fri, Sun; 5pm-2am Fri, Sat; *kitchen* 6-11pm daily (summer); 5-10pm daily (winter). **Map 1 B2**
Eel-baiting may have been a popular 'sport' along this canal before it was filled in at the turn of the century, but, fortunately, it's one thing you won't find on the menu at this vegetarian bar-restaurant. Small but glowingly cosy, this lesbian-owned place attracts a crowd of older locals, though the younger bar staff pull in a few admirers and contemporaries. The vicious cat is to be avoided.

### Vive la Vie
*Amstelstraat 7 (624 0114). Tram 4, 9, 14, 20.* **Open** 3pm-1am Mon-Thur, Sun; 3pm-3am Fri, Sat. **Map 5 E4**
On the edge of the bustling Rembrandtplein, this lively bar attracts a largely lipstick/femme clientele, though men are also welcome here. Don't be put off by the women dancing and singing along to the traditional Dutch music: it's guaranteed that by the end of the night – after a few beers, natch – you'll be joining in. Although the bar is a little on the small side, there are plans to extend it, and in the summer customers spill out on to the outside pavement terrace. In addition to the on-site events, owner Mieke Martelhof organises huge, commercial lesbian parties throughout the year at various locations: ask at the bar for details, or phone the AUB.

## One-off club nights

A few of Amsterdam's clubs hold one-off gay club nights; Hard and De Trut – listed below – are the biggest. *See also chapter* **Clubs***, page 175.*

### RoXY
*Singel 465 (620 0354). Tram 1, 2, 4, 5, 9, 14, 16, 20, 24, 25.* **Open** 11pm-4am Wed, Thur, Sun; 11pm-5am Fri, Sat. **Admission** ƒ12,50-ƒ20. **Map 5 D4**
Host to the weekly gay Hard Wednesday-nighter, which attracts a huge, mainly male, fashion-conscious crowd and a handful of women, as well as the lesbian Pussy Lounge, held every third Sunday of the month. The Original Pickwick Tea Dance, a swing night, also takes place here on the first

Sunday of the month (between September and May) from 4-9pm, costing ƒ20 (door) or ƒ15 (in advance). Hosted by Nickie Nicole, it always features a big band, plus special acts and '20s movies.

### De Trut
*Bilderdijkstraat 165 (612 3524). Tram 3, 7, 12, 17.* **Open** 11pm-4am Sun. **Admission** ƒ2,50. **Map 4 B5**
Probably the best gay club night in Amsterdam, attracting a good, mixed crowd. It's eternally popular, which means you have to start queueing outside around 10.40pm to ensure you get in: doors open at 11pm and shut when it's full, which could be just 20 minutes later. It's held in a bricked, industrial squat basement, and features innovative, quirky art works, UV lighting, videos and, occasionally, performances. The club is run on a non-profit basis – staff are all volunteers, and drinks are cheap – and proceeds are donated to suitably PC causes. Strictly no heterosexuals allowed.

## Sex parties

Apart from Wild Side events (*see below* **Other groups & organisations**), there are currently no women-only sex parties in Amsterdam, just occasional, mixed fetish parties. There are regular sex parties for men, with smaller parties generally taking place in bars on Warmoesstraat. The **Stablemaster Hotel** (Warmoesstraat 23; 625 0148) hosts jack-off parties almost every night, while SOS (Sex on Sunday) is held monthly at the Argos. **Club Jaecques** (Warmoesstraat 93; 622 0323) holds Naked Parties on every first Sunday of the month, and on every third Sunday of the month it's the Horsemen and Knights party. At the latter, admission is relative to, um, 'size': for most it's ƒ10, but it's free if you have more than 18 centimetres (roughly 7 inches) for you – or others – to play with.

Equally popular are the more regular and larger parties, at venues that offer a wide range of facilities from private cabins and sling and bondage rooms to golden shower areas. Held on the third Saturday of the month at the AMP (buses run from outside the Barbizon Hotel), **Club Trash** draws a big crowd; the dress code is leather/rubber, and tickets cost *f*25 in advance from MR B (*see below* **Leather-rubber/sex shops**). A less hardcore alternative is the **Hot Leather/Rubber Night**, held every two months at the COC on Rozenstraat (*see below* **Help & information**), while the irregular **Factory Parties** organised by GALA (616 1979) are both popular and steamy.

## Help & information

### COC (Amsterdam)

*Rozenstraat 14, 1016 NX Amsterdam (information 626 3087). Tram 13, 14, 17, 20.* **Open** *office* 9am-5pm Mon-Fri; *Info-Coffeeshop* 1-5pm Wed-Sat; *café* 8pm-midnight Wed; 8pm-3.30am Fri, Sat; *discos* 10pm-4am Fri, Sat. **Admission** *disco* *f*5. **Map 1 B3**
The Amsterdam branch deals with the COC's more social side. Many groups meet here, including the English-speaking **Wild Side** group, and **Love2Love** (*see below* **Other groups & organisations**), and the regular HIV café is also held here every Thursday, 8pm-midnight. In addition, the trendy-looking Info-Coffeeshop is a useful place to get help with any enquiries you may have about the COC or the gay scene in general, while the COC's weekly discos – mixed (with a male bias) on Fridays, lesbians only at the busy Saturday-nighter – draw people from all scenes.

### COC (National)

*Nieuwezijds Voorburgwal 68-70 (623 4596). Tram 13, 14, 17, 20.* **Open** 9am-5pm Mon-Fri. **Map 2 D2**
COC's head office, dealing with all matters relating to gays and lesbians; the organisation has strong social and activist tendencies. However, it's hard to have confidence in a gay and lesbian group that, in 1998, appointed an unashamedly heterosexual woman as chairperson. Cox Habbema justified her position to gay men by saying, 'You do it with men. Me too.' Er, quite. Its website is at *www.coc.nl*.

### Gay & Lesbian Switchboard

*Postbus 11573, 1001 GN Amsterdam (623 6565/text phone 422 6565/fax 638 0407).* **Open** 10am-10pm daily.
Whether it's information on the scene or safe sex you're after, the friendly, English-speaking Dutch men and women on this phone line are specially trained and well informed when it comes to giving information and advice on all gay and lesbian matters. Its website is at *www.dds.nl/~glswitch*.

### Het Vrouwenhuis (The Women's House)

*Nieuwe Herengracht 95 (625 2066/fax 638 9185). Tram 7, 9, 14, 20/Metro Waterlooplein.* **Open** *office* 10am-5pm Mon-Fri; *Info-Café* 5-8pm Tue (except school holidays); noon-5pm Wed, Thur. **Map 3 F6**
This multi-function emancipation centre for women is located in a canal-side building that was originally squatted by feminists in the '70s. There's a well-stocked library here, plus an Info-Café – where you can pick up all manner of leaflets, flyers and other, um, info – and a bar, which is usually most busy after many of the classes held here, including chess, politics and dance. A few autonomous women's organisations also operate from here. The website – at *www.dds.nl/~womenctr* – is good, though it is in Dutch.

## Archives

### Homodok

*Oudezijds Achterburgwal 185 (525 2601). Tram 4, 9, 14, 16, 20, 24, 25.* **Open** 10.30am-4.30pm Wed-Fri; by appointment Mon, Tue. **Map 2 D3**
This centre for lesbian and gay studies houses an extensive range of literature including books, journals, magazines,

newspaper articles and theses. The Homodok is currently located in a building at the University of Amsterdam, but in 1998 the university withdrew its funding, and the archives will be relocated from January 1999. Information on their new address will be available either on the Internet (*www.dds.nl/~gldocu*), or via e-mail (*homodok@sara.nl*).

### IIAV

*Obiplein 4 (665 0820). Tram 3, 6, 10, 14/bus 15, 22.* **Open** noon-5pm Mon; 10am-7pm Tue; 10am-5pm Wed-Fri.
Housed in a beautiful, listed neo-Byzantine church in the east of the city, this women's archive has a fascinating history. Confiscated during the World War II Nazi occupation, it was removed to Berlin where it then disappeared. In 1992 it was found in Moscow, but, in contravention of international law, the Russians are still refusing to return it. The current collection, started after the war, is officially an archive, but there is plenty of browsing potential for the lesbian bookworm.

### Lesbisch Archief

*1e Helmersstraat 17 (618 5879). Tram 1, 2, 3, 5, 6, 12.* **Open** *archives* 1-4.30pm Mon-Fri; *telephone enquiries* 9am-4.30pm Mon-Fri. **Map 5 C5**
The Lesbian Archives, housed in a building with other gay and lesbian organisations such as HIV Vereniging and Stichting GALA, specialises mainly in audio-visual material, but also holds selections of books, magazines and photos. Its website, like the Homodok, is at *www.dds.nl/~gldocu*.

## HIV/AIDS

The Netherlands were one of the first countries to pour money into research once the HIV virus was recognised. The Dutch government took a progressive approach towards HIV/AIDS, with active research complemented by high-profile fund-raising events and regular safe sex campaigns.

Recent reviews of governmental funding policies means that previously state-maintained HIV/AIDS organisations could lose their some or all of their funding. However, there are still a number of organisations dealing specifically with HIV/AIDS, that are as yet unaffected by cutbacks. On the social side, there is an HIV Café held at the **COC** (*see above* **Help & information**) every Thursday evening, often with informal, themed talks, while there is also an HIV Café held at **HIV Vereniging** every Sunday (*see below*).

Aside from the organisations listed below, the **AIDS Helpline** (06 022 2220/0800 022 2220; open 2-10pm Mon-Fri) offers advice by phone, while **HIVnet** has a wealth of advice on HIV and AIDS on its Dutch and English website (*www.hivnet.org*).

### HIV Vereniging

*1e Helmersstraat 17 (616 0160/fax 616 1200). Tram 1, 2, 3, 5, 6, 12.* **Open** 9am-5pm Mon-Fri. **Map 5 C5**
This, the Netherlands HIV Association, supports the individual and collective interests of all those who are HIV-positive, including legal help. It produces a bi-monthly Dutch magazine, *HIV Nieuws* (*f*50 per year, subscription only), which is also on line at *www.hivnet.org/hvn*. It also runs the Internet service, HIVNET (found at the aforementioned address), which has the latest HIV/AIDS information, and a help line, **HIVpluslijn** (685 0055). There's also an HIV Café for men and women every Sunday (4-8pm) and regular lunches and dinners for people with HIV; call for information and reservations.

### SAD-Schorerstichting

*PC Hooftstraat 5 (662 4206). Tram 2, 3, 5, 6, 7, 10, 12, 20.* **Open** *9am-5pm Mon-Fri.* **Map 5 D5**
This state-funded social agency offers psycho-social support, education and HIV prevention advice for gays and lesbians. One department is solely concerned with HIV/AIDS and related matters, including a buddy project, and it also runs a weekly clinic for 'men who have gay sexual contacts' and who would like anonymous medical help (7-9pm Fridays). Examinations and treatment of sexually transmitted diseases, including an HIV test, are free. The actual clinic is held at the city's health department, the **GG&GD** (Groenburgwal 44) but call the SAD-Schorerstichting (noon-2pm daily) to make an appointment. The staff speak English.

### Stichting AIDS Fonds

*Keizersgracht 390, 1016 GB Amsterdam (626 2669/fax 627 5221). Tram 1, 2, 5.* **Open** *9am-5pm Mon-Fri.* **Map 5 C4**
This active organisation, responsible for high-profile fundraising events such as the Amsterdam Diners (*see above* **The queer year**), was specifically set up to channel money into research and safer sex promotion, as well as providing grants for the more personal needs of people with AIDS. English information is available on its website at *www.aidsfonds.nl.*

## Other groups & organisations

### Amsterdam Stetsons

*(663 2402/683 7333).*
A country and western dance club for gays and lesbians, which meets regularly at the **Cruise Inn** at Zeeburgerdijk 271 (a pink, wooden building, and normally a straight rock 'n' roll dancing joint!). Open evenings are held every last Tuesday of the month at 8pm, while it also has a monthly Gay Western Salon and offers dance classes (beginners' courses start at *f*50 for ten lessons). Yee-haw!

### Dikke Maatjes

*c/o COC (Amsterdam): see above for address (625 5128).*
'Dikke Maatjes' means 'close friends,' though its literal translation is 'fat friends'. That's exactly what this gay club is for: chubbies, bears and their admirers. Based at the COC, the group organises various activities, from hunting bears in the local sauna to bear crawls (and, no doubt, bear tasting). Every summer they hold the Big & Bear Weekend.

### Groep 7152

*(035 524 3623).*
This national organisation for lesbians and bisexual women started with a classified ad (number 7152) placed in a publication back in 1971. In Amsterdam, they meet every third Sunday of the month (except June-August) for bridge (1-4pm), information and introductions (4-5.30pm), and dancing (4-8pm) at the **Crea Café** (Turfdraagsterpad 17). Entrance is *f*7,50 (members *f*5). On the whole, it's more of an older women's scene here, though more information on the group can be found on its English-language website, *www.geocities.com/westhollywood/stonewall/2591/engels.html.*

### Long Yang Club Holland

*Postbus 58253, 1040 HG Amsterdam (023 571 5788).*
The Dutch branch of this worldwide organisation for Asian and oriental gays and their friends meets regularly in town.

### Love2Love

*c/o COC (Amsterdam): see above for address (626 3087).*
A non-profit-making mixed gay and lesbian youth group based at the COC (*see above* **Help & information**). They meet there every Thursday (8pm-midnight) and put a lot of energy into creating themed evenings such as Abba parties or comedy nights, which are always well attended.

### Mama Cash

*Postbus 15686, 1001 ND Amsterdam (689 3634/fax 683 4647).* **Open** *9am-5pm Mon-Fri.*
Founder Marjan Sax put her *f*2.5 million inheritance into setting up this organisation supplying funding for women-run businesses (it has sponsored many lesbian organisations and events taking place in the city). Contact it for information on how to apply and ask for its English brochure, or see the website (*www.xxlink.nl/mamacash/0/home.htm*).

### Netherbears

*c/o Le Shako, Postbus 15495, 1001 ML Amsterdam (625 1400).*
This hairy men's club meets at **Le Shako** (Gravelandseveer 2) every second Sunday of the month from 5pm to 9pm.

### Sjalhomo

*Postbus 2536, 1000 CM Amsterdam (023 531 2318 evenings only).*
This national organisation for Jewish gays, lesbians and bisexuals – on the web at *www.worldaccess.nl/~lodewykz* – regularly organises cultural, social and political activities on and around Jewish feast days.

### Spellbound Productions

*(682 7228).*
A non-profit-making group of gays and lesbians that organises the Planet, a series of alternative, underground parties every few months. Gothic, electro and trance music combine with creative acts, slides and other art work. Location and frequency vary, so look out for flyers.

### Stichting Gay Arts Productions

*Postbus 3553, 1001 AJ Amsterdam (691 8347).*
A new association that actively supports and promotes gay artists, musicians and theatre bods.

### Stichting Tigertje

*Tigertje 10521, 1001 EM Amsterdam (673 2458).*
Tigertje organises a variety of sports activities for gays and lesbians, including an HIV swimming group.

### Wild Side

*c/o COC (Amsterdam): see above for address (626 3087).*
A social and educational support group for woman-to-woman SM. Every first Saturday of the month it holds SM workshops, and every third Saturday of the month there's an open business meeting. Wild Side organises regular 'play parties', and publishes the always-interesting *Wild Side News*, a free bi-monthly, bi-lingual newsletter that's a useful source for SM/fetish events; it's available from the COC (*see above* **Help & information**) and the Vrolijk bookshop (*see below* **Bookshops**). Its English-language website – *www.dds.nl/~wildside* – is also worth a look.

## Saunas

### Fenomeen

*1e Schinkelstraat 14 (671 6780). Tram 6.* **Open** *1-11pm daily; women's day Mon.* **Admission** *11am-6pm f*11; *6-11pm f*13,50.
Relaxed squat sauna, very popular with lesbians on Monday's women-only day. It's open-plan and split level with a sauna, steam bath, cold bath, chill-out room with mattresses, showers in the courtyard outside, and a café serving wholefood snacks, organic juices and herbal teas. Extras include massage and a sunbed.

*Be warned: stay out in the sun too long and you could look like this.*

### Thermos Day
*Raamstraat 33 (623 9158). Tram 1, 2, 5, 7, 10.* **Open**
noon-11pm Mon-Fri; noon-10pm Sat, Sun. **Admission**
*f*30; *f*22,50 under-24s with ID. **Map 5 C4**
Facilities at this relaxed sauna include a steam room, a dry-
heat room, a small cinema showing porn, private cubicles, a
bar and restaurant, hairdressers and a gym.

### Thermos Night
*Kerkstraat 58-60 (623 4936). Tram 1, 2, 5.* **Open** 11pm-
8am daily. **Admission** *f*30; *f*22,50 under-24s with ID.
**Map 5 D4**
Similar facilities to Thermos Day, with the addition of a
small Jacuzzi and a darkroom, but without a restaurant or
hairdressers. There is also a spacious bar, dry sauna and
steam room, and a maze of cubicles. Crowded on weekends.

## Shopping & services
## Accommodation

It's illegal for Amsterdam hotels to refuse accommodation to gays and lesbians, but those listed
below are all specifically gay-owned. The Gay &
Lesbian Switchboard can provide more information on hotels that are gay and lesbian friendly. *See*
*chapter* **Accommodation**, *page 89-102.*

### Black Tulip Hotel
*Geldersekade 16 (427 0933/fax 624 4281). Tram 1, 2, 4,
5, 9, 13, 16, 17, 20, 24, 25/Metro Centraal
Station/Nieuwmarkt.* **Rates** *single f190; double f250.*
**Credit** AmEx, DC, EC, MC, V. **Map 2 D2**
Located near Centraal Station, this recently opened men-only
hotel has mastered the art of serving the leather man: SM
facilities are included in all the rooms, as are a TV and VCR.
The fully equipped Black Body Fantasy Room costs a whop-
ping (or is that a whipping?) *f*290 a night.

### Hotel New York
*Herengracht 13 (624 3066/fax 620 3230). Tram 1, 2, 3,
5, 13, 14.* **Rates** *single f250; double f200; triple
f275.* **Credit** AmEx, DC, EC, MC, V. **Map 2 C2**
A beautiful, modernised seventeenth-century building on a
charming, picturesque canal-side location.

### ITC Hotel
*Prinsengracht 1051 (623 0230/fax 624 5846) Tram 4,
6, 7, 10.* **Rates** *single f80-f95; double f140-f170.* **Credit**
AmEx, DC, EC, MC, V. **Map 6 E4**
Located on the plushest canal in the city and close to the
Kerkstraat, Reguliersdwarsstraat and Amstel areas, this
canal-side house is a popular stopover for gay and lesbians.

### Orfeo Hotel
*Leidsekruisstraat 14 (623 1347/fax 620 2348). Tram 1,
2, 5, 6, 7, 10.* **Rates** *single f80-f150; double f115-f165;
twin f115-f165.* **Credit** AmEx, EC, MC, TC, V.
**Map 5 D5**
The Orfeo is handily located by the Leidseplein. Although
the breakfast area looks uninspiring – as were the staff when
we last visited, incidentally – the rooms are good value.

## Bookshops

Aside from the specialist bookshops listed below,
the **American Book Center** has a well-stocked
English language gay and lesbian section in its
basement, with a wide range of fiction and non-fiction titles, magazines (including porn) and postcards. And though **Waterstone's** has no actual

gay section, the occasional homo-erotic window
display has been spotted. (For information on both,
*see chapter* **Shopping**, *page 141.*) There are also
two charming second-hand women's bookstores in
the city in **Antiquariaat Lorelei** (Prinsengracht
495) and **Vrouwen in Druk** (Westermarkt 5):
both have a large number of titles in English.

### Intermale
*Spuistraat 251 (625 0009). Tram 1, 2, 5, 13, 14, 17, 20.*
**Open** 11am-6pm Mon; 10am-6pm Tue-Wed, Sat; 10am-
9pm Thur. **Credit** AmEx, EC, MC, V. **Map 2 C3**
This split-level gay men's bookstore is crammed with literature, porn and books on history and sexuality, as well as a
sexy selection of cards, magazines and newspapers.

### Vrolijk
*Paleisstraat 135 (623 5142). Tram 1, 2, 5, 13, 14, 17,
20.* **Open** 11am-6pm Mon; 10am-6pm Tue, Wed, Fri;
10am-9pm Thur; 10am-5pm Sat. **Credit** AmEx, DC, EC,
MC, V. **Map 2 C3**
A wide range of gay and lesbian books, from politics to fiction and anything in between. Many titles are in English –
some in the second-hand section – while there are also good
selections of international magazines, T-shirts, CDs by gay
and lesbian artists, and videos.

### Xantippe Unlimited
*Prinsengracht 290 (623 5854). Tram 1, 2, 5, 10, 13, 14,
17, 20.* **Open** 1-7pm Mon; 10am-7pm Tue-Fri; 10am-6pm
Sat. **Credit** AmEx, DC, EC, MC, V. **Map 5 C4**
After changing hands recently – and adding 'Unlimited' to
its name – this store has disposed of its '70s feminist bookstore image and gone for a designer look: it now considers
itself to be a general bookstore. Even so, Xantippe continues
to have a comprehensive Women's Studies section (mainly
of which are in English), as well as many international
women's/lesbian magazines.

## Hairdressers

### Cuts & Curls
*Korte Leidsedwarsstraat 74 (624 6881). Tram 1, 2, 5, 6,
7, 10.* **Open** 10am-6pm Mon, Wed; 10am-7pm Tue; 9am-
9pm Thur; 9am-6pm Fri; 9am-4pm Sat. **Credit** AmEx,
DC, EC, MC, V. **Map 5 D5**
Okay, so what male hairdresser isn't gay? But a butch hairdresser? There you go. Cuts & Curls leather men offer 'men's
cuts' and 'blockheads' for *f*33. No appointments.

## Leather-rubber/sex shops

Within the Red Light District lies the leather district, home to a handful of gay leather and rubber
shops such as **MR B** (Warmoesstraat 89; 422 0003)
and **Master Leathers** (Warmoesstraat 32; 624
5573). Rubber lovers should also visit **Black
Body**, a specialist rubber shop at Lijnbaansgracht
292 (626 2553). Other gay sex shops worth a look
include **The Bronx** (Kerkstraat 53-55; 623 1548),
**Drakes** (Damrak 61; 627 9544), and **RoB**
(Weteringschans 253; 625 4686).

Women's erotica can be found at **Female &
Partners** (Spuistraat 100; 620 9152) and **Mail &
Female** (Prinsengracht 489; 623 3916), while
**Demask** (Zeedijk 64; 620 5603) is popular with
both men and women. For these last two and other
such shops, *see chapter* **Shopping**, *page 144.*

# Media

**Though hardly a world leader in TV, radio or the press, Amsterdam is virtually streets ahead when it comes to the Net.**

*Read all about it in Amsterdam, but keep your phrasebook handy...*

Never fear, media junkies: just because Dutch reads like a bunch of bad Scrabble hands and sounds like it's descended from Klingon, there's still plenty to score when you're in town and in need of a media fix.

Amsterdam's traditional liberality, craftsmanship and readiness to make a buck have made the city a centre of printing and publishing since the Golden Age. These days, global giants such as Elseviers and VNU are based here, and the city is still pumping out some fine typography and book design. The Dutch flair for the visual maintains Amsterdam's strong international reputation for graphic design, while a small but creative local multimedia and online industry is flourishing. The city has also been fully cabled for years and has an excellent telecommunications infrastructure. When this is coupled with a cosmopolitan outlook and strong distribution skills (Euro editions of the *Economist* and *Time* are printed in the suburbs), it ensures a rich and varied media culture.

The city now even has its own Groucho Club. **Baby** opened its doors in June 1997 with the aim of becoming 'the most important creative bastion of the Netherlands'. Located in a former church at Keizersgracht 676 (530 6666), it's an expensive members-only meeting place and studio for professionals and upcoming talent in the fields of advertising, TV, film, photography, music, fashion, new media and design. Facilities include a restaurant, and libraries of literature and videos, the latter holding everything from movies to showreels and portfolios.

## Print

Like many Dutch social institutions, the newspaper business in the Netherlands is as much the product of historical and religious factors as political divisions and commercial imperatives. The events of the last war largely established the tone of the content, even if concentration of media ownership and long-term political coalition has eroded much of the difference. *De Telegraaf*, a one-time collaborationist and still right-wing daily, is Holland's biggest-selling paper, and the nearest the country has to a tabloid press. *Het Parool* was the main underground wartime journal, but is currently enjoying the fruits of a re-style and subsequent repositioning as a hip, afternoon local rag; its sister morning paper, *De Volkskrant*, also enjoys a relatively young, progressive readership.

*Trouw*, the other Amsterdam-published national daily, began life as a Protestant paper before going underground during the war; it's owned by Perscombinatie, the same company that owns *Het Parool* and *De Volkskrant*. For some socio-religious reason, Sunday papers have never taken off here.

Sadly, there's not a great deal news-wise for Anglophones, apart from the dull *Financieële Dagblad*: it stands at the functional end of the market and has a daily half-page business summary in English as well as a weekly English edition, *The Netherlander*. However, Dutch News Digest recently made an offer for the loss-making *Netherlander*, and its future is uncertain. The fortnightly *What's On In Amsterdam* (ƒ4), published by the VVV tourist office, might be rather turgid and insipid style-wise, but it's still the best printed guide to current events in English. In addition, comedy troupe **Boom Chicago** (*see chapter* **Theatre**, *page 221*) distributes an excellent free guide ten times a year, available from its theatre on Leidseplein and from bars around town; news on gay clubs and events can be found in *Queer Fish*, a photocopied freesheet found in assorted bars and clubs, and there's also a reach seam of information on the Internet (*see box* **Site & sound**, *page 199*).

Still on a positive note, there are a number of locally produced magazines that merit a look for their excellent design, styling and photography. *Blvd* (in Dutch) is the city's answer to *i-D*, while *Dutch* (also in Dutch, at *www.dag.nl/dutch*) covers culture, fashion and design. Of the English-language magazines, *ArtView* offers an interesting take on visual culture, while *Frame* is a new international journal on interior architecture. And after a two-year break during which it was only available online, *Mediamatic* (in Dutch and English, though the website – at *www.mediamatic.nl* – is only in English) offers classy critiques of new media and the wired-up revolution.

Wherever the Dutch press is available, you can also expect to find a wide range of foreign magazines and newspapers (British papers are available here, but are expensive at around ƒ4 for a daily and ƒ7 for a Sunday paper). Particularly good selections can be found around Spui: **Athenaeum** is a browser's dream, and 100 metres away, **Waterstone's** (formerly WH Smith) has all the main UK magazines, as well as five floors of English books, cards and videos. The **American Book Center** round the corner has four floors of US and British books, and its selections of New

# Caught in the Net

If anyone needed convincing that before too long, we'll all be living in cyberspace, then a visit to Amsterdam should prove the final straw. In a slightly scary development, the city now boasts a number of Internet terminals on the street, available for the public to use in much the same way as one would use a payphone. The sleek, silver-grey terminals are striking and easy to find: most are grouped alongside KPN's regular green phone booths. 'We originally had terminals in hospitals and the World Trade Centre, but they didn't get enough users,' explains Reineke van Meerten, a member of the working group at Amsterdam City Council that jointly developed the project from April 1996. 'The sites on the street have been very successful, and what started as an experiment has now been made permanent.'

As users of cash machines on sunny days will no doubt already be aware, an LCD screen can be hard to fathom if the sun shines, and these machines are no exception. But improvising shade with a coat or umbrella reveals a surprisingly high-quality colour screen, operating Microsoft Internet Explorer 3.0 at ISDN speed. Checking out the menu reveals a send-only e-mail capability and – a real downer, this – an operating system in Dutch only. The system is operated using a central track ball, though the layout is somewhat confusing at first. Similarly, the actual technology itself is far from perfect, though to expect otherwise is akin to expecting public toilets to be done out with brass taps and marble floors. The main disadvantage of the system is its inability to send any kind of e-mail attachment, because – due to fears of vandalism – the terminal has no floppy disk drive. There's also no sound card or Internet Relay Chat (IRC), but, surprisingly, it can print pages.

Street surfing doesn't come cheap: at 50 cents a minute and 25 cents for a printout (the stations don't accept cash, only phonecards), it's about 15 times the price of using a PC at home. Remember that payphones are enormously expensive compared to private phones, though, and it doesn't seem quite so unreasonable. And if you want a look at the shape of things to come, then one of these terminals is a pretty good place to start.

## KPN Internet Terminals

*Found on Spui, Centraal Station, Leidseplein, Paulus Potterstraat (near the Stedelijk Museum), at the newMetropolis Museum, and at assorted cafés in the city centre.*

Age literature and American magazines are unrivalled in town. You can also try Centraal Station or assorted branches of **Bruna** and **AKO** across the city for mainstream imports.

The best sources for alternative media are anarcho-political bookshop **Fort van Sjakoo**, and **Lambiek**, which specialises in comics and original cartoon art. For all these shops, *see chapter* **Shopping**, *pages 141-142.*

## Broadcast

Until 1992, a unique system of airtime allocation and strictly limited commercialisation had stranded Dutch television in a state of creative torpor. Three state channels had their hours divided among a number of stations according to the numbers of 'members' each channel had, a figure determined by sales of each channel's weekly TV guide. They were worthy but extremely dull; only the arty VPRO managed to produce anything of merit.

This arrangement began to crack when RTL4 started broadcasting commercial Dutch TV from Luxembourg. Reform has produced a number of new stations in recent years, including Veronica and SBS6 (glitzy and youth-oriented), TV10 (old repeats, such as *Black Adder*), RTL5 (series and films from the US), and the Music Factory (a Europop-heavy, Dutch-language MTV clone). But with several spectacularly complicated interactive, pay-per-view, TV-down-the-phone schemes mooted or already under way, the televisual media scene is changing as fast and as unpredictably as in the other mature consumer markets.

The city currently has ten commercial stations, most of which are as short on viewers as they are on style. Even RTL (which started the commercial revolution) has started losing money, and with the pay-per-view revolution heating up, it's now a volatile industry. The signs are that with 26 channels on cable, Amsterdammers are not willing to pay more for anything until standards are improved and prices fall.

Amsterdam's cable service has been fluctuating in recent years, as the operator, A2000, was privatised and now jockeys for position in the much-vaunted 'media convergence'. The basic package on cable includes the main Dutch channels, non-commercial stations in German, French, Italian and Belgian, various awful local channels, and English-language multinationals such as CNN and MTV. The basic also includes BBC1 and BBC2, so there's no need to miss out on *EastEnders*; you might also be relieved to know that some pubs in the city show the big football matches on Sky. The 'wall-to-wall porno' is an urban myth, so don't expect any late-night thrills unless your hotel has the 'extended service', which usually also features film channels, Discovery, the Cartoon Network, Eurosport and others.

Dutch radio is generally as bland as the TV: listeners of Veronica, the top commercial radio channel, have voted *Bohemian Rhapsody* number one in their annual 'best records ever' poll for the last few years, which should tell you something. Sadly, the ten-year-old squatters' pirate station Patapoe – a rare exception to the rule that Dutch radio is dull – was closed down in early '98, but has vowed to get back on the air. Without it, the airwaves are far less interesting.

## Advertising

Amsterdam is, as you'd expect, the centre of the Dutch ad biz. Following an era described by one commentator as 'art sponsored by clients', a more demanding commercial atmosphere has helped improve the quality: in 1996 a Dutch commercial – for Nestlé's Rolos – won a Grand Prix at the Cannes advertising festival. Today, the city boasts several creative partnerships that are highly rated abroad, such as KesselsKramer, the 'guerilla marketers' who grabbed the launch of Britain's Channel 5 from under the nose of the London ad industry.

Cinema ads in Holland are subject to looser regulations than in the UK, and are worth arriving early for. Meanwhile, the discreet billboards and *peperbussen* (ad-plastered 'pepperpots') adorn and inform rather than dominate the cityscape. In fact, perhaps the coolest thing about the Amsterdam media industry is its lightness of touch, producing a city less semiotically polluted than any other...

## New media

...Which is not such a problem in cyberspace, however: after all, Holland is the third busiest European country for Internet activity, after the UK and Germany. Just as the country's geographical position fostered a history of trade and an international outlook, so Amsterdam's virtual location as a major connection and distribution node for European transatlantic phone traffic has had a significant impact on its cyber development. And the industry, with 1,300 multimedia companies in the city employing 10,000 people, shows no signs of slowing down.

In the '80s, a large and skilled community of hackers flourished, based around Hacktic, one of Europe's most (in)famous bunches of anarchist techno-pranksters. Back in 1993, however, Hacktic morphed into Xs4all (that's 'Xs' as in 'access', not 'excess'), a low-cost Internet Service Provider for the masses. While its anarchic style has given way to a more responsible 'digital rights watchdog' role – they now have 40,000 subscribers – they've still proved they have more lead in their pencil than the commercial *parvenu* ISPs. The city also has ties with the less anonymous digerati: the likes of former editor of *Mondo 2000* RU Sirius and the late

Tim Leary have been frequent visitors to the city, while *Wired* magazine began life in 1988 as an Amsterdam bi-monthly, *Electric Word*.

This mix of home-spun and imported talent has made Amsterdam a major player in the digital revolution. Cultural centres, including **De Balie** (*see chapter* **Theatre**, *page 221*) and **Paradiso** (*see chapter* **Music: Rock, Roots & Jazz**, *page 208*), host events of international significance in critical media discourse, such as The Amsterdam Agenda (*www.dds.nl/p2p*), who focus on emerging practices in European media culture. In a similar vein, the Dutch Design Institute (*www.design-inst.nl*) has also established a strong reputation abroad with its Doors of Perception conferences on digital culture.

Another Hacktic initiative is the Digitale Stad (*www.dds.nl*), one of the first and most successful European 'electronic suburbs'. Based on the US Freenets, it offers access to city councillors,

# Site and sound

Checking beforehand what's going on during your visit is one of the great boons of online media. Just to help you out, here's our list of the top ten websites about Amsterdam...

**Amstel** *www.amstel.com*
An attractive and well-designed online guide, chatroom and news resource for and about Amsterdam.

**Amsterdam** *www.amsterdam.com*
Logically-titled city guide, packed to bursting with information and impressively designed to boot.

**Amsterdam Nightguide**
*www.logiclounge.com/nightguide*
A good round-up of the city's clubbing scene.

**Channels** *www.stad.com*
City-backed online self-promotion site.

**CliX** *www.clix.net*
Youth-orientated Amsterdam guide.

**De Digitale Stad** *www.dds.nl*
Excellent official site for the city, with plenty of links.

**Home Page of the Netherlands**
*www.dhp.nl*
Links to hundreds of other sites in Holland, including museums, clubs, institutes, galleries and arts centres.

**Netherlands Board of Tourism**
*www.nbt.nl*
Informative official site, with a handy search facility.

**Time Out** *www.timeout.co.uk*
Info on listings and events, updated weekly.

**UITweb** *www.aub.nl*
The AUB site provides details on what's on in town, and how to book tickets.

information about the city in Dutch and English, electronic art, and hundreds of home pages. It's a great starting point for the desktop traveller.

Despite the presence of several Internet cafés in the city – **Coffeeshop Internet**, **Freeworld** and the **Cyber Café** are the main three, with **Kalverstudio** (formerly Mystère 2000) acting as both Internet café and TV studio – Amsterdam's cyber scene had lacked any space for regular flesh-meets until the Society for Old and New Media opened in the refurbished **Waag** building at Nieuwmarkt in 1997 (*see chapter* **Cafés & Bars**, *page 125*). Aside from regular lectures, cyberarts installations, seminars and an informative website (*www.waag.nl*), the Society has set up a public reading room for old and new media in an attempt to revive the city's café society tradition. The atmospheric bar and restaurant is a good place to meet any cyber-friends you may have met on the Net. In 1997, the Society helped set up a network of public terminals around the city (*see box* **Caught in the Net**, *page 197*).

Finally, a word of warning. Laptop-toting visitors should note that Holland uses four-pin phone plugs. These fit a US-style jack; other adaptors are available at the airport and the usual retail outlets.

## New media centres

**Book 'n' Serve**
*Ferdinand Bolstraat 151-153 (664 3446/e-mail bns@euronet.nl). Tram 3, 12, 20, 24, 25.* **Open** noon-7pm Mon; 9.30am-7pmTue, Wed, Fri; 9.30am-9pm Thur; 9.30am-6pm Sat. **Price** ƒ2,50/15 mins. **Credit** EC.
**Map 6 E6**
*Disabled access (ground floor only).*

**Coffeeshop Internet**
*Prinsengracht 480 (638 4108). Tram 1, 2, 5, 6, 7, 10.* **Open** 10am-midnight Mon-Thur, Sun; 10am-1am Fri, Sat. **Price** ƒ2,50/15 mins. **Map 5 D5**
*Disabled access.*

**Cyber Café**
*Nieuwendijk 19 (623 5146/e-mail cyber@cybercafe.euronet.nl). Tram 1, 2, 5, 13, 17, 20.* **Open** 10am-1am Mon-Thur, Sun; 10am-3am Fri, Sat. **Price** ƒ3/20 mins. **Map 2 C2**

**Freeworld**
*Nieuwendijk 30 (620 0902/e-mail visitor1@cafe.euronet.nl). Tram 1, 2, 5, 13, 17, 20.* **Open** 10am-midnight Mon-Thur, Sun; 10am-1am Fri, Sat. **Prices** ƒ2,50/20 mins. **Map 2 D2**
*Disabled access (café only).*

**Kalverstudio**
*Singel 459 (620 2970/e-mail sala@euronet.nl). Tram 4, 9, 14, 16, 20, 24, 25.* **Open** noon-6pm Tue-Sat. **Prices** ƒ2,50/20 mins. **Map 4 D4**

**KPN Internet Centre**
*Weteringschans 165 (484 6196). Tram 6, 7, 10.* **Open** 9am-9pm Tue-Fri; noon-5.30pm Mon; 9am-5pm Sat. **Price** ƒ2,50/25 mins. **Map 6 E5**
Commercial Internet centre, with information on KPN's ISP (Hetnet) and ten IBM computers. *See box* **Caught in the Net**, *page 197*.

# Music: Classical & Opera

**How to tell your arse from your oboe.**

In an age when governments around the world are slashing arts funding in a frighteningly casual way, it's always a thrill when one finds a city in which the arts are not only fighting back, but holding their own. Amsterdam is such a city: the local arts scene is on the up-and-up; serious theatre is getting back on track again, despite competition from trashy musicals and the like; and classical music is most definitely alive and well, following the financial flux of the '80s.

Anyone with a half-decent classical music CD collection probably has at least one disc by the **Royal Concertgebouw Orchestra**. The famed ensemble – based at the **Concertgebouw**, naturally enough – has gone from strength to strength in recent years under Riccardo Chailly's direction. It's not all Chailly, though: despite the fact that the international conducting circuit is starting to get out of hand – how many guest appearances from 'star' conductors do audiences really need? – a roster of visiting baton-wielders that includes Michael Tilson Thomas, Bernard Haitink and Nikolaus Harnoncourt cannot fail to catch the eye.

Across town at the Beurs van Berlage, the **Netherlands Philharmonic**, directed by Hartmut Haenchen, plays a symphonic series alongside its regular productions at the **Netherlands Opera**, and is normally good value for a night out. The other major ensembles shouldn't be forgotten, either: the **Rotterdam Philharmonic Orchestra** has been taking great steps since the arrival of Valery Gergiev as chief conductor, while the **Radio Philharmonic Orchestra**, based in Hilversum but a regular visitor to Amsterdam, continues to work at the highest levels under the skilled baton of the internationally acclaimed Edo de Waart.

Almost everyone in Amsterdam has finally started to forget about the ruckus over the construction of the 'Stopera' building, which opened in 1985 and is now home to the **Netherlands Opera**. Good thing, too, for the company is presently on something of a roll under the artistic direction of Pierre Audi. Still, those after an evening of undemanding, frilly entertainment should pick their evening carefully, as the highly regarded Audi is currently trawling through Wagner's impossibly dense 'Ring' cycle.

## ENSEMBLES

Although it would be exaggerating to say that all small ensembles in Amsterdam fall into one of two camps, it's undeniable that two types of music stand out above all others in this city of extremes. On the one hand, there's the old school. Dutch musicians were the founders of authentic performance practice – performances using authentic period instruments – and the innovation has now almost become a tradition. Ton Koopman still holds the torch as harpsichordist and 'director who doesn't conduct' of the Amsterdam Baroque Orchestra, founded in 1979, while Marc Minkovski is still in charge of the Amsterdam Bach Soloists, formed by members of the Concertgebouw Orchestra. Recorder-player and director Frans Brüggen extends authentic practice into the classical era with his Orchestra of the Eighteenth Century, whose daring tempi, brilliant strings and valveless natural horns make for exciting performances. Look out for concerts organised by **Organisatie Oude Muziek** – literally, the 'Organisation for Old Music' – whose early music events at the Waalse are normally excellent.

On the flipside, there is a burgeoning modern music scene in Amsterdam. Holland's most important post-war composer Louis Andriessen still lives in the city, and his work is occasionally performed before mildly reverential audiences at the excellent **IJsbreker**, Amsterdam's nominal centre for new music. There are, in fact, around 20 new music ensembles based in the city: the Asko and Schönberg ensembles, in particular, are worth investigating, the latter often being directed by noted muso Oliver Knussen. Both the Nieuw Music Ensemble and the Nieuw Sinfonietta also make noises worth listening to, as do minimalist eccentrics Orkest de Volharding. Contemporary music fans should also keep an ear open for the Proms concerts. Kind of a low-down and dirty version of the British proms, it's a series of contemporary concerts held, oddly, in the grimy confines of the **Paradiso** (*see chapter* **Music: Rock, Roots & Jazz**, *page 208*).

# Tickets & information

Ticket prices in Amsterdam are reasonable compared with other European cities. However, this bonus is tapered by the fact that tickets for many of the larger venues are sold on a subscription system, and even though some concerts are announced up to a year ahead, it can be difficult to get tickets on an ad hoc basis if you're just in town for a few days. For the big concerts and operas, try to book as far in advance as you can, but if you're just passing through, it's always worth phoning up for returns.

For full listings information, pick up a copy of the free Dutch listings paper *Uitkrant*, published by the **AUB Ticketshop** (621 1211; *see chapter* **Directory**, *page 252*), which accepts all major credit cards, or call in at the VVV, which generally has information on upcoming concerts. Discounts on tickets are often available for students, over-65s and CJP card-holders.

## Concert halls

Where a telephone number is given in the listings below, tickets will be available from the venue's box office. Tickets are also available from the AUB Ticketshop (*see above*).

### Beurs van Berlage: AGA Zaal & Yakult Zaal

*Damrak 213 (627 0466). Tram 4, 9, 14, 16, 20, 24, 25.* **Open** *box office* 12.30-6pm Tue-Fri; 12.30-5pm Sat; also from 75 mins before performance for ticket sales and collection; closed June-mid-Aug. **Tickets** *f*15-*f*35; concessions with CJP card. **Map 2 D2**
This former stock exchange is now a cultural centre, housing a large exhibition hall, two concert halls, one of Holland's dedicated classical radio stations, the **Concertzender**, and the offices of the resident orchestras: the **Netherlands Philharmonic** and the **Netherlands Chamber Orchestra**. Entered from the Damrak, the medium-sized Yakult Zaal offers comfortable seating, a massive stage, and controllable but not ideal acoustics. The 200-seat AGA Zaal is an odd-looking free-standing glass box within the walls of a side room, which is sometimes referred to as the 'diamond in space'. *See chapters* **Architecture**, *p36, and* **Sightseeing**, *p42.*
*Disabled access & toilets.*

### Concertgebouw

*Concertgebouwplein 2-6 (reservations 671 8345 10am-5pm daily/24-hour information in Dutch 675 4411). Tram 2, 3, 5, 12, 16, 20.* **Open** *box office* 10am-7pm daily. **Tickets** *f*10-*f*250. **Credit** AmEx, DC, MC, V. **Map 5 D6**
The Concertgebouw is the favourite venue of many of the world's top soloists and orchestras, including its own **Concertgebouw Orchestra** (which, aside from its regular programme, plays a lovely Christmas matinée concert here every 25 December). The acoustics of the **Grote Zaal** (Great Hall) are second to none and a seat anywhere in the house offers great sound. The **Kleine Zaal** (Recital Hall) is less comfortable, but features top-class chamber groups and soloists, including the resident Borodin Quartet. Visiting stars push prices up, but for 75 per cent of the remaining concerts, tickets cost less than *f*30. The matinées on Saturdays at 3pm are renowned for concert performances of opera, and

the Sunday morning concert is a bargain at *f*20, or *f*10 for concessions (including half-price entry to the Rijksmuseum and Stedelijk Museum on the same day). Throughout July and August, tickets for the Robeco Summer Concerts – featuring high-profile artists and orchestras – are cheaper than usual: at *f*25, or *f*15 for concessions, they represent an excellent bargain.
*Disabled access & toilets.*

### IJsbreker

*Weesperzijde 23 (box office 693 9093/administration 668 1805). Tram 3, 6, 7, 10/Metro Weesperplein.* **Open** *box office* 9.30am-5.30pm Mon-Fri; also from 45 mins before start of performance weekends and evenings; *café* 10am-1am Mon-Thur, Sun; 10am-2am Fri, Sat. **Tickets** *f*12,50-*f*30; *f*12,50-*f*25 students. **Credit** EC, MC, V. **Map 7 G4**
An excellent contemporary music centre that has cemented its reputation as one of Europe's most innovative venues. Aside from its regular programme of ensembles and concerts, many of which feature obscure and avant-garde Dutch works and musicians, the venue co-produces several new music concerts with both the Holland Festival (*see chapter* **Amsterdam by Season**, *p10*) and the VARA-Matinée. The programme of free lunchtime concerts (*see below* **Lunchtime menus**) is also a great innovation: until recently, they were staged on Fridays, but at the time of going to press the IJsbreker was considering moving them to another day. Innovative electro-acoustic concerts take place in the space of the **Artis Planetarium** dome (*see chapter* **Museums**, *p83*), while the venue also programmes other concerts in both the **RoXY** and the **Melkweg** (for details of both, *see chapter* **Clubs**, *pp175-6*). The IJsbreker's café boasts some of the best outdoor terraces in town, with a fantastic view of the Amstel; it's open all day, every day, and after the concerts.
*Disabled access with assistance.*

*Chill out in the* **IJsbreker** *café.*

# Opera

### Koninklijk Theater Carré
*Amstel 115-125 (622 5225). Tram 4, 6, 7, 10, 20.* **Open**
*box office* 10am-7pm Mon-Sat; 1-7pm Sun. **Tickets** ƒ25-
ƒ100. **Credit** AmEx, DC, EC, MC, V. **Map 6 F4**
This former circus theatre hosts large-scale musicals such
as *Cats* and *La Cage aux Folles*, alongside reputable opera
and ballet companies on tour from the former Eastern bloc,
which perform popular classics.
*Disabled access & toilets.*

### Opera Muziektheater (Stopera)
*Waterlooplein 22 (625 5455). Tram 9, 14, 20/Metro
Waterlooplein.* **Open** *box office* 10am-6pm Mon-Sat;
11.30am-6pm Sun, or until start of performance. **Tickets**
ƒ25-ƒ110. **Credit** AmEx, DC, EC, MC, V. **Map 3 E3**
The modern Muziektheater is home to the **Nationale Ballet**
and the **Netherlands Ballet Orchestra** (*see chapter*
**Dance**, *p180*) as well as the **Netherlands Opera**, and visiting guest productions. The emphasis is on high-quality
opera and dance productions at reasonable prices. The big
staircases make an impressive sweep around the auditorium, which has floor-to-ceiling glass and marble-faced pillars,
giving a wonderful view of the Amstel. The stage's spa-
ciousness invites particularly ambitious ideas from world-
famous stage directors such as Willy Decker (*Wozzeck* and
*Werther*), Harry Kupfer (*Die Frau ohne Schatten*) and Peter
Sellars (*Pelléas et Mélisande*). Free lunchtime concerts are
held between September and May in the Boekman Zaal (*see
below* **Lunchtime menus**), with tours of the building given
on Wednesdays and Saturdays at 4pm during the same period, costing ƒ8,50. If you book in advance, the guide will come
prepared with English translations.
*Disabled access & toilets.*

### Stadsschouwburg
*Leidseplein 26 (624 2311). Tram 1, 2, 5, 6, 7, 10, 20.*
**Open** *box office* 10am-start of performance Mon-Sat; also
from 90 mins before performance Sun, public holidays.
**Tickets** ƒ15-ƒ45. **Credit** AmEx, EC. **Map 5 C5**
Because its productions are designed for portability, and
hence rarely get the chance to become established for any
length of time, the **Nationale Reisopera** (National
Travelling Opera) receives less attention than it deserves.
The Reisopera usually stages two or three performances of
each production in the red velvet surroundings of this municipal theatre, which also occasionally hosts other opera performances by visiting companies, often from abroad.
*Disabled access & toilets.*

# Churches

Many musicians in Amsterdam take advantage of
the monumental churches around the city. The
bonus for concertgoers is obvious: aside from hearing largely excellent music, you get a chance to see
the interiors of these wonderful buildings at the
same time. During the summer, the city's many
bell-towers resonate to the intricate tinkling of
their carillons: thumping the 'keyboard' mecha-
nism triggers a whole array of smaller bells into
surprisingly rapid renderings of tunes. But churches are not just for organ and carillon recitals. The

*The **Concertgebouw**, a pillar of the city's
classical music scene. See page 201.*

recently refurbished Amstelkerk and Lutherse
Kerk, and the intimate Bethanienklooster are also
used for concerts. Most churches have no box
office, but tickets and information are available
from the AUB Ticketshop (*see above* **Tickets &
information**).

### Engelse Kerk
*Begijnhof 48 (624 9665). Tram 1, 2, 4, 5, 9, 14, 16, 20,
24, 25.* **Map 5 D4**
Nestled in an idyllic courtyard, the Academy of the
**Begijnhof** (*see chapter* **Sightseeing**, *p50*) arranges weekly concerts of baroque and classical music at its English
Reformed Church, with particular emphasis on the use of
authentic period instruments in performances. The series of
free lunchtime concerts in July and August features
young players and new ensembles. The acoustics are vibrant
and clear.
*Disabled access.*

### Nieuwe Kerk
*Dam (information from Nieuwe Kerk Foundation 626
8168). Tram 1, 2, 5, 9, 13, 14, 16, 17, 20, 24, 25.*
**Open** 10am-5pm daily. **Tickets** ƒ12,50; ƒ10 students.
**Performances** 8pm. **Map 2 C3**
The Nieuwe Kerk has a magnificent sixteenth-century organ
and hosts organ concerts by top Dutch and international
players. Gustav Leonhardt, grandfather of baroque performance practice, is the resident organist. There's no regular
programme, but it's a popular venue for organ series. *See
chapters* **Architecture**, *p33*, and **Sightseeing**, *p42*.
*Disabled access.*

### Oude Kerk
*Oudekerksplein 23 (625 8284). Tram 4, 9, 14, 16, 20,
24, 25.* **Open** *15 Apr-15 Sept* 11am-5pm Mon-Sat; *16
Sept-14 Apr* 1-5pm Mon-Sat. **Tickets** ƒ7,50-ƒ15; ƒ5-
ƒ12,50 students. **Performances** June-Aug; carillon
concerts 4pm Sat. **Map 2 D2**
Jan Sweelinck, the Netherlands' most famous seventeenth-
century composer, was organist here. Concerts today include
organ and carillon recitals, choral and chamber music. The
Oude Kerk organises a summer 'wandering' concert series
(three pieces in three venues, with promenades and coffee
breaks) together with the Amstelkring Museum. *See chapter* **Sightseeing**, *p49*.
*Disabled access with assistance.*

### Waalse Kerk
*Oudezijds Achterburgwal 157 (information from
Organisatie Oude Muziek 030 236 2236). Tram 4, 9, 16,
20, 24, 25.* **Tickets** ƒ22,50; ƒ18,50 concessions.
**Map 2 D3**
Small, elegant and intimate, this was once the Huguenot
church for Amsterdam. Concerts here are now organised by
the Organisatie Oude Muziek, a group devoted to early music
played on period instruments that arranges upwards of 100
concerts in the country each year. Musicians from both the
Netherlands and abroad play here on a relatively regular basis.

# Out of town

### Anton Philipszaal, Den Haag
### (The Hague)
*Spuiplein 150 (box office 070 360 9810/information 070
360 7927). NS rail to Den Haag.* **Open** *box office* 10am-
6pm; also from 75 mins before performance. **Tickets**
ƒ30-ƒ80; concessions with CJP card, over-65s. **Credit**
AmEx, DC, EC, MC, V.
Home of The Hague's Residentie Orchestra since 1987, the
Anton Philipszaal is situated amid the modern architecture

of the city centre. Inside, it's a soundly designed hall with excellent acoustics.
*Disabled access & toilets.*

### De Doelen, Rotterdam
*Kruisstraat 2 (010 217 1717). NS rail to Rotterdam Centraal Station.* **Open** *box office* 10am-6pm Mon-Thur, Sat, Sun; 10am-9pm Fri. **Tickets** *ƒ20-ƒ150*; concessions for students. **Credit** AmEx, DC, EC, MC, V.
The Doelen, which is home to the **Rotterdam Philharmonic Orchestra** (RPO), contains both a large and small concert hall. The acoustics of the large hall are one of the reasons why the Rotterdam Philharmonic sounds so wonderful on tour: it has to work hard for a warm, expressive sound at home. The Doelen hosts about two dozen series a year, ranging from contemporary orchestral work to jazz and just about everything in between, including the RPO's own season. There are also plenty of concerts featuring visiting and guest orchestras from home and abroad.
*Disabled access & toilets.*

### Vredenburg Music Centre, Utrecht
*Vredenburgpassage 77 (box office 030 231 4544; 24-hour information 030 231 3144). NS rail to Utrecht.* **Open** *box office* noon-7pm Mon; 10am-7pm Tue-Sat; also from 45 minutes before performance. **Tickets** *ƒ25-ƒ55*. **Credit** AmEx, DC, EC, MC, V.
Worth the half-hour train ride from Amsterdam, as many performers make their only Dutch appearances here. Despite the horribly ugly setting – by a shopping mall, oddly – the Vredenburg attracts plenty of orchestras, with the Radio-Philharmonisch playing more than its fair share of concerts every year. Vredenburg remains 100 per cent government subsidised, which means that the ticket prices are cheaper that in Amsterdam. There are also occasional pop concerts held here, which tend to sell out very quickly.
*Disabled access & toilets.*

## Lunchtime menus

Many of Amsterdam's lunchtime concerts are free and run throughout the standard September to June season. Most venues have a weekly concert: among the best are the **Boekmanzaal** at the **Muziektheater** (*see above* **Opera**), which has a recital each Tuesday at 12.30pm. Most famous of all is the lunchtime concert at the **Concertgebouw** on Wednesdays at 12.30pm, with up-and-coming ensembles or soloists and even previews of evening concerts by visiting world-famous orchestras. Get there early to fight your way in. The **IJsbreker**'s programme of lunchtime concerts – held at 12.30pm every Friday, though there are plans to move them to another day – normally consists of intriguing and unknown works. In addition, the **Stedelijk Museum** (*see chapter* **Museums**, *page 77*) stages occasional concerts, often of innovative contemporary music, on Thursday and Saturday afternoons at 3pm. The **VVV** (*see chapter* **Directory**, *page 252*) have information regarding forthcoming concerts.

## Festivals & events

Further details on the events listed below can be obtained from the AUB Uitburo and the VVV. Two other festivals which feature a whole range

of arts including classical music are the **Holland Festival** and the **Uitmarkt** (for both, *see chapter* **Amsterdam by Season**, *page 10*).

### International Gaudeamus Music Week
*Postal and telephone enquiries Stichting Gaudeamus, Swammerdamstraat 38, 1091 RV Amsterdam (694 7349/fax 694 7258).* **Dates** first or second week in Sept. **Tickets** *ƒ15*.
An annual competition for young composers organised by the Centre for Contemporary Music, which includes a whole week of intense discussion of the state of the art plus performances of selected entries and works by already established composers. Also of interest is the International Gaudeamus Interpreter's Competition (14-24 October 1999, in **De Doelen, Rotterdam**; *see above*), a similar competition for performers of contemporary repertoire. Contemporary music devotees should not miss either; classicists, on the other hand, would do well to plug their ears and run as fast as their legs can carry them.

### Prinsengracht Classical Concert
*opposite Pulitzer Hotel, Prinsengracht 315-331 (523 5235).* **Date** third week of Aug. **Map 2 C3**
For one evening in August, musicians play a classical concert from a floating pontoon in front of the Pulitzer Hotel. Get there early for a good view. It's free, but is liable to be cancelled if it rains; always phone to check.

### Utrecht Early Music Festival
*Various venues in Utrecht; information from Stichting Oude Muziek, Postbus 734, 3500 AS Utrecht (030 236 2236).* **Dates** last week Aug-first week Sept. **Admission** *ƒ15-ƒ35*.
Top baroque and classical artists and ensembles from around the world, performing in churches and concert halls throughout the city. Many ensembles use period instruments, which satisfies the trainspotters no end. There's normally something interesting going on, and the festival is rightfully a popular one.

## Other organisations

### Network for Non-Western Music
*Pauwstraat 13A, 3512 TG Utrecht (030 233 2876).*
Indonesian, Turkish, African and Middle Eastern culture is brought to the Netherlands courtesy of this organisation. It arranges tours by visiting musicians. Expect six or seven concerts a year.

### STEIM (Stichting for Electro-Instrumental Music)
*Achtergracht 91, 1017 WL Amsterdam (622 8690).*
Amsterdam's electronic music institution is a unique research team examining the interface between man and music. Prototype MIDI controllers (Michel Waisvisz's gloved 'Hands' have the biggest claim to fame), novel sensors and hard- and software packages to convert any manner of signals into MIDI data. The five annual Rumori concerts at the **Frascati** (*see chapter* **Theatre**, *p222*) and its own intimate concerts give technophobes an intriguing glimpse into the future.

### Taller Amsterdam
*Keizersgracht 607, 1017 DS Amsterdam (624 6734).*
Founded by two visual artists, Taller is a 'total-theatre co-operative' that stages music workshop productions. The results mostly resemble music theatre with a political edge, created by themselves or contemporary composers. It normally has one big production a year, which it performs around the country, though there will not be one in 1998. *See chapter* **Art Galleries**, *p73*.

# Music: Rock, Roots & Jazz

**The liberal, anything goes vibe that Amsterdam is famous for has long attracted jazz musicians and rock groups. Even today, bands still flock to the city in droves.**

Amsterdam has always been a mecca to rock'n'roll types, who regard the city – with its casual vibe when it comes to, well, just about everything – as the nearest thing to rock heaven you're likely to find on God's merry earth. Unfortunately, the wicked weed so beloved of musicians from Hendrix to Cypress Hill doesn't lend itself to the tightest of tight-ass sets: it's common here to witness a visiting rock band enjoying themselves rather more than the audience. But when it comes to the more 'out there' rock and groove-fuelled types of music, such as jazz and reggae, the city usually manages to live up to its reputation as the magical centre of the universe. Hippie hype aside, Amsterdam is indeed one of the best cities in which on the planet to experience live music. Visiting musicians – those that aren't wasted, that is – tend to work extra hard in this town to put on a special performance.

In the 1950s, Zeedijk was the groovy hepcat strip of the day. After making their bread at the Concertgebouw earlier in the evening, jazz legends such as Gerry Mulligan, Count Basie and Chet Baker would gather and jam at one of the many after-hours places around here. The most famous is the **Casablanca**, whose spiritual void has been filled by the **Bimhuis**, the best place to catch current jazz legends in intimate confines.

Multimedia centres the **Melkweg** and the **Paradiso** came into being in the heady and revolutionary '60s. Condoned by the city as an alternative hangout for the hippies who were overrunning Vondelpark at the time, both clubs have always received huge council subsidies, allowing them to rise above the clouds of weed smoke and chart every new trend ever since, from hippie and punk to techno and drum 'n' bass.

With some of the world's best bands clamouring to play here, the many local outfits gagging to be heard are often forgotten. And since the general demise of the squat scene (*see box* **Squat thrusts**, *page 28*), there aren't many places where they can play, and few bands ever get beyond the Dutch club circuit. This is perhaps understandable given that some acts sing in Dutch (the cheek of it!), as is the case with the intense Raggende Manne and the hip hop Osdorp Posse. Most Amsterdam-based bands, though, either remain instrumental or opt for the more universal tongue of English.

The international respect garnered in the past by the likes of Urban Dance Squad, Bettie Serveert and the Ex, and the appearance of many promising new bands such as Junkie XL, Johan, Caesar and Solex – who runs a record shop in the city – suggest that the ongoing renaissance in the homegrown music scene shows no sign of letting up. It's all a very long way from traditional Dutch musical culture, which can be witnessed in many brown cafés in the Jordaan night after night. Incidentally, it's even further away from the live music sessions in the city's myriad Irish bars: for details on **O'Donnell's**, **O'Reilly's** and **Mulligan's**, the latter of which has the best Irish music in the city, *see chapter* **Cafés & Bars**, *pages 122-34*.

For full listings of all musical genres, check out the **AUB** ticket office on Leidseplein (*see chapter* **Directory**, *page 252*), Theater & Concert Online (*www.theater.nl*), the freebie Dutch-language listings newspaper *Uitkrant*, or the national music magazine *Oor*. Details of the town's bigger gigs are posted weekly on the *Time Out* International Agenda website (*www.timeout.co.uk*).

## General venues

Aside from those venues listed below, keep an eye out for news of **PH31**, an ex-squat bar featuring hardcore and experimental music that should be opening during 1998 or 1999 on Prinseneiland.

### Akhnaton
*Nieuwezijds Kolk 25 (624 3396). Tram 1, 2, 5, 13, 17, 20.* **Open** 11pm-5am Fri, Sat. **Admission** ƒ10-ƒ15. **Map 2 D2**
Akhnaton is renowned for its world music, hosting regular African dance nights and salsa parties, as well as providing recording studios and rehearsal facilities. Not exactly on the palatial side, the club is often bursting at the seams, so prepare to make like a sardine.

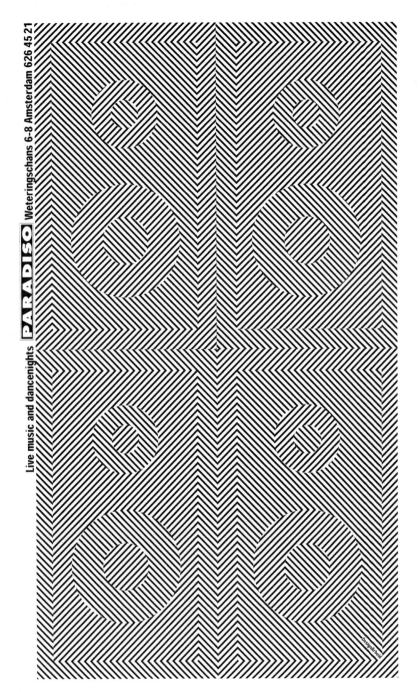

PARADISO Weteringschans 6-8 Amsterdam 626 45 21

Live music and dancenights

### AMP Studios
*KNSM-laan 13 (418 1111). Bus 28.* **Open** noon-1am daily. **Admission** free-ƒ15.
AMP Studios started out as a rehearsal space for bands, and now offers regular concerts and parties, an annual Battle of the Bands competition, full recording facilities (both analogue and MIDI), and a fully licensed café/bar. Their website is at *www.xs4all.nl/~ampmail*.

### Club Arena
*'s Gravesandestraat 51 (694 7444). Tram 3, 6, 7, 10, 14/Metro Weesperplein.* **Open** 11pm-4am Thur; 11pm-5am Fri, Sat. **Admission** ƒ10-ƒ15. **Map 7 G3**
The former Sleep-In hostel is now a sparkling new multimedia cultural centre (complete with a hostel, for which *see chapter* **Accommodation**, *p96*). Not to be confused with ArenA (*see below*), the much cosier Arena has an excellent alternative party venue in the old nuns' quarters high in the rafters, along with a small concert hall, which is currently relying solely on DJs. There are constant rumours that it may soon return to its glory days as a venue for up-and-coming local and international bands. Whether it does or not, the constant flux of a predominantly transient crowd means you're always guaranteed new faces.

### ArenA
*Bijlmermeer (311 1333). Metro Bijlmer.* **Open** times and dates vary. **Admission** ƒ40-60.
Amsterdam finally has its 50,000-seat mega-stadium for those mega-acts (U2, the Rolling Stones, Tina Turner, Michael Jackson et al) who occasionally deign to pass through town.

### De Buurvrouw
*Pieterpoortsteeg 9 (625 9654). Tram 4, 9, 14, 16, 20, 24, 25.* **Open** 8pm-3am Mon-Thur, Sun; 8pm-4am Fri, Sat. **Admission** free. **Map 2 D3**
Imaginative décor, frequent live performances from local rock bands and a particularly eclectic record collection make this pocket-sized watering hole stand out from the multitude of little bars that saturate the city. The place attracts a predominantly alternative rock clientele. *See chapter* **Cafés & Bars**, *p123*.

### Café IJburg
*Vrieshuis Amerika, Oostelijke Handelskade 25 (419 5209/2015). Bus 39.* **Open** 6pm-1am Wed-Sat. **Admission** free-ƒ10. **Map 3 F1**
Not content with being just a gallery and vegetarian restaurant, this bar – which is part of the squatted Vrieshuis Amerika (*see box* **Squat thrusts**, *p28*) – also plays host to quirky DJs during its dining hours. It occasionally has nights called 'Tegen' ('against'), featuring punk rock bands passing through town. When all's said and done, Café IJburg is an excellent alternative hangout – just a ten-minute walk from Centraal Station – that sadly may not be around much longer due to the council's assault on the squatting community. A sad sign of the times.

### Café Meander
*Voetboogstraat 5 (625 8430). Tram 1, 2, 5.* **Open** 8.30pm-3am Mon-Thur; 8.30pm-4am Fri-Sun. **Admission** ƒ5. **Map 5 D4**
This cosy bar in the heart of Amsterdam has found its niche by providing jazz dance, soul, funk, disco and trip hop for its enthusiastic crowds. The club is handily divided into three floors, which means there normally are three different vibes to choose from. Regular gigs by Saskia Laroo, New Cool Collective and DJ Graham B give the place a relaxed 'local' feeling. Monday and Tuesday are jazzy, Wednesday has a funky edge, Thursday is student night (complete with cheap beer), Friday and Saturday explore the funk in soul, and Sunday is salsa nights.
*Disabled access with assistance.*

### Caneçao Brazilian Bar
*Lange Leidsedwarsstraat 68-70 (638 0611). Tram 1, 2, 5.* **Open** 10pm-4am Mon-Thur, Sun; 10pm-5am Fri, Sat. **Admission** free. **Map 5 D5**
A buzzing bar that swings to the summery sounds of salsa and samba, transporting you from the city to far-off tropical beaches. The bar caters for a large South American and tourist clientele, and the drinks are a tad pricey but cheaper than a holiday. There's a live band every night at midnight.

### Cruise Inn
*Zeeburgerdijk 271-273 (692 7188). Tram 6, 10.* **Open** 9pm-3am Fri, Sat. **Admission** usually free.
James Dean clones twist the night away in this gloriously pink wooden club house: DJs and visiting bands often appear on Saturday nights. Brothel creepers abound, as do vintage clothes and quiffs and even more vintage motorbikes.

### Last Waterhole
*Oudezijds Armsteeg 12 (624 4814). Tram 4, 9, 16, 20, 24, 25/Metro Centraal Station.* **Open** noon-1am Mon-Thur, Sun; noon-3am Fri, Sat. **Admission** free. **Map 2 D2**
Hidden down a small side street in the heart of the Red Light District, this largish, well-known bar caters mainly for the Amsterdam chapter of the Hell's Angels. The many temporary residents of the adjoining youth hostel also venture in to play pool and listen to all sorts of native rockers getting up and jamming live, almost every night.

### Maloe Melo
*Lijnbaansgracht 163 (420 4592). Tram 7, 10, 13, 14, 17, 20.* **Open** 9pm-2am Mon-Thur, Sun; 9pm-3am Fri, Sat. **Admission** ƒ5. **Map 6 E5**
A cosy hangout for musicians and hangers-on escaping the chaotic revelry of the Korsakoff next door (*see box* **Squat thrusts**, *p28*). Wednesday, Friday and Saturday nights feature bands that explore the roots of rock and blues, while on other nights the stage plays host to blues jam sessions featuring shit-hot musicians, many of whom are of international stature and claim Melo's as their local when they're in town.

### Melkweg
*Lijnbaansgracht 234 (624 1777). Tram 1, 2, 5, 6, 7, 10, 20.* **Open** 7.30pm-late daily; *disco* 1-5am Fri, Sat. **Admission** ƒ7,50-ƒ27,50; includes admission to disco, theatre and cinema. **Membership** (compulsory) ƒ4,40/month; ƒ22,50/year. **Map 5 D5**
Once a dairy (the name means 'Milky Way'), the Melkweg opened in the late '60s as a hippie hangout, and over the years has evolved into a slickly run company. Completely remodelled in 1995 with the addition of the Pepsi-sponsored 'Max' hall – the opening of which coincided with the removal of its weed stall – the multimedia centre can now play host to a double helping of international acts of all imaginable genres, plus theatre, dance and film events. Thanks to the canny stepped design of the Max, this is now the only venue in town where people of normal height can see over the infamously lofty Netherlanders, and sound quality is extremely decent to boot. See its website – *www.melkweg.nl* – for more information, and *see chapters* **Art Galleries**, *p72*, **Clubs**, *p175*, **Film**, *p184*, and **Theatre**, *p222* for details on the Melkweg's other functions.

### OCCII
*Amstelveenseweg 134 (671 7778). Tram 2, 6.* **Open** 10pm-3am Fri, Sat; 9pm-2am Sun. **Admission** free-ƒ10.
A former squat venue, this cosy and friendly bar-cum-music hall makes you feel at home immediately and invites you to pull up a chair and take in some great local talent. Comfortably tucked away at the end of a delightful cycle ride through Vondelpark, it's a fine excuse to escape the hubbub of the city centre and catch an eclectic mix of quirky cabaret acts, flailing punk rock and world music.

## Paradiso

*Weteringschans 6-8 (623 7348). Tram 1, 2, 5, 6, 7, 10, 20.* **Open** 8.30pm-around 5am various days. **Admission** *f*10-*f*35. **Membership** (compulsory) *f*4,50/month. **Map 5 D5**

Like the Melkweg, the Paradiso has recently undergone an extensive refurbishment in an attempt to hide its hippie past. The weekly programme caters for a wide range of musical tastes, from local band nights to bigger names on tour: the Rolling Stones and the artist formerly known as Prince have both graced the 'Pop Temple' – as the Paradiso is also called – with their presence. The small upstairs podium and bar has lately undergone a renaissance as a venue for small, cultish bands. Its website is at *www.paradiso.nl*. *See chapters* **Clubs***, p176, and* **Music: Classical & Opera***, p208.*

## Tropeninstituut Kleine Zaal/Grote Zaal

*Linnaeusstraat 2/Mauritskade 63 (568 8500). Tram 9, 10, 14, 20.* **Open** *phone information & reservations* 10am-4pm Mon-Fri; *in person* noon-4pm Mon-Fri; *box office* from one hour before performance. **Admission** *f*15-*f*30. **Map 7 H3**

Two theatres attached to the Tropenmuseum, which exhibits artefacts from all over the world (*see chapter* **Museums***, p78*). The Tropeninstituut follows the same policy in its music programming, featuring international folk musicians in its formal, all-seater halls.

*Disabled access & toilets (Kleine Zaal only).*

## Vondelpark

*Vondelpark (673 1499). Tram 1, 2, 3, 5, 6, 7, 10, 12, 20.* **Open** dawn-dusk daily. **Map 5 C6**

Wander down to Vondelpark and spy on some of the more unusual examples of artistry and musicianship. And if the entertainment isn't entertaining enough, then just as much fun can normally be gleaned from staring at the mad people who frequent this popular green space. There is an organised agenda of entertainment for the permanent outdoor podium; flyers and posters are usually plastered over trees and gates in the park. Check the website for more details on the events in Vondelpark – *www.theater.nl/vondelpark/frame.html* – and *see chapters* **Amsterdam by Season***, p9, and* **Sightseeing***, p62-3.*

## Winston Kingdom

*Warmoesstraat 123-129 (625 1380). Tram 4, 9, 16, 20, 24, 25.* **Open** 8pm-3am Mon-Thur, Sun; 8pm-4am Fri, Sat. **Admission** free-*f*10. **Map 2 D3**

Part of the Winston Hotel (*see chapter* **Accommodation***, p99*), this bar attracts a mixture of residents, locals and wandering tourists. A wonderfully quirky booking policy means that on any given week one might luck upon a '70s disco party, a local band, a poetry reading and an underrated international legend (the late Townes van Zandt strummed one of his last concerts here).

# Jazz venues

Throughout the year, venues play host to big international stars, while local groups and jam sessions sneak into the early hours in snug bars on most nights of the week.

## Alto Jazz Café

*Korte Leidsedwarsstraat 115 (626 3249). Tram 1, 2, 5, 6, 7, 10, 20.* **Open** 9pm-3am Mon-Thur, Sun; 9pm-4am Fri, Sat. **Admission** free. **Map 5 D5**

A cosy and relaxed traditional brown bar in an otherwise commercialised tourist area just off Leidseplein. Live jazz and blues is played every night of the week by the in-house musicians and guests.

## Bamboo Bar

*Lange Leidsedwarsstraat 66 (624 3993). Tram 1, 2, 5, 6, 7, 10, 20.* **Open** 9pm-3am Mon-Thur, Sun; 9pm-4am Fri, Sat. **Admission** free. **Map 5 D5**

A small bar with a friendly crowd of regulars enjoying Brazilian and world music. Squeeze in for local blues and jazz every night except Sunday.

## Bimhuis

*Oudeschans 73-77 (623 1361/3373). Tram 9, 14, 20/Metro Waterlooplein.* **Open** *box office* 11am-1pm, 2-4pm Mon-Fri. **Admission** *f*15-*f*25. **Map 3 E2**

Opened in 1974, the city's major jazz venue stages a mixture of well-known international artists and avant-garde local talent in a subdued and reverent atmosphere. It's often hard to get a seat, so arrive early. There is a free (in terms of both cost and style) jazz workshop on Monday and Tuesday, while Thursday through Saturday has the gigs. Tickets are available on the day from the **AUB** or **VVV** tourist offices (*see chapter* **Directory***, p252*), or on the door one hour before performances. There's talk of Bimhuis moving to the eastern docklands in 2000, so keep an eye out for news.

## Bourbon Street

*Leidsekruisstraat 6-8 (623 3440). Tram 1, 2, 5, 6, 7, 10.* **Open** 10pm-4am Mon-Thur, Sun; 10pm-5am Fri, Sat. **Admission** *f*2,50 Mon-Thur; *f*5 Fri-Sun. **Map 5 D5**

A spacious bar with a podium for jazz most nights of the week and a very late licence. The friendly staff and customers will make you feel right at home. Performances can border on the poetic.

## Casablanca

*Zeedijk 26 (625 5685). Tram 4, 9, 16, 20, 24, 25.* **Open** 8pm-1am Mon-Thur, Sun; 10pm-3am Fri, Sat. **Admission** free-*f*10. **Map 2 D2**

This formerly legendary home to jamming junkie jazz musicians has sadly lost its edge: it now has karaoke from 10pm until closing from Thursday to Saturday. However, it still has something going for it: Sunday to Wednesdays night are dedicated to live jazz, from big band to trio. Candy's hip dad Hans Dulfer leads a jam session every first Tuesday of the month between 9pm and 1am.

## IJsbreker

*Weesperzijde 23 (668 1805). Tram 3, 6, 7, 10/Metro Weesperplein.* **Open** *box office* 9.30am-5.30pm Mon-Fri, from 45 mins before performance; *café* 10am-1am Mon-Thur, Sun; 10am-2am Fri, Sat. **Admission** *f*12,30-*f*30.

Situated on the picturesque banks of the Amstel, this venue is especially pleasant on summer evenings. The programming – details of which can be found at *www.ysbreker.nl* – concentrates on contemporary classical music and experimental jazz. It's worth a visit for the bar alone, even when there's no live performance. *See chapter* **Music: Classical & Opera***, p201.*

*Disabled access with assistance.*

# Festivals

Maybe it's the flat terrain. Maybe it's the Netherlands' festival-friendly narcotics legislation. It certainly ain't the weather. Whatever the reasons, Holland is host to a myriad of music festivals, held throughout the year and catering for all tastes. Tickets for most festivals are available from

Hang with the Hell's Angels at the **Last Waterhole**. See page 207.

# Tales of the city
## Rock'n'roll Babylon

The long-clichéd unholy trinity of sex, drugs and rock'n'roll may not define Amsterdam as well as it used to, but the city's cobblestoned streets still reverberate with tales of quality excess. Its past as a port meant that the city was used to lusty excess well before rock'n'roll came along. And by the eighteenth century, the rich and famous had joined in: even Peter the Great was said to have trashed a hotel room on Herengracht. (OK, so it was a house, but who's counting?)

However, it was 150 years before Amsterdam gained worldwide infamy as a haven for the Great Junkies of Jazz. Perhaps the most famous of 'em all is the tragic Chet Baker, who, on 13 May 1988, toppled from a balcony in the Prins Hendrik Hotel on to a bollard below, never to blow his horn again. But you have to look to the **Melkweg** and the **Paradiso** (*see pages 207-08*) for the juiciest tales of extra-curricular frolics. Before the advent of coffeeshops, these two venues were among the first places where drugs were openly sold. One oft-told tale relates of when the Hog Farm – an American commune – and the caterers at Woodstock – came to the Paradiso. The audience, reduced to a strobing and affectionate mass of drool following the starter, an LSD-spiked soup, were then treated to the sight of a woman in a pudding-filled plastic suit porcupined with straws. This was, back then, an average night out in Amsterdam. However, all the big clubs cleaned up their acts long ago, and their heady beginnings have slipped into history as standards of hippie misbehaviour and decadence.

As the hippies burnt out, punk rock bloomed. Skins and Punks did battle. Hell's Angels forced an apology out of Iggy Pop for calling the audience 'sissies'. The late D Boon of the Minutemen used his ample mass to put the fear into heckling skinheads with a stage-dive. The Thompson Twins were booed off stage. Well, some things never change. It's just a matter of befriending an employee of the Melkweg or the Paradiso to hear an infinity of similar mythologised facts.

With the rise of E culture, the city has lost some of that much-sentimentalised radical edge that once inspired explosions of absurdity during live performances. Perhaps the audiences have become less rock'n'roll. Perhaps they've seen it all before. Even so, musicians around the world still think of Amsterdam – Absurdam – as the best place to indulge their dreams of rock'n'roll excess. And even if you're not up for the weed, the city still provides ample opportunities to witness your favourite artists at their most damaged.

*Has the **Melkweg** lost its cutting edge? This kid seems to think so.*

**VVV** offices and the **AUB** (for both, *see chapter* **Directory**, *p252*).

## Amsterdam Pop Prijs/Wanted R&B & Hip Hop Prijs Finals

*(information 420 8160)*. **Date** May-June, Sept. **Admission** *Pop Prijs f15; Wanted f20*.
Local music talent (pop, R&B and hip hop) can be watched – and heard – around town during these events. The Pop Prijs competition is held in May and June, and the Wanted R&B/Hip Hop competition in June. The finals of Pop Prijs are held at the Melkweg on the fourth Saturday of June, while those of you wanting to see the finals of Wanted R&B & Hip Hop will have to hang on until September, when it's featured as part of the Bassline night at the Paradiso.

## Amsterdam Roots Festival

*(information/tickets 621 1211/624 1777)*. **Date** June. **Admission** free- *f60*.
A new festival, initiated by the Melkweg, Tropeninstituut, Concertgebouw and Holland Festival. Different venues will feature some of the greatest 'world music' acts on the planet, while a 'world village' in Oosterpark, with a collection of different podiums, will host a selection of lesser-known names.

## Blues Festival

*Meervaart, Meerenvaart 300 (610 7498). Tram 1, 17/bus 19, 23, 64, 68*. **Admission** phone for details.
The Meervaart's blues festival is gradually growing in status, staging a mix of young names and cult legends. Although it has previously taken place in March, the date may change when the venue reopens following renovation work, due to finish in September 1999.

## A Camping Flight to Lowlands

*(information 015 284 0740/tickets 0900 300 1250; also at post offices). NS rail to Lelystad*. **Admission** *three-day pass f150*. **Date** last weekend of August.
The 'alternative' festival of the year – basically a Dutch Glastonbury – where tens of thousands descend to many metres below sea level on the polder (reclaimed land) of Walibi Park, Flevoland, for three days to camp and groove to the hippest bands and DJs. The price includes camping, and a bus to the site from Lelystad train station: for full details on the Dutch rail system, *see chapter* **Beyond Amsterdam**, *pp224-5*.

## Drum Rhythm Festival

*Westergasfabriek, Haarlemmerweg (information 015 215 7756). Tram 3, 10/bus 18, 22*. **Date** mid-May. **Admission** *day f55; two days f100*. **Map 1 A1**
This annual festival of rhythm and roots takes place on four different stages in the Westergasfabriek (*see chapter* **Theatre**, *p222*). It often features well known bands and artists in its proudly eclectic line-ups: one year, for example, it managed to slot George Clinton, Lee 'Scratch' Perry and Youssou N'Dour together on the same bill.

## Dynamo Open Air Festival

*Kunstijsbaan, Eindhoven (information 040 211 7878). NS rail to Eindhoven, then shuttle bus to festival*. **Date** end May or mid-Jun. **Tickets** around *f100*.
Undoubtedly the loudest three days in a field you're ever likely to experience. With a turnout of roughly nine billion stage-diving, skateboarding adolescent devotees of MTV culture, the Dynamo Open Air Festival may give visitors the distinct impression that the Dutch language contains at least 50 per cent American slang. Two tips: don't wear anything smart (you'll stand out like a pork chop in a kosher shop), and if you tend to rely on the use of all major limbs, it's probably not wise to head for the area directly in front of centre stage when Machine Head are due on. The venue may change in future years: phone for details.

## Halfway Amsterdam

**Date** early to mid-June. **Tickets** around *f60*.
A great day out to get you in full festival swing, this event takes place halfway between Amsterdam and Haarlem (hence the name), at the Spaarnwoude recreation ground. Local talent such as Bettie Serveert and De Dijk groove along with the likes of Sheryl Crow, Galliano and Paul Weller. Organisers have resisted strong public pressure to rename the festival 'Mudbath Amsterdam'.

## North Sea Jazz Festival

*Netherlands Congress Centre, Churchillplein 10, Den Haag (The Hague) (information 015 215 7756/tickets 010 591 9000/ England 0171 439 0747). NS rail to Den Haag Centraal Station, then tram 7, 8 or bus 4, 14; NS rail to Den Haag HS, then tram 8*. **Date** second weekend of July. **Admission** *in advance f95; on the door f100; three-day pass f255; whole festival f495*.
This three-day mega-event in The Hague, reputedly the biggest jazz festival in the world, is a fantastic opportunity to see a hatful of bona fide jazz legends: up to a thousand artists perform each year and hoping to land one of the special awards. The three-day pass covers the main hall, where the big names – from the instrumental twiddlings of Oscar Peterson and Lionel Hampton to the triumphant croonings of Tony Bennett and James Brown – take curtain call after curtain call for educated audiences. The pass for the entire festival covers the whole shebang: shows by the big names, plus the entry to all the smaller halls and fringe stuff. *Disabled access*.

## Parkpop

*Zuiderpark, Den Haag (0900 340 3505 [VVV]). NS rail to Den Haag Centraal Station*. **Date** late June. **Admission** free.
The biggest of the numerous free, one-day festivals held each year in Holland, Parkpop is one of the few festivals that caters for both Dutch and international music in equal amounts. The crowd is very mixed, due largely to the fact that the festival is basically a family day out: the music is just thrown in for good measure. The eclectic programming reflects this, and often comes up with bills you're unlikely to find anywhere else: Buju Banton, Robbie Williams and the Hellacopters all played in 1998. Its website, offering information on line-ups and the like, is at *www.parkpop.nl*.

## Pink Pop

*Landgraaf (046 475 2500). NS to Landgraaf, then shuttle bus to festival*. **Date** late May/early June. **Tickets** *one day around f75; three days around f120*.
Held near Landgraaf, a small village in the south of Holland, this increasingly popular three-day outdoor festival usually has an impressive line-up of famous Dutch and international pop stars. Expect to find a diverse mixture of artists: Garbage, Roni Size, Teenage Fanclub, Bad Religion, Ozric Tentacles, the Verve and Spiritualized all played in 1998.

## Sonic Acts

*Paradiso, Weteringschans 6-8 (623 7348). Tram 1, 2, 5, 6, 7, 10*. **Date** end Aug. **Admission** *f17,50*. **Map 5 D5**
The Paradiso (*see above* **General venues**) hosts this three- or four-day festival for new electronic music, which in the past has featured Stockhausen, Scanner, David Toop and Zoviet France as guests. Workshops and an Image and Sound lab for remixing completes the cutting-edge ambience.

## Tracks and Traces

*Paradiso, Weteringschans 6-8 (626 4521) Tram 1, 2, 5, 6, 7, 10*. **Date** start Mar. **Admission** *f17.50*.
Another cutting-edge festival organised by the Paradiso (*see above* **General venues**), this time dedicated to 'unusual music', an open term that may include unique DJs (à la David Shea), postrockers (such as Rex or Kriedler) or any other inspired mutants from the world of music.

# Sport & Fitness

*Excellent facilities mean there's no excuse to slack in Amsterdam.*

When it comes to sport, the Dutch are a contradiction. Despite the surfeit of leisure facilities in the country, they are, apparently, a nation of couch potatoes. And while the Dutch passion for football is well known, they're also obsessed with the skate and the cycle. Still, the popularity of the latter two sports is largely landscape-driven: the flat Dutch terrain is ideal for cycling, while the abundance of water and cold winters has meant that skating has become embedded in the national consciousness.

Below we list the main spectator sports, and the best and most popular leisure and fitness facilities in Amsterdam. For further information on what's available, call the city's **Sport and Recreation Department** on 552 2490, or look in the relevant sections of the *Amsterdam Yellow Pages*. To get an overview of sports past and present in Holland, take a trip to the **Nederlands Sport Museum** in Lelystad (Museumweg 10; 0320 261010; open 10am-5pm Tue-Fri, noon-5pm Sat, Sun; admission ƒ7,50, ƒ5 with Museum Card, under-12s). Aside from all the usual exhibits, it holds comprehensive archives of books, cuttings and photos, open by appointment.

## Spectator sports

### American football

American football has been played in the Netherlands for some time. The Admirals are the city's pro team, while the Amsterdam Crusaders represent the city in the amateur league, and can be reached on 617 7450. The season runs from March to June. Full details of American football in the Netherlands can be gleaned from the governing body, the NAAF, on 0299 414123.

**Amsterdam Admirals**
*Amsterdam ArenA, Arena Boulevard 29 (465 4545).
Metro Strandvliet/Metro & NS Bijlmer.* **Admission** ƒ25-ƒ60. **Matches** 7pm Sat. **Credit** AmEx, EC, MC, V.
Members of the NFL Europe League that was launched in 1995, the Admirals regularly draw crowds of 15,000.
*Disabled access.*

### Baseball

There are around a dozen baseball (*honkbal*) and softball clubs in and around Amsterdam operating at all levels. The season runs from April to October. For details, contact the regional KNBSB on 023 539 0244.

## Cricket

Cricket is now taken seriously in the Netherlands: there are now some 100 clubs affiliated to the Royal Dutch Cricket Board (KNCB), and in recent years the national side, rated just below the test match countries, has enjoyed notable victories over English, Australian and South African sides. Although the Dutch didn't qualify for the 1999 World Cup, there will be a World Cup match here when South Africa play Kenya on 26 May 1999 at the VRA's ground in Amstelveen.

There are several clubs in Amsterdam, the best of which are the VRA: they can be reached on 645 9816. Most Dutch clubs have junior, veteran and women's teams as well as their main sides, and welcome new players. Interested parties should contact the KNCB, based at the VRA (645 1705/fax 645 1715; open 10am-1pm Mon-Thur).

## Cycling

The Netherlands is a cycling nation, and produces many pro cyclists, both sprinters and, in particular, climbers: the Dutch still talk with awe and affection about Joop Zoetemelk who, after finishing second six times, finally won the Tour in 1985.

There's plenty to watch, too: Dutch cycling fans turn out for stage, *criterium* (road circuit) and one-day road races, plus track, field, cyclo-cross and ATB/mountain biking. The biggest Dutch races are the Amstel Gold Race around Limburg in late April; the RAI Derny Race, held at the RAI in Amsterdam in mid-May; the popular Acht van Chaam, a 100-kilometre *criterium* held in Noord Brabant on the first Wednesday after the Tour de France (late July or early August); and the Tour de Nederland, a five-day race – it passes through Amsterdam – held in late August. For details on all types of cycle racing, contact the KNWU (Dutch Cycle Racing Association) at Postbus 136, 3440 RC Woerden (0348 484084/fax 0348 411437), or the Amsterdam rep, Bert de Bruin, on 496 3621.

If you have a racing bike and are looking for competition, head for Sportpark Sloten. Two cycle clubs are based here – ASC Olympia (617 7510/secretary 617 3057), the oldest cycling club in Europe, and WV Amsterdam (secretary 619 3314) – and there is a 2.5-kilometre (1.5-mile) circuit round the park. The 200-metre track has also recently been rebuilt as a hyper-modern velodrome. If it's information on recreational cycling you're after, contact the ENFB, a national cyclists' group: the Amsterdam branch can be reached on 685 4794.

## Darts

Darts? Just a pub game, right? Well, no, at least not in Holland. After Amsterdam's own Raymond 'Barny' van Barneveld won the world title in 1998, there has been a surge of interest in the sport. The Dutch Darts Federation (NDF) looks after the sport nationally, but much of the organisation is done by regional affiliates: 150 cafés in Amsterdam boast 180 teams and 1,300 members affiliated to DORA (662 0247), which organises leagues from September to May, and smaller summer games. The ADB (682 1970) is smaller, but still has 400 members who play in cafés in and around the city.

It's normally easy to find a café to play, but if you're serious, try Muralto Bar (Theophile de Bockstraat 1), De Vluchtheuvel (Van Woustraat 174), or Matchroom Sloten (Slimmeweg 8).

## Football

Just as in other countries, there's a huge gap between the big football clubs in the Netherlands and the smaller teams. After Ajax, PSV and Feyenoord, it's a long way down to the rest. In recent years even Feyenoord have fallen away, finishing fourth or fifth in the league.

The Dutch season runs from late August until late May, with a break from Christmas until early February. Pleasingly, you can still watch the big games on network TV: plans to broadcast games on a commercial subscription sender collapsed in 1998, and highlights can still be seen Saturday and Sunday nights in Studio Sport on network TV. *See also box* **Pre-millennial tension** *below.*

### Ajax
*Amsterdam ArenA, Arena Boulevard 29 (311 1444). Metro Standvliet/Metro & NS Bijlmer.* **Matches** 2.30pm Sun. **Admission** from ƒ35. **Credit** AmEx, DC, EC, MC, V (advance bookings only).
Fancy going to an Ajax game? Think again: tickets for Ajax are worth more than their weight in gold. The team are

# Pre-millennial tension

Dutch football should, in theory, be entering a halcyon period. The national team is going from strength to strength; Ajax have high hopes of doing well in future European club competitions; and Euro 2000 – to be held in the Netherlands and Belgium – will be the biggest sporting event ever staged in Holland, surpassing even the 1928 Olympics. The eyes of the world will be on the country, and the KNVB – the Dutch football association – is keen to impress.

Yet Dutch football is in turmoil. The main problem is the resurgence of hooliganism: numerous fights have broken out between supporters of rival teams at grounds across the country. The worst of these was a pre-arranged confrontation in March 1997 on isolated terrain between so-called fans of Ajax and Feyenoord, which left one dead and several injured. As a result, fans have been banned from matches, kick-off times and dates have been rescheduled and, in some cases, matches have even been moved: one play-off game between Groningen and Leeuwarden for promotion to the Eredivisie (Premier League) took place behind closed doors at the KNVB headquarters.

In an attempt to control the hooliganism, the KNVB introduced a Club Card for the Eredivisie: only those with a Club Card were able to purchase tickets for a match, and even then it was only for games played by the club that issued

the card. And, as if that weren't enough, this system looks set to be tightened still further: from the 1998-9 season, the card will be known as the Personal Club Card and will carry the owner's photo. Even this is not sufficient to allay the fears of some clubs: Vitesse, for one, will now only admit season-ticket holders to its games.

For the neutral, visiting football enthusiast – especially one wanting to see a game on the spur of the moment – prospects look bleak, particularly for Euro 2000. Regulations being drawn up by the Dutch and Belgian governments and FAs will only result in more restrictions: most importantly, it looks like ticket sales will be principally for groups, with individual sales restricted.

On the other hand, where Dutch football is ahead of the game is with ground facilities: generally speaking, the quality of stadia is on the up, partly because of the need to get facilities in tip-top condition for Euro 2000. Ajax's home stadium the ArenA – complete with retractable roof – is a real gem (despite a few teething problems with the playing surface), but even this has been overshadowed by Arnhem's Gelredome, with its retractable playing surface. Still, what's the use of all this if just about no one gets access to the tickets? Good question. In fact, cynical visitors might be forgiven for thinking that the closest it's possible to get to top Dutch football is the (admittedly splendid) Ajax Museum at the ArenA…

*Gym'll fix it for you at* **The Garden**, *near Waterlooplein.*

dominating Dutch football once again and won the league and cup double in 1998. *See also chapter* **Museums**, *p84. Disabled access & toilets.*

### Feyenoord

*De Kuip, Van Zandvlietplein 3, Rotterdam (010 292 8888/information 0900 049 4000). NS rail to Rotterdam Centraal Station, then bus 46.* **Matches** 2.30pm Sun. **Admission** ƒ27,50-ƒ42,50. **Credit** EC.

Feyenoord's form in recent years means the 52,000 capacity stadium isn't usually full, unless the visitors are Ajax or PSV. *Disabled access.*

### PSV

*Philips Stadium, Frederiklaan 10A, Eindhoven (040 250 5501). NS rail to Eindhoven, then bus 4, 13.* **Matches** times vary. **Admission** ƒ35-ƒ70. **Credit** EC.

After a successful 1996-7 season, PSV fell away in '98. However, the team is rebuilding, hopes are high, and tickets are increasingly hard to come by. *Disabled access & toilets.*

### Other teams

Though the stadiums may not be full, the *personen verbonden clubkaart* (*see box* **Pre-millennial tension***, page 213*) is sure to prove a big obstacle for any visitors wanting to see a Premier League game. Instead, try the First Division, which has a rather more flexible policy on the card. Failing that, some of the top amateur clubs in the city (such as Blauw Wit, DGC and Elinkwijk) play surprisingly decent and attractive football. For information on these and other clubs, or if you fancy a game yourself, contact the Amsterdam area KNVB on 487 9130.

## Hockey

Both the Dutch men's and women's teams are up at the top of world hockey, and the game here is hugely popular. The 7,000-capacity Wagener Stadium in Amsterdam is used for both club games and internationals. The many hockey clubs in the area welcome players and spectators; details of the local teams are available from Mr A Flokstra of the North Holland district of the KNHB (644 3830), or from the KNHB Bunnik (030 656 6444). The season runs from September until May.

## Kaatsen

A forerunner to tennis, using the hands to hit the ball, kaatsen was banned between 1500 and 1750 because of the nuisance it caused. However, this authentic Dutch sport – played on a 60m by 32m field, with two teams of three players – is still popular in Friesland, where many competitions are held. Contact Mr L Bierma (611 2680) of the Amsterdam KNKB for details of events in the city.

## Korfball

A shotgun marriage of netball and volleyball indigenous to Holland, korfball is hugely popular here. The season has three stages: from September to mid-November and from April to June, games are played outdoors, while from mid-November to March, it heads indoors. Contact the North Holland KNKV (075 635 4065) for more details.

## Motor sport

### TT Races
*De Haar Circuit, Assen (0592 321321/race day information 0592 380367). Exit Assen south off A28, then follow signs.* **Date** *Grand Prix* fourth Sat in June. **Admission** *circuit ƒ55; ƒ20 children; stands ƒ75-ƒ85.* **Credit** EC.
More than 100,000 people come to the TT, with the Grand Prix races for sidecars and assorted bikes particularly popular. Tickets can be booked in advance from TT Assen, Postbus 150, 9400 AD Assen.

### Zandvoort
*Exploitatie Circuit Park Zandvoort, Burgermeester Van Alphenstraat (023 574 0740/information 023 574 0750). NS rail to Zandvoort.* **Admission** usually ƒ15-ƒ40. **Credit** AmEx, DC, EC, MC, V.
This racing track, 40 minutes' drive from Amsterdam, was once a venue for Formula One racing. A programme of international races runs roughly every other weekend from March to October, with tickets available from 8am on the day.

## Rugby union

Rugby is flourishing in the Netherlands, with nearly 100 clubs throughout the country. The Dutch have high hopes for the future: the National Rugby Centre in Amsterdam was opened in September 1997, and the country is confident of qualifying for the 1999 World Cup. There are four clubs in and around the city, who play from September to May. Details on these – and on the Amsterdam Heineken Rugby Sevens tournament – are available from the National Rugby Board on 480 8100.

## Volleyball

Thanks to the success of both men's and women's national teams, volleyball is on the up and up in Holland. For details of events and local clubs, contact the NeVoBo on 0348 411994 (national office) or 693 6458 (Amsterdam office).

### Fitness & leisure
## Athletics

There are four athletics tracks in Amsterdam: Elzenhagen, Olympiaplein, Ookmeer and Chris Bergerbaan. The *Trimloopboekje*, published every August, lists all running events in the Netherlands. The four big events in Amsterdam are the Vondelparkloop in January; June's Grachtenloop round the city's canals; the Dam tot Damloop from Amsterdam to Zaandam in late September; and the Amsterdam Marathon, held in early November. Further details on athletics in Holland are available from the KNAU on 030 608 7300.

## Badminton

There are several badminton clubs in Amsterdam: call the national NBB office (0251 233416) or the Amsterdam representative, Ms Gerda Dekker (642 7441), for more details on the sport in the city.

## Basketball

Until the Museumplein redevelopments, you could dunk for free in the centre of town. However, there are several clubs in Amsterdam who welcome players: call the NBB Amsterdam district office on 675 0462 (open 3-7pm Mon-Thur) for information.

## Golf

Golf has become quite popular in Holland, though it is still considered elitist by most Dutch people. You can play at a private club if introduced by a member, or if you belong to a British club; otherwise, there are several public courses open to everyone. For details, see the *Amsterdam Yellow Pages*, or contact the Nederlands Golf Federation (030 662 1888).

### De Hoge Dijk
*Abcouderstraatweg 46, Amsterdam ZO (0294 281241/285313). Metro Nieuw Gein; from Holendrecht stop, take bus 120, 126 to Abcoude.* **Open** dawn-dusk daily. **Cost** *ƒ60; club hire ƒ15 half-set.*
A public 18-hole polder course on the edge of Amsterdam. Reservations necessary.

### Sloten
*Sloterweg 1045 (614 2402). Bus 145.* **Open** 8.30am-dusk Mon-Fri; *mid-Jun-mid-Aug* also 8.30am-8pm Sat, Sun. **Cost** *weekdays* daytime *ƒ20;* evening *ƒ15; weekends ƒ25; driving range ƒ6,50 (incl 60 balls); club hire ƒ10 half-set.*
A nine-hole public course, with a driving range and practice green. Booking is advisable on weekends.

### Spaarnwoude
*Het Hogeland 2, Spaarnwoude (023 538 5599). Bus 82.* **Open** *summer* 7.30am-8.30pm Mon-Fri; 6.30am-7.30pm Sat, Sun; *winter* 8.30am-4pm daily. **Cost** *18-hole course ƒ44; nine-hole courses ƒ18/ƒ22; pitch &putt ƒ10.*
An 18-hole course, with two short courses and a pitch and putt. Reservations can be made up to three days ahead.

## Health & fitness

Look under 'Fitnesscentra' in the *Amsterdam Yellow Pages* for a full listing of health centres.

### A Bigger Splash
*Looiersgracht 26 (624 8404). Tram 7, 10, 17, 20.* **Open** 7am-midnight daily. **Admission** day *ƒ35;* week *ƒ67;* two weeks *ƒ98;* month *ƒ140.* **Credit** AmEx, DC, EC, V.
**Map 5 C5**
Facilities at A Bigger Splash include a weights room, Turkish baths, a massage service and a sauna, all included in the price. There are ten aerobics classes daily, and personal trainers are available.

### The Garden
*Jodenbreestraat 158 (626 8772). Tram 9, 14, 20/Metro Waterlooplein.* **Open** 9am-11pm Mon, Wed, Fri; noon-11pm Tue, Thur; 11am-6pm Sat; 10am-7pm Sun. **Admission** *training & shower* day *ƒ15;* month *ƒ97,50;*

*training & sauna* day ƒ22,50; ten visits ƒ155; *sauna* day ƒ17,50; month ƒ117,50. **Credit** EC. **Map 3 E3**
The cheapest all-in-one price in town gives you the choice of high- and low-impact and step aerobics, bodyshape, callisthenics and stretching. There's also a sun studio and hairdressers, and masseurs are available.

### Sporting Club Leidseplein
*Korte Leidsedwarsstraat 18 (620 6631). Tram 1, 2, 5, 6, 7, 10, 20.* **Open** 9am-midnight Mon-Fri; 10am-6pm Sat, Sun. **Admission** day ƒ25; week ƒ55; month ƒ110. **Map 5 C5**
A central health club with weights, aerobics classes and a sauna. Individual training programmes can be put together.

## Horse riding

The two main centres – De Amsterdamse Manege (643 1342) and Nieuw Amstelland Manege (643 2468) – both offer rides daily in the Amsterdam Bos at ƒ30 an hour for adults; lessons are available for kids. For more details, see 'Maneges' in the *Amsterdam Yellow Pages*.

## Saunas

Dutch saunas are mixed, so shed your inhibitions along with your clothes. See also the *Amsterdam Yellow Pages* under 'Saunas', **Health & fitness** *above*, and *chapter* **Gay & Lesbian**, *pages 192-5*.

### Deco Sauna
*Herengracht 115 (623 8215). Tram 1, 2, 5, 13, 17, 20.* **Open** 11am-11pm Mon-Sat; 1-6pm Sun. **Cost** ƒ26,50 up to five hours; ƒ18,50 Mon-Fri before 2pm; quiet children tolerated: half-price for under-12s before 8pm. **Map 2 C2**
The most beautiful sauna in town, with art deco glass panels and murals. Facilities include a Turkish bath, a Finnish sauna, a cold plunge bath and a solarium, while massages, Shiatsu, and skin and beauty care are by appointment.

### Oibibio
*Prins Hendrikkade 20-21 (553 9311). Tram 1, 2, 4, 5, 9, 13, 17, 20, 24, 25/Metro Centraal Station.* **Open** 10am-midnight daily. **Cost** ƒ23,50 before 5pm; ƒ29 after 5pm; ƒ19 children, students, over-60s Mon-Fri. **Map 2 C2**
The sauna in this New Age centre has all usual facilities, plus mud baths, bubble baths with added essential oils, and massages. There's also a beauty salon.

## Skateboarding, inline & rollerskating

Although the skateboard ramps at Museumplein are scheduled to disappear when the square is renovated, inliners and rollerskating enthusiasts are well-catered for here, with new places appearing all the time: check the *Amsterdam Yellow Pages* (under 'Sport en Spelartikelen') for a complete list. Those more interested in watching than doing should note that the 1998 World Inline Finals are being held at the RAI on 19 and 20 December.

### Balance
*Overtoom 464 (489 4723). Tram 1, 6.* **Open** 1-6pm Mon; 10am-6pm Tue, Wed, Fri; 10am-9pm Thur; 9.30am-5pm Sat. **Cost** *inline/roller skates* ƒ17,50/day; *skeelers* ƒ22,50/day (rates incl wrist, elbow and knee protection); *helmet* ƒ2.50; *deposit* ƒ300 with ID.

### Rent A Skate
*Vondelpark; entrance at Amstelveenseweg (06 5466 2262). Tram 1, 2, 3, 5, 6, 12, 20.* **Open** Mar-Nov 11am-9.30pm Mon-Fri; 10.30am-8pm Sat, Sun. **Cost** ƒ7,50/hr; ƒ15/three hrs; ƒ25/day; *deposit* ƒ50 with ID. **Map 5 C6**
There are two branches in Vondelpark: one at the café by the Amstelveenseweg, the other at the Melkgroothuis.

## Skating

Skating in the Netherlands is all about blades, not wheels, and we're not talking figure skating either. Dutch skating is about long-distance treks and tours, and it's not for the faint-hearted. However, conditions are rarely right nowadays: the scenes depicted by the old masters of people skating on the canals are, in general, a thing of the past.

If conditions are right – the ice must be very thick – look out for the **Elfstedentocht**, a 200-kilometre (124-mile) jaunt round Friesland (*see chapter* **The Provinces**, *page 239*). With up to 10,000 people taking part – starting early, and finishing by dusk – it's a massive national event. You must be a member of the Elfstedenvereniging association to compete, and even then, lots are drawn as numbers are limited. However, exceptions are sometimes made for foreigners.

If the canals freeze over in Amsterdam and you fancy a skate, then be careful: the ice is often weak, particularly under the bridges. If in doubt, ask one of the locals, or head to the **Jaap Edenhal** 400-metre ice track at Radioweg 64 (694 9894). Some of the ponds and lakes in and around Amsterdam may offer safer opportunities: contact the KNSB in Amersfoort (0334 621784) for information on conditions and organised events.

## Snooker & carambole

There are several halls in Amsterdam where you can play snooker or pool fairly cheaply. Carambole, played on a table without pockets, is a popular variation. Traditionally, biljart (billiards) has been associated with cafés: outside the centre of town, there are many cafés with biljart and pool tables. A full listing of clubs can be found in the *Amsterdam Yellow Pages* under 'Biljartzalen'.

### Snooker & Pool Club OudWest
*Overtoom 209 (618 8019). Tram 1, 6/bus 171, 172.* **Open** noon-1am Mon-Thur, Sun; noon-2am Fri, Sat. **Cost** *opening-2pm* ƒ10/hr; *2pm-close* ƒ15/hr. **Membership** ƒ50/year. **Map 4 B6**
The atmosphere in this former church is quiet, making it a club for the serious snooker player. Members pay ƒ2,50 less an hour.

### Snooker & Poolcentrum Bavaria
*Van Ostadestraat 97 (676 4059). Tram 3, 12, 20, 24, 25.* **Open** 11am-1am Mon-Thur, Sun; 11am-2am Fri, Sat; pool tables open from 2pm. **Cost** *snooker* ƒ15/hr; *pool* ƒ13,50/hr; *carambole* ƒ10/hr.
Spread over four floors here, the Bavaria boasts one carambole table, 26 billiards tables) and seven snooker tables, with the first floor a pool hall. Some nights are reserved for members only.

*Play with your balls at the* **Snookercentrum de Keizer**.

## Snookercentrum de Keizer

*Keizersgracht 256 (623 1586). Tram 13, 14, 17, 20.*
**Open** noon-1am Mon-Thur, Sun; noon-2am Fri, Sat. **Cost**
*noon-7pm* ƒ10/hr; *7pm-1am* ƒ16/hr; *match tables* ƒ13/hr
after 3pm. **Membership** ƒ100/year. **Map 2 C3**
There are seven snooker tables and two professional-size
pool tables here, all of which are in separate rooms. There
are phones in all rooms, so players can phone orders down
to the bar and have drinks or sandwiches sent up. Members
pay less for tables, but all are welcome. The most civilised
snooker club in Amsterdam.

## Sports centre

### Borchland Party & Sportcentrum

*Borchlandweg 8-12 (696 1441). Metro Strandvliet.* **Open**
7.30am-midnight Mon-Sat; 8.30am-midnight Sun. **Cost**
varies with activity: phone for details **Credit** AmEx, DC,
EC, MC, V.
The only big *omni-sportcentrum* (sports centre) in
Amsterdam – a Metro journey out of the centre – offering
squash, outdoor and indoor tennis, ten-pin bowling, badminton and, on a non-sporting level, a restaurant. It's impossible to list all the prices here, but rates are higher in the
evening and at weekends.

## Squash

For details of local clubs, phone Ms AP Bokma of
the Nederlands Squash Rackets Bond on 079 361
5400. Details of squash courts can be found in the
*Amsterdam Yellow Pages* under 'Squashbanen'.

### Dicky Squash

*Gustav Mahlerlaan 16 (646 2266). Tram 5, Metro
51/bus 63, 69.* **Open** 9.30am-midnight Mon-Fri; 9.30am-
8pm Sat, Sun. **Cost** *court hire 9.30am-4pm* ƒ15/half-
hour; ƒ25/hr; *4pm-close* ƒ17,50/half-hr; ƒ27,50/hr.
**Membership** ƒ395-ƒ595.
This wonderfully named place caters for experienced players, with 12 courts and a sauna.

### Squash City

*Ketelmakerstraat 6 (626 7883). Bus 18, 22.* **Open**
8.45am-midnight Mon-Fri; 8.45am-9pm Sat, Sun. **Cost**
*court hire 8.30am-5pm* ƒ13,50 per person/45 mins; *5pm-
close* ƒ35 per person/45 mins (prices incl sauna for two
persons). **Credit** AmEx, EC, MC, V.
The place to head if you see squash as more of a hobby than
a battle. There are 12 courts, a sauna, a weights room and
two aerobics rooms.

# Swimming

The opening times of both indoor and outdoor pools in Amsterdam vary hugely, with hours set aside for various groups. And while it's best to phone ahead, most pools set aside lanes for swimming lengths in the early morning, mid-afternoon and evening. Look in the *Amsterdam Yellow Pages* under 'Zwembaden' for a full list of pools.

### Brediusbad (outdoor)

*Spaarndammerdijk 306 (682 9116). Bus 22, 35.* **Open** *mid-May-Aug* 7.30am-9am, 10am-5.30pm Mon-Fri; 10am-5.30pm Sat, Sun. **Admission** *ƒ4,50; ƒ3,50 3-15s.*
A 1950s-style pool with high diving boards, children's pools and sunbathing area.

### Flevoparkbad (outdoor)

*Zeeburgerdijk 630 (692 5030). Tram 14.* **Open** *May-early Sept* times vary. **Admission** *ƒ4,75; ƒ4,25 3-15s; ƒ3,50 over-65s; from one hour before closing ƒ2,50.*
Two huge pools with kids' areas, a playground and a sunbathing area.

### Marnixbad (indoor)

*Marnixplein 9 (625 4843). Tram 3, 7, 10.* **Open** times vary Mon-Sat; 10am-5pm Sun. **Admission** *ƒ4,25; ƒ3,75 under-18s; ƒ2,75 over-65s.* **Map 1 B3**
As well as a 25m indoor pool with water slides and a whirlpool, Marnixbad also boasts a sauna.

### De Mirandabad (indoor & outdoor)

*De Mirandalaan 9 (622 8080/644 6637). Tram 15/bus 169.* **Open** *indoor* times vary; *outdoor* May-Sept 7am-9pm daily. **Admission** *ƒ5,75; ƒ4,50 4-17s; ƒ4 over-65s.*
The only sub-tropical pool in Amsterdam, De Mirandabad is very clean, with a stone beach and a wave machine. It's not good for swimming lengths, but there's fun to be had on the waterslide and in the whirlpool and outdoor pool. *Restaurant. Squash courts.*

### Zuiderbad (indoor)

*Hobbemastraat 26 (671 0287). Tram 2, 16, 24, 25.* **Open** times vary; call for details. **Admission** *ƒ4,75; ƒ4,25 4-11s; ƒ3 over-65s; ƒ2,75 1-3s.* **Map 5 D5**
The Zuiderbad was built in 1912 and is one of Holland's oldest pools. Exhibitionists should note that there's nude swimming from 4pm to 5pm on Sundays.

# Table tennis

For full details of clubs and facilities, contact the Nederlandse Tafeltennis Bond on 079 341 4811.

### Tafeltennis Centrum Amsterdam

*Keizersgracht 209 (624 5780). Tram 13, 14, 17, 20.* **Open** 1.30-6pm Mon; 1.30pm-1am Tue-Sat; 1-8pm Sun. **Cost** *table hire ƒ12.50/hr (inc bats and balls).* **Map 2 C3**
One of the few places where you can ping pong in town. Booking is advisable, and there are showers and a bar.

# Tennis

For information on competitions – including the Dutch Open in Hilversum in August – and clubs, call the KNTLB Amsterdam Office on 301 0743 (open 11am-3pm Mon-Fri); the national office can be reached on 035 626 4100. A full listing of courts can be found in the *Amsterdam Yellow Pages* under 'Tennisparken en -hallen'.

### Amstelpark

*Koenenkade 8 (301 0700). Bus 170, 171, 172 from Amsterdam Centraal Station; 169 from Amstel Station.* **Open** 8am-11pm daily. **Cost** *court hire ƒ35/hr; racket hire ƒ5.* **Membership** *Apr-Sept ƒ260.*
All in all, 42 courts: during the summer, there are ten indoor courts, and in the winter six of the outdoor courts are also covered over. There are also 12 squash courts, a Turkish bath, a sauna, a swimming pool and a shop.

### Kadoelen Tenniscentre

*Sportpark Kadoelen 5, Kadoelenweg (631 3194). Bus 92.* **Open** 9am-11pm daily. **Cost** *winter, indoor courts ƒ30/hr 9am-4pm Mon-Fri; ƒ40 4-11pm Mon-Fri, all day Sat, Sun; summer, outdoor courts ƒ25/hr.*
Kadoelen is subsidised by the local council, so the nine indoor courts cost less to hire than elsewhere. Tennis lessons can be arranged in advance.

# Ten-pin bowling

Several places mentioned above, such as the Borchland sports centre, have lanes; see the *Amsterdam Yellow Pages* under 'Bowlingbanen'. Phone the Nederlandse Bowling Federatie on 040 251 3515 (open 8.30am-5pm Mon-Fri) for more details.

### Knijn Bowling

*Scheldeplein 3 (664 2211). Tram 4.* **Open** 10am-1am Mon-Thur, Sun; 10am-2am Fri, Sat. **Cost** *10am-5pm Mon-Sat ƒ29,50/hr; 5pm-1am Mon-Thur, all day Sun ƒ39,50/hr; Fri, Sat 5pm-2am ƒ42.50/hr.* **Lanes** 18; max six persons per lane.

# Watersports

Holland has loads of water, and watersports are accordingly very popular: sailboards are normal holiday luggage for the Dutch. If you want to go sailing, visit Loosdrecht (25km/15 miles south-east of Amsterdam) or go to the IJsselmeer. Catamarans can be rented in Muiden (20km/12 miles east of Amsterdam). For details on canoeing, phone the NKB on 033 462 2341. Most watersports schools ask for a deposit and ID when you rent a boat.

### ROWING

There are rowing clubs on the Amstel and at the Bosbaan (the former Olympic rowing course) in the Amsterdam Bos. For full details, call the Dutch Rowing Union (KNRB) on 646 2740.

### Duikelaar

*Sloterpark, Noordzijde 41 (613 8855). Tram 13, 14/bus 19, 64.* **Open** times vary with weather. **Cost** *sailing boat hire ƒ15/hr; one-/two-person canoes ƒ7,50/hr per person; sailboard/wetsuit ƒ15/hr; deposit ƒ50 with ID.*
You can rent small sailing boats, canoes and sailboards on the banks of the Sloterplas lake next to the Sloterpark swimming baths. The season runs from May to October; from November to April, only canoes are available for hire.

### Gaasperplas Park

*Gaasperplas Park. Metro Gaasperplas/bus 59, 60, 174.* **Open** 24 hours daily.
Tucked away behind the Bijlmermeer in Amsterdam South-East, this park's large lake is a centre for watersports and windsurfing. There's also a campsite.

# Theatre

*All of Amsterdam's a stage... from international musicals to improv and summer festivals.*

The Dutch theatrical tradition dates back to the Middle Ages, and developed through the seventeenth century when theatre companies used to perform all over Europe (back then, Dutch was the international language of trade). Hooft, Bredero and Vondel were the most popular playwrights of the time, and their plays are sometimes performed even today, both classically and in modern productions. During the eighteenth and nineteenth centuries, theatre was still performed by and for the people, and it was not until the end of the 1800s that it became an élitist affair: something for those with an 'education', actors and public alike. The Dutch still tend to have a slightly snooty attitude, though ticket prices are actually less than in London's West End or on Broadway in New York.

## KETCHUP TIME

In the late '60s, young actors and directors who wanted to introduce new ideas and forms into the theatre started the 'tomato action'. At the time, Dutch theatre was controlled by a small, exclusive group of actors and directors, an establishment set-up the upstarts resented hugely. The radicals decided – reasonably enough – that the theatrical revolution they'd long dreamed about would only happen if they took to hurling tomatoes at their older, established colleagues during performances.

Curiously, it worked. As is the way of these things, those who once threw tomatoes at the establishment now make up the establishment themselves. Still, they didn't lose their enthusiasm for the medium in the transition: over the past few decades, there's been a move away from Dutch plays and towards works from elsewhere in the world. The influx of talent from Eastern Europe has been another notable and noticeable trend, as has the increase in the number of co-productions.

It's amazing how few original Dutch-language productions are currently being staged in the city. Even so, all but a few productions in Amsterdam are performed in Dutch – often translated from English – including work from many avant-garde companies, the most innovative of which are Nieuw West, Orkater, De Trust, Art & Pro and Mexicaanse Hond. But the real forte of Dutch the-

*Performances at **De Balie** often turn convention back to front. See page 221.*

*The beautiful **Felix Meritis** building.*

atre is design: sets, lighting and costumes are often striking and innovative, while Dutch acting, certainly in the more commercial, mainstream companies, tends towards the declamatory.

Sadly, in the mid-1980s, the government initiated a programme of cutbacks in arts support. As in the classical music world, several companies were forced to merge, and a few have disappeared altogether. So-called 'serious' theatre has, at least financially, lost out to more popular forms of entertainment, such as cabaret and musicals. Still, there's more than enough happening on the stages of Amsterdam to keep locals and visitors interested, even if the latter are somewhat hampered by the predominance of Dutch-language productions.

## DRAMATIC EVENTS

Many of the larger Dutch cities host their own theatre festivals (*see below* **Festivals & events**). Location theatre is another new development: it's not unheard of for the venues themselves – which could be anything from a fortress to a factory – to form an integral part of some performances. Look out for shows by Griftheater, Dogtroep, and choreographer/theatre-maker **Shusaku Takeuchi** (*see chapter **Dance**, page 181*).

## ENGLISH-LANGUAGE THEATRE

Because virtually everyone in Amsterdam speaks English, there is a large potential audience for English-language theatre in the capital. Unfortunately, because of massive competition, there's quite a quick turnover of companies staging productions in English, so it's always best to check what's on near the time. That said, there are some safe bets. **Badhuis Theater de Bochel**, based in a former bathhouse, is normally good value, while Panache typically co-produces

or manages two or three productions a season, usually in the summer. There is also a handful of groups – the Amsterdam Chamber Theatre (ACT), the Euro-American Theatre and Yell Theatre – who, though they produce plays less frequently, help keep the flow of English-language theatre constant.

One thing anglophones can enjoy is stand-up comedy, which is becoming increasingly big in the capital. Massively popular American troupe **Boom Chicago** are the kings of this particular form of entertainment, with their own theatre right on Leidseplein. The wide variety of theatre elsewhere in the Netherlands, meanwhile, is reflected in the range and number of venues offering quality work, and you're just as likely to find enjoyable productions at the small, off-the-beaten-track theatres as you are at the larger, more established, subsidised venues.

## INFORMATION & BOOKINGS

*Uitkrant* is a monthly freesheet with listings for almost every venue in Amsterdam; it's available in most theatres, bookshops and tourist information centres. For information – but not reservations – about performances, phone the **AUB** information line (621 1211; open 9am-9pm Mon-Sat). *What's On In Amsterdam* (ƒ4 from VVV tourist offices) gives details of selected events in English, and you can also find details on Amsterdam theatre and other events on the *Time Out* website at *www.timeout.co.uk*. Check local press for details of fringe productions.

Tickets can be bought from theatre box offices, or from the **AUB Uitburo** (open 10am-6pm Mon-Wed, Fri, Sat; 10am-9pm Thur; *see chapter* **Directory**, *page 252*). There's a ƒ2 booking fee, or ƒ6 for credit card bookings made by phone. You can also reserve or purchase tickets from VVV tourist offices, or through their phone reservation service (06 3403 4066/0900 400 4040); there is a ƒ3,50 booking fee. Unless otherwise stated, credit cards are not accepted at the venues listed. For details on the CJP card, a discount card for under-26s, *see chapter* **Directory**, *page 252*.

*Get your tickets from the **AUB**.*

*Have a laugh with **Boom Chicago** at their newly renovated theatre on Leidseplein.*

# Venues

## Badhuis Theater de Bochel
*Andreas Bonnstraat 28 (668 5102). Tram 3, 6, 7, 10, 20.* **Open** *box office* 7pm-start of performance; reservations taken until 30 mins before start of performance. **Performances** times vary. **Tickets** *f*12,50-*f*17,50. **Map 7 G4**
Once a public bathhouse, this theatre now plays host to a variety of guest artists and performers who often work in English. As well as reworking established scripts, these guests tend to produce a lot of their own offbeat creations. The atmosphere is relaxed and friendly, and generally appeals to a mixed bunch of nationalities. East European work is also often staged here.
*Café.*

## De Balie
*Kleine Gartmanplantsoen 10 (553 5151). Tram 1, 2, 5, 6, 7, 10, 20.* **Box office** 5-8.30pm Tue-Sat. **Performances** times vary. **Tickets** *f*10-*f*17,50. **Map 5 D5**
This cultural centre stages theatre, music and literature events, as well as lectures, debates, discussions and special projects, all of which informally influence Amsterdam's sometimes-controversial political opinions and lifestyle.
*Café. Disabled access.*

## Bellevue
*Leidsekade 90 (530 5301). Tram 1, 2, 5, 6, 7, 10, 20.* **Box office** 11am-6pm Mon; 11am-8.30pm Tue-Sun. **Performances** 8.30pm; some lunchtime shows. **Tickets** *f*17,50-*f*25. **Credit** AmEx, DC, EC, MC, V. **Map 5 C5**
Bellevue hosts dance and serious spoken theatre by state-subsidised companies such as the Ro Theater, lesser-known interesting companies including Het Volk, and physical comedy by the likes of Carver. Here's where you'll find many Dutch cabaret artistes as well as modern dance companies such as Krisztina de Châtel (*see chapter* Dance, *p180*).
*Café. Disabled access by arrangement.*

## Boom Chicago
*Leidseplein Theater, Leidseplein 12 (423 0101). Tram 1, 2, 5, 6, 7, 10, 20.* **Box office** 11am-11pm daily. **Performances** *show* 8.15pm daily; dinner & seating from 6.30pm daily; *late show* midnight Sat; seating from 11.15pm. **Open** *bar* 11am-1am Mon-Thur, Sun; 11am-3pm Fri, Sat; *restaurant* 11am-midnight daily. **Tickets** *f*27,50 (fourth person free Sun-Thur); *late show* *f*15. **Credit** AmEx, MC, V. **Map 5 D5**
A funny, fast-paced American improv comedy show in a laid-back setting. The Boomsters recently renovated and moved into the Leidseplein Theater, and now has various shows throughout the year. While some of the sketches are rehearsed, others are based on audience suggestions, though thanks to the largely foreign audience, a lot of them revolve around predictable Amsterdam clichés such as dope and sex. Still, the performers are excellent, the jokes (usually) right on the money, and with dinner and drinks served throughout the performance, it all adds up to a great evening out. Boom Chicago also organises boat trips.
*Bar. Restaurant.*

## De Brakke Grond
*Nes 45 (626 6866). Tram 4, 9, 14, 16, 20, 24, 25.* **Box office** 1-6pm Mon-Sat; 1-8.30pm performance days; 1-7.30pm if performance is in Frascati, Mon-Sat; 12.30pm-8.30pm. **Performances** 8.30pm. **Tickets** *Rodezaal* *f*18; *Expozaal* *f*21; *studio* *f*15. **Map 2 D3**
Just like its neighbour the Frascati, with which it shares a box office (*see below*), De Brakke Grond places more emphasis on Flemish productions. Exhibitions are also regularly held here.
*Café.*

## Cosmic Theater
*Nes 75 (622 8858). Tram 4, 9, 14, 16, 20, 24, 25.* **Box office** *phone* 2-5pm Mon-Sat. **Performances** 8.30pm. **Tickets** *f*17,50. **Map 2 D3**
The programming at Cosmic Theater is geared towards the new, multicultural Europe. Productions by its own company are staged here, but work by other groups also features.
*Café.*

## De Engelenbak
*Nes 71 (626 3644/reservations 626 6866).Tram 4, 9, 14, 16, 20, 24, 25.* **Box office** 1pm-start of performance. **Performances** 8.30pm. **Tickets** *f*15; *f*12,50 students. **Map 2 D3**
This theatre is best known for 'Open bak', an open stage each Tuesday where virtually anything goes. It's the longest-running theatre programme in the Netherlands, where everybody gets their 15 minutes of potential fame. So get out there with your juggling, singing or bicycle repair skills and become a star. Or not, as the case may be. Arrive at least an hour early to reserve a spot.
*Café.*

## Felix Meritis
*Keizersgracht 324 (623 1311). Tram 1, 2, 5, 13, 17, 20.* **Box office** 10am-5pm Mon; 10am until time of last performance Tue-Sat. **Performances** usually 8.30pm. **Tickets** *f*26; *f*20 students. **Map 5 C4**
This beautiful, early nineteenth-century building was the centre of fringe theatre in the early 1970s, and the multicultural programme now covers theatrical performances, dance, music, video and seminars: some of the Netherlands' best dance has premièred here, including the work of the first lady of Dutch dance, Truus Bronkhorst. However, budget cuts in recent years have resulted in changes in programming policy, and the theatre has suffered as a result.
*Café.*

### Frascati

*Nes 63 (626 6866). Tram 4, 9, 14, 16, 20, 24, 25.* **Box office** *see* De Brakke Grond *above.* **Performances** times vary. **Tickets** *Zaal 1 f18; Zaal 2 & 3 f15;* concessions with CJP card, over-65s. **Map 2 D3**
One of Amsterdam's better venues for interesting new work, with one large auditorium (*zaal*) and two smaller spaces. *Café.*

### Gasthuis Werkplaats & Theatre

*Marius van Bouwdijk Bastiaanstraat 54; entrance opposite 1e Helmerstraat 115 (616 8942 noon-5pm Mon-Fri). Tram 1, 3, 6, 12.* **Box office** one hour before start of performance. **Performances** 9pm. **Tickets** *f15; f7,50 under-18s,* art students. **Map 1 B6**
The complex housing this alternative theatre workshop used to be a hospital, but – thankfully – the smell of disinfectant has been banished. It provides a stage for smaller (co-)productions, often of an experimental nature.

### Koninklijk Theater Carré

*Amstel 115-125 (622 5225). Tram 4, 6, 7, 10, 20.* **Box office** 10am-7pm Mon-Sat. **Performances** 8pm. **Tickets** *f25-f100.* **Credit** AmEx, DC, EC, MC, V. **Map 6 F4**
Once home to a circus, Carré now hosts some of the best Dutch comedians and cabaret artistes. If mainstream theatre is more your thing, though, look out for the Dutch versions of popular British and American musicals – such as *Phantom of the Opera, Les Misérables* and *Cats* – which almost invariably end up here. Other offerings include folk dance and revues, while you can also take a backstage tour Wednesdays or Saturdays (3pm; *f5;* phone for reservations).

### Melkweg

*Lijnbaansgracht 234A (624 1777). Tram 1, 2, 5, 6, 7, 10.* **Box office** 1-5pm Mon-Fri; also from 7.30pm Wed-Sun; 4-6pm Sat, Sun; *phone reservations* noon-5pm Mon-Fri. **Performances** times vary. *membership (compulsory)* one month *f4,50;* three months *f7,50;* year *f22,50.* **Map 5 C5**
This multimedia centre on the site of a former milk factory, opened its doors in 1970. The symbol of Amsterdam liberalism and tolerance in the '70s, the Melkweg has managed to retain its reputation as a cultural meeting place; in 1983, it became a founder member of Transeuropehalles, an international network of multimedia cultural groups. Now, it's one of the few places where 'new dance' can be seen, and foreign touring companies, of both dance and movement theatre, often make a brief stop here. *See also* chapters **Galleries,** *p72,* **Film,** *p184,* and **Music: Rock, Roots & Jazz,** *p207.*
*Café.*

### De Nieuw Amsterdam

*Grote Bickersstraat 2/4 (627 8672/8699). Tram 1, 2, 5, 14, 17.* **Box office** 10am-5pm Mon-Fri; also 7.30pm-start of performance. **Performances** times vary. **Tickets** *f15; f12,50* students.
The brainchild of renowned director Rufus Collins, De Nieuw Amsterdam (DNA) is a network of artists of many nationalities staging 'non-western' productions, both in its own space and on tour. It's a multicultural theatre, and also runs a school programme for young people set on becoming the next big thing.

### De Stadsschouwburg

*Leidseplein 26 (624 2311). Tram 1, 2, 5, 6, 7, 10, 20.* **Box office** 10am-start of performance Mon-Sat; from one and a half hours before performances Sun, public holidays. **Performances** 8.15pm. **Tickets** prices vary. **Credit** AmEx, EC, MC, V. **Map 5 C5**
The Stadsschouwburg (Municipal Theatre) is into its third incarnation: the first two buildings were destroyed by fire in

the seventeenth and eighteenth centuries. The present theatre, opened in 1894 and recently refurbished, is a beautiful and impressive baroque building built in the traditional horseshoe shape and seating about 950. Director Cox Habbema is responsible for a policy that not only nurtures traditional Dutch theatre but also stages a wide variety of contemporary national and international productions. The Bovenzaal space plays host to small-scale productions that are often in English.
*Café.*

### Westergasfabriek

*Haarlemmerweg 8-10 (information & tickets from AUB; 621 1211). Tram 10/bus 18, 22.* **Performances** times vary. **Tickets** prices vary. **Map 1 A1**
As unlikely as this may sound, the Westergasfabriek is a former gas factory complex turned into a theatrical breeding ground. On any given evening, there may be up to five different performances, in just as many disciplines. It's ideal for location projects and repertory theatre alike.

## Bookshop

### International Theatre & Film Books

*Leidseplein 26 (in the Stadsschouwburg building, to the right of the main entrance; 622 6489). Tram 1, 2, 5, 6, 7, 10, 20.* **Open** noon-6pm Mon; 10am-6pm Tue-Sat. **Credit** (min *f100*) AmEx, DC, EC, MC, V. **Map 5 C5**
The ITFB stocks a wide variety of international magazines and books on stage and screen. There are books on everything from history to theatre management – often in English – as well as texts of current productions, a few of which are in English.

## Festivals & events

*See also* **Theatermuseum** (*chapter* **Museums,** *page 83*); and the **Holland Festival** and **Vondelpark Openluchttheatre** (*chapter* **Amsterdam By Season,** *pages 9, 10*).

### International Theatre School Festival

*Reservations can be made at the specific venues. (information 527 7614/information & reservations 626 6866).* **Tickets** *f15; f12,50* students.
A festival of theatre school productions from all over the world takes place at the end of June in theatres located on Nes, including De Brakke Grond, Cosmic Theater, De Engelenbak, Frascati and the Stadsschouwburg (*for all, see above*).

### Over Het IJ Festival

*NDSM shipyard, Neveritaweg, Amsterdam North. Ferry from Centraal Station/bus 35 from Centraal Station (stop Atatürk)/bus 38 from Molenwijk (stop Klaprozenweg)/bus 94 from Centraal Station (stop Klaprozenweg). Reservations & information from AUB (credit card hotline & information 621 1211).* **Tickets** *f25-f30; f20* with CJP card, students.
This summer-long outdoor festival of larger location projects is one of the most exciting events in Amsterdam, with all performances held on the other side of the IJ channel in northern Amsterdam (hence the name). Look out, in particular, for productions by Dogtroep, which performs around the world and was part of the 1998 festival. Other highlights from 1998 included Sèmola from Spain; *Crossroads* by Urban Dance; and Accrorap, which featured a rapper, an opera singer, a percussionist, a DJ and a cello player and was infinitely better than you might expect from that description. There's also an on-site restaurant serving a limited three-course dinner. Tickets are sold on the door, with other discounts available; phone for details. Their website is at *www.ijfestival.nl.*

# Trips Out of Town

# Beyond Amsterdam

***So you can't stand the heat and want to get out of the proverbial kitchen? Here's the lowdown on how to get around.***

There's more to the Netherlands than just Amsterdam. That much everyone knows. But what about the rest of the country? The national borders enclose 12 distinctive provinces, each with its own character. But the whole country covers just 41,864 square kilometres (16,000 square miles) and even the remotest corners are less than a day's drive or train ride away. Many towns and cities worth visiting in the Netherlands are under an hour's drive from Amsterdam.

Due to the importance of the region of Holland in Dutch history, the entire country has confusingly become widely known by that name, instead of the Netherlands. In fact, Holland accounts for just two of the 12 provinces: Noord (North) and Zuid (South) Holland. Amsterdam lies in the south of Noord Holland and is a quick day trip away from most of the classic Dutch attractions.

## Travel information

The **Netherlands Board of Tourism** (Vlietweg 15, 2266 KA, Leidschendam; 070 3705 705) which has branches outside of Holland, can help with general information. Throughout the following three chapters, we've listed the VVV tourist office for each area, which can suggest and book accommodation, as will **Netherlands Reserverings Centrum** (Postbus 404, 2260 AK Leidschendam; 070 419 5500). For all national transport information and timetables (trains, buses and Metro), call the **OV Reisinformatie** information line (0900 9292; open 6am-midnight Mon-Fri; 7am-midnight weekends, public holidays); calls are charged at 75c per minute. Those connected to the Internet can go to *www.ns.nl*, though most of the website is only in Dutch.

## On the road

The Netherlands' extensive network of motorways and roads is well-maintained, and clearly signposted. For suggested maps and details of the motoring organisation **ANWB**, *see chapter* **Directory**, *page 254*.

## Buses & coaches

The national bus service is reasonably priced, but not as easy to negotiate as the railway (*see below*). For bus information and timetables, phone **OV Reisinformatie** (*see above*). Private coach companies offer good value half and full-day excursions (from ƒ30 per person for local trips, to ƒ60 per person to Belgium); ask the VVV for details.

## Cycling

The Netherlands is flat (but windy), so it's no surprise that the bike is the country's favourite mode of transport. Cycle paths can be found in abundance and the VVV and ANWB sell cycle tour maps. Most major railway stations have bike hire depots. You'll need proof of identity and a cash deposit (ranging from ƒ50 to ƒ200). Rail ticket holders with a bike ticket bought at the station are entitled to a discount. Bicycles cost around ƒ9,50 per day and ƒ36 per week, but for mountain bikes, the rent goes up to around ƒ25 per day and ƒ85 per week, with the deposit around ƒ300).

During the summer months, you should reserve a bike at least a day in advance. Bicycles cannot be taken on Dutch trains at peak times (6.30-9am, 4.30-6pm, Mon-Fri). It costs ƒ10 one way and ƒ17,50 return to take them on board when travelling up to 80km (50 miles), and slightly more for longer trips. You can also take your bike on international trains for only ƒ20. Throughout July and August, there are no time restrictions.

## Netherlands Railway (NS)

*The prices listed below are a rough guide: fares are updated in January each year.*
The extensive NS (Nederlandse Spoorwegen) rail network is efficient, clean, punctual and inexpensive in comparison to other European countries. Services are frequent, so reservations are unnecessary unless you're on an international train. First class travel is one-and-a-half times the cost of going second class. Credit cards are not accepted

at ticket offices. Departure and arrival times are displayed on yellow station posters; a national timetable can be bought at stations and most news agents, and the **OV Reisinformatie** (*see above*) can help with any departure and arrival information. For full details on international departures and arrivals, phone **NS Internationaal Reisinformatie** on 0900 9296 (open 8am-9pm Mon-Fri; 10am-6pm weekends, public holidays); calls cost 50c a minute. Those with access can go to its Internet site (*www.ns.nl*). Travellers from the UK may be interested in **Holland Rail** (01962 773646), the UK ticket agent for NS.

As a rule, tickets are valid for one day only: if you make a return journey spanning more than one day you need two singles. Bear this in mind when travelling from Schiphol Airport to the city. If you are returning on the same day, you pay a cheaper rate if you ask for a day return ticket (*dagretour*). A weekend return ticket is the exception to the rule: it's valid from Friday night until Sunday night for the price of a normal return ticket.

## Special offers

**Dagkaarten (Day Tickets)** offer unlimited travel anywhere in the country: a second-class ticket costs *f*71,50, first-class *f*110,75. A 40 per cent reduction is possible with a special discount pass (*see below*). For an extra *f*8 you can upgrade to an **OV Dagkaart (OV Day Ticket)**, which also lets you travel on buses, trams and Metros nationwide.

A **Euro Domino** ticket gives you unlimited travel on any three-, five- or ten-day period within one month. Prices vary per European country, but for second-class travel in the Netherlands and Belgium, a pass costs *f*115 for three days, *f*135 for five days and *f*250 for ten days. Those under 26 receive a discount of approximately 25 per cent.

In July and August, you can use the **Zomertoer (Summer Tour)** ticket to travel through the Netherlands for any three days within a period of ten consecutive days. It costs *f*99 for second-class travel, or *f*129 for two people.

If you're travelling to the Frisian Islands it's wise to buy a special **Waddenbiljet (Wadden Ticket)**, an open-return train, bus and boat ticket all in one. Prices from Amsterdam start at around *f*100, depending on which island you visit.

For group travel, the **Meermanskaart (Multi Rover)** offers unlimited travel on one day for up to six people (not available before 9am from Monday to Friday from September to June). Prices for second-class travel range from *f*108 for two people to *f*186 for six.

The perfect discount card for those who intend to stay longer is the **Voordelenurenkaart (Off-peak Card)**. Depending on your age, you can buy the **Jongerenkaart** (under-26s), the **Rail-Aktiefkaart** (26-59) and the **60+ Seniorenkaart**

(over-60s). It costs *f*99 a year, but after only a few trips you'll break even. The card gives a 40 per cent discount on single, return and day tickets after 9am Monday to Friday, travelling first or second class. It entitles you to special discounts such as an evening return ticket for the cost of a single. You also get a **Museumjaarkaart**, which gives you free or reduced admission to almost every museum in the Netherlands (*see chapter* **Museums**, *page 74*). However, this bonus only applies to those who agree to buy a new off-peak card annually.

**Inter-Rail** tickets are valid in the Netherlands, but a supplement is payable on Eurocity trains.

## Rail Idee

NS offers around 200 all-inclusive **Rail Idee** excursions (discount rail and other travel, admission to sights and occasional extras) to destinations all over the Netherlands. Details can be found in the (Dutch) brochure *Er-op-Uit!* (*f*6,25), available at tourist offices, stations, bookshops and post offices.

## Night Net

**Night Net** is the night train network: a loop train that runs hourly every night (1am to 5am) in a loop between Utrecht, Rotterdam, Delft, Den Haag (The Hague), Leiden Centraal Station, Schipol Airport, Amsterdam Centraal Station and back to Utrecht. Timetables are available from NS stations.

## Children

Children under four travel free; four- to 11-year-olds can pay a fixed fare of *f*2,50 (regardless of class) with a **Railrunner** pass, but must be accompanied by a fare-paying adult. Four- to 11-year-olds travelling alone pay 60 per cent of the standard fare.

## Disabled travellers

Any passenger who may need special assistance during their journey (such as wheelchair provision) should phone **030 230 5566** (8am-4pm Mon-Fri) at least 24 hours before day of travel to ensure that help will be provided. NS produces a booklet called *Rail Travel for the Disabled* (in English), available from all main stations or by from the above number. There is disabled access to refreshment rooms and toilets at all stations.

## Trains & cabs

There are 111 train stations in the Netherlands that offer the services of a **Treintaxi**, a special cab that allows you to take a taxi for only *f*7 when you have a valid train ticket (without a ticket, the price is *f*9). The Treintaxi takes you from the station to any destination within a fixed area (usually the city limits) and vice versa. For more information, phone **OV Reisinformatie** (*see above*).

# Excursions in Holland

**History, tradition, architecture... and a whole bunch of cheese.**

The majority of the Netherlands' stereotypical sights are concentrated in the two provinces around Amsterdam: Noord and Zuid Holland. Both provinces are small, and many of the sights are close to each other and easily reached by public transport or as part of special tours (*see chapter* **Beyond Amsterdam**, *pages 224-5*).

## Cheese

The Dutch export well over 400,000 tonnes of cheese every year, and the summer cheese markets, museums and traditional farms capture the flavour of how this commodity used to be made and sold. The most famous market is at **Alkmaar**, a synonym for the cheese trade for over 700 years, while a lesser-known but equally authentic farmers' cheese market is held every Tuesday throughout the year in the village of **Bodegraven**, between Gouda and Utrecht.

There are many thatched-roof *kaasboerderijen* (cheese farms) near Gouda, several of which are on the picturesque River Vlist. If you're passing through, keep your eyes peeled for signs reading *kaas te koop* ('cheese for sale'): this indicates a farm shop where you may be able to look behind the scenes as well as buy freshly made Gouda.

### Alkmaar

**Getting there** *by car* 37km (22 miles) north-west; *by rail* direct from Amsterdam Centraal Station.
**VVV** *Waagplein 2 (072 511 4284).* **Open** 9am-5.30pm Mon-Wed; 9am-9pm Thur; 9am-6pm Fri; 9am-5pm Sat.
Alkmaar cheese market, which runs every Friday from 10am to noon between mid-April and mid-September, is as much a ritual for tourists as it is for members of the cheese porters' guild. Garbed in pristine white uniforms and straw hats, with coloured ribbons denoting the competing guilds, the porters weigh the cheeses and carry them on wooden trays hung from their shoulders. Buyers then test a core of cheese from each lot, before the ceremony itself, which takes place at the **Waag** (weigh house); here you can also find open-air craft stalls and a **Cheese Museum** (072 511 4284; open 10am-4pm Mon-Thur, Sat; 9am-4pm Fri; admission *f*5).

But the city has more to offer than just cheese. The VVV offers a written walking tour of the medieval centre, dating from 935, which often resounds to the sound of a carillon concert. There's a beer-tasting cellar at the **Biermuseum** (Houttil 1; 072 511 3801; open Apr-Oct 10am-4pm Tue-Fri, 1-4pm Sat, 1.30-4pm Sun; Nov-Mar Tue-Sat 1-4pm, 1.30-4pm Sun; admission *f*4, *f*2,50 7-14s, over-65s); and an impressive

art and toy collection at the **Stedelijk Museum** (Doelenstraat 5; 072 511 0737; open 10am-5pm Tue-Fri, 1-5pm Sat, Sun; admission *f*3, free with Museum Card, 10-17s).

### Edam

**Getting there** *by car* 10km (5 miles) north; *by bus* 110, 112, 114 from Amsterdam Centraal Station.
**VVV** *Stadhuis, Damplein 1 (0299 315125/fax 0299 374236).* **Open** Mar-Oct 10am-5pm Mon-Sat; July, Aug also noon-4.30pm Sun; Nov-Mar 10am-2pm Mon-Sat.
This tiny town was a prosperous port during the Golden Age and has some exquisite façades and bridges. However, it suffers fewer tourist hordes than Volendam (*see below*), which is a short bus ride away. The famous red-skinned cheese is sold at the cheese market, held every Wednesday in July and August from 10am until noon. Other attractions in the town include the remarkable stained glass at the 400-year-old **Grote Kerk** (open May-Sept 2-4.30pm daily), and the **Municipal Museum** on Damplein (0299 372644; open 10am-4.30pm Tue-Sat, 1.30-4.30pm Sun).

### Gouda

**Getting there** *by car* 29km (18 miles) south-west; *by rail* direct from Amsterdam Centraal Station.
**VVV** *Markt 27 (0182 513666).* **Open** 9am-5pm Mon-Sat; July, Aug also noon-3pm Sun.
Golden wheels of cheese are traded at the cheese market every Thursday from 10am in July and August in front of the 1668 Waag – whose gablestone depicts cheese-weighing – and the Gothic city hall of 1450. But though the cheese is justly famed the world over, Gouda does have other points of interest other than the yellow stuff. Its other famous products include clay pipes and pottery, which can be seen in the **De Moriaan Museum** (Westhaven 29; 0182 588444; open 10am-5pm Mon-Fri, 10am-12.30pm, 1.30-5pm Sat, noon-5pm Sun; combined admission for De Moriaan and Caterina Gasthuis *f*4,25, *f*2 5-15s); interested visitors shouldn't miss the hugely popular pottery festival, held each year in the second week of May. Gouda's candles are another city classic: 20,000 of them illuminate the square during the Christmas tree ceremony.

Elsewhere, St Janskerk has 70 antique stained-glass windows, while the **Stedelijk Museum Caterina Gasthuis** (Oosthaven 9; 0182 588440; open 10am-5pm Mon-Sat, noon-5pm Sun; *see* **De Moriaan Museum** for admission), which was a hospice and hospital from 1320 to 1910, has heaps of Golden Age silver and modern art on display. The general market that (Thursdays and Saturdays) is worth a visit.

### Purmerend

**Getting there** *by car* 26km (15 miles) north-east; *by rail* direct from Amsterdam Centraal Station; *by bus* 100, 106 from Amsterdam Centraal Station.
**VVV** *Kerkstraat 9 (0299 425365).* **Open** 1-5.30pm Mon; 9am-5.30pm Tue-Fri; 9am-4.30pm Sat.
Not much doing here, if we're honest. Still, the cattle and general markets every Tuesday morning – where deals are sealed by a handclap – is a nice little diversion, while the dis-

*Flowers go under the hammer at the **Aalsmeer Flower Auction**. See page 228.*

plays around local history in the **Purmerend Museum** are interesting, if unspectacular (Kaasmarkt 20; 0299 428755/472718; open 10am-4pm Tue-Fri, 1-5pm Sat, Sun; admission ƒ3,50, ƒ2,50 under-13s, free with Museum Card). If you're driving, the most rewarding return route to Amsterdam is on country roads via Den Ilp and Landsmeer.

## Flowers

Ask any visitor what springs to mind when they hear the word 'Holland', and you can be pretty sure that tulips will be top of the list or thereabouts. But that's not the end of the story: the Netherlands produces 70 per cent of all the world's flowers, and many types of blooms can be seen all year round in markets, botanical gardens, auctions and flower parades. For export rules on bulbs and flowers, *see chapter* **Shopping**, *pages 149-50*.

## Floral calendar

### Spring
The flower trade's year kicks off in mid- to late February with the indoor **Westfriese Flora** (0228 511644) at Bovenkarspel, near Enkhuizen. From late March to late May, the bulb district from Den Helder to The Hague is carpeted with blooms of the principal crops: daffodils, crocuses, gladioli, hyacinths, narcissi, and – of course – tulips.

### Summer
In mid- to late May, golden fields of rapeseed brighten Flevoland, Friesland and Groningen (*see chapter* **The**

Provinces, *pp238-43*). In The Hague, the Japanese Garden at **Clingendael Gardens** is in full flower from early May to mid-June, while the rose garden in **Westbroek Park** (which contains 350 varieties) bursts into colour during July and August. In late June, there's the **Floralia** exhibition at the Zuider Zee Museum in Enkhuizen (*see below* **Traditions: West Friesland**).

### Autumn
Heather purples the landscape – especially in Gelderland's Veluwe (*see chapter* **The Provinces**, *p240*) – during August and September, when greenhouse flowers also emerge. Autumn is also flower parade season (*see below*).

### Winter
In November, the public and florists from all over the world view new varieties at the Professional Flower Exhibition at **Aalsmeer Flower Auction** (*see below*). At Christmas, there's the **Kerstflora** show at Hillegom near Lisse.

## Flower parades

### Bloemen Corso (Flower Parade)
*(0297 325100)*. **Parade** Aalsmeer (9.30am) to Amsterdam (4pm). **Date** first Sat of Sept.
The Aalsmeer to Amsterdam Parade is Europe's largest flower procession; floats can be viewed in Aalsmeer Auction Hall (*see below* **Flower auctions**) from 3pm until 10pm on the Friday preceding the parade, and from 9am until 5pm on the following Sunday. The highlights include the parade down Amstelveenseweg before lunch, the 4pm reception at Dam Square in Amsterdam (for which, *see chapter* **Amsterdam by Season**, *p11*), and the hour-long illuminated cavalcade through Aalsmeer, which runs from 9pm to 10pm.

### Noordwijk-Haarlem Parade

*(0252 434710).* **Parade** Noordwijk (10am) via Sassenheim (1pm) to Haarlem (7pm). **Date** first Sat after 19 Apr.
The floats are on show at Lisse and Hobahohallen all day for the two days preceding the parade.

### Rijnsburg Parade

*(071 409 4444).* **Parade** Rijnsburg (11am) via Leiden (1pm) to Noordwijk (4pm). **Date** first weekend of Aug.
The floats show at the Boulevard in Noordwijk on Saturday evening and Sunday.

## Flower auctions

### Aalsmeer Flower Auction

*Legmeerdijk 313 (0297 393939).* **Getting there** *by car* 15km (9 miles) south-west; *by bus* 172 from Amsterdam Centraal Station. **Open** 7.30-11am Mon-Fri. **Admission** *ƒ7,50;* free under-12s.
Each year, more than 3.5 billion cut flowers and 370 million pot plants are handled, mostly for export, at the Verenigde Bloemenveilingen Aalsmeer, the world's biggest flower auction. The perishable nature of the flowers demands high speed action, the result being a chaotic scene. To bid, dealers push a button to stop a 'clock' that counts from 100 down to one: unusually, the price is lowered, rather than raised, until a buyer is found. Bidders risk either overpaying or not getting the goods if time runs out. This procedure gave rise to the English phrase 'Dutch auction'. The best action before here is usually before 9am, except on Thursdays when very little happens.

### Broeker Veiling

*Museumweg 2, Broek-op-Langerdijk (0226 313807).*
**Getting there** *by car* 36km (22 miles) north; *by rail* from Amsterdam Centraal Station to Alkmaar, then bus 155; from Amsterdam Centraal Station to Heerhugowaard, then taxi. **Open** *Apr-Nov* 10am-5pm Mon-Fri; noon-5pm Sat, Sun. **Admission** *auction & museum ƒ9,25; ƒ5,50 under-15s; auction, museum & boat trip ƒ15,50; ƒ8,50 under-15s.*
The oldest auction in the world is a bit of a tourist trap, though bidding is done as at a professional auction. The admission price includes a museum of old farming artefacts, and – for a small extra fee – a boat trip round the area.

## Nurseries & gardens

Over 100 botanical gardens serve as research centres for the industry, notably the **Hortus Botanicus** at Leiden, and the **Hortus Bulborum** in Heiloo, which, from mid-April to mid-May, has offshoots of the original tulips introduced from Turkey.

### Frans Rozen Nursery

*Vogelenzangseweg 49, Vogelenzang (023 584 7245).*
**Getting there** *by car* 25km (16 miles) west; *by rail* from Amsterdam Centraal Station to Heemstede, then bus 90 to Café Rusthoek. **Open** *late Mar-May* 8am-6pm daily; *Aug-Sept* 9am-5pm Mon-Fri. **Admission** *ƒ2;* under-14s free.
The enormous greenhouse and extensive fields of this 200-year-old nursery are open to the public, and allow you to gain an insight into commercial cultivation and the meticulous development of new hybrids. You can also purchase bulbs for export, and there's a tulip show in April and May.

### Keukenhof Bulb Gardens

*Keukenhof, near Lisse (0252 465555).* **Getting there** *by car* 27km (17 miles) south-west; *by rail* from Amsterdam Centraal Station to Leiden, then bus 54. **Open** *mid-Mar-*

*mid-May* 8am-7.30pm daily *(ticket office* 8am-6pm daily).
**Admission** *ƒ17,50; ƒ8,50* 4-12s.
Since 1949, it's been flowers, flowers everywhere at the Keukenhof Bulb Gardens. This former fifteenth-century royal 'kitchen garden' contains over 500 varieties of tulip and over six million bulbs in 32 hectares (80 acres), but the new glass flower pavilion – all 6,500sq m (70,480sq ft) of it – is just as interesting, as are the various statues and works of art. With the help of a VVV map, you can tour the bulb district (in bloom from March to late May), from which over half of the world's cut flowers and pot plants originate. The gardens and café get overrun, so arrive early with a picnic lunch.
The bulb district's history is covered at the **Museum de Zwarte Tulp** in Lisse (Grachtweg 2A; 0252 417900; open 1-5pm Tue-Sun; admission *ƒ4, ƒ2* under-12s).
*Café. Wheelchairs and pushchairs for hire (by arrangement).*

## Traditions

A few Dutch diehards still wear local costume or keep to their old ways. Some make a genuine effort to preserve traditions, while others pander to tourists looking for the 'authentic' Holland by hauling out their lace caps and turning on windmills *(windmolens)* for special days.

### Bunschoten-Spakenburg

**Getting there** *by car* 40km (25 miles) south-east; *by rail* from Amsterdam Centraal Station to Amersfoort, then bus 116. **Dates** *mid-July-mid-Aug* Wed.
About one-fifth of Bunschoten-Spakenburg residents still wear traditional dress on special market days, and many of the older folk wear it every day. Costumes are also worn at the markets in Hoorn, Medemblik and Schagen (*see below* **West Friesland**), and sometimes on Sundays in Urk, Flevoland, and on market days – Thursdays during July and August – in Middelburg, Zeeland (*see chapter* **The Provinces**, *p243*). Fashion fans may also be interested in the **Kostuum Museum** in The Hague (*see chapter* **The Randstad**, *p233*).

### Kinderdijk Windmills

*Molenkade, Alblasserdam (078 691 4300).* **Open** *Apr-Sept* 9.30am-5.30pm daily. **Admission** *ƒ3; ƒ1,75* 6-14s; under-6s free.
**Getting there** *by car* 60km (37 miles) south-west; *by rail* from Amsterdam Centraal Station via Rotterdam to Dordrecht, then bus 152 to Alblasserdam, then bus 154.
**VVV** *Cortgene 2, inside City Hall, Alblasserdam (078 692 1200).* **Open** 10am-noon Mon-Fri; also 2-4pm Mon, Wed.
The sight of these 19 windmills under sail is spectacular, particularly when they're illuminated during the second week in September. To drain water from reclaimed land, windmills were usually clustered in a co-ordinated group called a gang. This gang now operates purely for the benefit of tourists every Saturday afternoon (2.30-5.30pm) during July and August; you can look around inside Nederwaarde mill, or go on a boat trip around the windmills.

### Schoonhoven

**Getting there** *by car* 48km (30 miles) south; *by rail* from Amsterdam Centraal Station to Gouda, then bus 197.
**VVV** *Stadhuisstraat 1 (0182 385009).* **Open** *May-Sept* 1.30-5pm Mon; 9am-5pm Tue-Fri; 10am-3pm Sat; *Oct-Apr* 10am-noon, 2-4pm, Tue-Fri; 10am-3pm Sat.
Schoonhoven has been famous since the Middle Ages for its silversmiths, who crafted items such as filigree jewellery, miniatures and ornaments to be worn with traditional costume. You can see antique pieces in the **Nederlands Goud Zilver en Klokkenmuseum** (Gold, Silver and Clock

Museum; Kazerneplein 4; 0182 385612; open noon-5pm Tue-Sun; admission *f*4,50, *f*2,50 under-12s) and the **Edelambachthuis** (Museum of Antique Silverware; Haven 13; 0182 382614; open 10am-5pm Tue-Sat; admission *f*1). There's also an annual silver market on Whit Monday, but the standard silver shops are open all year round. Starting at **Silverhuys** (Silver House; Haven 1-3) is a row of buildings full of silver and pewter collectibles, many of traditional design, while the **Klokkenhuys** (Clock House) at Haven 9 stocks barometers and timepieces. Olivier van Noort, the first Dutchman to sail around the world (1598-1601) and Claes Louwerenz Blom, who introduced the windmill to Spain in 1549, are buried in **St Bartholomaeus Kerk** (1354), the tower of which leans 1.6m (5ft) off-centre and offers great views. Finally, the carillon of the 1452 Stadhuis has 50 bells made from the guns of van Noort's ship.

## Witches' Weigh House, Oudewater

*Leeuweringerstraat 2 (0348 563400)*. **Open** *Apr-Oct* 10am-5pm Tue-Sat; noon-5pm Sun, public holidays. **Admission** *f*3; *f*2,50 with Museum Card, over-65s; *f*2 4-16s; free under-5s.
**Getting there** *by car* 29km (18 miles) *south*; *by rail* from Amsterdam Centraal Station to Gouda, then bus 180.
**VVV** *Markt 8 (0348 564636)*. **Open** *Apr-Oct* 10am-4.30pm Tue-Sat; 1-4.30pm Sun; *Nov-Mar* 10am-1pm Tue-Sat.

Dating from 1000, Oudewater (north of Schoonhoven; *see above*) was once known for cheese, rope-making and its particularly honest merchants. However, an epidemic of witch-hunting broke out in 1487, lasting until the beginning of the seventeenth century. It was during this period that Oudewater achieved fame for its honest weighing of suspected witches and warlocks in the **Witches' Weigh House** (Heksenwaag) after Charles V attended a witch trial in Polsbroek where the (bribed) weighmaster declared that the woman suspect weighed only 2.5kg (5.5lb); at Oudewater she was found to weigh 50kg (110lb), and was consequently acquitted. Each of the accused witches received a document verifying that she was too heavy to travel by broom; today's (free) certificate comes in six languages for the swarms of tourists who step on to the scales. The Weigh House also has a small, informative museum on witchcraft.

# Waterland

Until the IJ tunnel was built in 1956, the Waterland district north of Amsterdam was accessible mainly by ferry and steam railway to Volendam. This isolation preserved much of the area's heritage, which is best enjoyed from the seat of a bicycle. For nearby Edam and the Museum Waterland in Purmerend, *see above* **Cheese**.

## Broek-in-Waterland

**Getting there** *by car* 10km (6 miles) north-east; *by bus* 111 from Amsterdam Centraal Station.
**VVV** *See Monnickendam.*
Full of eighteenth-century charm, this town has Waterland's greatest collection of old wooden buildings. Even rich Amsterdam merchants declined to build their country homes in stone for fear of them sinking.

## Marken

**Getting there** *by car* 15km (9 miles) north-east; *by rail* with NS Rail Idee ticket (including Volendam); *by bus* 110 from Amsterdam Centraal Station to Volendam, then boat to Marken; *bus* 111 from Amsterdam Centraal Station to Marken, or 111 to Monnickendam, then boat to Marken.
**VVV** *See Monnickendam or Volendam.*
Now reached via a causeway, Marken was once full of

fishermen, but is now bursting with costumes, souvenir shops and tourists. However, it's bearable out of season and is far more attractive and authentic than Volendam (*see below*), a boat ride away. The **Marker Museum** (Kerkbuurt 44-47; 0299 601514; open 10am-5pm Mon-Sat, noon-4pm Sun, public holidays; admission *f*4, *f*2 under-12s) offers an interesting glance at the island's history, while you can see *klompen* (clogs) being carved – and buy a souvenir pair, if you so wish, – at the shoemaker's at Kets 52 (0299 601630; open 9am-6pm Mon-Sat).

## Monnickendam

**Getting there** *by car* 12km (72 miles) north-east; *by bus* 111 from Amsterdam Centraal Station.
**VVV** *De Zarken 2 (0299 651998)*. **Open** 10am-5pm Mon-Sat.
The most remarkable thing about Monnickendam is the proportion of ancient buildings that have been preserved, from Golden Age merchants' houses to herring smokehouses. History lovers should enjoy the collection of music boxes at the **Stuttenburgh** fish restaurant at Haringburgwal 2-5 (0299 651869), and there's a delightful antique carillon on the bell-tower of the old town hall.

## Volendam

**Getting there** *by car* 18km (11 miles) north-east; *by rail* with NS Rail Idee ticket (including Volendam); *by bus* 110 from Amsterdam Centraal Station.
**VVV** *Zeestraat 37 (0299 363747)*. **Open** *mid-Mar-Oct* 10am-5pm daily; *Nov-mid-Mar* 10am-3pm Mon-Sat.
Volendam was such a successful fishing village that its flag flew at half-mast when the Zuider Zee was enclosed in 1932, cutting off access to the sea. The village's enterprise was soon applied to creating a theme park from its historic features, but, unfortunately, the gaily garbed locals can barely be seen for the coachloads of tourists that are dumped there on a daily basis.

## De Zaanse Schans

*(information from VVV below)*. **Open** *Oct-Mar* 8.30am-5.30pm Mon-Sun; *Apr-Sept* 8.30am-6pm Mon-Sun. **Admission** free-*f*5; free-*f*4 under-12s.
**Getting there** *Near Zandijk; by car* 14km (9 miles) north; *by rail* with NS Rail Idee ticket (includes cruise on River Zaan, admission to windmill museum, pancake and cup of coffee); *by bus* 89 from Marnixstraat.
**VVV** *Gedempte Gracht 76 (075 616 2221)*. **Open** 9am-5.30pm Mon-Fri; 9am-4pm Sat.
De Zaanse Schans is a reconstructed museum village with a difference: people actually live in it. The Zaan district was once noted for industrial windmills that powered the manufacture of paint, flour and lumber: here you can buy mustard produced in one of the five working mills. Amid the gabled homes – largely green with white trim – are an old-fashioned Albert Heijn grocery store, a former merchant's home and a cheese house. Boat trips on the adjacent Zaan River provide another perspective on the village.

# West Friesland

Facing Friesland across the northern IJsselmeer is West Friesland. Although the area was part of Noord Holland for centuries, it has its own customs – and, incidentally, slightly fewer visitors – than its near neighbour. One particularly nice and scenic way to get there is to take a train to Enkhuizen, then a boat to Medemblik. From here, head on to Hoorn via the **Museum Stoomtram** (steam railway; *see below* **Hoorn** for information); there's an all-inclusive NS Rail Idee ticket for this route.

**Muiderslot**, *where Count Floris V was muidered in 1296.*

## Enkhuizen

**Getting there** *by car* 45km (28 miles) north-east; *by rail* direct from Amsterdam Centraal Station; with NS Rail Idee ticket.

**VVV** *Twee Havens 1 (0228 313164)*. **Open** *Apr-Oct* 9am-5pm daily; *Nov-Mar* 9am-5pm Mon-Fri; 9am-2pm Sat.

**Zuider Zee Museum** *Wierdijk 18 (0228 351111)*. **Open** *Binnenmuseum* 10am-5pm daily; *Buitenmuseum Apr-Oct* 10am-5pm daily; *July, Aug* 10am-7pm daily. **Admission** *f*17,50; *f*12,50 4-12s; *f*12 over-65s.

This once-powerful fishing and whaling port has many relics of its past, but most people come here for the remarkable **Zuider Zee Museum**, which celebrated its fifteenth anniversary in 1998. It comprises two separate plots: the indoor Binnenmuseum, which features a nice section on seafaring life and crafts, and an open-air reconstructed village, the Buitenmuseum. To make good use of the one-way crowd control system, start with the Buitenmuseum. Take a guided tour, or just wander around the hundred or so homes, shops and other buildings transplanted from towns around the Zuider Zee and authentically arranged.

## Hoorn

**Getting there** *by car* 33km (20 miles) north-east; *by rail* with NS Rail Idee ticket.

**VVV** *Veemarkt 4 (0229 218343)*. **Open** *Sept-May* 1-5pm Mon; 9.30am-5pm Tue-Sat; *Jun-Aug* 1-6pm Mon; 9.30am-6pm Tue-Fri; also 7-9pm Thur; 9.30am-5pm Sat; *Apr-Aug* also 1-5pm Sun.

**Museum Stoomtram Hoorn-Medemblik** *Tickets from Van Dedemstraat 8, Hoorn (0229 214862), or any rail station*. **Admission** *f*14-*f*44.

This extremely pretty port, dating from 1311, grew rich on the Dutch East Indies trade; its success is reflected in its grand and ancient architecture. Local costume and crafts can be seen in the weekly folklore celebrations called Hartje Hoorn, held from 10am to 5pm every Wednesday during July and August, while the grandly named **Museum van de Turintigste Eeuw** (Museum of the Twentieth Century; Bierkade 4; 0229 214001; open 10am-5pm Tue-Sun; admission *f*5, *f*4 5-16s, over-65s) has a permanent exhibition of daily life from the last hundred or so years. The baroque former Staten-College (council building) of 1632 now houses the **Westfries Museum** (Rode Steen 1; 0229 280028; open 11am-5pm Mon-Fri, 2-5pm Sat, Sun; admission *f*5, *f*2,50 under-15s, over-65s), which focuses on art and interior décor with a display on the region's past. Older still is the **Hoofdtoren** (harbour tower) and **St Jansgasthuis**, a hospital from 1563 until 1922 and now an exhibition centre.

## Medemblik

**Getting there** *by car* 45km (28 miles) north; *by rail* with NS Rail Idee ticket.

**VVV** *Dam 2 (0227 542852)*. **Open** *Nov-Mar* 10am-noon, 2-4pm Mon-Sat; *Apr-Oct* 10am-5pm Mon-Sat; *July, Aug* also noon-5pm Sun.

An ancient port dating from AD334, dominated by the Gothic St Bonifacius Kerk and Radboud Kasteel. Built in 1289, the castle is smaller than when it defended Floris V's realm, but still retains its knights' hall, towers, dungeon and a cellar tavern. Charming traditional costume is worn at the Saturday market (held during July and August), when goods are brought in by barges. Nearby is the circular village of Opperdoes, built on a terp mound, and the 'long village' of Twisk, complete with its pyramid-roofed farm buildings.

## Schagen

**Getting there** *by car* 48km (30 miles) north; *by rail* direct from Amsterdam Centraal Station.
**VVV** *Markt 22 (0224 298311).* **Open** 10am-2pm Tue-Sat.
Schagen is situated right between Alkmaar and Den Helder, which makes it an excellent base from which to explore the traditions of this part of the Netherlands. Costumed dancers entertain tourists at the cattle and crafts markets in the summer, and there's also a museum farm where ancient trades are performed. Near the cosy city square are the remnants of two medieval castle towers, now converted into a so-so World War I museum. Apart from horse-drawn carriage races, Schagen also boasts several music festivals that attract visitors from all over the area.

## Castles

The Netherlands is studded with 400 castles, and many fortress towns retain large parts of their defences. Some of the best are in the province of Utrecht, within half an hour of Amsterdam; for those further afield, *see chapter* **The Provinces**, *page 243*. No less than 80 of the castles are open for tourists or business conferences; the fifteenth-century **NJHC Slot Assumberg** at Heemskerk, between Haarlem and Alkmaar, is a youth hostel (025 123 2288); while the ultimate power lunch can be had at either **Château Neercanne** in Maastricht (043 325 1359) or **Kasteel Erenstein** in Kerkrade (045 546 1333).

### De Haar

*Kasteellaan 1, Haarzuilens, Utrecht (030 677 1275/tour bookings 030 677 3804).* **Open** *Jan-mid-Aug, mid-Oct-mid-Nov* 11am-4pm Mon-Fri; 1-4pm Sat, Sun.
**Admission** *castle & grounds* f15; f10 5-12s (no under-5s); *grounds only* f5.
**Getting there** *by car* 30km (19 miles) south; *by rail* from Amsterdam Centraal Station to Utrecht, then bus 127.
De Haar looks like the quintessential medieval castle. However, its romantic embellishments are relatively recent neo-Gothic re-creations: in 1887, the baron who inherited the ruins of De Haar married a Rothschild and together they re-created the original building on a majestic scale, commissioning the Rijksmuseum's architect, PJH Cuypers, and moving the entire village of Haarzuilens 2km (1.2 miles) to make room for the outstanding formal grounds. The whole process took over 20 years. The castle, the largest in the Netherlands, had previously been completed in 1391, destroyed in 1482, rebuilt in 1505 and damaged again, by the French, in 1672 and 1673. The lavish interior boasts ancient tapestries, Louis XIV-XVI furniture and Far Eastern art, with spectacular stone carvings and stained glass in the hall.

### Muiden (Stichting Rijksmuseum Muiderslot)

*Herengracht 1, Muiden (0294 261325).* **Open** *Apr-Oct* 10am-5pm Mon-Fri; 1-5pm Sat, Sun; *Nov-Mar* 1-4pm Sat, Sun. **Admission** f7,50; f5 under-12s, over-65s; free with Museum Card. Group discounts (by arrangement).
**Getting there** *by car* 12km (7.5 miles) south-east; *by bus* 136 from Amstel Station.
The Muiderslot is a legendary place: many Dutch historical events took place in this moated rectangular castle, strategically situated at the mouth of the River Vecht. It was originally built in 1280 for Count Floris V, who was murdered here in 1296 (*see chapter* **History**, *p13*). Rebuilt in the fourteenth century, the fortress has been through many

sieges and frequent renovations. The seventeenth-century furnishings may seem out of context, however: in fact, they originate from the period of its most illustrious occupant, the Dutch poet and historian PC Hooft, who entertained the Muiden circle of writers, musicians and scholars in the castle's splendid halls. You can only look around as part of a guided tour (in English by arrangement). You can also see falconers in action during summer, and wander through the beautiful gardens at your leisure.

### Naarden

**Getting there** *by car* 20km (12 miles) south-east; *by rail* direct from Amsterdam Centraal Station; *by bus* 136 from Amsterdam Centraal Station.
**VVV** *Adriaan Dortsmanplein 1B (035 694 2836).* **Open** *May-Sept* 10am-5pm Mon-Fri; 10am-3pm Sat; noon-3pm Sun, Easter and autumn holidays; *Nov-Apr* 10am-2pm Mon-Sat.
**Vestingmuseum Turfpoortbastion** *Westvalstraat 6 (035 694 5459).* **Open** *Easter-Oct* 11am-5pm Mon-Fri; noon-5pm Sat, Sun, public holidays. **Admission** f10; f9 over-65s; f7,50 4-16s; free with Museum Card, under-4s.
Naarden is a double-moated, star-shaped stronghold with arrowhead-shaped bastions, and one of Europe's most perfectly preserved fortified towns: it was in active service as recently as 1926. The defences are explained in the **Vestingmuseum**, located partly underground in the Turfpoort (Peat Gateway) bastion; admission includes a boat trip around the *vesting* (fortress). Every day, from April to September, cannons are fired by men in sixteenth-century soldiers' uniforms. The fortifications themselves date from 1675, after the inhabitants were massacred by the Duke of Alva's son in 1572: the slaughter is depicted above the door of the **Spaansehuis** (Spanish House), now a part-time conference venue. Music buffs should be sure to catch Bach's *St Matthew Passion*, presented in the gorgeous **Grote Kerk** on the Sunday (2.30pm), Thursday (7pm), Friday and Saturday (first part at 11.30am, second part at 2.30pm) before Easter. Phone 030 251 3413 for more information on this terrific concert.

### River Vecht tour

**Getting there** *by car* 35km (22 miles) south-east; *by rail* to Utrecht from Amsterdam Centraal Station.
**Utrecht Canal Touring Co** *Oudegracht, opposite no.85 (030 272 0111/030 231 9377).* **Times** *mid-May-Sept* leaves Utrecht 9.30am Tue, 10.30am Fri to Loenen, returning 6pm and 7pm respectively. **Tickets** f31; f27 under-13s.
Meandering upstream from Muiden (*see above*) into Utrecht province (*see chapter* **The Provinces**, *p243*), you reach Loenen, a charming town with cobbled streets, a leaning church spire and the restored castle of Loenersloot, the latter complete with a thirteenth-century keep. Gracing the river banks are seventeenth- and eighteenth-century mansions, built as retreats by Amsterdam merchants. At Breukelen – which gave its name to Brooklyn, New York – is the elegant, classical house of Gunterstein (rebuilt in 1681); just beyond it, on the other bank, is Nijenrode, a medieval castle destroyed in 1672 and subsequently rebuilt, neglected again, and finally restored in 1907 in seventeenth-century style. Across the river is Oudaen, a country house which dates, in part, from 1303; a detour east around the Loosdrechtse Plassen lake leads to **Sijpesteyn**, a castle museum. Built on the foundations of a manor house that was destroyed in about 1580, the castle was rebuilt at the turn of the century in medieval style. You can now take tours of the castle between Easter and October (035 582 3208; open 10am-5pm Tue-Fri, noon-5pm Sat, Sun; admission f7, f4 4-14s). Back on the Vecht, between De Haar castle (*see above*) and the city of Utrecht, is **Slot Zuylen** at Maarssen. Surrounded by woods and a moat, it dates from about 1300, but has an eighteenth-century façade and is well worth a look.

# The Randstad

## Amsterdam isn't the only city in the Netherlands...

The Randstad – or 'Edge City', named for its coastal location on the Netherlands' western edge – is essentially a ring-shaped conurbation bounded by Amsterdam, Delft, Haarlem, The Hague, Leiden, Rotterdam and Utrecht, though in recent years, Gouda (*see chapter* **Excursions in Holland**, *page 226*) and Dordrecht have also come to be considered part of the Randstad. Although separately administered and fiercely independent, the individual towns work together by choice for their common good. Somewhat surprisingly, it's also one of the most densely populated areas in the world: no less than 40 per cent of the Dutch population inhabit this urban sprawl.

The road, rail and waterway networks are impressive, and the area's strong economy accounts for at least half of the national turnover. The Randstad's importance is based on several factors: Rotterdam's port, which handles more tonnage than any other in the world; Amsterdam's Schiphol airport and the city's role as financial and banking centre; the seats of government and royalty at The Hague; and a huge agricultural belt.

Regarded with awe and sometimes resentment by the outlying provinces, the Randstad is often accused of monopolising government attention and funds. However, it has no formally defined status and is still prone to bitter rivalries between cities and municipalities. The cities mentioned below are all part of the night train network (*see* chapter **Beyond Amsterdam**, *pages 224-5*), and train times given are all approximate.

## Delft

Almost everything you might want to see in this compact city is located along the Oude Delft, as are the best views. Delft's loss in trade has been Rotterdam's gain, but it has meant that the city's centuries-old gables, humpback bridges and shady canals remain unchanged. To get an idea of how little has altered, go to the **Hooikade**, where Vermeer painted the *View of Delft* that now hangs in Mauritshuis (*see below* **The Hague**).

Delft is most famous for its blue and white pottery and tiles, and there are still a few factories open to visitors. For a historical perspective, though, the **Museum Lambert van Meerten**, a nineteenth-century mansion, houses fine pieces of tin-glazed earthenware, as well as a vast collection of magnificent ebony-veneered furniture. The huge range of tiles – depicting everything from battling warships to copulating hares – compares startlingly with today's mass-produced trinkets.

Museums in Delft have the air of private residences and are thankfully devoid of crowds. **Het Prinsenhof** on Sint Agathaplein has permanent exhibitions on William the Silent (assassinated here in 1584) and about the building's role as the Convent of St Agatha until 1572, while opposite, in another convent wing, is the ethnographic collection of the **Nusantara Museum**. Delft also has two spectacular churches that can be seen for miles around. The **Nieuwe Kerk**, in the Markt opposite De Keyser's 1618 Stadhuis, contains the mausoleums of William the Silent and lawyer-philosopher Hugo de Groot. Not to be outdone, Gothic **Oude Kerk**, with its picturesque tilting tower, is the last resting place of Vermeer (1632-75).

## Essential information

### Getting there
*by car* 60km (37 miles) south-west on A4, then A13; *by rail* one hour, changing at The Hague if necessary.

### VVV
*Markt 83-85 (015 212 6100).* **Open** *Apr-Oct* 9am-6pm Mon-Fri; 9am-5.30pm Sat; *Nov-Mar* 9am-5.30pm Mon-Sat.

## Accommodation

**De Ark** (Koornmarkt 59-65; 015 214 0552/215 7999) is up-market, with single rooms priced at ƒ140-ƒ175 and doubles at ƒ175-ƒ235. **Dish** (Kanaalweg 3; 015 256 9358) is more reasonable, with singles at ƒ140,50, doubles at ƒ183 and triples at ƒ245,50. Budget travellers should try **De Kok** (Houttuinen 14; 015 212 2125), where singles cost ƒ95-ƒ125 and doubles ƒ125-ƒ150.

## Restaurants, cafés & bars

In summer, delicious sandwiches are served on a canal barge at **Klijwegs Koffiehuis** (Oude Delft 133; 015 212 4625). Across the water, **Rumours** (Oude Delft 78; 015 215 8689) serves excellent meals priced anywhere from ƒ9,50 to ƒ40. Other bars, *eetcafés* and restaurants are situated around the Beestenmarkt, Delft's nicest square.

## Museums

### Het Prinsenhof
*Sint Agathaplein 1 (015 260 2358).* **Open** 10am-5pm Tue-Sat; 1-5pm Sun, public holidays. **Admission** ƒ5; ƒ2,50 12-16s.

### Museum Lambert van Meerten
*Oude Delft 199 (015 260 2358).* **Open** 10am-5pm Tue-Sat; 1-5pm Sun. **Admission** ƒ3,50; ƒ1,75 12-15s.

The city of **Rotterdam**, an exciting mix of the old and the new. See page 236.

**Nusantara Museum**

*St Agathaplein 4 (015 260 2358).* **Open** 10am-5pm Tue-Sat; 1-5pm Sun. **Admission** ƒ3,50; ƒ1,75 12-15s.

## Delftware factories

### Delft Pottery de Delftse Pauw

*Delftweg 133 (015 212 4920).* **Open** *mid-Apr-mid-Oct* 8.30am-4.30pm daily; *mid-Oct-mid-Apr* 8.30am-4.30pm Mon-Fri; 11am-1pm Sat, Sun.

### Royal Delftware Factory: 'De Porceyleyne Fles'

*Rotterdamseweg 196 (015 256 9214).* **Open** *Apr-Oct* 9am-5pm Mon-Sat; 9.30am-5pm Sun; *Nov-Mar* 9am-5pm Mon-Sat. **Admission** ƒ5. Group discounts (min 20 persons).

## The Hague (Den Haag)

Once the hunting ground of the Counts of Holland, The Hague was founded in 1250 when William II built a castle on the site of the present **Binnenhof** parliament buildings. The buildings have retained a bastion-like appearance to this day, though a modern hall was added in 1994. The only evidence of the building's unruly past is the Gevangenpoort (prison gate) across the Hofweg, where political prisoners were once jailed; it's also where the brothers De Witt were lynched after being accused of conspiring to kill William of Orange. Every year on Prinsjesdag (the third Tuesday of September), the Queen arrives at the Binnenhof in a golden coach for the state opening of parliament. Guided tours of the Binnenhof are organised daily when the buildings are not in use (Binnenhof 8A; 070 364 6144; tours ƒ6, ƒ5 under-12s, over-65s).

Sadly, The Hague's palaces – **Voorhout Paleis** and **Paleis Noordeinde** at either end of the fashionable Lange Voorhout avenue, and Queen Beatrix's residence, **Huis ten Bosch**, at the far end of the Haagse Bos – are no longer open to visitors. However, the **Mauritshuis** (*see chapter* **Museums**, *page 86*), a former regal home, is now open to the public and houses an excellent art collection including works by Rubens, Rembrandt, Van Dyck, Vermeer and even Warhol.

One of the greenest cities in Europe, The Hague has a number of parks. **Clingendael** has a Japanese garden; **Meijendael**, a little further out of town, is part of the ancient forest; and the **Scheveningse Bosje** is big enough to get lost in, and is flanked by the **Madurodam** miniature city (*see chapter* **Children**, *page 172*) and the **Haags Gemeentemuseum**. Notable for its art nouveau architecture and its works by Mondrian and other modern masters, the museum incorporates the Dutch costumes, clogs and caps of the **Kostuum Museum** (National Costume Museum), and is linked to the **Museon**, a hi-tech ethnological display, and the **Omniversum**, a state-of-the-art planetarium. Between the Scheveningse Bosje and the city is **Vredes Paleis** (the Peace Palace), built in 1907 to host peace conferences; it's now the UN's Court of International Justice. More cultural diversions are the **Anton Philipzaal** concert hall (*see chapter* **Music: Classical & Opera**, *page 203-204*) and the **North Sea Jazz Festival**, held around town in early July (*see chapter* **Music: Rock, Roots & Jazz**, *page 211*).

Just past Scheveningse Bosje is **Scheveningen**, a former fishing village. It's now a huge resort with high-rise hotels and, in summer, a massive choice of beach cafés. The architectural highlight of the beach is the **Kurhaus**: built in 1887, it's a legacy of Scheveningen's days as a bathing place for European high society. The main salon, with its enormous chandeliers and awesome glass cupola, is a wonderful and intimidating place to take tea.

Back in The Hague, more history can be had at the **Mesdag Museum**, which holds paintings of the Scheveningen coast by members of The Hague School, including HW Mesdag. Close by is the **Panorama Mesdag**, where you can see Mesdag's remarkable 360-degree painting of Scheveningen village in 1880.

## Essential information

### Getting there
*by car* 50km (31 miles) south-west on A4, then A44; *by rail* 50 mins to Den Haag Centraal Station, changing at Leiden if necessary.

### VVV
*Koningen Julianaplein, at Centraal Station (06 3403 5051/0990 340 3505).* **Open** 9.30am-5.30pm Mon-Fri; 10am-5pm Sat; *Jul, Aug* also 10am-5pm Sun.

## Accommodation

**Des Indes Intercontinental** (Lange Voorhout 54-56; 070 363 2932) is the most luxurious hotel in town, with prices to match: singles cost ƒ415, with doubles at ƒ530. The **City Hotel** (Renbaanstraat 1-3; 070 355 7966) has singles for ƒ65-ƒ100 and doubles at ƒ125-ƒ135, while the youth hostel **NJHC City Hostel Den Haag** (Scheepmakersstraat 27; 070 315 7878) charges ƒ32,50-ƒ36,50 per person, including ƒ5 membership.

## Restaurants, cafés & bars

**Luden** (Frederikstraat 36; 070 360 1733) serves expensive Dutch food with a French panache, while **Schlemmer** (Lange Houtstraat 17; 070 360 8580) has a medium-priced restaurant frequented by Dutch politicians, plus a trendy café upstairs.

Of the city's bars, **De Zwarte Ruiter** (Grote Markt 27; 070 364 9549) is a stylish brown café popular with students, though homesick Brits may enjoy English pub **De Bok** (36 Papenstraat; 070 364 2162). Clubs include **Artizz** on Kettingstraat, or **Asta Movement**, an old cinema on Spui.

## Museums

### Haags Gemeentemuseum
*Stadhouderslaan 41 (070 338 1111).* **Open** 11am-5pm Tue-Sun. **Admission** ƒ10; ƒ5 12-17; free under-12s. Group discounts (min 15 persons).

### Mesdag Museum
*Laan van Meerdervoort 7F (070 362 1434).* **Open** noon-5pm Tue-Sun, public holidays. **Admission** ƒ5; ƒ2,50 under-18s.

### Panorama Mesdag
*Zeestraat 65 (070 364 4544).* **Open** 10am-5pm Mon-Sat; noon-5pm Sun, public holidays. **Admission** ƒ6; ƒ3 under-14s; ƒ2 under-14s. Group discounts (min ten persons).

Lying between Amsterdam and Zandvoort, Haarlem is a busy Dutch coastal resort that attracts flocks of Amsterdammers and more than its fair share of Germans during the summer. All trace of Haarlem's origins as a tenth-century set-tlement on a choppy inland sea disappeared with the draining of the Haarlemmermeer in the mid-nineteenth century. However, the town hasn't lost its appeal: the centre, for example, is simply beautiful, and around the old market square, you'll find old canals lined with characterful houses.

To catch up with Haarlem's history, head to **St Bavo's Church**, which dominates the main square. It was built in around 1313, but suffered severe fire damage in 1328, and due to lack of funds it took another 150 years to complete the restoration work. It's surprisingly bright inside: cavernous, white transepts stand as high as the nave and make for a stunning sight. Music buffs will swoon at the sight of the famed Müller organ (1738): boasting an amazing 5,000 pipes, it's been played by both Handel and the young Mozart.

Haarlem residents have given its **Grote Markt** the nickname 'living room of Haarlem', mainly since it's so cosy: indeed, it's one of the loveliest squares in the Netherlands. A short walk from the square is Groot Heiligland, a building that currently houses the **Frans Hals Museum** (*see chapter Museums, page 85-6*). Though it holds a magnificent collection of seventeenth-century portraits, still lifes, genre paintings and landscapes – including works by Pieter Claesz, Jacob van Ruisdael and Adriaan van Ostade – the highlight is Frans Hals's eight group portraits of militia companies and regents. (Hals, incidentally, is buried in the aforementioned St Bavo's Church.) The museum also houses a large collection of period furniture, Haarlem silver and ceramics, an eighteenth-century apothecary with Delftware pottery, and an extensive modern collection.

Though it's rather in the shadow of the Frans Hals Museum – and understandably so – the **Teylers Museum** is equally excellent. Founded in 1778, it's the Netherlands' oldest museum and has a proverbial mixed bag of exhibits: fossils and minerals sit alongside antique scientific instruments in a passable imitation of an alchemist's workshop, while there's also a superb collection of 4,000 drawings dating from the sixteenth to nineteenth century by masters such as Rembrandt, Michelangelo and Raphael.

Haarlem is more than a city of nostalgia, of course. The **Patronaat** at Zijlsingel 2 (023 532 6010) is a fine rock music venue: it's Haarlem's answer to the Melkweg in Amsterdam, though without the really big bands.

## Essential information

### Getting there
*by car* 20km (12 miles) west on A5; *by rail* 20 mins, direct.

### VVV
*Stationsplein 1 (023 531 9059).* **Open** *Apr-Sept* 9am-5.30pm Mon-Sat; *Oct-Mar* 9am-5.30pm Mon-Fri; 9am-4pm Sat.

## Accommodation

The beautiful **Carlton Square Hotel** (Baan 7; 023 531 9091) is as pricey as Haarlem gets, with single and double rooms at ƒ390 and triples at ƒ465. The **Waldor** (Jansweg 40; 023 531 2622) is more reasonable, with rates currently standing at ƒ65 for a single room, ƒ75 for a double and ƒ125 for a triple, while the **NJHC Hostel Jan Gijzen** (Jan Gijzenpad 3; 023 537 3793) offers bed and breakfast at ƒ29,75 (non-members) or ƒ24,75 (members).

## Restaurants, cafés & bars

The best Greek food in town can be had at **Zorba de Griek** (Smedestraat 47; 023 531 5188), while **Pamukkale** (Gedempte Oudegracht 29; 023 532 6300) is a Turkish joint that has the added bonus of live music Thursday to Sunday nights. One of the tiniest restaurants in town, **De Keuken** (Lange Veerstraat 4; 023 534 5343) offers European cuisine in a quiet atmosphere, though if you have money to burn, don't miss **De Componist** (Korte Veerstraat 1; 023 532 8853), where main courses start at ƒ37.

## Museum

### Teylers Museum
*Spaarne 16 (023 531 9010).* **Open** 10am-5pm Tue-Sat; noon-5pm Sun. **Admission** ƒ7,50; ƒ3,50 5-15s.

## Leiden

Leiden is home to the Netherlands' oldest university, founded in 1581 after the city stood up to the Spanish during the Dutch Revolt in 1574. The siege almost starved the population into submission, but the city was rescued when William of Orange opened dykes to flood central Holland, so his ships could sail up to the town walls. Leidens Ontzet (the Relief of Leiden) is still celebrated with a carnival-like festival every 3 October, when commemorative dishes – stew, herring and white bread – are consumed in vast quantities.

In the late sixteenth and seventeenth centuries, Leiden heard the first cries from the mouths of a trio of Dutch painters: Rembrandt was born here, as were Jan van Goyen and Jan Steen. The university can boast some fine alumni: both Descartes and American president John Quincy Adams, among others, have graced its hallowed cloisters. The main student quarter today is around **Sint Pieterskerk**, the home of the Pilgrim Fathers before they sailed to America via Plymouth on the *Mayflower*. Their leader, John Robinson, stayed and is buried in the church; for more history, visit the **Pilgrims' Documentation Centre** at Vliet 45.

Leiden's **Rijksmuseum van Oudheden** houses the largest archaeological collection in the Netherlands: the extensive collection of Egyptian mummies, in particular, should not be missed. Of the other notable museums, the recently refurbished **Rijksmuseum voor Volkkunde** (National Museum of Ethnology) has art from all over the world, while the **Stedelijk Museum de Lakenhal** includes paintings by famous Dutch artists in a building that once housed the clothmakers' guild. Fans of Dutch clichés could do a lot worse than visit the **Molenmuseum de Valk** (Windmill Museum), where you can explore the inside of a typical Dutch windmill and absorb the view of Leiden from the balcony. An even better view of the city and surrounds can be had from the top of the **Burcht**, a twelfth-century fort on an ancient artificial mound reached via the fifteenth-century **Korenbeursbrug** ('Corn Exchange Bridge'), the only covered bridge in Leiden. The latest addition to Leiden's many sights is the already hugely popular **Biological Museum Naturalis**, which has displays including full-scale dinosaurs, minerals and stuffed animals.

## Essential information

### Getting there
*by car* 40km (24 miles) south-west on A4; *by rail* 35 mins, direct.

### VVV
*Stationplein 210 (0900 222 2333).* **Open** 9am-5.30pm Mon-Fri; 10am-2pm Sat.

## Accommodation

Top of the range is the **Golden Tulip** (Schipholweg 3; 071 522 1121), which has singles at ƒ162-ƒ255 and doubles at ƒ190-ƒ285. Cheaper is the **Mayflower** (Beestenmarkt 2; 071 514 2641), which offers singles for ƒ125-ƒ150 and doubles for ƒ170 (both including breakfast), while the **Bik Bed & Breakfast** (Witte Singel 92; 071 512 2602; closed Oct) is cheaper still, at ƒ40 for a single and ƒ80 for a double.

## Restaurants, cafés & bars

**Annie's Verjaardag** (Hoogstraat 1A; 071 512 5737) is a food bunker/café underneath a bridge, though the main selling point is the boat deck and canal barge terrace; expect to pay around ƒ23. For a more easygoing dining experience, try **La Bota** (Herensteeg 9; 071 514 6340). Very popular with students, it offers a great variety of good-value meals. Another option is **Einstein** (Nieuwe Rijn 19; 071 512 5370).

Leiden is a student city, so you're always just around the corner from a half-decent bar. Two good, slightly alternative examples are **De WW** (Wolsteeg 6; 071 512 5900) and **Sus Antigoon** (Oude Vest 81; 071 512 1090).

## Museums

### Biological Museum Naturalis
*Darwinweg (071 568 7600).* **Open** noon-6pm Tue-Sun. **Admission** ƒ12,50; ƒ5 6-12s.

### Molenmuseum de Valk
*2E Binnenvestgracht 1 (071 516 5353).* **Open** 10am-5pm Tue-Sat; 1-5pm Sun. **Admission** ƒ5; ƒ3 6-15s.

### Rijksmuseum van Oudheden
*Rapenburg 28 (071 516 3163).* **Open** 10am-5pm Tue-Fri; noon-5pm Sat, Sun. **Admission** ƒ7; ƒ6 6-17s.

### Rijksmuseum voor Volkkunde
*Steenstraat 1 (071 521 1824).* **Open** 10am-5pm Tue-Fri; noon-5pm Sat, Sun. **Admission** ƒ7; ƒ5 4-17s.

### Stedelijk Museum de Lakenhal
*Oude Singel 28-32 (071 516 5360).* **Open** 10am-5pm Tue-Fri; noon-5pm Sat, Sun. **Admission** ƒ5; ƒ2,50 6-17s.

## Rotterdam

Rotterdam is the eternal second city of the Netherlands, but don't ever say that to a local. It certainly isn't a place for agoraphobics: practically the whole of Rotterdam's old city centre was destroyed by bombs in May 1940 and, with commendable daring, the authorities decided to start afresh rather than try to reconstruct its former maze of canals. Perch on the **Willemsbrug** bridge for a magnificent view of the futuristic skyline, or, if you can stomach the expense and the height, go up the **Euromast** for an overview of the immense Rhine-Maas Delta. This huge tower is situated in **Het Park**, where many Rotterdammers spend time when the weather is good.

Not every bomb site was developed immediately after World War II, in part because the city first wanted to plan its future. One of the success stories is the **Old Harbour**, a lesson in imaginative modernism that has given the world Piet Blom's witty **Kijk-Kubus**. These tilted, cubic houses on stilts are popular with tourists, who can visit the recently renovated no.70 (phone 010 414 2285 for information).

In a country dense with history, it's hardly surprising that the few buildings that survived the war have become major attractions. The heavily restored **St Lawrence Church** originally dates from 1646, while a solitary row of merchants' houses on Wijnhaven is also pretty. Best of all, though, is **Schielandshuis** off Beursplein, a seventeenth-century mansion that doubles as an excellent city museum. Displaying re-creations of scenes in Rotterdam from late medieval times – when Erasmus was born here – to the construction of the Nieuwe Waterweg, it makes for a lovely afternoon out. Another architectural delight is the new, trouble-ridden **Erasmusbrug**, an astounding masterpiece of bridge-building. Stand in the middle and see Rotterdam in all its magnificent splendour before walking to another architectural highlight, the former warehouse of the Holland-America Lijn. Although it's off the beaten track, it's worth a visit since it was renovated to house the fantastic **Hotel New York** (*see below* **Accommodation**).

The city's deep-water channel to the sea facilitated the creation of the world's biggest harbour, **Europoort**: in 1997 alone, the harbour handled an incredible 310.1 million tonnes of goods. Take one of the various SPIDO boat tours (010 275 9988) from Willemsplein to check the place out. If you're in the city at the start of September, don't miss the Wereldhavendagen (World Harbour days), a three-day festival where a myriad of activities related to the harbour are organised all over the city.

Just downstream from Europoort is **Delfshaven**, where genuinely old buildings are currently being restored. These include the former warehouses that now contain the **Museum de** **Dubbelde Palmboom**, which covers working life in the Meuse estuary. A plaque on the quay marks where the Pilgrim Fathers left for America in 1620, having held a final service at the nearby **Oude Kerk**, where they are also commemorated. The best museum in Rotterdam is the recently renovated **Museum Boymans-Van Beuningen** (*see chapter* **Museums**, *page 86*), which reopens in January 1999, but try and find time to visit the **Maritime Museum Prins Hendrik**, a startling piece of architecture with stunning river views, and a pretty decent maritime museum, too.

## Essential information

### Getting there
*by car* 73km (45 miles) south on A4, then A13; *by rail* one hour, direct.

### VVV
*Coolsingel 67 (0900 403 4065).* **Open** 9.30am-6pm Mon-Thur; 9.30am-9pm Fri; 9.30am-5pm Sat; noon-5pm Sun.

## Accommodation

The proverbial lap of luxury is best experienced at the **Hotel New York** (Koninginnenhoofd 1; 010 439 0500), where you can stay in the wonderfully preserved boardroom for ƒ350; other double rooms cost from ƒ145-ƒ350. Rates at the **NJHC Youth Hostel** (Rochussenstraat 107-109; 010 436 5763) – ƒ27,50 members, ƒ32,50 non-members – include breakfast.

## Restaurants, cafés & bars

**De Tuin** (Plaszoom 354; 010 452 7743), in the lovely Kralingse park, serves pretty decent traditional dishes in beautiful surroundings. The film-café **De Consul** (Westersingel 28; 010 436 3323) is a great bar/restaurant combination, where you can eat in a beautiful tropical garden: meals cost around ƒ17,50, and the bar is open very late. Rotterdam institution **Rotown** (Nieuwe Binnenweg 19; 010 436 2669) serves good meals and occasionally has live music, though jazz lovers should go to **Dizzy's** ('s Gravendijkwal 127; 010 477 3014), one of the best live jazz venues in the entire country.

## Museums

### Maritime Museum Prins Hendrik
*Leuvehaven 1 (010 413 2680).* **Open** 10am-5pm Tue-Sat; 11am-5pm Sun. **Admission** ƒ6; ƒ3 4-15s. Group discounts (min 15 persons).

### Museum de Dubbelde Palmboom
*Voorhaven 12 (010 476 1533).* **Open** 10am-5pm Tue-Fri; 11am-5pm Sat, Sun. **Admission** ƒ6; ƒ3 4-16s. Group discounts (min 15 persons).

## Utrecht

Utrecht (*see chapter* **The Provinces**, *page 243*) takes its name from the *oude trecht* ('old ford') founded by the Romans in AD 48 as a crossing on the Rhine. It later became a big Christian centre after Holland's patron saint, St Willibrord, chose it as a base from which to convert the Netherlands to Christianity in around AD 700.

But there's more to Utrecht than just history and picturesque scenery. **Utrecht University** is the largest in the Netherlands, and as a result, the city centre has a relaxed atmosphere and plenty of cafés. The city also boasts the largest shopping centre in Holland and one of the country's biggest eyesores, the **Hoog Catharijne**. Combined with Utrecht railway station, it's so large that you can easily get lost and spend a whole day in the building. Luxury lovers should head for **La Vie**, the shopping centre opposite, while others may prefer the **markets** at Vredenburg (Wednesdays and Saturdays) and St Jacobsstraat (Saturday mornings), or the flower and plant markets at Janskerkhof and Oudegracht on Saturdays.

Utrecht is a very compact city, with practically everything within walking distance. A good place to start a walk around town is the **Domtoren** (Dom Tower), an imposing structure that, at over 100 metres (328 feet) high, is the tallest church tower in the country. The views from the top of the fourteenth-century tower are breathtaking – on a clear day you can see Amsterdam – but with 465 steps to climb, it's not a place for those with weak hearts or an aversion to exercise. Guided tours are available, but don't expect too much from them.

From the tower you can see the **Domkerk**, which also dates from the fourteenth century. Originally a Catholic church, it became Protestant after the Reformation. Outside is the **Pandhof**, a cloister garden planted with many medicinal herbs. The garden, with its lovely decorative fountain, is a lovely, quiet place to sit and contemplate before you continue on your travels.

Another good place to explore is the **Oudegracht**, the canal that runs through the centre of Utrecht. Its waterside footpaths and cellars are unique: unlike Amsterdammers, who winched their goods up by a pulley into their houses, the residents of Utrecht had goods delivered across the quays into the basement of their canalside houses. Many of these cellars now house cafés and shops, and are excellent places to get a snack and watch the boats navigate their way through the narrow bridges. There are regular boat trips, and *waterfietsen* ('water bikes') can also be hired.

Of Utrecht's several museums, the magnificent **Rijksmuseum het Catharijneconvent** has the largest collection of medieval art in Holland and gives a fascinating account of the country's religious history. The **University Museum**, meanwhile, spotlights the world of science, both past and present, and has a special lab where youngsters can do optical experiments. Other museums include the **Nederlands Spoorwegmuseum** (Dutch Railway Museum), which is housed in buildings dating from 1874, and the **Rijksmuseum van Speelklok tot Pierement**, which has a collection of automated musical instruments from the eighteenth century to the pre-

sent day (for both, *see chapter* **Children**, *page 172*). Finally, a short ride out of Utrecht is the fascinating **Rietveld-Schröderhuis**, designed in 1924 by architect and designer Gerrit Rietveld for a wealthy acquaintance, Truus Schröder. When she died in 1985, this expensive architectural commission was put into the hands of a foundation so that others would benefit from it. Visiting is by appointment only (phone 030 236 2310 for details).

## Essential information

### Getting there
*by car* 40km (25 miles) south-east; *by rail* 30 mins, direct.

### VVV
*Vredenburg 90 (06 3403 4085/0990 414 1414).* **Open** 9am-6pm Mon-Fri; 9am-5pm Sat.

## Accommodation

The **Holiday Inn** (Jaarbeursplein 24; 030 291 0555) charges ƒ350 for doubles and ƒ315 for singles, though better value – and more characterful – is the **Parkhotel** (Tolsteegsingel 34; 030 251 6712), a budget hotel with a swimming pool and double rooms from ƒ83. Travellers on a shoestring should try the **Bunnik Youth Hostel** (Rhijnauwenselaan 14, Bunnik; 030 656 1277), only ten minutes from the centre by bus. B&B costs ƒ24,25 with an IYH card, ƒ29,25 without.

## Restaurants, cafés & bars

The appallingly named **Moustache** (Drieharingenstraat 18; 030 231 8953) is a fairly expensive French restaurant run by the well-known culinary Fagel family, with meals from ƒ35. Budget travellers are better off in De Zakkendragerssteeg, a tiny street close to the station. This is where you'll find **Restaurant de Zakkendrager** (030 231 7578), a cosy place overlooking a garden. **Pancake Bakery de Oude Munt Kelder** (Oudegracht aan de Werf 12; 030 231 6773) offers pancakes from ƒ6,50 and a lovely view of the canal.

Most of the bars in the city centre are in the brown café league and are overrun by students. **Kafé België** (Oude Gracht 196; 030 231 2666) is a welcome exception: it's a nice Belgian beer café with over 200 bottled beers and 20 on tap. At the end of Oude Gracht is **Café Ledig Erf** (Tolsteegbrug 3; 030 231 7577), one of the better places in the city. Chess lovers are challenged to solve the problem above the bar.

## Museums

### Nederlands Spoorwegmuseum
*Maliebaanstation (030 230 6206).* **Open** 10am-5pm Tue-Fri; 11.30am-5pm Sat, Sun. **Admission** ƒ13,50; ƒ9 4-12s, free with Museum Card.

### Rijksmuseum het Catharijneconvent
*Nieuwegracht 63 (030 231 7296).* **Open** 10am-5pm Tue-Fri; 11am-5pm Sat, Sun, public holidays. **Admission** ƒ7; ƒ3,50 7-17s.

### Rijksmuseum van Speelklok tot Pierement
*Buurkerkhof 10 (030 231 2789).* **Open** 10am-5pm Tue-Sat; noon-5pm Sun. **Admission** ƒ9; ƒ5 4-12s; ƒ2,25 over-65s. Group discounts (min 37, max 50 persons).

### Universiteits Museum
*Lange Nieuwstraat 106 (030 253 8008).* **Open** 10am-5pm Tue-Fri; 1-5pm Sat, Sun. **Admission** ƒ7; ƒ3,50 under-18s, students.

# The Provinces

**Charming and rural, or flat and dull? Read on and find out...**

The ancient arrogance of urbanites dictates their belief that life in their country ends at the borders of the big cities. The Netherlands is no exception to the rule: people from the Randstad like to scorn residents of the Provinces as being a bunch of farmers living in boring places where the only goal in life seems to be getting drunk. However, this is not exactly true. These outlying regions are excellent places to spend a couple of days when Amsterdam's insanity gets to be a bit too much.

Visitors should note that many of the VVV tourist offices listed below only accept postal and phone enquiries. There's a basic map of Holland on page 289; for a scale map, the Falk Plan tourist map has a useful place index.

### PROVINCIAL CHARM

The people of the largely Protestant northern provinces of Friesland, Groningen and Drenthe are renowned for stubbornness, loyalty and hard work. **Friesland** was once an independent tribal nation that reached along the coast from North Holland to eastern Germany, and whose people were called 'unconquerable' by Pliny the Elder. Neighbouring **Groningen**, a staid, rural and conservative area, has a surprisingly liberal university, though graduates don't usually stay around long. The fens, moors and forests of pagan place **Drenthe**, meanwhile, is worlds apart, inhabited since the Palaeolithic age. Saxons initially occupied the hillier **Overijssel** east of Amsterdam.

The largest province, **Gelderland**, borders Germany and is sandwiched between north and south. Its terrain of wild countryside, orchards and commercial rivers has been fought over for centuries. Gelderland became land-locked when part of the Zuider Zee was drained to form **Flevoland**. Today, the enormous and impressive Afsluitdijk connects North Holland with Friesland.

Another victory over the sea was the building of the Delta Works flood barrier to protect the islands of **Zeeland**, once isolated in the river delta bordering Belgium. Caricatures of the Dutch come unstuck in the Catholic south ('below the rivers'), where there are even a few small hills. The entire **Noord Brabant** village of Eersel sometimes gathers for weddings in a large tent at the market-place, savouring milk and brandy with sugar. Wedged between Belgium and Germany, the rolling landscape of **Limburg** is also home to *bons vivants*, who thrive on its famous cuisine.

*The rural beauty of **Drenthe**.*

## Drenthe

Drenthe's affectionate nickname – 'Het Oude Landschap' ('the old landscape') – might go back centuries, but not as far back as the area itself: humans have lived here for no less than 50,000 years. The best place to appreciate what much of the countryside looked like as little as 20 years ago is in Orvelte at the **Oud Saksisch Kijkdorp** (Old Saxon Village; Dorpstraat 3; 0593 322335; open Apr-Oct 10am-5pm Mon-Fri, 11am-5pm Sat, Sun, public holidays; admission ƒ12,50, ƒ10 over-65s, ƒ8 4-12s, free under-4s).

To find out more about the province's past, start at the magnificent **Drents Museum** in **Assen** (Brink 1; 0592 312741; open 11am-5pm Tue-Sun; admission ƒ7,50, ƒ2,50 5-15s), which features a fascinating display of prehistoric artefacts. The surrounding area is full of ancient sites, though the most impressive monuments are the *hunebedden* (megaliths), towards the German border. Burials took place between 3400BC and 2300BC in this string of megalithic burial sites, constructed from boulders shed by the nearby Hondsrug, a moraine on which most of Drenthe is built. The history of the monuments is explained at the **National Hunebedden Information Centre** in **Borger** (Bronnegerstraat 12; 0599 236374; open Feb-Dec 10am-5pm Mon-Fri, 1-5pm Sat, Sun).

The Drenthe countryside is the perfect backdrop to the megalithic tombs. Rivulets run through peat cuttings (look for villages whose names end in 'veen', which means 'peat bog') on huge heaths such as the Fochtelooer Veen near Assen. There's also a lovely forest, the **Drentse Wold**, near Uffelte, and another, **Ellertsveld**, west of the *hunebedden.* Near Ellertsveld is a chilling reminder of the past, the Nazi transit camp at Westerbork.

### VVV tourist offices

**Provincial Office** *Postbus 10012, 9400 CA Assen (0592 373755).* **Open** *phone enquiries* 9am-5pm Mon-Fri. **Assen** *Brink 42, 9401 HV (0592 314324).* **Open** 1-6pm Mon; 9am-6pm Tue-Thur; 9am-9pm Fri; 9am-5pm Sat; *22 Jun-24 Aug* open at 11am.
**Emmen** *Marktplein 17, 7811 AM (0591 613000).* **Open** 9am-5.30pm Mon-Fri; 9am-4pm Sat.

## Flevoland

Slightly north-east of Amsterdam, Flevoland only became a province in its own right in 1986 when the polders (essentially, pieces of reclaimed land) of South Flevoland and East Flevoland were combined with the north-east polder (formerly in Overijssel, for which *see below*). The province is the most recent stage in the Netherlands' massive, land-reclamation process. Drained between 1950 and 1957 to create more room for the population, Flevoland offered little to entice new residents. Its capital, **Lelystad**, should have been a planner's dream. However, while development there is refreshingly low-level, it's hard to get to and sits hunched on the windy outer edge of the province. By contrast, the space-age city of **Almere**, intended as a satellite to Lelystad, is almost embarrassingly successful. Now an outpost of Amsterdam, it has attracted thousands of the capital's commuters.

Reminders of Flevoland's past as a sea bed are often unearthed, and remains of vessels, anchors and cannonballs are displayed in the **Museum Schokland** in Ens (Middelbuurt 3; 0527 251396; open Nov-Mar 11am-5pm Sat, Sun, Apr-Jun, Sept, Oct 11am-5pm Tue-Sun, July, Aug 11am-5pm daily; admission *f*4,50; *f*3 6-12s). Lelystad's **NISA** – the Netherlands Institute for Ships and Underwater Archaeology – opens in late 1998 (Oostvaardersdijk 0104; 0320 269700; open 10am-5pm daily; admission *f*17,50, includes entry to Batavia Wharf). Modern attractions include a the **Walibi Flevo** adventure park in Biddinghuizen, (Spijkweg 30; 0321 329900; open mid-Apr-Nov 10am-5pm Mon-Sat, 10am-6pm Sun; admission *f*32,50, free under-4s, two-day pass *f*48).

### VVV tourist offices

**Provincial Office** *Stationsplein 86, 8232 VT Lelystad (0320 243444).* **Open** 9am-5pm Mon-Wed, Fri; 9am-5pm, 6.30-9pm Thur; 9am-3pm Sat.
**Almere** *Spoordreef 20, 1315 GP Almere (036 533 4600).* **Open** 9.30am-6pm Mon-Wed, Fri; 9.30am-9pm Thur; 9.30am-5pm Sat.
**Urk** *Raadhuisstraat 2, 8321 EP (0527 684040).* **Open** *Apr-Oct* 10am-5pm Mon-Fri; 10am-1pm Sat.

## Friesland

Friesland, in the far north, has always been regarded by southerners as a windswept barbarian outpost. It has its own language (*never* say 'dialect'!), a highly unusual landscape and the nearest thing to provincial nationalism you're likely to find in the country. Because of its vast network of lakes and canals, the region used to be cut off. Nowadays, the water is a major attraction: the lakes are packed with yachts and motor cruisers in summer, with boating focused on the town of **Sneek**. The best way to explore the waterways is to go on an excursion or rent a boat and stop off at fishing towns like **Grouw**, **Terhorne**, **Heeg** and **Sloten**.

The best feature of the province is its landscape, but the capital, **Leeuwarden**, also boasts a picturesque centre within a star-shaped moat. Like Groningen (*see below*), Friesland is dotted with beautiful brick churches, built on *terpen* (mounds) to escape flooding. The best examples, such as that at **Hogebeintum**, west of Dokkum, are in the far north of the province. Friesland is also the setting for a great Dutch tradition: **De Elfstedentocht** ('eleven cities tour'), a skating marathon on natural ice that leads the skaters through almost the entire province (*see chapter* **Sport***, page 216*).

### VVV tourist offices

**Provincial & Leeuwarden Office** *Stationsplein 1, 8911 AC Leeuwarden (06 3202 4060/0900 202 4060).* **Open** 9am-5.30pm Mon-Fri; 10am-1pm Sat.
**Hindeloopen** *Postbus 4, 8713 ZG (0514 522550).* **Open** 1-3pm Mon; 10.30am-12.30pm, 1.30-4pm Tue-Fri; 10.30am-12.30pm, 1.30-3pm Sat.
**Noordoost-Friesland Office** *Grote Breedstraat 1, 9100 KH Dokkum (0519 293800).* **Open** 1-5pm (*July, Aug* 11am-5pm) Mon; 9am-6pm Tue-Thur; 9am-6pm, 7-9pm Fri; 9am-5pm Sat.
**Sneek** *Marktstraat 18, 8601 CV (0515 414096).* **Open** 9am-12.30pm, 1-5.30pm Mon-Fri; 9am-12.30pm, 1-5pm Sat.

## The Frisian Islands

The five sparsely populated Frisian Islands (or Wadden Islands) are frequented more by migrant birds and grey seals than by human visitors. It's possible to island-hop between the first three islands (Texel, Vlieland and Terschelling), but Ameland and Schiermonnikoog can only be reached by ferry from the mainland.

The biggest island, **Texel**, is in fact administered by Noord Holland and reached via Den Helder. The beautiful nature and bird reserves (De Slufter and De Muy) make it a good place for long walks, though animal lovers should also visit the seal sanctuary at the resort of De Koog. A good place to learn about the island's history is the **Maritiem En Jutters Museum**: apart from displays on island history, it has an impressive collection of weird refuse gathered by beachcombers (Barentszstraat 21; 0222 314956; open Sept-Jun 10am-5pm Tue-Sun; July, Aug 10am-5pm daily; admission *f*8; *f*7 over-65s; *f*4 4-13s).

**Vlieland** is the most deserted island – no cars are allowed – though since some of its beaches are reserved for bombing practice by the Dutch Air

Force, this is hardly surprising. **Terschelling**, on the other hand, is the most picturesque island. Apart from the beautiful nature, beaches and fishing villages, the island boasts the **Brandaris**, the most famous lighthouse in the country, and Hessel, an eccentric rock legend who runs the Café de Groene Weide in the small village of Hoorn.

The fourth island, **Ameland**, is good for walking and cycling tours, particularly since it has an impressive collection of rare plants and birds, plus a huge rabbit population. The least inhabited island is **Schiermonnikoog**, with only one village, built in 1760. Most of this island is now a nature reserve, and cars are not allowed.

### VVV tourist offices

**Ameland** *Rixt van Doniastraat 2, 9163 GR Nes (0519 546546)*. **Open** 8.30am-12.30pm, 1.30-6.30pm Mon-Fri; 10am-4pm Sat.
**Schiermonnikoog** *Reeweg 5, 9166 ZP (0519 531233)*. **Open** 9am-1pm, 2-6pm Mon-Fri; 9am-1pm, 2-4.30pm Sat.
**Terschelling** *Willem Barentszkade 19a, Postbus 1, 8880 AA Terschelling-West (0562 443000)*. **Open** 9.30am-5.30pm Mon-Sat.
**Texel** *Emmelaan 66, 1791 AV Den Burg (0222 312847)*. **Open** *Dec-Mar* 9am-6pm Mon-Fri; 9am-5pm Sat; *Apr-Nov* 9am-6pm Mon-Thur; 9am-9pm Fri; 9am-5.30pm Sat; *July, Aug* also 1am-1.30pm Sun.
**Vlieland** *Havenweg 10, Postbus 1, 8899 ZN Vlieland (0562 451111)*. **Open** 9am-5pm Mon-Fri; 9am-12.30pm Sat (phone enquiries); also when ferry arrives Sat, Sun.

Gelderland is the largest of the provinces. Nearly a third is covered by the **Veluwe** (Bad Land), a 4,600-hectare (11,400-acre) stretch of forest and moorland. In the south of the Veluwe near **Arnhem** is the Netherlands' biggest national park, the **Hoge Veluwe** (entrances at Otterlo, Schaarsbergen and Hoenderloo; visitors' centre 0318 591627; open daily (phone for details); admission *f*7, *f*3,50 6-12s, free under-6s, cars *f*8,50), where wild animals such as boars and deer wander around freely. Stroll among the trees near the park's Otterlo entrance, though, and you'll find the fascinating **Rijksmuseum Kröller-Müller** (0318 591041; open 10am-5pm Tue-Sun). It holds an impressive collection, including the most important Van Goghs outside Amsterdam, plus works by Mondrian and the Dutch symbolists; the sculpture park outside includes pieces by Rodin, Moore, Hepworth and Giacometti. Not far from Hoge Veluwe is **Paleis Het Loo**, a gorgeous building originally built as a hunting lodge by William III in 1685-92 and now open to the public (Amersfoortseweg, Apeldoorn; 055 577 2400; open 10am-5pm Tue-Sun; admission *f*12,50, *f*10 5-18s).

Moving away from the park, you may come across the **Betuwe** (Good Land), the south-west region of fertile land sandwiched between the River Waal, the River Maas and the River Lek further north. The countryside to the east and

*Peace and quiet isn't hard to find on* **Texel**.

towards Germany, the **Achterhoek**, is dominated by commercial waterways.

Arnhem and **Nijmegen**, the province's biggest city, both have several good museums: Nijmegen's **Bevrijdingmuseum** (Liberation Museum; Wylerbaan 4; 024 397 4404; open 10am-5pm Mon-Sat, noon-5pm Sun) will appeal to history buffs, as will the **Nederlands Openluchtmuseum** in Arnhem (Schelmseweg 89; 026 357 6123; open Apr-Oct 10am-5pm daily; admission *f*17, *f*15,50 over-65s, *f*11,50 4-12s), an open-air folklore collection. However, the best things about both cities are their imposing Gothic churches – Nijmegen's church survived the Allied bombs – and riverside views.

### VVV tourist offices

**Provincial Office** *Postbus 142, 6860 AC Oosterbeek (026 333 2033)*. **Open** phone/postal enquiries 8.30am-5pm Mon-Fri.
**Arnhem** *Stationsplein 45, Postbus 552, 6811 KL Arnhem (06 3202 4075/0900 2024075)*. **Open** 11am-5.30pm Mon; 9am-5.30pm Tue-Fri; 10am-4pm Sat.
**Nijmegen** *St Jorisstraat 72, Postbus 175, 6500 AD (06 9112 2344/0900 1122344)*. **Open** 9am-5pm Mon-Fri; 10am-5pm Sat.

All roads in this province lead to the city of Groningen, the province's capital and namesake. The province's history is explained in the

**Groninger Museum** (Museumeiland 1; 050 366 6555; open 10am-5pm Tue-Sun; admission ƒ8, ƒ6 5-15s, over-65s), which also holds modern art exhibitions. The city also has a beautiful fifteenth-century church, the **Martinikerk**. The views from the top of the six-tiered church tower are wonderful: the lush agricultural landscape is sprinkled with eighteenth-century *kop-romp* (head-trunk) farmhouses, a combination of tall, stuccoed villas and wide barns built for heavy harvests.

However, it's the rural churches that are the real glory of the province. Beautifully proportioned and, generally speaking, with high, saddleback towers peeping over a ring of trees, they're best seen in the morning mist or under a thick blanket of snow. **Garmerwold, Ten Boer, Stedum, Loppersum, Appingedam, Bierum, Spijk,** and **Uithuizen** all have lovely houses of worship dating from up to 700 years ago. Uithuizen also boasts one of the loveliest country houses in the Netherlands: the fortified fifteenth-century **Menkemaborg** (Menkemaweg 2; 0595 431970; open 10am-noon, 1-5pm Mon-Sun; admission ƒ5, ƒ4 over-65s, ƒ3 under-15s). The **Het Hoogeland** open-air museum at **Warffum** is also worth a visit (Schoolstraat 2-4; 0595 422233; open Apr-Oct 10am-5pm Tue-Sat, 1-5pm Sun).

### VVV tourist offices
**Provincial & Groningen Office** *Gedempte Kattendiep 6, 7911 PN Groningen (06 3202 3050/0900 2023050).* **Open** 9am-5.30pm Mon-Fri; 10am-5pm Sat.
**Appingedam** *Wijkstraat 38, 9901 AX (0596 620300).* **Open** 10am-5pm Mon-Fri; 2-5pm Sat, Sun.
**Uithuizen** *Mennonietenkerkstraat 13, 9981 BB (0595 434051).* **Open** 10am-noon, 1-5pm Mon-Fri; 1-4pm Sat.
**Winschoten** *Stationweg 21A, 6970 AC (0597 412255).* **Open** 9am-5.15pm Mon-Fri; 9am-12.45pm Sat.

## Limburg

Limburg, a southern spur of Dutch territory wedged between Belgium and Germany, is the antidote to all those clichés about the Netherlands being flat. The valley of the Geul, a small stream which drives waterwheels and clatters past black and white half-timbered farmsteads, is dominated by **Valkenburg**, a fortified town with prehistoric caves and Roman catacombs, and dotted with picturesque villages. Nearby **Heerlen** has Roman baths in the **Thermenmuseum**.

**Maastricht**, best known for the European treaty that bears its name, is the provincial capital of Limburg. A town of contrasts, it's a wonderful town to explore: head for the tiny shop-packed streets jostling for attention around the Markt, then stroll along the southern ramparts for a breathtaking view of the river. The glorious stone **Basilica of St Servatius** dates from the eleventh century but is not Maastricht's oldest building: that honour is held by the Romanesque **Basilica of Our Lady**.

Maastricht, though, is not the only town in Limburg worth a visit: be sure to make time for a trip to **Roermond**, and specifically the city's part-Romanesque, part-Gothic **Munsterkerk**, built in 1220. Fans of geographical oddities will prefer **Vaals**, however. The town boasts two three-country points where Holland is connected with its neighbours Belgium and Germany. Vaals also has the **Labyrint Dreilandandenpunt**, a maze that adults and kids find delightful (Viergrenzenweg 79; 043 306 5200; open Apr-Oct 10am-5pm daily; admission ƒ5, ƒ4,50 over-65s, ƒ4 3-12s).

### VVV tourist offices
**Provincial Office** *Kerkstraat 31, Postbus 811, 6300 AV Valkenburg (043 601 7321).* **Open** 9am-5pm Mon-Fri; 10am-1pm Sat.
**Heerlen** *Honingmanstraat 100, 6411 LM (045 571 6200).* **Open** 9.30am-6pm Mon-Wed, Fri; 9.30am-8pm Thur; 9.30am-2pm Sat.
**Maastricht** *Kleine Straat 1, 6211 ED (043 325 2121).* **Open** 9am-6pm Mon-Sat; 11am-4pm Sun.
**Roermond** *Kraanpoort 1, 6041 EG (0900 202 5588).* **Open** *Apr-Sep* 9am-6pm Mon-Fri; 9am-4pm Sat; *Oct-Mar* 9am-5pm Mon-Fri; 10am-2pm Sat.
**Vaals** *Maastrichterlein 73a, 6291 EL (043 306 2918).* **Open** 9am-5.30pm Mon-Fri; 10am-3pm Sat.
**Valkenburg** *Theo Dorrenplein 5, 6301 DV (043 609 8600/8518).* **Open** 9am-6pm Mon-Fri; 9am-5pm Sat; 10am-2pm Sun.

## Noord Brabant

Noord Brabant, which borders Belgium in the south, was one of the last provinces to turn against Spain during the Dutch Revolt at the start of the seventeenth century, and one of the most reluctant to forget its Burgundian past. Consequently, its character has been shaped to a large extent by its Catholic population, who in 1867 commissioned PJH Cuypers and G van Swaay to build a replica of Rome's St Peter's Basilica in Oudenbosch, east of Breda. Five centuries earlier, the **Cathedral of St Jan** had been built at the provincial capital **'s-Hertogenbosch**. It's now the only example of pure Gothic architecture in Holland.

Den Bosch, the common name for the provincial capital, is also one of the two main Dutch centres of carnival (the other is Maastricht), held the weekend before Lent. Although carnival is celebrated all over the country, the south is the place to experience it, though the Mediterranean-style celebrations are slightly – and comically – marred by the severe cold weather in this part of the world.

The nearby city of **Eindhoven** is, if we're being honest, nothing special. Still, it is home to three places of interest: Stationsplein, where a statue of electronics pioneer AF Philips stands; the **Stedelijk Van Abbemuseum**, an excellent modern art museum (Vonderweg 1; 040 275 5275; open 11am-5pm Tue-Sun; admission ƒ8, ƒ4 7-15s, over-65s); and football club **PSV Eindhoven**. After taking in the Van Abbe, art-lovers should head a few miles north to **Nuenen**. Van Gogh's family lived in the town's vicarage, and displays of memorabilia have made it a place of pilgrimage for fans of the artist. Move further north-east towards Germany and you'll find De Groote Peel, a nature reserve, and the **National War and Resistance Museum** at Overloon (Museumpark 1; 0478 641250; open Sep-May 10am-5pm daily; Jun-Aug 9.30am-6pm daily; admission ƒ11, ƒ9 over-65s, ƒ7 under-18s).

Noord Brabant is also home to two of the most famous tourist attractions in the country: the **Safaripark Beekse Bergen** in Hilvarenbeek, and **De Efteling Theme Park** in Kaatsheuvel. The Safaripark is a wonderful park inhabited by no less than 1,000 animals; refreshingly, it's possible to do the safari by boat, bus, car or on foot, with or without a guide (Beekse Bergen 31; 0900 233 5732; open 10am-3.30pm daily; admission ƒ22,50, ƒ19,50 3-11s, over-60s, free under-3s, cars ƒ5). Kids will also love De Efteling, an amazing theme park originally designed by Dutch artist Anton Pieck (Europalaan 1; 0416 288111; open Apr-Jun & Oct 10am-6pm, Jul-Sept 10am-9pm; admission ƒ35, under-3s free).

### VVV tourist offices

**Provincial Office** *Stadhuisplein 128, 5003 DG Tilburg (013 535 1135).* **Open** 9am-5.30pm Mon-Fri; 10am-4pm Sat (telephone and postal enquiries only).
**Bergen-op-Zoom** *Beursplein 7, 4611 JG (0164 266000).* **Open** noon-5.30pm Mon; 9am-5.30pm Tue-Fri; 9am-5pm Sat.
**Breda** *Willemstraat 17, 4811 AJ (076 522 2444).* **Open** 9am-6pm Mon-Fri; 9am-5pm Sat.
**Eindhoven** *Stationsplein 17, 5611 AC (0900 112 2363).* **Open** 10am-5.30pm Mon; 9am-5.30pm Tue-Thur; 9am-8.30pm Fri; 9am-5pm Sat.
**'s-Hertogenbosch (Den Bosch)** *Markt 77, 5211 JX (073 612 2334).* **Open** 11am-5.30pm Mon; 9am-5.30pm Tue-Fri; 9am-4pm Sat.

## Overijssel

Also known as the Garden of the Netherlands, Overijssel is crisscrossed by long, winding rivers and 400 kilometres (249 miles) of canoe routes. A superb spot for watersports, it's dotted with holiday homes and cabins. The VVV even provides self-drive, horse-drawn carts, which you can sleep in.

Most visitors head for the Lake District, comprising the **Weerribben** and **Wieden** districts. Between the two runs the road linking **Steenwijk** and **Blokzijl**, both fortified towns, the latter with a marina in its old harbour. Wieden's highlights include the huge **Beulaker Wijde/Belter Wijde** lake, and the watersports centre of **Wanneperveen**, with its thatched farmsteads and thousands of eager boaters.

Hidden among the reedlands is the village of **Giethoorn**, also known as the 'green Venice' for reasons that will become obvious upon first sight. The residents get around this charming village mostly by boat: only foot bridges connect the individually marooned houses. August is a good time to visit: the town holds a pair of music festivals – **Jazz Inn** and **Blues Inn** – on a platform erected in the lake, with a procession of flower-decked boats staged the following Saturday.

Further up the IJssel lie the Hanse towns of **Kampen, Hasselt, Zwolle, Hattem, Deventer, Zutphen** and **Doesburg**. The history of the seven towns goes back to the twelfth century, when the 129-km (80-mile) long IJssel river used to act as the trade freeway between the Rhine and the Zuiderzee. Tradesmen dealing the same goods within a city joined together in organisations known as Hansas and, eventually, Hanse.

Of the Hanse towns, Kampen, with a wealth of historic buildings and a particularly beautiful waterfront, is probably the most attractive, though the province's capital, Zwolle, does have a lovely town hall, parts of which date from 1448. Deventer, meanwhile, is best known for its domed tower of **St Lebuinuskerk**, while Zutphen holds its own medieval games during the summer.

Almost every town in Overijssel has a summer carnival. **Raalte** holds its harvest festival in the third week of August (Wed-Sat); vehicles parade through **Lemelerveld** during **Bloemen Corso** (Flower Parade, early August); and sheepdogs herd sheep around **Hellendoorn** (mid-August).

East along the River Vecht from Zwolle is the superb fishing centre of **Ommen**. Visitors can collect a fishing licence from the post office, and find out about the best baits and fishing spots in the first-class tackle shop, **Beste Stek** (Vrijthof 1; 0529 154972). Stretching south are the **Salland Hills**, rising to 81 metres (266 feet) at Holterberg. Near here is **Hellendoorn Adventure Park** (Luttenbergerweg 22; 0548 655555; open Apr-Oct 10am-6pm daily; admission ƒ28,50; free 0-2s).

**Twente**, the district stretching up to Germany, is dominated by **Enschede**, the province's biggest city. It's home to **Rijksmuseum Twenthe**, a modern art museum (Lasondersingel 129-131; 053 435 8675; open 11am-5pm Tue-Sun; admission ƒ7,50, ƒ5 under-17s, over-65s); and **Los Hoes**, a large renovated farm showing how people and animals used to live together in barns back in the days when warmth was more important than smell (Ledeboerpark, Hengelostraat; 0534 351825; open by appointment; admission free). Some of the district's Saxon farms can still be seen on an NS day excursion (including travel in a horse-drawn covered wagon), or on a six-day cycle tour organised by the VVV. Some of the finest farms are near **Ootmarsum**, a knot of narrow streets lined with timber buildings, and **Denekamp**, with its thirteenth-century sandstone church.

### VVV tourist offices

**Provincial Office** *Postbus 500, 7600 AM Almelo (0546 535535).* **Open** 10am-5pm Mon; 8.30am-5pm Tue-Fri.

**Enschede** *Oude Markt 31, 7511 GB (053 432 3200).*
**Open** 10am-5.30pm Mon; 9am-5.30pm Tue-Fri;
9am-2pm Sat.
**Giethoorn** *boat at Beulakerweg 114a, 8355 AL (0521
361248).* **Open** *mid-May-mid-Sept* 9am-6pm Mon-Sat;
10am-5pm Sun; *mid-Sept-Oct, Mar-mid-May* 9am-5pm
Mon-Sat; *Nov-Feb* 9.30am-5pm Mon-Fri, 10am-1pm Sat.
**Ommen** *Markt 1, 7731 DB (0529 451638).* **Open** 9am-
5pm Mon-Fri; 10am-5pm Sat; 2-5pm Sun.
**Raalte** *Varkensmarkt 8, 8102 (0572 352406).* **Open**
9am-5pm Mon-Fri; 9am-2pm Sat.
**Zwolle** *Grote Kerkplein 14, 8011 PK (0900 112 2375).*
**Open** 9am-5.30pm Mon-Fri; 9am-4pm Sat.

## Utrecht

If you go anywhere in the Netherlands over land,
the chances are you'll go through the city of
**Utrecht**, the country's main rail and road junction
just south of Amsterdam (*see chapter* **The
Randstad**, *page 237*). Earlier travellers, who
came down the Lek river, chose the province in AD
863 as the location for Europe's largest trading
post, **Dorestad**, and it's now the site of **Wijk-bij-
Duurstede**, which still has many ancient buildings. In either direction along the Lek, old towns
such as **Rhenen** and **Culemborg** have remained
virtually unchanged for hundreds of years.

Between Amsterdam and Utrecht are the 2,500-
hectare (6,200-acre) **Loosdrechtse Plassen** and
smaller **Vinkeveense Plassen**. These fan-
shaped lakes have narrow strips of land radiating
into them and are now used mainly for fishing and
watersports. The area groans with private wealth,
as testified by the many villas dotted around the
picturesque old villages of **Oud-Loosdrecht**,
**Westbroek** and **Breukeleveen**. A few kilometres away in Noord Holland is **Hilversum**, home
of Dutch radio and television.

For a taste of more ancient times, wander down
the **Vecht**, which flows north between the *plassen*.
It's the Netherlands' prettiest navigable river,
overshadowed by iron bridges, grand, decaying
estates at **Loenen**, **Vreeland** and **Breukelen**,
and the province's almost unavoidable castles (*see
chapter* **Excursions in Holland**, *page 231*). In
the east of the province, **Soestdijk** is home to the
country's former Queen (now Princess) Juliana,
and at **Austerlitz**, Napoleon's army built a huge
sand pyramid purely because they had nothing
else to do at the time. Best of all, though, is
**Amersfoort**, a beautifully-preserved medieval
town set in a ring of canals on the edge of the
**Leusder Heide**.

### VVV tourist offices

**Amersfoort** *Stationsplein 9-11, 3800 RK (0900 112
2364).* **Open** 9am-5.30pm Mon-Wed, Fri; 9am-8pm Thur;
10am-4pm Sat.
**Utrecht** *Vredenburg 90, 3511 BD (06 3403 4085).*
**Open** 9am-6pm Mon-Fri; 9am-5pm Sat.
**Wijk-bij-Duurstede** *Markt 24, 3961 BC (0343
575995).* **Open** 9.30am-4.30pm Mon-Thur; 9.30am-
4.30pm, 7-9pm Fri; 9.30am-4.30pm Sat; noon-3pm Sun.

## Zeeland

The massive storm floods of 1953 swept away
many of the old buildings and farms in Zeeland,
until then one of the most old-fashioned areas in
the country. Now, though, you'd never know that
the place was threatened at all: salt-water damage
and tide-marks, seen on the medieval churches of
**Kruiningen** (on the isthmus to Beveland Island)
and **Brouwershaven** (on Schouwen Island), are
the only reminders. For this, we can thank the
**Delta Works**, the world's biggest flood barrier.
Completed in 1986, it took 30 years to build, and
cost a staggering ƒ14 billion: the revolutionary
technology is explained at the **Delta Expo** on
**Neeltje Jans**, an island along the Oosterschelde
Dam (Postbus 19, 4328 ZG Burghamsteede; 0111
652702; open Apr-Oct 10am-5.30pm daily, Nov-
Mar 10am-5pm Wed-Sun; admission Nov-Mar
ƒ12,50, ƒ7,50 5-12s; Apr-Oct ƒ14,50, ƒ12,50 5-12s).
Along at **Expo Haringvliet** in **Stellendam**, kids
can watch a cartoon that explains the history of
Holland, while adults can witness how the enormous waterworks do their stuff (Haringvlietplein
3; 0187 499913; open Apr-Nov 10am-6pm daily).

Seafood is available all over Zeeland, but the best
hauls of the day often find their way to restaurants
in **Yerseke** (a town near Kruiningen named after
the Dutch for 'oyster'). In season (September to
April), you can take a tour of the oyster beds.
Elsewhere in Zeeland, the port of **Vlissingen** is the
birthplace of the heroic Admiral de Ruyter, whose
statue in the Rotunda surveys the dramatic
seascape. Among the artefacts in the **Stedelijk
Museum** (Bellamypark 19; 0118 412498; open
10am-5pm Mon-Fri, 1-5pm Sat, Sun; admission
ƒ2,50, ƒ1,50 4-11s, over-65s) is a copy of De Ruyter's
portrait by Ferdinand Bol, the original of which is
held – alongside tapestries depicting sea battles –
in Middelburg's **Zeeuws Museum** (Abdij; 0118
626655; open 11am-5pm Mon-Sat, noon-5pm Sun;
admission ƒ8, ƒ6,50 over-65s, ƒ2 7-12s).

Just north of Middelburg is the most beautiful
town in Zeeland: **Veere**, where elegant flèche
spires and the towering Church of Our Lady can
be seen across the flats for miles. The churches in
the province, many of which were used as light-
houses, are worth a tour in themselves, though the
churches at **Kapelle**, **Zoutelande** and **'s-Heer
Arendskerke** are perhaps the most attractive.

### VVV tourist offices

**Provincial Office** *Nieuwe Burg 42, 4331 AH
Middelburg (0118 659965).*
**Open** 9.30am-5pm Mon-Fri.
**Goes** *Stationsplein 3, 4461 HP (0900 168 1666).* **Open**
noon-5pm Mon; 9am-5pm Tue-Fri; 9am-noon Sat.
**Veere** *Oudestraat 28, 4351 AV (0118 501365).* **Open**
11am-4pm Mon-Sat.
**Vlissingen** *Nieuwendijk 15, 4381 BV (0118 412345).*
**Open** 9am-5pm Mon-Sat.
**Yerseke** *Kerkplein 1, 4401 ED (0113 571864).*
**Open** 10am-noon, 12.30-4.30pm Tue-Fri; 9am-noon Sat.

# Directory

# Directory

## Essential Information

Before you arrive

### Visas

A valid passport is all that is required for a stay of **up to three months** in Holland if you are an EU national or from the USA, Canada, Australia or New Zealand. If you are a national of any other country, apply for a tourist visa from your country of origin.

For stays of longer than three months, you need to apply in advance from your country of origin for a **residents' permit** (MVV visa), regardless of your country of origin (though it is generally harder to get one if you're not from one of the countries listed above). When you have a fixed address in Holland, you need to get an application form from the **Bureau Vreemdelingen-politie** (the Aliens' Police). Once they receive your form they will give you an interview date about five weeks from then. You must take the following to the interview: personal ID, an employment contract or written confirmation that you're a student in Holland, written proof of accommodation (a rent agreement or a written letter from the person you're staying with, plus a copy of their passport and a copy of their accommodation status) and colour passport photos. When moving from one locality to another within the city, you must sign off from the locality you're leaving before registering with the one you're moving to.

**Bureau Vreemdelingenpolitie (Aliens' Police)**

*Johan Huizingalaan 757 (559 6214). Tram 2/bus 19, 63.* **Open** 8am-5pm Mon-Fri.

### ID

Regulations concerning identification require that everyone carries some form of ID when opening accounts at banks or other financial institutions, when looking for work, when applying for benefits, when found on public transport without a ticket, and when going to a professional football match. You then have to register with the local council, which is in the same building as the Aliens' Police.

Customs

EU nationals over the age of 17 may import limitless goods into the Netherlands for their personal use. Other EU countries may still have limits on the quantity of goods they permit on entry. For citizens of non-EU countries, the old limits still apply. These are:
• 200 cigarettes or 50 cigars or 250g (8.82oz) tobacco;
• 1 litre (1.76 pints) of spirits (over 22 per cent alcohol) or 2 litres of fortified wine (under 22 per cent alcohol) or 2 litres of non-sparkling wine;
• 50g (1.76oz) of perfume;
• 500g (1.1lb) coffee;
• 100g (3.52oz) tea;
• Other goods to the value of ƒ380.

The import of meat or meat products, fruit, plants, flowers and protected animals is illegal.

### Insurance

EU countries have reciprocal medical treatment arrangements with the Netherlands. British citizens will need form E111, which can be obtained by filling in the application form in leaflet SA30, available in all Department of Social Security (DSS) offices and the Post Office. Make sure you read the small print on the back of form E111 so you know how to obtain medical or dental treatment at a reduced charge: you'll probably have to explain this to the Dutch doctor or dentist who treats you. If you need treatment, photocopy your insurance form and leave it with the doctor or dentist who treats you. Not all treatments are covered by these forms, so it's best to take out private travel insurance to cover both health and personal belongings.

Citizens of other EU countries should make sure they have obtained one of the forms E110, E111 or E112. Citizens of the following non-EU countries can also receive medical treatment at reduced rates by producing the appropriate form: Morocco, form MN111; states of the former Yugoslavia, YN111; Tunisia, TUN/N111; Turkey, TUR/N111. Citizens from all other countries should take out private medical insurance before their visit. Dutch medical treatment costs about half of what it would in the USA, which is still more than enough to make travelling without insurance unwise.

# Basic vocabulary

## Pronunciation guide

**ch** – like 'ch' in 'loch'
**ee** – like 'ay' in 'hay'
**g** – similar to 'ch' (*above*) ('ch' is like 'ch' in 'loch')
**ie** – like 'ea' in 'lean'
**ei** – like 'i' in 'line'
**j** – like 'y' in 'yes' except when preceded by 'i', in which case it should be pronounced as a 'y' (*see below*)
**oe** – like 'o' in 'who'
**oo** – like 'o' in no
**ou, au, ui** – like 'ow' in 'cow' (have to be heard to be imitated)
**tie** – like 'tsy' in 'itsy bitsy'
**tje** – like 'ch' in 'church'
**v** – like 'f' in 'for'
**w** – like 'w' in 'which', with a hint of the 'v' in 'vet' thrown in
**y/ij** – (written as either) a cross between 'i' in 'hide' and 'ay' in 'way'

## Words & phrases

**hello** – hallo (hullo) or dag (daarg)
**goodbye** – tot ziens (tot zeens)
**bye** – dag (daarg)
**yes** – ja (yah)
**Yes please** – Ja, graag (ya, graag)
**no** – nee (nay)

**No thank you** – Nee, dank je (nay, dank ye)
**please** – alstublieft (als-too-bleeft); also commonly used to replace the phrase 'there you are' when exchanging items such as money with others
**thank you** – dank u (dank-oo)
**thanks** – bedankt
**excuse me** – pardon (par-don)
**Excuse me, do you speak English?** – Sorry, spreekt u Engles? (sorry, spraykt oo Engels?)
**I'm sorry, I don't speak Dutch** – Het spijt me, ik spreek geen Nederlands (et spite meh, ik spraykhane nayderlants)
**I don't understand** – Ik begrijp het niet (ik begripe et neet)
**What is that?** – Wat is dat? (Vot is dat?)
**My name is…** – Mijn naam is…(mine naam is…)
**I want…** – ik wil graag…
**how much is…?** – wat kost…?
**could I have a receipt?** – mag ik een bonnetje alstublieft?
**how far is it to…?** – hoe ver is het naar…?
**waiter** – ober
**nice, tasty** (only food) – lekker (lecker)
**nice** (non-food) – mooi (moy)
**open** – open

**closed** – gesloten/dicht
**inside** – binnen
**outside** – buiten (bowten)
**left** – links
**right** – rechts (reks)
**straight ahead** – rechtdoor
**far** – ver (fair)
**near** – dichtbij (dikt-bye)
**street** – straat (straart)
**canal** – gracht
**square** – plein (pline)
**good** – goed
**bad** – slecht
**big** – groot
**small** – klein (kline)

## Numbers

**0** – nul; **1** – een; **2** – twee; **3** – drie; **4** – vier; **5** – vijf; **6** – zes; **7** – zeven; **8** – acht; **9** – negen; **10** – tien; **11** – elf; **12** – twaalf; **13** – dertien; **14** – veertien; **15** – vijftien; **16** – zestien; **17** – zeventien; **18** – achttien; **19** – negentien; **20** – twintig; **21** – eenentwintig; **22** – tweeëntwintig; **30** – dertig; **31** – eenendertig; **32** – tweeëndertig; **40** – veertig; **50** – vijftig; **60** – zestig; **70** – zeventig; **80** – tachtig; **90** – negentig; **100** – honderd; **101** – honderd een; **110** – honderd tien; **200** – tweehonderd; **201** – tweehonderd een; **1,000** – duizend

## Climate

Amsterdam's climate is very changeable, and often wet and windy. January and February are coldest, with summer often humid. The average daytime temperatures are: January, February 5°C (41°F); March 8°C (47°F); April 12°C (54°F); May 16°C (61°F); June 19°C (66°F); July, August 21°C (69°F); September 18°C (64°F); October 14°C (57°F); November 9°C (48°F); December 6°C (42°F). If you understand Dutch, try the 24-hour recorded information weather line on 0900 8003.

## Communications

### Public phones

Public phone boxes are mainly glass with a green trim. There are also telephone poles all over the city, some of which are next to Internet terminals (*see box* **Caught in the Net**, *page 197*). These are identifiable by their blue and green KPN Telecom logo. Most phones take phonecards rather than coins (those that do take coins take 25c, ƒ1 and ƒ2,50 coins). Phonecards are available from post offices, the VVV, stations and tobacconists: ƒ10 (with five free units) or ƒ25 (15 free units). Ask about special discount cards. You can use credit cards in many public phones.

### The telephone system

The phone system in Holland is in the midst of a large overhaul. Many big businesses such as banks and institutions are switching to ISDN lines, and are changing their phone numbers. Where possible, we've listed the new number, but more are bound to change.

Until recently, numbers beginning with 06 were either information numbers (most of these were 06 followed by four digits) or mobile phone numbers. In order to standardise codes across Europe, public information numbers are gradually switching over to 0800 (free information lines) or 0900 (charged information lines). Until 31 December 1999, both the 06 number and its new 0800 or 0900 'equivalent' will be in use, but note that aside from most 06 plus four digit numbers, it's not always simply a case of using 0800 or 0900 instead of the 06. From January 2000, only the 0800 and 0900 numbers will be in use, and 06 numbers will only be for mobile phones. There is a helpline – 0800 022 6788 (8am-5.30pm Mon-Fri) – set up specifically to cope with any problems, though it is only in operation until 31 December 1999. You can also ask Internal directory enquiries (0900 8008).

All Amsterdam numbers within this book are listed without the city code, which is **020**. To call Amsterdam from within Amsterdam, you don't need the code: just dial the seven-digit number. To call an Amsterdam number from elsewhere in the Netherlands, add 020 at the start of the listed number. Numbers in Holland outside of Amsterdam are listed complete with their code in this Guide.

## Post

Previously, PTT Post and PTT Telecom were the same company. Now they are both privatised and called **KPN Telecom** (the telephone part; phone 0800 0404) and **TPG** (the post part), which is split into business units, including **PTT post** (the normal postal service), and courier services such as TNT and EMS.

For post destined for outside Amsterdam, use the *overige bestemmingen* slot in letter boxes. The logo for the national postal service is *ptt post* (white letters on a red oblong). Most post offices – recognisable by their red and blue signs – are open 9am-5pm, Monday to Friday. The postal information phoneline is 0800 0417 (8am-8pm Mon-Fri; 9am-1pm Sat). Housed in every post office is the **Postbank**, a money-changing facility.

### Stamps

At the time of writing, it costs 80c to send a postcard from Amsterdam to anywhere in Europe (ƒ1 to the USA) and ƒ1 for letters weighing less than 20g. To send post elsewhere, prices vary according to weight and destination. Stamps (*postzegels*) can also be bought with postcards from many tobacconists and souvenir shops.

### Main Post Office

*Singel 250 (556 3311/fax 556 3382). Tram 1, 2, 5, 13, 14, 17, 20.* **Open** 9am-6pm Mon-Wed, Fri; 9am-8pm Thur; 10am-1.30pm Sat. **Map 2 C3**
In addition to usual services, facilities include phones, self-service faxes, directories, maps, stamp machines, counters where you can buy packaging for parcels and a counter for collectors' stamps and stationery.

### Centraal Station Post Office

*Oosterdokskade 3-5 (622 8272). Tram 1, 2, 4, 5, 9, 13, 16, 17, 20, 24, 25.* **Open** 9am-9pm Mon-Fri; 9am-noon Sat. **Map 2 D1**
Only this and the main post office (*see above*) deal with large parcels.

### Post Restante

*Post Restante, Hoofdpostkantoor, Singel 250, 1016 AB Amsterdam.* **Map 2 C3**
If you're not sure where you'll be staying in Amsterdam, people can send your post to the above address. You'll be able to collect it from the main post office (*see above*) with ID.

## Telegrams

**Telegrams** can be sent from post offices for a basic charge of ƒ23,50, plus 49c per word under 11 letters (including address and signature) inside the Netherlands; ƒ27,50 plus 89c per word under 11 letters elsewhere. There's a ƒ2,50 to ƒ5 surcharge if you send it from a post office. Details are available on 0800 0409.

### Disabled

The most obvious difficulty people with mobility problems face in the Netherlands is negotiating the winding cobbled streets of the older towns. Poorly maintained and broken pavements are widespread, and canal houses, with their narrow doorways and steep stairs, can also present access problems. But the pragmatic Dutch don't have preconceptions about people with disabilities, and any problems are generally solved quickly and without fuss.

Most of the large museums have reasonable facilities for disabled users but little for the partially sighted and hard of hearing. Most cinemas and theatres also have an enlightened attitude and are accessible. In this Guide we list establishments that claim to have disabled access, but it's advisable to check in advance.

The **metro** is accessible to wheelchair users who 'have normal arm function'. There is a **taxi service** for wheelchair users (*see below* **Getting around**). Most trams are inaccessible to wheelchair users, especially because of their high steps. For rail travel for the disabled, *see chapter* **Beyond Amsterdam**, *pages 224-5.*

The AUB and the VVV (*see above* **Essential information**) produce brochures listing accommodation, restaurants, museums, tourist attractions and boat excursions with facilities for the disabled.

### Electricity

The voltage in the Netherlands is 220, 50-cycle AC, so it's compatible with British equipment, but because Holland uses two-pin continental plugs you'll need an adaptor. American visitors need to convert their equipment or buy a transformer, plus a new plug: Dutch sockets require a larger plug than those used in the USA.

### Embassies & Consulates

The VVV offices have lists of embassies and consulates; most are based in The Hague (Den Haag).

### American Consulate General

*Museumplein 19, 1071 DJ Amsterdam (664 5661/679 0321). Tram 3, 5, 12, 16, 20.* **Open** 8.30am-5pm Mon-Fri for US citizens; 8.30-noon Mon-Fri for visa applications. **Map 5 D6**

# Useful phone numbers

## Phone codes

Dial the relevant code, then the number.

### From Holland

Dial the following code, then the number:
**To Australia**: 00 61
**To Irish Republic**: 00 353
**To UK**: 00 44, plus number (drop first '0' from area code)
**To USA**: 00 1

### To Holland

Dial the relevant international access code listed below, then the Dutch country code **31**, then the number; drop the first '0' of the area code, so for Amsterdam use 20 rather than 020. To call 06 and 0900 numbers from abroad there is no city code: just drop the first '0' from the 06 or 0900. 0800 numbers cannot be reached from abroad.
**From Australia**: 00 11
**From Irish Republic**: 00
**From UK**: 00
**From USA**: 011

### Within Holland

**Internal directory enquiries**: 0900 8008 (24 hours, 60c charge).
**International directory enquiries**: 0900 8418 (24hrs, ƒ1,05 charge).
**Local & international operator**: 0800 0410 (24 hrs, free).

## Making a call

Listen for the dialling tone (a low-pitched hum), insert phone card (look for the small red arrow to see which side up it should go) or money (a minimum of 50c), dial the appropriate code (no code is required for calls within Amsterdam), then dial the number. A digital display on public phones shows the credit remaining, but only wholly unused coins are returned. Phoning from a hotel room is, of course, more expensive.

### International phone calls

International calls can be made from all phone boxes. Off-peak rates apply, 8pm-8am Monday to Friday and all weekend. For more information on off-peak rates, phone international directory enquiries (0900 8418).

### Telephone directories

Found in post offices (*see below*). When phoning information services, taxis or train stations you may hear the recorded message, '*Er zijn nog drie [3]/twee [2]/een [1] wachtende(n) voor u.*' This tells you how many people are ahead of you in the telephone queueing system.

## Emergencies

### Emergency Switchboard (112)

A 24-hour switchboard for ambulance, fire and police. In phone boxes, you don't have to insert coins or a card to dial this number.

### Afdeling Inlichtingen Apotheken (694 8709)

A 24-hour service that can direct you to your nearest chemist.

### Doktorsdienst (0900 503 2042)

A 24-hour English-speaking line offering advice about medical symptoms. Sympathetic to people who've overdone it on the weed.

### TBB (570 9595)

A 24-hour service which refers callers to a dentist. Operators can also give details of chemists open outside normal hours.

### Lost or stolen credit cards

Use the following relevant 24-hour number:
**American Express** (504 8666)
**Diner's Club** (557 3407)
**Mastercard/Eurocard** (030 283 5555 if your card was issued in Holland; freephone 06 022 5821 if your card was issued outside of Holland)
**Visa** (660 0611 if your card was issued in Holland; freephone 06 022 4176 if your card was issued outside of Holland)

### Rape & sexual abuse

**De Eerstelijn** (613 0245/fax 613 3341). **Open** 10.30am-11.30pm Mon-Fri; 3.30-11.30pm Sat, Sun.
Formerly called TOSG, this helpline is for women who are the victims of rape, assault, sexual harassment or threats. Unfortunately, the line is often very busy in the daytime, so try calling in the evening or weekend or faxing.
**Meldpunt Vrouwenopvang** (Women's refuge; 611 6022). **Open**. 9.30-11pm Mon-Fri; 4-11pm Sat, Sun.
Women who are being abused will be referred to a safe house or safe address within Amsterdam.

### Australian Embassy

*Carnegielaan 4, 2502 ES The Hague (070 310 8200).* **Open** 8.30am-4.50pm Mon-Fri; visa enquiries 8.45-11.15am Mon-Fri.

### British Consulate General

*Koningslaan 44, 1075 AE Amsterdam (676 4343/675 8121). Tram 2, 6.* **Open** 9am-noon, 2-3.30pm Mon-Fri.

### British Embassy

*Lange Voorhout 10, 2514 ED Den Haag (070 364 5800).* **Open** 9am-1pm, 2.15-5.30pm Mon-Fri.

### Canadian Embassy

*Sophialaan 7, 2514 JP Den Haag (070 311 1600).* **Open** 9am-1pm, 2-5.30pm Mon-Fri.

### Eire Embassy

*Dr Kuyperstraat 9, 2514 BA Den Haag (070 363 0993).* **Open** 10am-12.30pm, 3-5pm Mon-Fri.

### New Zealand Embassy

*Carnegielaan 10, 2517 KN Den Haag (070 346 9324).* **Open** 9am-12.30pm, 1.30-5pm Mon-Fri.

## Language

Most of the people you will encounter in Amsterdam, both in formal and informal situations, will have at least a basic grasp of English, though they always appreciate it if you at least attempt a few niceties; *see below* **Translations**, and **Interpreters**, and *box* **Basic vocabulary**, *page 247.*

# MODERN PAINTERS

*Major British and American writers contribute to the U.K.'s most controversial art magazine:*

- ■ JULIAN BARNES

- ■ WILLIAM BOYD

- ■ A.S.BYATT

- ■ PATRICK HERON

- ■ HILTON KRAMER

- ■ JED PEARL

- ■ CHARLIE FINCH

- ■ MATTHEW COLLINGS

- ■ DAVID SYLVESTER

*Britain's best-selling quarterly journal to the fine arts.*

## Maps

This book has comprehensive maps of the centre of Amsterdam, plus a tram map, on pages 275-290. However, if you require more detail, the Falk Pocket Book Map (ƒ10) and the Falk fold-out map (ƒ7) are useful and accurate, and have a full street index on the back. Cheaper and smaller, but perfectly adequate, is Falk's small fold-out plan (ƒ5,50). All these can be bought from newsagents and bookshops (*see* chapter **Shopping**, *page 141*).

## Money

The unit of Dutch currency is the guilder (or occasionally, florin), variously abbreviated as ƒ, fl or Hfl. Throughout this Guide, the abbreviation 'ƒ' is used. The guilder is divided into 100 cents, abbreviated to c. Coins in use are 5c, 10c, 25c, ƒ1, ƒ2,50 and ƒ5. The 5c coin is copper; 10c, 25c, ƒ1 and ƒ2,50 coins are silver-coloured and the ƒ5 coin is gold-coloured (it closely resembles the £1 coin). The 5c coin is also known as a *stuiver*, the 10c coin as a *dubbeltje*, 25c as a *kwartje* and the ƒ2,50 coin is called a *rijksdaalder*. Notes come in ƒ10, ƒ25, ƒ50, ƒ100, ƒ250 and ƒ1,000 denominations. The ƒ10 note is blue, ƒ25 pink, ƒ50 yellow, ƒ100 brown, ƒ250 purple and ƒ1,000 green. Since the Dutch no longer have 1c or 2c coins, prices are rounded up or down to the nearest 5c.

Amsterdammers prefer to use cash for most transactions, though larger hotels, shops and most restaurants will accept some credit cards. Many will also take Eurocheques with guarantee cards, and travellers' cheques with ID. The single European currency, to which the Dutch have signed up, will not really affect casual travellers until 2002, when new coins and notes will be delivered to retailers across Europe.

## Banks

Banks and bureaux de change offer similar rates of exchange, but banks tend to charge less commission. Most banks are open from 9am to 4pm Monday to Friday. As yet, no banks open on Saturdays, but exchange facilities are available at the bureaux de change listed below. Dutch banks buy and sell foreign currency and exchange travellers' cheques and Eurocheques, but few give cash advances against credit cards. For a full list of banks, *see below* **Business** or consult the *Amsterdam Yellow Pages* (*Gouden Gids*), under 'Banken'.

## Bureaux de change

Bureaux de change can be found throughout the city centre, especially on Leidseplein, Damrak and Rokin. Those listed below offer reasonable rates, though they charge more commission than banks. Hotel and tourist bureau exchange facilities (*see below* **Tourist information**) are generally more expensive.

### American Express
*Damrak 66 (504 8777). Tram 4, 9, 14, 16, 20, 24, 25.* **Open** 9am-5pm Mon-Fri; 9am-noon Sat. **Map 2 D2**
A number of facilities here.

### Change Express
*Damrak 86 (624 6681/624 6682). Tram 4, 9, 14, 16, 20, 24, 25.* **Open** 8am-11.30pm daily. **Map 2 D2**
**Branch:** Leidseplein 123 (622 1425); **open** 8am-11.30 daily. **Map 5 C5**

### GWK
*Centraal Station (627 2731). Tram 1, 2, 4, 5, 9, 13, 16, 17, 20, 24, 25.* **Open** 24 hours daily. **Map 2 D1**
**Branches:** Amsterdam Schiphol Airport (in the railway station; 653 5121); **open** 24 hours daily.

### Thomas Cook
*Dam 23-25 (625 0922). Tram 4, 9, 14, 16, 20, 24, 25.* **Open** 9am-8pm Mon-Sat; 10am-6pm Sun. **Map 2 D3**
**Branches:** Damrak 1-5 (620 3236); **open** 8am-noon Mon-Sat; 8.30am-1pm Sun. **Map 2 D2**
Leidseplein 31A (626 7000); **open** 8.30am-6pm Mon-Sat; 10am-4pm Sun. **Map 5 C5**
There's no charge for cashing Thomas Cook travellers' cheques.

## Opening hours

For all our listings in this Guide we give full opening times, but as a general rule, shops are open from 1pm to 6pm on Monday; 9am to 6pm on Tuesdays, Wednesdays and Fridays; 9am to 9pm on Thursdays; and 9am to 5pm on Saturdays. Smaller, specialist shops tend to open at varying times; if in doubt phone first. For shops that are open late, *see* chapter **Shopping**, *pages 153-4*.

The city's bars open at various times during the day and close around 1am throughout the week, except for Fridays and Saturdays, when they stay open until 2am. Restaurants are generally open in the evening from 5pm until 11pm (though some close as early as 9pm); some are closed on Sunday and Monday.

## Police & security

The Dutch police are under no obligation to grant a phone call to those they detain – they are entitled to hold people for up to six hours for questioning if the alleged crime is not too serious, 24 hours for major matters – but they will phone the relevant consulate on behalf of a foreign detainee.

If you are a victim of theft or assault, report it to the nearest police station. In the case of a serious incident or an emergency, phone the emergency switchboard on 112 and ask for the police.

### Hoofdbureau Van Politie (Police Headquarters)
*Elandsgracht 117 (559 9111). Tram 7, 10, 20.* **Open** 24 hours daily. **Map 5 C4**

## Public holidays

Called 'Nationale Feestdagen' in Dutch, they are: New Year's Day; Good Friday; Easter Sunday and Monday; Koninginnedag (Queen's Day, 30 April; *see chapter*

**Amsterdam By Season**, *pages 7-8*; Remembrance Day; 5 May; Ascension Day; Whit (Pentecost) Sunday and Monday; Christmas Day, and the day after Christmas.

## Public toilets

… are few and far between, basically. It's more than likely that you'll have to use the facilities of museums, hotels and cafés. Some cafés and bars will charge you a nominal fee to do so, even if you're a patron.

## Time

Amsterdam, like all of continental Europe, is one hour ahead of Greenwich Mean Time (GMT). All clocks on Central European Time (CET) now go back and forward on the same spring and autumn dates as GMT. For the speaking clock in Dutch, phone 0900 8002.

## Tipping

Although by law a service charge is included in hotel, taxi, bar, café and restaurant bills, most Amsterdammers generally round up the change to the nearest five guilders for large bills and to the nearest guilder for smaller ones,

leaving the extra in small change rather than putting it on a credit card. In taxis, the most common tip is around ten per cent for short journeys.

## Tourist information

The national tourist information organisation is the VVV (pronounced 'vay vay vay'). It is a private company, though many individual offices are subsidised by local councils.

There are three VVV offices in Amsterdam and about 450 throughout Holland, all offering services similar to those listed below. In larger branches, staff speak English, German and French; English is spoken by almost all staff in the smaller offices..

### AUB Uitburo

*Leidseplein 26 (621 1211). Tram 1, 2, 5, 6, 7, 10, 20.* **Open** 9am-9pm daily. **Map 5 C5**
AUB Uitburo provides information and advance tickets for theatre, concerts and other cultural events. It's possible to make a reservation over the phone if you have a credit card, though they charge a fee. You can also get the **CJP** (Cultureel Jongeren Passport) here (*f*20): it's valid for a year and entitles under-26s to discounts on museum entrance fees and cultural events nationally. You can also buy an annual **Museumjaarkaart** (*see chapter* **Museums**, *page 74*), costing *f*45 or (*f*32,50 for under-18s and pensioners).

### Dutch Tourist Information Office

*Damrak 35 (638 2800). Tram 4, 9, 14, 16, 20, 24, 25.* **Open** 8am-10pm Mon-Sat; 9am-10pm Sun. **Map 2 D2**
This Dutch office concentrates on car and bike hire, hotels and day-trips.

### Pro-Amsterdam

*Leidseplein 12 (06 5577 1435). Tram 1, 2, 5, 6, 7, 10, 20.* **Open** *Apr-Sept* noon-5pm daily. **Map 5 C5**
A new, laid-back independent service in the lounge of Boom Chicago, Pro-Amsterdam is aimed at young-minded travellers. Friendly staff offer unbiased hints on, for example, how to avoid the tourist traps and where to find the best nightlife. The service is free, but tips (average *f*5) are appreciated. A nice idea.

### VVV

*Stationsplein 10 (24-hour recorded information in Dutch, English, German and French 06 340 34066/0900 400 4040). Tram 1, 2, 4, 5, 9, 13, 16, 17, 20, 24, 25.* **Open** 9am-5pm daily. **Map 2 D1**
The main office of the VVV is right by Centraal Station. English-speaking staff can change money and provide details on transport, entertainment, exhibitions, and day-trips in Holland. They also arrange theatre and hotel bookings for a fee of *f*5, and excursions and car hire for free. There is a good range of brochures for sale detailing walks and cycling tours, as well as cassette tours, maps and, for *f*4, the English-language listings magazine *What's On In Amsterdam*. The VVV runs a premium-rate information line on the above number, which features an English-language service. **Branches**: Leidseplein 1; **open** 8am-9pm daily; Centraal Station; **open** 8am-9pm daily.

# Getting to Amsterdam

You're spoiled for choice when it comes to getting to Amsterdam. There are plenty of operators in addition to those listed below, and it's always worth keeping your eye out for special offers in the press and at travel agents. It's best to do a bit of research before you decide.

## By air

Generally, flying is still the most expensive way to get to the city, but the short flight – just 45 minutes from London – more than

compensates. Amsterdam's Schiphol Airport is located 18km (11 miles) south-west of the city; for details about connections to the centre of town, *see below* **To & from the airport**. For airlines that operate to and from Amsterdam, *see below* **Airline information**.

## By bus or coach

Cheap but tiring, basically.

### Eurolines

*(UK 01582 40 45 11).* **Open** 8am-8pm Mon-Sat; 10am-2pm Sun;

answerphone service after hours. **Credit** AmEx, MC, V.
Departs from London Victoria coach station, arrives at Amstel Station, which has connections to the centre of Amsterdam. The ferry crossing is from Dover to Calais or Ramsgate to Ostend; there's also a hovercraft Hoverspeed City Sprint (Dover-Calais). Both of these have at least two daily services in summer (more in July and August) and three a day in winter.

## By rail

### Eurostar

Waterloo to Brussels takes just 2 hrs 40 mins; from here, there are train connections on to Holland. There are ten trains a day Monday to Friday, 11 on Saturday and eight on Sunday.

## Waterloo International Terminal

*(01233 617575/local rate charges within the UK 0345 881881).* **Open** 7am-10pm Mon-Fri; 7am-9pm Sat; 9am-5pm Sun. **Credit** AmEx, DC, MC, V.

Prices from London to Brussels start at £65 mid-week for a special non-exchangeable deal and rise to £280 for an all-the-works first-class return trip.

## Eurotunnel

Formerly Le Shuttle, Eurotunnel can transport you and your car from Cheriton Park on the M20 near Folkestone to Coquelles near Calais in just 35 minutes. From there you can drive to

Amsterdam. It's a 24-hour service with up to four shuttles an hour departing from Folkestone. Tickets can be bought from a travel agent, Le Shuttle direct or on arrival.

## Eurotunnel

*(UK 0990 353535).* **Open** 7am-10pm Mon-Fri; 8am-6pm Sat, Sun. **Credit** AmEx, DC, MC, V.

Five-day returns are around £120 for daytime travel; £95 in the evening. Single tickets cost around £95.

## By sea

### Hoverspeed

*(01304 240241).* **Open** 8am-7.30pm Mon-Fri; 8am-5.30pm Sat; 9am-5pm Sun. **Credit** AmEx, MC, V, DC.

Dover to Calais by hovercraft takes a mere 35 minutes (about 14 services a day); 50 by SeaCat. There's a train service from London Charing Cross to Amsterdam Centraal Station, making

the sea crossing by Sea Cat from Dover to Ostend. This service runs three times a day, and the adult return fare is £75.

### Sally Lines

*(UK 0845 600 2626).* **Open** 7am-11pm daily. **Credit** AmEx, MC, V.

Sally Lines has a service from Ramsgate to Ostend in Belgium. There are two services a day Monday to Friday, and one a day at weekends. A car plus driver is £25 return (if return is within 24 hours); £5 each additional passenger; £5 foot passengers.

### Stena Sealink

*(UK 0990 707070).* **Open** 24 hours daily. **Credit** AmEx, DC, MC, V.

Nederlandse Spoorwegen (NS), in conjunction with Stena Sealink and British Rail, operates a twice-daily boat-train service from London to Amsterdam (Centraal Station) via Harwich and the Hook of Holland (Hoek van Holland). The standard adult return is £75; under-26s can go for £57 return.

# Getting Around

Getting around Amsterdam is fairly easy. The city has an efficient and reasonably priced tram and bus system, though if you're staying in the centre of town, most places are easily reachable on foot. Amsterdammers tend to get around by bike: the streets are busy with bike traffic all day and most of the evening. There are also pleasure boats, commercial barges and water taxis on the canals.

If you're thinking of bringing a car to Amsterdam for a short stay, don't. The roads aren't designed for them, and parking places are elusive and expensive. Unfortunately, public transport provision for those with disabilities is dire: though there are lifts at all Metro stations, the staff can't always help people in wheelchairs.

Tram 20, also known as the Circle Line tram, departs from two stops outside Centraal Station. Its route stays within a fairly central area but is convenient for all the major museums and sights.

Note that Metro 51, 53 and 54 are, confusingly, fast trams that run on Metro lines. This is not the same as the number 5 tram, actually called a *sneltram* (which translates literally as 'fast tram').

## To & from the airport

### KLM Hotel Bus Service

*Main exit, Schiphol Airport (649 1393).* **Times** buses at 30-minute intervals 6.30am-3pm, then on the hour until 10pm daily. **Tickets** *single* ƒ17,50; *return* ƒ30.

This service is available to anyone; you don't need to have travelled on the airline or be staying at one of the hotel stops. The route starts at Schiphol, then goes to the Golden Tulip Barbizon (Leidseplein), Pulitzer (Westermarkt-Keizersgracht), Krasnapolsky (Dam Square), Holiday Inn and Renaissance (Nieuwezijds Voorburgwal), Barbizon Palace (Zeedijk) and back to Schiphol again. There is also a route that leaves from the south of the city: details are available from the above number or from the VVV.

### Schiphol Airport Rail Service

*Schiphol Airport/Centraal Station (information 06 9292/0900 9292).* **Times** Trains daily at 15-minute

intervals 4am-midnight; then hourly from 12.44am. **Tickets** *single* ƒ6.25; ƒ2,50 under-12s with adult; free under-4s; *return* ƒ10,50; ƒ2,50 under-12s with adult; free under-4s.

The journey to Centraal Station takes about 20 minutes. You'll probably want a single ticket; a day return is valid only for that day.

## Taxis

There are always plenty of taxis outside the main exit. It's pricey, however: at the time of writing, about ƒ70 from the airport into Amsterdam is average, and even more at night.

## Airline information

For general airport enquiries ring Schiphol Airport on **06 3503 4050/0900 0141**. Major airlines can be reached at the following addresses. Staff will normally speak English.

### British Airways

*Neptunusstraat 31, Hoofddorp (reservations 023 554 7555/Schiphol 601 5413).* **Open** 5.30am-9pm Mon-Fri; 5.30am-7.30pm Sat; 5.30am-9pm Sun. **Credit** AmEx, DC, EC, MC, V.

You can also book tickets on the British Airways Schiphol information number.

### British Midland

*Ticket desk, Schiphol Airport (604 1459/reservations 662 2211).* **Open** 6am-9.30pm Mon-Fri; 6am-7.30pm Sat; 8am-9.30pm Sun. **Credit** AmEx, DC, MC, V.

### KLM

*Ticket desk, Schiphol Airport (474 7747).* **Open** *phone* 24 hours daily; *ticket desk* 6am-10.15pm daily. **Credit** AmEx, DC, MC, V. **Map 5 D6**

### Transavia Airlines

*Postbus 7777, 1118 ZM, Schiphol Airport (604 6518).* **Open** 9am-5.30pm Mon-Fri; 10am-4pm Sat. **Credit** AmEx, DC, MC, V.

### TWA

*Singel 540 (627 4646).* Tram 4, 9, 14, 16, 20, 24, 25. **Open** 9am-12.30pm, 1.30-5pm Mon-Fri. **Credit** AmEx, DC, MC, V. **Map 5 D4**

## Left luggage

There is a staffed left-luggage counter at Schiphol Airport, open 7am-10.45pm daily; the charge is *f*5 per item per day. There are also lockers in the arrival and departure halls, costing *f*5 and *f*8 per day, while in Amsterdam itself, there are lockers at Centraal Station with 24-hour access, costing *f*4 and *f*6.

## Cycling

Cycling is widely considered the most convenient means of getting from A to B in Amsterdam: there are bike lanes on most roads, marked out by white lines and bike symbols. Some drivers insist on using bike lanes (which are often paved red) as parking spaces, but most motorists are used to the abundance of cyclists and collisions are rare. Remember, though, that cycling two abreast is illegal, as is going without reflector bands on both front and back wheels.

Never leave your bike unlocked: there's a minor trade in stolen bikes. Use a sturdy lock: some thieves are equipped with powerful cutters which will make short work of thin chains. Always lock your

bike to something unmovable, preferably using two locks: one round the frame and one through the front wheel. If someone in the street offers you a bike for sale ('fiets te koop'), don't be tempted: it's almost certainly stolen, and there's no shortage of firms where a good bike can be hired for about *f*10 a day. Aside from the bike hire firms listed below, check the *Amsterdam Yellow Pages* (*Gouden Gids*) under 'Fietsen en Bromfietsen Verhuur'.

### Bike City

*Bloemgracht 68 (626 3721).* Tram 10, 13, 14, 17, 20. **Open** 9am-6pm daily. **Cost** *f*12,50 first day, *f*10 extra days, *f*50 per week, plus *f*50 deposit (basic bikes; others are more expensive) and passport or credit card imprint. **Credit** AmEx, DC, EC, MC, V. **Map 1 B3**
Opening times may vary slightly in winter.

### Rent-A-Bike

*Damstraat 22 (625 5029).* Tram 4, 9, 14, 16, 20, 24, 25. **Open** 9am-6pm daily. **Cost** *f*12,50 per day, plus *f*50 deposit and passport/ID card or credit card imprint. **Credit** AmEx, DC, MC, V. **Map 2 D3**
Rent-A-Bike offers a ten per cent discount (excluding deposit) to anyone mentioning that they heard of them through *Time Out*.

### Take-A-Bike

*Centraal Station, Stationsplein 12 (624 8391).* Tram 1, 2, 4, 5, 9, 13, 16, 17, 20, 24, 25. **Open** 6am-10pm Mon-Fri; 7am-10pm Sat; 8am-10pm Sun. **Cost** *f*8 per day (8am-10pm) or *f*32 per week, plus *f*200 deposit. **Map 2 D1**
Here you can either hire a bike (until 10pm) or store one (up to midnight).

## Driving

If you absolutely, positively must bring a car to the Netherlands, be sure to join a **national motoring organisation** beforehand. These provide international assistance booklets, which explain what to do in the event of a breakdown in Europe. To drive in the Netherlands you'll need a valid national driving licence, although the Dutch motoring club, **ANWB** (*see*

*below*) and many car hire firms favour an **international driving licence**, available from branches of national motoring organisations. In Britain, take your full licence and a passport photo to a branch of the AA or RAC and they will process it in minutes.

Major roads are usually well-maintained and clearly sign-posted. Motorways are labelled 'A'; major roads 'N'; and European routes 'E'. Brits in particular should note that the Dutch drive on the **right**, while everyone should remember that drivers and front-seat passengers must always wear seatbelts. Speed limits are 50km (31 miles) an hour within cities, 70km (43 miles) an hour outside, and 100km (62 miles) an hour on motorways. If you're driving in Amsterdam, look out for cyclists. Many Amsterdam streets are now one-way.

To bring your car into the Netherlands, you'll need an international identification disk, a registration certificate, proof of the vehicle having passed a road safety test in its country of origin, and insurance documents.

### Royal Dutch Touring Club (ANWB)

*Museumplein 5 (070 314 1420/24-hour emergency line 0800 0888).* Tram 2, 3, 5, 12, 16, 20. **Open** 9am-5.30pm Mon-Fri; 9am-4pm Sat. **Credit** foreign currency, EC, MC, TC, V. **Map 5 D6**
If you haven't already joined a motoring organisation, you can enroll here for around *f*140, which covers the cost of assistance should your vehicle break down. If you're a member of a foreign motoring organisation, you're entitled to free help, providing you can present membership documents. You may find emergency crews don't accept credit cards or cheques at the scene.

## Car hire

Dutch car hire (*auto-verhuur*) companies generally expect at least one year's driving experience and will want to see a valid national driving licence and passport. All companies will require a deposit through an international credit card, and you'll generally need to be over 21. Prices given below are for one day's hire of the cheapest car available at the time of writing, excluding insurance unless otherwise stated.

### Adam's Rent-a-Car
*Nassaukade 344-346 (685 0111).* *Tram 7, 10, 17, 20.* **Open** 8am-6pm Mon-Wed; 8am-9pm Thur-Sat. **Credit** AmEx, DC, MC, V. **Map 5 C5** Hire for a day costs from ƒ75; the first 100km (62 miles) are free, and after that the charge is 35c/km.

### Dik's Autoverhuur
*Van Ostadestraat 278-280 (662 3366). Tram 3, 4.* **Open** 8am-7.30pm Mon-Sat; 9am-12.30pm, 8-10pm Sun. **Credit** AmEx, DC, MC, V. **Map 6 F6** Prices start at ƒ55 per day, plus 51c/km including tax.

### Hertz
*Overtoom 333 (612 2441). Tram 1, 6.* **Open** 8am-6pm Mon-Thur; 8am-7pm Fri; 8am-4pm Sat; 9am-2pm Sun. **Credit** AmEx, DC, MC, TC, V. **Map 4 B6** Prices start at ƒ74 per day including insurance; the first 200km are free, with subsequent mileage charged at 33c/km.

### Ouke Baas
*Van Ostadestraat 362-372 (679 4842). Tram 3, 4.* **Open** 7am-8pm Mon-Fri; 7.30am-9pm Sat; 8am-1pm, 7-10.30pm Sun. **Credit** AmEx, DC, MC, TC, V. **Map 7 G5** Inclusive of VAT and the first 100km (62 miles), Ouke Baas' cheapest car costs ƒ74 per day. After the first 100km it costs 22c/km.

## Clamping & fines

Amsterdam's wheel-clamp (*wielklem*) teams are swift to act and show little mercy if they see a car parked illegally. A yellow sticker on the windscreen informs you where to go to pay

the fine (ƒ126). Once you've paid, return to the car and wait for the traffic police to remove the clamp. Luckily, the declampers normally arrive promptly.

If you park illegally or fail to pay your parking fine within 24 hours, your car will be towed away. It'll cost over ƒ400 – plus parking fine – to reclaim it from the pound if you do so within 24 hours, and ƒ90 for every 12 hours thereafter. The pound is at Cruquiuskade 25 (*see below*). Take your passport, licence number and enough cash or personal cheques to pay the hefty fine. All major credit cards are accepted. If your car has been clamped or towed away, this is where to go to pay the ƒ121 fine:

### Head office
*Weesperstraat 105A (553 0300). Tram 6, 7, 9, 10, 14, 20.* **Open** 8.30am-5pm Mon-Fri. **Map 3 F3**

### Branches
*Bakkersstraat 13 (533 0333). Tram 4, 9, 14, 16, 20, 24, 25.* **Open** 24 hours daily. **Map 3 E3** *Cruquiuskade 25 (533 0333). Tram 6, 10.* **Open** 24 hours daily. *Ceintuurbaan 159 (533 0333). Tram 3.* **Open** 8am-8pm Mon-Sat. **Map 6 F6** *Kinkerstraat 17 (533 0333). Tram 1, 3, 6, 12.* **Open** 8-11pm Mon-Sat. **Map 4 B5**

## Parking

Parking in central Amsterdam is a nightmare: the whole of the town centre is metered from 9am to 7pm and meters are difficult to see. Meters will set you back ƒ4 an hour, and illegally parked cars get clamped or towed away without any warning (*see*

*above*). Car parks (*parkeren*) are indicated by a white 'P' on a blue square. After 7pm, parking at meters is free. Below is a list of central car parks where you're more likely to find a space during peak times. Be sure to empty your car completely of all valuables and the radio: cars with foreign number plates are particularly vulnerable to break-ins.

### ANWB Parking Amsterdam Centraal
*Prins Hendrikkade 20A (638 5330).* **Open** 24 hours daily. **Cost** ƒ4 per hour; maximum ƒ45 per day; week-card (runs from noon Sat-noon following Sat) ƒ195. **Map 2 D2** Hotels in the surrounding neighbourhood give 20% discount on parking at this car park near Centraal Station.

### Europarking
*Marnixstraat 250 (623 6694).* **Open** 6.30am-12.30am Mon-Thur; 6.30am-1.30am Fri, Sat; 7am-12.30am Sun. **Cost** *winter* ƒ2,50 per hour; *summer* ƒ3. **Map 4 B4**

### De Kolk Parking
*Nieuwezijds Voorburgwal 12 (427 1449).* **Open** 24 hours daily. **Cost** ƒ4 per hour; ƒ50 24 hours. **Map 2 C2**

### Kroon & Zn
*Under the Stadhuis-Muziektheater, Waterlooplein 1 (638 0919).* **Open** 24 hours daily. **Cost** ƒ2,50 per hour; ƒ45 for 24 hours. **Map 3 E3**

### Prinsengracht 540-542
*(625 9852).* **Open** 24 hours daily. **Cost** ƒ4 per hour; ƒ40 for 24 hours. **Map 5 D5**

## Petrol

The main 24-hour petrol stations (*benzinestations*) within the city limits are at Gooiseweg 10-11, Sarphatistraat 225, Marnixstraat 250, and Spaarndammerdijk 218.

# Public transport

A basic map of the tram network is on page 290. For information, tickets, maps and an English-language guide to the city's ticket system, visit the GVB, Amsterdam's Municipal Transport Authority.

### GVB (Amsterdam Municipal Transport Authority)
*Stationsplein 15 (06 9292/0900 9292). Tram 1, 2, 4, 5, 9, 13, 16, 17, 20, 24, 25.* **Open** *phones for enquiries* 6am-midnight Mon-Fri; 7am-midnight Sat, Sun; *office (personal callers)* 7am-10.30pm

Mon-Fri; 8am-10.30pm Sat. **Map 2 D1** The GVB runs Amsterdam's Metro, bus and tram services, and can provide information on all. **Branches:** GVB Head Office, Prins Hendrikkade 108; Amstel Railway Station, Julianaplein.

## Metro

The Metro system in Amsterdam uses the same ticketing system as trams and buses (*see box* **Tickets please**), and serves suburbs to the south and east. There are three lines, all terminating at Centraal Station (which is sometimes abbreviated to CS). Trains run from 6am Mon-Fri (6.30am Sat, 7.30am Sun) to around 12.15am daily.

## Trams & buses

As a visitor to Amsterdam, you will find buses and trams a particularly good way to get around the city centre. Tram services run from 6am Monday to Friday, 6.30am on Saturday and 7.30am on Sunday, with a special night bus service taking over after midnight. Night buses are numbered from 71 to 79; all go to Centraal Station, except 79. Night bus stops are indicated by a black square at the stop with the bus number printed on it. Night buses run 1-5.30am from Monday to Friday, and until 6.30am on weekends.

Yellow signs at tram and bus stops indicate the name of the stop and further destinations. There are usually maps of the entire network in the shelters and diagrams of routes on board the trams and buses, and the city's bus and tram drivers are generally courteous and will give directions if asked; most are sufficiently fluent to do this in English.

The yellow and decorated varieties of tram are as synonymous with Amsterdam as the red double-decker bus is with London. The vehicles make for fast and efficient travel, but other road users should be warned that they will stop only when absolutely necessary. Cyclists should listen out for tram warning bells, and motorists should avoid blocking tramlines: cars are allowed to venture onto

them only if they're turning right. Cyclists, too, should be careful to cross tramlines at an angle that avoids the front wheel getting stuck.

To get on or off a tram, wait until it has halted at a stop and press the yellow button by the doors, which will then open. On some trams you can buy a ticket from the driver at the front; on others from either a machine in the middle, or a conductor at the back.

## Trains

From Centraal Station, one of the biggest railway terminals in Europe, you can get direct trains to most major cities across the continent. The ornate neo-Renaissance station, designed by PJH Cuypers, is one of Amsterdam's most imposing structures and gives a bustling first impression of the city. All conceivable needs of the newly-arrived visitor are catered for here, from showers and restaurants inside the station to hotel, travel and booking services on Stationsplein outside. As most of the city's bus and tram services begin and end here, it's also an ideal starting point for trips around the city. On the down side, beware of pickpockets, street hustlers and rip-off merchants. For more details on rail travel, and for the **Night train network**, *see chapter* **Beyond Amsterdam**, *page 224-5*.

You must reserve tickets for international trains, and be warned: the office gets very crowded during the summer season. Tickets can be reserved over the phone (620 2266), but this should be done at least a week ahead of travel.

### Centraal Station Information Desk

*Stationsplein 13 (information 06 9292/0900 9292). Tram 1, 2, 4, 5, 9, 13, 16, 17, 20, 24, 25.* **Open** *information desk* 6.30am-10pm daily; *reservations office* 6.30am-10pm daily. **Credit** MC, V. **Map 2 D1**

## Taxis

As with any major city, there are a few ground rules that visitors would do well to follow. First of all, be sure to check that the meter initially shows no more than the minimum charge (ask the driver for an estimate of how much the journey will cost before setting out). Even short journeys are expensive: after paying an initial $f5,80$, it works out at $f2,85$ per kilometre between 6am and midnight and rises to $f3,25$ per kilometre thereafter. On the narrow streets around the main canals, you may get stuck behind an unloading lorry and end up paying a fortune for the privilege.

If you feel you have been ripped off, ask for a receipt, which you are legally entitled to see before handing over any money. If the charge is extortionate, phone the central taxi office (677 7777) or contact the police. Such rip-offs are relatively rare.

Awkwardly, you're not supposed to hail a taxi in the street – though occasionally one may stop – as there are ranks dotted around the city. The best places to find taxis are outside Centraal Station, the bus station at the junction of Kinkerstraat and Marnixstraat, Rembrandtplein, and Leidseplein. You can't book cabs in advance, but if you call Amsterdam's 24-hour central taxi control on 677 7777, a taxi will arrive almost immediately. The line is often busy on Friday and Saturday nights, but there's a telephone queueing system.

Wheelchairs will only fit in taxis if folded. If you're in a wheelchair, phone the car transport service for wheelchair users on 633 3943 (generally open 9am-6pm, Monday to Friday). You'll need to book your journey one or two days in advance and it costs around $f3$ per kilometre.

## Tours

### Bike tours

Cycling may be the best way to get around Amsterdam, but be careful of resident cyclists and car drivers who delight in cutting up tourists (*see above* **Cycling**). However, stick with one of the tours, being careful to follow the guide's instructions, and you should be okay. Rental of a bicycle for the duration of

the tour is included in the prices listed below.

#### Yellow Bike

*Nieuwezijds Voorburgwal 66 (620 6940). Tram 1, 2, 5, 13, 17, 20.* **Open** Apr-Nov 9am-5pm daily. **Map 2 C2** Glide past Amsterdam's main sights with Yellow Bike's City Tour: it takes three hours, departs at 9.30am and 1pm every day from Nieuwezijds Kolk 29, and costs ƒ30. The Waterland Tour takes you further afield and lasts about two hours: the trip includes a visit to a cheese factory and a clockmaker and a return or

outward bus journey. Waterland Tours depart at 9am daily from the Beurs van Berlage, or at noon from Centraal Station, and cost ƒ30.

### Helicopter tours

#### KLM Helicopter Tours

*(649 2041).* **Open** 9am-5pm Mon-Fri. If you're keen to get an aerial view of Amsterdam and its surroundings, you can charter a helicopter through KLM. However, it'll set you back ƒ4,500 (ten passengers) or ƒ5,500 per hour (25 passengers). Thankfully, they take major credit cards.

# Tickets please

Beware of travelling on a bus or tram without a ticket. Uniformed inspectors make regular checks and passengers without a valid ticket – or an exceptional excuse – will be asked for ID and fined ƒ60 on the spot. Playing the ignorant foreigner rarely works.

### STRIP TICKETS (STRIPPENKAARTEN)

A strip ticket system operates on trams, buses and the Metro in Amsterdam: it's initially confusing, but ultimately good value for money. Prices range from ƒ3 for a strip with two units to ƒ11,50 for 15 units and ƒ33,75 for 45 units; children under four travel free, and older children (aged 4-18) pay reduced fares (ƒ6,75 for a 15-strip card).

Ticket prices increase every year. Tickets can be bought at GVB (Public Transport) offices, post offices, train stations and many tobacconists. The tickets must be stamped upon boarding a tram or bus and on entering a Metro station. The city is divided into five zones: Noord (north), West, Centrum, Oost (east) and Zuid (south); most of central Amsterdam falls, not surprisingly, within zone Centrum. Strip tickets are also valid on trains that stop at Amsterdam train stations, with the exception of Schiphol.

For travel in a single zone, two units must be stamped, while three are stamped for two zones, four for three zones and so on. In trams you can stamp your own tickets in the yellow box-like contraption near the doors: fold the ticket so the unit you need to stamp is at the end. On buses, drivers stamp the tickets, and on the Metro there are stamping machines at the entrance to stations. An unlimited number of people can travel on one card, but the appropriate number of units must be stamped

for each person. The stamps are valid for one hour, during which time you can transfer to other buses and trams without having to stamp your card again. If your journey takes more than an hour you have to stamp more units, but no single tram journey in central Amsterdam is likely to take that long. There is no set expiry date on *strippenkaarten*.

### DAY TICKETS (DAGKAARTEN)

A cheaper option for unlimited travel in Amsterdam, a day ticket costs ƒ10, two days cost ƒ15 and three days ƒ19, with each additional day costing an extra ƒ4. Only Dutch pensioners and the unwaged are eligible for cheaper travel, but for a child (aged four to 18) a two-day ticket costs ƒ9 and three days ƒ11,50, with each additional day costing a further ƒ2. Child day tickets are valid on night buses. A day ticket is valid on trams, buses and Metro on the day it is stamped until the last bus or tram runs. You need to buy a new ticket for night buses. Only the one-day ticket can be bought from drivers on trams and buses. After stamping the day ticket on your first journey, you do not need to stamp it again.

### SEASON TICKETS (STERABONNEMENT)

These can be bought from GVB offices, tobacconists and post offices, and are valid for a week, a month or a year. A weekly pass for the central zone (Centrum) costs ƒ17,25, a monthly one ƒ57,25 and a yearly one ƒ572,50. Children aged between 4 and 18 get cheaper season tickets: ƒ10 for a day, ƒ35,25 a month and ƒ352,50 for a year. You'll need a passport photo to get a season ticket.

# Water, water everywhere

## Boat tours

The best way to see Amsterdam is undoubtedly from the water, so try not to be put off by the hordes of coach parties lining up to get on board one of the various tour boats. There are plenty of tour operators in the city, with most boat tours leaving from points along Rokin and opposite Centraal Station. All the tours cover the same canals, give the same information and carry the same bunch of gawping tourists: the only real choice is whether to take a boat with a live guide or one where you just listen to a pre-recorded, disembodied voice announcing the points of interest as you pass them.

Whatever the time of day and whatever the company, you can expect to take a pretty standard route, albeit in different directions. Whatever the start point, however, the tours generally meander up and down the Herengracht and down through the Amstel, before chugging around the IJ behind Centraal Station, giving plenty of opportunities for nosey peeks into some of Amsterdam's 3,000 houseboats. On sunny days, try and grab a seat in the open air at the back of the boat. The noise of the engine will drown out the voice of the guide, though this is often no bad thing, and the loss of a commentary is more than compensated for by a lovely wind-in-your-hair, sun-on-your-back feeling.

### The Best of Holland
*Damrak 34; cruises depart from Rederij Lovers landing stage, opposite Centraal Station (623 1539). Tram 4, 9, 16, 20, 24, 25.* **Open** *Apr-Oct* 9am-10pm daily; *Nov-*
*Mar* 9am-5.30pm daily. **Cruises** *day cruise* approx every 30 mins, 9am-6pm daily; *candlelight cruise* (reservation required) 9pm daily (summer); 9pm Wed, Fri, Sat (winter).* **Duration** *day cruise* one hour; *candlelight cruise* two hours. **Tickets** day cruise *f*12; *f*8 under-13s; candlelight cruise *f*42,50; *f*17,50 under-13s. **Credit** AmEx, EC, MC, V, TC. **Departs Map 2 D2**

### Holland International
*Prins Hendrikkade 33A; cruises depart from opposite Centraal Station (622 7788). Tram 1, 2, 4, 5, 9, 13, 16, 17, 20, 24, 25.* **Cruises (summer)** approx every 20 mins, 9am-6pm, every 45 mins 6-10pm daily; *brunch cruise* (reservation required) 11am Wed, Sat, Sun; *candlelight cruise* (with wine & cheese; stop-off at bar; reservation required) 9.30pm daily; *dinner cruise* (four-course dinner; reservation required) 8pm daily - lasts 3 hrs; **(winter)** approx every 30 mins, 10am-6pm daily; *brunch cruise* 11am Sun; *candlelight cruise* 8pm daily; *dinner cruise* 7pm Tue, Fri, Sat. **Duration** *day cruise* one hour; *brunch cruise* three hours; *candlelight cruise* two hours, *dinner cruise* three hours. **Tickets** *day cruise f*15; *f*7,50 under-13s; *brunch cruise f*55; *f*50 under-13s; *candlelight cruise f*47,50; *f*25 under-13s; *dinner cruise f*145; *f*115 under-13s. **Credit** AmEx, MC, V. **Departs Map 2 D2**
One of the most commercial companies, which attracts coach parties by the score. Prices for most winter cruises may rise slightly in the near future, and there are plans for an extra brunch cruise in winter; phone to check.

### Lindbergh
*Damrak 26 (622 2766). Tram 4, 9, 16, 20, 24, 25.* **Cruises** *day cruise* Mar-Oct approx every 15 mins, 10am-6pm daily; Nov-Apr approx every 30 minutes, 9am-4pm daily; *dinner cruise* 7.30pm daily; *candlelight cruise* (wine & cheese) 9pm daily (May-Oct); 9.30pm Wed, Sat (Nov-Apr). **Duration** day cruise one hour; dinner cruise two hours; candlelight cruise two hours. Tickets day cruise *f*13; *f*8 4-13s; dinner cruise *f*99; *f*79 4-13s; candlelight cruise *f*42,50; *f*21,25 4-13s. Credit AmEx, DC, MC, TC, V. **Departs Map 2 D2**

## Walking tours

Amsterdam is a great city to explore on foot, though its uneven streets and tramlines mean it isn't the world's best city if you're wearing stilettos, pushing pushchairs or sat in a wheelchair. The VVV has a series of brochures (in English) outlining easy-to-follow walks. Tours can be given in English.

### Archivisie
*Postbus 14603, 1001 LC Amsterdam (625 8908/fax 620 6791).*
Archivisie organises tailor-made architectural tours, and runs regular theme tours. Phone for appointments and details of charges.

### Mee in Mokum
*Hartenstraat 18 (625 1390). Tram 13, 14, 17, 20.* Tours (last two to three hours) 11am Tue-Fri, Sun. **Cost** *f*4; free under-12s. **Map 2 C3**
Long-time residents of Amsterdam, all over 55, give highly personal and individual tours of the old part of the city and the Jordaan: each guide has his or her own route and his or her own story to tell about the city (in English as well as Dutch). Tours leave from the Amsterdams Historisch Museum; advance booking is necessary.

## Travel from Amsterdam

*See also chapter* **Beyond Amsterdam,** *pages 224-225.*

## Hitch-hiking

An accepted practice, but caution is advised.

### International Lift Centre
*Oudezijds Achterburgwal 169 (622 4342). Tram 4, 9, 14, 16, 20, 24, 25.* **Open** 9am-5pm Mon-Fri; 11am-3pm Sat. **Map 2 D3**
*f*10 for 12 months, about *f*15 if a lift is found, and then a maximum of 6c/km payable to the driver.

### Starting points
**Towards The Hague/Rotterdam:** between RAI station and the RAI on Europa Boulevard, by the motorway. **Towards Utrecht:** the corner of Rijnstraat and President Kennedylaan. **Towards Arnhem & Germany:** at Gooiseweg, by Amstel rail station.

### Lovers

*Prins Hendrikkade (opposite 25-27), by Centraal Station (622 2181). Tram 1, 2, 4, 5, 9, 13, 16, 17, 20, 24, 25.* **Cruises** *day cruise* approx every 30 minutes, 9am-6pm daily; *dinner cruise* (reservation required) 7.30pm daily; *candlelight cruise* (reservation required) 9pm daily. **Duration** *day cruise* one hour; *dinner cruise, candlelight cruise* two hours. **Tickets** *day cruise* ƒ15; ƒ10 under-13s; *dinner cruise* ƒ99; ƒ48 under-13s; *candlelight cruise* ƒ42,50; ƒ21,25 under-13s. **Credit** AmEx, DC, EC, MC, TC, V. **Departs Map 2 D2**
A range of tours for all the honeymooners and romantically inclined couples who drift into Amsterdam. Instead of a guide, they have talking video monitors.

### Rondvaarten

*Kooy BV Rokin (opposite 125), at the corner of Spui (623 3810). Tram 4, 9, 16, 20, 24, 25.* **Cruises** *Mar-mid-Oct* every 30 minutes 9am-10pm daily; *mid-Oct-Feb* every 30 minutes 10am-5pm daily; *candlelight cruise* Apr-mid-Oct 9pm daily. **Duration** one hour; *candlelight cruise* two hours. **Tickets** ƒ13; ƒ8 under-14s; *candlelight cruise* (wine & cheese) ƒ40. **Departs Map 2 D3**
Rondvaarten's boats are slightly more upmarket than some of those sitting outside Centraal Station and seem to attract fewer coach parties. The guides speak an impressive four languages.

### Boats to rent

So you reckon you could do it better yourself? Well, here's your chance: there are firms in Amsterdam who'll quite happily rent you a boat or pedalo and let you loose on the water. Fun, if you like that sort of thing.

### Canal Bike

*Weteringschans 21 (626 5574).* **Open** 10am-6pm daily. **Moorings** Leidsekade at Leidseplein, between Marriott and American Hotels; Stadhouderskade, opposite Rijksmuseum; Prinsengracht, by Westerkerk; Keizersgracht, on the corner of Leidsestraat. **Hire rates** *four-person pedalo* if one or two people, ƒ12,50 per person per hour; if three or four people, ƒ10 per person per hour. **Deposit** ƒ50 per canal bike. **Credit** TC. **Office Map 5 D5**

### Roell

*Mauritskade 1, by the Amstel (692 9124). Tram 6, 7, 10.* **Open** *Apr-Sept* 11am-9pm Wed-Sun; closed Mon, Tue; *Oct-Feb* 10am-6pm Wed-Sat; also by appointment. **Hire rates** *two-person pedalo* ƒ27,50 per hour; *four-person pedalo* ƒ35 per hour; *four-person motor boat* ƒ55 for one hour (ƒ95 for 2 hours); group boat (Mar-Dec only; max 30 persons; incl captain): ƒ225 1 hour; ƒ200 per hour for subsequent hours. **Deposit** *pedalos* ƒ50; *motor boat* ƒ250 (ID required). **Map 6 F4**

## Canal buses

### Canal Bus

*Weteringschans 24 (623 9886). Tram 6, 10.* **Open** 9am-6pm Mon-Sat. **Cost** *day ticket* ƒ22; ƒ15 under-12s; *two-day ticket* ƒ29,75; *combination one-day ticket incl entrance to Rijksmuseum* ƒ32. **Map 5 D5**
These 52-seater canal buses are the latest addition to Amsterdam's water transport system. They provide a regular service on the canals from the Rijksmuseum to Centraal Station, stopping at Leidseplein, Leidsestraat/ Keizersgracht and Westerkerk/Anne Frankhuis. The service operates every day between 10am and 6pm at 30-minute intervals.

## Water taxis

Only the extravagant use the city's water taxi network regularly. However, it is possible to hire a taxi – with guides, food and drink provided by the company at extra charge – and use it for your own personal tour or party.

### Water Taxi Centrale

*Stationsplein 8 (622 2181). Tram 1, 2, 4, 5, 9, 13, 16, 17, 20, 24, 25.* **Open** 8am-midnight daily. **Cost** eight-person boat ƒ90 for first half-hour, then ƒ30 per 15 minutes; 16-person boats ƒ180 for first half-hour, then ƒ60 per 15 minutes; 35-person boat ƒ210 for first half-hour, then ƒ75 per 15 minutes. **Credit** AmEx, DC, EC, MC, TC, V (accepted only prior to boarding). **Map 2 D1**
Advance booking is advisable as the service is usually busy, particularly in high season. Water taxis can be hailed as they're sailing along a canal – but it's unlikely there'll be much room on board.

# Business

## Information

Many of the agencies listed below are in The Hague (Den Haag), though they are able and willing to deal with basic enquiries on the telephone or by post. For full information country embassies, and consulates, *see above* Embassies.

### American Chamber of Commerce

*Van Karnebeeklaan 14, 2585 BB Den Haag (070 365 9808).* **Open** 9am-5pm Mon-Fri.

### British Embassy, Commercial Department

*Lange Voorhout 10, 2514 ED Den Haag (070 364 5800).* **Open** 9am-1pm, 2.15-5.30pm, Mon-Fri.
This office cooperates with the British Department of Trade and Industry to assist British companies operating in the Netherlands.

### Centraal Bureau voor Statistiek (CBS)

*Prinses Beatrixlaan 428, 2273 XZ Voorburg (070 337 3800).* **Open** 9am-noon, 2-5pm Mon-Fri.
The Central Bureau for Statistics provides statistics on every aspect of Dutch society, and the economy.

### Commissariaat voor Buitenlandse Investeringen Nederland (Netherlands Foreign Investment Agency)

*Bezuidenhoutseweg 2, 2594 AV Den Haag (070 379 7233/fax 070 379 6322).* **Open** 8am-6pm Mon-Fri.
The Commissariaat is probably the most useful first port of call for business people wishing to relocate to the Netherlands.

### Douane Amsterdam (Customs)

*Leeuwendalersweg 21 (586 7511). Tram 12, 14/bus 21, 68, 80.* **Open** 8am-5pm Mon-Fri.

## Douane Rotterdam (Customs)

*West Zeedijk 387, Rotterdam (010 244 2333).* **Open** 8am-4.30pm Mon-Fri.

## Economische Voorlichtingsdienst, EVD (Netherlands Foreign Trade Agency)

*Bezuidenhoutseweg 181, 2594 AH Den Haag (070 379 8933).* **Open** 9am-4pm Mon-Fri.
A useful library and information centre for business people. It incorporates the Netherlands Council for Trade Promotion (NCH), another handy source of information.
*Disabled access.*

## Kamer van Koophandel (Chamber of Commerce)

*De Ruijterkade 5 (531 4000). Tram 1, 2, 4, 5, 9, 13, 16, 17, 24, 25.* **Open** 8.30am-4pm Mon-Fri. **Map 2 C1**
Amsterdam's Chamber of Commerce has lists of import/export agencies, government trade representatives and companies by sector. They will also advise on legal procedure, finding an office and hiring locals.
*Disabled access.*

## Ministerie van Economische Zaken (Ministry of Economic Affairs)

*Bezuidenhoutseweg 30, 2594 AV Den Haag (070 379 8911).* **Open** 9am-4pm Mon-Fri.
The Ministry of Economic Affairs can provide answers to general queries concerning the Dutch economy. More detailed enquiries tend to be referred to the **EVD** (Netherlands Foreign Investment Agency; *see above*).
*Disabled access.*

## Ministerie van Buitenlandse Zaken (Ministry of Foreign Affairs)

*Bezuidenhoutseweg 67, Postbus 20061, 2500 EB Den Haag (070 348 6486).* **Open** 10am-4.30pm Mon; 9am-4.30pm Tue-Fri.
General queries only. As with the Ministry of Economic Affairs, detailed enquiries will probably be referred to the **EVD** (Netherlands Foreign Investment Agency; *see above*).
*Disabled access and toilets.*

## Netherlands-British Chamber of Commerce

*Oxford House, Nieuwezijds Voorburgwal 328L (421 7040/fax 421 7003). Tram 1, 2, 5, 13, 14, 17.* **Open** 9am-5pm Mon-Fri; trade enquiries in person by appointment only 10am-noon, 2-4pm Mon-Fri. **Map 2 D3**

The branches listed below are head offices. Most do not have general banking facilities, but staff will be able to provide a list of branches that do. For information about foreign exchanges, *see above* **Money**.

## ABN-Amro

*Vijzelstraat 68 (629 2940). Tram 6, 7, 10, 16, 24, 25.* **Open** 9am-5pm Mon-Fri. **Map 5 D4**
The main offices of this super-bank.
*Disabled access.*

## Citibank NA

*Hoogoorddreef 54 B (651 4211). Metro Bijlmer/Sneltram 51, 52, 53/bus 62, 137, 158, 163, 164, 174, 175, 176, 187, 188, 189.* **Open** 9am-5pm Mon-Fri.
Affiliated to the US Citibank, dealing with business transactions only.
*Disabled access.*

## Credit Lyonnais Bank Nederland NV

*Strawinskylaan 3093 (504 7070). Tram 5/NS rail to RAI station.* **Open** 9am-6pm Mon-Fri.
Again, this deals with business transactions only.
*Disabled access.*

## Generale Bank

*Buitenveldertselaan 3a (404 0510). Tram 5/Metro 51.* **Open** 9am-4.30pm Mon-Fri.
The Generale Bank also deals with the consumer banking department of the Credit Lyonnais Bank Nederland.
*Disabled access.*

## ING Group

*Bijlmerplein 888 (563 9111). Bus 59, 60, 62, 137/Metro Bijlmer.* **Open** 9am-4pm Mon-Fri.
The ING Group incorporates the 50 Amsterdam branches of the post office bank, with banking and exchange services.
*Disabled access.*

## Lloyds Bank

*Gatwickstraat 17-19, 1043 GL Amsterdam (524 9300). Tram 12/NS rail to Sloterdijk.* **Open** 9am-6pm Mon-Fri (by appointment only). **Map 5 C5**
Business transactions only.
*Disabled access.*

## Postbank

*Singel 250 (556 3311/information 0800 0400)* **Open** 9am-6pm Mon-Wed, Fri; 9am-8pm Thur; 10am-1.30pm Sat.
There is a Postbank housed in every Post Office in Amsterdam.
*Disabled access.*

## Rabobank

*Dam 16 (530 4630). Tram 1, 2, 5, 9, 13, 14, 16, 17, 20, 24, 25.* **Open** 9.30am-5.30pm Mon-Thur; 10am-2pm Sat.
29 branches in Amsterdam.
*Disabled access.*

## Verenigde Spaarbank (VSB)

*Singel 548 (624 9340). Tram 4, 9, 14, 16, 20, 24, 25.* **Open** 1-5pm Mon; 9.30am-5pm Tue-Fri. **Map 5 D4**
Full banking facilities in their 41 Amsterdam branches.
*Disabled access.*

In October 1998, the following three exchanges will be merging onto one premises (Beursplein 5; 550 4444).

## Effectenbeurs (Stock Exchange)

*Beursplein 5 (550 4444). Tram 4, 9, 14, 16, 20, 24, 25.* **Open** for free tours (mainly groups only; phone for details). **Map 2 D2**
Stock for officially listed Dutch companies is traded here. Phone to arrange a guided tour.

## Nederlandse Termijnhandel

The commodity exchange for trading futures in potatoes and pigs.

## Optiebeurs (European Options Exchange)

The EOE opened in 1987 and is now the largest options exchange in Europe. Trading share, gold and silver options as well as bond and currency options, it books about 55,000 transactions daily. Tours are possible by appointment.

Most major hotels offer full conference facilities and the city's main congress centre, the **RAI** (*see below*) hosts some 65 international events a year. Specialist conference organisers can arrange these events.

## Congrex Convention Services

*AJ Ernststraat 595 K (504 0200/fax 504 0225). Tram 5/Metro 51.* **Open** 9am-5.30pm Mon, Wed, Thur; 8.30am-5.30pm Tue; 9am-5pm Fri. **Credit** AmEx, DC, EC, MC, V. **Map 6 E4**
These specialists in teleconferencing will organise and supply equipment

for congresses and seminars at reasonable rates.
*Disabled access.*

### Grand Hotel Krasnapolsky
*Dam 9 (554 8081/fax 554 7010). Tram 1, 2, 4, 5, 9, 14, 16, 20, 24, 25.* **Map 2 D3**
This recently refurbished hotel (*see chapter* **Accommodation***, p91*) has the most comprehensive in-hotel meeting facilities.
*Disabled access.*

### RAI Congresgebouw
*Europaplein 8-22 (549 1212; exhibition centre and restaurant: fax 646 4469/e-mail mail@rai.nl). Tram 4, 25/NS rail to RAI Station.*
A self-contained congress and trade fair centre in the south of the city. The building contains 11 halls totalling 87,000sq m of covered exhibition space and 19 conference rooms which can seat between 40 and 1,750 people.
*Disabled access.*

### Stichting de Beurs van Berlage (Berlage Exchange Foundation)
*Damrak 277 (530 4141/fax 620 4701). Tram 4, 9, 14, 16, 20, 24, 25.* **Open** office and enquiries noon-5pm Mon; 9am-5pm Tue-Fri.
**Map 2 D2**
This building is now used for cultural events and smaller trade fairs (up to 2,500 visitors can be provided with buffet dinners). Berlage Hall is a stylish conference venue for between 50 and 200 people.
*Disabled access.*

### World Trade Center
*Strawinskylaan 1 (575 9111/Congress Centre 575 2035/fax 662 7255). Tram 5/NS rail to RAI Station.* **Open** 9am-5pm Mon-Fri.
Facilities include an international press centre, small studios for top-level meetings and 14 business-class rooms seating from four to 40 people. A conference room seating up to 250 costs *f*1,750 per full day of 8am-11pm (excluding VAT and services). *See also below* **Office services***.*
*Disabled access.*

You can send faxes from some district post offices and from **Telehouse** (Raadhuisstraat 48-50) 24 hours daily, though the future of this business is uncertain. Lots of tobacconists and copy shops also have fax facilities. Major hotels have fax services for guest, but prices are high. The **World Trade**

**Center** (*see below* **Office hire**) also has full reception and transmission facilities. For photocopy centres, *see chapter* **Services***, page 166.*

## Couriers & shippers

### EMS (Emergency Couriers Nederland)
*(0800 1234).*
You can send packages within Holland by EMS by either taking it yourself to the post office or it can be picked up from you.

### Fedex
*Berquellaan 20-22, Oudemeer (0800 022 2333).* **Open** 8am-6.30pm Mon-Fri.
Even from Amsterdam, packages can be delivered to the US by 10.30am the next morning. Your package will be picked up by a multilingual driver.

### International Couriers Amsterdam
*Coenhavenweg Loods 8, Pier Asia (686 7808/7805). Bus 40.* **Open** 24 hours daily.
This worldwide courier service will transport packages across Amsterdam within an hour for *f*22,50. Rates for London (arriving before noon the following day) start at *f*80 for up to 0.5kg/1.1lb.

### TNT Post Group
*(24-hour phoneline 0800 1234).*
Documents of up to 500g/18oz can be delivered to London within 24 hours for *f*113 (*f*121 for parcels up to 1kg/2.2lb). Overnight delivery in the Netherlands costs *f*35 plus *f*0,25 per kilogram before noon; *f*25 after noon. Packages have to be picked up by a TNT agent.

## Forwarding agents

### Geytenbeek Europe BV
*De Rutherfordweg 51, 3542 CN Utrecht (030 241 2416/fax 030 241 5181).* **Open** office times 8.30am-5.30pm Mon-Fri.
A business removals and exhibition delivery service, Geytenbeek deals with all customs formalities.
**Branch:** RAI Congresgebouw, Europaplein 8 (644 8551).

## Mailing services

### Mail & More
*Nieuwezijds Voorburgwal 86 (638 2836/fax 638 3171). Tram 1, 2, 5.* **Open** 9am-5.30pm Mon-Fri.
**Map 2 C2**
Mail & More will deal with your mail requirements, and can also provide a message service, fax and

photocopying services and word processing facilities.

## Printing & duplicating

### Grand Prix Copyrette
*Weteringschans 84A (627 3705). Tram 16, 24, 25.* **Open** 9am-6pm Mon-Fri. **Map 5 D5**
There are a number of branches of this firm around the city. Each offers both colour and monochrome copying, ring binding, fax services and laser printing.
**Branch:** Amsteldijk 47 (671 4455).

### Multicopy
*Weesperstraat 65 (520 0720/fax 520 0722). Tram 4, 9, 14, 20/ Metro Waterlooplein.* **Open** 8am-7pm Mon-Fri; noon-4pm Sat.
**Map 3 F3**
As in many copy centres, the machines here are metered: rather than fidgeting around with coins and changes, you pay a total on your way out. You can make colour and monochrome copies in A4, A3 and A2 sizes, on white or coloured paper.

## Translations (Vertalingen)

### Berlitz Language Center
*Rokin 87 (639 1406/fax 620 3959). Tram 4, 9, 14, 16, 20, 24, 25.* **Open** 8.15am-9pm Mon-Thur; 8.15am-6pm Fri; 9am-1pm Sat. **Map 2 D3**
Specialists in commercial, technical, legal and scientific documents. All European languages are translated, plus Japanese and Arabic. English/Dutch translation costs a minimum of *f*150.

### Krasilovsky and Sons
*Ten Katestraat 67 (618 5080/fax 412 0488).Tram 7, 17.* **Map 1 B1**
Dutch/English copy and translations. Other services include copywriting, scriptwriting and editing. Specialities are film, television, theatre and the arts in general.

### Mac Bay Consultants
*PC Hooftstraat 15 (24-hour phoneline 662 0501/fax 662 6299). Tram 2, 3, 5, 12, 20.* **Open** 9am-5pm Mon-Fri. **Map 5 C6**
Specialises in translating financial documents. Dutch/ English translations cost *f*220 an hour. Other languages are also translated and there is a copywriting service.

### Tibbon Translations
*Utrechtsedwarsstraat 18 (420 1007/fax 420 0047). Tram 4.* **Open** 9am-5pm Mon-Fri.
Dutch/English translations. Tibbons also offers a copywriting and editing service.

## Interpreters (Tolken)

### Congrestolken-Secretariaat

*Prinsengracht 993 (625 2535/fax 626 5642). Tram 4, 16, 20, 24, 25.* **Open** 9am-5.30pm Mon-Fri. **Map 6 E4**

Highly specialised staff for conference interpreting. Languages offered include amongst others Arabic, Japanese, Cantonese and all European languages.

## Office services
### Equipment hire

### Avisco

*Stadhouderskade 156 (671 9909). Tram 6, 7, 10.* **Open** 7am-5pm Mon-Fri. **Map 6 F5**

Slide projectors, video equipment, screens, cameras, overhead projectors, microphones and tape decks hired out or sold.

### Decorum Verhuur

*Jarmuiden 21 (611 7905). Bus 42, 82.* **Open** 8am-5pm Mon-Fri. Office furniture hire.

### Office hire

### Euro Business Center

*Keizersgracht 62 (520 7500/fax 520 7510). Tram 13, 14, 17, 20.* **Open** 8.30am-5.30pm Mon-Fri. **Credit** AmEx, DC, MC, V. **Map 2 C2**

Fully equipped offices for hire (long- or short-term) which include the use of fax, photocopier, phone and mailbox services plus multilingual secretaries. For a minimum of three months, fully-equipped offices cost between *f*1,550-*f*5,000 per month. Private offices cost around *f*125-*f*200 per day.

### Jan Luyken Residence

*Jan Luykenstraat 58 (573 0730/fax 676 3841). Tram 2, 3, 5, 12, 20.* **Open** *office* 9am-5pm Mon-Fri. **Credit** AmEx, DC, EC, MC, V. **Map 5 D6**

Three fully equipped offices for hire, long- or short-term. Projectors, videos, phones, fax and mailbox are among the services that can be provided. Small temporary offices cost *f*350 per day. Conference rooms cost *f*450-*f*600 per day.

### World Trade Center

*Strawinskylaan 1 (575 9111/fax 662 7255). Tram 5/NS rail to RAI Station.* **Open** *office and enquiries* 9am-5pm Mon-Fri.

Office space in the World Trade Center is let by the Dutch Business Center Association Strawinskylaan 305 (571 1800/fax 571 1801). Offices can be hired long- or short-term. Audio and projection equipment is also for hire. Secretarial services, fax and photocopying facilities are offered. *See above* **Conferences**. *Disabled access.*

### Relocation

### Formula Two Relocations

*Stadionweg 131 (672 2590/fax 672 3023). Tram 24.* **Open** 8.30am-5.30pm Mon-Fri. **Map 5 C6**

This is an independent company, established in 1983, offering a comprehensive relocation service to companies and individuals moving to into and out of the Netherlands. *Disabled access.*

### Home Abroad

*Weteringschans 28 (625 5195/fax 624 7902). Tram 6, 7, 10.* **Open** 10am-5.30pm Mon-Fri. **Map 6 E5**

A company that assists in all aspects of living and doing business in the Netherlands. There's a fixed hourly rate of *f*95 for advice and assistance; rates for other services, such as seminars on the Dutch way of doing business, are negotiable. *Disabled access.*

## Employment agencies (Uitzendbureaus)

### Content Uitzendbureau

*Nieuwezijds Voorburgwal 156 (625 1061). Tram 1, 2, 5, 13, 17.* **Open** 8.30am-5.30pm Mon-Thur; 8.30pm-6pm Fri. **Map 2 C3**

A firm with office, secretarial, medical and technical staff on their books. There are nine branches in Amsterdam; the one listed above is their head office.

### Manpower

*Van Baerlestraat 41 (664 4180). Tram 3, 5, 12.* **Open** 8.30am-5.30pm Mon-Thur; 8.30am-6.30pm Fri. **Map 5 C6**

A large employment agency with 12 branches in Amsterdam. Staff can be provided for general office, secretarial, computer and other work.

### Randstad

*Leidseplein 1-3 (420 5843). Tram 1, 2, 5, 6, 7, 10, 20.* **Open** 8.30am-5.30pm Mon-Fri. **Map 5 D5**

There are 22 branches of Randstad scattered around Amsterdam supplying office and secretarial staff, specialist translators and data-entry staff.

### Tempo Team

*Rokin 118 (622 9393). Tram 4, 9, 14, 16, 20, 24, 25.* **Open** 8.30am-5.15pm Mon-Fri. **Map 2 D3**

Secretarial, hotel and catering, medical, technical and academic staff are on Tempo's books.

# Students

Amsterdam is an intellectual place. With around one in ten of its inhabitants in higher education, it is one of the Netherlands' main student cities. Its two major universities are the **UvA** (Universiteit van Amsterdam), which currently has around 27,000 students, and the **VU** (Vrije Universiteit), with about half that. Many of the UvA buildings scattered across town are historic and listed (you can recognise them by their red and black plaques),

whereas the VU has just one big building at de Boelelaan, in the south of Amsterdam.

Dutch higher education is divided in two sectors: Institutes of Higher Education (HBO), and universities. Only students between the ages of 18 and 27 are eligible for the four-year grant (or five years for technical studies courses). Students must pass at least half of their courses each year, otherwise they have to pay the grant back to the government.

Students are often entitled to discounts at shops, clubs, museums, attractions, cinemas and entertainment venues; presenting an ISIC card is often enough, but CJP cards (available from the Uitburo, for which *see* **Tourist information** *above*) are more frequently used.

## Student unions

Student unions tend to have a low volume of members. Nevertheless, the following are

excellent sources of help
and advice.

### AEGEE

*Herengracht 516 (525 2496). Tram
1, 2, 5.* **Open** *2-5pm Mon-Thur.*
**Map 6 E4**
The Association des Etats Généraux
des Etudiants de l'Europe basically
organises seminars, workshops,
summer courses and sporting events
in Amsterdam and around 170 other
European university cities.

### ASVA-OBAS

*Binnengasthuisstraat 9
(accommodation agency 623 8052).
Tram 4, 9, 14, 16, 20, 24, 25.* **Open**
*union and accommodation agency*
12.30-4pm Mon-Wed, Fri; 12.30-6pm
Thur; *July, Aug* 11am-4pm Mon-Fri.
**Map 2 D3**
ASVA offers assistance to foreign students. Its accommodation agency can
find you a room for about *f* 350 per
month, charging a *f* 10 deposit. An
accommodation lottery is held daily at
4pm and at 6pm on Thursdays.
Anyone with an ASVA card (*f* 25 for
a year) can enter.

### SRVU

*De Boelelaan 1183A (444 9424).
Tram 5/Metro 51.* **Open** *July-mid-
Aug* irregular hours (message in
English on answerphone); *mid-Aug-
June* 12.30-3.30pm Mon-Fri.
SRVU is the union for VU students.
Its accommodation service can also
help foreign students find a place to
stay, and offer general advice.
Membership is *f* 17,50 per year.

## Student life

Students are well catered for in
Amsterdam. Although open to
all, the bars listed below are
essentially student hangouts.

## Cafés & bars

### Café Het Paleis

*Paleisstraat 16 (626 0600). Tram 1,
2, 5, 20.* **Open** 11am-1am Mon-Thur;
1pm-1am Sun; 11am-2am Fri, Sat;
*food* 6-11pm daily. **Credit** AmEx,
DC, EC, MC, V. **Map 2 C3**
Het Paleis has been popular with
students for years. The food is
excellent, and the terrace is lovely.

### Café Maarten

*Handboogstraat 15 (622 1254).
Tram 1, 2, 5.* **Open** 9.30pm-3am
Mon-Wed, Sun; 9.30pm-4am Thur-
Sat. **Map 5 D4**
This long, narrow café has two
entrances, one on Voetboogstraat and
one on Handboogstraat, and is
popular with student union members.

### Crea Café

*Grimburgwal (627 3890). Tram 9,
14, 16, 20, 24, 25.* **Open** 9.30am-
1am Mon-Fri; 10am-1am Sat; noon-
7pm Sun. **Credit** EC. **Map 2 D3**
This café seems to attract the more
arty, upmarket type of student.

### Nota Bene

*Voetboogstraat 4 (624 7461). Tram
1, 2, 5.* **Open** 8pm-3am Mon-Thur,
Sun; 8pm-4am Fri, Sat. **Map 5 D4**
Plus points here include late opening
hours and friendly bar staff.

### Schutter Café

*Voetboogstraat 13-15 (622 4608).
Tram 1, 2, 5.* **Open** *bar* 11am-1am
Mon-Thur, Sun; 11am-2am Fri, Sat;
*food* noon-2.45pm, 5.45-10pm daily.
**Credit** EC. **Map 5 D4**
A café frequented by students and
tourists alike, selling snacks and 40
different types of beer, including

several British varieties. Meals are
also available.

## Mensae

Amsterdam has several mensae
(student restaurants), where the
food is good and the prices low.
They are subsidised and open
to the public, but are generally
only patronised by students.
University refectories are
another cheap and reliable bet.

### Agora

*De Roetersstraat 11 (525 5270
switchboard). Tram 7, 20.* **Open**
11.30am-2pm, 5-7pm, Mon-Fri.
**Average** *f* 8. **Map 3 F3**
A new, stylish mensa serving
reasonable food at affordable prices to
hungry students.

# Losing your religion?

### Catholic

**St John and St Ursula** *Begijnhof 30 (622 1918). Tram 1, 2, 4, 5,
16, 20, 24, 25.* **Open** 1-6pm Mon; 8.30am-6pm Tue-Sat. **Services** in
Dutch, English and French (phone for details). **Map 5 D4**

### Dutch Reformed Church

**Oude Kerk** *Oudekerksplein 33 (625 8284). Tram 4, 9, 16, 20, 24, 25.*
**Open** 11am-5pm Mon-Sat; 1-5pm Sun. **Services** *Dutch* 11am Sun.
**Map 2 D2**

### Jewish

**Liberal Jewish Community Amsterdam** *Jacob Soetendorpstraat 8
(642 3562/office rabbinate 644 2619). Tram 4.* **Open** 9am-3pm Mon-
Fri; *office rabbinate* 10am-3pm Mon-Thur. **Services** 8pm Fri; 10am Sat.
Times may vary, so phone ahead to check.
**Orthodox Jewish Community Amsterdam** *Postbus 7967, Van der
Boechorststraat 26 (646 0046). Bus 69, 169.* **Open** 9am-5pm Mon-Fri
by appointment only.
Information on orthodox synagogues and Jewish facilities.

### Muslim

**THAIBA Islamic Cultural Centre** *Kraaiennest 125 (698 2526).
Metro Gaasperplas.*
Phone for details of prayer times and cultural activities.

### Quaker

**Religious Genootschap der Vrienden** *Voissiusstraat 20 (679
4238). Tram 1, 2, 5.* **Open** 11am-4pm Tue; on other days call *070 363
2132.* **Service** 10.30am Sun.

### Reformed Church

**English Reformed Church** *Begijnhof 48 (624 9665). Tram 1, 2, 4,
5, 9, 16, 20, 24, 25.* **Open** *May-Sept* 2-4pm Mon-Fri. **Services** *English*
10.30am Sun; *Dutch* 7pm Sun. **Map 5 D4**
The main place of worship for Amsterdam's English-speaking community.

### Salvation Army

**National Headquarters** *Oudezijds Armsteeg 13 (520 8408). Tram 4,
9, 16, 20, 24, 25.* **Open** 9am-5pm Mon-Fri. **Map 2 D2**
Information on Salvation Army Citadels in Amsterdam.

## Atrium

*Oudezijds Achterburgwal 237 (525 3999). Tram 4, 9, 14, 20, 16, 24, 25/Metro Nieuwmarkt.* **Open** *lunch* noon-2pm, *dinner* 5-7pm, Mon-Fri. **Average** *f*10. **Map 2 D3**

A buffet/self-service restaurant where a starter and main course can be had for as little as *f*8,25.

## Mensa VU

*De Boelelaan 1105 (444 5897). Tram 5/Metro 51.* **Open** 10am-7pm Mon-Fri. **Dinner** 5-7pm Mon-Fri. **Average** *f*7,50.

This large, spacious mensa offers a choice of four meals Monday-Thursday, and three on Friday.

## Courses

A number of UvA departments offer international courses and programmes for postgraduates, graduates and undergraduates, all taught in English. Details are available from the **Foreign Relations Office** (Spui 25, 1012 SR Amsterdam). Most postgraduate institutes of the UvA also take foreign students. *See also above* **Visas**.

## Amsterdam Summer University

*Felix Meritis Building, Keizersgracht 324 (620 0225). Tram 1, 2, 5.* **Courses** last week of July-end first week of Sept. **Map 5 C4**

The ASU offers an annual summer programme of courses, workshops, training and seminars in the arts and sciences, plus international classes.

## Crea

*Turfdraagsterpad 17 (626 2189). Tram 4, 9, 14, 16, 20, 24, 25.* **Open** 10am-11pm Mon-Fri; 10am-5pm Sat; 11am-5pm Sun; closed July. **Map 2 D3**

Offers inexpensive creative courses, lectures and performances, covering theatre, radio, video, media, dance, music, photography and fine art. Courses are not in English.

## Foreign Student Service (FSS)

*Oranje Nassaulaan 5 (671 5915). Tram 2.* **Open** 9am-5pm Mon-Fri.

The FSS promotes the well-being of foreign students, providing personal assistance and general information on studying in the Netherlands. It also runs the International Student Insurance Service (ISIS) and organises social activities.

## UvA Service & Information Centre

*Binnengasthuisstraat 9 (information 525 8080 9am-5pm Mon-Fri). Tram 4, 9, 16, 20, 24, 25.* **Open** 10am-4pm Mon-Wed, Fri; 10am-7pm Thur. **Map 2 D3**

Personal advice on studying and everything that goes with it. The documentation centre stocks all the information you need to find a course for you in Holland or abroad.

## VU Student Information

*(office 444 7777/direct line 444 5000).* **Open** 9am-4.30pm Mon-Fri.

This is the helpline for the Vrije Universiteit, and can provide help and advice on courses, studying and accommodation.

## University libraries

Both libraries below cover many academic titles and also provide access to the Internet.

## UvA Main Library

*Singel 465 (525 2301/information 525 2326). Tram 1, 2, 5.* **Open** *for study* 9am-midnight Mon-Fri; 9.30am-5pm Sat; *for borrowing* 11am-4.30pm Mon; 9.30am-8pm Tue, Thur; 9.30am-4.30pm Wed, Fri; 9.30am-12.45pm Sat. Closed 1 Jul-15 Aug. **Map 5 D4**

To borrow books you need a UB (Universiteit Bibliotheek-University Library) card (*f*40): foreign students can also get one if they're in Amsterdam for three months or more, though a passport is needed as ID.

## VU Main Library

*De Boelelaan 1105 (444 5200). Tram 5/Metro 51.* **Open** *for study* 9am-9pm Mon-Thur; 9am-5pm Fri (July-Aug open only 9am-5pm Mon-Fri); *for borrowing* 10am-4pm Mon-Fri. **Membership** *f*30 per year (also for foreign students).

This isn't one big library, but several small ones. The books are spread over different floors, which can make them hard to track down, and some sciences such as mathematics, chemistry and biology have their own library in a building next door. Patience will reap dividends

## Student bookshops

Because English textbooks are widely used in Dutch colleges, they are sold everywhere, often cheaply. *See chapter* **Shopping**, *pages 140-42.*

## Allert de Lange

*Damrak 62 (624 6744). Tram 4, 9, 16, 20, 24, 25.* **Open** 1-6pm Mon; 10am-6pm Tue-Sat; noon-5pm Sun. **Credit** EC, MC, V. **Map 2 D2**

*The* place to go for books on the language, literature, history and culture of France, Germany and England. You'll also find sections devoted to philosophy, history, the history of art, film, travel and photography.

## VU Academic Bookshop

*De Boelelaan 1105 (644 4355). Tram 5/Metro 51.* **Open** 9am-7pm Mon-Fri; 10am-3.30pm Sat. **Credit** AmEx, EC, MC, V.

The VU Academic Bookshop (or VU Boekhandel, as the Dutch call it) has a large selection of books relating to all sciences, plus a good and varied collection of novels, tourist guides and children's books.

# Resources

## Drugs

The Amsterdam authorities have a relaxed attitude towards **soft drugs**, but you should note that smoking isn't acceptable everywhere in the city, so use some discretion. Many bars and cafés will not tolerate the practice and will eject offenders. Outside Amsterdam, public consumption of cannabis is largely unacceptable. For full details, *see chapter* **Coffeeshops**, *pages 135-8.*

Foreigners found with any amount of **hard drugs** – cocaine, speed, ecstasy, LSD and especially heroin – should expect prosecution. Organisations offering advice to users can do little to assist foreigners with drug-related problems, though the **Drugs Prevention Centre** is happy to provide help in several languages, including English. Its helpline, on 626 7176 (1-5pm Mon-Tue, Thur), offers advice and information on drugs and alcohol abuse. Visitors caught dealing in drugs are likely to be swiftly prosecuted and repatriated.

If you're suffering from too much dope, go to a hospital out-patients' department or see a doctor, who will be well-acquainted with the symptoms.

## Health

For **emergency services** and **medical or dental referral agencies**, *see above* **Emergencies**. For AIDS/HIV information, *see chapter* **Gay & Lesbian**, *pages 191-2*.

In the case of minor accidents, try the outpatients' departments at the following hospitals (*ziekenhuis*), all of which are open 24 hours a day, 365 days a year.

### Academisch Medisch Centrum

*Meibergdreef 9 (566 9111/566 3333). Bus 59, 60, 61, 62, 120, 126, 158. Metro Holendreschp.*

### Boven IJ Ziekenhuis

*Statenjachtstraat 1 (634 6346). Bus 34, 36, 37, 39.*

### Onze Lieve Vrouwe Gasthuis

*'s Gravesandeplein 16 (599 9111). Tram 3, 6, 10.* **Map 7 G4**

### St Lucas Andreas Ziekenhuis

*Jan Tooropstraat 164 (reception 510 8911/first aid 510 8164). Tram 13/bus 19, 47, 64, 80, 82, 97.*

### VU Ziekenhuis

*De Boelelaan 1117 (444 4444). Bus 23, 48, 64, 65, 173/Metro Amstelveenseweg.*

## Dentists

For a dentist (*tandarts*), phone the dentist administration bureau on 06 821 2230/0900 821 2230. An operator can put you in touch with your nearest dentist; lines are open 24 hours daily. The Central Medical Service may also be of help (*see above* **Emergencies**).

### AOC

*Wilhelmina Gasthuisplein 167 (616 1234). Tram 1, 2, 3, 5, 6, 12.* **Open** 8am-4pm Mon-Fri. **Map 4 B5** Emergency dental treatment.

## Prescriptions

Chemists (*drogist*) sell toiletries and non-prescription drugs and usually open 9.30am-5.30pm Monday-Saturday, although many close all day on Tuesday. For prescription drugs go to a pharmacy (*apotheek*), usually open 9.30am-5.30pm Mon-Fri.

Outside these hours, phone the **Afdeling Inlichtingen Apotheken** (*see above* **Emergencies**) or consult the daily newspaper *Het Parool*, which publishes details of which *apotheken* are open late that week. Details are also post-ed at local *apotheken*.

## Contraception & abortion

### MR '70

*Sarphatistraat 620-626 (624 5426). Tram 6, 9, 10, 14. Bus 22.* **Open** 9am-4pm Mon-Thur; 9am-1pm Fri. **Map 7 G2** An abortion clinic which offers help and advice.

### Polikliniek Oosterpark

*Oosterpark 59 (693 2151). Tram 3, 6, 9.* **Open** 9am-5pm for advice services. *Phonelines* **open** 24 hours a day. **Map 7 H4** Information and advice on contraception and abortion. Abortions are carried out (on Tue and Fri only), though non-residents without appropriate insurance will be charged from ƒ600 for the operation. The process is prompt and backed up by sympathetic counselling.

### Rutgersstichting

*Aletta Jacobshuis, Overtoom 323 (616 6222). Tram 1.* **Open** by appointment 9am-4.30pm Mon-Fri; 6-9pm Tue, 7-9pm Thur. **Fee** ƒ42,50. **Map 5 C6** Besides giving information on health issues, the staff at this family planning centre can help visitors with prescriptions for contraceptive pills, morning-after pills and condoms, IUD fitting and cervical smear tests. Prescription costs vary.

## Helplines

### Alcoholics Anonymous

*(625 6057).* **Open** 24-hour answerphone. A lengthy but informative message details times and dates of meetings, and also gives contact numbers for counsellors.

### SOS Telephone Helpline

*(675 7575).* **Open** 24 hours daily. A counselling service – comparable to the Samaritans in the UK and Lifeline in the US – for anyone with emotional problems, run by volunteers. English isn't always understood at first, but keep trying and someone will be able to help you.

### Narcotics Anonymous

*(662 6307).* **Open** 24-hour answerphone message with direct numbers of counsellors.

## Legal & immigration

### ACCESS

*Plein 24, 2511 CS Den Haag (070 346 2525).* **Open** 9.30am-3.30pm Mon-Fri; answerphone outside office hours. The Administrative Committee to Coordinate English Speaking Services is a non-profit organisation, which provides assistance in English through a telephone information line, workshops and counselling.

### Bureau Voor Rechtshulp

*Spuistraat 10 (626 4477). Tram 1, 2, 5.* **Open** by appointment 12.30-5pm Mon; 9am-12.30pm, 1.30-5pm Tue; 9am-12.30pm Wed; 9am-12.30pm, 4.30-7pm Thur; 9am-12.30pm Fri. **Map 2 D3** This legal advice centre has qualified lawyers who give free legal advice on matters of tenancy, social security, immigration, insurance, consumer complaints and disputes with employers.

### Legal Advice Line

*(444 6333).* **Open** 9pm-1pm Mon; 1-5pm Tue; 9am-1pm Wed, Fri; 9am-5pm Thur. Free advice from student lawyers; a relaxed, friendly service. They deal mainly with civil law queries and problems, but will occasionally be able to help with minor criminal law matters. Most speak English.

## Libraries

You'll need to present proof of residence in Amsterdam and ID if you want to join a library (*bibliotheek*) and borrow books. It costs ƒ34 (23-64s) or ƒ20,50 (18-23s, over-65s) per year and is free for under-18s. However, in the public libraries (*openbare bibliotheek*) you can read books, newspapers and magazines without membership or charge. For university libraries, *see above* **Students**.

### American Institute
*Plantage Muidergracht 12 (525 4380). Tram 7, 9/Metro Waterlooplein.* **Open** 10am-4pm Mon, Wed, Fri. **Map 7 G3**

### British Council Education Centre
*Oxford House, Neuwizijds Voorburgwal 328L (421 7040/fax 421 7003). Tram 1, 2, 5, 13, 14, 17.* **Open** *telephone enquiries* 9.30am-5pm Mon-Thur; *in person* 1-5pm Tue, Wed; 1am-6pm Thur. **Map 2 D3**

### Centrale Bibliotheek
*Prinsengracht 587 (523 0900). Tram 1, 2, 5.* **Open** 1-9pm Mon; 10am-9pm Tue-Thur; 10am-5pm Fri, Sat; *Mar-Oct* also 1-5pm Sun. **Map 5 C4**
Anyone is welcome to use this, the main public library, for reference purposes. There is a variety of English-language books and newspapers and a small coffee bar. *Disabled access.*

## Lost property

For the sake of insurance, report lost property to the police immediately; *see below* **Police & security**. If you lose your passport, inform your embassy or consulate as well. For

anything lost at the Hoek van Holland ferry terminal or Schiphol Airport, contact the company you're travelling with. For lost credit cards, *see above* **Emergencies.**

### Centraal Station
*NS Lost Property Information, Stationsplein 15 (557 8544). Tram 1, 2, 4, 5, 9, 13, 16, 17, 20, 24, 25.* **Open** 24 hours. **Map 2 D1**
Items found on trains are kept here for four days and then sent to *NS Afdeling Verloren Voorwerpen, Tweede Daalsedijk 4, 3500 HA Utrecht (030 235 3923; open 2-4pm Mon-Fri).*

### GVB Lost Property
*Prins Hendrikkade 108-114 (460 5858). Tram 1, 2, 4, 5, 9, 13, 16, 17, 20, 24, 25.* **Open** 9am-4pm Mon-Fri. **Map 2 C1**
Where to head for items lost on a bus, metro or tram. If you're reporting a loss from the previous day, phone after 2pm to allow time for the property to be sorted.

### Police Lost Property
*Stephensonstraat 18 (559 3005). Tram 12/bus 14/Metro Amstel station.* **Open** 9.30am-3.30pm Mon-Fri; *phone* noon-3.30pm Mon-Fri.
For items lost in the streets or parks. Report any loss to the police station in the same district: they generally hold

items for a day or so before sending them here for up to three months.

## Washing & cleaning

A comprehensive list of launderettes (*wassalons*) can be found in the *Yellow Pages* (*Gouden Gids*). For dry-cleaners, *see chapter* **Services**, *page 164.*

### Baths & showers

#### Marnixbad
*Marnixplein 9 (625 4843). Tram 3, 10.* **Open** for baths or showers 4-7.30pm Mon-Fri; 1-4.30pm Sat. **Cost** *f*2,75 per shower; *f*3 per bath. **Map 1 B3**
The best place in town for a wash; there's also a bar. Bring a towel.

#### Stichting De Warme Waterstaal
*Da Costakade 200 (612 5946). Tram 3, 7, 12, 17.* **Open** 1-6.30pm Tue; 10am-4.30pm Sat. **Cost** *f*3 per shower; *f*5 per bath. Sauna 2-10.30pm Mon, Tue (women's day), Thur-Sat; 2.30-10.30pm Sun. **Cost** 2-6pm *f*11; after 6pm *f*14; Sun *f*14. **Map 4 B5**
Bring your own towel or rent one for *f*1. Treat yourself to a massage or a sunbed session.

# Further Reading

## Literature

**Van Dantzig, Rudi** *For a Lost Soldier*
Autobiographical story set in the years following 1944.
**De Moor, Margriet** *First Grey, Then White, Then Blue*
Compelling story of perception, love and mortality.
**Irving, John** *The Widow for One Year*
1998 novel from the esteemed American author, a large part of which is set in the Red Light District.
**Joris, Lieve** *Back to the Congo*
Historical novel about Belgium and its ex-colony.
**Krabbé, Tim** *The Vanishing*
A man's search for his vanished lover. Twice made into a feature film.
**Minco, Marga** *Bitter Herbs*
Autobiographical masterpiece about a Jewish family falling apart during and after the war.
**Morley, John David**
*The Anatomy Lesson*
Novel about two very different American brothers growing up in Amsterdam.

**Mulisch, Harry** *The Assault*
A boy's perspective of the last war.
**Multatuli** *Max Havelaar or the Coffee Auctions of the Dutch Trading Company*
The story of a colonial officer and his clash with the corrupt government.
**Nooteboom, Cees**
*The Following Story*
An exploration of the differences between platonic and physical love. Other Nooteboom books worth investigating include *Rituals, Philip and the Others, In The Dutch Mountains, The Knight Has Died* and *A Song of Truth.*
**Rubinstein, Renate** *Take It Or Leave It*
Diary of one of the Netherlands' most renowned journalists and her battle against multiple sclerosis.
**Welsh, Irvine** *The Acid House*
A book of short stories by the celebrated Scottish author, one set in Amsterdam's druggy underworld.
**van der Wetering, Janwillem**
*The Japanese Corpse*
Marvellously off-the-wall police proce-dural set in Amsterdam. On of an excellent series.

## Architecture

**Fuchs, RH** *Dutch Painting*
A comprehensive guide.
**Groenendijk, Paul** *Guide to Modern Architecture in Amsterdam*
Exactly what the title suggests.
**Kloos, Maarten (ed)** *Amsterdam, An Architectural Lesson*
Architects and town planners on the development of the city.
**Overy, Paul** *De Stijl*
Amsterdam's modern art examined.
**Wit, Wim de** *The Amsterdam School Dutch Expressionist Arcitecture*
Early twentieth-century architecture.

## History

**Andeweg, Rudy B, & Irwin, Galen A** *Dutch Government & Politics*
An introduction to Dutch politics which assumes no prior knowledge.
**Boxer, CR** *The Dutch Seaborne Empire*
The Netherlands' wealth and what happened to it.

**Directory**

**Burke, Peter** *Venice and Amsterdam*
A succinct comparative history.
**Gies, Miep and Gold, Alison Leslie** *Anne Frank Remembered*
The story of the woman who helped the Frank family during the war.
**Israel, Jonathan I** *The Dutch Republic and the Hispanic World 1606-1661*
How the Dutch Republic broke free.
**Kussmann, EH** *The Low Countries 1780-1940*
Good background reading.
**Parker, Geoffrey** *The Thirty Years' War; The Dutch Revolt*
The fate of the Netherlands and Spain in descriptive, analytical history.

**Schama, Simon** *The Embarassment of Riches*
Lively, witty, social and cultural history of the Netherlands.
**Schetter, William Z** *The Netherlands in Perspective*
An essential book which goes beyond the usual stereotypes.

## General interest

**Blyth, Derek** *Amsterdam Explored*
Nine walks around the city.
**Frank, Anne** *The Diary of Anne Frank*
The war-time diary of the young Anne Frank. Compulsively readable.

**Herbert, Zbigniew** *Still Life with a Bridle*
The Polish poet and essayist meditates on the Golden Age.
**Van Straaten, Peter** *This Literary Life*
Highly amusing collection of one of the Netherlands' most popular cartoonist's works.
**Various** *Dedalus Book of Dutch Fantasy*
Anthology of contemporary Dutch short stories.
**White, Colin & Boucke, Laurie** *The Undutchables*
Everything you ever wanted to know about the Dutch (and that they'd rather you never found out).

# Size conversion chart for clothes

| Women's clothes | | | | | | | | | |
|---|---|---|---|---|---|---|---|---|---|
| British | 8 | 10 | 12 | 14 | 16 | • | • | • | • |
| American | 6 | 8 | 10 | 12 | 14 | • | • | • | • |
| French | 36 | 38 | 40 | 42 | 44 | • | • | • | • |
| Italian | 38 | 40 | 42 | 44 | 46 | • | • | • | • |
| **Women's shoes** | | | | | | | | | |
| British | 3 | 4 | 5 | 6 | 7 | 8 | 9 | • | • |
| American | 5 | 6 | 7 | 8 | 9 | 10 | 11 | • | • |
| Continental | 36 | 37 | 38 | 39 | 40 | 41 | 42 | • | • |
| **Men's suits/overcoats** | | | | | | | | | |
| British | 38 | 40 | 42 | 44 | 46 | • | • | • | • |
| American | 38 | 40 | 42 | 44 | 46 | • | • | • | • |
| Continental | 48 | 50/52 | 54 | 56 | 58/60 | • | • | • | • |
| **Men's shirts** | | | | | | | | | |
| British | 14 | 14.5 | 15 | 15.5 | 16 | 16.5 | 17 | • | • |
| American | 14 | 14.5 | 15 | 15.5 | 16 | 16.5 | 17 | • | • |
| Continental | 35 | 36/37 | 38 | 39/40 | 41 | 42/43 | 44 | • | • |
| **Men's shoes** | | | | | | | | | |
| British | 8 | 9 | 10 | 11 | 12 | • | • | • | • |
| American | 9 | 10 | 11 | 12 | 13 | • | • | • | • |
| Continental | 42 | 43 | 44 | 45 | 46 | • | • | • | • |
| **Children's shoes** | | | | | | | | | |
| British | 7 | 8 | 9 | 10 | 11 | 12 | 13 | 1 | 2 |
| American | 7.5 | 8.5 | 9.5 | 10.5 | 11.5 | 12.5 | 13.5 | 1.5 | 2.5 |
| Continental | 24 | 25.5 | 27 | 28 | 29 | 30 | 32 | 33 | 34 |

**Children's clothes**

In all countries, size descriptions vary from make to make, but are usually based on age or height.

# Index

# Advertisers' Index

# Maps

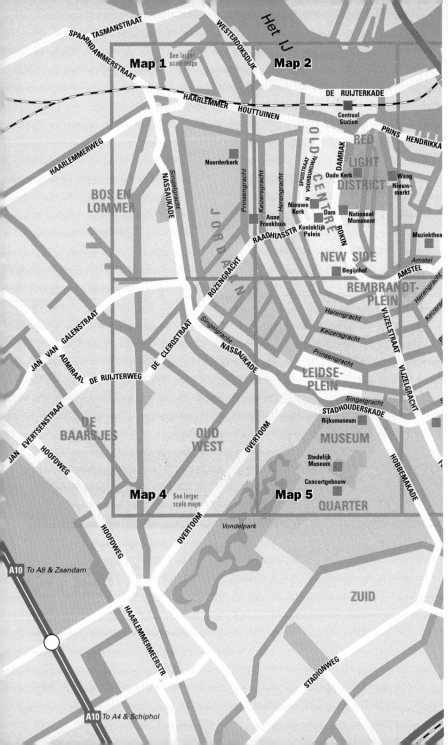

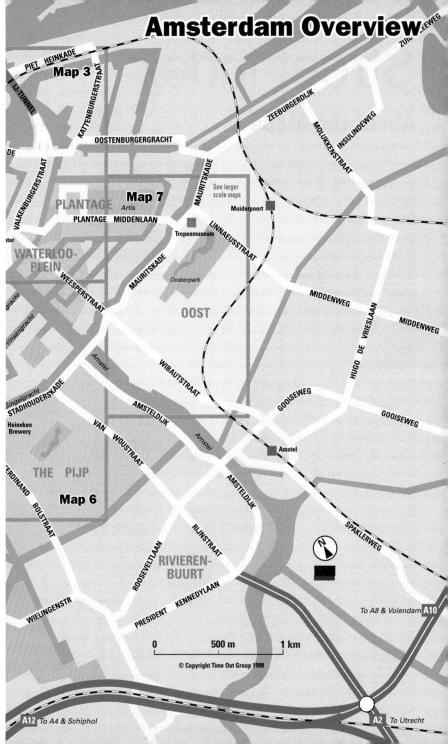

# Street Index

## About the Maps

Each street that is included on the maps in this book has been given a map reference, comprising a map number and a grid reference. 'Achtergracht - 6 F4', for example, means that Achtergracht can be found on Map 6, grid reference F4. The map numbers tally with the grid references as follows:

**Map 1**: A1-3, B1-3.　　**Map 2**: C1-3, D1-3.
**Map 3**: E1-3, F1-3.　　**Map 4**: A4-6, B4-6.
**Map 5**: C4-6, D4-6.　　**Map 6**: E4-6, F4-6.
**Map 7**: G2-5, H2-5.

Due to the crowded layout of Amsterdam, the length of many of the street names and the size of this book, not all street names have been listed on the map itself. However, all are alphabetised and referenced below. Where a street name has not been able to be fitted on to the map, it has been referenced and marked with an asterisk (*) so as to differentiate it from those that are fully marked on the map.

This index has been designed to tie in with other commercially available maps of Amsterdam, and certain principles of the Dutch language have been followed for reasons of consistency and ease of use:
● Where a street is named after a person – Albert Cuypstraat, for example – it is alphabetised by surname. Albert Cuypstraat, therefore, is listed under 'C'.
● Where a street is numbered, it has been listed under the name of the street, rather than the number. 1e Goudbloemdwarsstraat, then, is alphabetised under 'G'.
● The following prefixes have been ignored for alphabetisation: Da, De, Den, 's, Sint (St), 't, Van, Van der. Where street names contain one of these prefixes, they have been alphabetised under the subsequent word. For example, Da Costakade can be found under 'C', and Van Breestraat is listed under 'B'.
● In Dutch, 'ij' is the same as 'y'. Streets containing 'ij' – Vijzelstraat, for example – have been alphabetised as if 'ij' was a 'y'.

Oudekerksplein - 2 D2
Oudemanhuispoort - *2 D3
Oudeschans - 3 E2/3 E3
Oudezijds Achterburgwal - 2 D3/2 D2
Oudezijds Armsteeg - 2 D2
Oudezijds Kolk - 2 D2
Oudezijds Voorburgwal - 2 D2/2 D3
Overtoom - 4 B6/5 C6

**Paardenstraat** - 3 E3
Paleisstraat - 2 C3
Palmdwarsstraat - 1 B2
Palmgracht - 1 B2
Palmstraat - 1 B2
Papenbroeksteeg - *2 D3
Passeerdersgracht - 5 C4
Passeerdersstraat - 5 C4
Pastoorsstraat, Willem - 6 F6
Pieterspoortsteeg, St - 2 D3
Pieterssteeg, St - *5 D4
Planciusstraat - 1 A1
Plantage Badlaan - 7 G3
Plantage Doklaan - 3 F2/7 G2
Plantage Kerklaan - 3 F3
Plantage Lepellaan - 7 G3
Plantage Middenlaan - 3 F3/7 G3
Plantage Muidergracht - 3 F3/7 G3
Plantage Parklaan - 3 F3
Plantage Westermanlaan - 7 G3
Platanenweg - 7 H5
Polaklaan, Henri - 3 F3
Populierenweg - 7 H4
Potgieterstraat - 4 B4
Potterstraat, Paulus - 5 D6
Pretoriusstraat - 7 H4
Prinseneiland - 1 B1
Prinsengracht - 1 B2/6 E4
Prinsenstraat - 2 C2
Pijlsteeg - 2 D3

**Quellijnstraat** - 6 E5/6 E6

**Raadhuisstraat** - 2 C3
Raamgracht - 3 E3
Raamstraat - 5 C4
Ramskooi - *2 D2
Rapenburg - 3 E2
Rapenburgerplein - 6 E4/3 F2
Rappenburgerstraat - 3 F3
Recht Boomssloot - 3 E2/6 E5
Reestraat - 2 C3
Reguliersbreestraat - 6 E4
Reguliersdwarsstraat - 5 D4
Reguliersgracht - 6 E4
Reigersbergenstraat, Van - 4 A4
Reijstraat, De la - 7 H5
Reinwardtstraat - 7 H3
Reitzstraat - 7 H4
Rembrandtplein - 6 E4
Retiefstraat - 7 H4
Rhijnspoorplein - 7 G4
Roetersstraat - 3 F3/7 G3
Rokin - 2 D3/5 D4
Roomolenstraat - 2 C2
Rosmarijnsteeg - *2 D3
Rozenboomsteeg - *2 D3
Rozengracht - 1 B3
Rozenstraat - 1 B3/4 B4
Runstraat - 5 C4
Rusland - 2 D3
Rustenburgerstraat - 6 F6
Ruyschstraat - 7 G4
Ruysdaelkade - 6 E6
Ruysdaelstraat - 6 E6
Ruijterkade, De - 2 C1/3 E1

**Saenredamstraat** - 6 E6

Sajetplein - 7 G3
Sarphatikade - 6 F4
Sarphatipark - 6 F5/6 F6
Sarphatistraat - 6 F4/7 G2
Schaepmanstraat - 1 A3
Schapensteeg - 6 E4
Schimmelstraat - 4 A5
Schippersgracht - 3 F2
Schippersstraat - *3 E2
Scholtenstraat, Fannius - 1 A2
Schoolmeesterstraat - 4 B5
Schoorsteenvegerssteeg - *2 C3
Schoutensteeg - *2 D3
Schwartzestraat, Therese - 6 F6
Servetsteeg - 2 D3
Simonszstraat, Fokke - 6 E5
Singel - 2 C2/5 D4
Singelgracht - 1 A2/7 H3
Slatuinenweg - 4 A5
Sloterdijkstraat - 1 B1
Slijkstraat - 2 D3
Smaksteeg - *2 C2
Spaarndammerstraat - 1 A1
Spaarpotsteeg - *2 D3
Speijkstraat, Van - 4 A5
Spiegelgracht - 5 D5
Spinhuisdwarssteeg - *2 D3
Spinhuissteeg - 2 D3
Spinozastraat - 7 G4
Spitsbergenstraat - 1 A1
Spooksteeg - *2 D2
Sprenglerstraat, Anna - 4 B6
Spui - 2 D3/5 D4
Spuistraat - 2 C2/2 C3
Staalkade - 3 E3
Staalstraat - 3 E3
Stadhouderskade - 5 C5/6 F5
Stalpertstraat, Daniel - 6 E6
Stationsplein - 2 C2/2 D2
Steenhoudersteeg - *2 D3
Steenstraat, 1e Jan - 6 E6
Steenstraat, 2e Jan - 6 F5
Steynplant, President - 7 H5
Stormsteeg - 2 D2
Stromarkt - 2 C2
Suikerbakkerssteeg - *2 C2
Swammerdamstraat - 7 G4
Sweelinckstraat - 6 F5/6 F6
Swindenstraat, 1e Van - 7 H3
Swindenstraat, 2e Van - 7 H3

**Taksteeg** - *2 D3
Teerketelsteeg - 2 C2
Teniersstraat - 5 D6
Tesselschadestraat - 5 C5
Texstraat, Den - 6 E5
Theronstraat, Danie - 7 H5
Thorbeckeplein - 6 F4
Tichelstraat - 1 B2
Tilanusstraat - 7 G4
Tolbrugstraat - 4 A5
Tollensstraat - 4 B5
Torensteeg - 2 C3
Torontobrug - 6 F4
Transvaalkade - 7 H5
Tripstraat, Lodewijk - 1 A2
Tugelaweg - 7 H4/7 H5
Tuindwarsstraat, 1e - 1 B3
Tuinstraat - 1 B3/1 B2
Tulpplein, Professor - 6 F4

**Uilenburgergracht** - 3 E2
Utrechtsedwarsstraat - 6 E4
Utrechtsestraat - 6 E4

**Vaalrivierstraat** - 7 H5
Valckenierstraat - 6 F4/7 G3

Valkenburgerstraat - 3 E3
Valkensteeg - *2 D3
Veldestraat, Van der - 5 D6
Vermeerstraat, Johannes - 5 D6
Verversstraat - 3 E3
Viljoenstraat, Ben - 7 H5
Vinkenstraat - 1 B1
Visscherstraat, Roemer - 5 C5
Visseringstraat - 1 A3
Visserplein, Meester - 3 E3
Voetboogstraat - 5 D4
Vondelpark - 5 C6
Vondelstraat - 4 B6/5 C6
Vondelstraat, Anna van der - 5 C5
Voormalige Stadstimmertuin - 6 F4
Vossiusstraat - 5 C5
Vredenborgersteeg - *2 D2
Vrolikstraat - 7 G4/7 H4
Vijzelgracht - 6 E5
Vijzelstraat - 5 D4

**Waalseilandsgracht** - 3 E2
Wagenaarstraat - 7 H3
Wagenstraat - *3 E3
Wanningstraat - 5 D6
Warmoesstraat - 2 D2/2 D3
Waterlooplein - 3 E3
Waterpoortsteeg - *2 D2
Watersteeg - 2 D3
Weesperplein - 6 F4
Weesperstraat - 3 F3
Weesperzijde - 7 G5
Wenslauerstraat - 4 A5
Westeinde - 6 F5
Westelijk Martkanaal - 4 A4
Westerdok - 1 B1
Westerdoksdijk - 2 C1
Westerdokskade - 2 C1
Westerpark - 1 A1
Westerstraat - 1 B3/4 B4
Weteringdwarsstraat, 1e - 5 D5
Weteringdwarsstraat, 2e - 5 D5
Weteringdwarsstraat, 3e - 5 D5
Weteringschans - 5 D5/6 E5
Weteringstraat - 5 D5
Wibautstraat - 7 G4/7 H5
Wilheminastraat - 4 A6/4 B6
Willemsparkweg - 5 C6
Willemstraat - 1 B2
Willibrordusstraat, St - 7 G5
Withstraat, Witte de - 4 A6
Witsenkade, Nicolaas - 6 E5
Witsenstraat, Nicolaas - 6 E5
Wittenkade, De - 1 A2
Wittenstraat, De - 1 A2
Wolffstraat, Elisabeth - 4 A5
Wolvenstraat - 5 C4
Woustraat, Van - 6 F5
Wijde Enge Lombardsteeg - 2 D3
Wijde Heisteeg - 5 C4
Wijde Kapelsteeg - *2 D3
Wijdesteeg - *2 C3
Wijttenbachstraat - 7 H3

**Zaandijkstraat** - 1 A1
Zaanstraat - 1 A1
Zandbergplein - 5 D6
Zandpad - 5 C5
Zandstraat - 3 E3
Zeedijk - 2 D2
Zeldenruststraat, Mary - 7 G4
Zesenstraat, Von - 7 H2
Zieseniskade - 5 D5
Zoukeetsgracht - 1 B1
Zoutsteeg - 2 D2
Zwanenburgwal - 3 E3
Zwarte Handsteeg - *2 C3

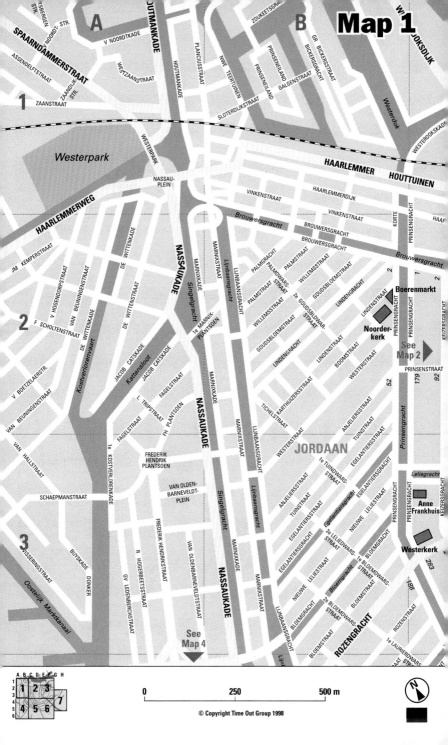

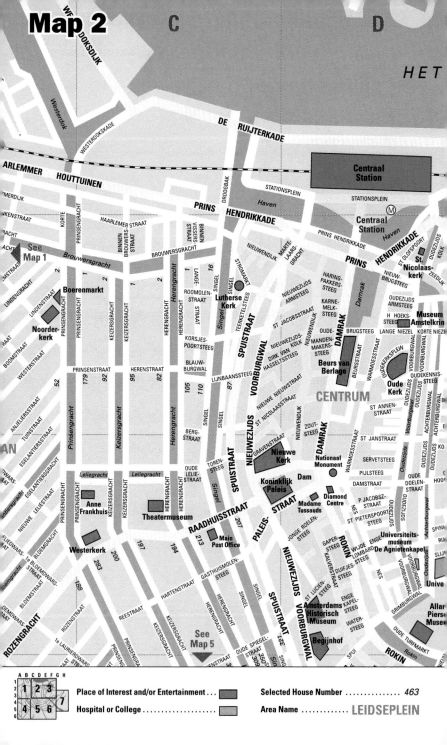

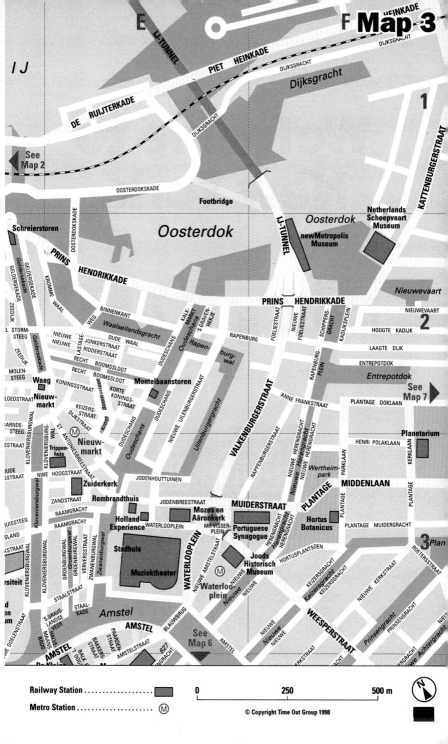

# Welcome to New York.

# Now get out.

**The obsessive guide to impulsive entertainment**

On sale at newsstands in New York

Pick up a copy!

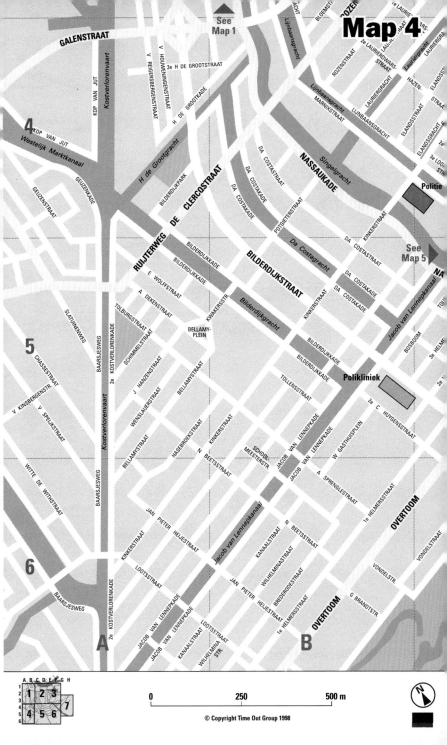

# Map 5

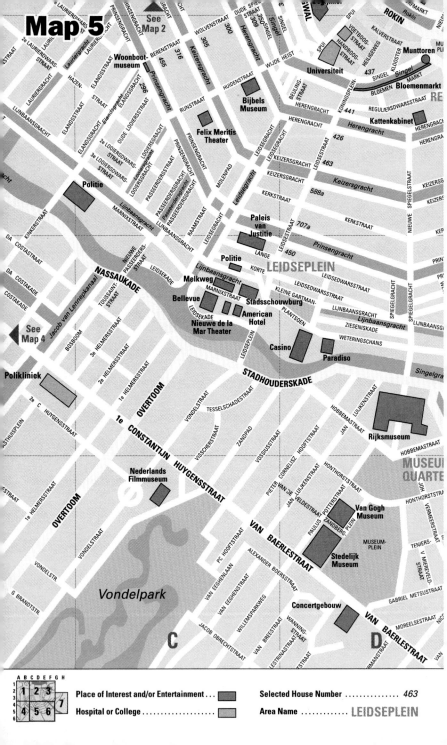

See
Map 2

LAURIERDWARS
LAURIERDWARS-STRAAT
2e LAURIERDWARS-STRAAT
2e LAURIER.
STRAAT

PRINSENGRACHT
PRINSENGRACHT
GRACHT

WOLVENSTRAAT 300
OUDE SPIEG
SPIEG
STRAAT
309
Singel
Singel
SPUI

VOETBOOG-
STRAAT
HANDBOOG-
STRAAT
HEILIGEWG

ROKIN
Rokin

FMARKT

SPUI

KALVERSTRAAT

BERENSTRAAT 316
455
455

KEIZERSGRACHT
305
300

HERENGRACHT

WIJDE HEIST

Universiteit

KONINGSPLEIN

Munttoren

MU
PLI

Woonboot-
museum

LAURIERGRACHT
HAZEN.

ELANDSGRACHT
296
ELANDSSTRAAT
Elandsgracht

HUIDENSTRAAT

RUNSTRAAT

Bijbels
Museum

BELLING-
STRAAT

SINGEL
BLOEMEN.
STRAAT
437

KLOOSTER.

MARKT

Bloemenmarkt

RE

LIJNBAANSGRACHT
ELANDSGRACHT
ELANDSSTRAAT
2e LOOIERSDWARS.
STRAAT
3e LOOIERDWARS.
STRAAT

OUDE LOOIERSSTRAAT
LOOIERSGRACHT

PRINSENGRACHT

Felix Meritis
Theater

LEIDSEGRACHT

HERENGRACHT

HERENGRACHT
426

REGULIERSDWARSSTRAAT

441

HERENGRACHT

Kattenkabinet

HERENGRA

LAURIERGRACHT
LINKERSTRAAT
DA COSTASTRAAT
DA COSTAKADE

Politie

PASSEERDERSGRACHT
PASSEERDERSGRACHT
PASSEERDERSGRACHT

LIJNBAANSGRACHT
MARNIXSTRAAT

RAAMSTRAAT

MOLENPAD

LEIDSEGRACHT

LEIDSEGRACHT
KEIZERSGRACHT
463

KEIZERSGRACHT
588a

KEIZERSGRACHT

KERKSTRAAT

KERKSTRAAT

KERKSTRAAT

NIEUWE SPIEGELGRACHT
SPIEGELGRACHT

KEIZERS

NASSAUKADE

NIEUWE
PASSEERDERS-
STRAAT

Paleis
van
Justitie

LANGE

LEIDSESTRAAT
707a
450

Prinsengracht

PRINSENGRACHT

PRIN

SPIEGELGRACHT

LEIDSEGRACHT

Politie

KORTE

LEIDSEPLEIN

LEIDSEDWARSSTRAAT

LIJNBAANSGRACHT

COSTAKADE

Melkweg

Lijnbaansgracht

MARNIXSTRAAT

Bellevue

LEIDSEKADE

Stadsschouwburg

KLEINE GARTMAN.
LEIDSEDWARSSTRAAT

LIJNBAANSGRACHT

LIJNBAANSGRACHT

Lijnbaansgracht

SPIEGELGRACHT
LIJNBAANSGR

See
Map 4

Jacob van Lennepkanaal

BOSBOOM

TOUSSAINT.
STRAAT

3e HELMERSSTRAAT

Nieuwe de la
Mar Theater

LEIDSEKADE

American
Hotel

LEIDSEPLEIN

PLAN'TSOEN

ZIESENISKADE

WETERINGSCHANS

Casino

Paradiso

Singelgr

Polikliniek

2e C

HUYGENSSTRAAT

2e HELMERSSTRAAT

1e HELMERSSTRAAT

OVERTOOM

STADHOUDERSKADE

VONDELSTRAAT

TESSELSCHADESTRAAT

HOBBEMAKADE

JAN LUIJKENSTRAAT

HOBBEMASTRAAT

Rijksmuseum

HOBBEMASTRAAT

MUSEU
QUARTE

THUISPLEIN

1e CONSTANTIJN HUYGENSSTRAAT

VISSERSTRAAT

ZANDPAD

VOSSIUSSTRAAT

PIETER CORNELISZ. HOOFTSTRAAT

JAN VAN DE VELDESTRAAT

JAN LUIJKENSTRAAT

HONTHORSTSTRAAT

HONTHORSTSTRAAT

VERMEERSTRAAT

1e HELMERSSTRAAT

OVERTOOM

Nederlands
Filmmuseum

VONDELSTRAAT

PC HOOFTSTRAAT

PAULUS POTTERSTRAAT

Van Gogh
Museum

VAN DER
PLEIN

MUSEUM-
PLEIN

TENIERS-
STRAAT

V MIEREVELD.
STRAAT

VONDELSTR

VAN BAERLESTRAAT

ALEXANDER BOERSSTRAAT

Stedelijk
Museum

GABRIEL METSUSTRAAT

G BRANDTSTR

Vondelpark

VAN EEGHENLAAN

WILLEMSPARKWEG

VAN EEGHENSTRAAT

JACOB OBRECHTSTRAAT

VAN BREESTRAAT

WANNING-
STRAAT

Concertgebouw

VAN BAERLESTRAAT

MOREELSESTRAAT

C

D

ESTRINASTRAAT

MANSTRAAT

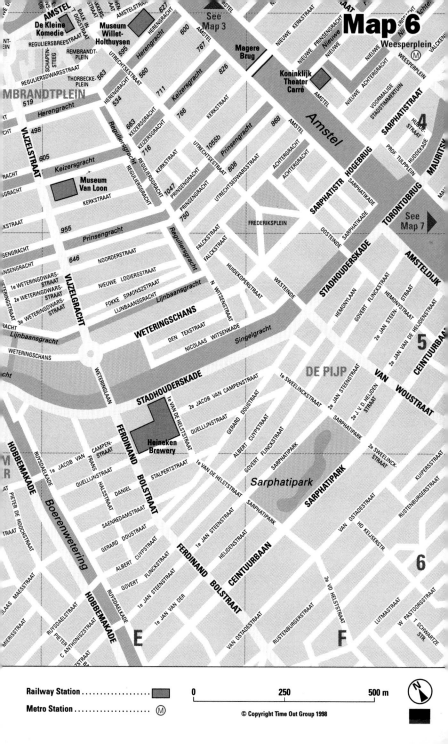

# Map 6

**Weesperplein** Ⓜ

**4**

**5**

**6**

**E**

**F**

MBRANDTPLEIN

DE PIJP

*Sarphatipark*

SARPHATIPARK

De Kleine Komedie

Museum Willet-Holthuysen

Magere Brug

Koninklijk Theater Carré

Museum Van Loon

Heineken Brewery

See Map 3

See Map 7

Amstel

VIJZELSTRAAT

VIJZELGRACHT

HOBBEMAKADE

FERDINAND BOLSTRAAT

STADHOUDERSKADE

CEINTUURBAAN

VAN WOUSTRAAT

AMSTELDIJK

Boerenwetering

SARPHATISTRAAT

HOGEBRUG

TORONTOBRUG

WETERINGSCHANS

Singelgracht

FREDERIKSPLEIN

Railway Station ................
Metro Station ..................... Ⓜ

0    250    500 m

© Copyright Time Out Group 1998

N

# The Netherlands

© Copyright Time Out Group 1998

# AMSTERDAM PUBLIC TRANSPORT

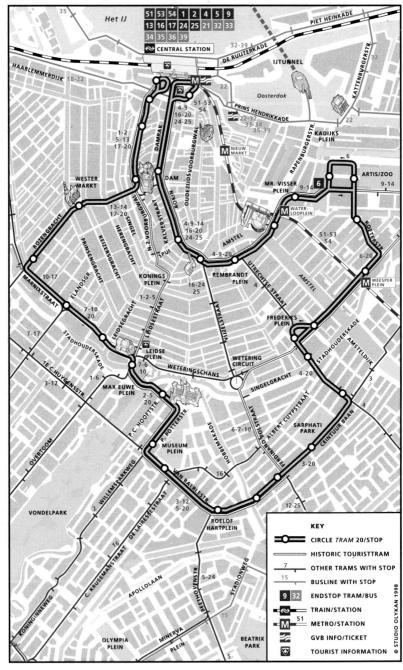

**KEY**

| | |
|---|---|
| ⊙━━⊙ | CIRCLE TRAM 20/STOP |
| | HISTORIC TOURISTTRAM |
| ━7━ | OTHER TRAMS WITH STOP |
| ─15─ | BUSLINE WITH STOP |
| **9** **32** | ENDSTOP TRAM/BUS |
| ⌇ | TRAIN/STATION |
| M **51** | METRO/STATION |
| ⌇ | GVB INFO/TICKET |
| ⌇ | TOURIST INFORMATION |

© STUDIO OLYKAN 1998